I0727816

ARCHITECTURE AND DESIGN

REVIEW

THE ULTIMATE INSPIRATION – FROM INTERIOR TO EXTERIOR

ARCHITECTURE AND DESIGN

REVIEW

THE ULTIMATE INSPIRATION – FROM INTERIOR TO EXTERIOR

EDITED BY
Cindi Cook

CONTRIBUTING EDITOR
Martin Waller

TEXTS BY
Frank Wagner

teNeues

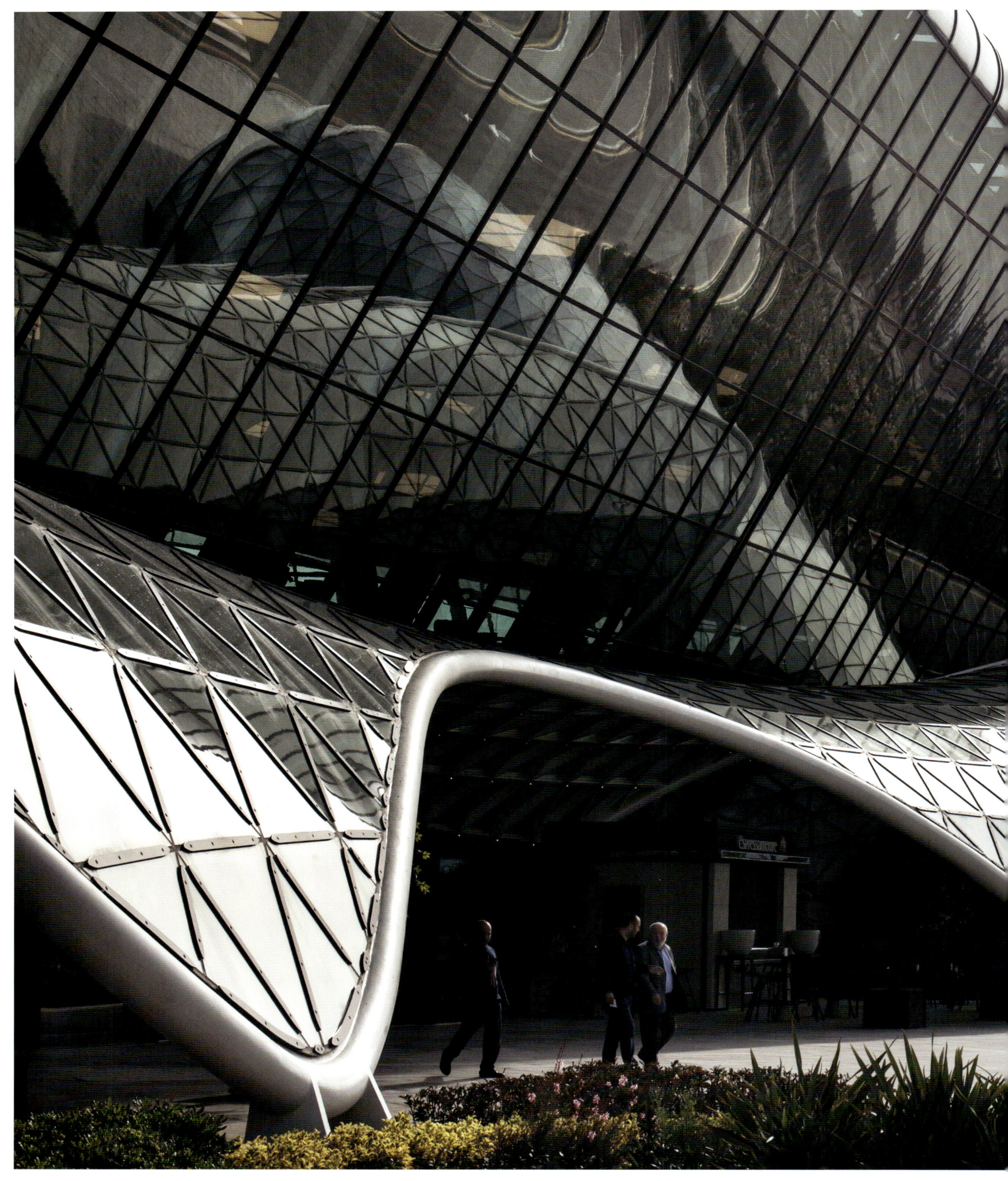

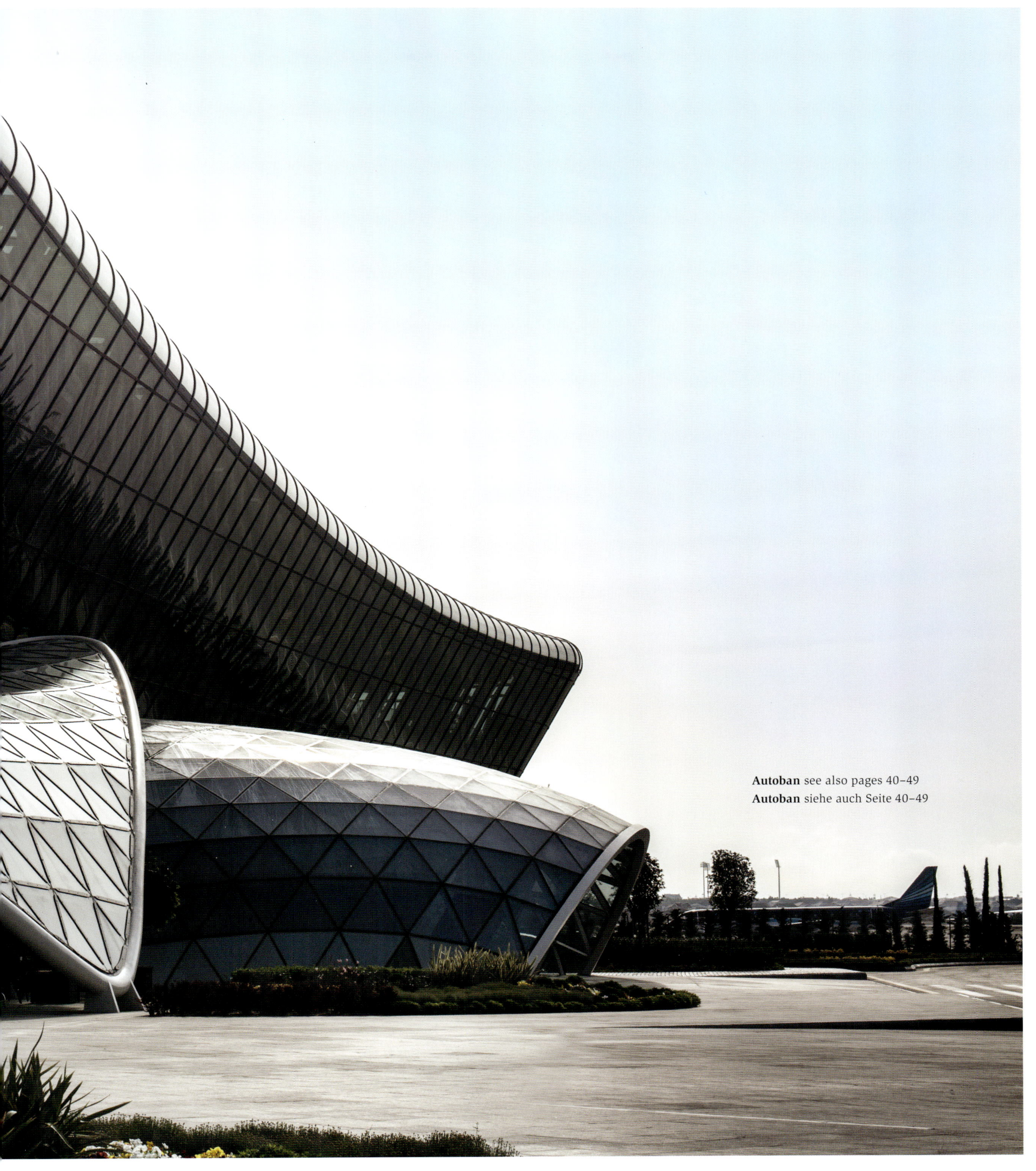

Autoban see also pages 40–49
Autoban siehe auch Seite 40–49

CONTENTS

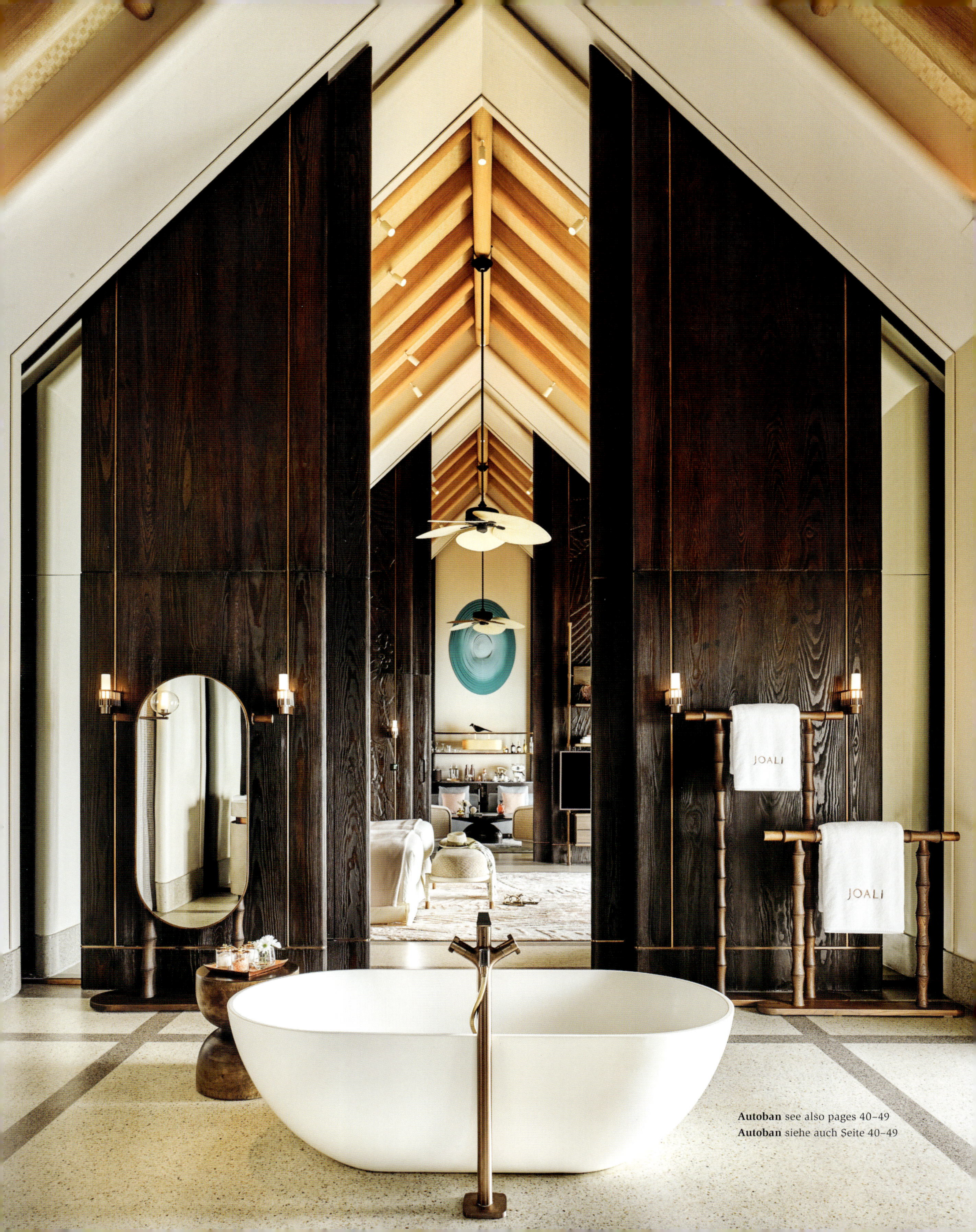

Autoban see also pages 40–49
Autoban siehe auch Seite 40–49

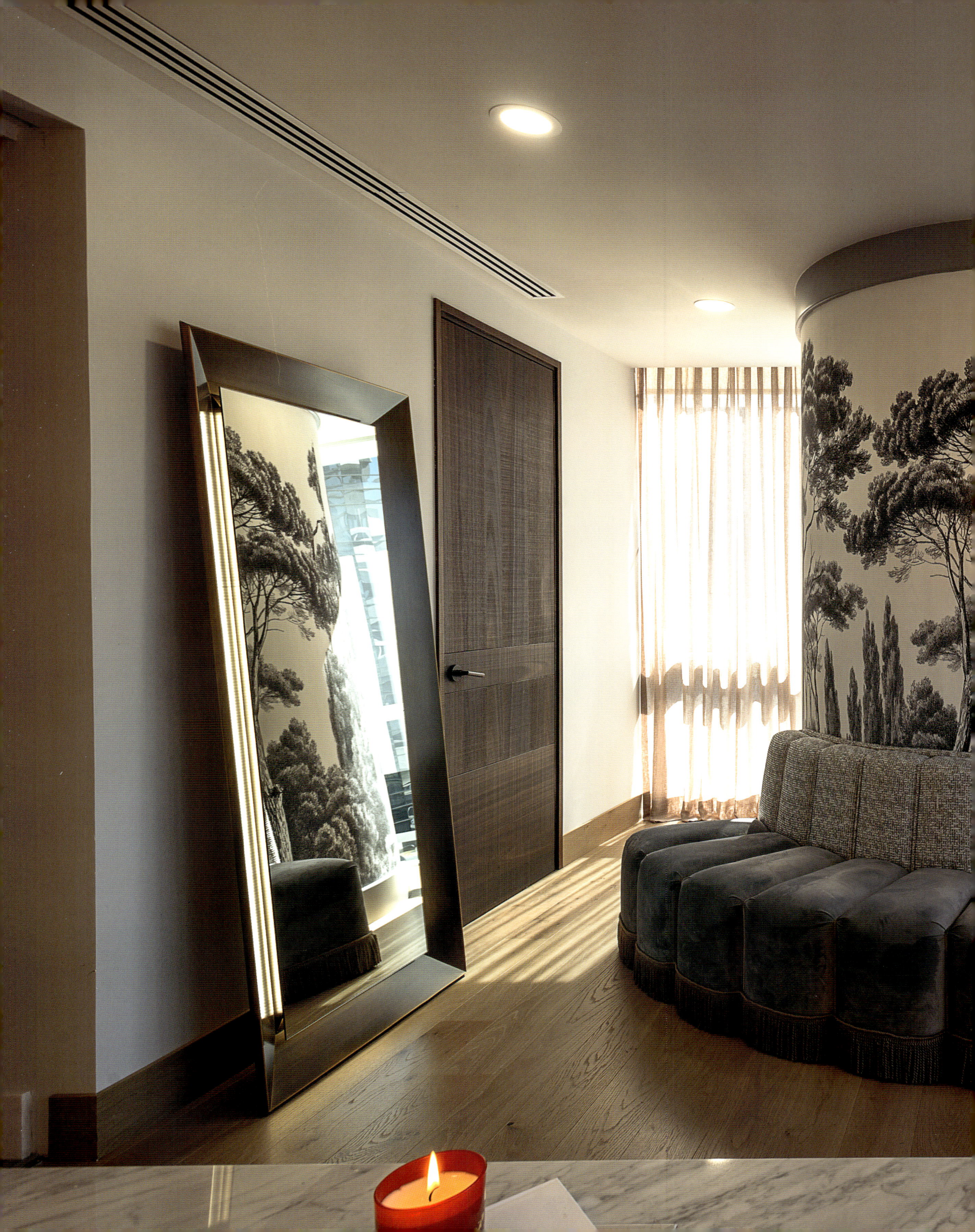

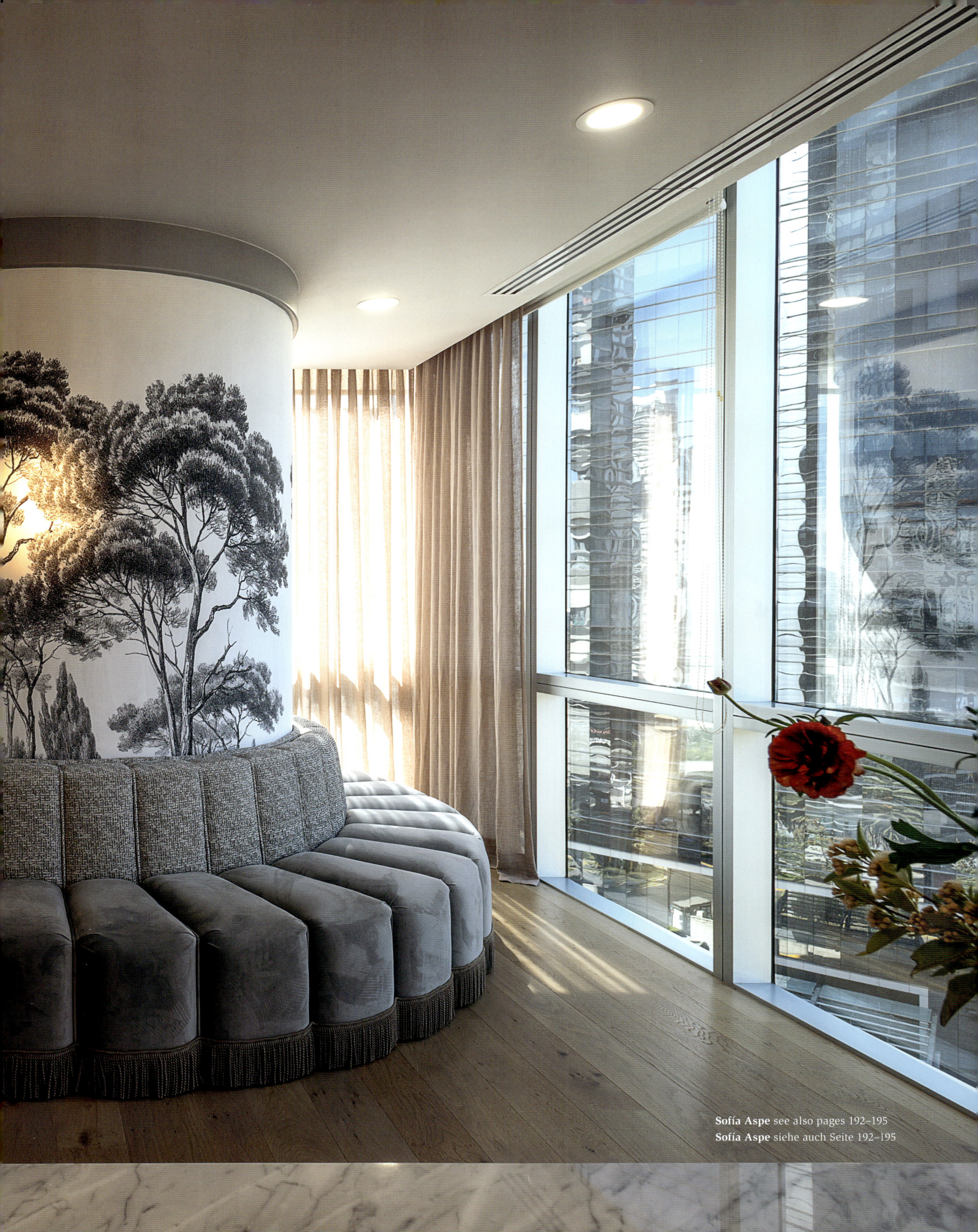
Sofía Aspe see also pages 192–195
Sofía Aspe siehe auch Seite 192–195

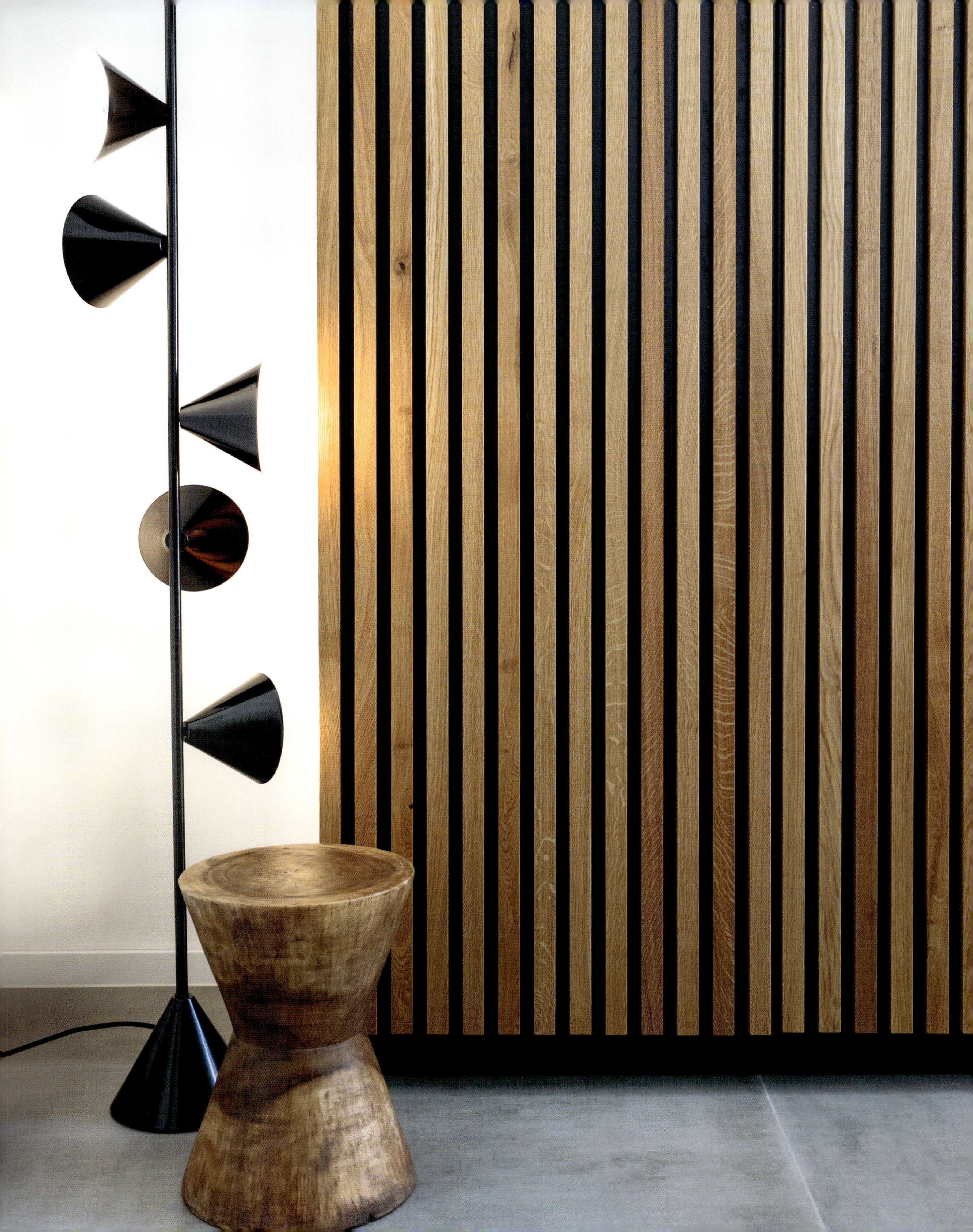

FOREWORD

You are holding the latest edition of the *Architecture & Design Review* in your hands—a book you will enjoy browsing through and reading at your leisure. This issue will once again take you on a journey to the conceptual worlds and dreams, as well as to the existing real-life achievements of the leading designers, artisans, architects, and interior designers of our time. Much of what has been captured on camera will amaze, astound, or simply entertain you.

This most recent edition is well worth a closer look, as you are invited into some extraordinary apartments, houses, and properties which vary in scope and style. Seize the opportunity to explore the remarkably designed spaces which would otherwise remain hidden behind the walls, windows, and doors of private owners or companies.

High-quality, professional photographs accompanied by short, pertinent texts, provide easy access to this fascinating world. The new *Architecture & Design Review* brings you the latest insights into the current, state-of-the-art scene of international interior design.

As one would of course expect, the US interior design professionals such as Rebekah Caudwell, Matthew Frederick, and GWdesign feature prominently also in this edition. Many of the designers presented this time around are, however, based in Europe, for example Christine Kröncke or Sebastian Zenker from Germany, Feyrsinger from Austria, Alexandra de Garidel from Switzerland, Nicky Dobree from the United Kingdom, Stock Dutch Design from the Netherlands, Icazar Architects from Spain, and Autoban from Turkey, to name but a few. Also included are successful designers from Canada, Mexico, Taiwan, Russia, as well as the Indian company, Mancini Enterprises.

Generally, however, geographical location plays a minor role in international interior design: the women, men, couples, and teams in this compelling industry work wherever they find exciting spaces to design and interested clients to commission them. Borders are crossed effortlessly and lose their importance.

Discover, regardless of their whereabouts, the skills and artistry of these top international designers, whose unique talents soon become evident, even for the layperson. Hardly any style resembles another—and the results of their work are as unique and inspiring as the stories of the people behind them.

Finally, this book may also stimulate your imagination and trigger new ideas that will enhance your own personal home environment for a long time to come. Most importantly, however, please just sit back and relax with this brand-new edition of the *Architecture & Design Review.*

Sebastian Zenker see also pages 188–191
Sebastian Zenker siehe auch Seite 188–191

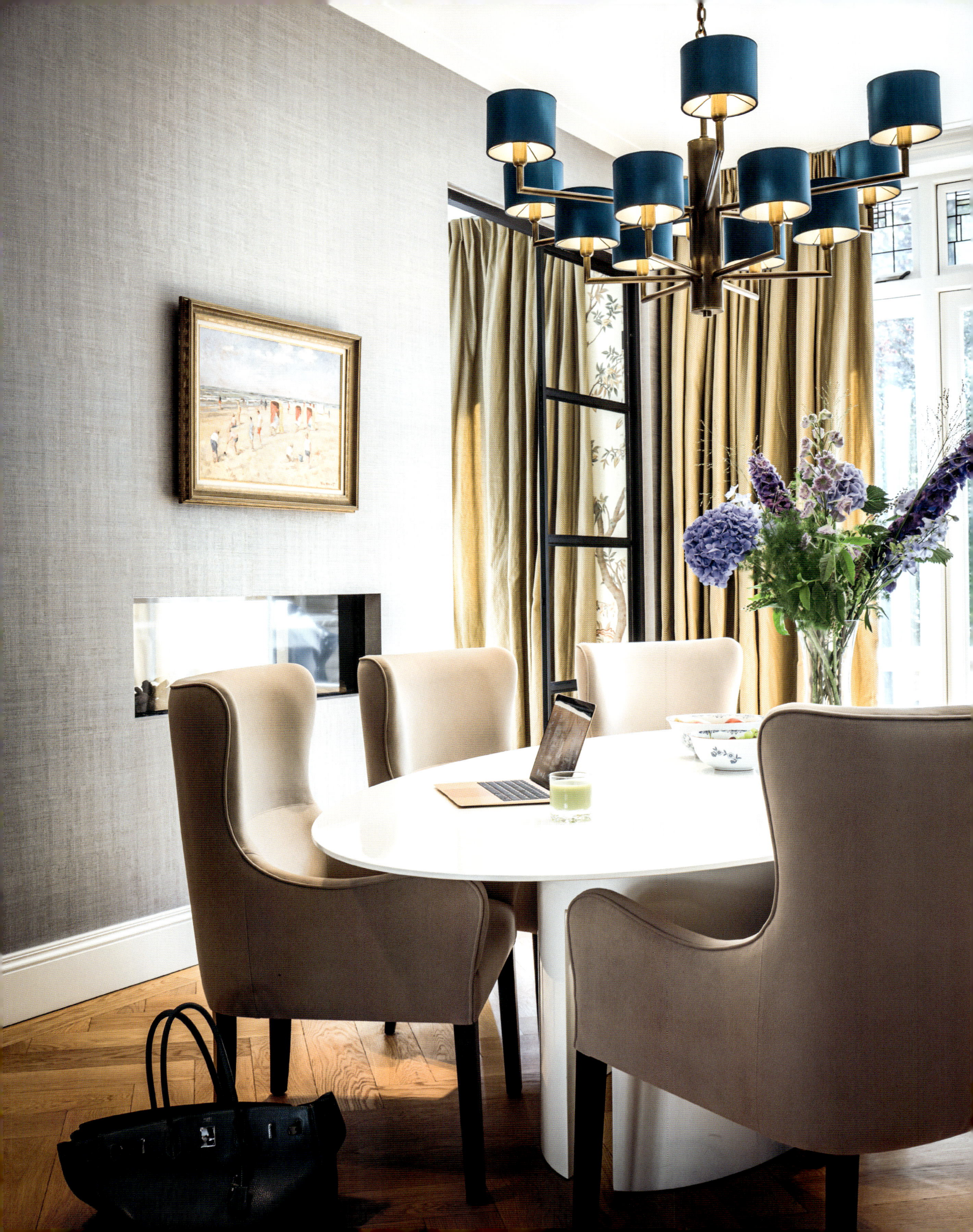

VORWORT

Eine neue Ausgabe des *Architecture & Design Review* liegt in Ihren Händen, und Sie können sich darauf freuen, sie in Ruhe durchzublättern, zu lesen, zu genießen. Auch dieser Band will Sie wieder mitnehmen in die Gedankenwelten, Träume und ganz realen Arbeiten der Top-Gestalter, Handwerker, Architekten, Innenarchitekten und Interior Designer unserer Zeit. Vieles von dem, was hier fotografiert wurde, wird Sie zum Staunen bringen, in Bewunderung versetzen oder einfach gut unterhalten.

Das Stöbern lohnt sich auch diesmal wieder, denn Sie sind eingeladen in ganz besondere Wohnungen, Häuser und Anwesen unterschiedlicher Größenordnung. Nutzen Sie die Gelegenheit, beeindruckend gestaltete Räume zu erkunden, die sonst meist hinter den Mauern, Fenstern und Türen der privaten Besitzer oder Unternehmen verborgen bleiben.

Qualitativ hochwertige, professionelle Aufnahmen, erläutert durch treffende kurze Texte, bringen Ihnen die Faszination meisterhafter Innengestaltung unkompliziert näher. So gewinnen Sie mit dem neuen *Architecture & Design Review* einen aktuellen Eindruck, was im internationalen Interior Design State of the Art ist.

Klassischerweise spielen Interior-Profis aus den USA wieder eine große Rolle, exemplarisch seien hier Rebekah Caudwell, Matthew Frederick oder GWdesign genannt. Viele der in diesem Band vorgestellten Designerinnen und Designer haben ihren Firmensitz aber auch in Europa: etwa Christine Kröncke oder Sebastian Zenker aus Deutschland, Feyrsinger aus Österreich, Alexandra de Garidel aus der Schweiz, Nicky Dobree aus Großbritannien, Stock Dutch Design aus den Niederlanden, Icazar Architects aus Spanien oder die Firma Autoban aus der Türkei, um nur einige Namen und Länder zu nennen. Hinzu kommen erfolgreiche Gestalterinnen und Gestalter aus Kanada, Mexiko, Taiwan, Russland – oder auch aus Indien wie das Unternehmen Mancini Enterprises.

Im Grunde aber spielen räumliche Entfernungen im internationalen Interior Design eine untergeordnete Rolle: Die Frauen, Männer, Paare oder Teams dieser faszinierenden Branche arbeiten nämlich in der Regel überall, wo sie spannende Räume zum Gestalten und interessierte Kunden als Auftraggeber finden.

Grenzen von Ländern und Kontinenten werden schließlich auch für Sie als Leser dieses Buchs ganz mühelos übersprungen und an Bedeutung verlieren. Entdecken Sie überall auf der Welt das Talent und die Kunstfertigkeit dieser internationalen Top-Designer, deren einzigartige Begabungen selbst für den Laien in der Regel sehr schnell deutlich werden. Denn kaum ein Stil gleicht dem anderen, die Ergebnisse ihrer Arbeit sind ebenso besonders und spannend wie die Biografien der Menschen, die dahinterstehen.

Und schließlich soll dieser Band auch Anregungen für Ihre eigene Realität geben. Vielleicht löst das eine oder andere Kapitel ja einen Impuls aus, der Ihre ganz persönlichen Wohnwelten dauerhaft bereichern wird. Aber die Hauptsache soll sein, dass Sie Ihre Stunden des Schauens und Lesens genießen – mit dieser neuen Ausgabe des *Architecture & Design Review*.

Stock Dutch Design see also pages 196–203
Stock Dutch Design siehe auch Seite 196–203

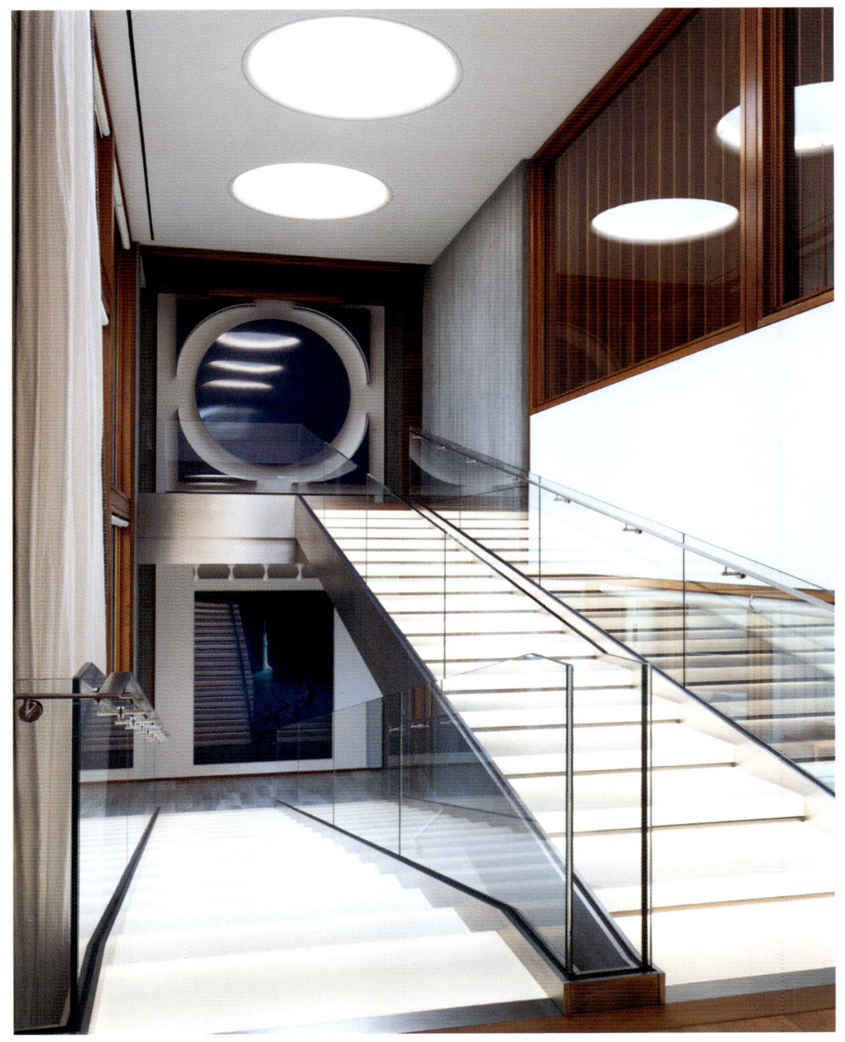

ALEXANDRA DE GARIDEL
Interior Artistic Director for Avilda
VANDŒUVRES / SWITZERLAND

Breathtakingly Cozy | Atemberaubend wohnlich

'A perfect blend of Swiss precision, modernity and an eye for detail,' is how the journalist Ian Phillips describes the work of Alexandra de Garidel, and with it the secret to the interior designer's success and that of her firm Avilda. International companies, alongside private clients throughout the world, appreciate Alexandra de Garidel's architectural knowledge, interior design style and taste in art. The projects presented here on the US coast and in Switzerland are perfect examples of her unique signature: within the breathtaking architecture she has created a delightfully cozy space.

„Eine perfekte Mischung aus Schweizer Präzision, Modernität und Liebe zum Detail", so beschreibt der Journalist Ian Phillips die Arbeit von Alexandra de Garidel und damit das Erfolgsgeheimnis der Innenarchitektin und ihrer Firma Avilda. Internationale Unternehmen, aber auch private Auftraggeber weltweit schätzen das architektonische Wissen, den Interior-Design-Stil sowie den Kunstgeschmack Alexandra de Garidels. Die hier gezeigten Projekte an der US-Küste und in der Schweiz sind perfekte Beispiele für ihre unverwechselbare Signatur, mit der sie in einer atemberaubenden Architektur einen wunderbar wohnlichen Ort geschaffen hat.

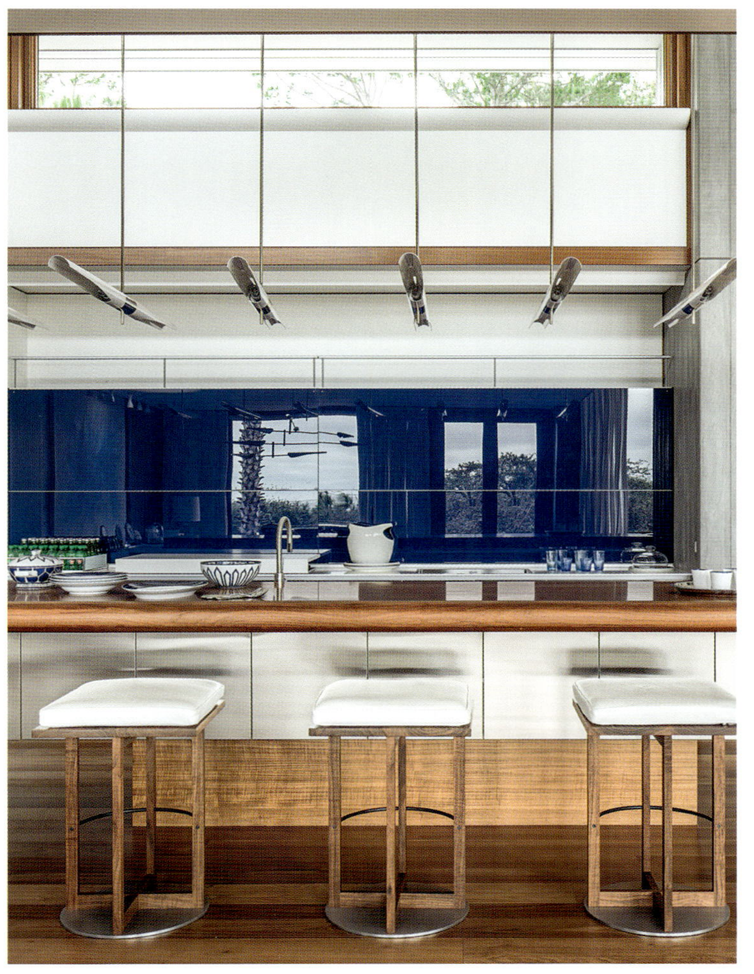

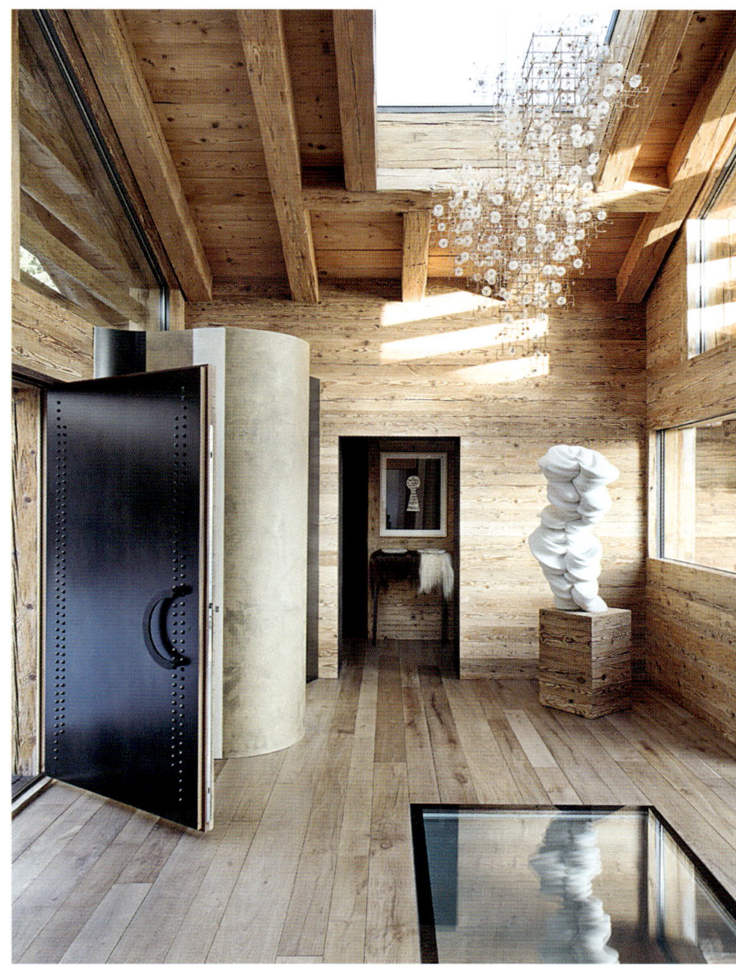

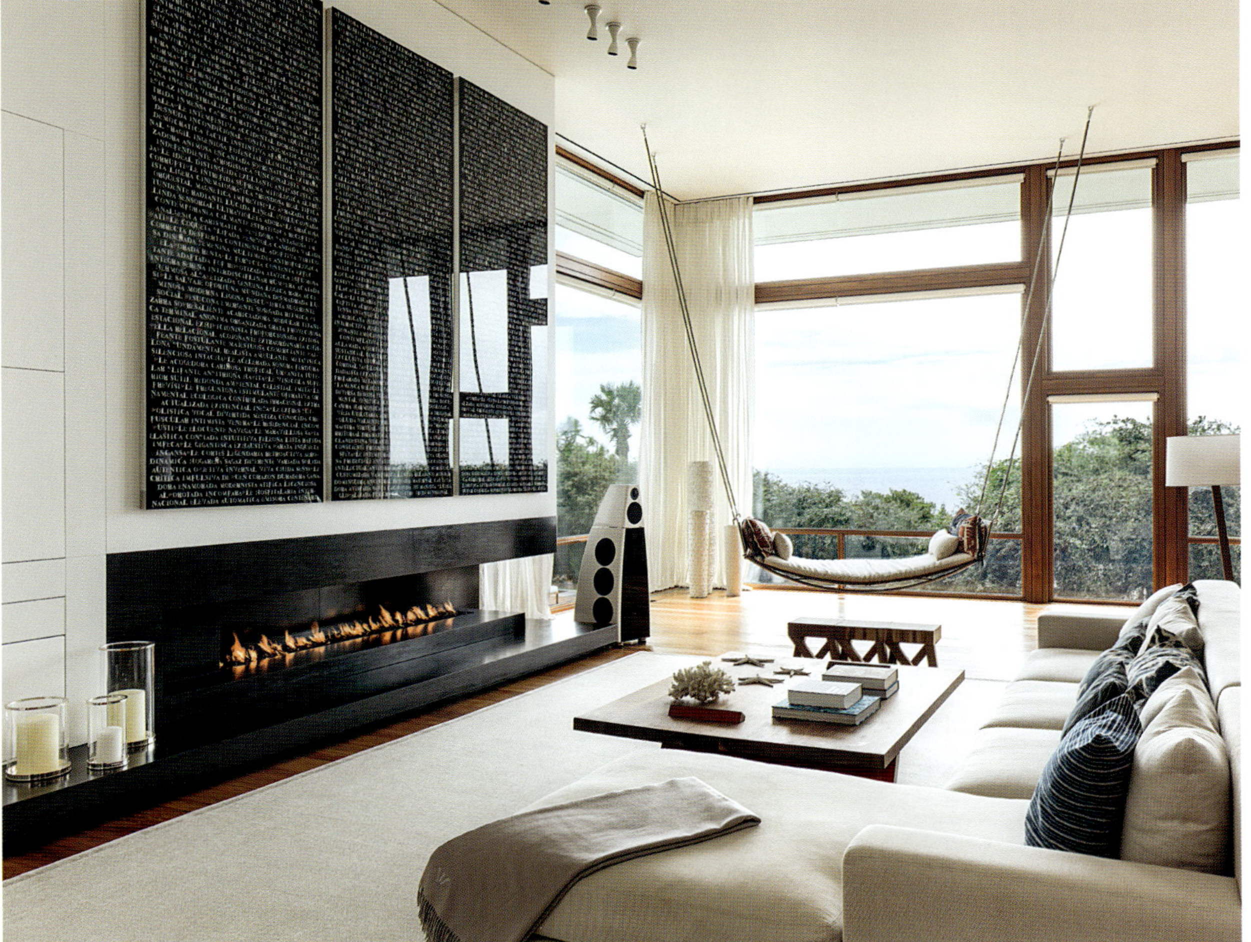

Blue and white are the dominant colors on the stairway (opposite page) and in the kitchen (above left). Unexpected features are the long, low fireplace and a hammock in the living room window (left). Art objects stand and hang in a chalet entrance hall in the Swiss Alps (top right).

Blau und weiß sind die Leitfarben im Treppenhaus (Seite gegenüber) und in der Küche (oben links). Überraschende Elemente sind der lange, niedrige Kamin und eine Hängematte im Fenster des Wohnzimmers (links). Stehende und hängende Kunstobjekte finden sich im Eingangsbereich eines Chalets in den Schweizer Alpen (oben rechts).

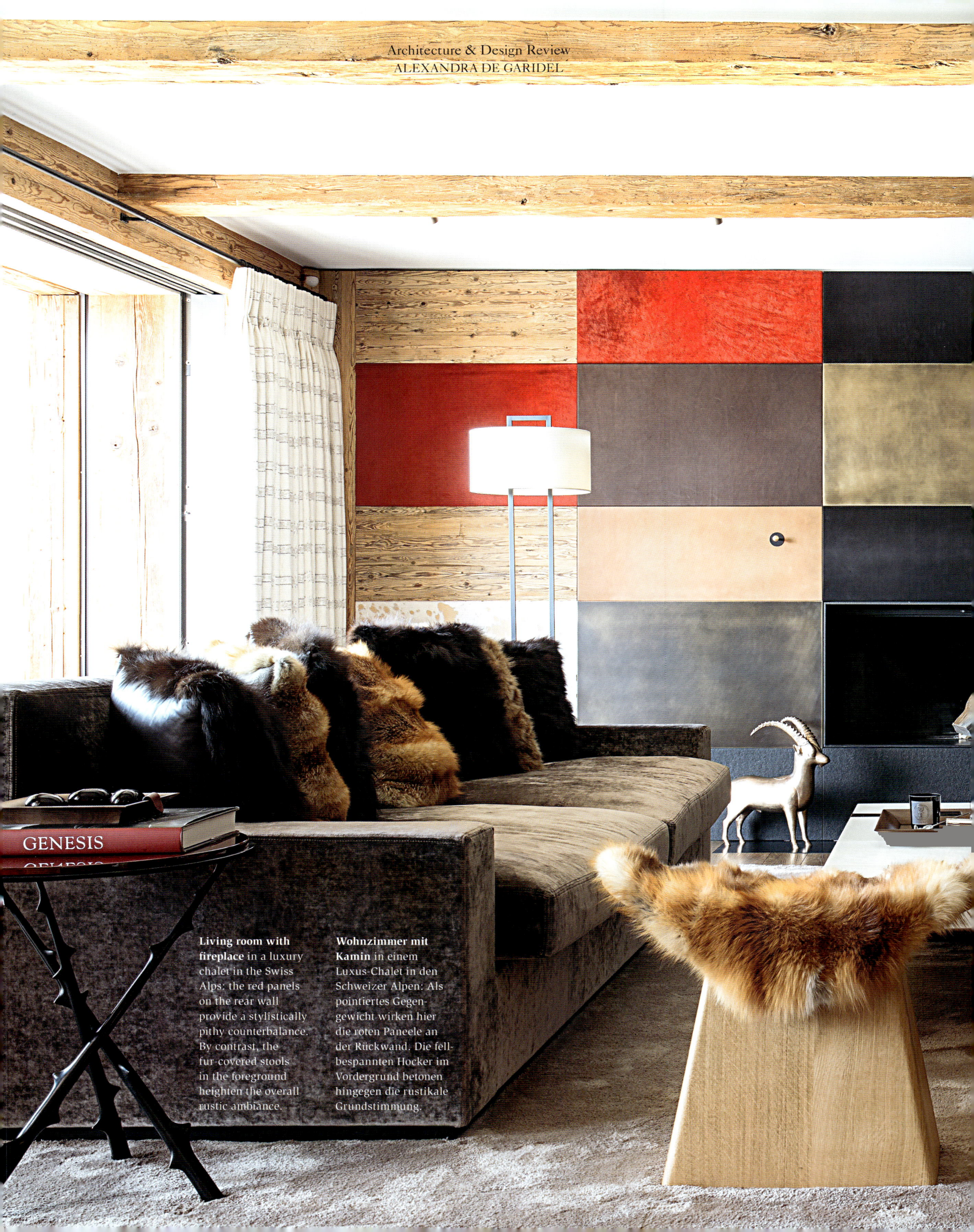

Living room with fireplace in a luxury chalet in the Swiss Alps: the red panels on the rear wall provide a stylistically pithy counterbalance. By contrast, the fur-covered stools in the foreground heighten the overall rustic ambiance.

Wohnzimmer mit Kamin in einem Luxus-Chalet in den Schweizer Alpen: Als pointiertes Gegengewicht wirken hier die roten Paneele an der Rückwand. Die fellbespannten Hocker im Vordergrund betonen hingegen die rustikale Grundstimmung.

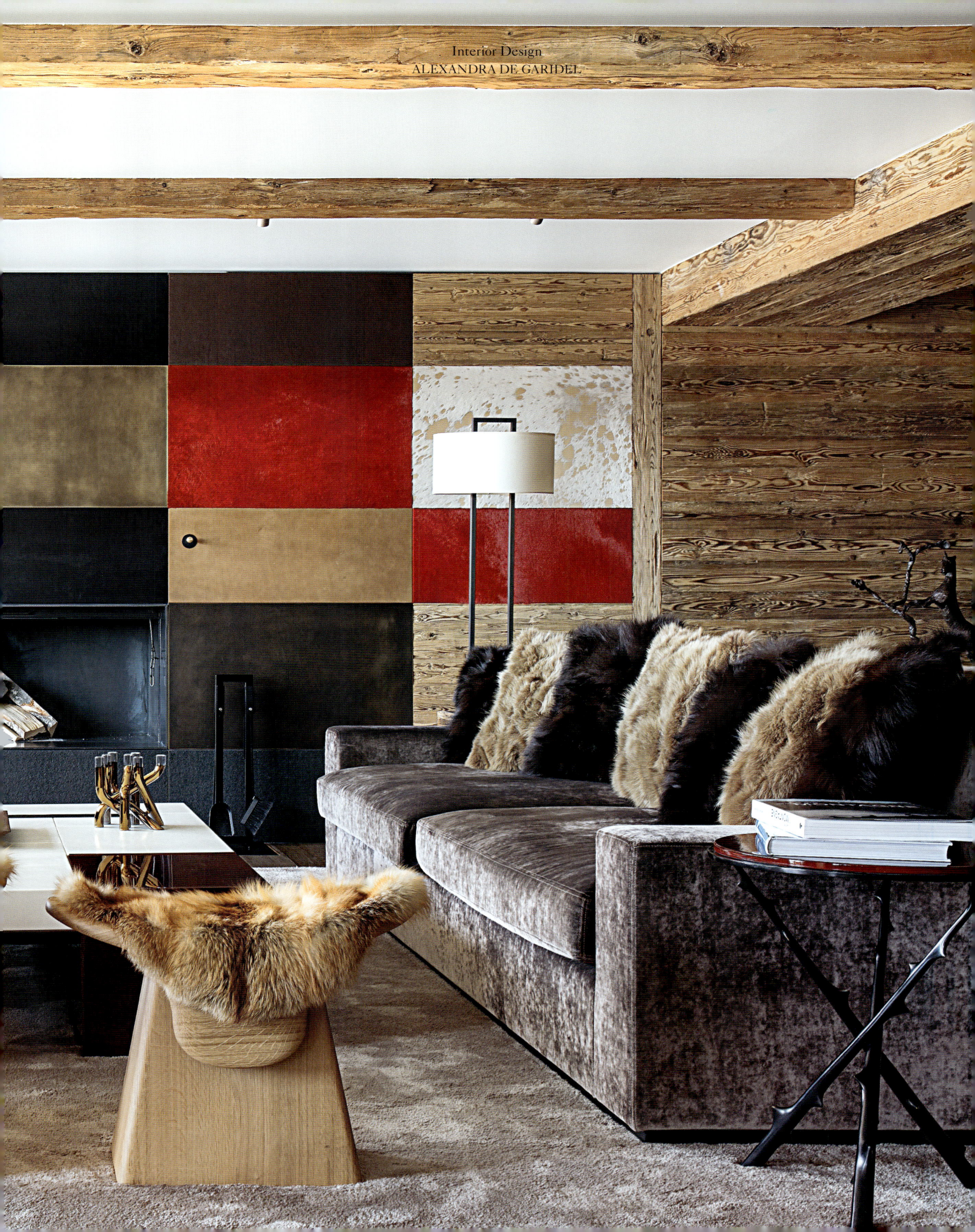
Interior Design
ALEXANDRA DE GARIDEL

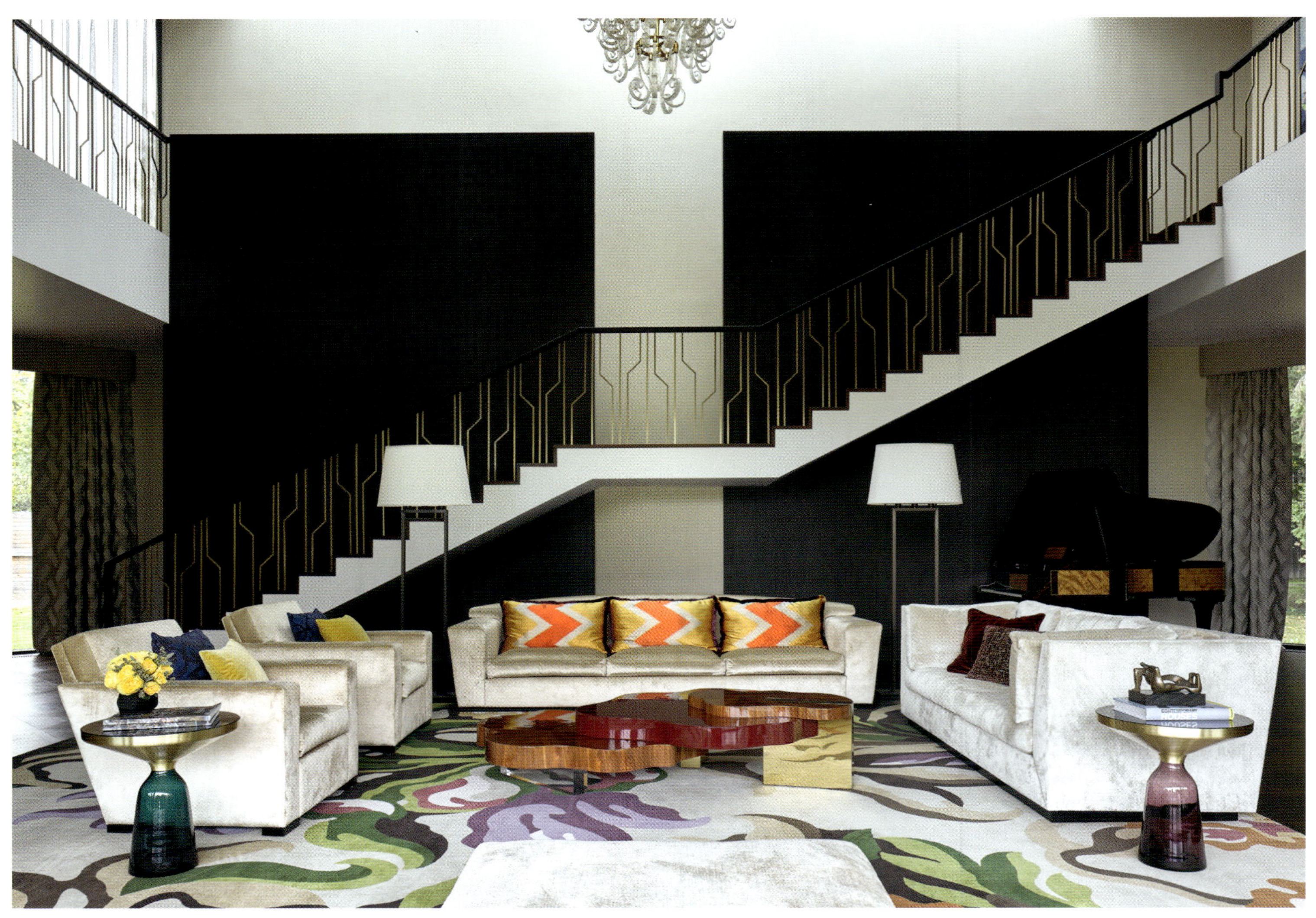

ANGELINA ASKERI

MOSCOW / RUSSIA

Variety and Comfort | Vielfalt und Komfort

The expertise of the Moscow firm Angelina Askeri Interiors extends to both residential and commercial property. Designer Angelina Askeri established the company in 2008, following her graduation from the Istituto Europeo di Design in Milan. Today she works on different projects throughout Europe. The photos show a 2000 square meter property in the Greater Moscow area: the owner's wish was for an elegant, yet comfortable family home. Angelina Askeri opted for an eclectic style featuring elements of American Art Deco. She designed the house with a blend of boiserie, bespoke furniture and a large collection of modern art.

Wohn- und Geschäftsobjekte sind das Spezialgebiet des Moskauer Unternehmens Angelina Askeri Interiors. Designerin Angelina Askeri gründete die Firma 2008, nachdem sie ihr Studium am Istituto Europeo di Design in Mailand abgeschlossen hatte. Heute arbeitet sie europaweit an unterschiedlichen Projekten. Die Fotos zeigen ein 2000 Quadratmeter großes Anwesen im Raum Moskau: Der Eigentümer wünschte sich ein elegantes, aber komfortables Heim für seine Familie. Angelina Askeri entschied sich für einen eklektischen Stil mit Elementen des amerikanischen Art déco, unter anderem mit Paneelen, maßgefertigten Möbeln sowie einer großen Sammlung moderner Kunst.

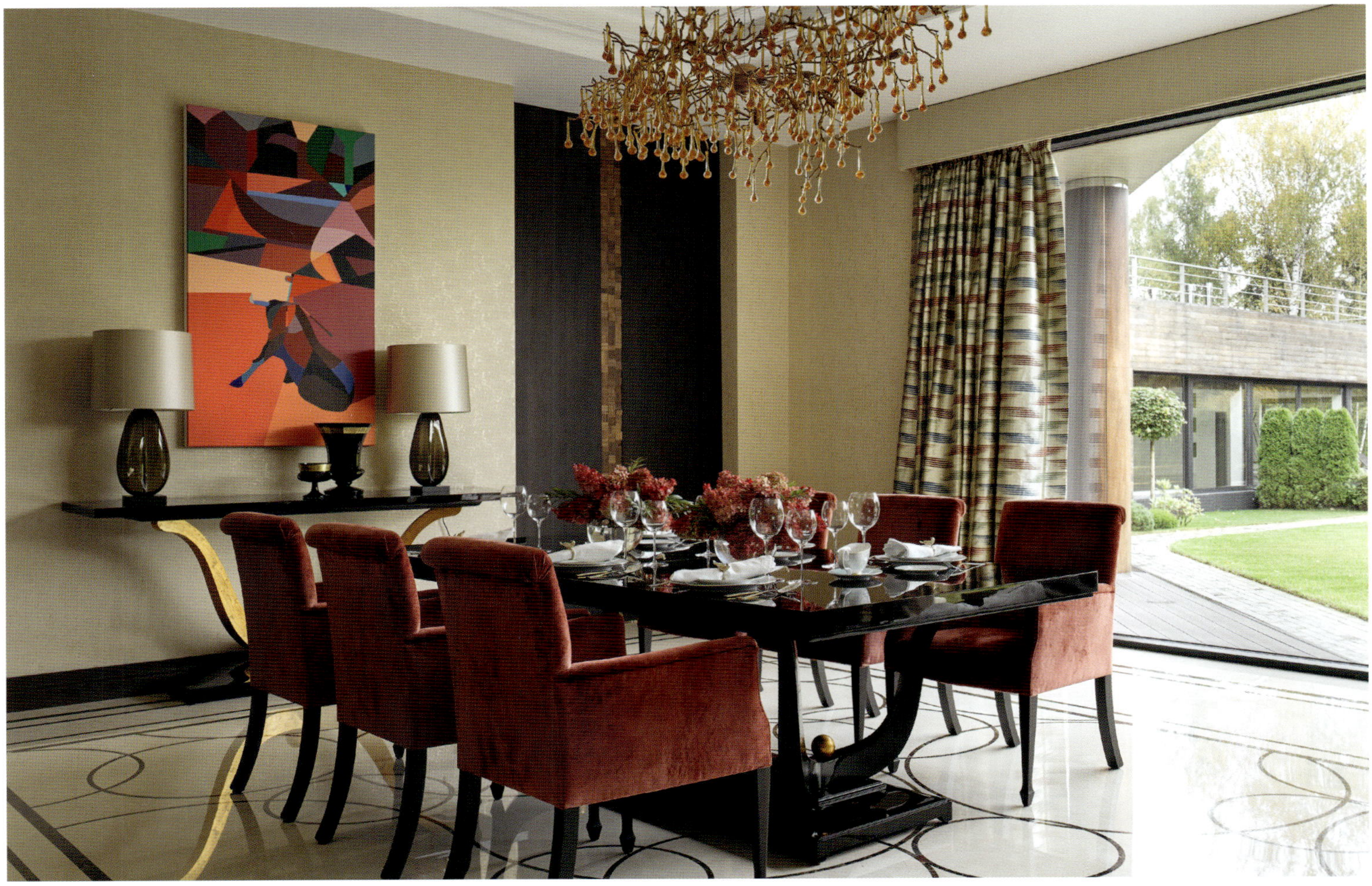

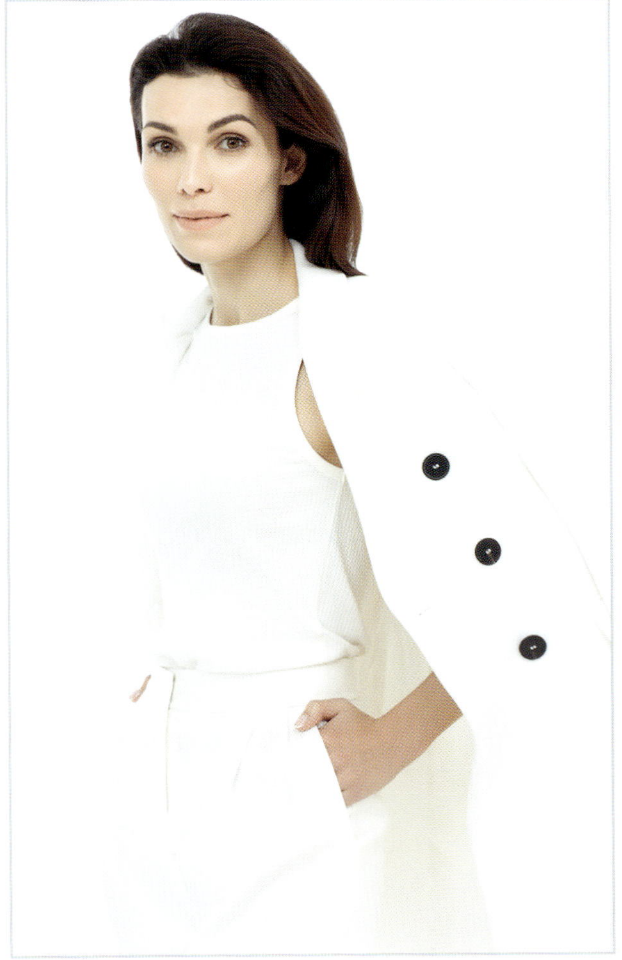

Design, Angelina-Askeri-style: living room (opposite page) with a bright, contrasting carpet and a stairway with a brass banister. A dining room with bright accents (above). Guest bedroom (below).

Gestaltet im Angelina-Askeri-Stil: Wohnzimmer (Seite gegenüber) mit hellem, kontrastierendem Teppich und Treppe mit Messinggeländer. Hell akzentuiertes Esszimmer (oben). Gästeschlafzimmer (unten).

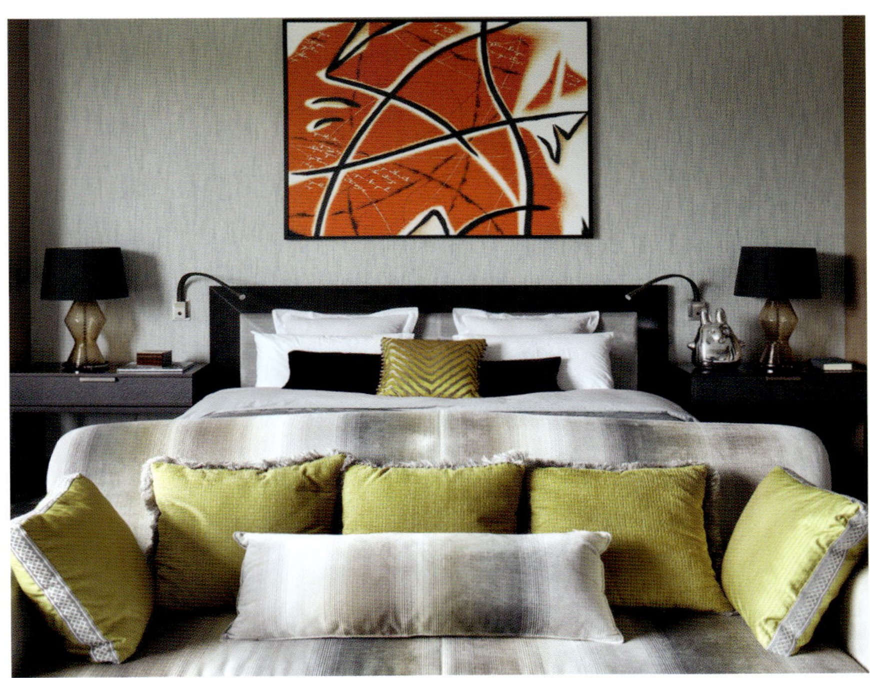

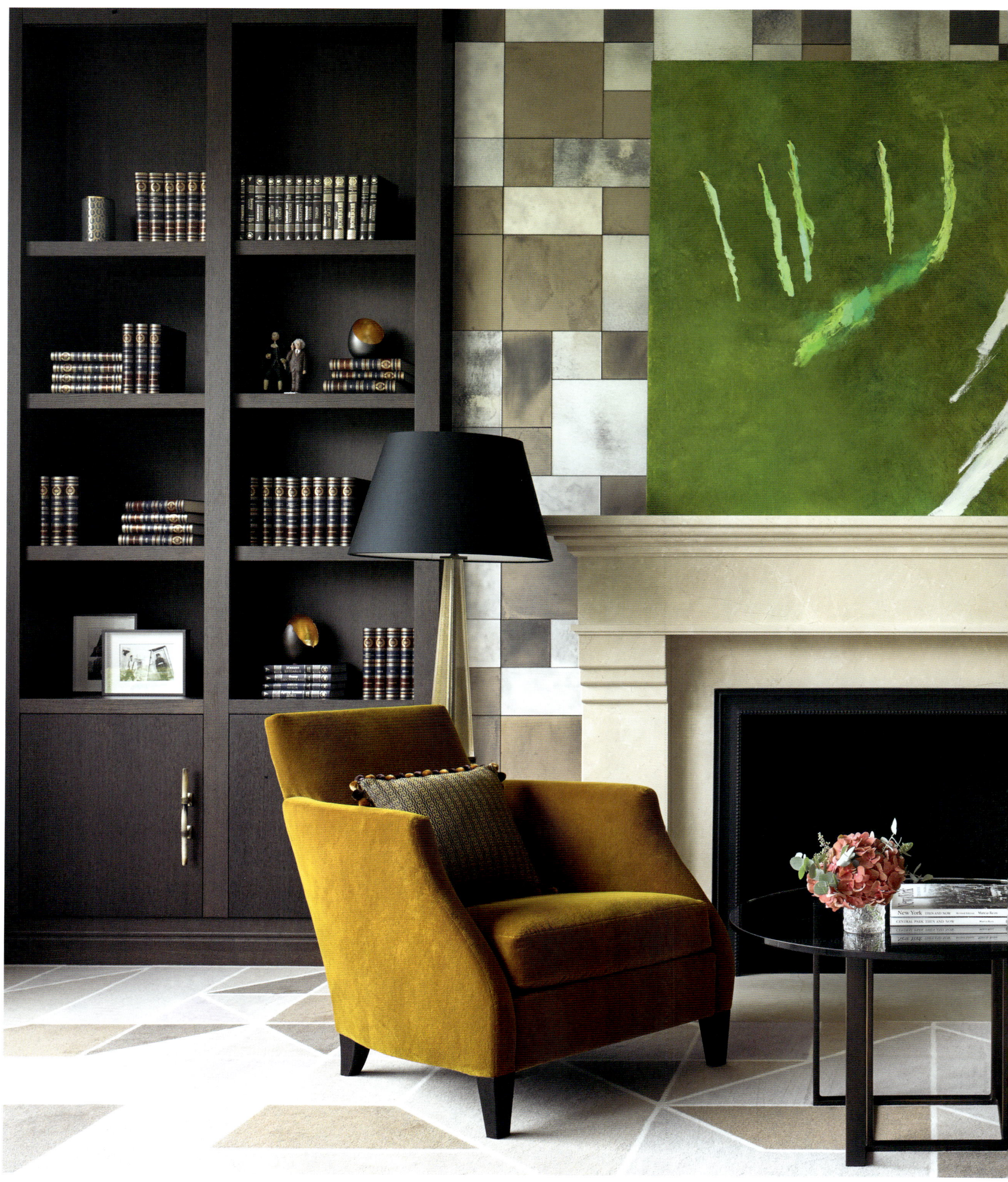

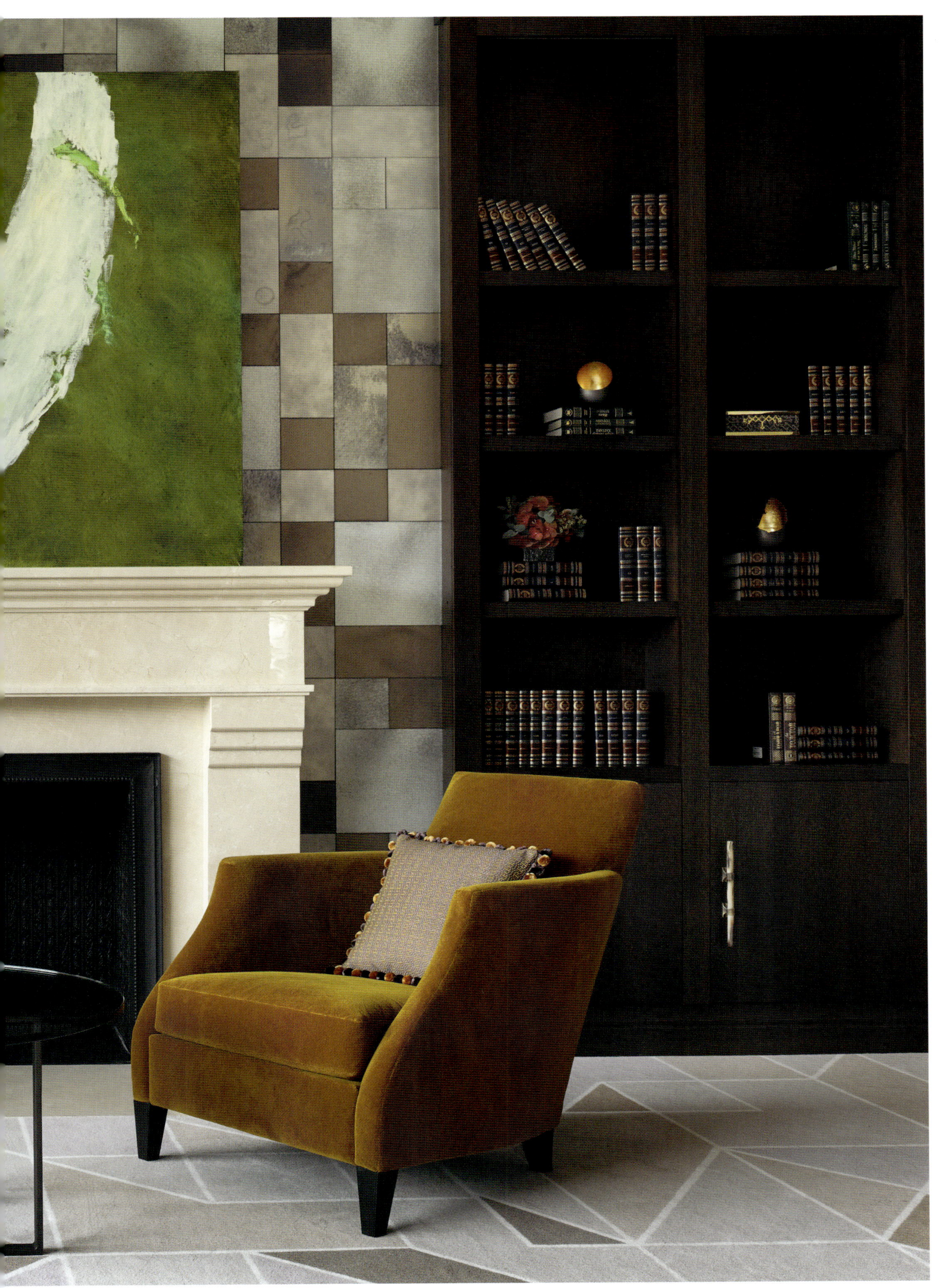

Bookcases and a painting turn this master bedroom sitting area into a place of cultivated relaxation, while the light marble fireplace creates a calm, cozy ambiance. The matching carpet was manufactured in Germany based on Askeri's custom designs.

Bücherregale und ein Gemälde machen diese Sitzecke im Hauptschlafzimmer zu einem Ort kultivierter Entspannung, während der Kamin aus hellem Marmor ein heiteres, gemütliches Ambiente schafft. Der passende Teppichboden wurde nach individuellen Entwürfen Askeris in Deutschland hergestellt.

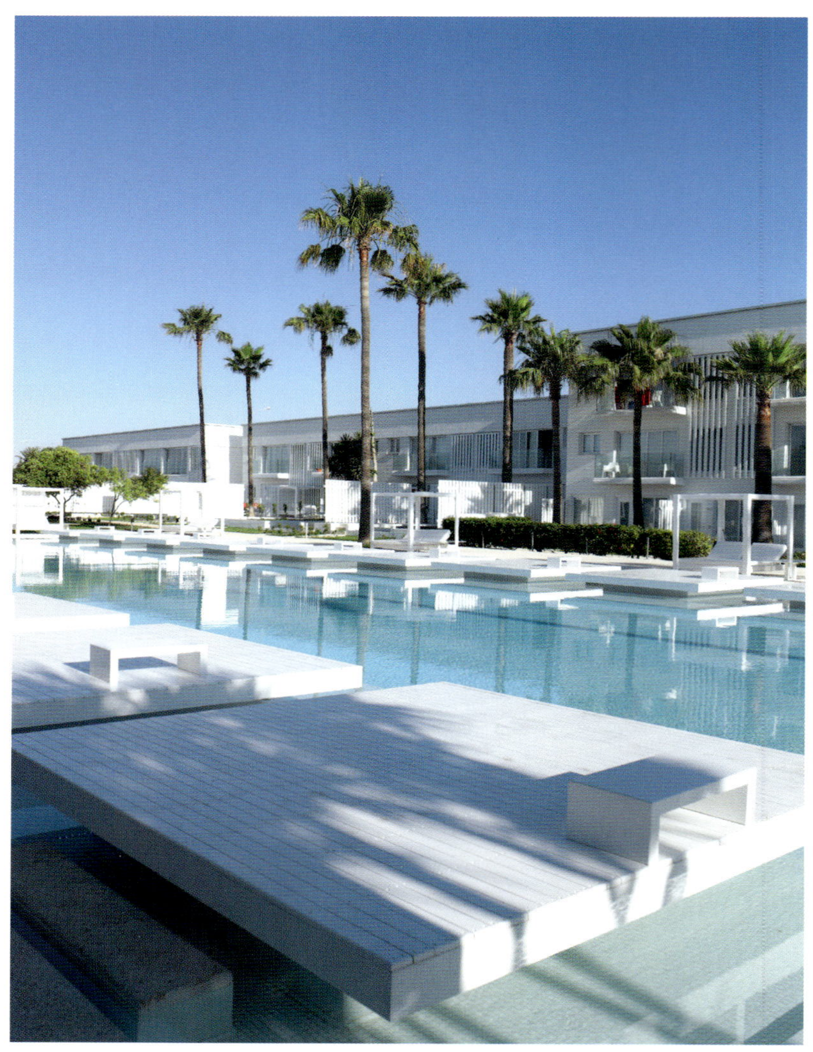

ANGELOS ANGELOPOULOS ASSOCIATES DESIGN

ATHENS / GREECE

Better Quality of Life | Mehr Lebensqualität

Architecture, landscaping, home decor, as well as façade, furniture and lighting design, are all part of the portfolio of Angelos Angelopoulos Associates. In addition to private residential projects, the firm focuses primarily on hotels and restaurants, as well as residential and urban development. Angelopoulos lives in Athens but works in the most diverse locations throughout Europe and the US. His firm has, among other things, designed the interiors of more than a hundred hotels. Angelopoulos always regards interior design as a tool for improving our quality of life and even our way of thinking.

Architektur, Fassaden- und Landschaftsgestaltung, Möbel- und Lichtdesign, Innenarchitektur – das alles gehört zum Portfolio von Angelos Angelopoulos Associates. Der Schwerpunkt liegt neben privaten Wohnprojekten jedoch vor allem auf Hotels und Restaurants sowie auf der Wohn- und Stadtentwicklung. Angelopoulos lebt in Athen, ist aber an den verschiedensten Orten Europas und der USA tätig. Sein Unternehmen hat unter anderem die Innenausstattung von über hundert Hotels entworfen. Angelopoulos begreift die Innenarchitektur dabei immer auch als ein Werkzeug, das die Lebensqualität und sogar unsere Art zu Denken verbessern kann.

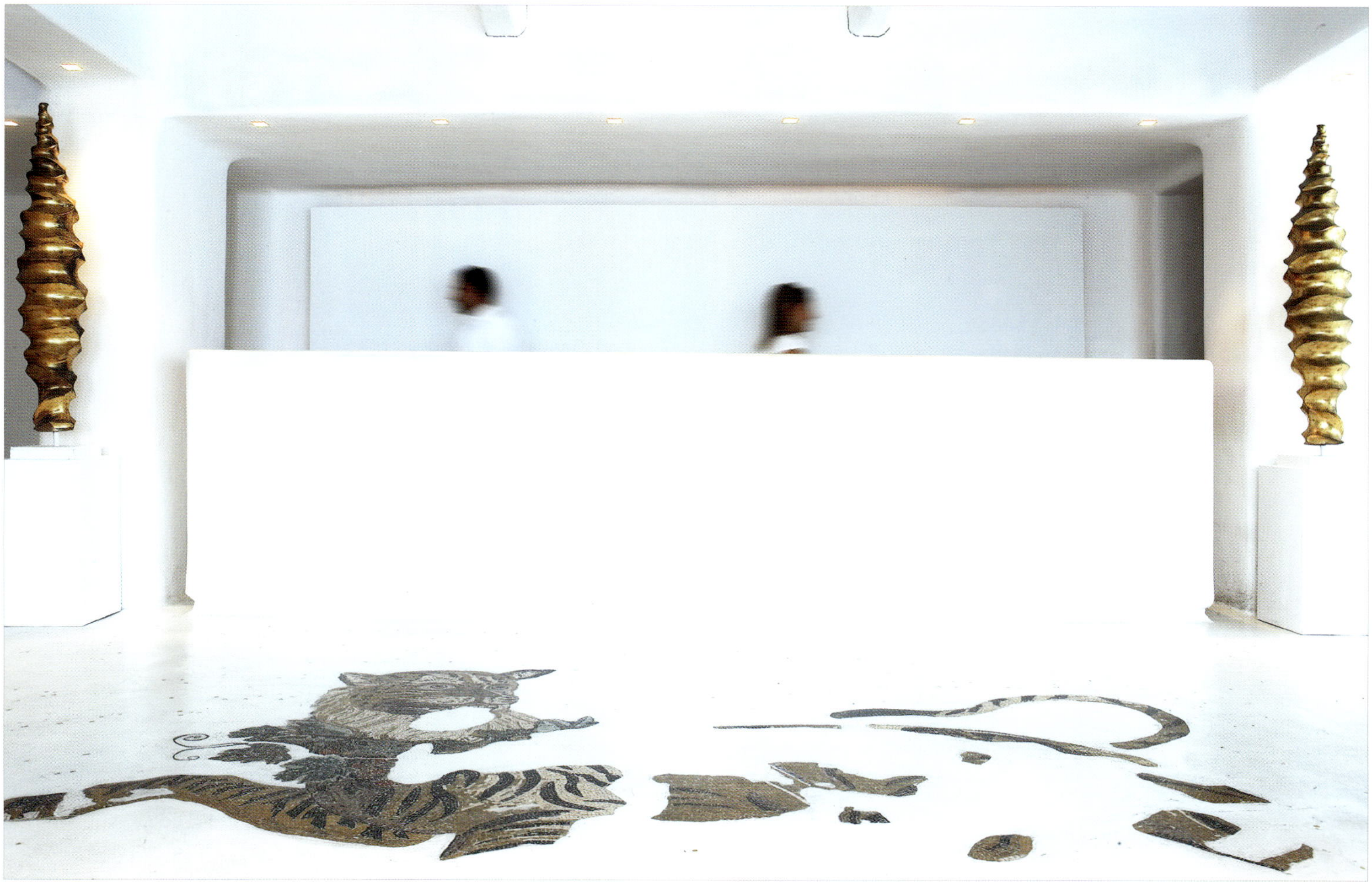

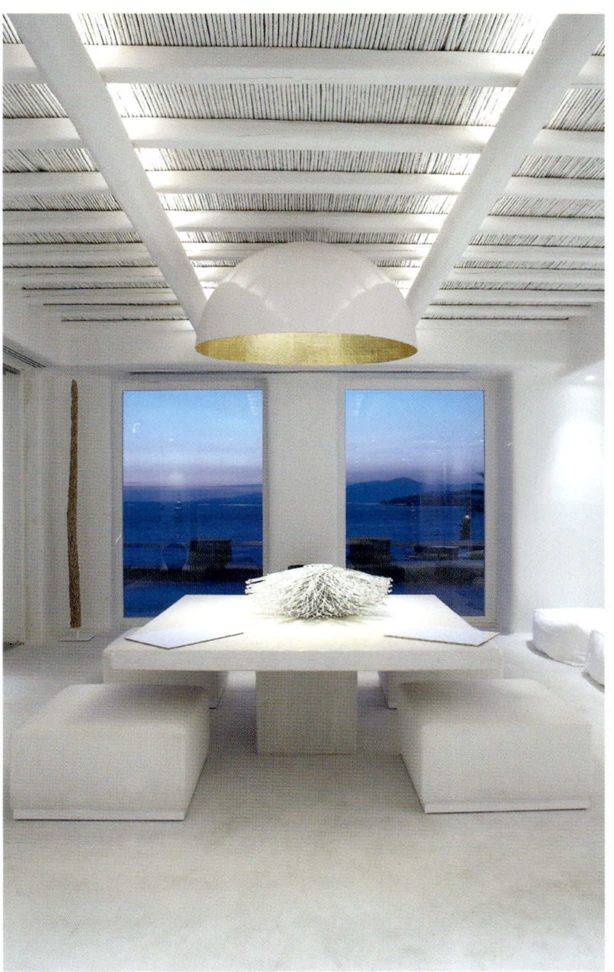

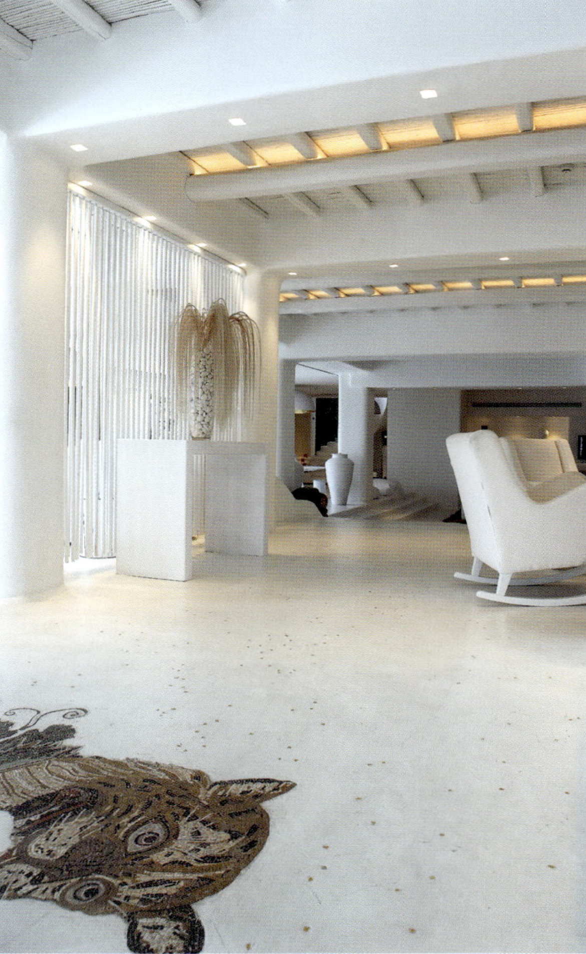

Hotel Cavotagoo on the island of Mykonos: white elegance also dominates Angelos Angelopoulos' design when it comes to exteriors (opposite page). And as for interiors, the pervasive base color is set off by carefully selected counterpoints, as achieved here by the gold of the art objects and lamps, as well as the floor mosaic in the foyer (left).

Hotel Cavotagoo auf Mykonos: Auch im Außenbereich dominiert edles Weiß das Design von Angelos Angelopoulos (Seite gegenüber). Im Innern wird die allgegenwärtige Grundfarbe durch sorgfältig gewählte Kontrapunkte betont, wie hier vom Gold der Kunstobjekte, Lampen und dem Bodenmosaik im Foyer (links).

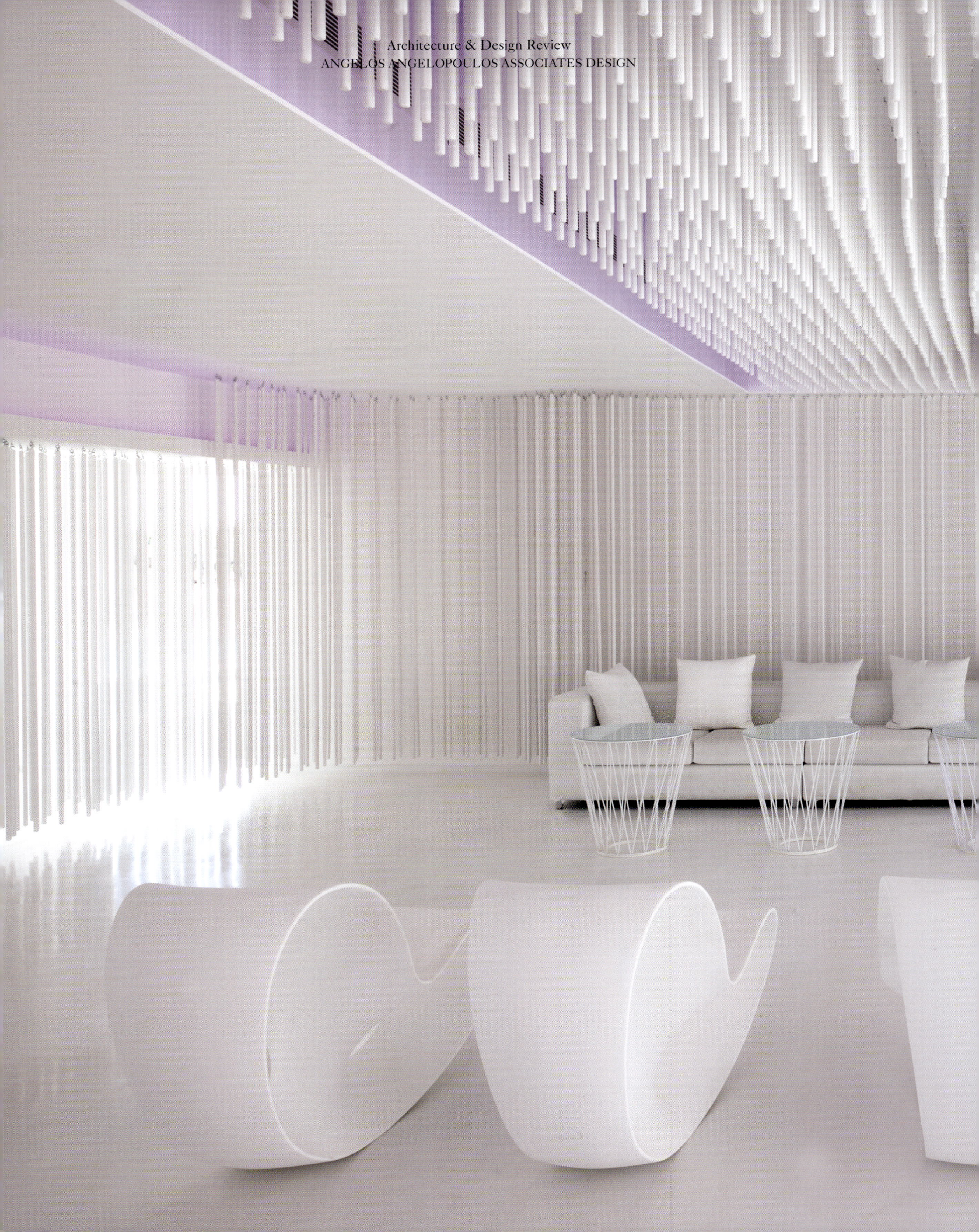

Architecture & Design Review
ANGELOS ANGELOPOULOS ASSOCIATES DESIGN

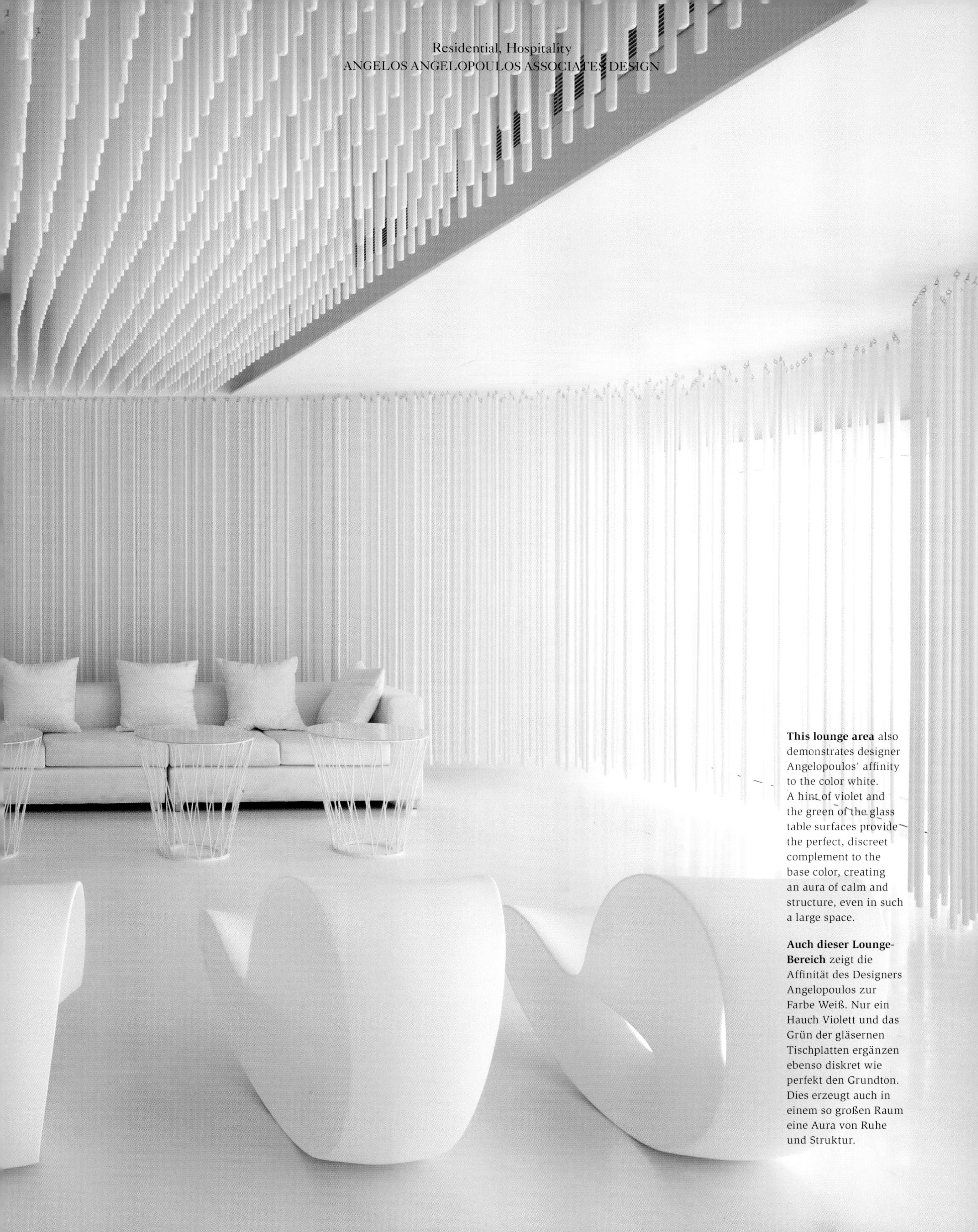

This lounge area also demonstrates designer Angelopoulos' affinity to the color white. A hint of violet and the green of the glass table surfaces provide the perfect, discreet complement to the base color, creating an aura of calm and structure, even in such a large space.

Auch dieser Lounge-Bereich zeigt die Affinität des Designers Angelopoulos zur Farbe Weiß. Nur ein Hauch Violett und das Grün der gläsernen Tischplatten ergänzen ebenso diskret wie perfekt den Grundton. Dies erzeugt auch in einem so großen Raum eine Aura von Ruhe und Struktur.

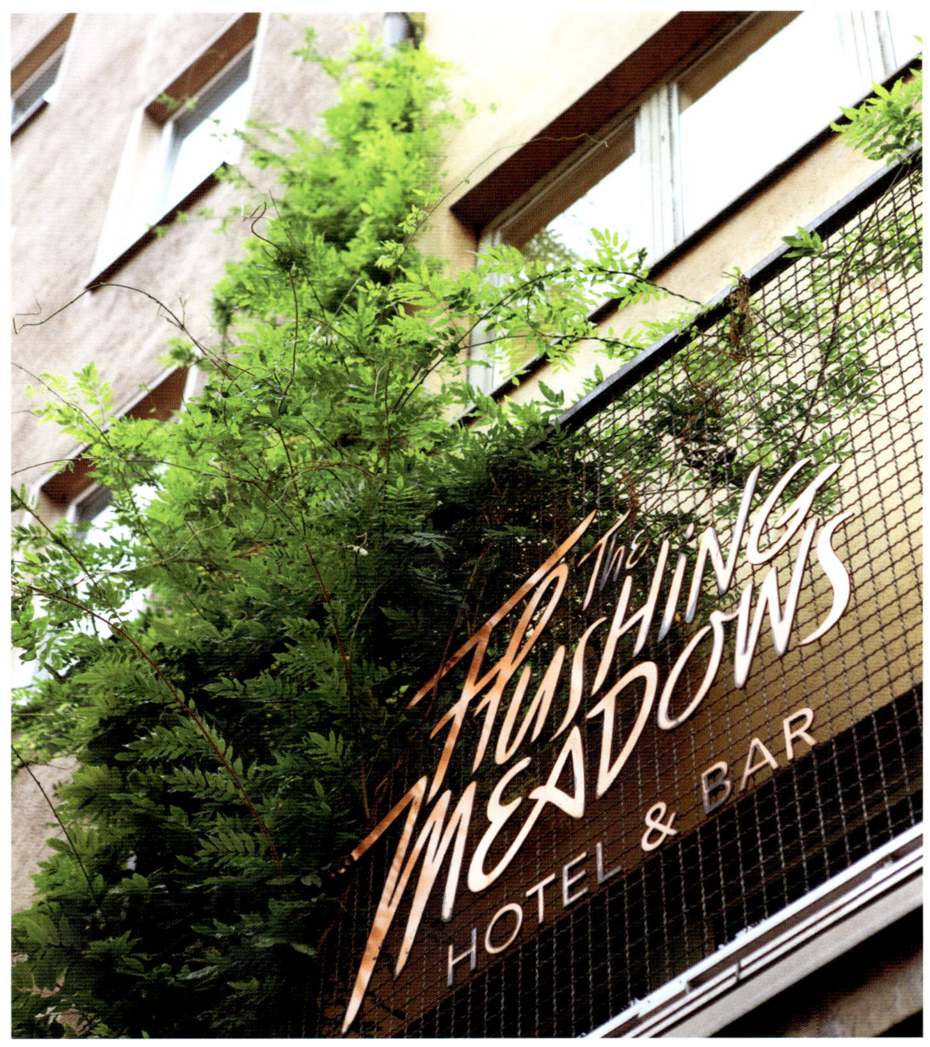

ARNOLD / WERNER

MUNICH / GERMANY

Well-conceived Details | Durchdachte Details

The Munich firm Arnold / Werner is a byword for architecture and interior design that has been thought through in detail without losing sight of the big picture. The firm handles the development and detailed drafting of the projects—from the building's shell to the interior and individual rooms. The team also specializes in sustainable and environmentally-friendly construction. A former 1970s technical building in Munich's Glockenbach district was converted into the Flushing Meadows Hotel & Bar in cooperation with the design studio Fantomas. There are eleven loft studios on the third floor and five penthouse studios on the fourth, as well as an open rooftop bar for all visitors.

Architektur und Innenarchitektur, bis ins Detail durchdacht, ohne das große Ganze aus den Augen zu verlieren – dafür stehen Arnold / Werner. Von der Gebäudehülle über die Innenräume bis hin zum Interieur übernimmt das Münchner Unternehmen die Entwicklung und detaillierte Ausarbeitung der Projekte. Zudem ist die Firma Spezialist für nachhaltiges, klimapositives Bauen. Im Münchner Glockenbachviertel wurde in Zusammenarbeit mit dem Designstudio Fantomas ein ehemaliges Technikgebäude aus den 1970er-Jahren zum Flushing Meadows Hotel & Bar umgebaut: elf Loft-Studios im dritten und fünf Penthouse-Studios im vierten Stock sowie eine für alle Besucher offene Rooftop-Bar.

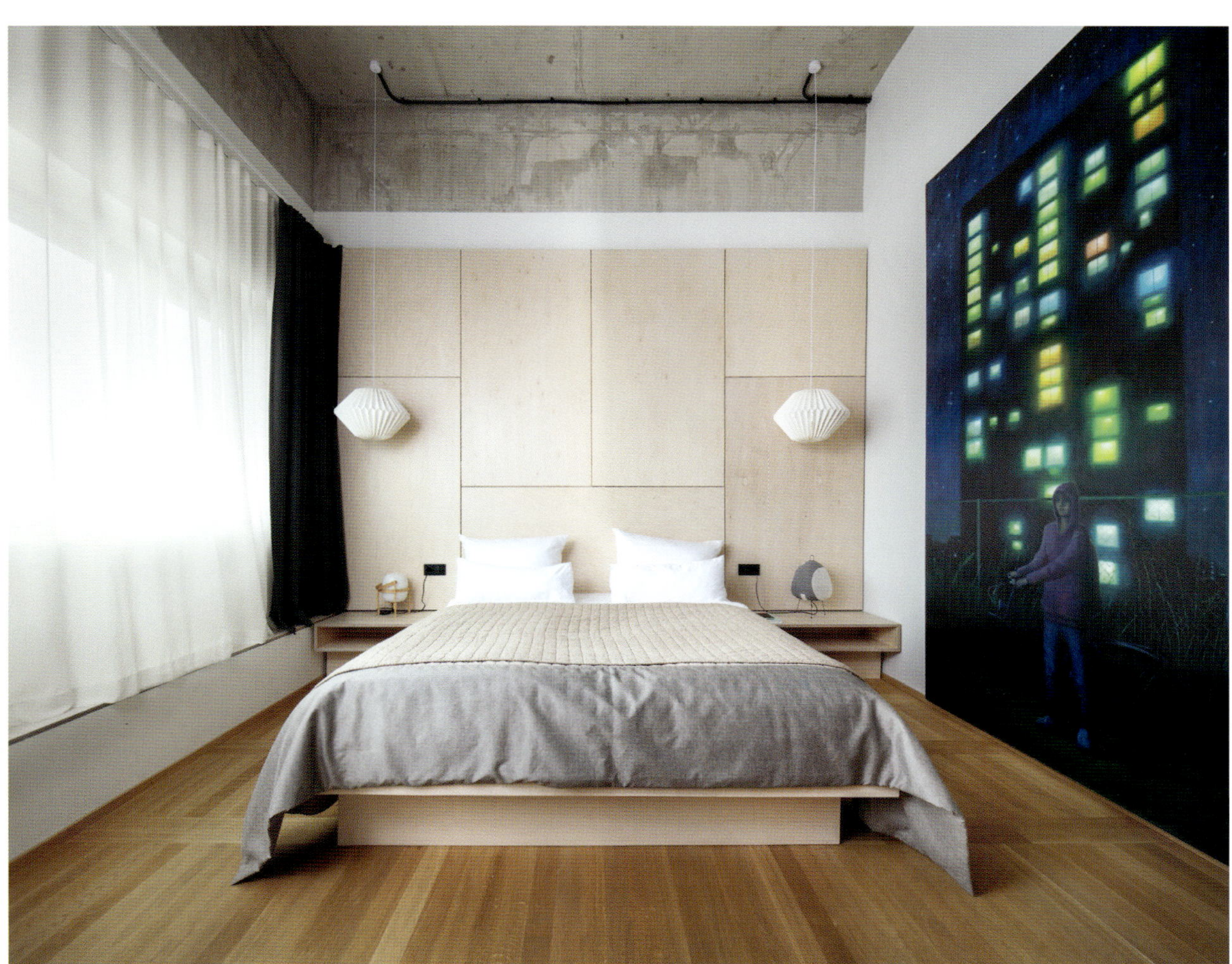

Some of the studios (left) were custom-designed together with personalities from the fields of music, theatre, design, fine dining, fashion, sport, and art. Warm colors, wooden surfaces, fabric wall panels, and the open wood stove create a welcoming atmosphere in the bar (below).

Einige der Studios (links) wurden gemeinsam mit Persönlichkeiten aus Musik, Schauspiel, Design, Gastronomie, Mode, Sport und Kunst jeweils individuell gestaltet. Der Barraum (unten) schafft durch warme Farbtöne, Holzoberflächen, Wandpaneele aus Stoff sowie den offenen Holzofen eine einladende Atmosphäre.

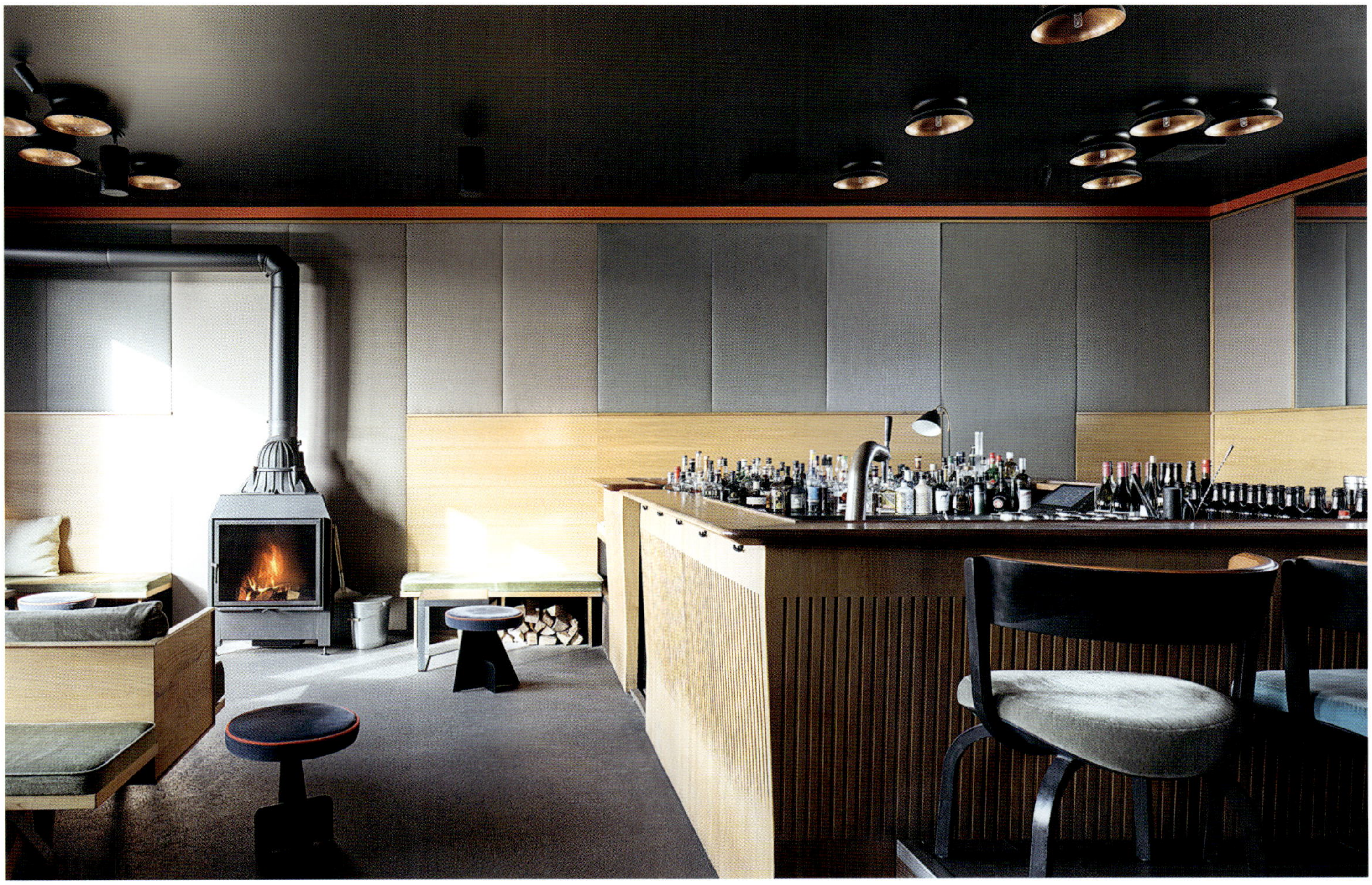

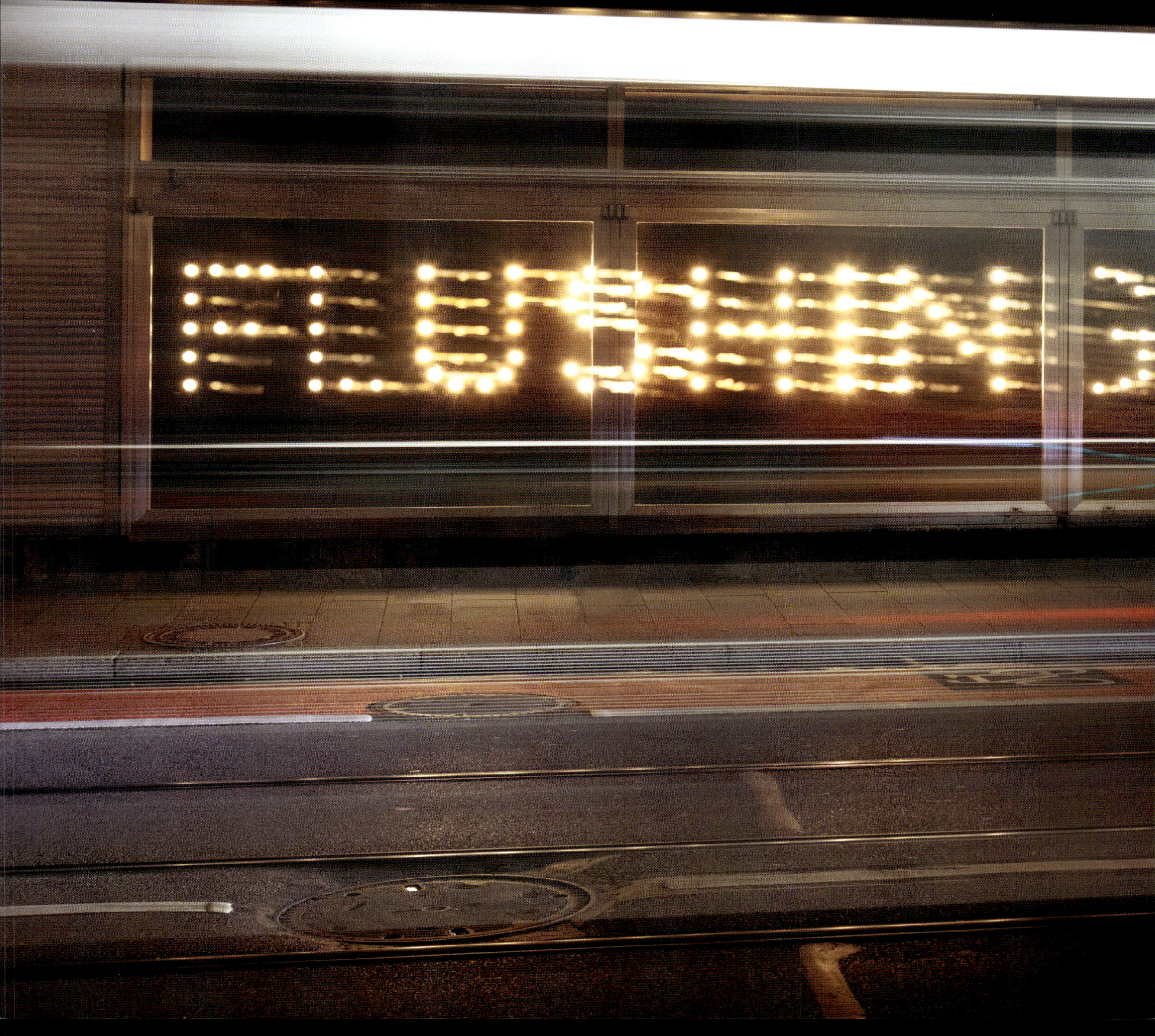

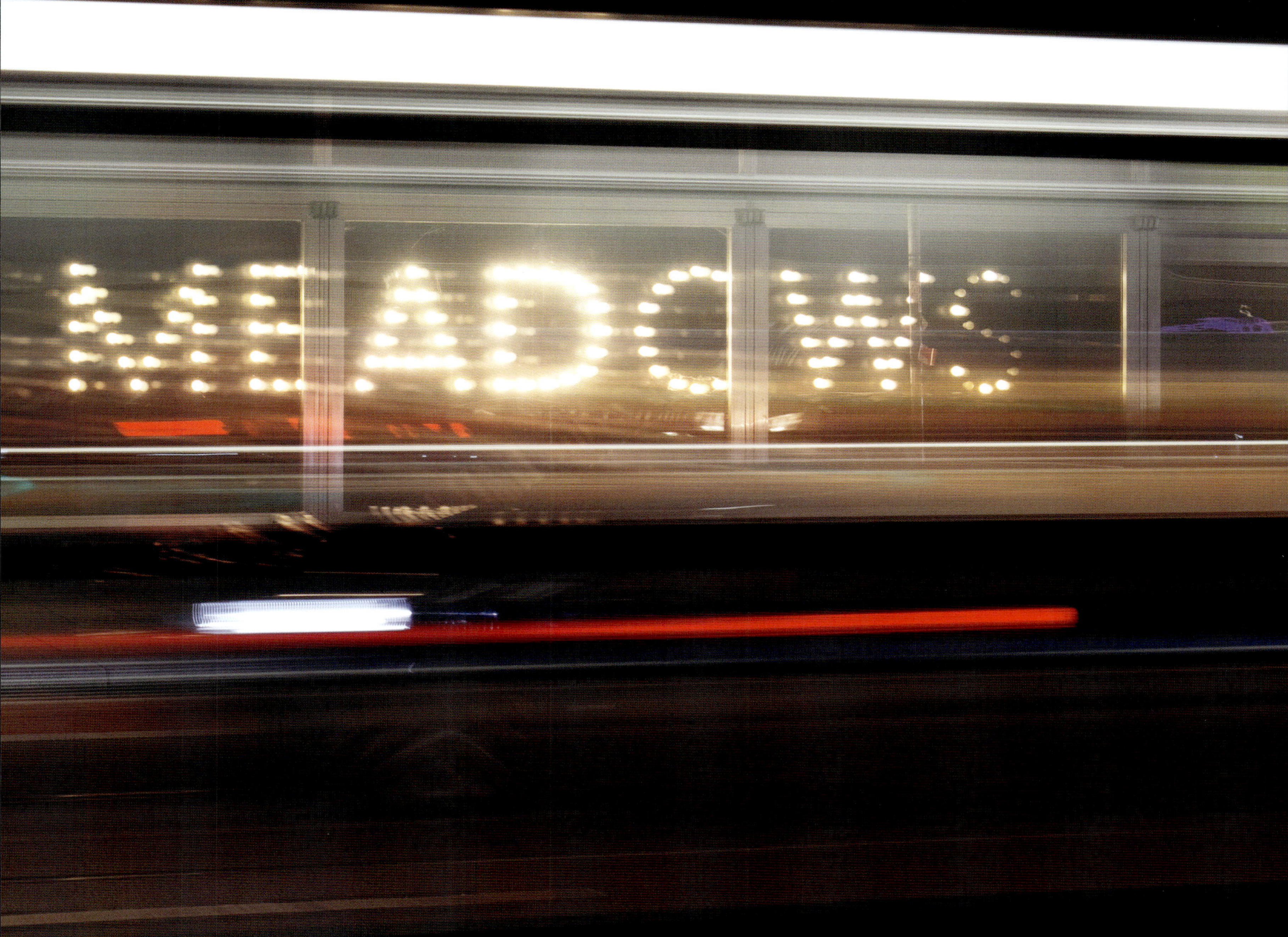

MEADOWS

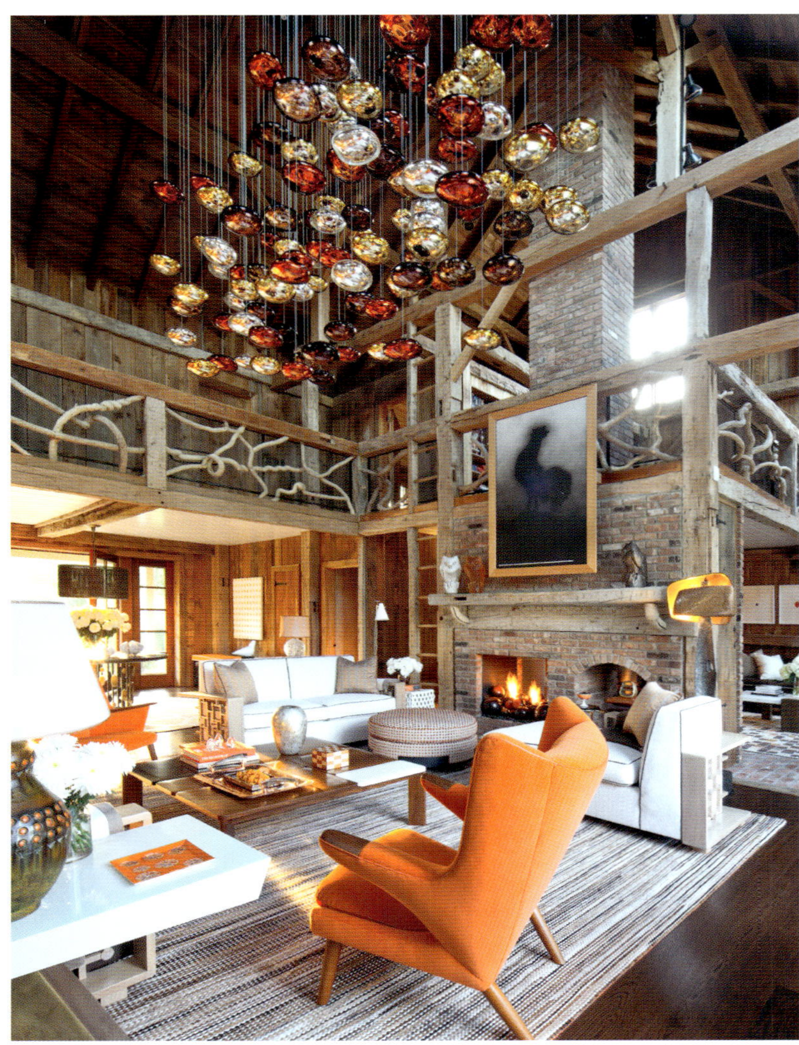

ARTHUR DUNNAM
FOR JED JOHNSON STUDIO

NEW YORK / USA

Design with Personality | Design mit Persönlichkeit

The company Arthur Dunnam for Jed Johnson Studio was established in 2016 to continue the successful work of Jed Johnson Associates, for which Mr. Dunnam served as Design Director since the founder's untimely death in 1996. Arthur had worked alongside Mr. Johnson for ten years prior to becoming Design Director of the firm. The photos present two typical properties: a barn conversion in the Hamptons and a recently designed holiday home in Palm Beach. One of the designer team's greatest strengths is its close cooperation with clients, thereby allowing the latter's personalities, wishes, and dreams to become part of the projects.

Das Unternehmen Arthur Dunnam for Jed Johnson Studio wurde Ende 2016 gegründet, um die erfolgreiche Arbeit des Designstudios Jed Johnson Associates fortzusetzen. Arthur Dunnam hatte mit Jed Johnson bereits zehn Jahre lang zusammengearbeitet und war nach dessen tragischem frühen Tod 1996 Design Director von Jed Johnson Associates geworden. Die Fotos zeigen zwei typische Objekte: Eine umgestaltete Scheunenwohnung in den Hamptons sowie eine frisch designte Saisonwohnung in Palm Beach. Eine große Stärke des Designerteams ist die enge Zusammenarbeit mit den Kunden, denn so fließen deren Persönlichkeiten, Wünsche und Träume in die Projekte ein.

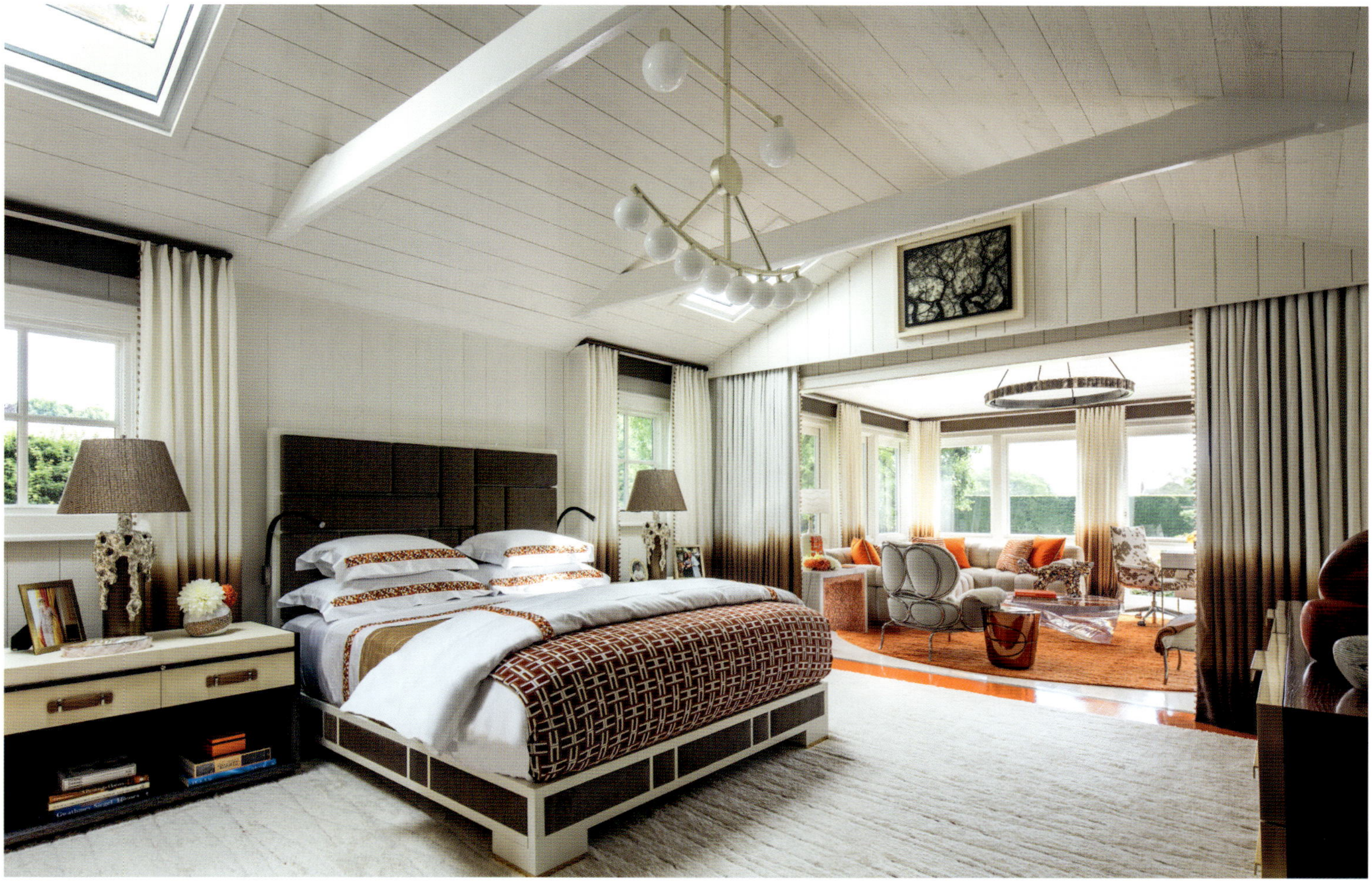

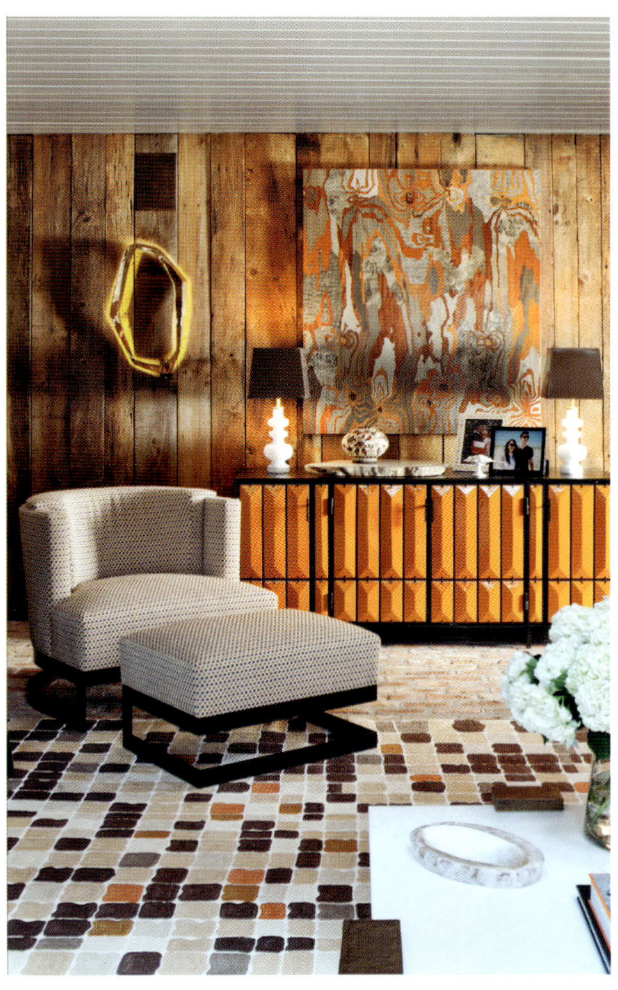

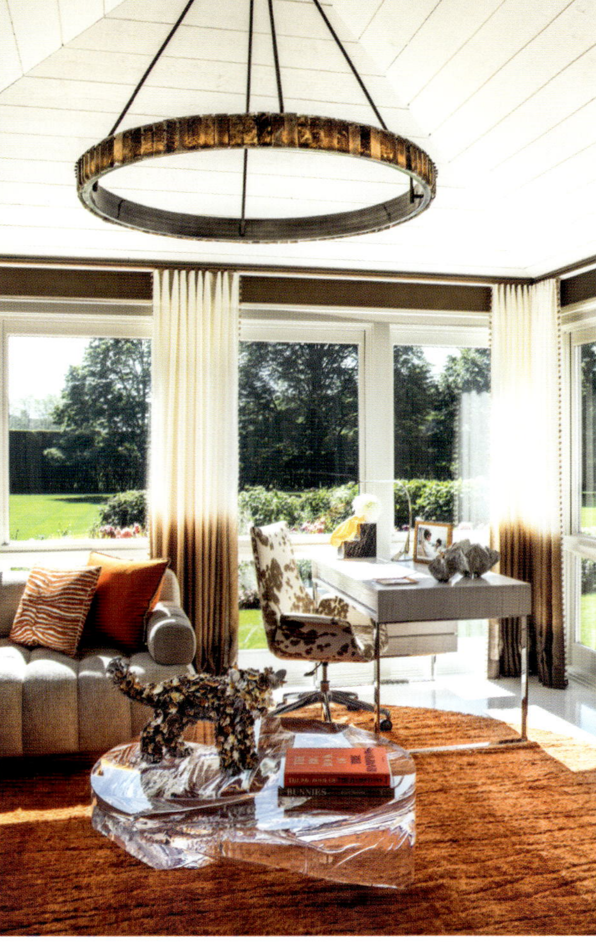

This project involved the conversion of an eighteenth century barn that was in need of a 'new breath of fresh air.' The original character of this relatively modest historic residence was, however, to be maintained. Almost without exception, the dark and uncomfortable furniture was replaced by designer pieces.

Kern dieses Projekts war die Umgestaltung einer Scheune aus dem 18. Jahrhundert, die „viel frischen Wind" benötigte. Der ursprüngliche Charakter einer relativ einfachen historischen Wohnstätte sollte jedoch erhalten bleiben. Bis auf wenige Ausnahmen wurden hier dunkle und unbequeme Möbel durch Designerstücke ersetzt.

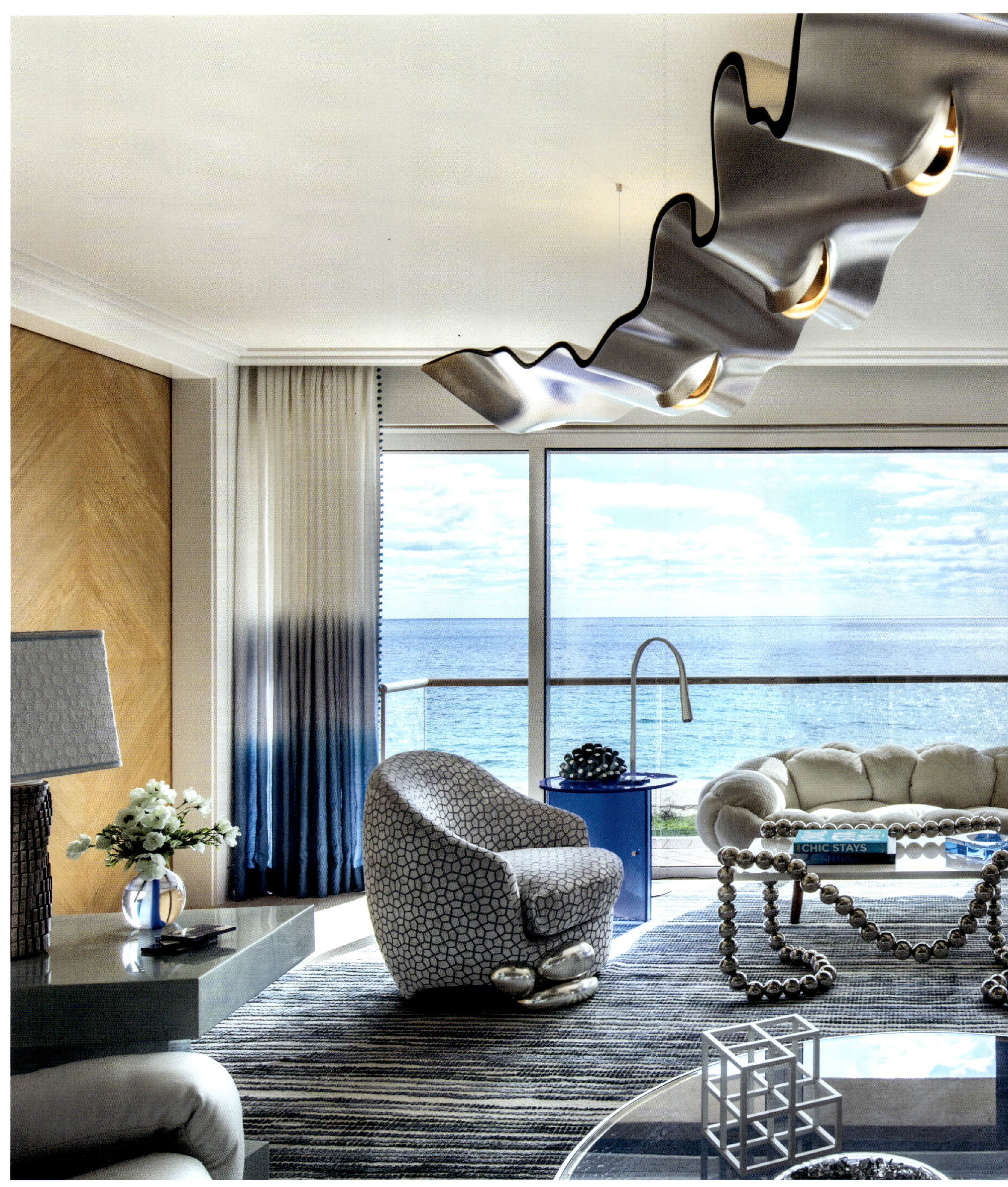

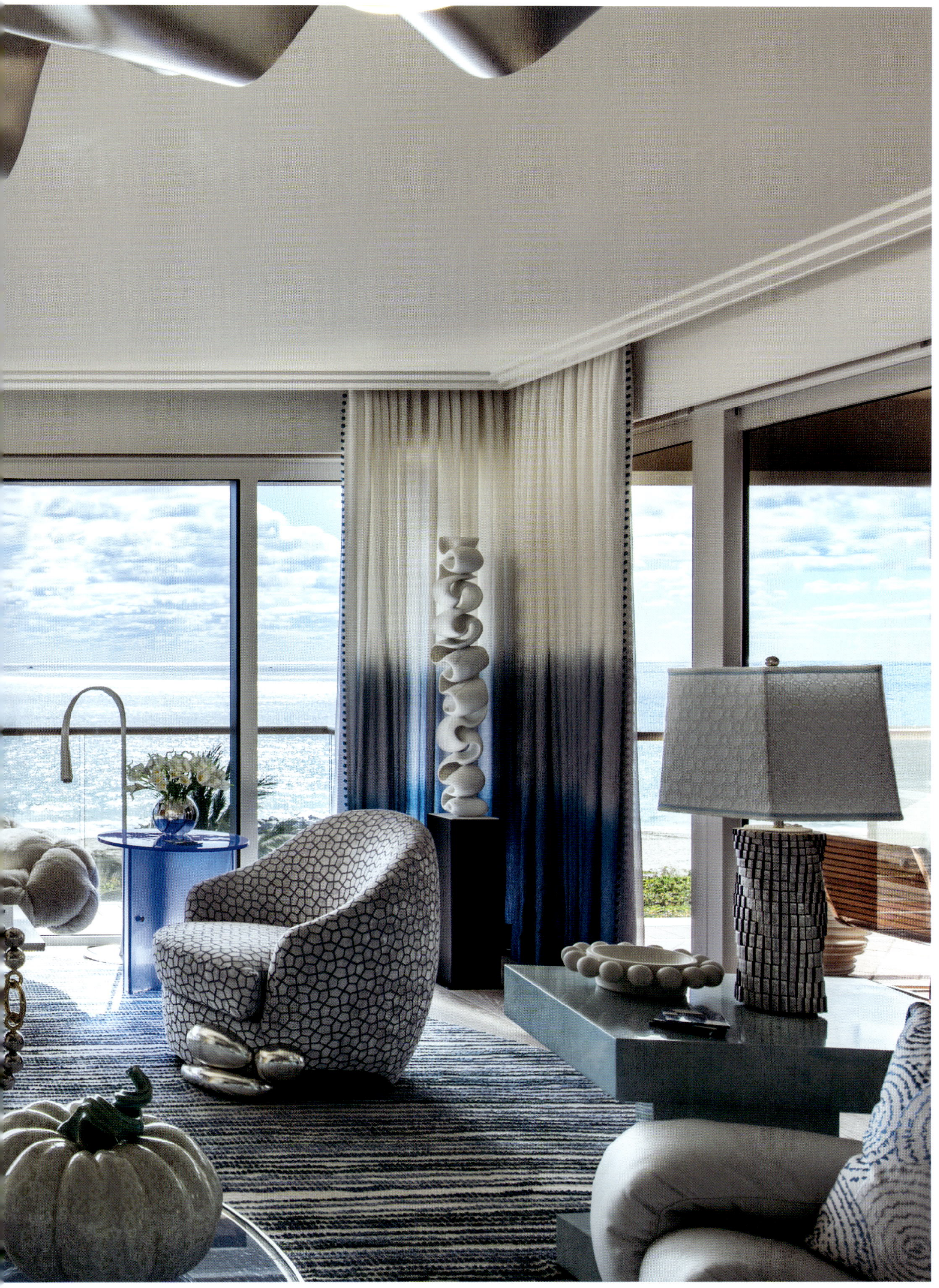

Holiday home in Palm Beach: with all of the windows looking out directly onto the white Atlantic beach, a pallet of blue and white was an ideal choice for the interior furnishings. In addition, the client requested some shades of gray to provide greater peace and complexity. As the many glass walls left little space for artworks, a greater focus was placed on furniture and lamps as functional and sculptural pieces. The s-shaped Ingo Maurer Palladium Ribbon light, which is more than five meters in length, was manufactured specially for this space.

Ferienwohnung in Palm Beach: Alle Fenster sind direkt auf den weißen Atlantikstrand ausgerichtet, sodass Blau- und Weißtöne für die Inneneinrichtung gut passen. Zusätzlich wünschte sich der Kunde graue Akzente für etwas mehr Komplexität und Ruhe. Da wegen der zahlreichen gläsernen Wände viele Kunstobjekte nicht infrage kamen, rückten Möbel und Lampen als funktionale und skulpturale Objekte in den Fokus. Die s-förmige, über fünf Meter lange Palladiumbandleuchte von Ingo Maurer wurde speziell für diesen Raum hergestellt.

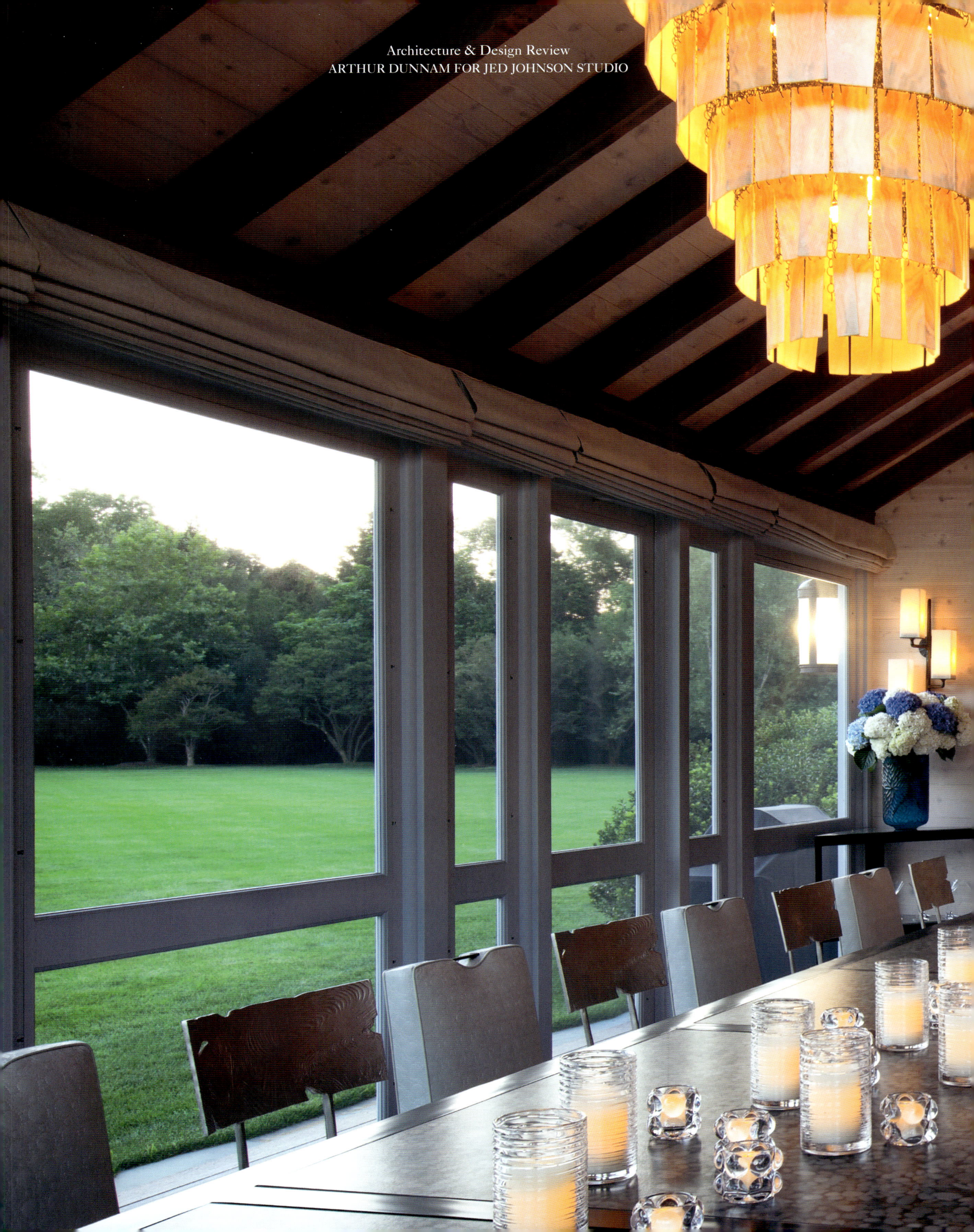

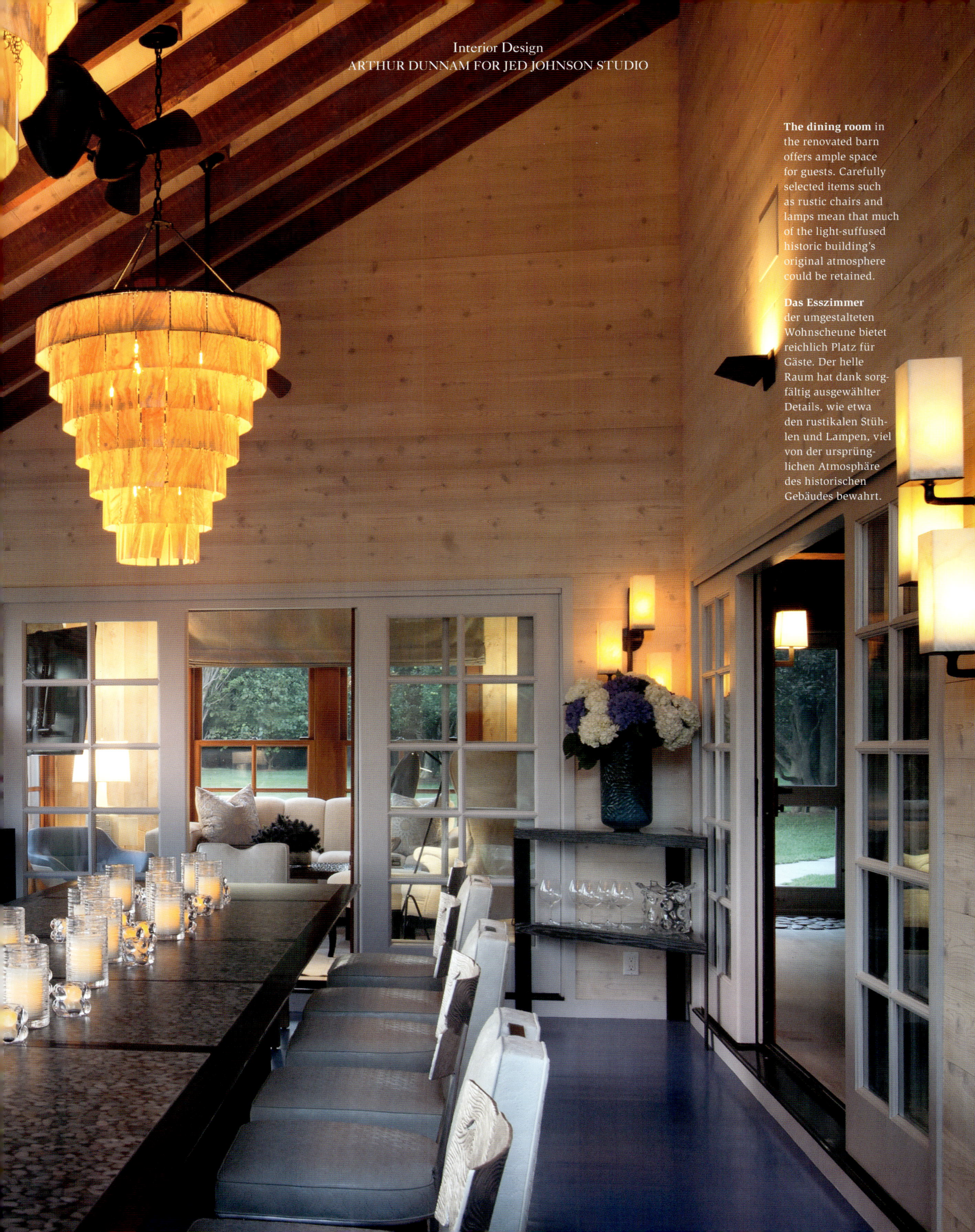

Interior Design
ARTHUR DUNNAM FOR JED JOHNSON STUDIO

The dining room in the renovated barn offers ample space for guests. Carefully selected items such as rustic chairs and lamps mean that much of the light-suffused historic building's original atmosphere could be retained.

Das Esszimmer der umgestalteten Wohnscheune bietet reichlich Platz für Gäste. Der helle Raum hat dank sorgfältig ausgewählter Details, wie etwa den rustikalen Stühlen und Lampen, viel von der ursprünglichen Atmosphäre des historischen Gebäudes bewahrt.

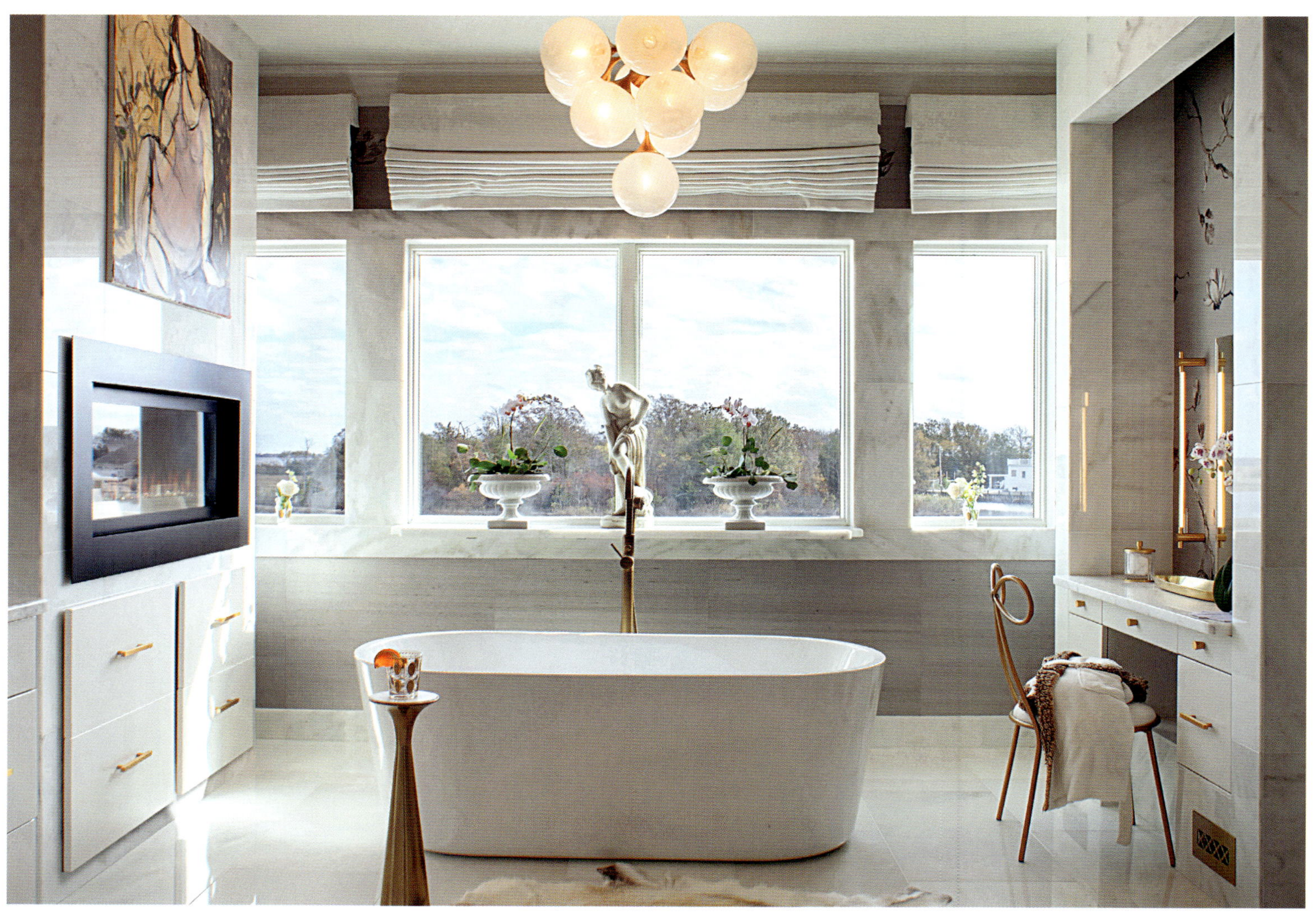

ATELIER DURANTE

NEW YORK / USA

A Dream Made of Marble | Ein Traum in Marmor

Pamela J. Durante had already been working for many years as an interior designer, coordinator and project manager for prestigious luxury hospitality companies when she established her firm, Atelier Durante Interior Design PLLC, in New York in 1994. The unique service that she offers her clients draws on this valuable experience and her close contacts to leading designers. Durante always attaches particular importance to her sophisticated design style in her projects. The bathroom refurbishment in a house on the New Jersey coast depicted here provided Durante and her team with the opportunity to work mainly with marble, one of their favorite materials.

Schon viele Jahre hatte Pamela J. Durante als Interior-Designerin, Koordinatorin und Projektleiterin in namhaften Häusern der Luxusgastronomie gearbeitet, als sie 1994 ihr Unternehmen Atelier Durante Interior Design PLLC in New York gründete. Auf diesem Erfahrungsschatz und engen Kontakten zu Top-Designern beruht der einzigartige Service, den sie ihren Kunden bietet. Bei ihren Projekten legt Durante immer großen Wert auf einen anspruchsvollen Designstil. Das abgebildete Bad wurde in einem Haus an der Küste New Jerseys neu gestaltet. Durante und ihr Team konnten und sollten dabei vor allem mit Marmor arbeiten, eines ihrer Lieblingsmaterialien.

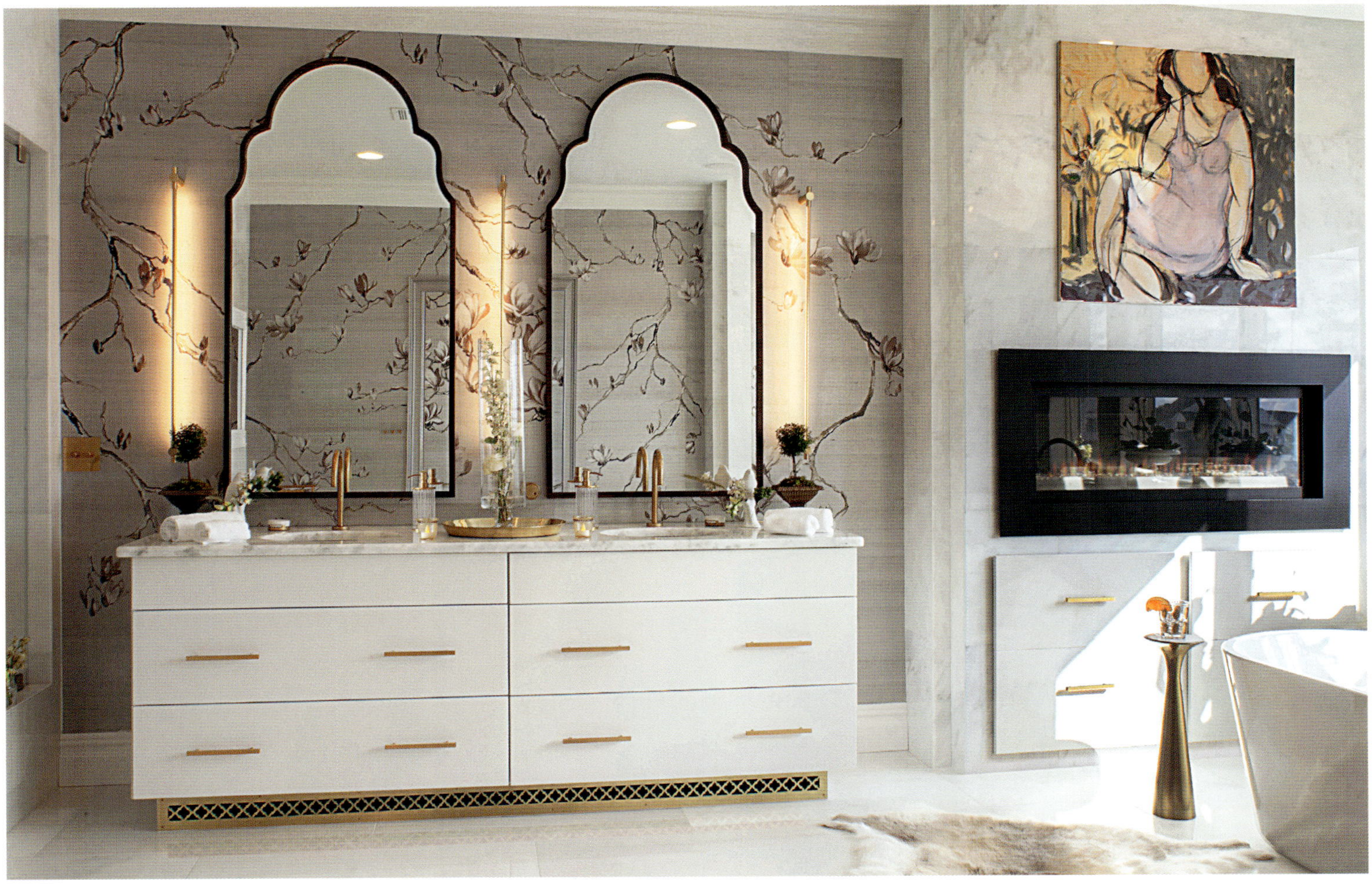

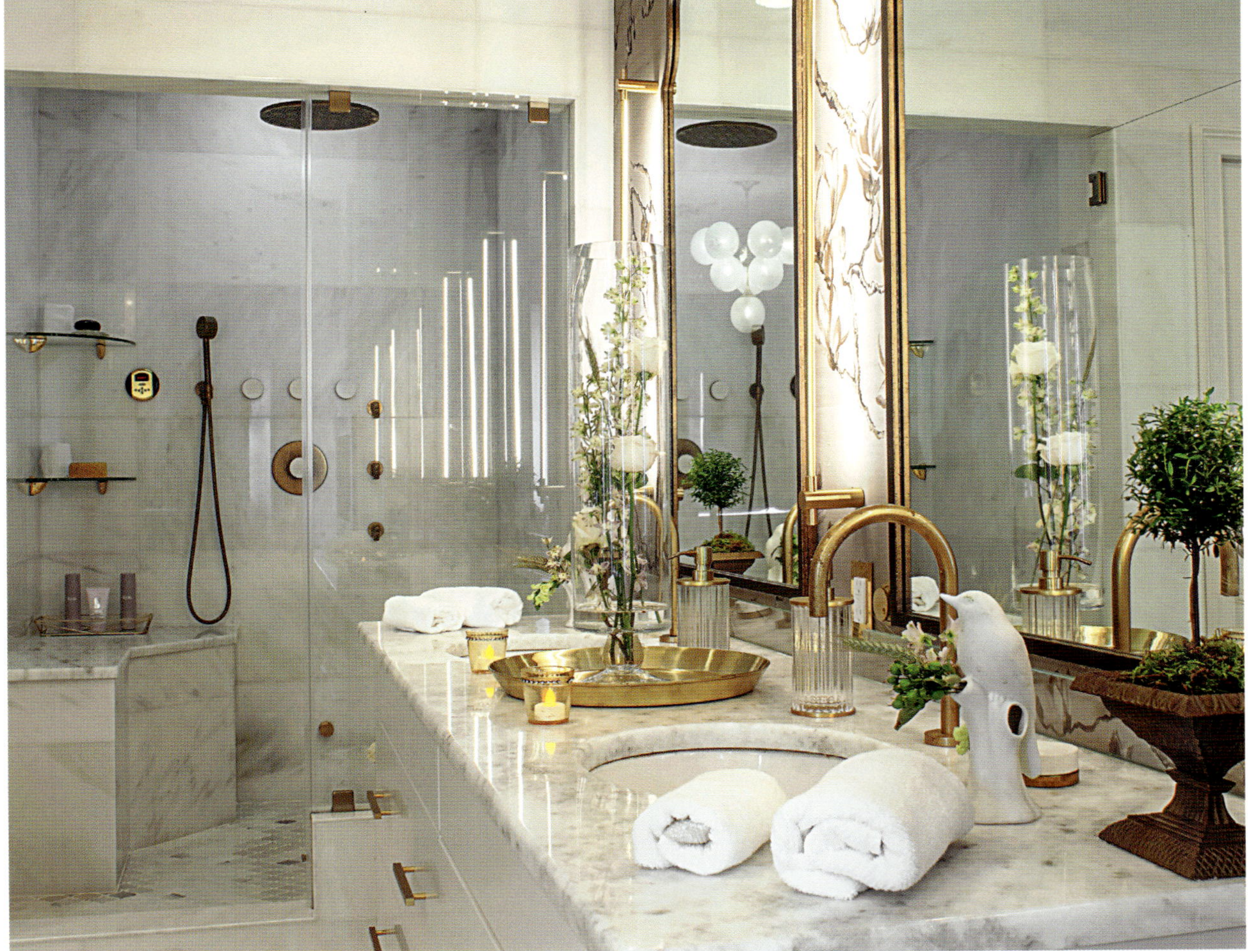

The client wanted the new bathroom to be brighter, hence the choice of white marble. As this would have given the room a rather cold feel, however, a silk wall covering was selected to lend some color. A fireplace, TV, sound system, sophisticated lighting, elegant brass accessories and a painting provide the finishing touches to the luxury bathroom.

Der Kunde wollte das neue Badezimmer vor allem heller, also in weißem Marmor. Das hätte den Raum aber sehr kalt wirken lassen, deshalb setzt eine seidene Wandverkleidung einen Farbakzent. Kamin, TV, Soundsystem, ausgeklügelte Beleuchtung, edles Messing und ein Gemälde runden das Luxusbad ab.

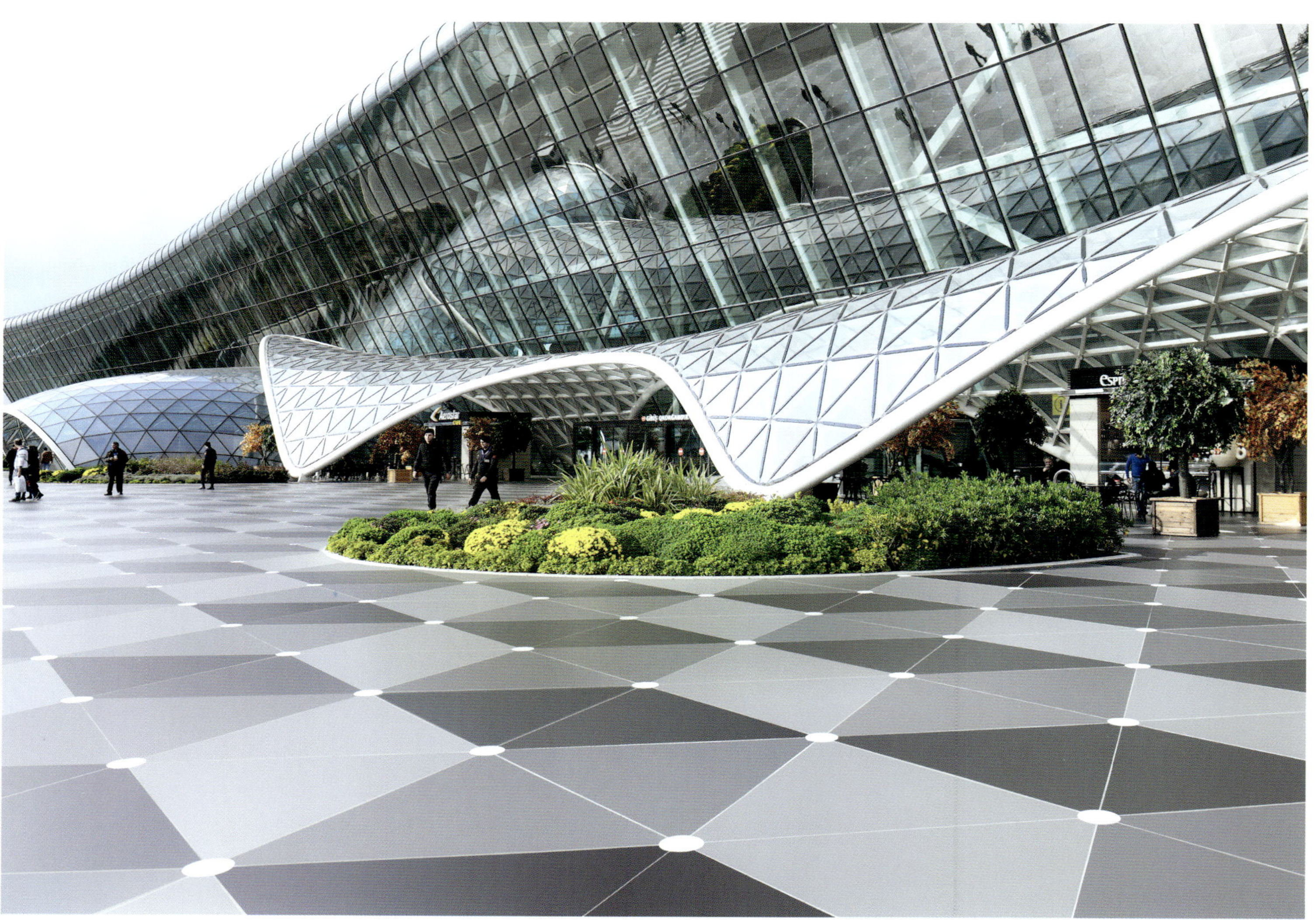

AUTOBAN

ISTANBUL / TURKEY

Lively and Contemporary | Lebendig und zeitgemäß

Seyhan Özdemir and Sefer Çağlar established Autoban in 2003, with Efe Aydar also joining later on. The firm's portfolio includes transportation, commercial, retail and office projects that have redefined the urban landscape, not only in Istanbul, but also elsewhere. In the meantime, their work in the fields of architecture, interior architecture, as well as product and experience design, are to be found in London, Manchester, Malta, Hong Kong, the Maldives, Thailand and several other cities. The company's furniture and lamp assortment is sold in more than sixty locations throughout the world. Reinterpreting familiar shapes and materials in a vital and lively way is a hallmark of Autoban's style.

Seyhan Özdemir und Sefer Çağlar gründeten das Studio Autoban im Jahr 2003, später stieß auch Efe Aydar dazu. Im Portfolio der Firma finden sich Verkehrs-, Geschäfts-, Einzelhandels- und Büroprojekte, die nicht nur das Stadtbild Istanbuls neu definiert haben. Die Arbeiten aus den Bereichen Architektur, Innenarchitektur, Produkt- und Erlebnisdesign sind inzwischen in London, Manchester, Malta, Hongkong, den Malediven, Thailand und vielen anderen Städten zu finden. Das Möbel- und Leuchtensortiment des Unternehmens wird weltweit an über sechzig Orten verkauft. Typisch für Autoban sind vertraute Formen und Materialien, die auf lebendige Weise neu interpretiert werden.

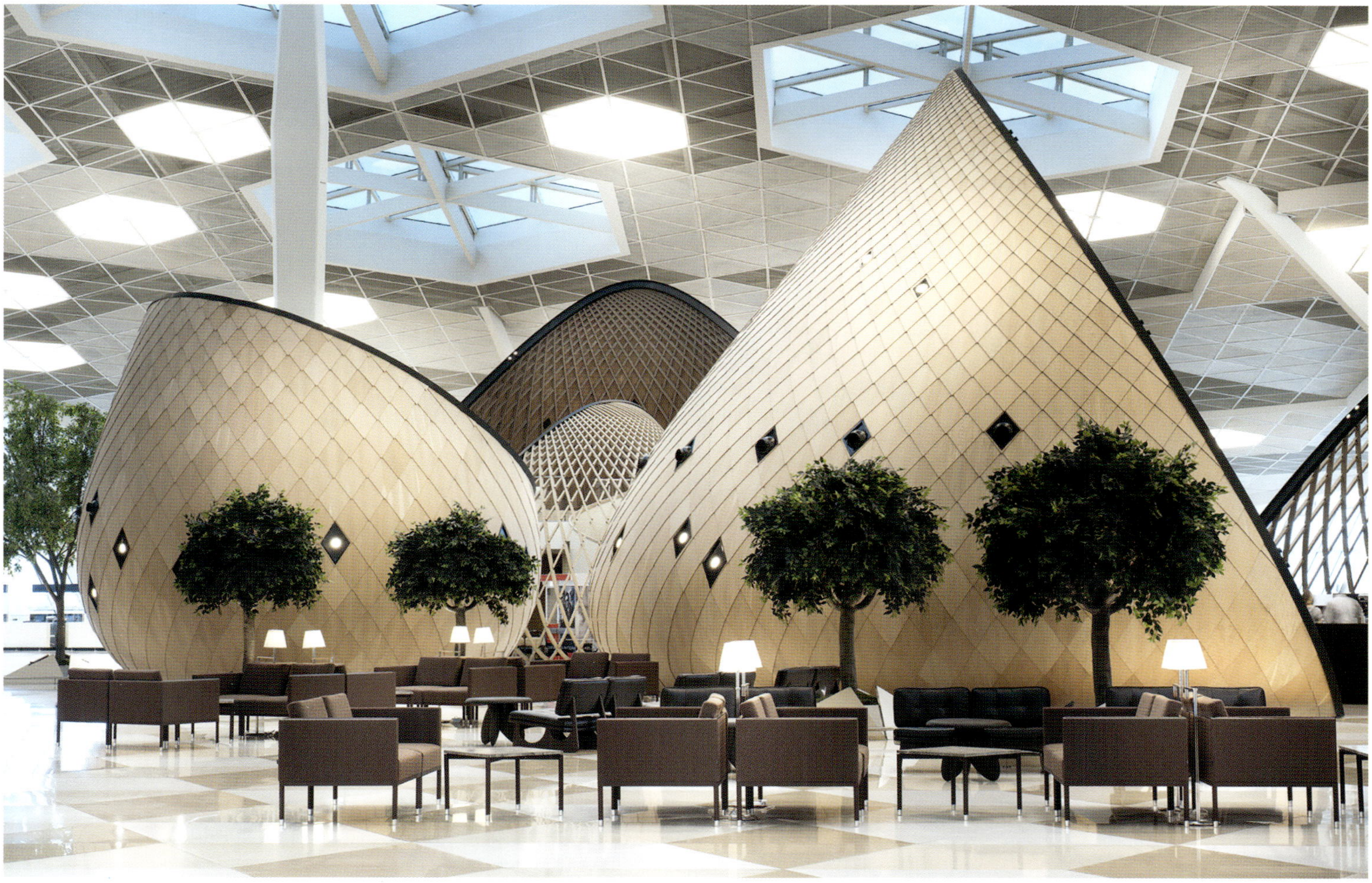

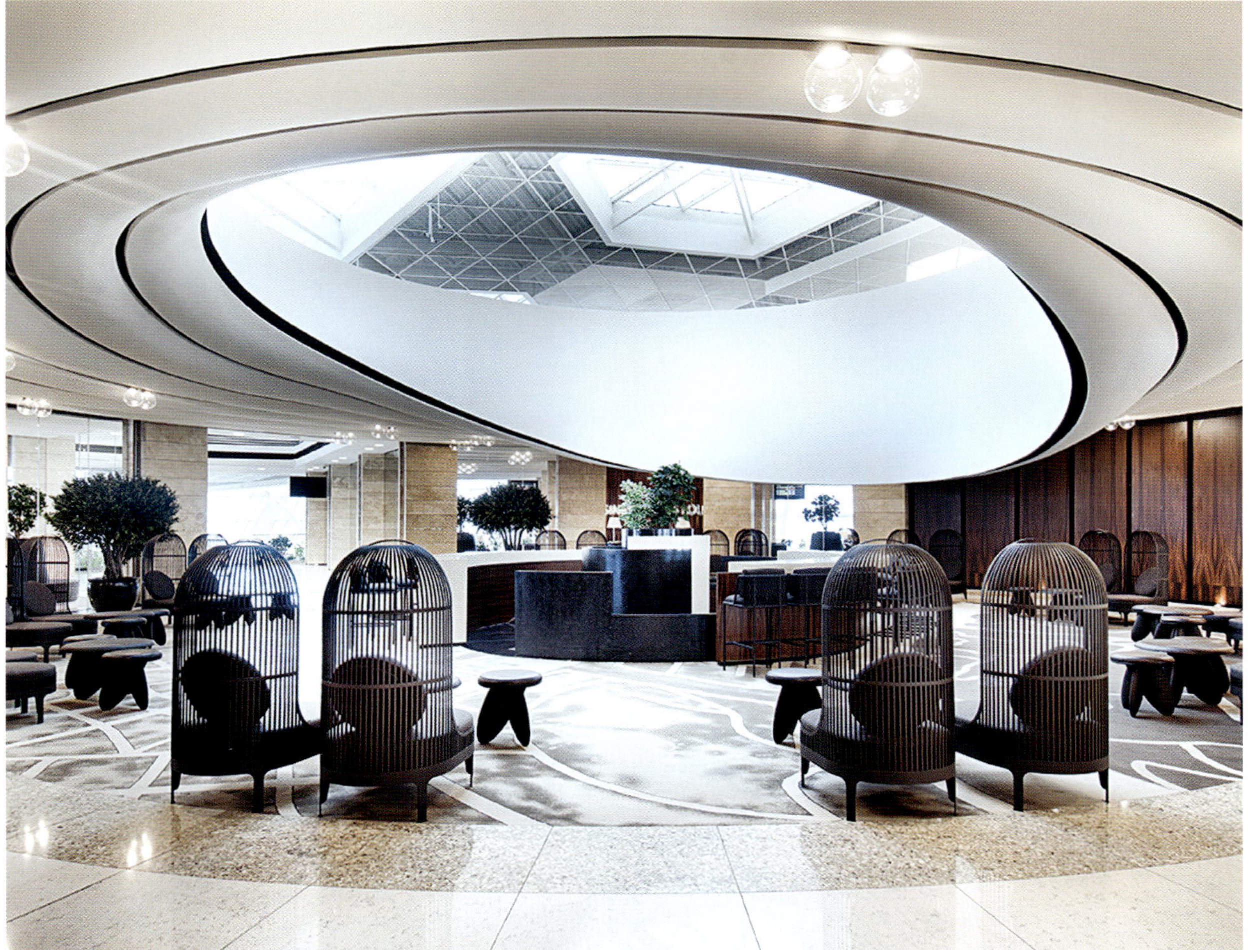

Heydär Äliyev
International Airport
in Baku, Azerbaijan:
since 2014, the 65,000
square meter airport
has been handling
several million pas-
sengers every year. Its
design has attracted
considerable interest
from the international
specialized press, with
Autoban being decora-
ted with both the Red
Dot Design Award and
the A+Award.

Heydär Äliyev
International Air-
port in Baku, Aser-
baidschan: Auf dem
65 000 Quadratmeter
großen Flughafen wer-
den seit 2014 jährlich
mehrere Millionen
Passagiere abgefertigt.
Seine Gestaltung fand
in der internationalen
Fachpresse großes
Interesse. Autoban
wurde dafür mit dem
Red Dot Design Award
und dem A+Award
ausgezeichnet.

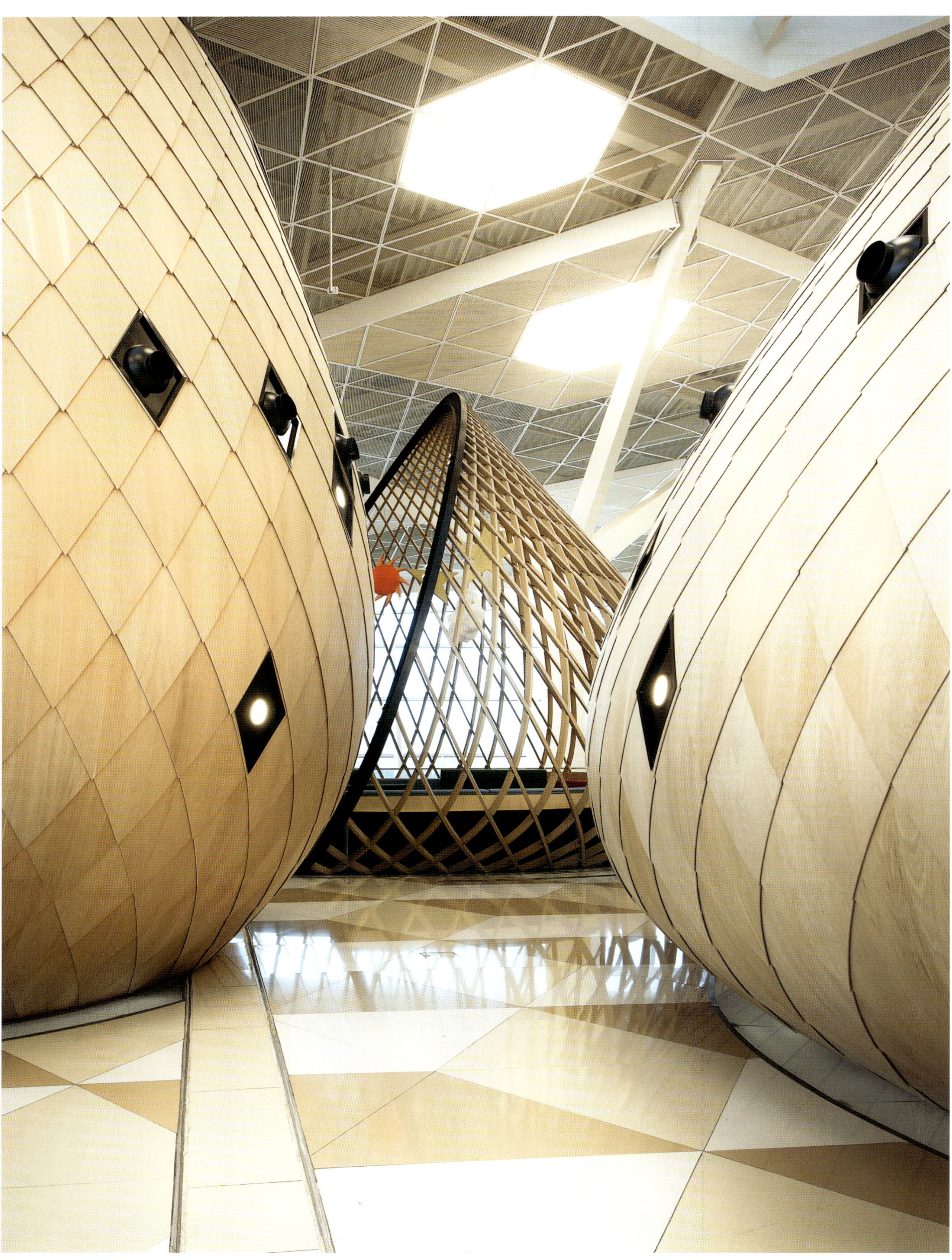

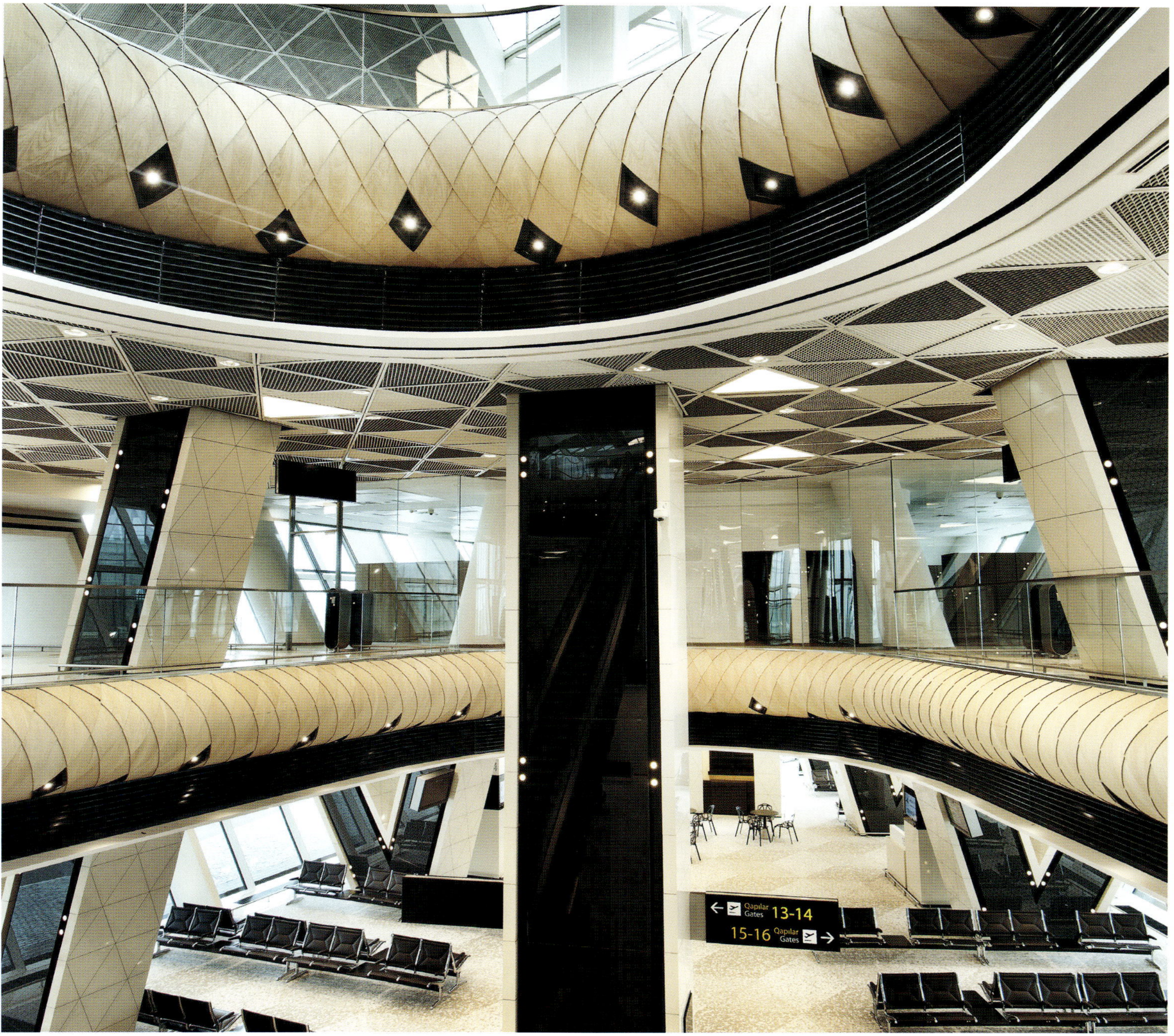

Organic-shaped wooden cocoons, ranging from 6.2 to 10.5 meters in height, house amenities of the Heydär Äliyev Airport, such as cafés and ticket counters. Indirect, warm lighting emphasizes the natural materials. The cocoons counterbalance the technical environment of a state-of-the-art airport in a pleasing and unexpected way.

In organisch geformten Holzkokons mit Höhen von 6,2 bis 10,5 Metern finden sich unter anderem Cafés und Ticketschalter des Heydär Äliyev Airport. Indirekte, warme Beleuchtung betont die Naturmaterialien. Die Kokons bilden so ein überraschendes, angenehmes Gegengewicht zur technischen Umgebung des hochmodernen Flughafens.

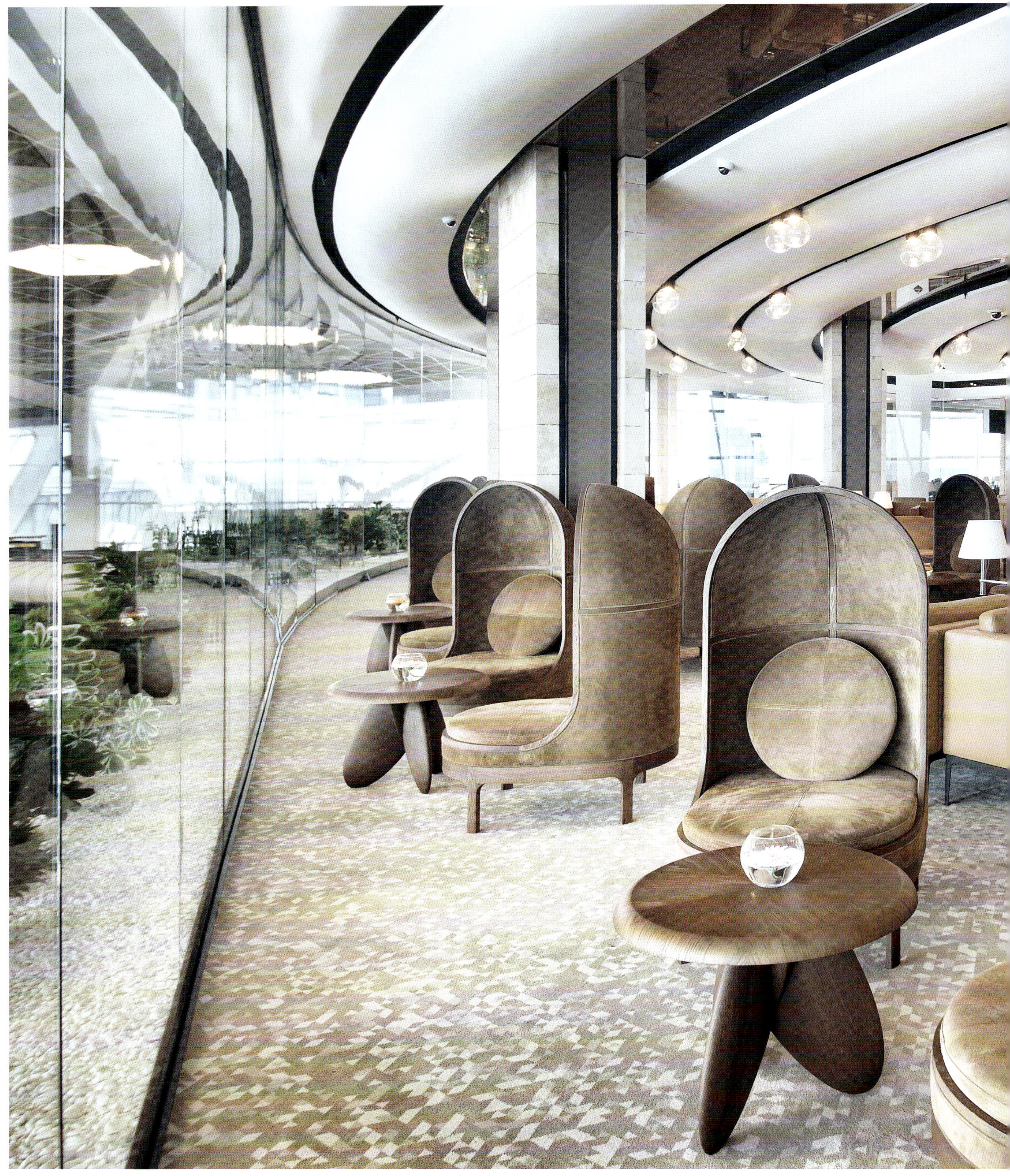

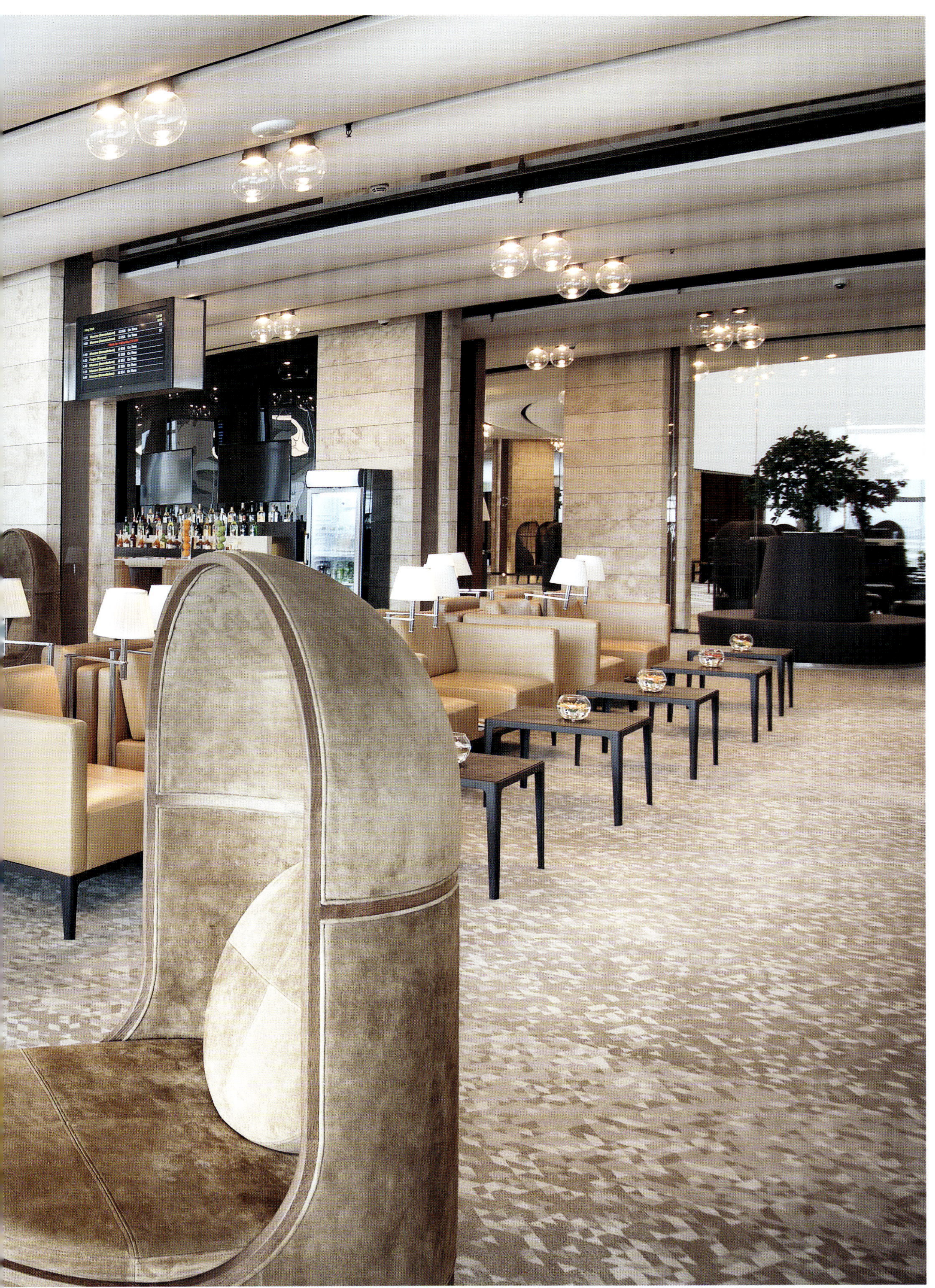

A further insight into one of the lounge and waiting areas at the Heydär Äliyev terminal in Baku: the closed version of the designer chairs offers even greater comfort and relaxation, yet still places guests and travelers at the heart of the action.

Ein weiterer Einblick in einen der Lounge- und Wartebereiche des Heydär Äliyev-Terminals in Baku: Die geschlossene Variante der Designersessel ermöglicht noch mehr entspannte Geborgenheit und trotzdem ein „Mittendrin" für Gäste und Reisende.

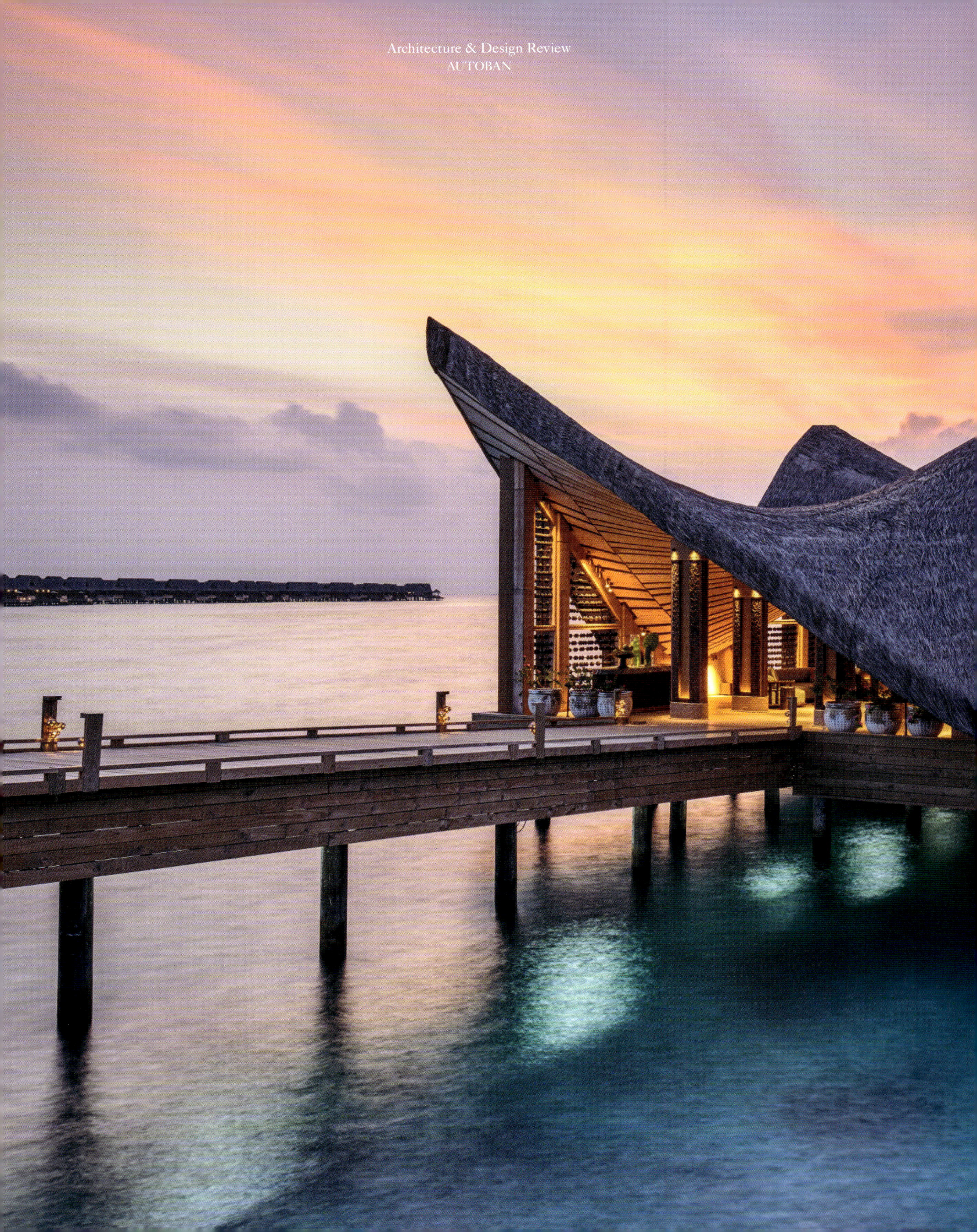

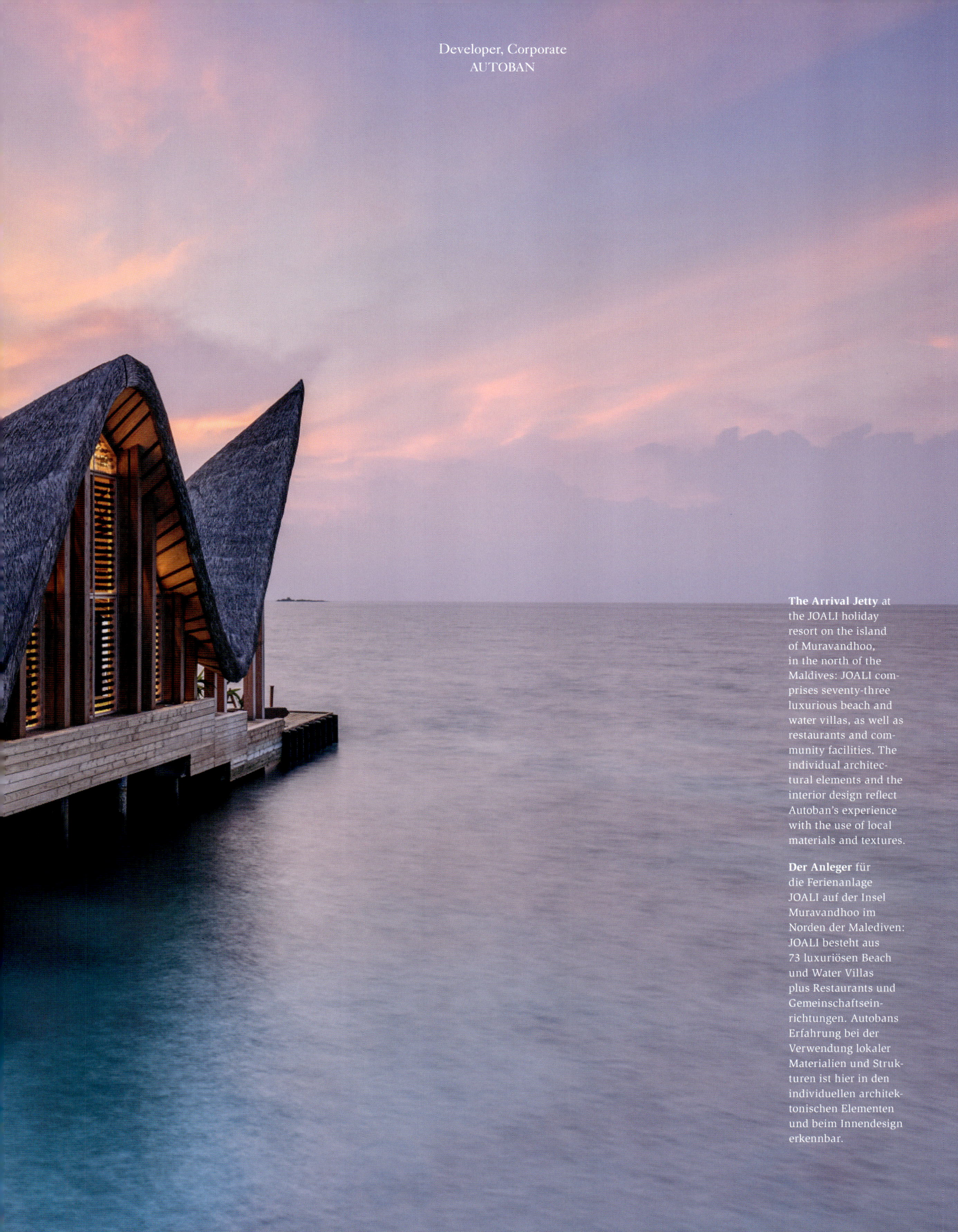

The Arrival Jetty at the JOALI holiday resort on the island of Muravandhoo, in the north of the Maldives: JOALI comprises seventy-three luxurious beach and water villas, as well as restaurants and community facilities. The individual architectural elements and the interior design reflect Autoban's experience with the use of local materials and textures.

Der Anleger für die Ferienanlage JOALI auf der Insel Muravandhoo im Norden der Malediven: JOALI besteht aus 73 luxuriösen Beach und Water Villas plus Restaurants und Gemeinschaftseinrichtungen. Autobans Erfahrung bei der Verwendung lokaler Materialien und Strukturen ist hier in den individuellen architektonischen Elementen und beim Innendesign erkennbar.

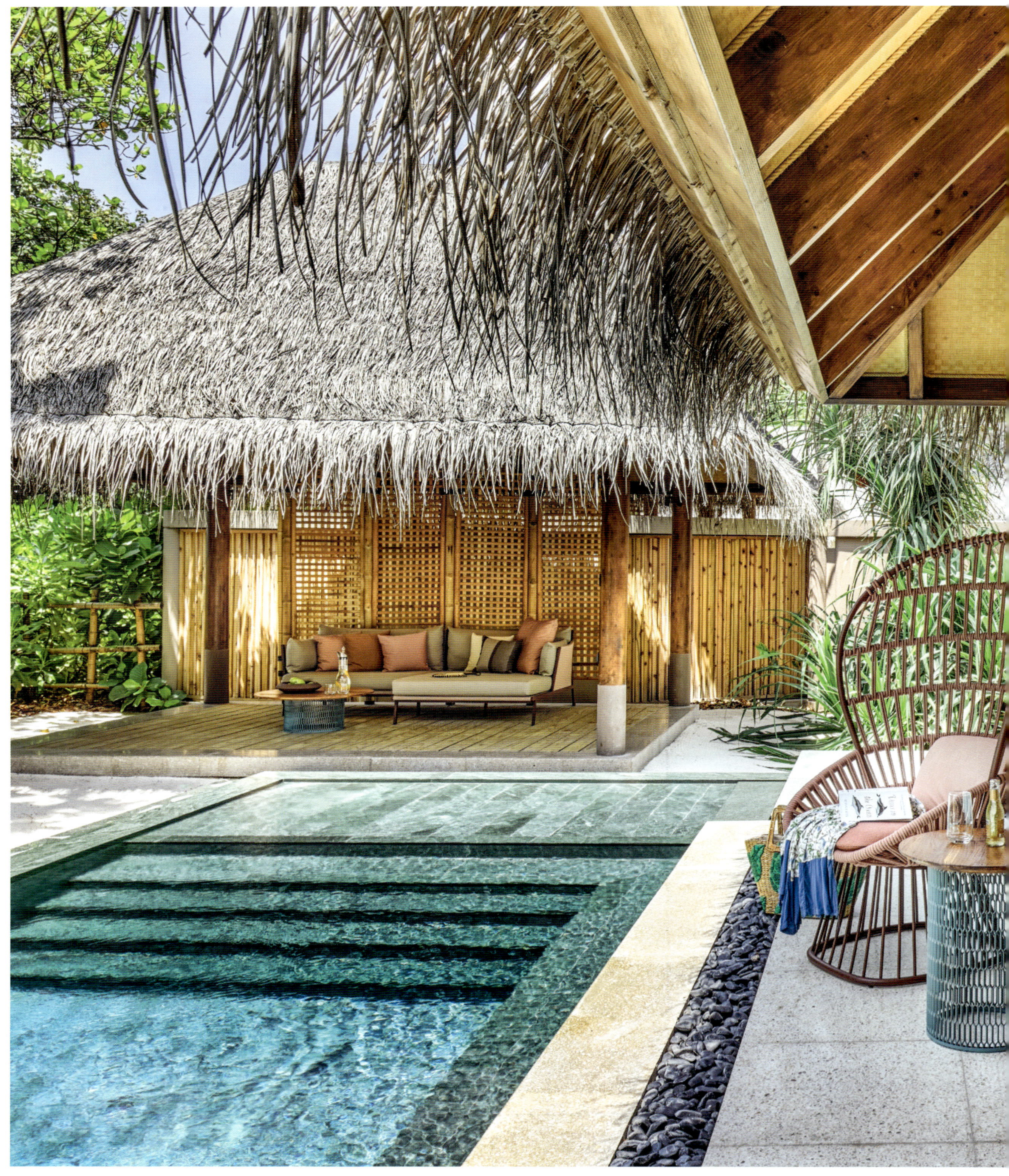

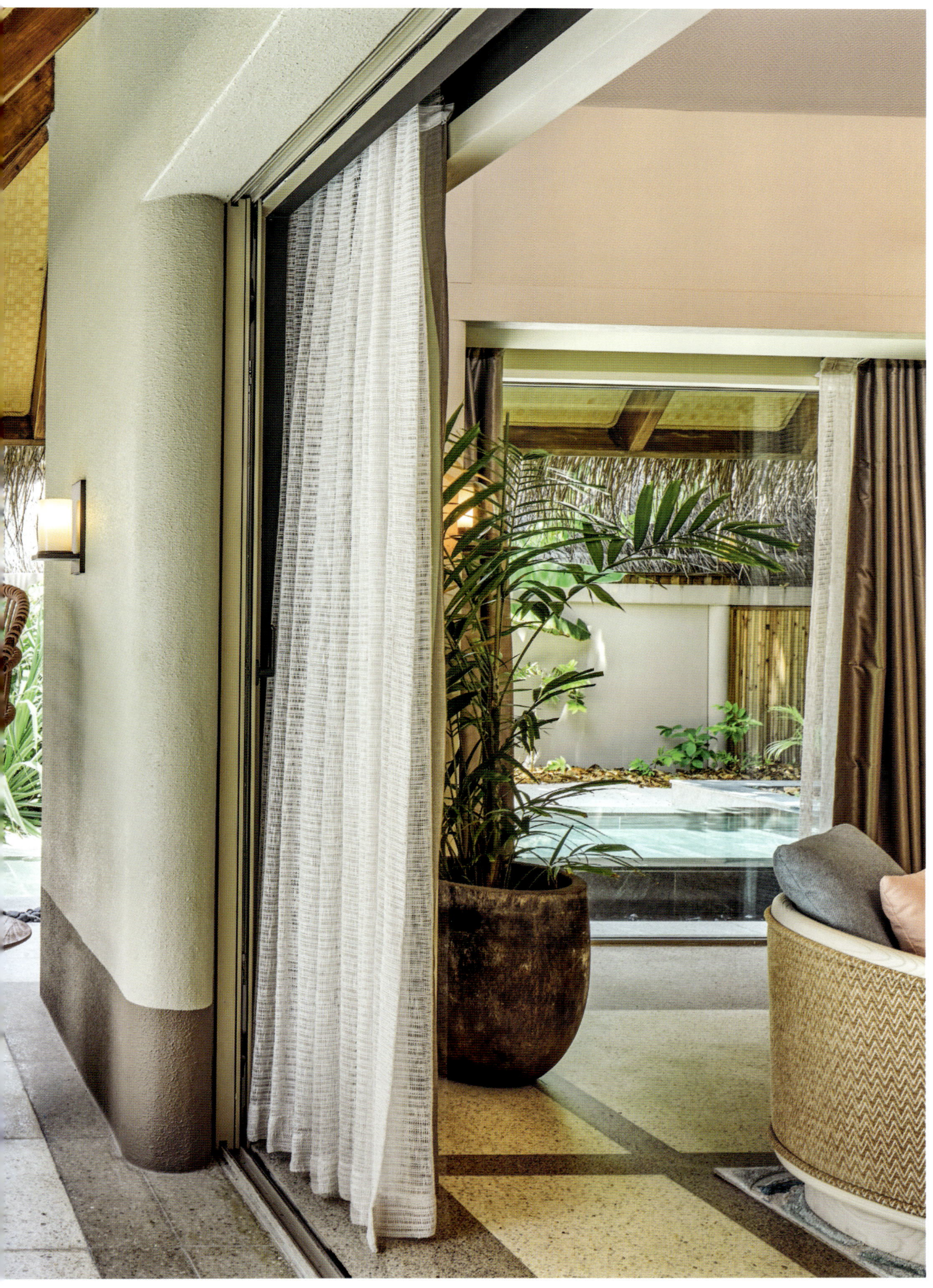

One of the outdoor areas at the JOALI holiday resort on the island of Muravandhoo. Every element is inspired by very individual stories and designed in a way that takes guests on a rich, sensorial journey. Handcrafted comforts, curated libraries in the rooms as well as sophisticated design and luxurious art objects all contribute to JOALI's perfect, unconventional luxury.

Einer der Außenbereiche in der Ferienanlage JOALI auf Muravandhoo: Jedes Element ist von ganz individuellen Geschichten inspiriert und so gestaltet, dass die Gäste auf eine vielfältige sensorische Reise mitgenommen werden. Handwerkliche Annehmlichkeiten, kuratierte Bibliotheken in den Zimmern, durchdachtes Design und luxuriöse Kunstgegenstände sorgen im JOALI für perfekten unkonventionellen Luxus.

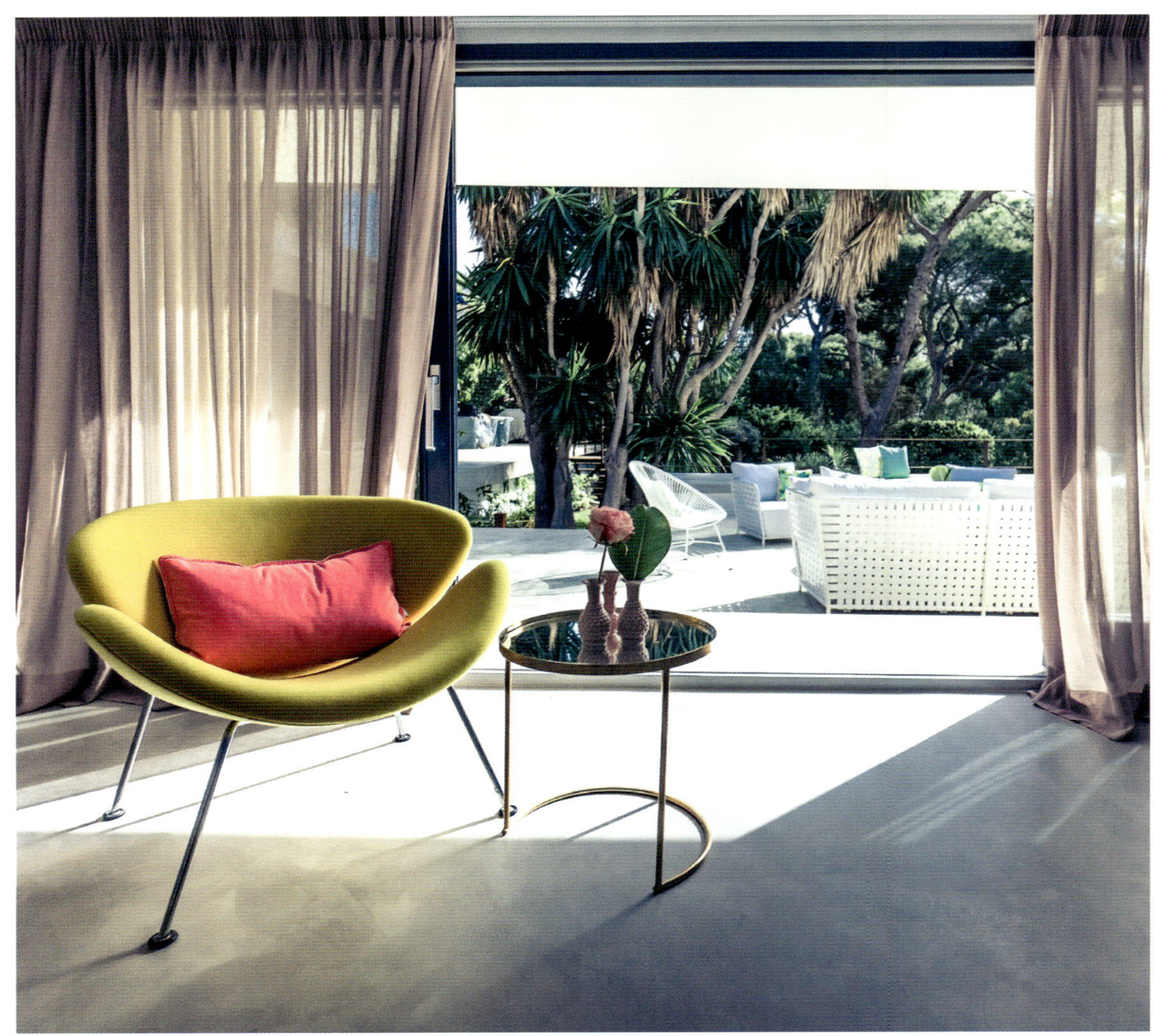

bconnected

PALMA DE MALLORCA / SPAIN

Light and Color | Licht und Farbe

'**Every new client and project** provides a fresh challenge. The planning, design, and construction of residential spaces is one of the most satisfying professions,' enthuses Christine Leja, the founder of the bconnected group. She enjoys taking on the task of understanding her clients' needs, wishes and dreams, in order to design a new home for them. In the project presented, however, the future resident was none other than the visionary designer herself. Could that work out? All that was clear at the outset was that the property should be a midcentury modern bungalow with the typical L.A. spirit. This idea provided Leja with sufficient scope to make a success of her own personal project.

„**Mit jedem neuen Kunden und Projekt** gibt es eine neue Herausforderung. Die Planung, Gestaltung und der Bau von Wohnräumen ist einer der schönsten Berufe", schwärmt Christine Leja, Gründerin der Unternehmensgruppe bconnected. Immer wieder nimmt sie die Aufgabe an, die Bedürfnisse, Wünsche und Träume der Kunden herauszufinden, um ihnen ein neues Zuhause zu gestalten. Bei dem hier gezeigten Projekt war die Visionärin allerdings selbst die zukünftige Bewohnerin. Konnte das klappen? Klar war zunächst nur, dass es ein Mid-century-Bungalow mit typischem L.A.-Spirit sein sollte. Doch diese Idee ließ genügend Raum, um Lejas persönliches Projekt zum Erfolg zu führen.

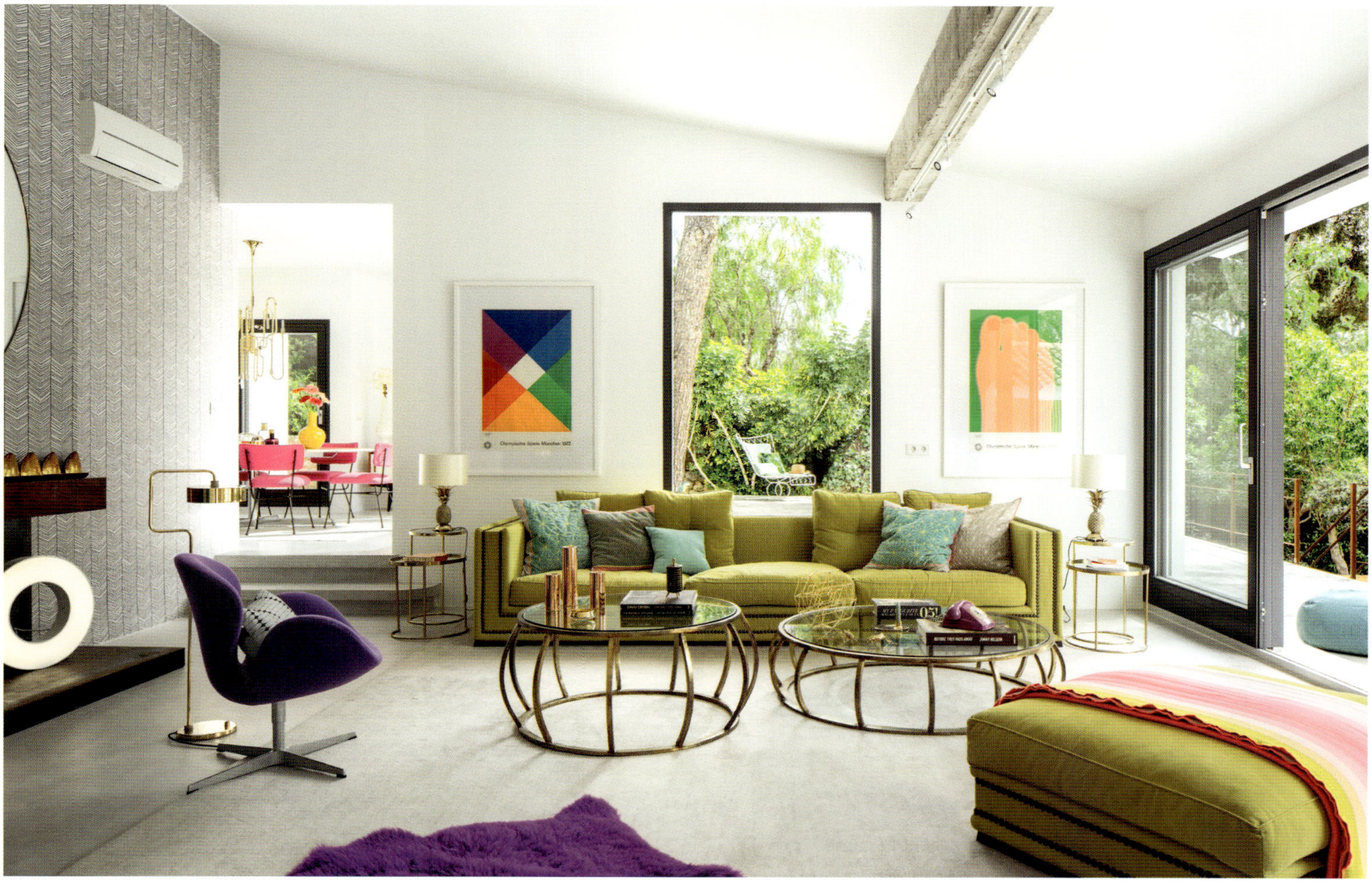

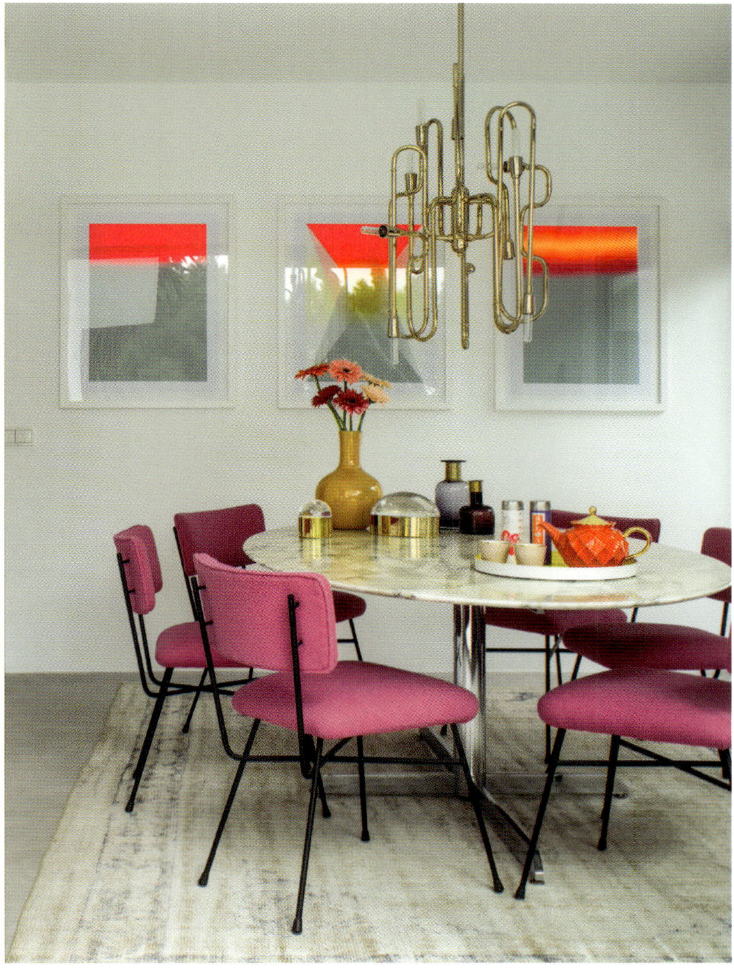

Colorful and positive:
Wallpaper from all over the world, marble from Italy, shutters from Poland, lamps from Portugal, as well as collector items such as the Egg Chair: this exciting selection has enabled Christine Leja to realize her own personal vision, while creating a unique designer home to meet her own requirements.

Bunt und positiv:
Tapeten aus allen Teilen der Welt, Marmor aus Italien, Fensterläden aus Polen, Lampen aus Portugal, dazu Sammlerstücke wie der Egg Chair: Mit einer solchen spannenden Auswahl hat Christine Leja eine persönliche Vision verwirklicht und sich selbst ihr privates Designerhaus ganz nach eigenen Bedürfnissen geschaffen.

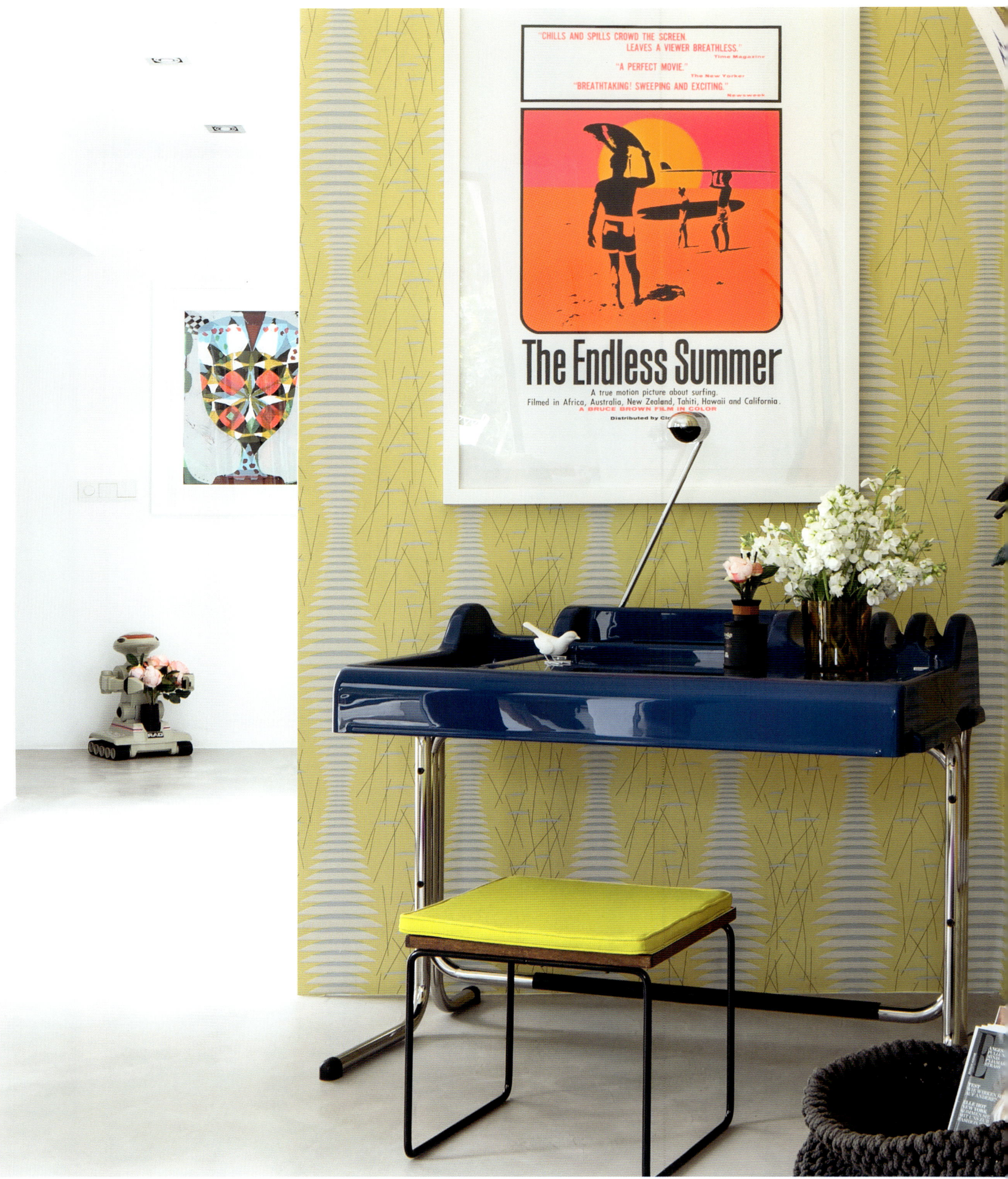
"CHILLS AND SPILLS CROWD THE SCREEN.
LEAVES A VIEWER BREATHLESS."
Time Magazine
"A PERFECT MOVIE."
The New Yorker
"BREATHTAKING! SWEEPING AND EXCITING."
Newsweek
The Endless Summer
A true motion picture about surfing.
Filmed in Africa, Australia, New Zealand, Tahiti, Hawaii and California.
A BRUCE BROWN FILM IN COLOR
Distributed by Cinema

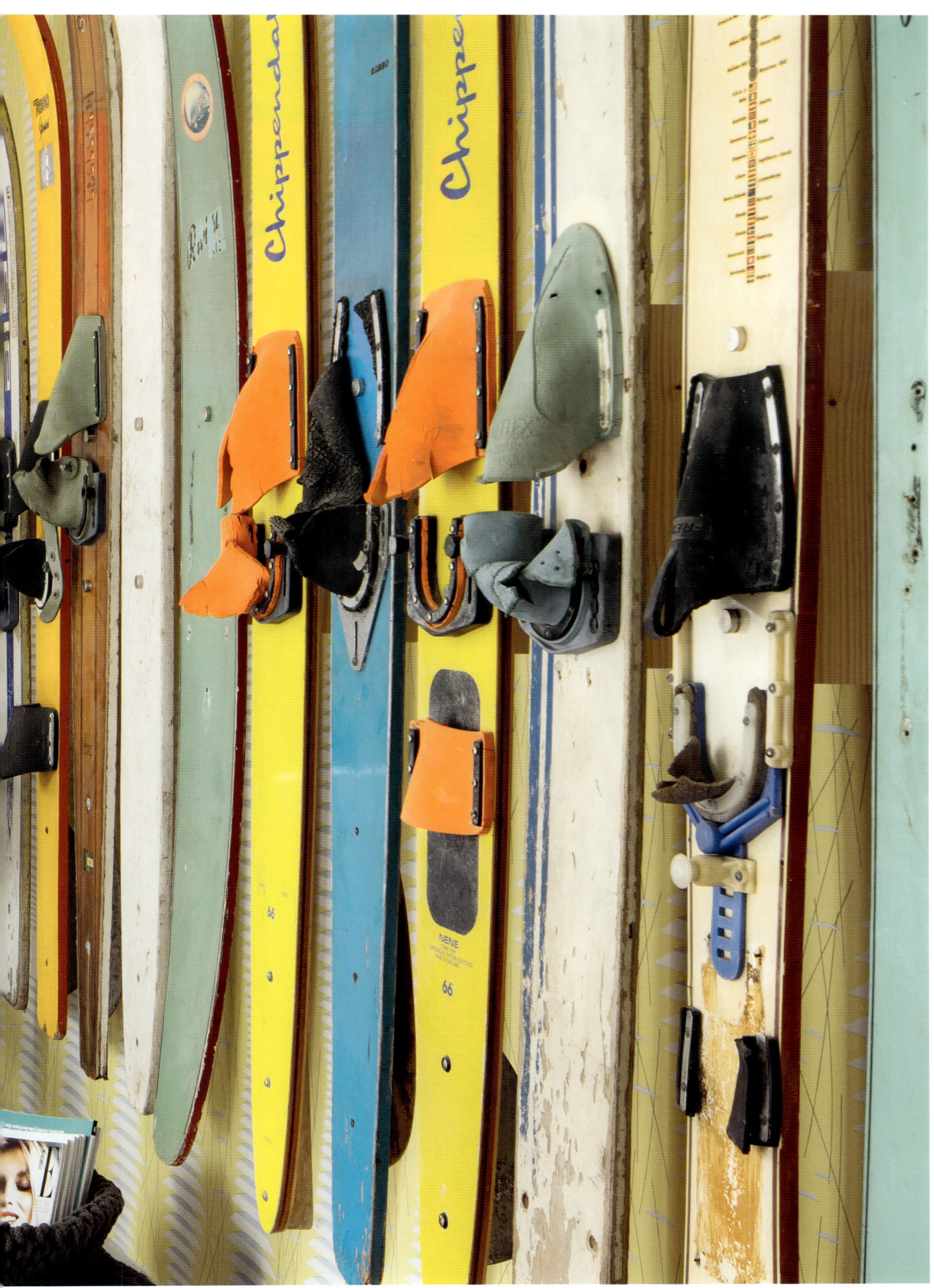

Christine Leja has a talent for finding themes and imbuing them with a life of their own by sharing her perception of them. A few selected items, such as this antique waterski collection, suitably combined with other objects, allow an otherwise unremarkable area of the house to suddenly take on its own special character.

Christine Leja besitzt das Geschick, Themen zu finden und in erlebbare Atmosphäre umzusetzen. Ein paar ausgewählte Objekte wie diese Kollektion alter Wasserskier, gut kombiniert mit anderen Gegenständen, lassen eine unscheinbare Ecke im Haus plötzlich zu einem ganz besonderen Wohnbereich werden.

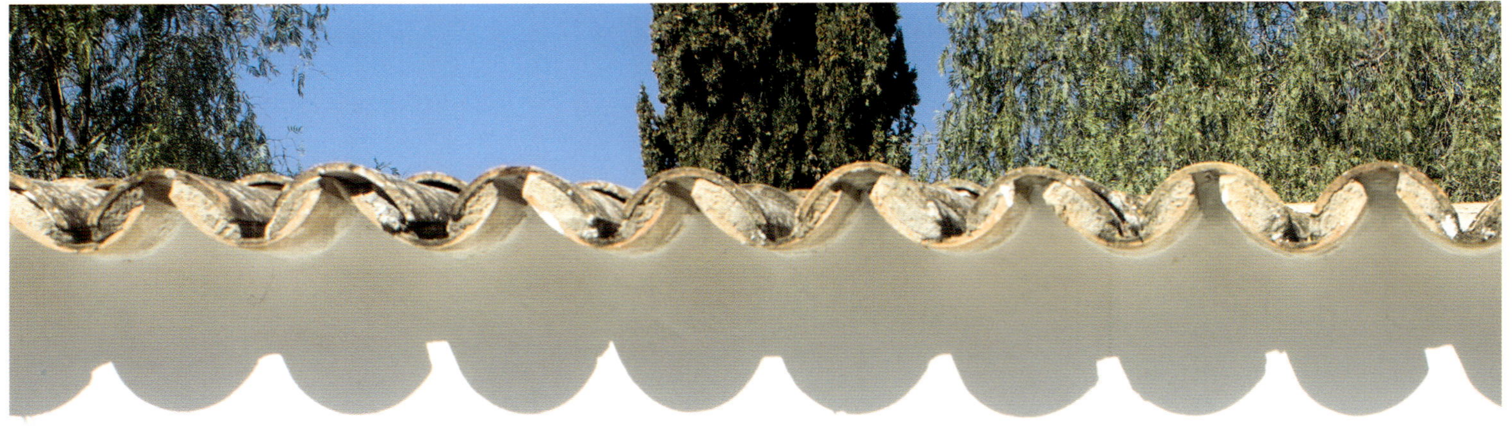

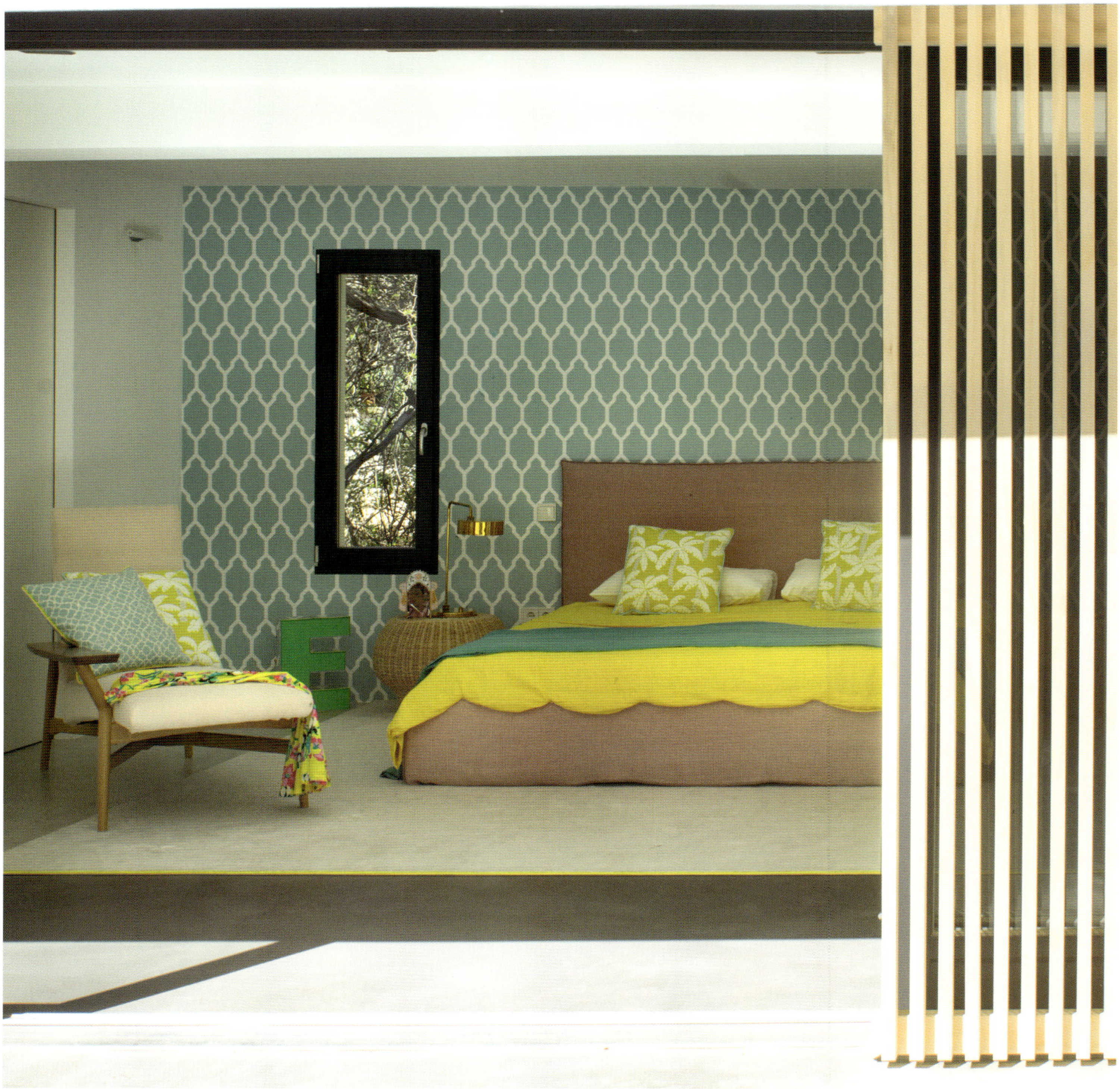

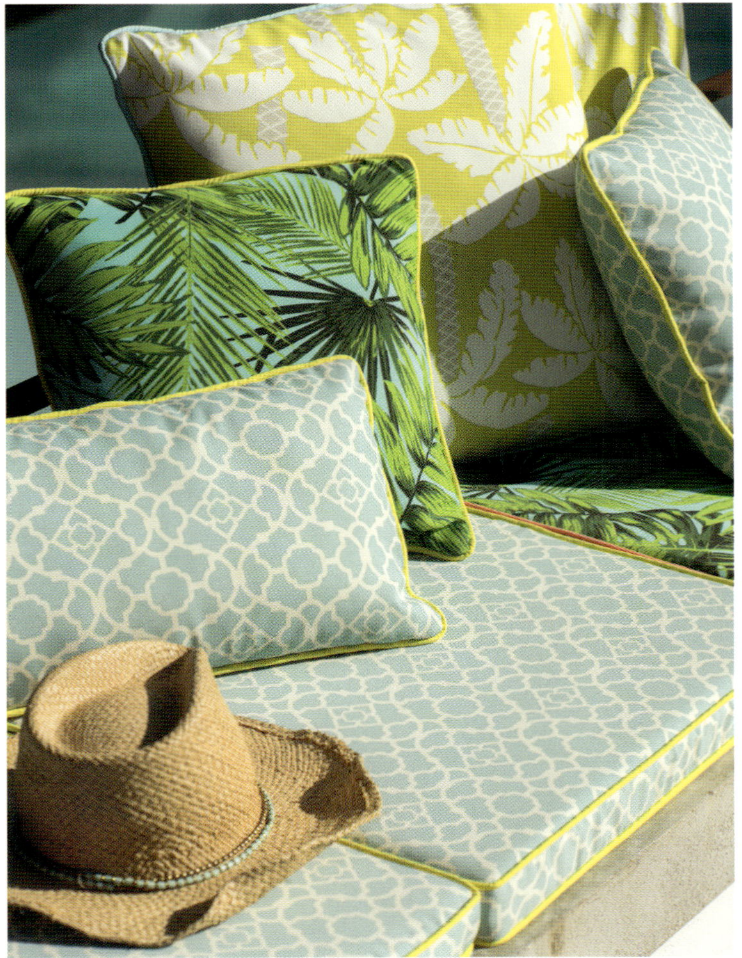

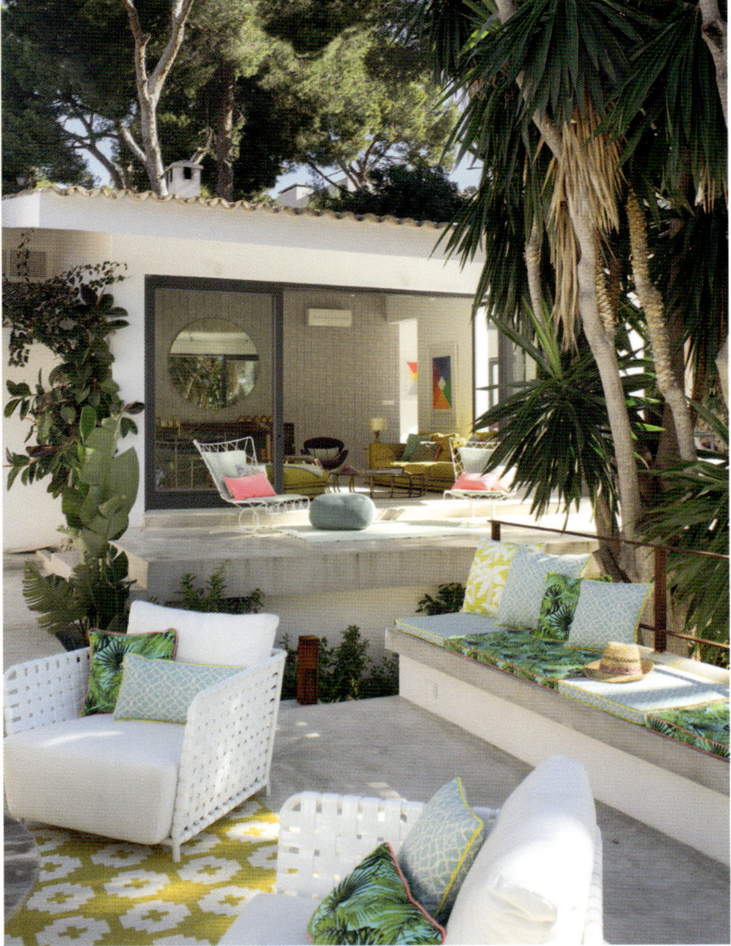

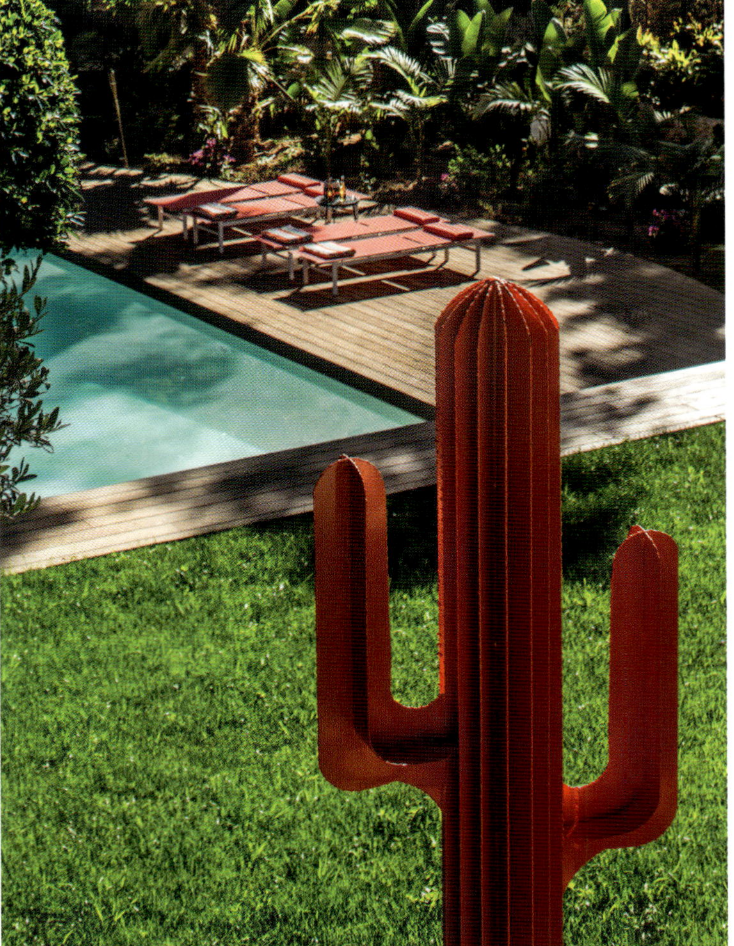

Christine Leja was obliged to respect the existing shell of the 1960s building—no changes could be made to its shape, or to the roof. She clearly needed, however, to allow much more light into the house if she was to convert it into a modern, open living space. For this reason, she took down more than half the façade to create sufficiently large openings. She also removed almost all the interior walls to make the house and its rooms clear and transparent.

Christine Leja musste den Baukörper aus den 1960er-Jahren unangetastet lassen – die Gebäudeform und das Dach konnten nicht verändert werden. Dennoch war klar, dass sie viel mehr Licht im Haus brauchte, wenn sie ein modernes offenes Wohnkonzept umsetzen wollte. Deshalb wurde über die Hälfte der Fassade für ausreichend große Öffnungen aufgerissen. Auch ließ sie fast alle Innenwände entfernen, um Haus und Räume transparent und klar zu machen.

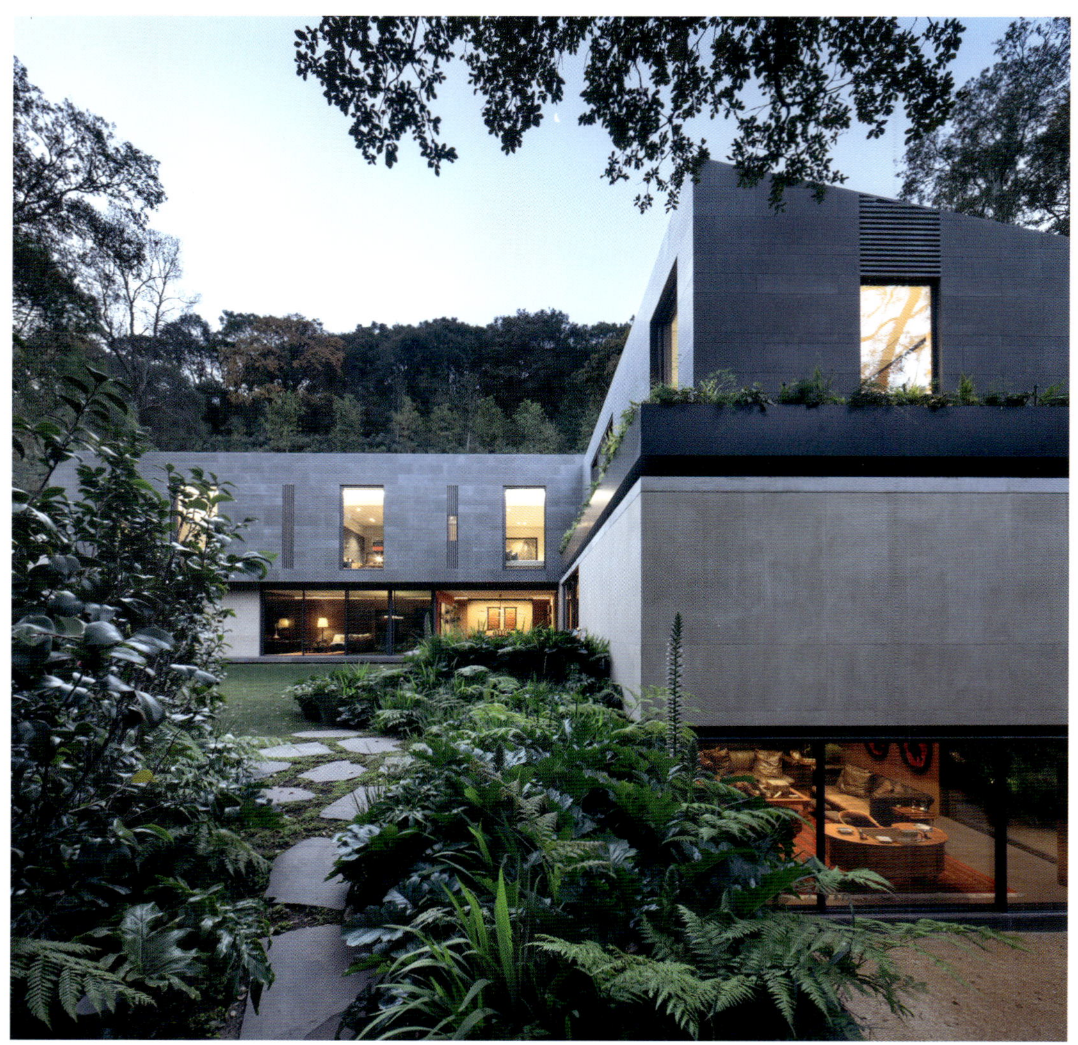

BERNARDI + PESCHARD ARQUITECTURA

MEXICO CITY / MEXICO

Exceptional Attention to Detail | Besondere Liebe zum Detail

The experience gained by twenty years of creative accomplishments has enabled the award-winning firm of architects, with its main offices in Mexico City, to strike a successful balance between its own creativity and the needs of its clients. Trust is key to this success, with several business relationships becoming lasting friendships. Spearheaded by Alejandro Bernardi Gallo and Beatriz Peschard Mijares, the firm has become a byword for contemporary design in Mexico. Its portfolio comprises private apartments, culinary establishments, commercial buildings, and shipbuilding. All projects are characterized by elegance, luxury, and a particularly close attention to detail.

Mit der Erfahrung von zwanzig Jahren kreativer Leistungen hat das preisgekrönte Architekturbüro mit Sitz in Mexico City eine erfolgreiche Balance zwischen den eigenen Ideen und den Bedürfnissen der Kunden gefunden. Kennzeichen dieses Erfolgs ist Vertrauen – aus Geschäftsbeziehungen wurden nicht selten dauerhafte Freundschaften. Angeführt von Alejandro Bernardi Gallo und Beatriz Peschard Mijares, steht die Firma exemplarisch für aktuelles Design in Mexiko. Das Portfolio umfasst Privatwohnungen, Gastronomiebetriebe, Firmengebäude und Schiffbau. Alle Projekte zeichnen sich durch Eleganz, Luxus und eine besondere Liebe zum Detail aus.

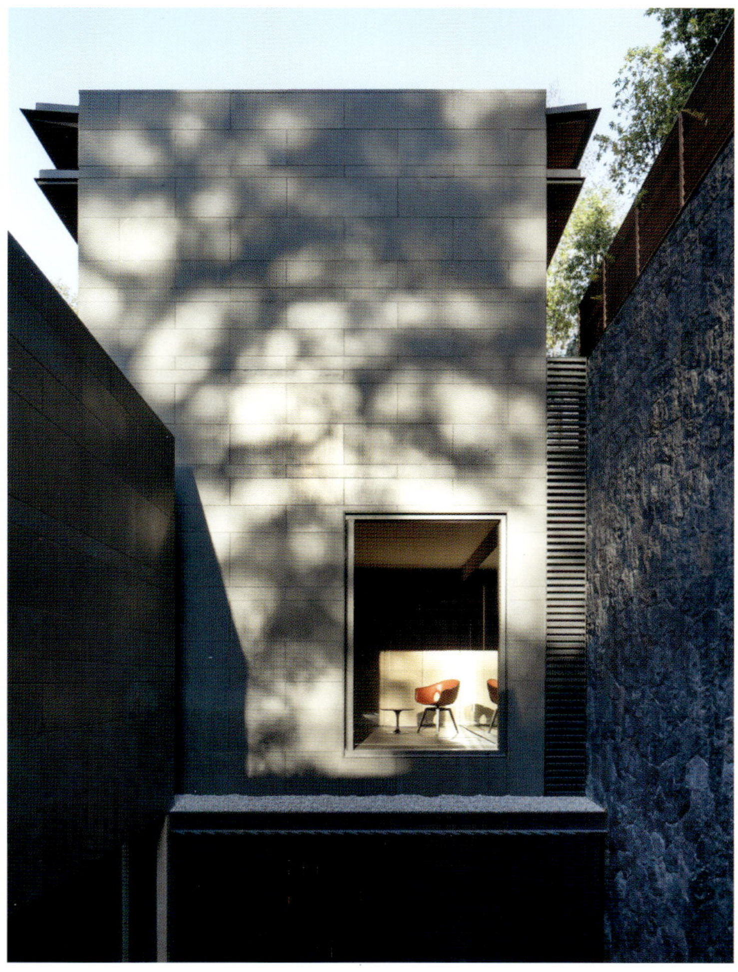

This house's beautiful location in a calm woodland area on Mexico City's western periphery offers an extremely private, privileged setting for a perfect family home. The clear separation between private and communal areas enables the residents to balance independent needs and family life.

Die schöne Lage dieses Hauses in einem ruhigen Waldgebiet am westlichen Rand von Mexiko-Stadt bietet sehr private und privilegierte Voraussetzungen für ein perfektes Familiendomizil. Die klare Trennung der individuell und gemeinsam genutzten Bereiche ermöglicht ein Gleichgewicht zwischen Unabhängigkeit und Familienleben.

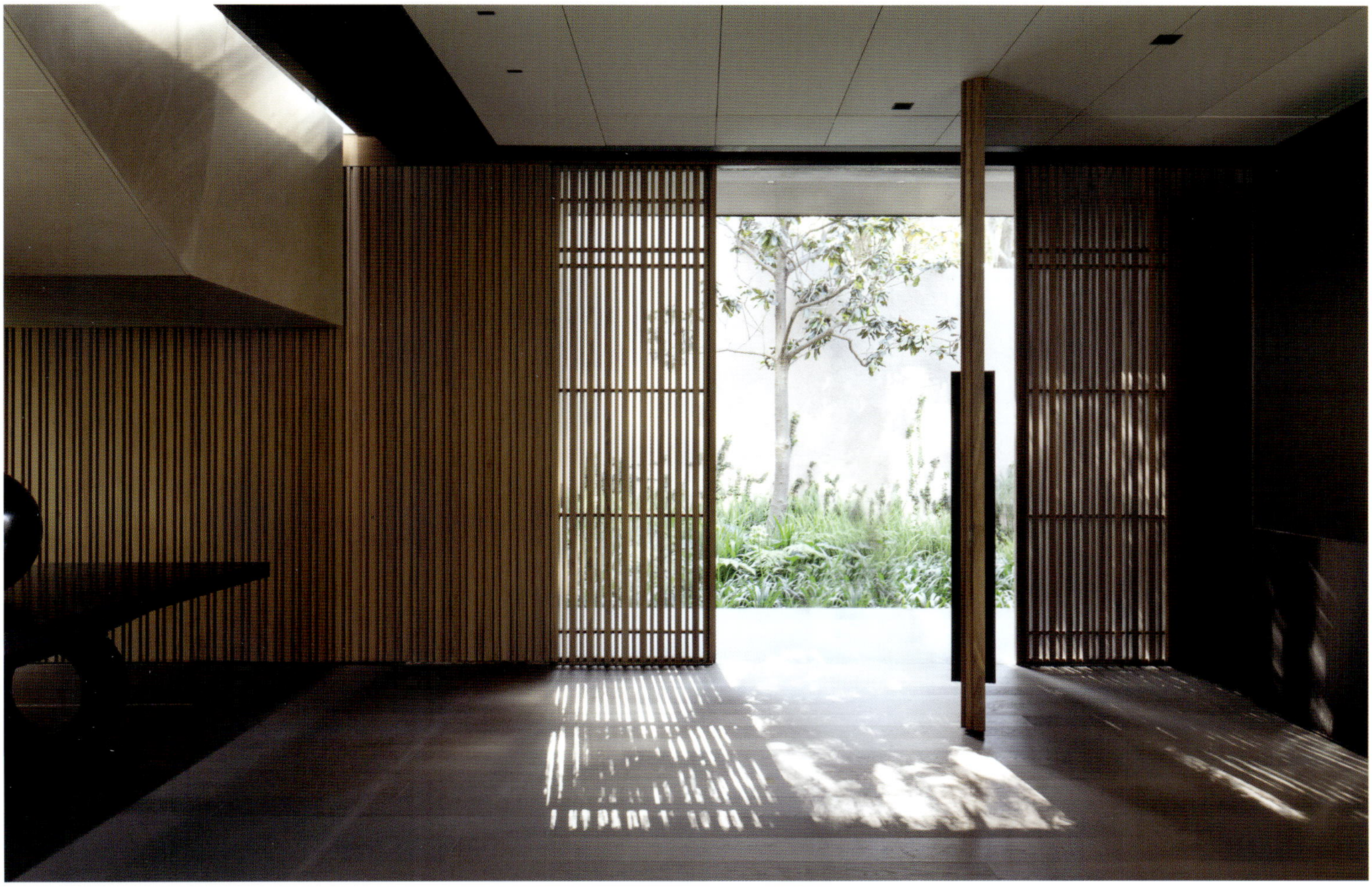

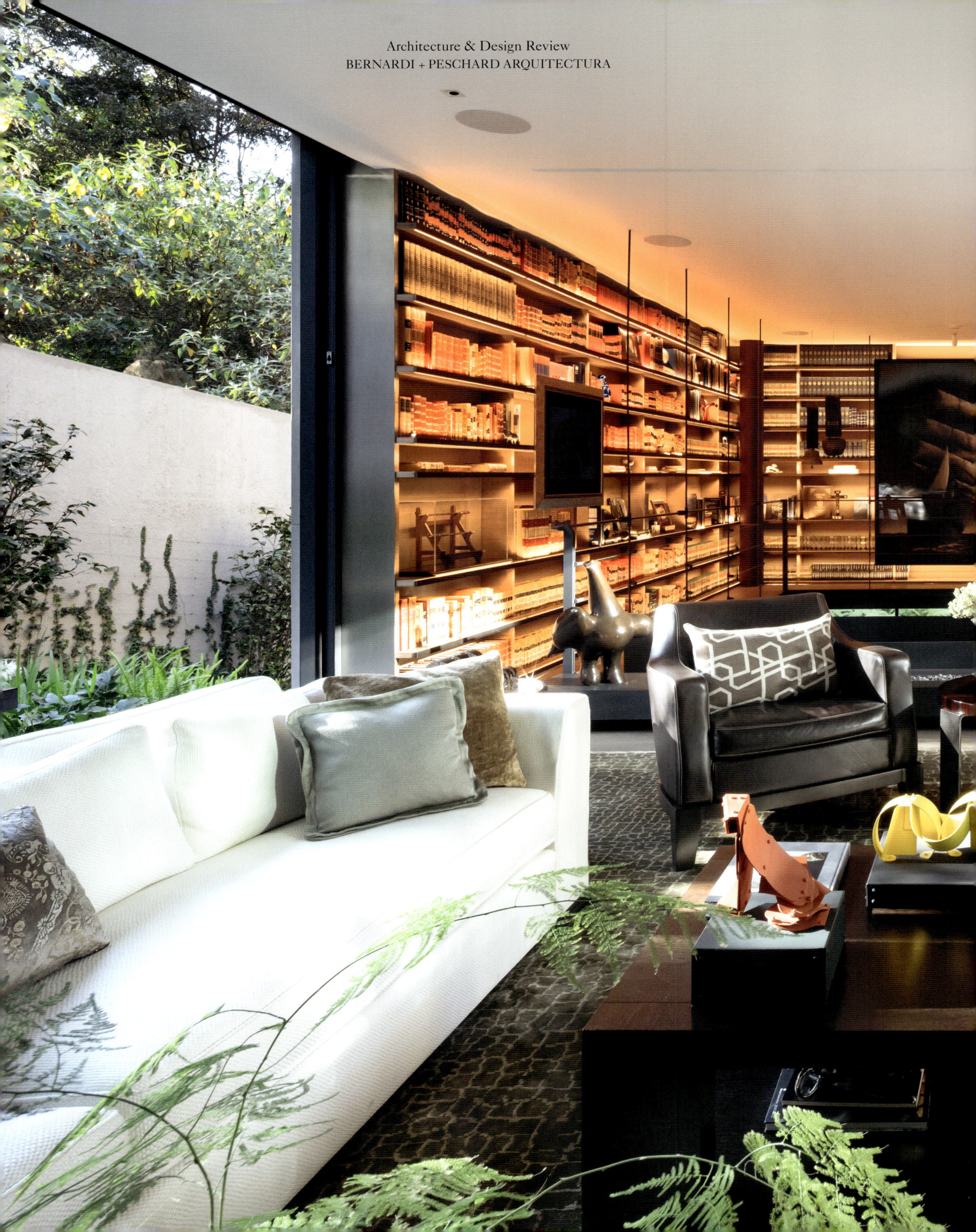

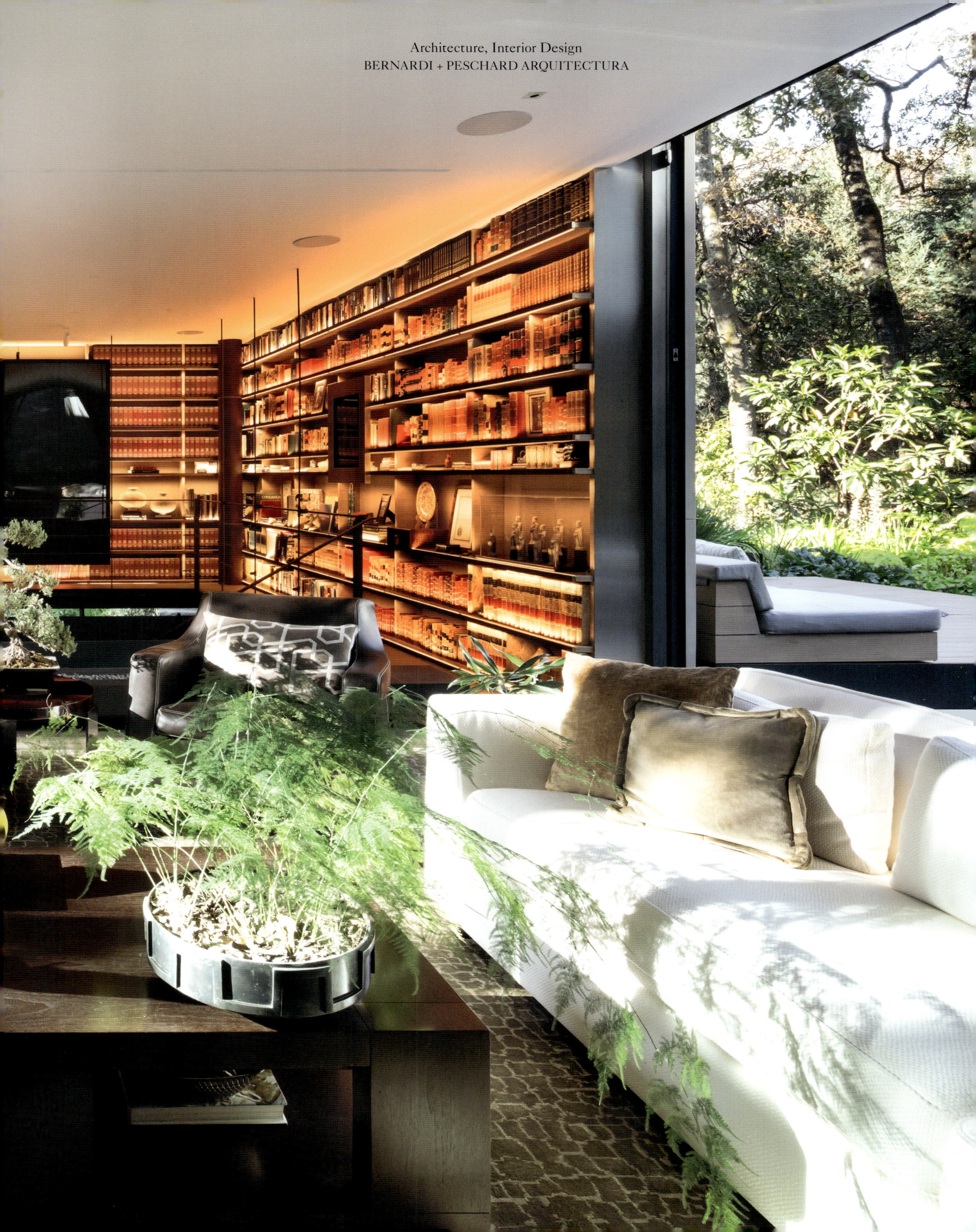

Architecture, Interior Design
BERNARDI + PESCHARD ARQUITECTURA

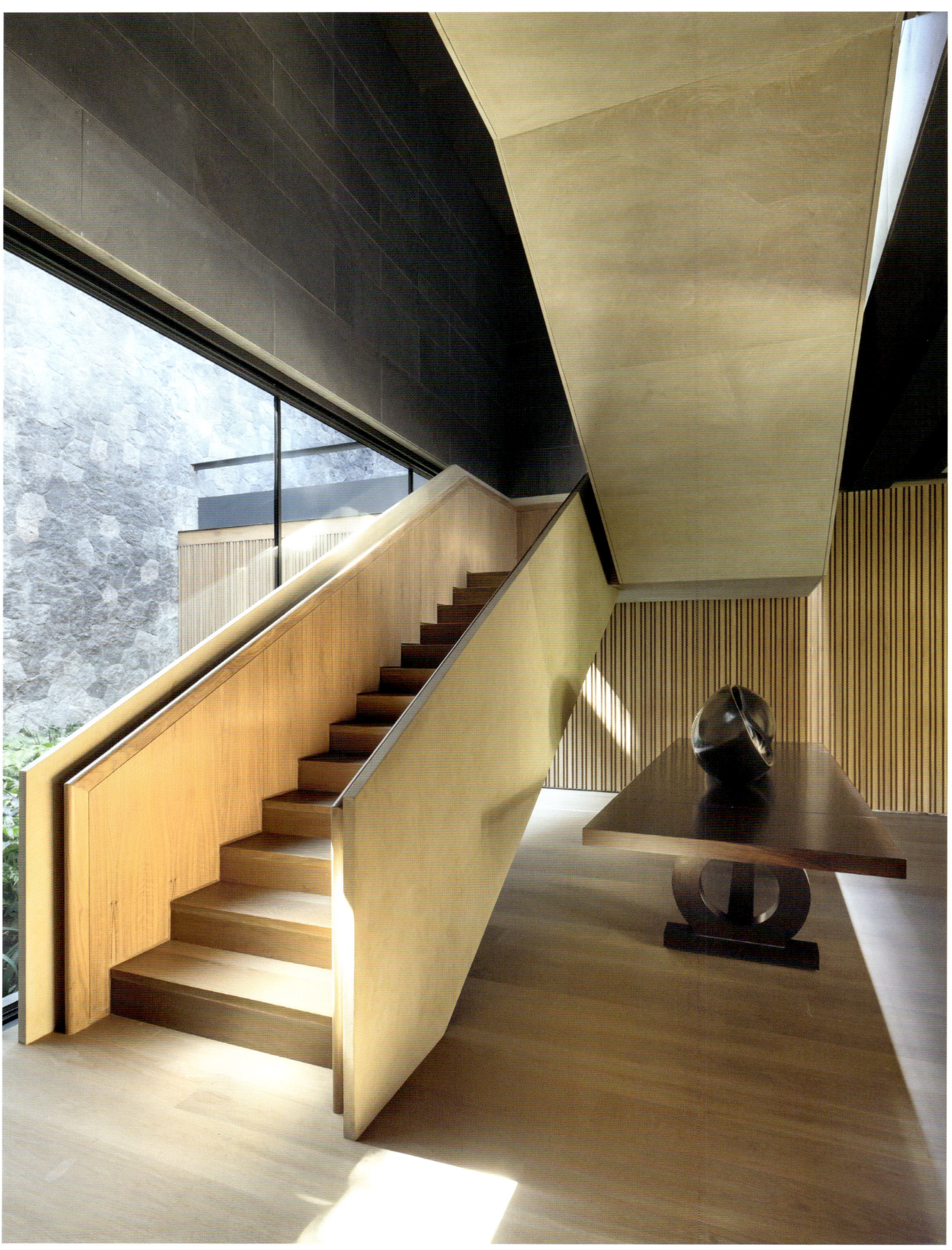

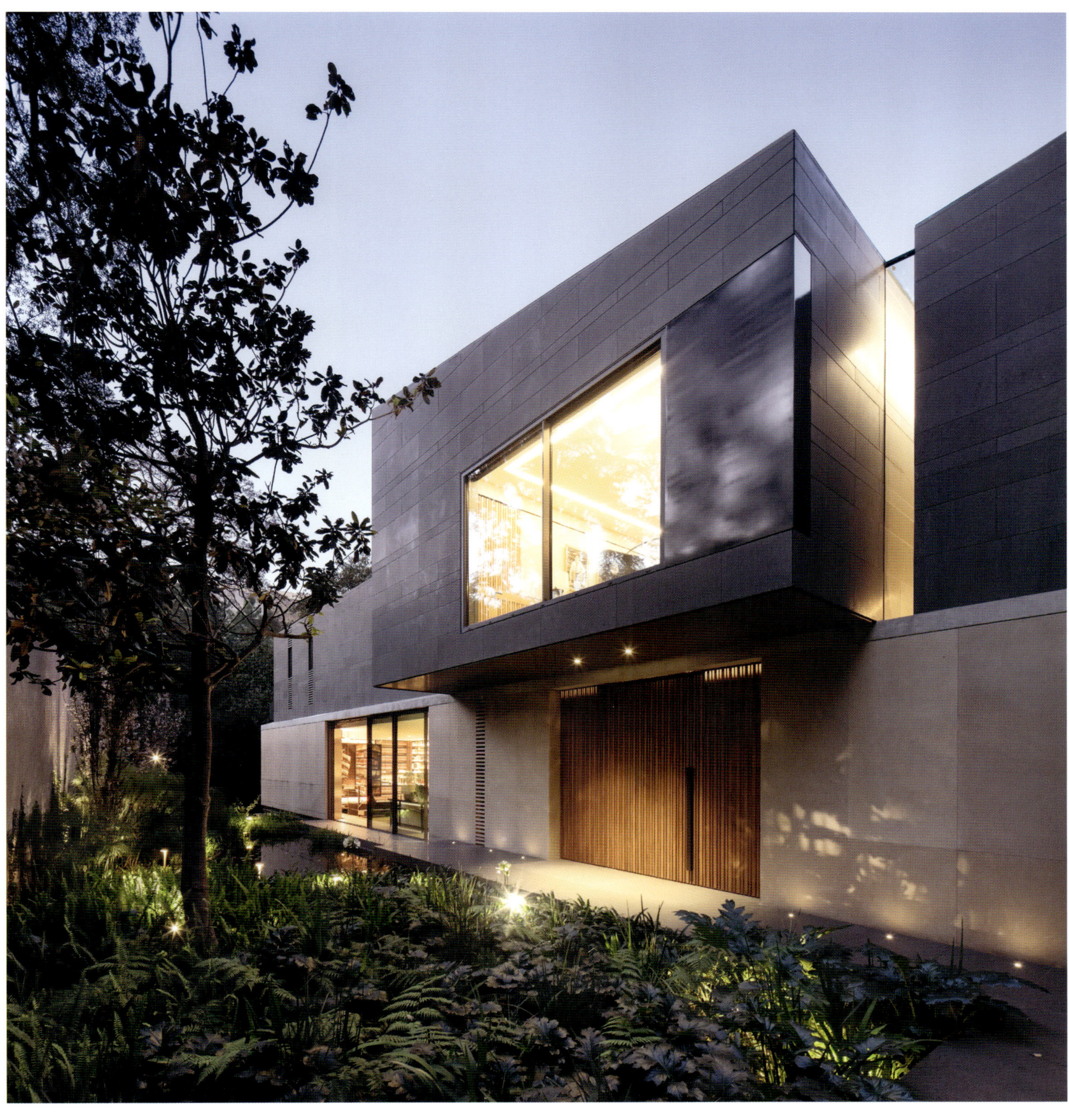

The staircase lies at the apex of the L-shaped cross-section (opposite page), which provides the structure for the building on all levels. The communal first-floor rooms are surrounded by the garden (pages 58–59). Large glass surfaces create a high degree of transparency, with the blending of internal and external areas demonstrating the rigorous functionalism of the firm's architectural philosophy. At one end of the house, the rooms are twice as high as those at the other (above). The library, atelier, and private main bedroom are somewhat secluded. The transition to the upper floor is lent further emphasis by using different materials and design elements in the façade.

Im Scheitelpunkt des L-förmigen Querschnitts liegt das Treppenhaus (Seite gegenüber). Hierdurch wird das Gebäude auf allen Ebenen strukturiert. Die gemeinschaftlich genutzten Räume des Erdgeschosses sind vom Garten umgeben (Seite 58–59). Durch die großen Glasflächen entsteht viel Transparenz. Solche Verschmelzungen von Innen- und Außenbereichen zeigen den entschlossenen Funktionalismus des architektonischen Konzepts. An einem Ende des Hauses sind die Raumhöhen verdoppelt (oben). In einer gewissen Abgeschiedenheit befinden sich hier Bibliothek, Atelier und privates Hauptschlafzimmer. Der Übergang zum Obergeschoss wird zudem durch unterschiedliche Materialien und Gestaltungselemente in der Fassade betont.

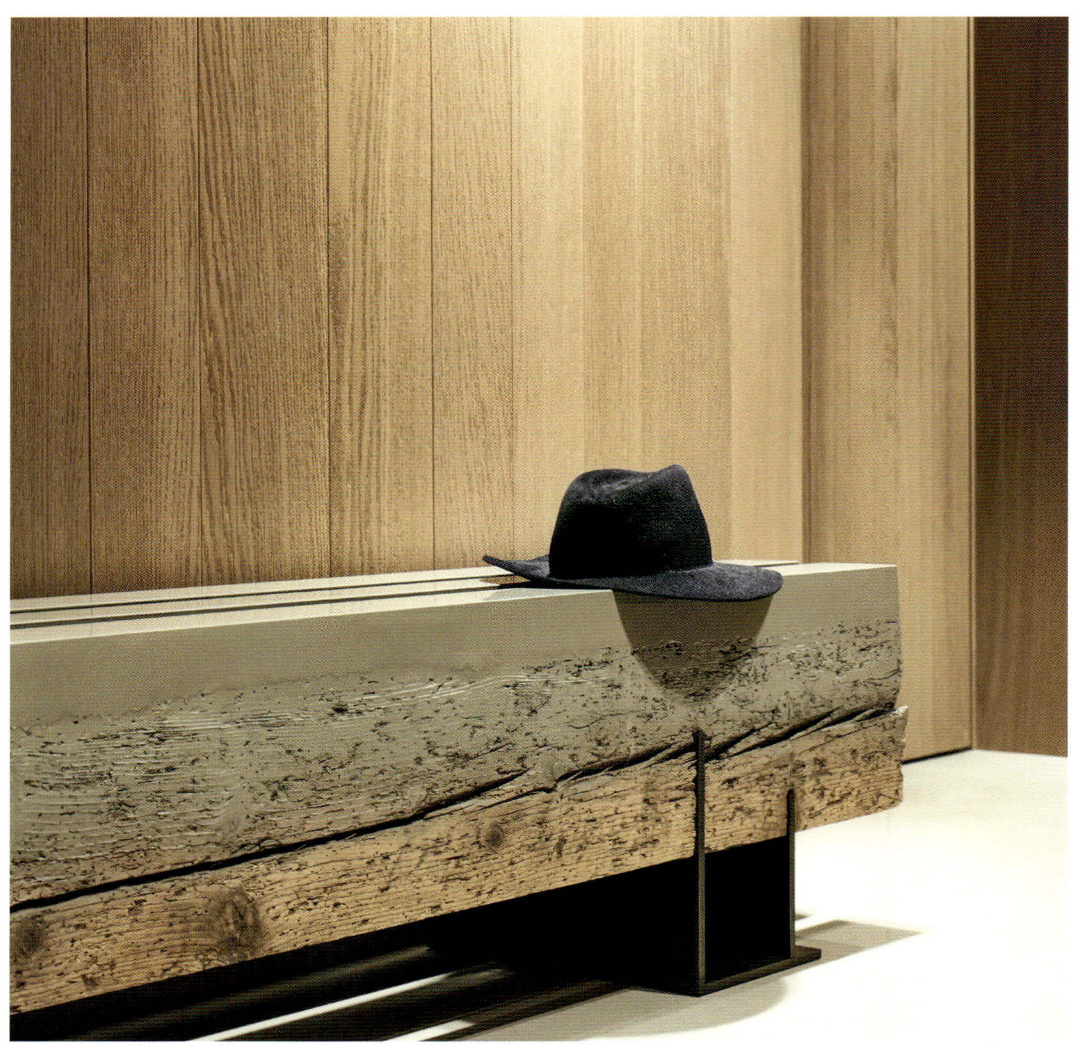

BERND GRUBER GMBH

STUHLFELDEN / AUSTRI

Strong Local Roots | Starke heimische Wurzeln

When Bernd Gruber took over his father's carpentry workshop in Stuhlfelden in the state of Salzburg in 1992, he soon became aware of the high standard of craftsmanship in his surrounding area. What the young man considered lacking, however, was a liaison with conceptional interior design. Gruber therefore acquired and embraced traditional skills and knowledge but also questioned certain aspects of them. With his intuitive grasp of contemporary design, and aided by his wife Ruth and creative director Philipp Hoflehner, he was able to steadily develop, expand and modernize the production facility in Stuhlfelden: what started as a traditional carpenter's workshop went on to become an international design company with a studio in Aurach, close to Kitzbühel.

Als Bernd Gruber 1992 die väterliche Tischlerwerkstatt in Stuhlfelden im Salzburger Land übernahm, erkannte er bald das hoch qualitative Handwerk in seinem Umfeld. Was der junge Mann jedoch vermisste, war eine Verbindung zum konzeptionellen Interior Design. Gruber machte sich also das traditionelle Können und Wissen zu eigen, stellte aber auch manches infrage. Mit einem intuitiven Gespür für zeitgemäßes Design und unterstützt von seiner Frau Ruth sowie Creative Director Philipp Hoflehner konnte er die Produktionsstätte in Stuhlfelden beständig weiterentwickeln, erweitern und modernisieren: Aus der Traditionstischlerei wurde ein internationales Interior-Design-Unternehmen mit einem Atelier in Aurach-Kitzbühel.

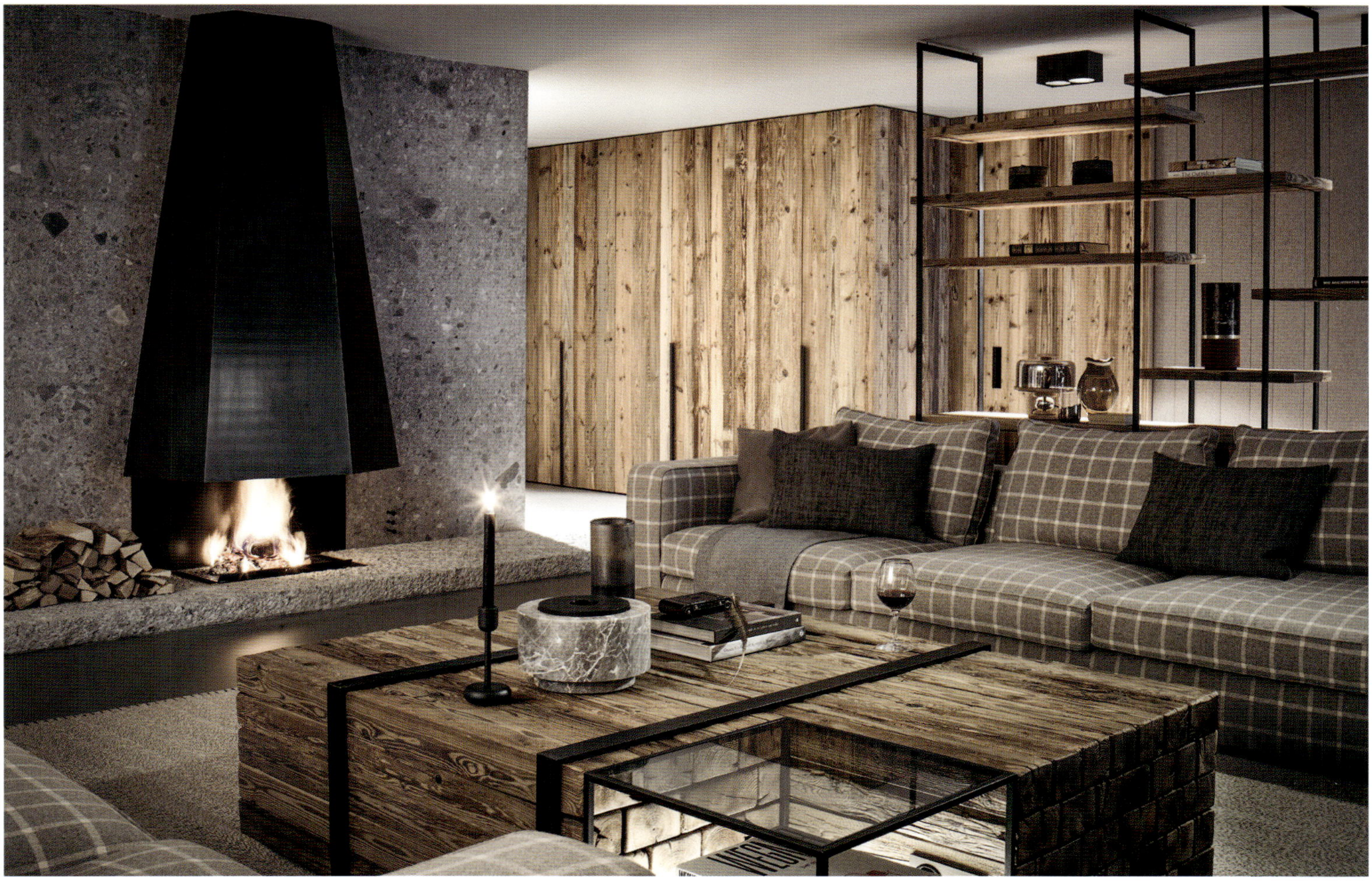

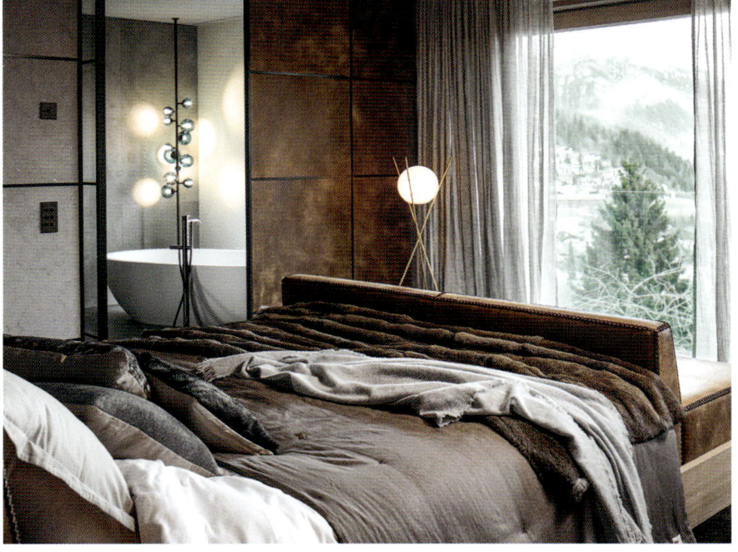

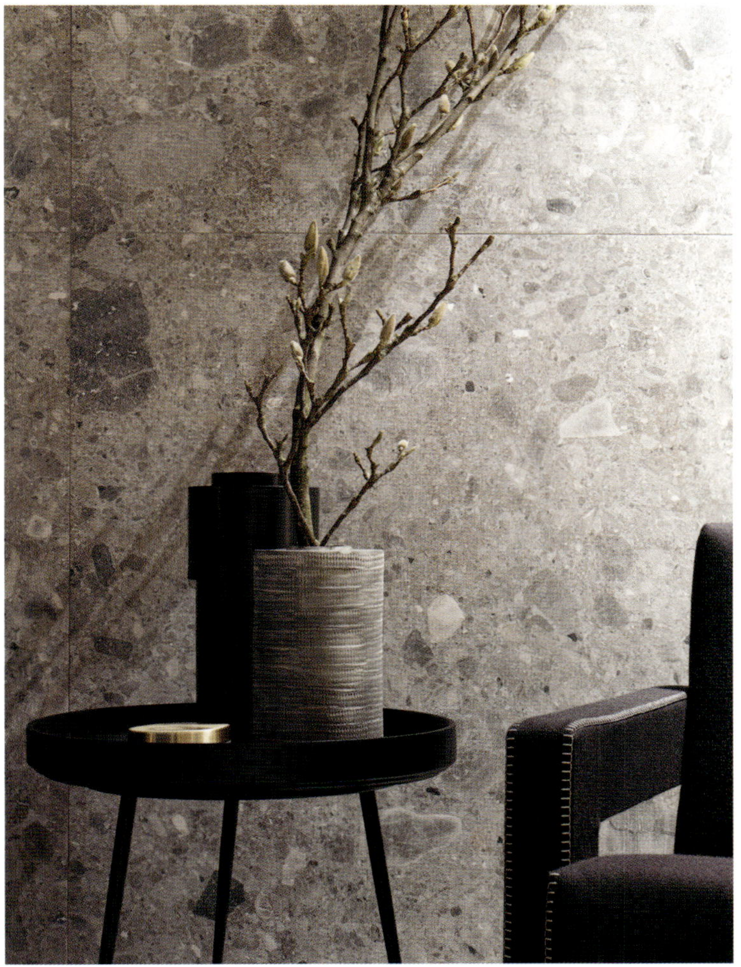

Grison apartment: this apartment is located at an altitude of more than 1000 meters in the Grison Alps. The approximately 700 square meter surface area can either be used as an individual loft or—thanks to its movable partitions—as four separate units.

Apartment Graubünden: Über 1000 Meter hoch liegt dieses Apartment in den Bündner Alpen. Die rund 700 Quadratmeter können als ein einziges Loft oder – dank beweglicher Unterteilungen – in vier separaten Einheiten genutzt werden.

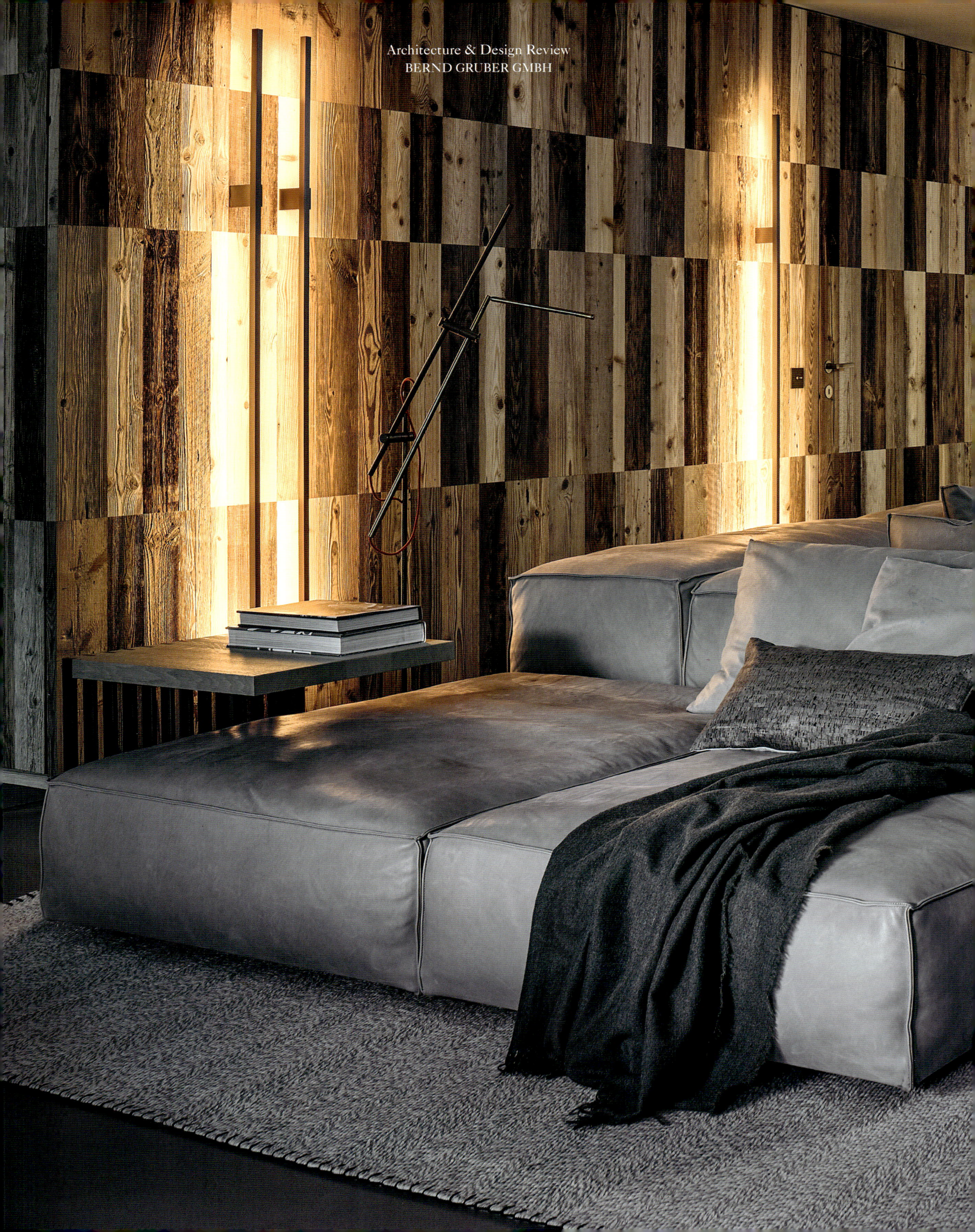
Architecture & Design Review
BERND GRUBER GMBH

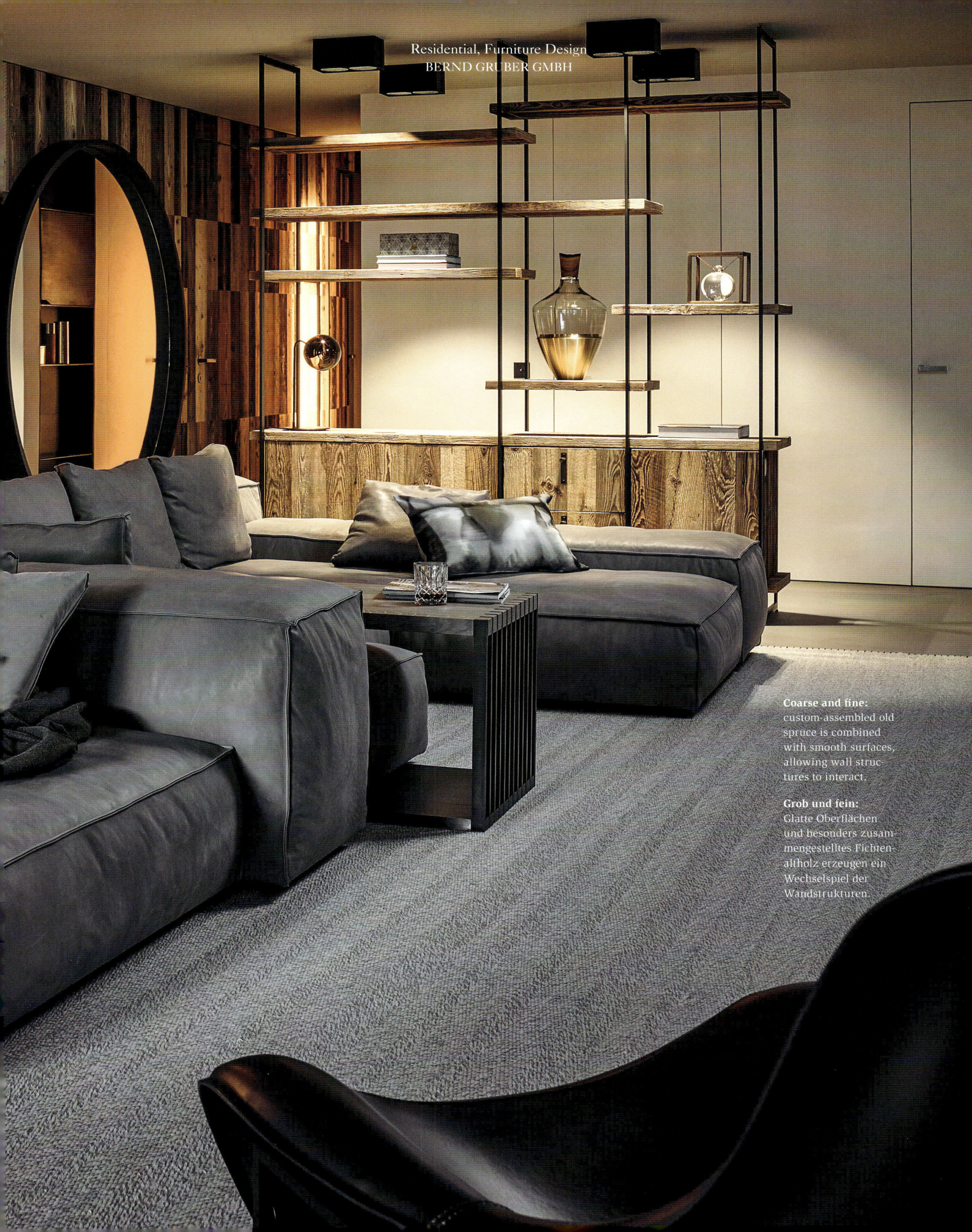

Coarse and fine: custom-assembled old spruce is combined with smooth surfaces, allowing wall structures to interact.

Grob und fein: Glatte Oberflächen und besonders zusammengestelltes Fichtenaltholz erzeugen ein Wechselspiel der Wandstrukturen.

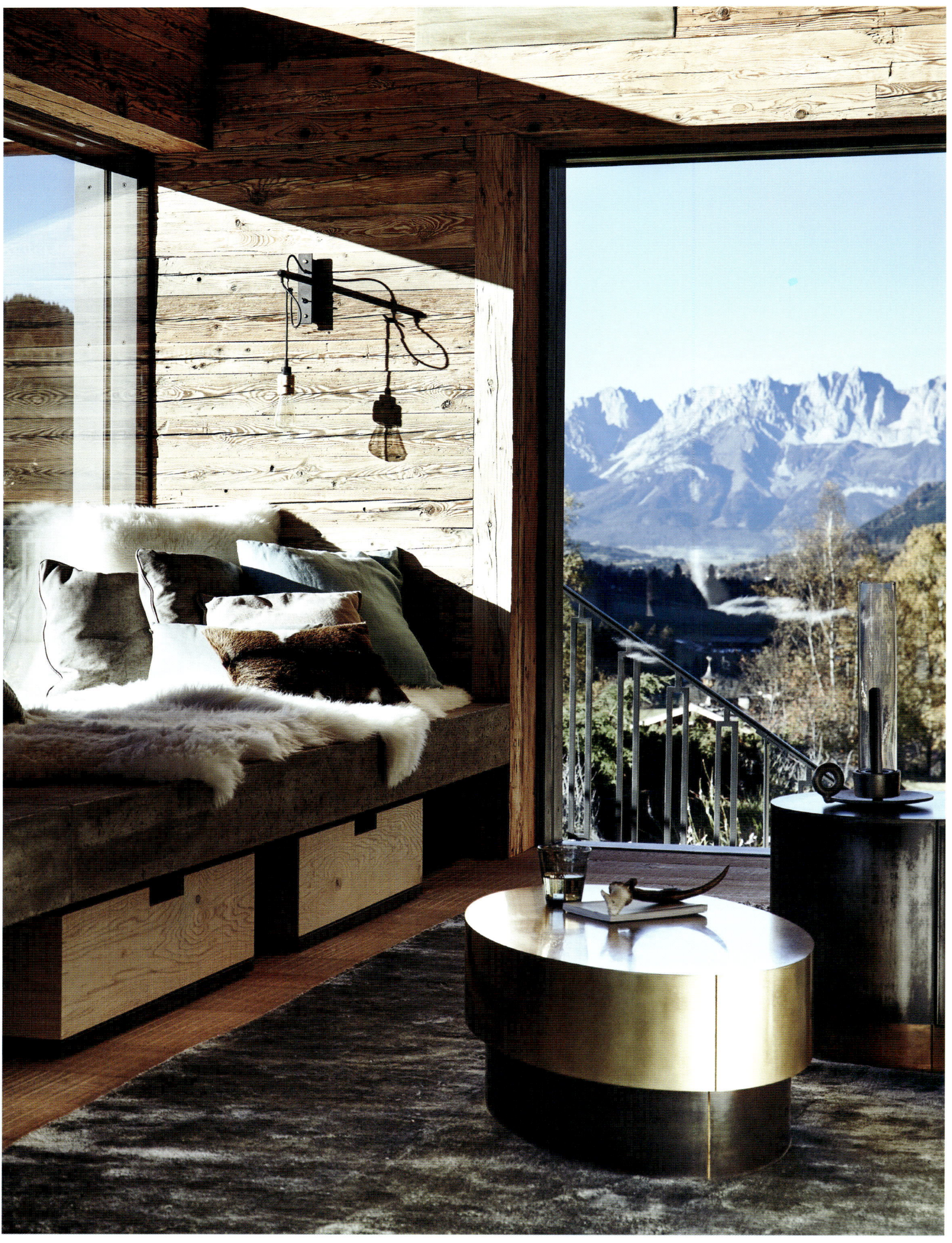

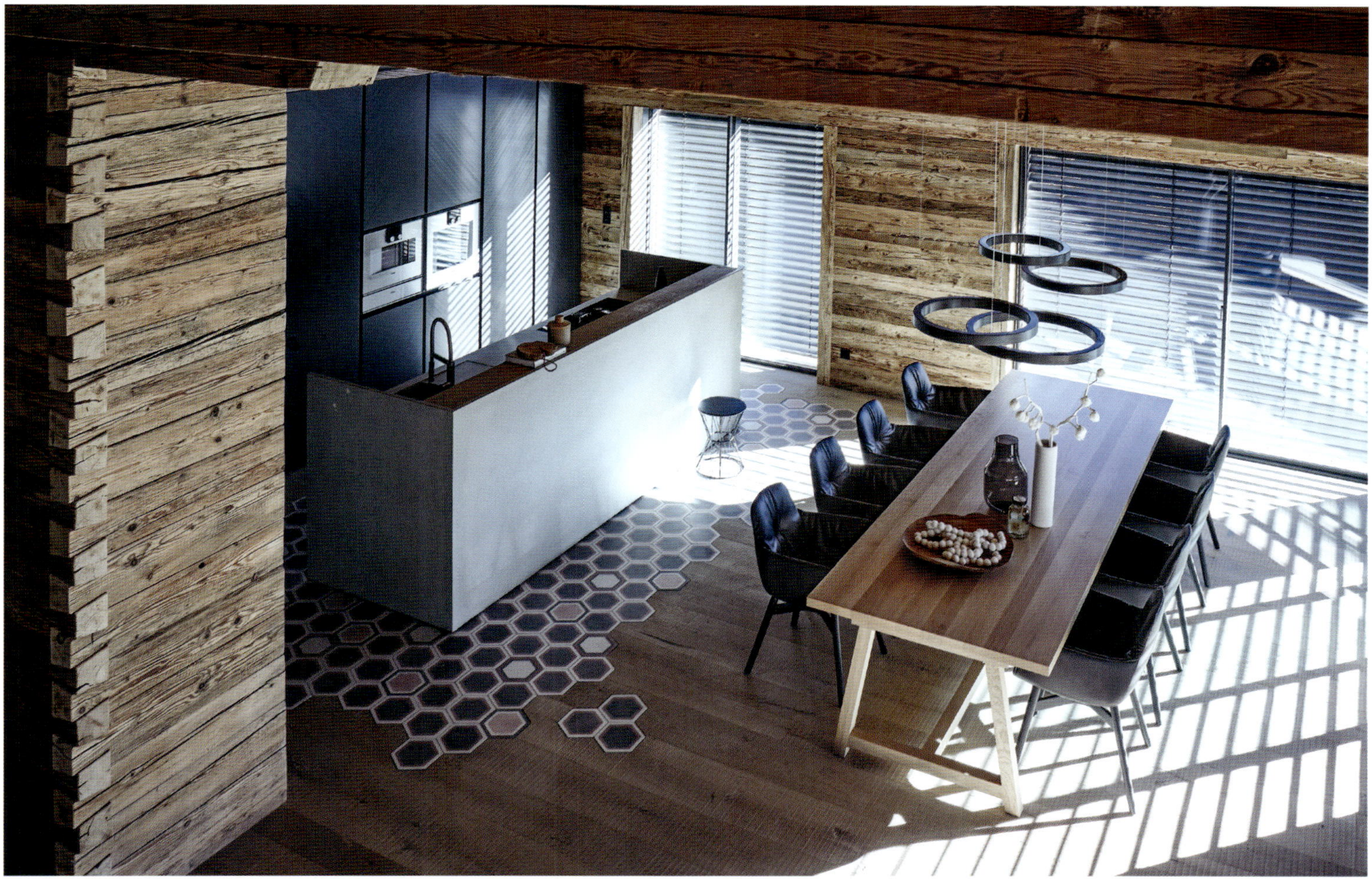

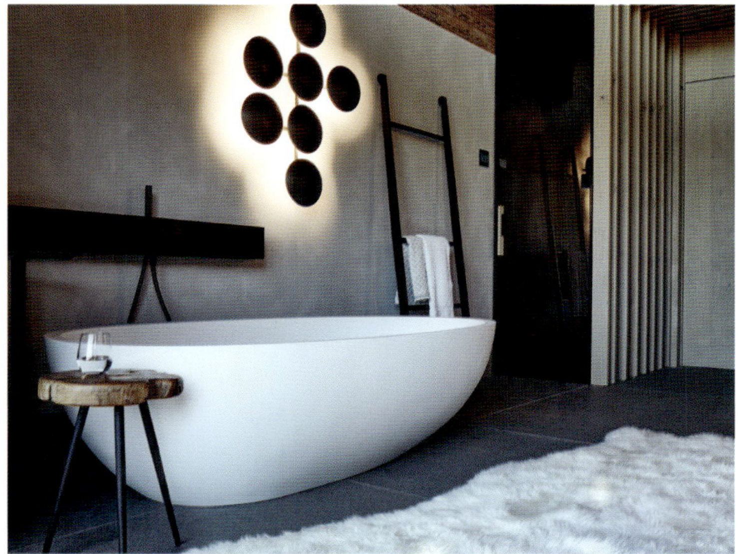

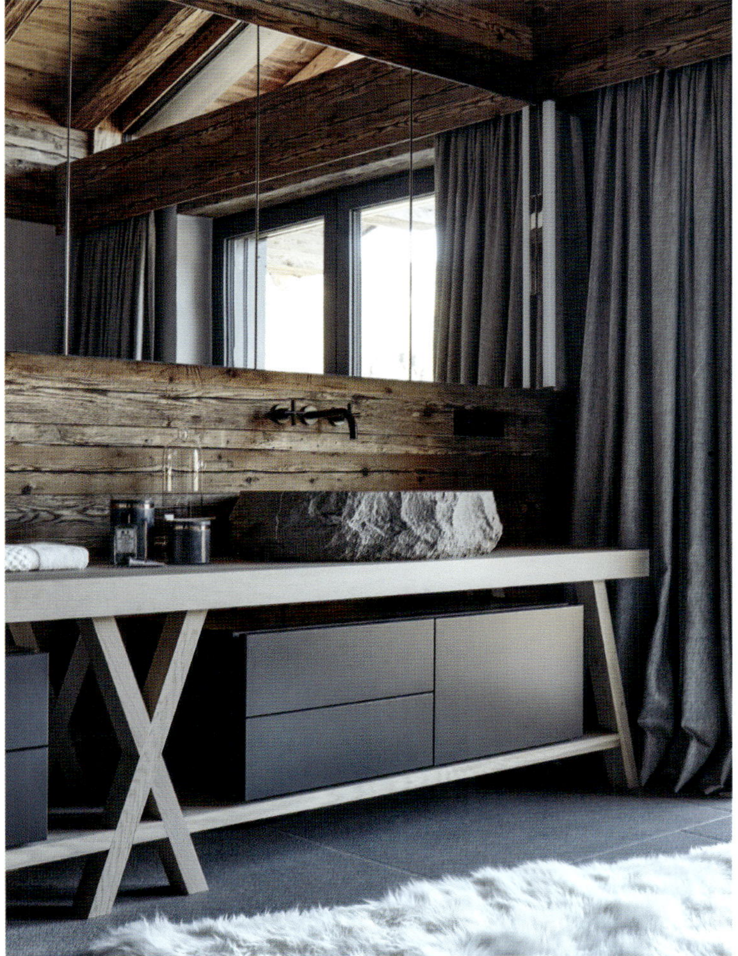

Chalet Leitenweg Jochberg: in line with the surrounding mountain scenery, a harking-back to nature was the guiding design principle here. Bernd Gruber accompanied the client for two years in his search for this location.

Chalet Leitenweg Jochberg: Entsprechend der umgebenden Berglandschaft war die Rückbesinnung auf die Natur Leitgedanke der Ausgestaltung. Bernd Gruber hatte den Bauherrn zwei Jahre lang auf der Suche nach diesem Ort begleitet.

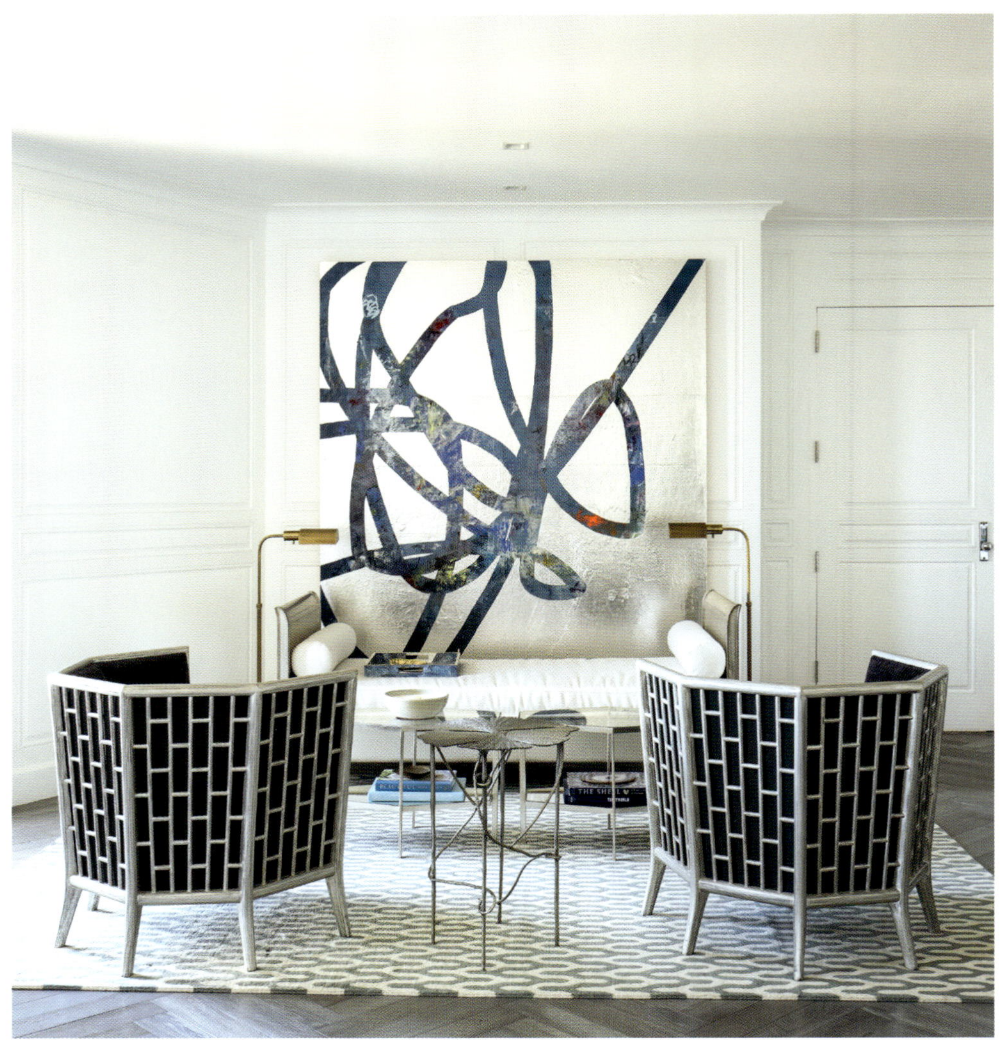

BLUE CARREON

NEW YORK / USA

Clear Design Philosophy | Klare Designphilosophie

Blue Carreon's work as a fashion and lifestyle journalist brought him into contact with the world of interior architecture. His work includes the book *Conversations,* a collection of interviews with icons from the fields of fashion, design, and art. Blue Carreon has gone on to apply his knowledge of interior design to projects in the Philippines, Hong Kong and New York. He has also taken a bold decision to launch his own design brand. All of the products of Blue Carreon Home are hand made by artisans, and his collections of furniture, decorative objects and home accessories are consistent with a design philosophy defined by modern elegance.

Mit der Welt der Innenarchitektur kam Blue Carreon durch seine Arbeit als Mode- und Lifestyle-Journalist in Kontakt. Er ist unter anderem Autor des Buches *Conversations,* das Interviews mit Ikonen aus Mode, Interior Design und Kunst versammelt. Seine Innenarchitektur-Kenntnisse konnte Blue Carreon dann bei Projekten auf den Philippinen, in Hongkong und in New York anwenden. Schließlich hat er sich mit einer eigenen Marke in die Welt des Designs gewagt. Jedes Produkt von Blue Carreon Home ist handgefertigt, und seine Kollektionen von Möbeln, dekorativen Objekten und Wohnaccessoires folgen konsequent einer Designphilosophie moderner Eleganz.

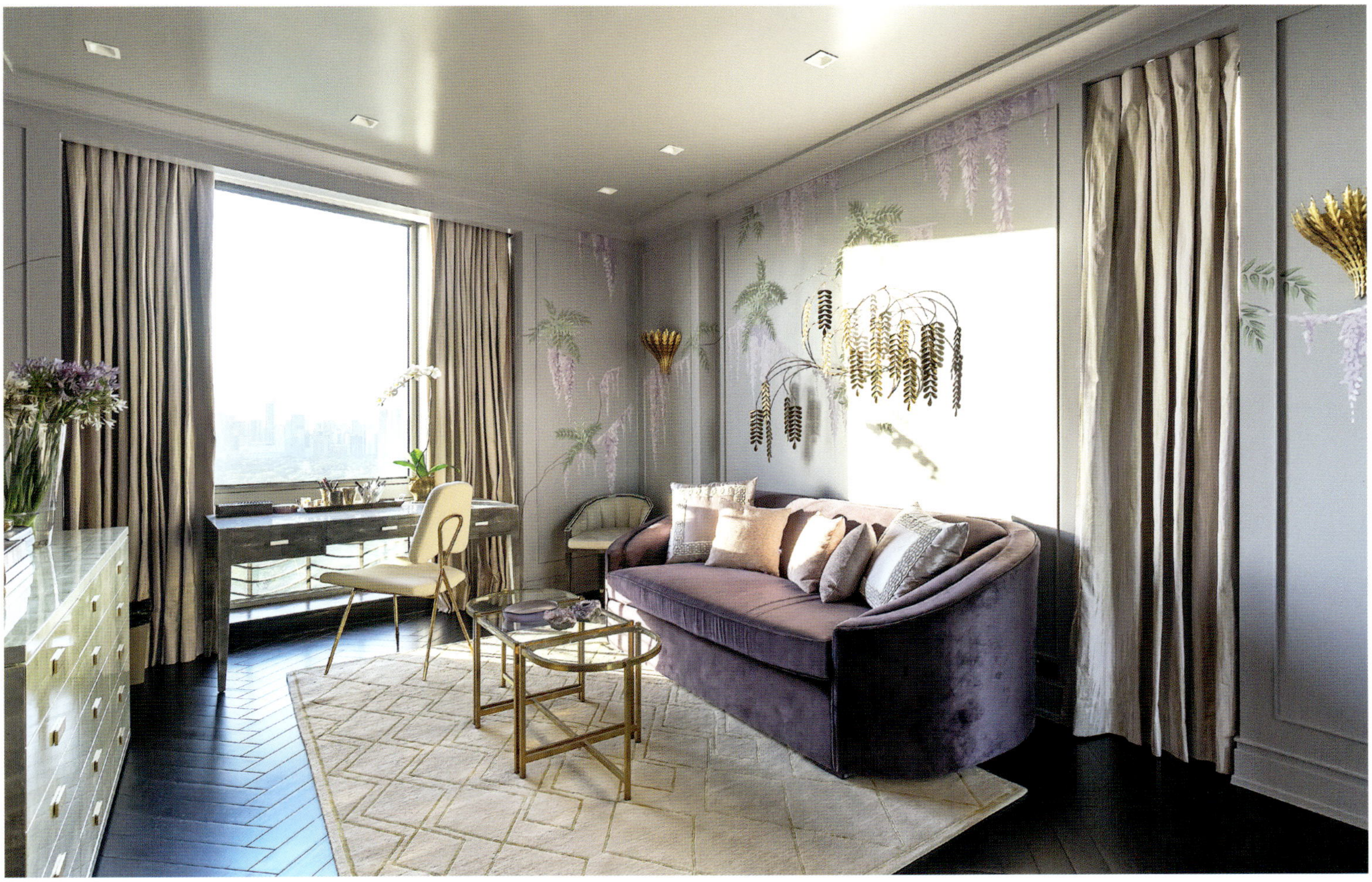

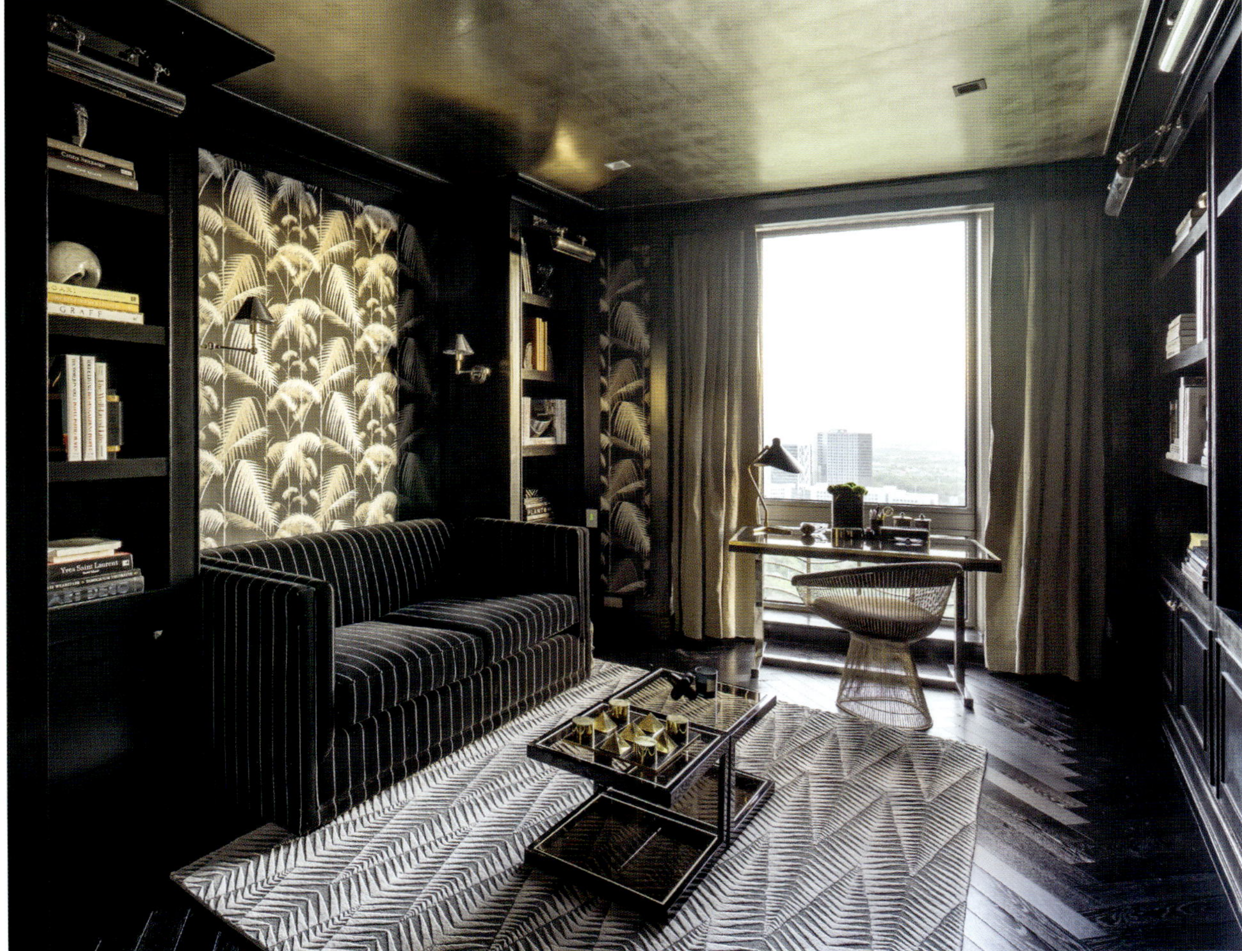

Apartment in Manila, Philippines (opposite page): seating area with a painting by Hugo McCloud and custom-made chairs covered in Donghia. The boudoir (above) impresses with its hand-painted walls. The library (left) is dominated by Art Deco elements which are set off by Cole & Son's tropical palm-leaf print wallpaper.

Wohnung in Manila, Philippinen (Seite gegenüber): Sitzbereich mit Gemälde von Hugo McCloud und maßgefertigten Stühlen mit Donghia-Stoff. Das Boudoir (oben) beeindruckt mit handbemalten Wänden. In der Bibliothek (links) dominiert Art déco im Kontrast mit tropischen Palmblattdruck-Tapeten von Cole & Son.

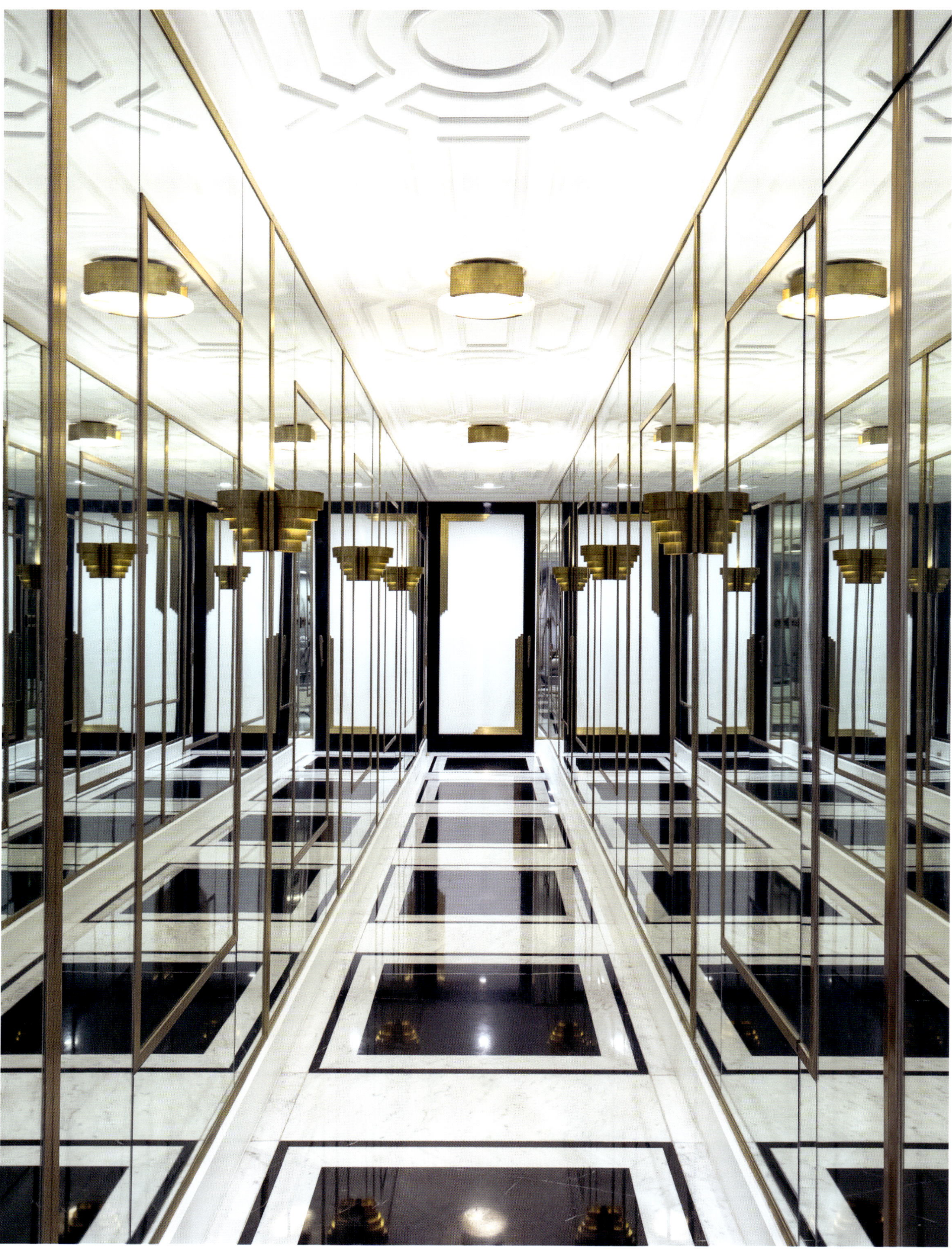

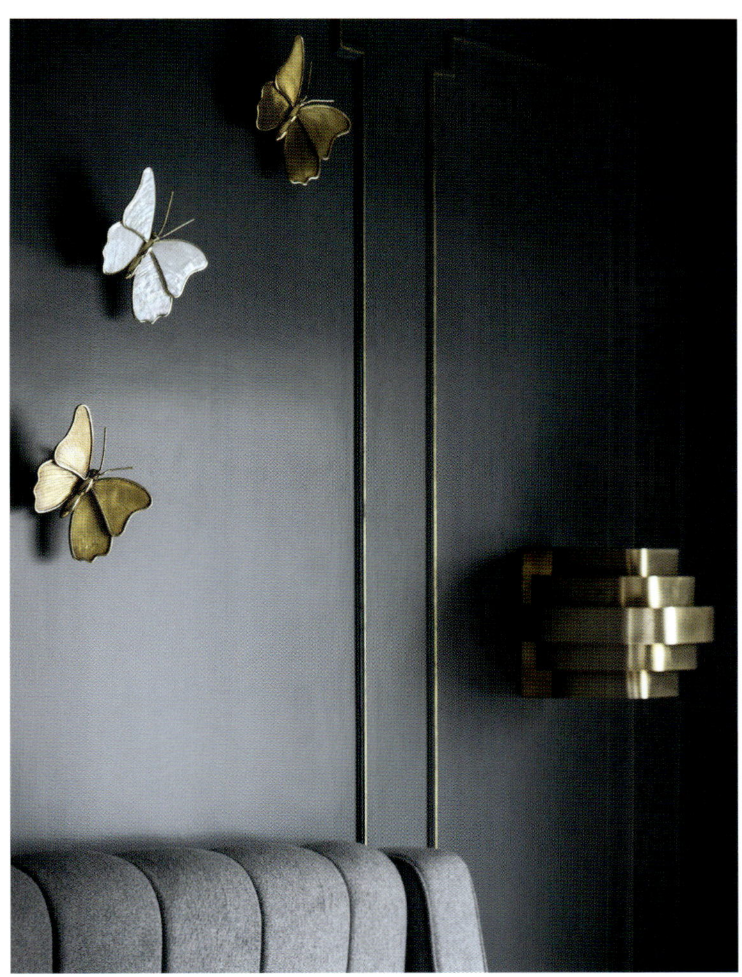

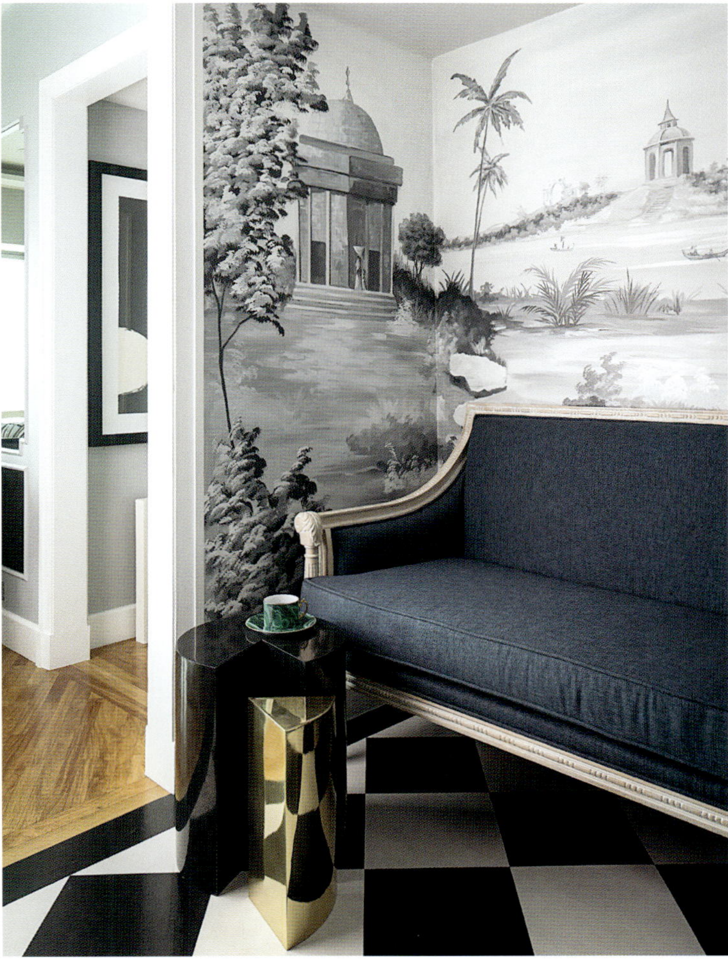

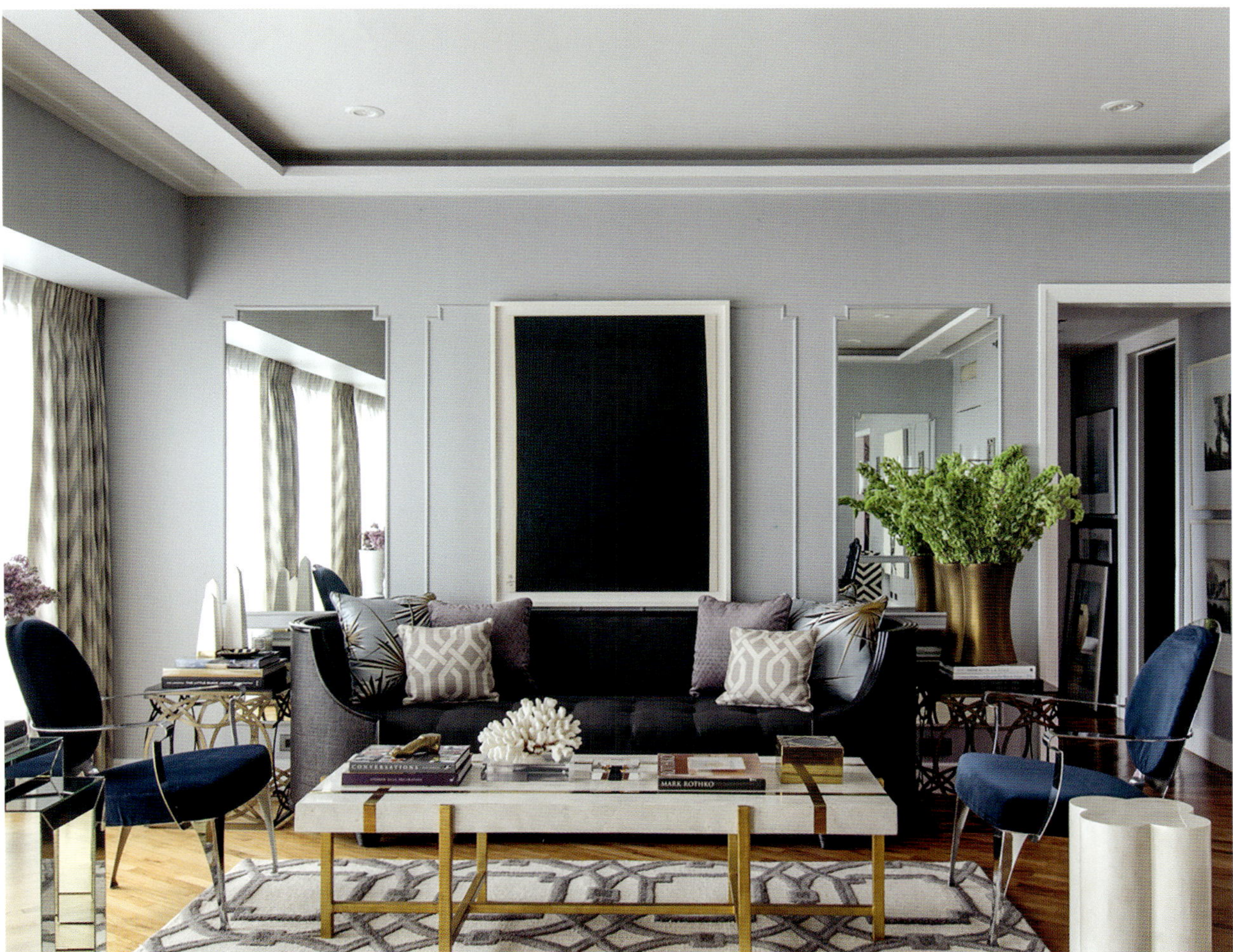

A mirror enfilade with hidden doors to connect two apartments (opposite page). Blue Carreon's own apartment features a hand-painted grisaille foyer with varnished wooden floors (top right). Butterfly sculptures on a dark bedroom wall (top left). A modern French-style living room (left).

Spiegel-Enfilade mit verborgenen Türen zur Verbindung zweier Wohneinheiten (Seite gegenüber). Blue Carreons Apartment verfügt über ein hand-bemaltes Grisaille-Foyer mit lackierten Holzböden (oben rechts). Schmetter-lingsskulpturen auf dunkler Schlafzimmer-wand (oben links). Wohnzimmer im modernen französi-schen Stil (links).

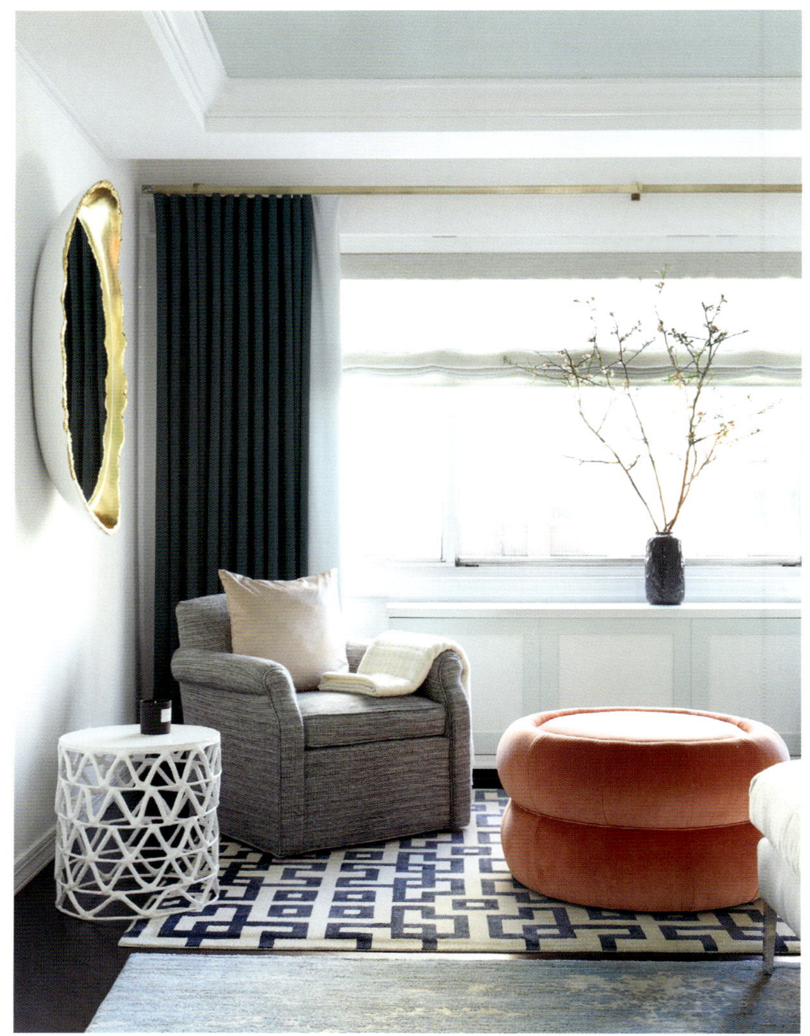

BROOKE MOORHEAD DESIGN

NEW YORK / USA

Purposeful and Contemporary | Zielstrebig und zeitgemäß

Brooke Moorhead creates interiors where her clients genuinely 'feel at home.' After careers in both finance and law within a stone's throw of Wall Street, Moorhead did an about-face, enrolling at the New York School of Interior Design. Shortly thereafter, she became an entrepreneur as well as a mother. In so doing, she has inherently brought sophistication juxtaposed with practicality to her projects—all of which boast clean lines, contemporary elements, and artful details. Above all, Brooke relies on both passion and partnership to design beautiful spaces that help clients realize their dream homes.

Brooke Moorhead gestaltet Innenräume, in denen sich ihre Kunden wirklich zu Hause fühlen. Nach Karrieren in der Rechts- und Finanzbranche ganz in der Nähe der Wall Street warf Moorhead das Steuer herum und schrieb sich an der New York School of Interior Design ein. Bald wurde sie sowohl Unternehmerin als auch Mutter, was mit sich brachte, dass ihre Projekte nicht nur von Raffinesse, sondern auch von Praktikabilität geprägt sind. Alle zeichnen sich durch klare Linien, moderne Elemente und kunstvolle Details aus. Es sind vor allem aber Engagement und Partnerschaftlichkeit, mit denen Brooke schöne Räume gestaltet, damit die Wohnträume ihrer Kunden Wirklichkeit werden.

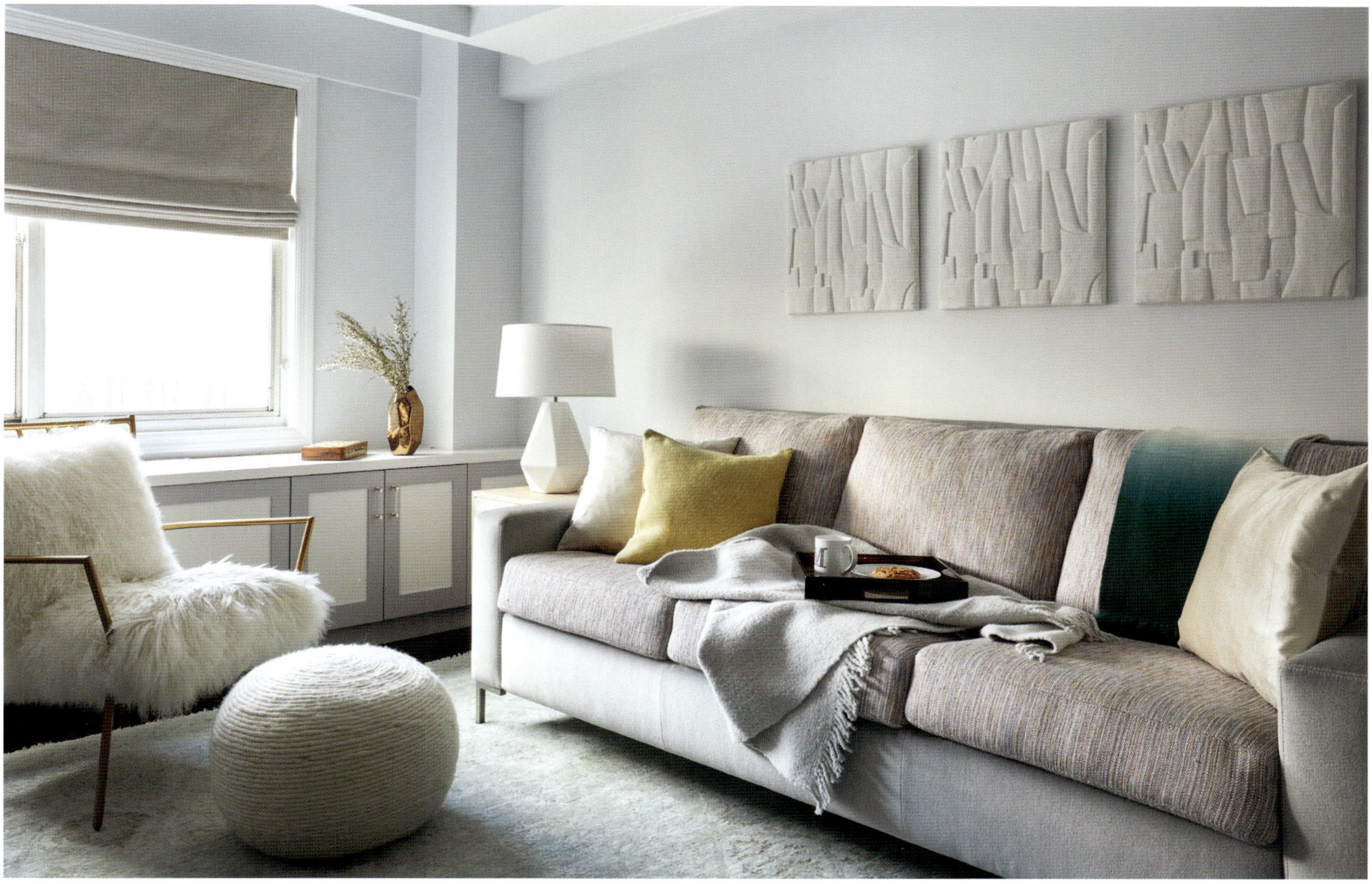

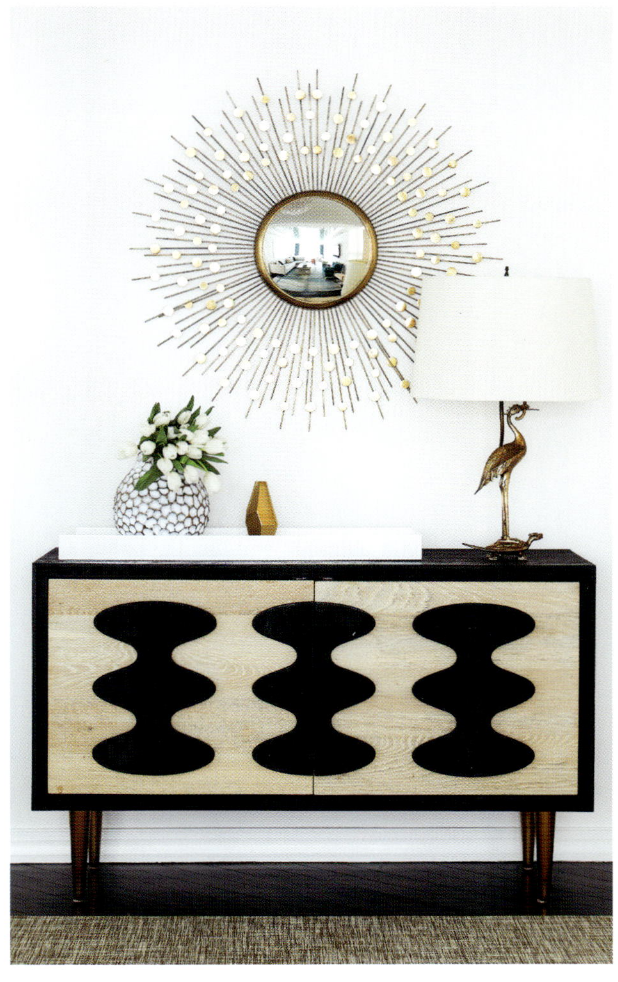

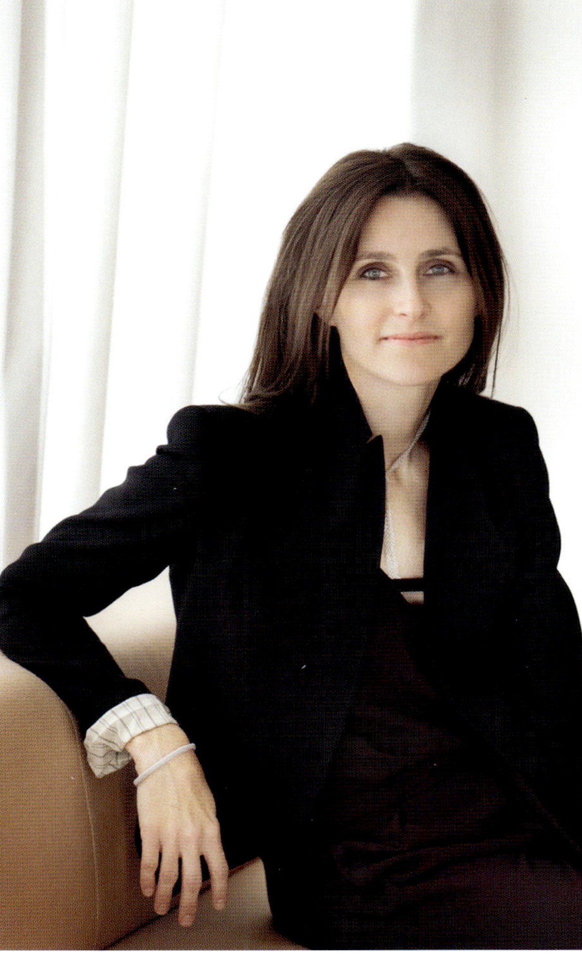

The team surrounding Brooke Moorhead is dedicated to providing a comprehensive personalized experience, supporting the client from planning to completion. No detail is left undone, and the design is achieved with unerring dedication to style and contemporary taste.

Das Team um Inhaberin Brooke Moorhead ist darauf spezialisiert, seine Auftraggeber individuell und umfassend zu unterstützen, vom Entwurf bis zur Fertigstellung. Ein unfehlbares Gespür für Stil und zeitgemäßen Geschmack prägt die Gestaltung in allen Einzelheiten.

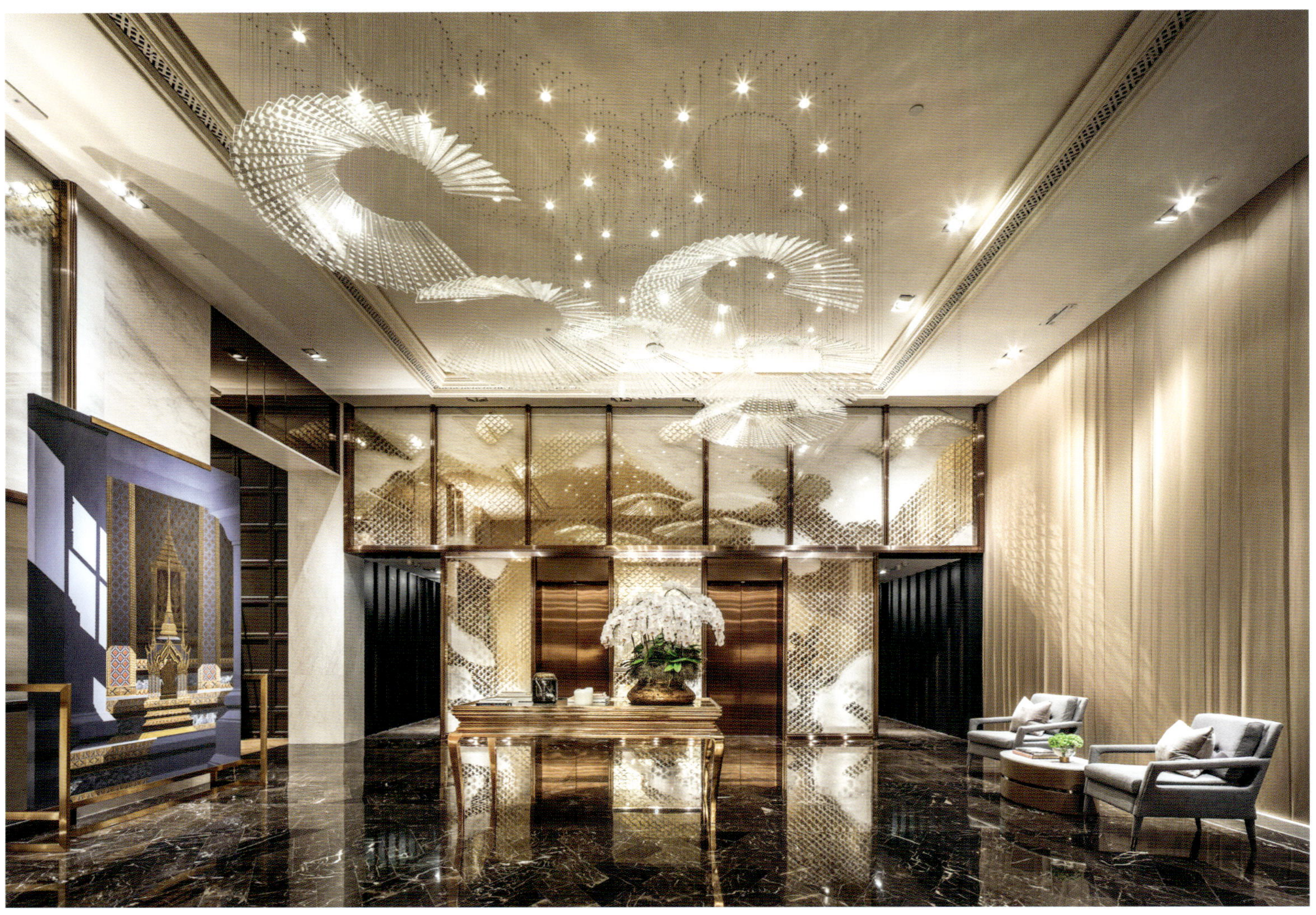

CELIA CHU DESIGN & ASSOCIATES

TAIPEI / TAIWAN

Award-winning Design | Preisgekröntes Design

Celia Chu Design & Associates especially enjoys working on unusual hotel projects. The dynamic and creative interior architecture firm from Taiwan attaches particular importance to its Asian identity, even though it operates, of course, internationally. The photos presented here show the award-winning interior design of the thirty-floor Rosewood Hotel in Bangkok, Thailand, which was constructed in 2019. Capturing the richness of Thai culture, from the building's external design right down to the window blinds, without neglecting international standards of comfort and furnishings, represented a special challenge for Celia Chu.

Außergewöhnliche Hotelprojekte sind etwas, womit sich Celia Chu Design & Associates besonders gern beschäftigt. Das dynamisch-kreative Innenarchitekturbüro aus Taiwan legt dabei Wert auf seine asiatische Identität, obwohl natürlich international gearbeitet wird. Die abgebildeten Fotos zeigen das preisgekrönte Innendesign des 2019 erbauten dreißigstöckigen Rosewood Hotel in Bangkok, Thailand. Für Celia Chu war es eine besondere Herausforderung, von der äußeren Gestaltung des Gebäudes bis zu den Fensterläden den Reichtum der thailändischen Kultur einzufangen, ohne dabei internationale Komfort- und Ausstattungsstandards zu vernachlässigen.

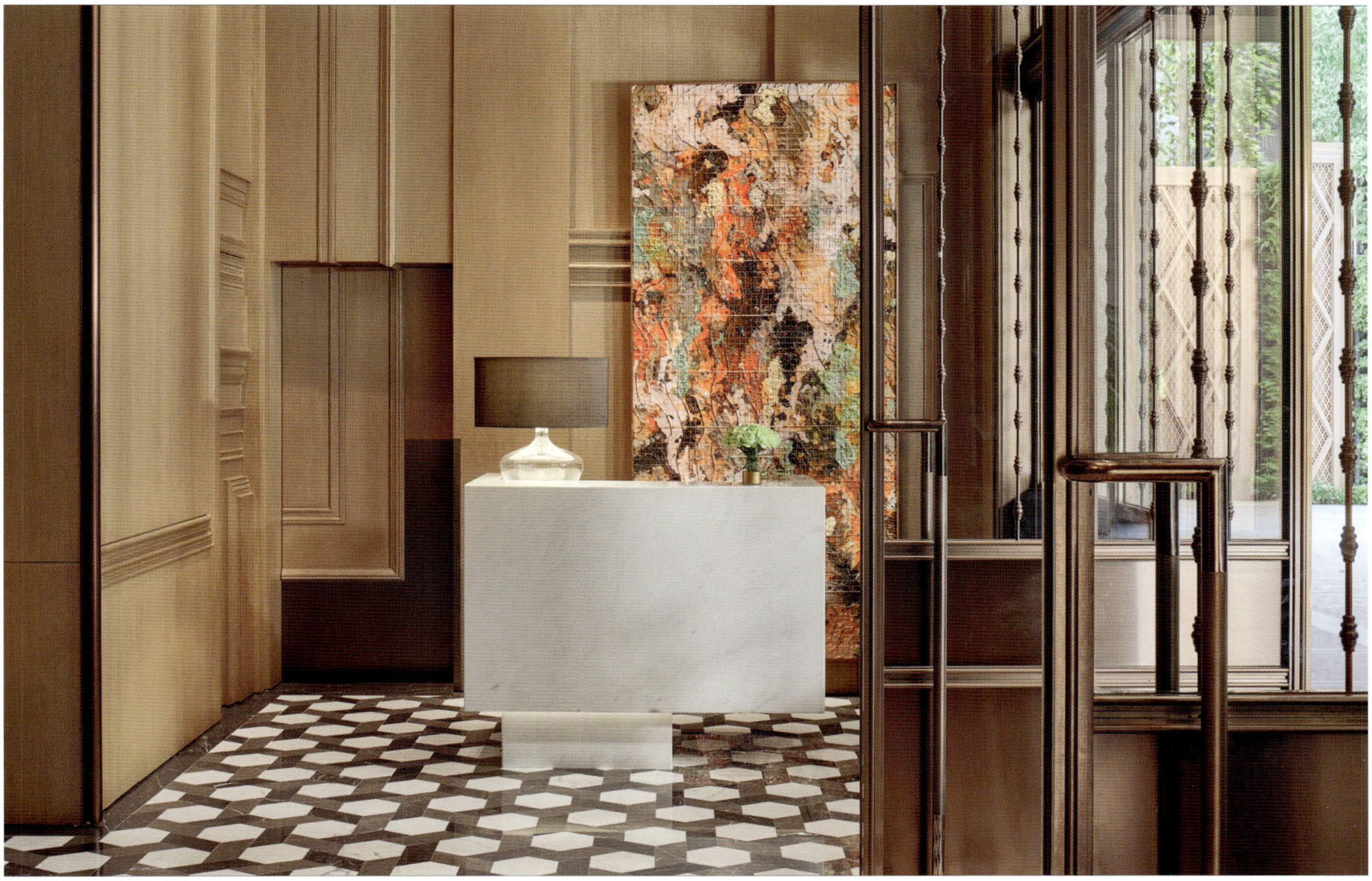

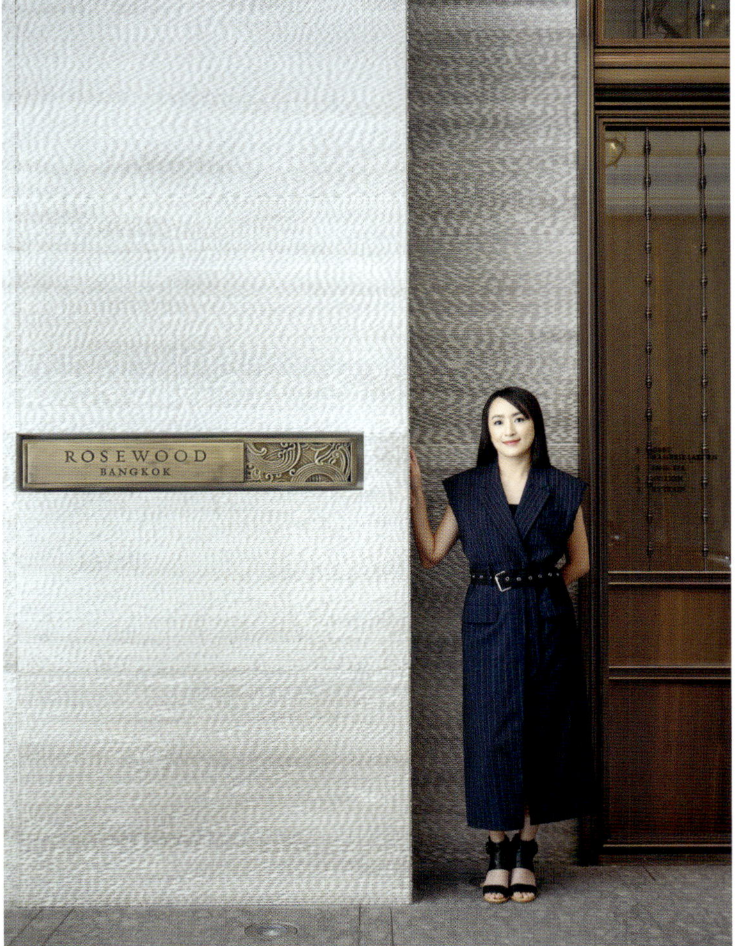

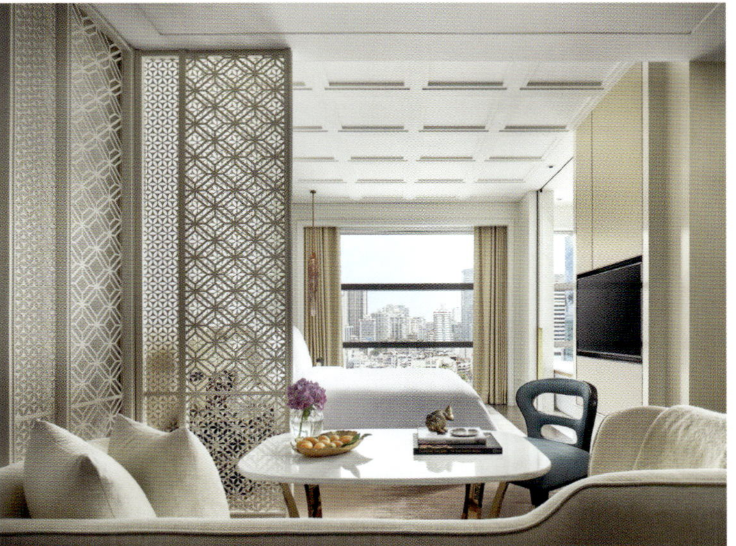

Blending contemporary and classical design is the concept behind Celia Chu's success. Unusual surfaces, materials and textures, brought to the fore by bespoke lighting, combine to create an oasis of relaxation.

Gegenwärtige und klassische Designs harmonisch zu verbinden ist Celia Chus erfolgreiches Konzept. Außergewöhnliche Oberflächen, Materialien und Texturen, betont durch individuelle Beleuchtung, erschaffen ein Wunderland der Entspannung.

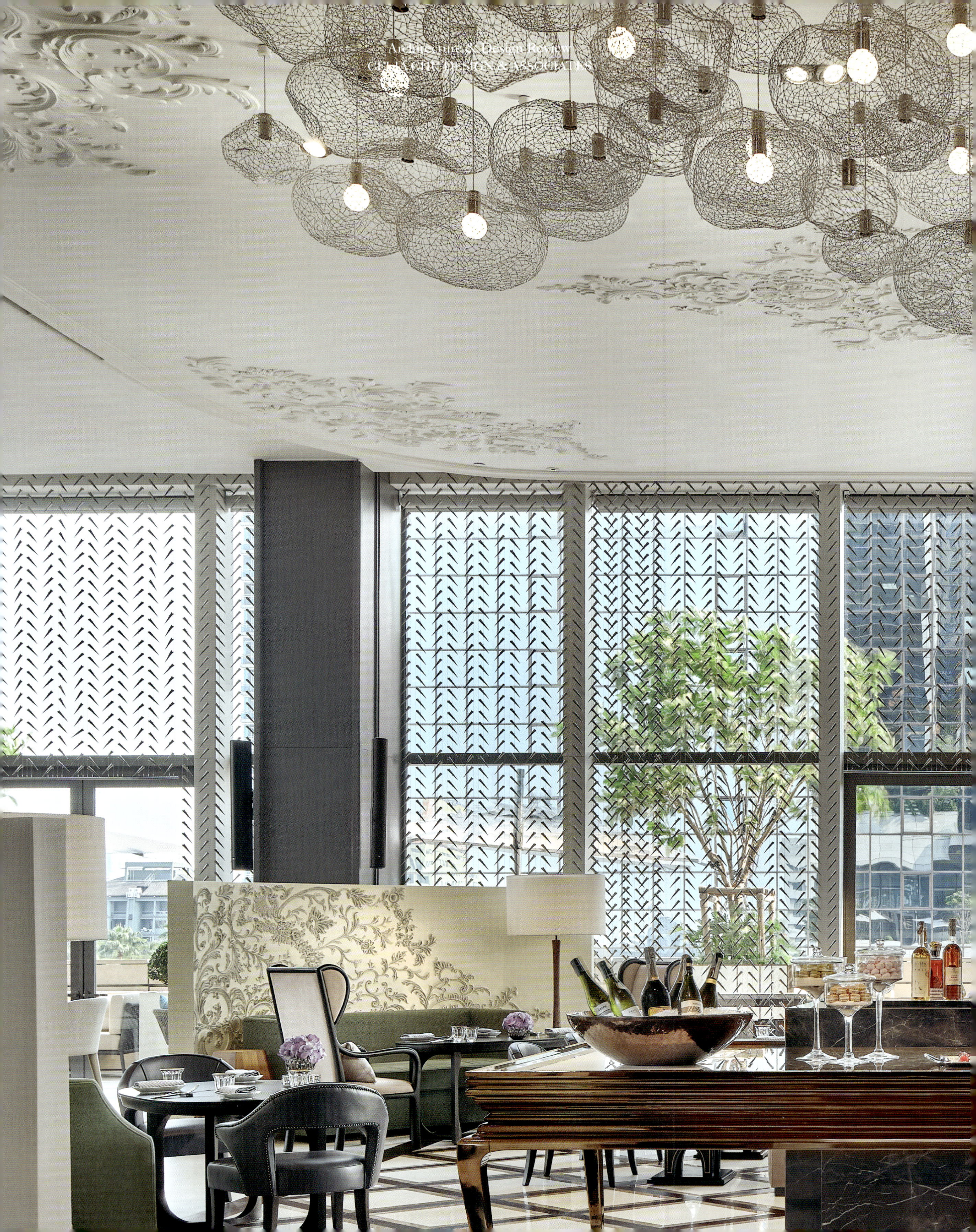

Architecture & Design Review
CELIA CHU DESIGN & ASSOCIATES

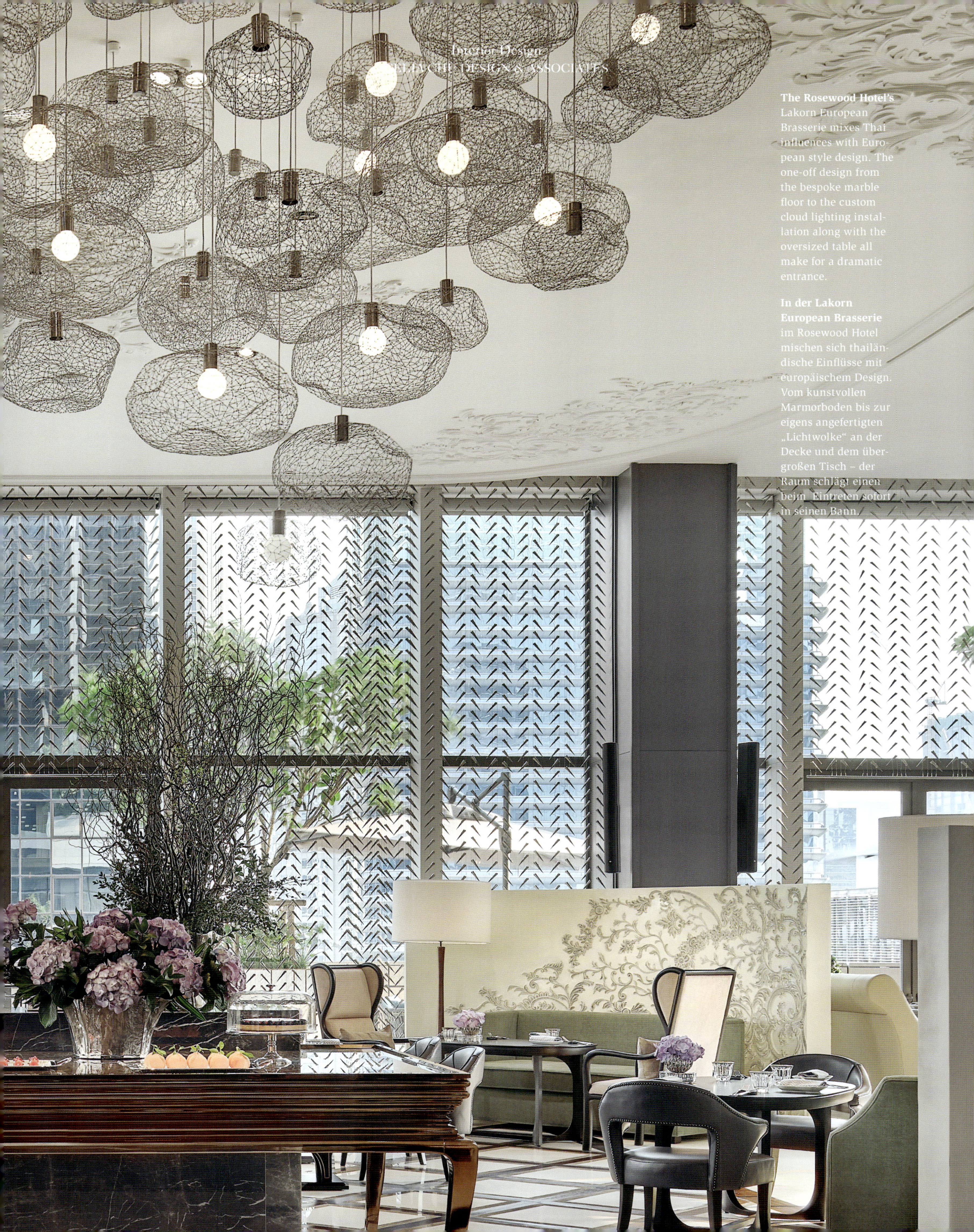

The Rosewood Hotel's Lakorn European Brasserie mixes Thai influences with European style design. The one-off design from the bespoke marble floor to the custom cloud lighting installation along with the oversized table all make for a dramatic entrance.

In der Lakorn European Brasserie im Rosewood Hotel mischen sich thailändische Einflüsse mit europäischem Design. Vom kunstvollen Marmorboden bis zur eigens angefertigten „Lichtwolke" an der Decke und dem übergroßen Tisch – der Raum schlägt einen beim Eintreten sofort in seinen Bann.

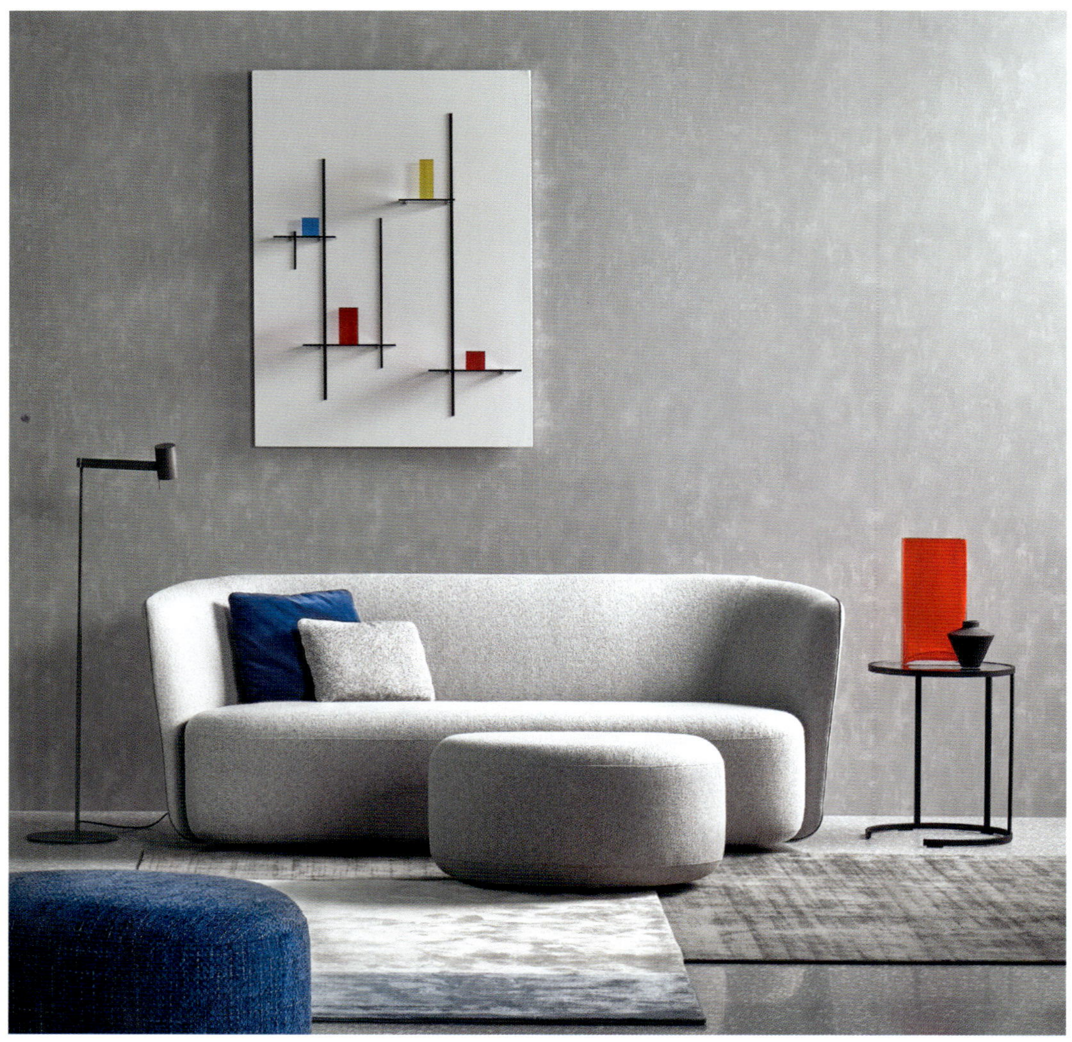

CHRISTINE KRÖNCKE
INTERIOR DESIGN

MUNICH / GERMANY

Taste and Experience | Geschmack und Erfahrung

The Munich firm Christine Kröncke Interior Design has enjoyed a good reputation in the industry for many years. Since 1974, Kröncke, the founder, and her team have been known for their stylish interiors and personal advice. One of the design professionals' key insights is that good taste cannot be bought. It is, however, still important to discuss—and when furnishing a property, nothing, of course, should be left to chance. For more than four decades, Christine Kröncke Interior Design's mission has been to ensure careful planning and that the client's personality is reflected in the living environments it creates.

Das Münchner Unternehmen Christine Kröncke Interior Design hat seit Langem einen guten Namen in der Interior-Szene. Denn bereits seit 1974 sind Gründerin Kröncke und ihr Team für stilvolles Interieur und ihre individuelle Beratung bekannt. Eine der Erkenntnisse der erfahrenen Designprofis dabei: Geschmack kann man nicht kaufen. Aber man sollte natürlich trotzdem darüber diskutieren, und selbstverständlich darf beim Einrichten nichts dem Zufall überlassen werden. Genau dafür, dass dies nicht geschieht und sich schließlich die Persönlichkeit der Kunden in den geschaffenen Lebenswelten widerspiegelt, steht Christine Kröncke Interior Design seit über vier Jahrzehnten.

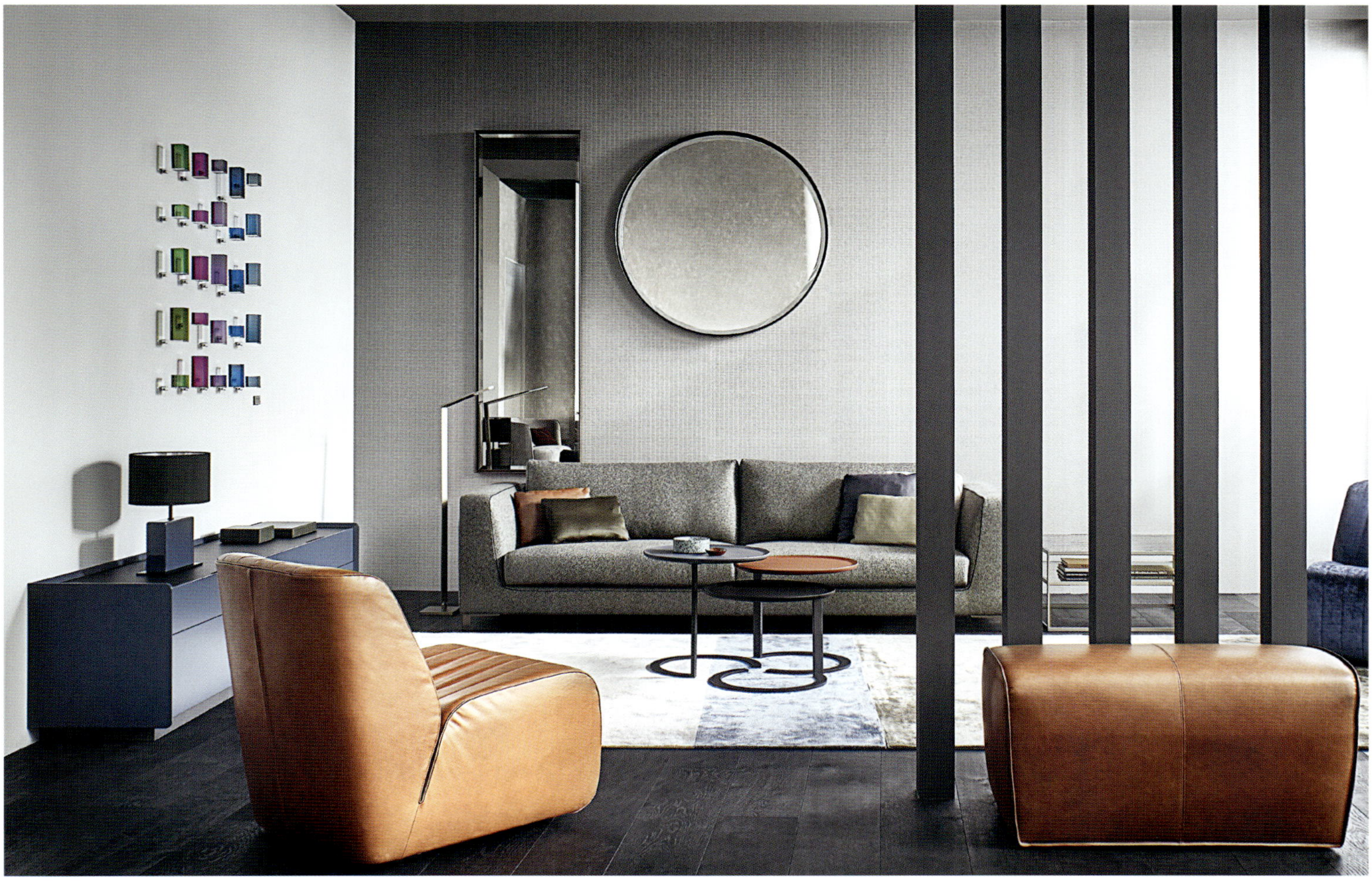

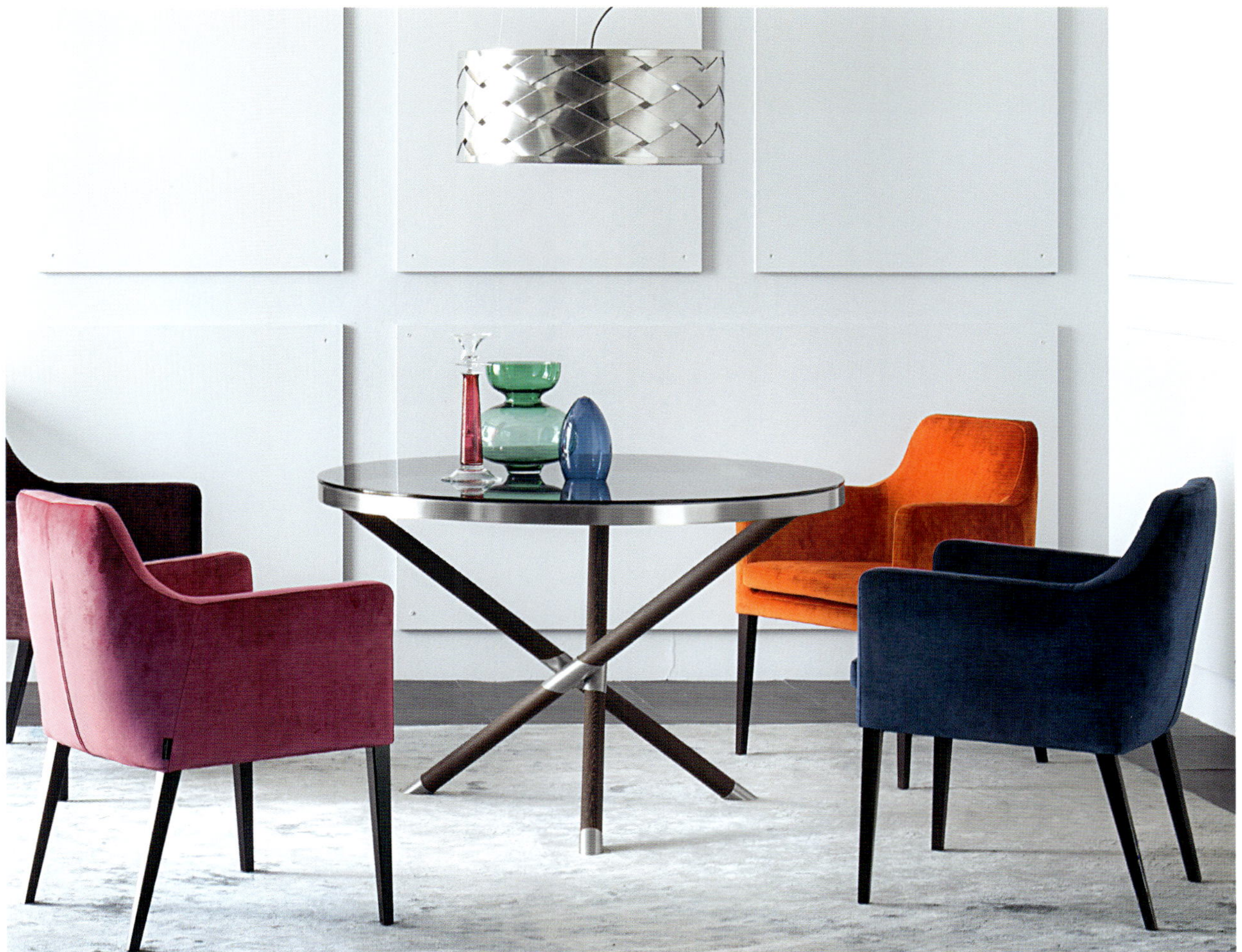

Christine Kröncke
Interior Design regards the furnishing of homes as a varied and dynamic process that is never complete. Almost everything is to be found in the designers' work, ranging from an inviting sofa to the furnishing of an entire house—and always in the incomparable Kröncke style.

Für Christine Kröncke
Interior Design ist „Einrichten" ein abwechslungsreicher, vitaler Prozess, der nie abgeschlossen ist. In der Kollektion der Gestalter findet sich dafür alles: vom einladenden Sofa bis zur ganzen Hauseinrichtung, und das immer im unvergleichlichen Kröncke-Style.

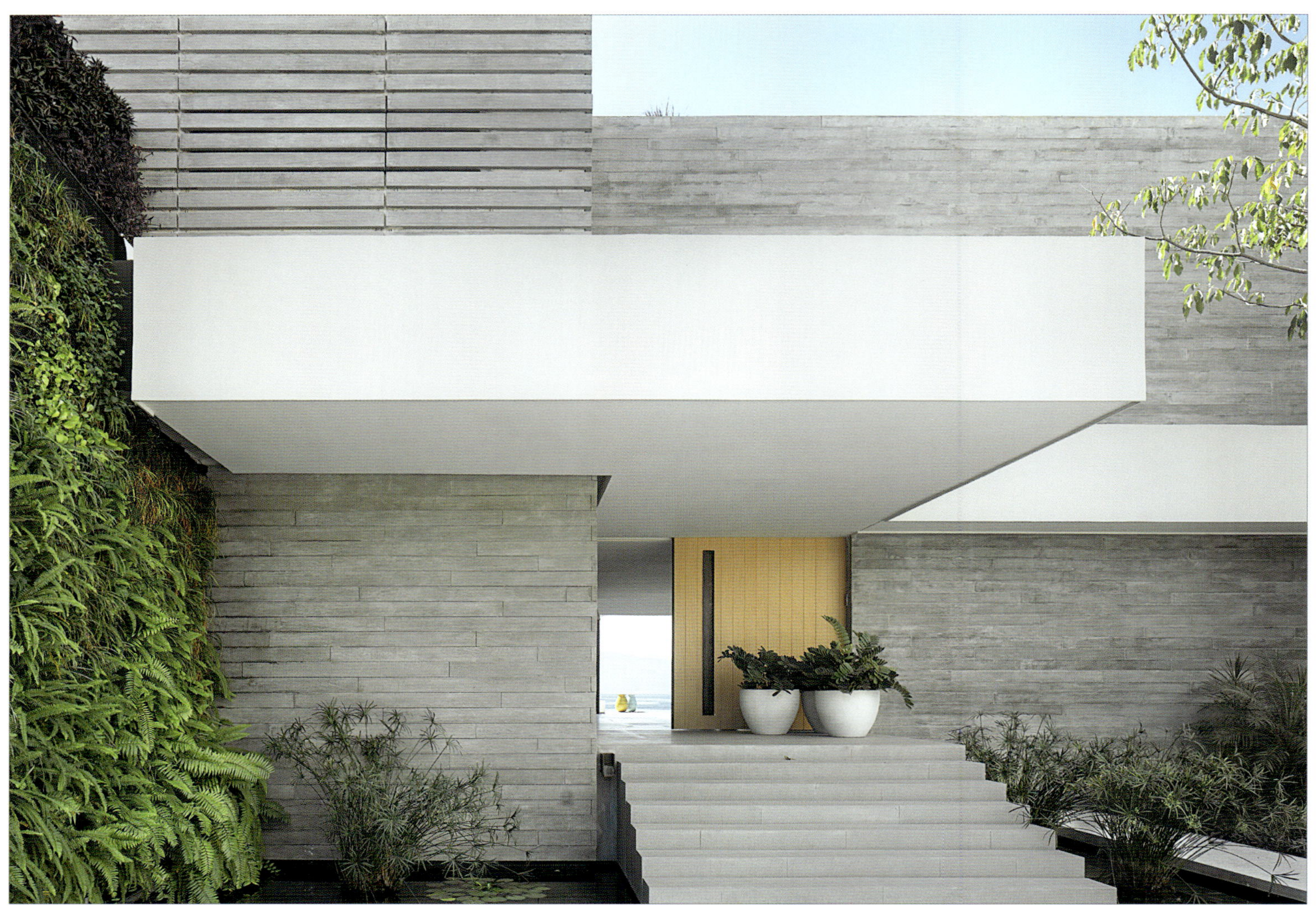

EZEQUIEL FARCA +
CRISTINA GRAPPIN

LOS ANGELES / USA

Warmth and Functionality | Wärme und Funktionalität

The architecture firm and product and interior design studio, founded by Ezequiel Farca in 1995, acquired even more prestige when design partner Cristina Grappin came on board in 2016. In their Los Angeles, Milan, and Mexico City branches, Ezequiel Farca + Cristina Grappin now employ a team of specialists. For projects in the fields of culture or catering, the partners are often inspired by their Mexican heritage and enjoy working with traditional craftspeople. Natural materials lend spaces a timeless universality and convey a feeling of warmth and comfort. The property depicted here in Puerto Vallarta, Mexico, is a good example of their work.

Das 1995 von Ezequiel Farca gegründete Studio für Architektur, Produkt- und Innendesign gewann durch Designpartnerin Cristina Grappin 2016 noch einmal an Bedeutung. In den Niederlassungen Los Angeles, Mailand sowie Mexiko-Stadt beschäftigen Farca + Grappin heute diverse Spezialisten. Für ihre Projekte, etwa im Kultur- und Gastronomiebereich, lassen sie sich oft von ihrem mexikanischen Erbe motivieren und arbeiten gern mit traditionellen Handwerkern zusammen. Natürliche Materialien machen ihre Räume zeitlos-universell und vermitteln das Gefühl komfortabler Wärme. Das abgebildete Anwesen in Puerto Vallarta, Mexiko, ist ein gutes Beispiel für ihre Arbeit.

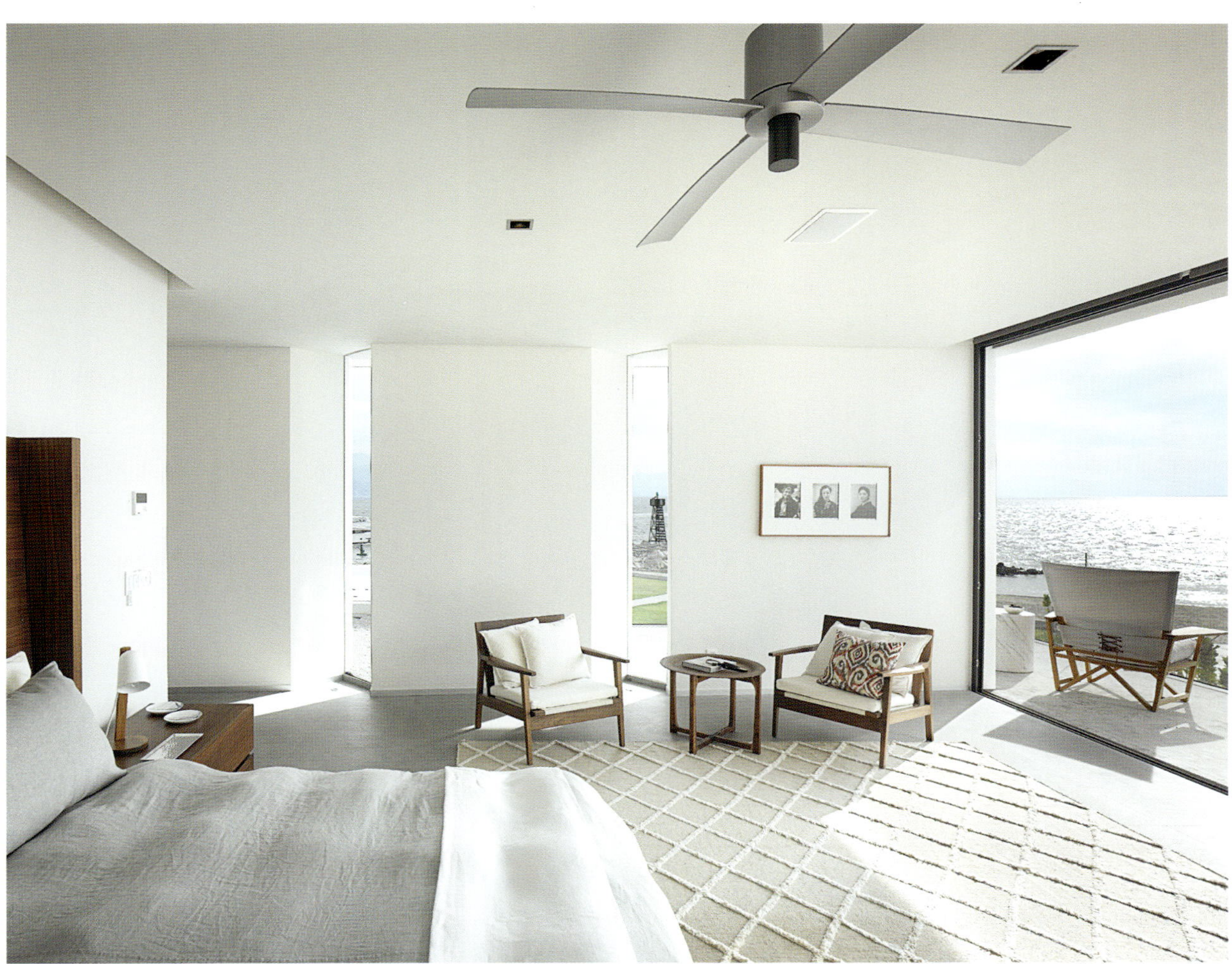

At the front of the Vallarta House several walls were planted with greenery to create a 'vertical garden' (opposite page). In the interior, linen lends an aura of freshness and comfort, with vintage accessories providing counterpoints of elegance and nostalgia (left). The cool ambiance evolving from the use of natural stone and concrete with a wood grain texture underline the overall impression (below).

An der Frontseite des Vallarta House wurden mehrere Wände als „vertikaler Garten" begrünt (Seite gegenüber). Im Innern schafft Leinen frische Behaglichkeit, Vintage-Accessoires bilden elegant-nostalgische Kontrapunkte (links). Kühlender Naturstein und holzgemaserter Beton prägen den Gesamteindruck (unten).

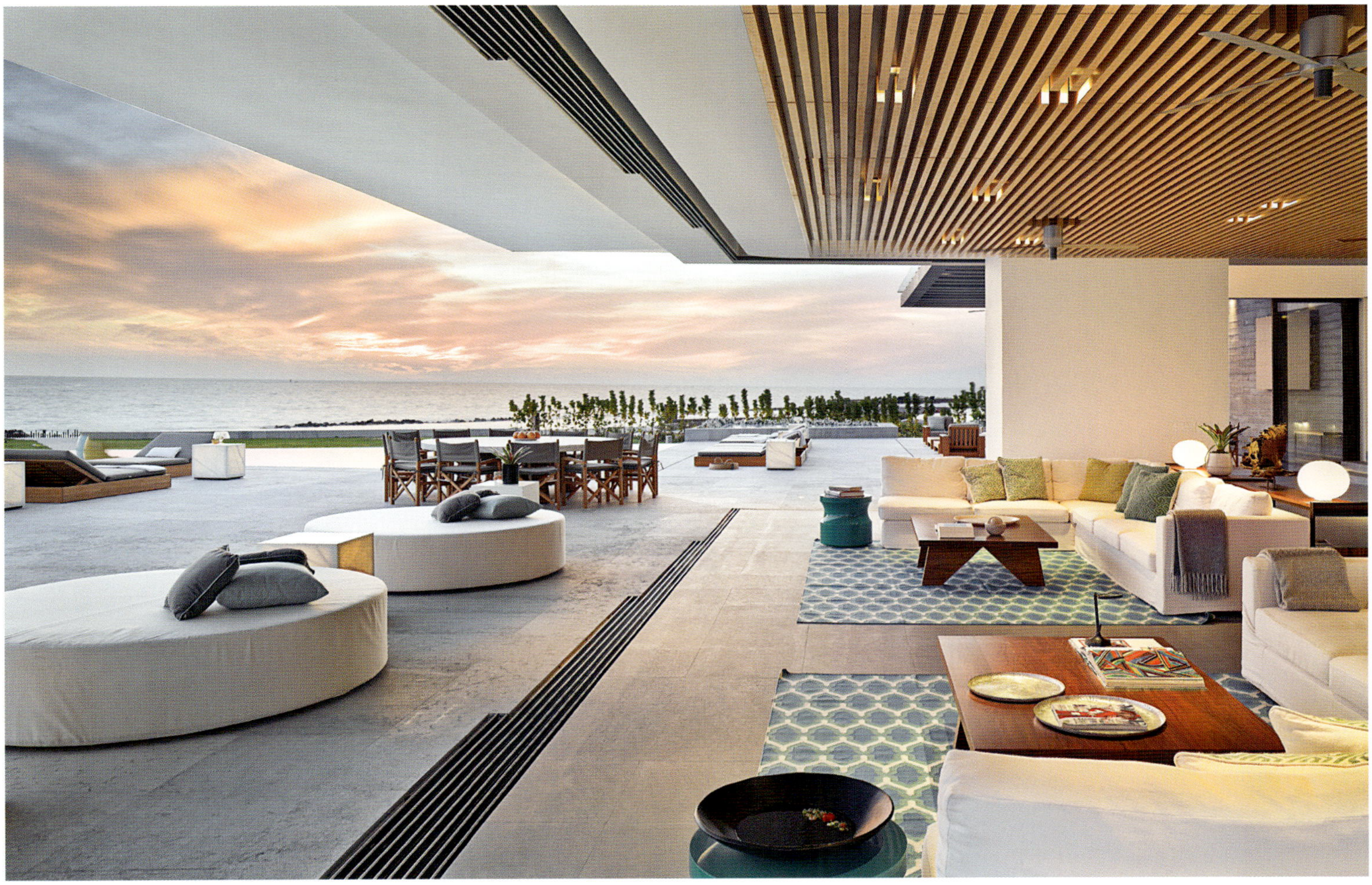

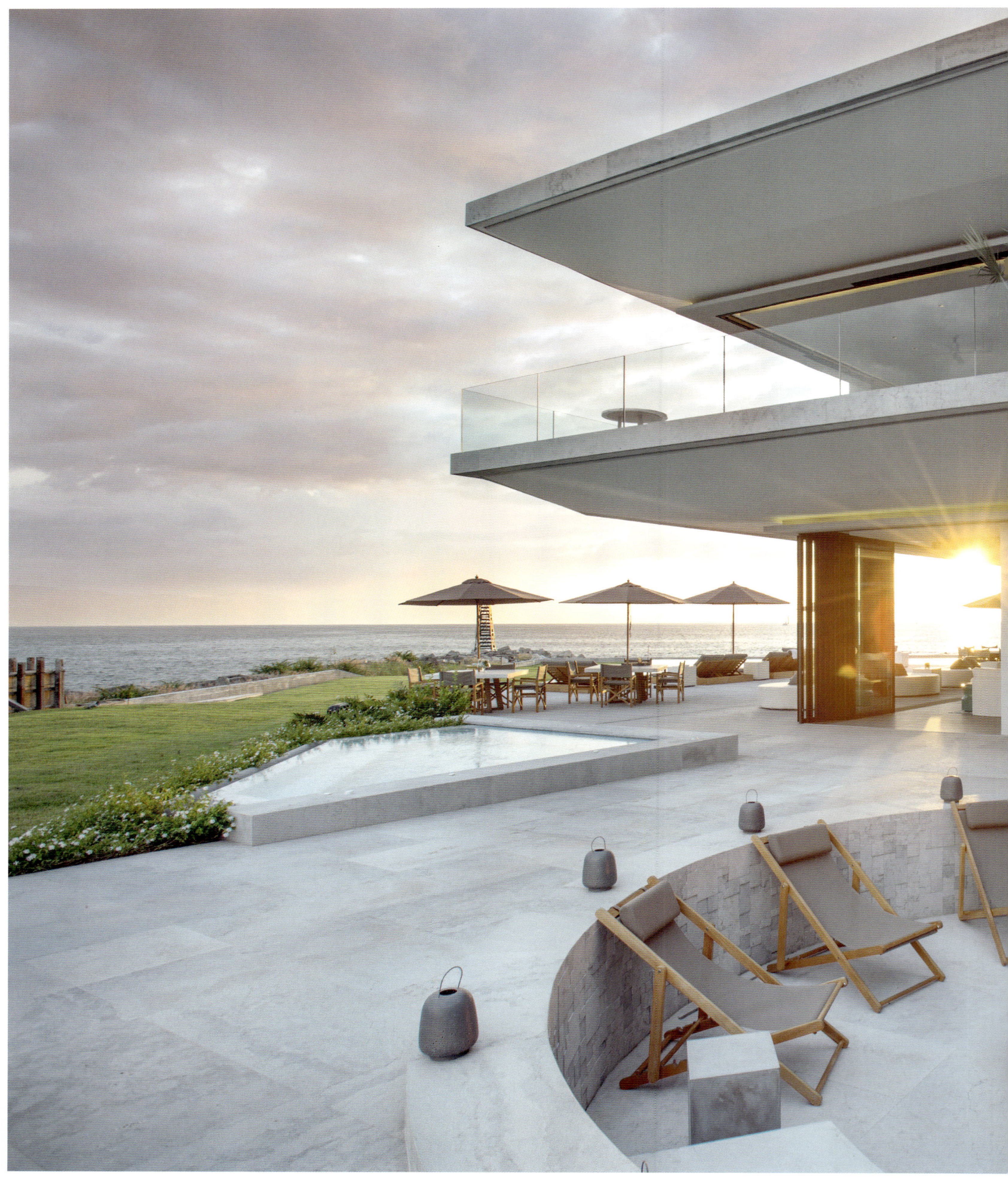

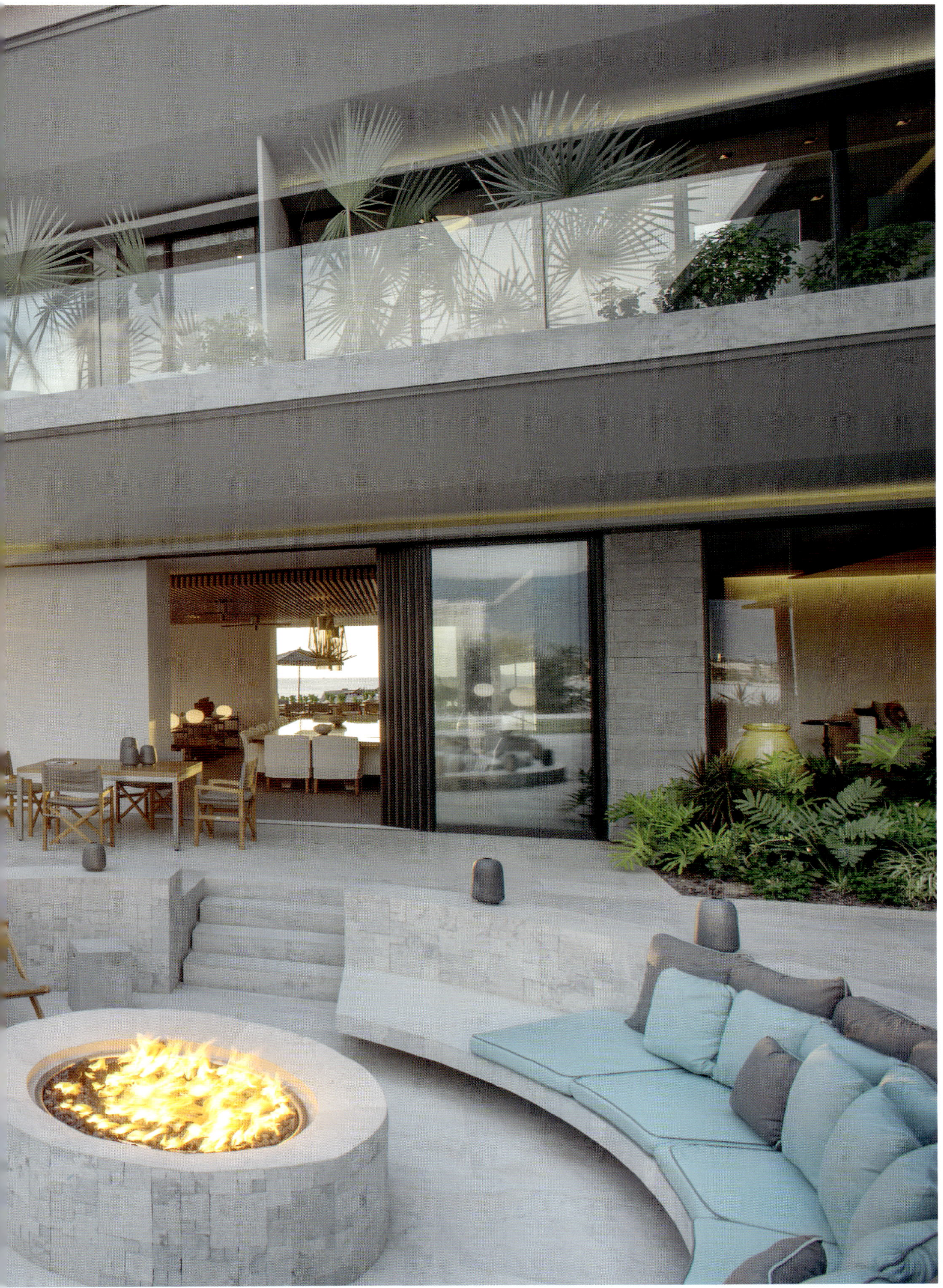

Vallarta House

is located close to the Puerto Vallarta yacht marina in the delightful Banderas Bay. Farca + Grappin's vision was to blend the property with its surroundings, allowing the landscape to mingle with the residence while simultaneously protecting the occupants' privacy. Inspired by California beach houses, the contemporary architecture melds with features from the 1950s. To ensure a sweeping, pervasive view over the bay, floor-to-ceiling windows looking out on to the terrace and balcony were fitted on both floors.

Vallarta House

liegt in der Nähe des Jachthafens von Puerto Vallarta in der traumhaften Banderas-Bucht. Ezequiel Farca + Cristina Grappin wollten das Anwesen so in die Umgebung einfügen, dass die Landschaft in die Residenz mit einfließt, ohne die Privatsphäre der Hausbewohner zu verletzen. Zeitgenössische Architektur mischt sich mit Elementen der 1950er-Jahre, inspiriert von kalifornischen Strandhäusern. Um überall einen weiten Blick auf die Bucht zu ermöglichen, wurden in beiden Stockwerken deckenhohe Fenster eingebaut, die auf die Terrasse bzw. den Balkon hinausgehen.

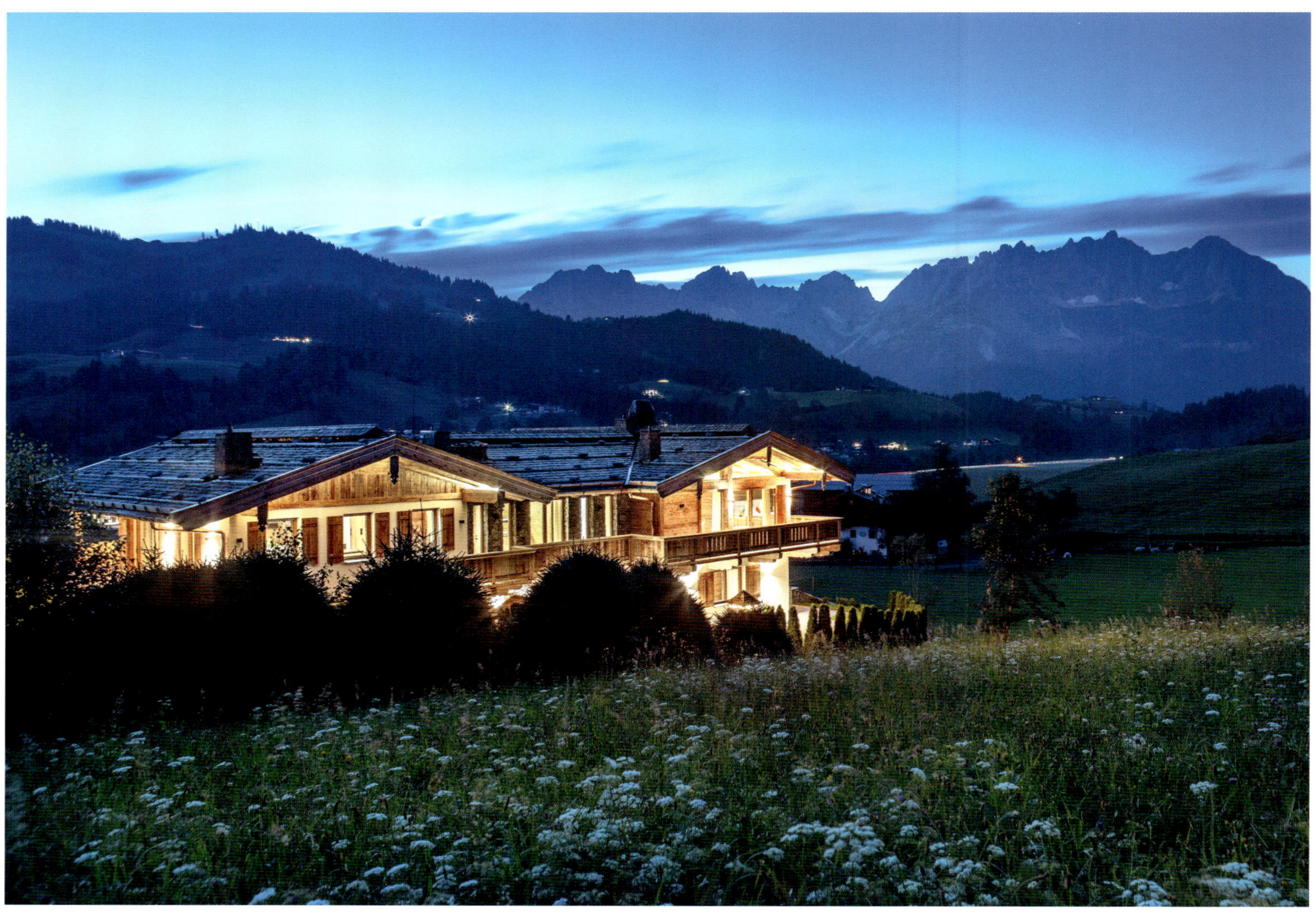

FEYRSINGER BAUTRÄGER

KITZBÜHEL / AUSTRIA

Investing in Life | Investitionen ins Leben

'Quality, exclusiveness, comfort, and harmony across generations,' is how Feyrsinger describes its company philosophy. Founded in 1981 in Reith close to Kitzbühel, the property developer has made a name for itself with the conception and execution of high-end real estate projects. Behind each project is a basic concept and theme that is reflected in its name. This forms the basis for the overall design and all construction phases—such as the Chalet Infinity – The Endless Experience depicted here. Feyrsinger's blend of integrity, punctuality, and enthusiasm enables it to create exclusive, aesthetically rounded, high-value properties.

„Qualität, Einmaligkeit, Komfort und Harmonie über Generationen hinweg", so beschreibt die Firma Feyrsinger die Prinzipien ihrer Arbeit. 1981 in Reith bei Kitzbühel gegründet, hat sich der Bauträger mit der Entwicklung und Umsetzung hochwertiger Immobilienprojekte einen Namen gemacht. Für jedes Projekt gibt es eine Grundidee, ein Thema, das sich im Namen niederschlägt und das Fundament für die gesamte Konzeption und alle Bauphasen bildet – wie das hier abgebildete Chalet Infinity – The Endless Experience. Mit Seriosität, Pünktlichkeit und Begeisterung schafft Feyrsinger exklusive Immobilien von vollendeter Ästhetik und wirtschaftlichem Wert.

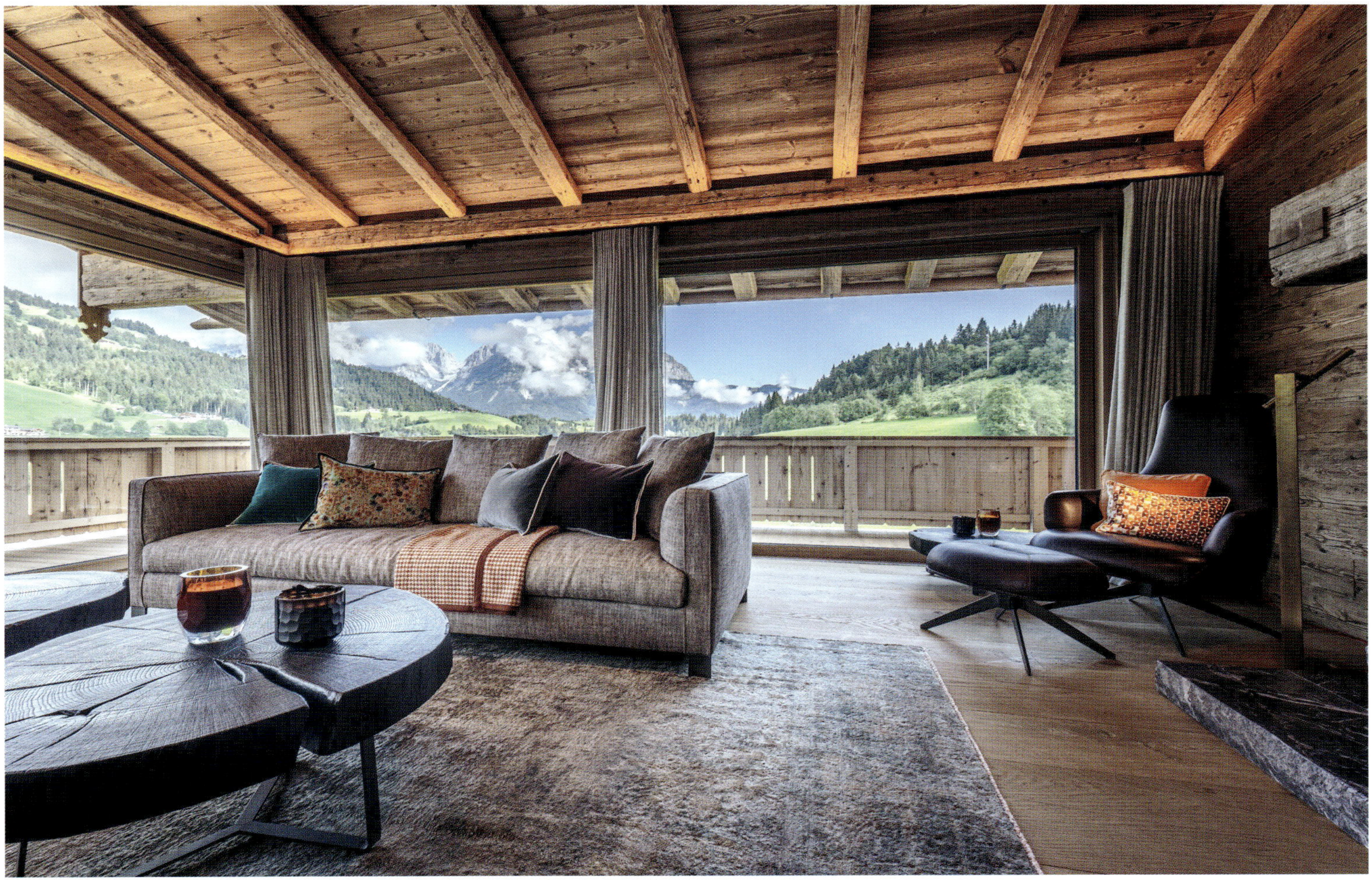

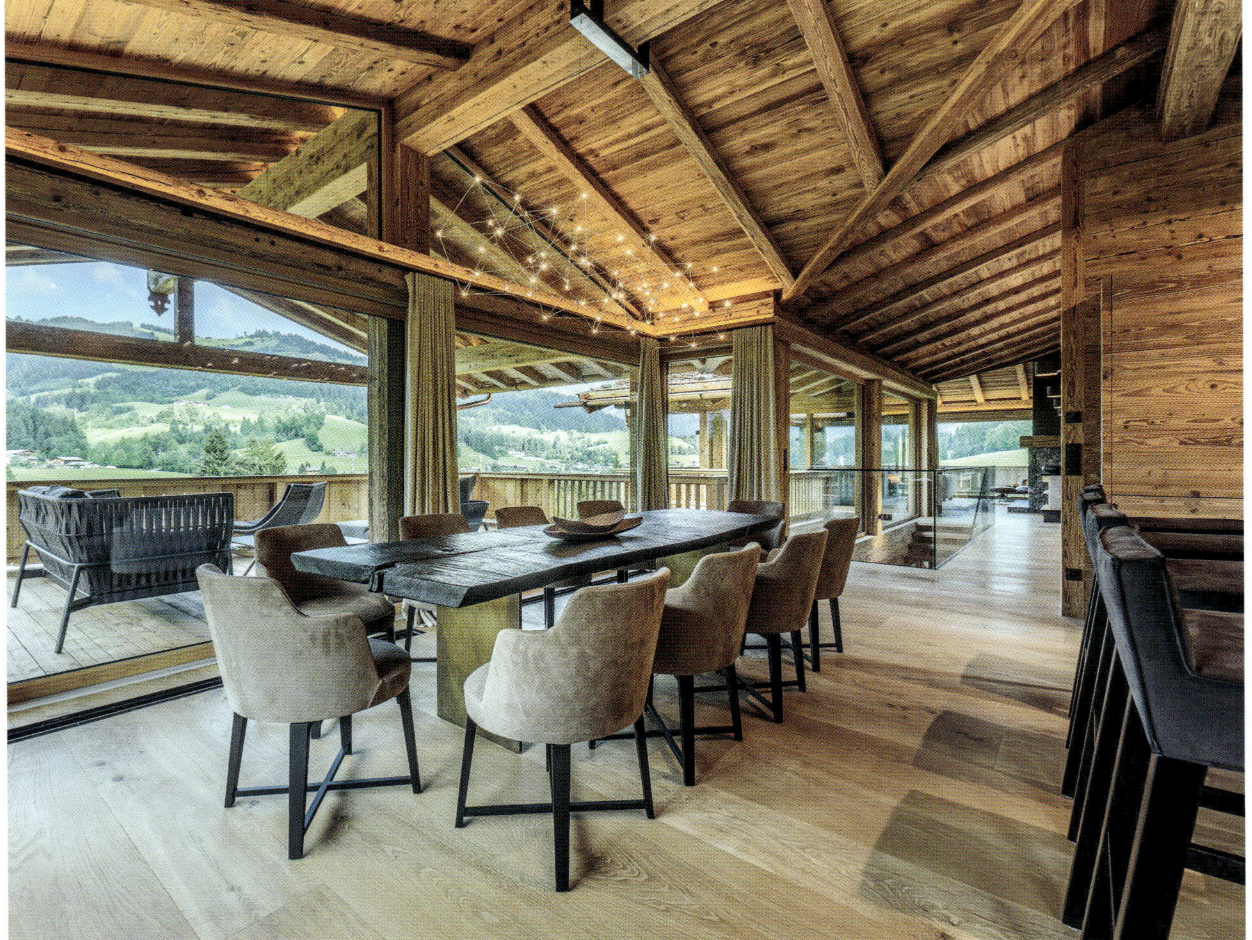

Modern building techniques and a close attention to detail are combined to reinterpret the traditional Tyrolian architectural style. Whether in the living room (above) or the pool (pages 86–87), high-quality materials such as fine woods and stone floors reside alongside exclusive designer pieces such as the Luster Quasar table in the dining room (left).

Der traditionelle Tiroler Baustil wurde hier mit moderner Bautechnik und Liebe zum Detail neu interpretiert. Vom Wohnzimmer (oben) bis zum Pool (Seite 86–87) finden sich hochwertige Materialien wie edle Hölzer und Steinböden und exklusive Designerstücke wie der Tisch Luster-Quasar im Esszimmer (links).

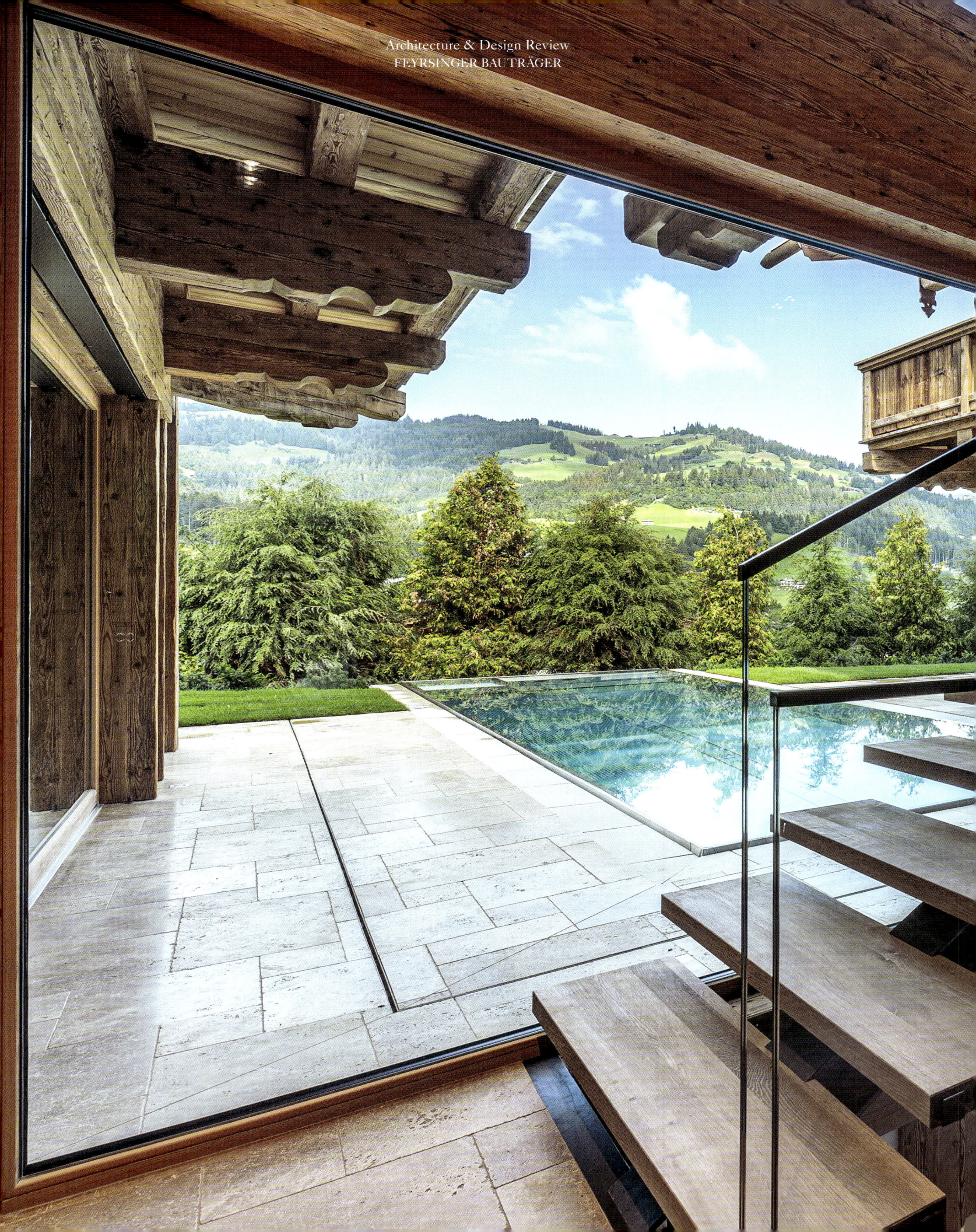

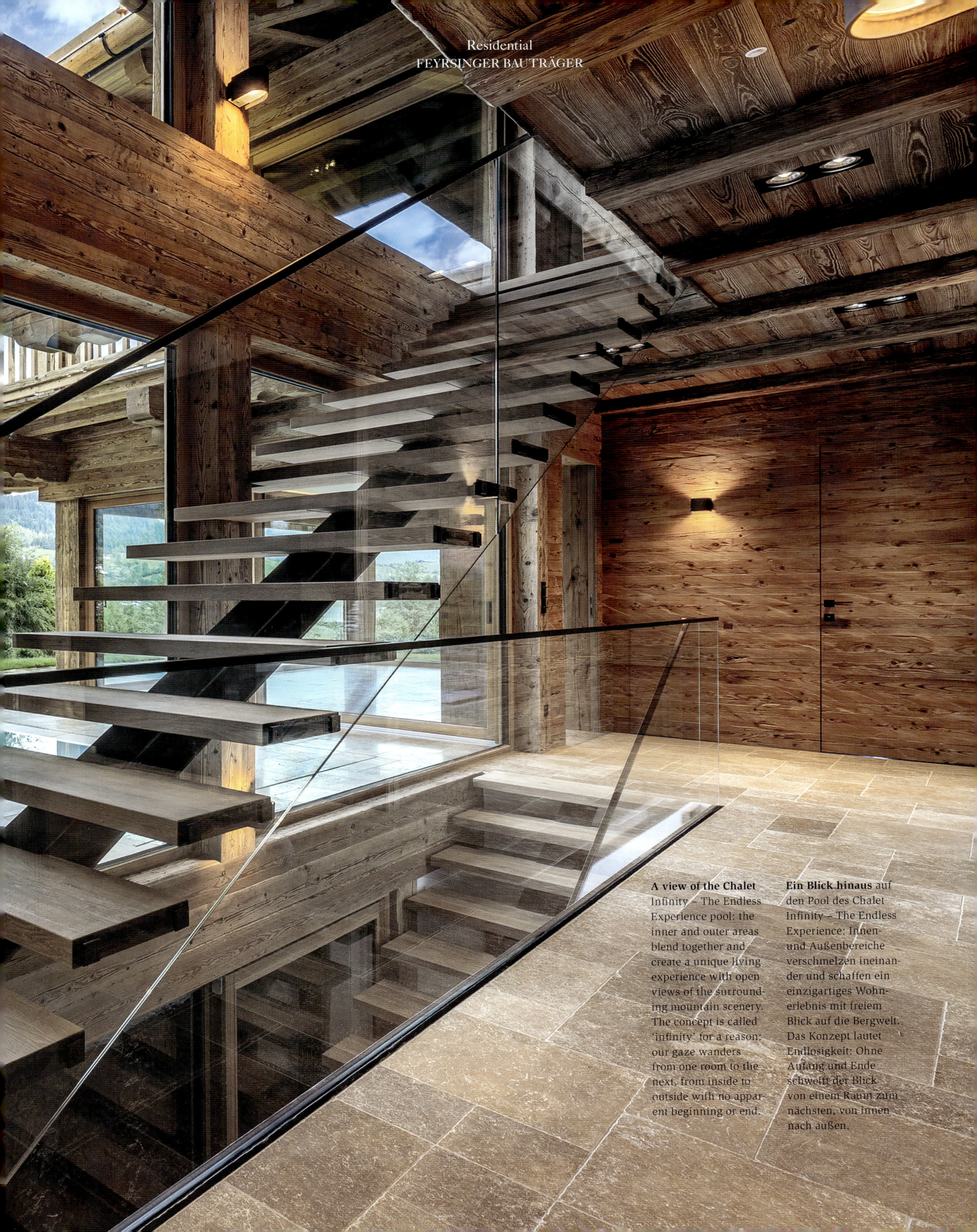

A view of the Chalet Infinity – The Endless Experience pool: the inner and outer areas blend together and create a unique living experience with open views of the surrounding mountain scenery. The concept is called 'infinity' for a reason: our gaze wanders from one room to the next, from inside to outside with no apparent beginning or end.

Ein Blick hinaus auf den Pool des Chalet Infinity – The Endless Experience: Innen- und Außenbereiche verschmelzen ineinander und schaffen ein einzigartiges Wohnerlebnis mit freiem Blick auf die Bergwelt. Das Konzept lautet Endlosigkeit: Ohne Anfang und Ende schweift der Blick von einem Raum zum nächsten, von innen nach außen.

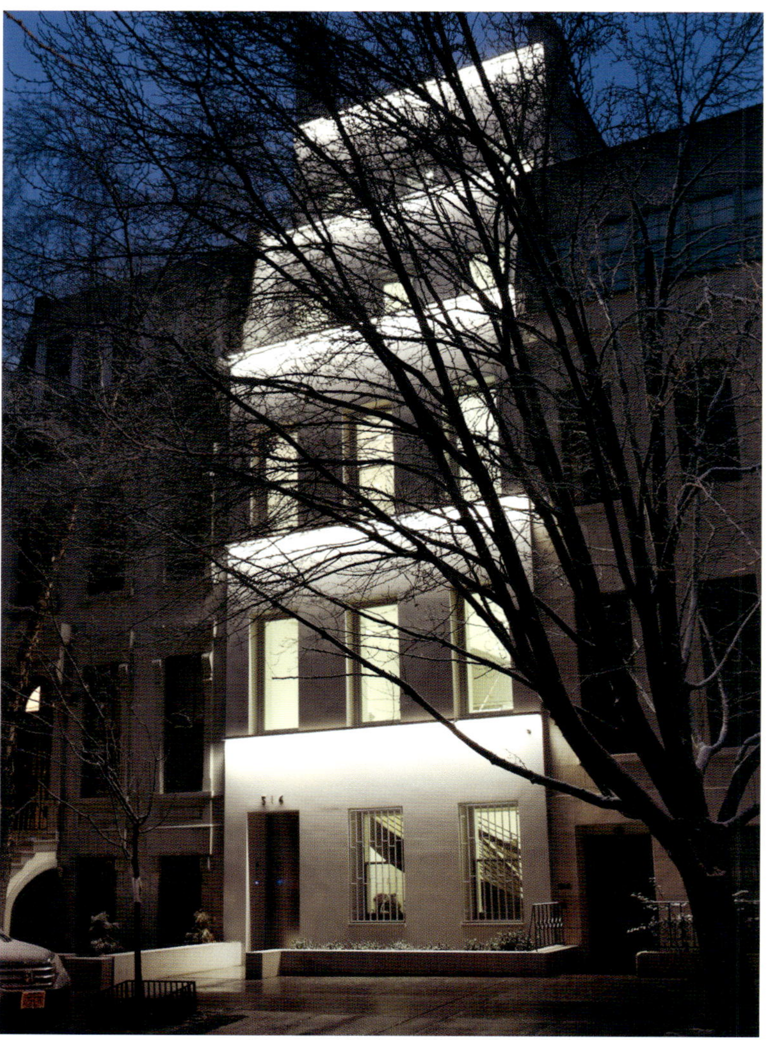

THE FRACTAL GROUP
Upper East Side Townhouse
NEW YORK / USA

Perfectly Executed Interiors | Perfekt ausgewogene Räume

The architect Ulises Liceaga is the founder and director of the design firm The Fractal Group LLC with headquarters in New York. He and his team focus primarily on the refurbishment of listed buildings. Convinced that successful design should reflect the needs of modern life and culture, the Fractal Group's craft builds a bridge between the past and the present. The result is a combination of perfectly executed and intriguing interiors, an example of which is the townhouse on Manhattan's Upper East Side, depicted here. It was transformed between 2009 and 2019 into a living oasis covering more than 460 square meters.

Der Architekt Ulises Liceaga ist Gründer und Direktor der Designfirma The Fractal Group LLC mit Sitz in New York. Er und sein Team beschäftigen sich bevorzugt mit der Neugestaltung denkmalgeschützter Gebäude. In der Überzeugung, dass erfolgreiches Design den Bedürfnissen des modernen Lebens und der modernen Kultur entsprechen muss, schlägt die Designsprache der Fractal Group eine Brücke zwischen Vergangenheit und Gegenwart. So entstehen ausgewogene und spannende räumliche Erfahrungen. Ein Beispiel ist das abgebildete Stadthaus in der Upper East Side in Manhattan, das zwischen 2009 und 2019 in eine über 460 Quadratmeter große moderne Wohnoase verwandelt wurde.

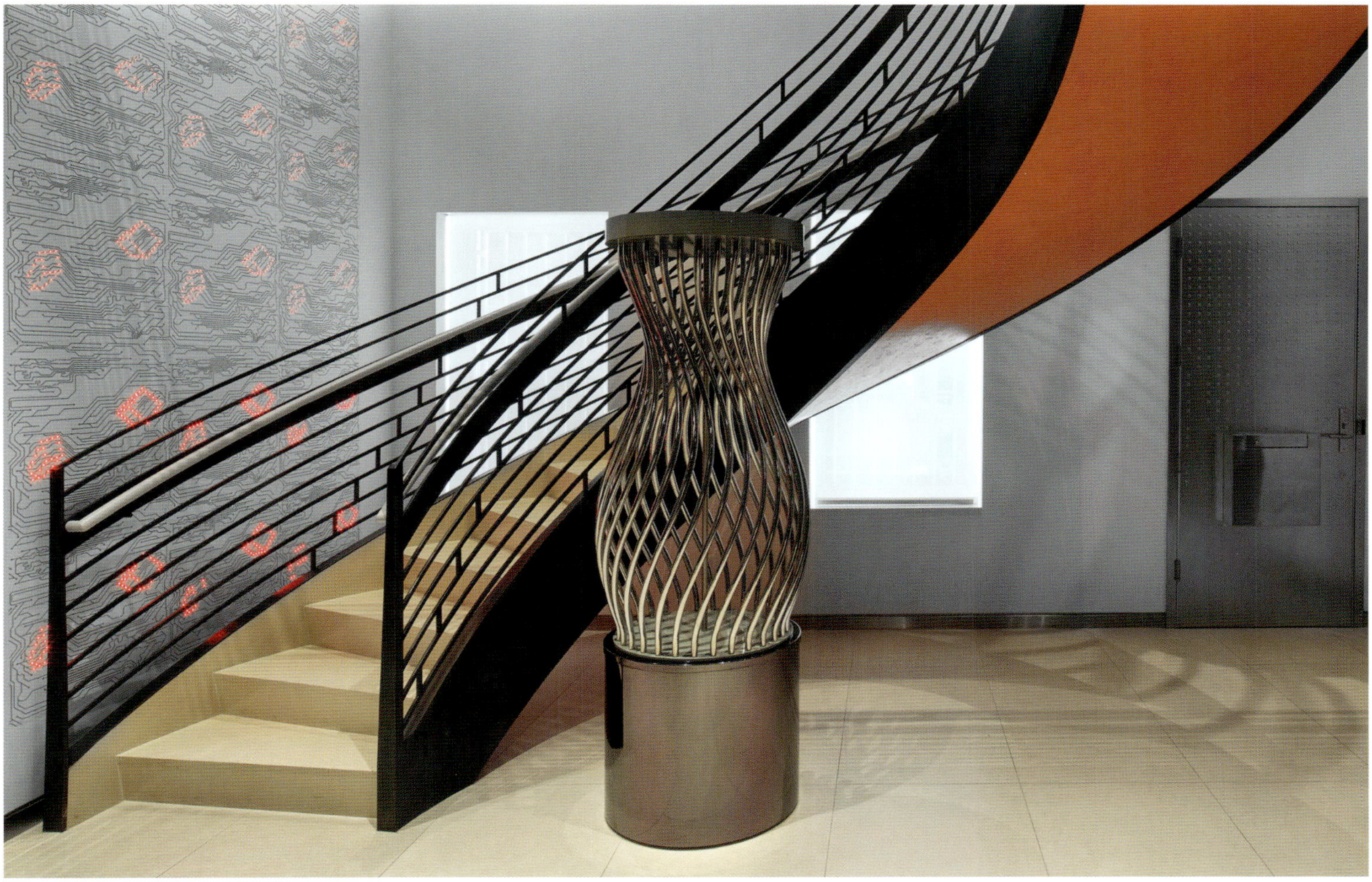

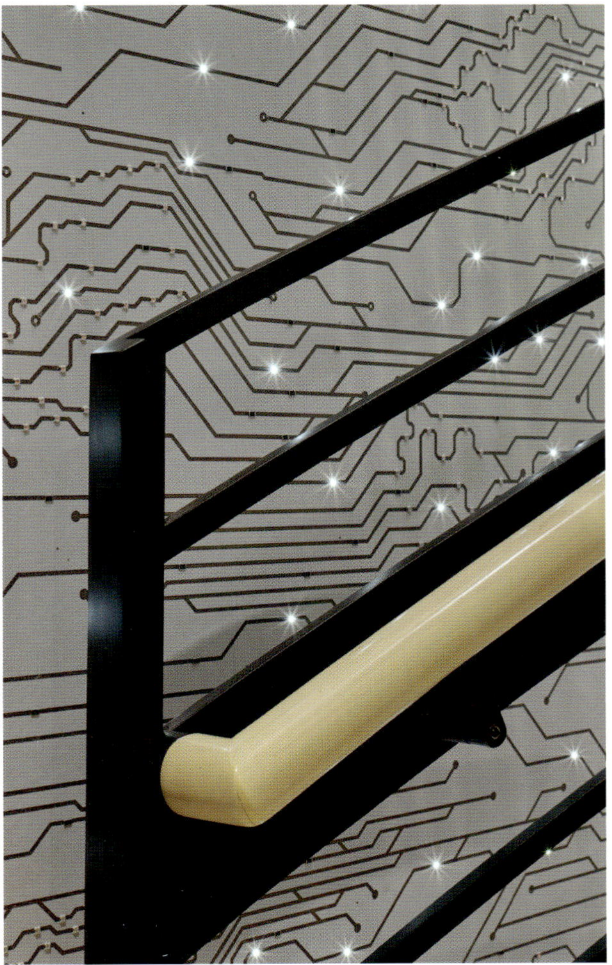

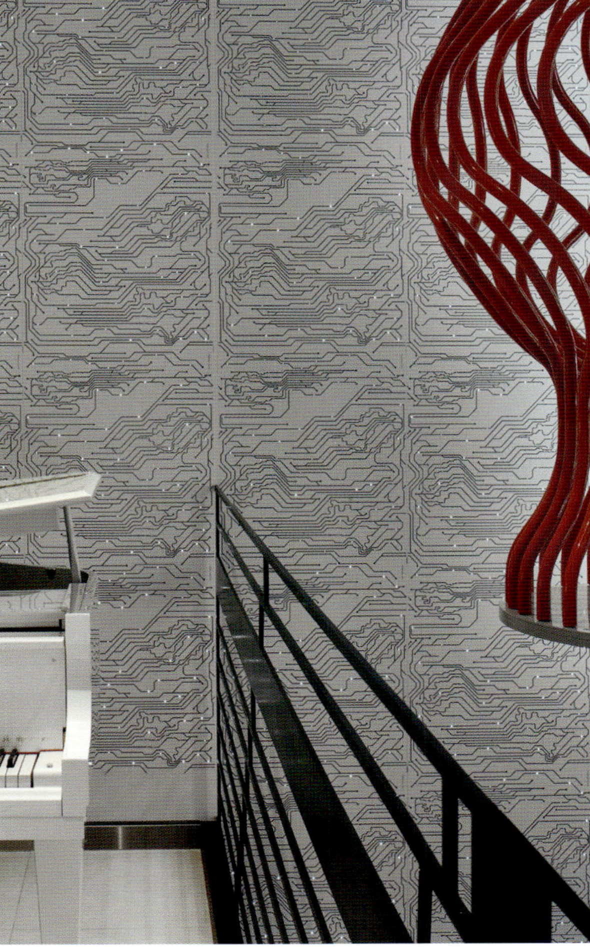

Although equipped with an elevator, all of the townhouse's four floors can be reached via staircases in the living room and foyer. A modern sculpture as well as wallpaper with stylized electrical circuits, which doubles as a source of lighting, provide the backdrop to the dramatic spiral staircase.

Trotz des Aufzugs sind die vier Stockwerke des Stadthauses auch über Treppen im Wohnzimmer und im Foyer erreichbar. Die passende Umgebung für die dramatische Wendeltreppe in diesem Foyer schaffen eine moderne Skulptur sowie, gleichzeitig als Beleuchtung, eine Tapete mit stilisierten Stromkreisen.

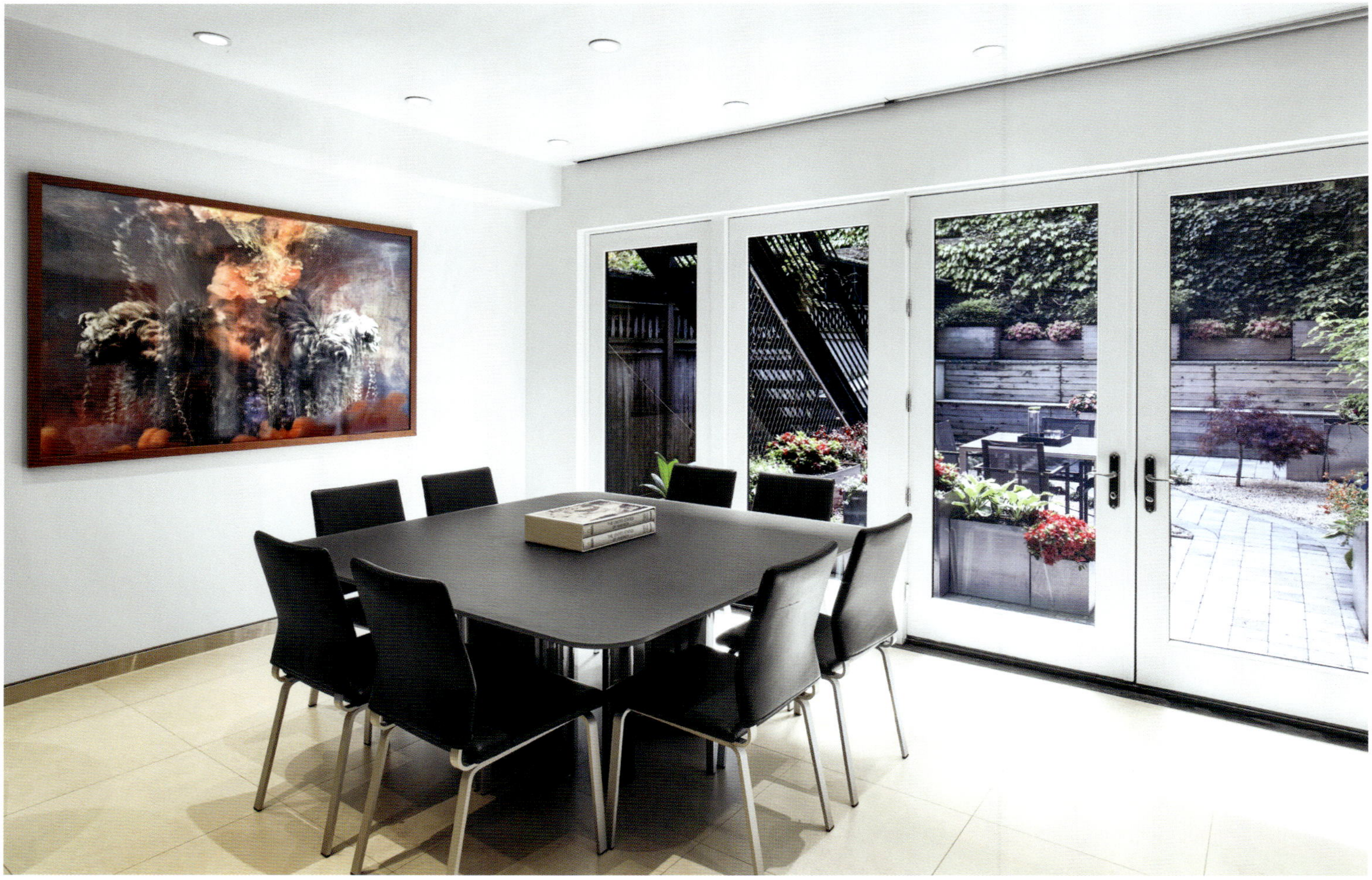

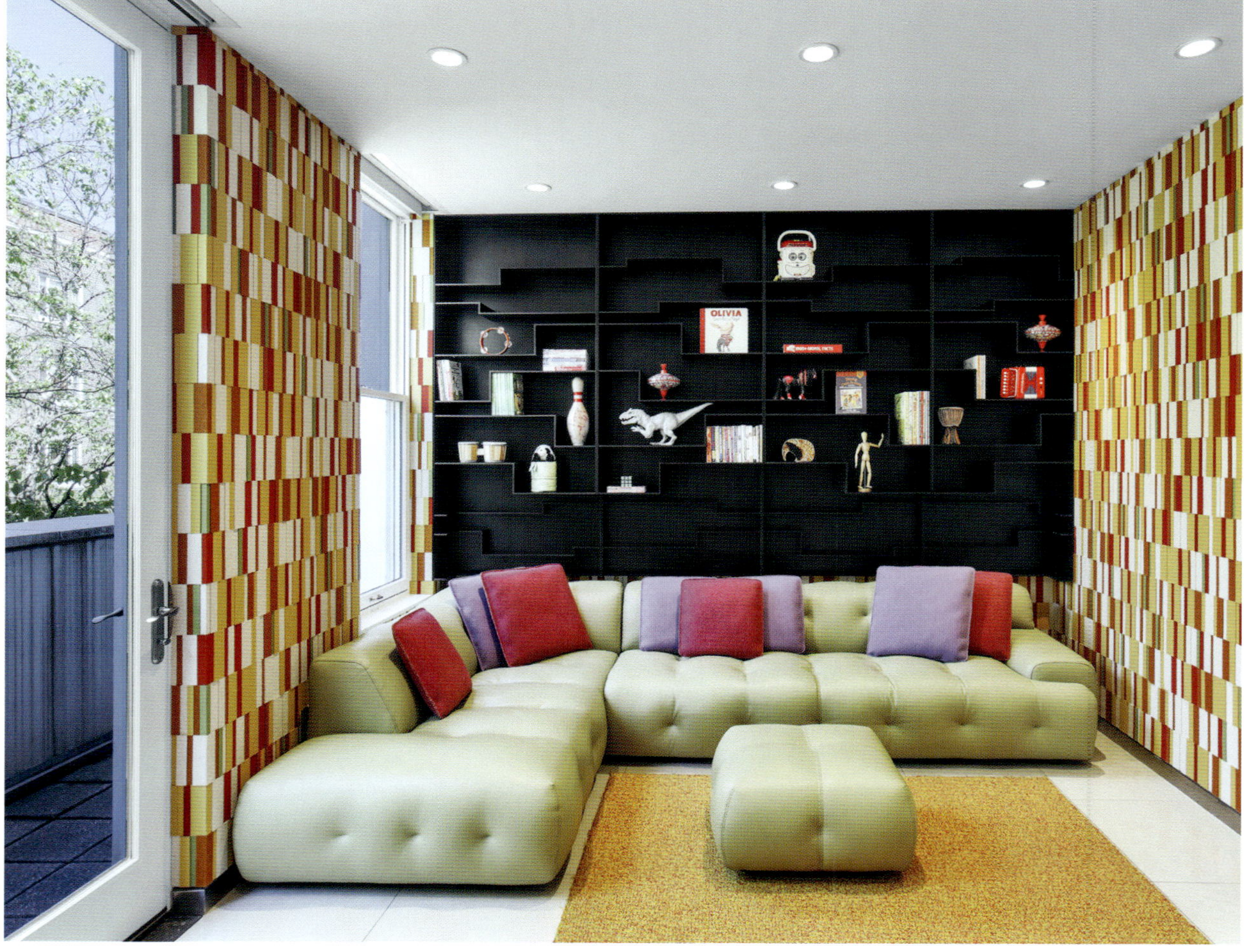

A coltish, colorful living area with upholstered furniture and shelving (left). A terrace connects the light dining area (above) to a Zen garden. The previously insensate backyard was transformed into a comfortable place for reflection by the addition of climbing ivy, flowering bushes, evergreen shrubs and potted plants (right page).

Ein bunt-verspielter Wohnbereich mit Polstermöbeln und Regal (links). Vom hellen Essbereich (oben) geht es über eine Terrasse in den „Zen-Garten": Der einst leblose Hinterhof wurde durch kletternden Efeu, blühende Büsche, immergrüne Sträucher und Topfpflanzen in einen Ort der Besinnung und des Komforts verwandelt (rechte Seite).

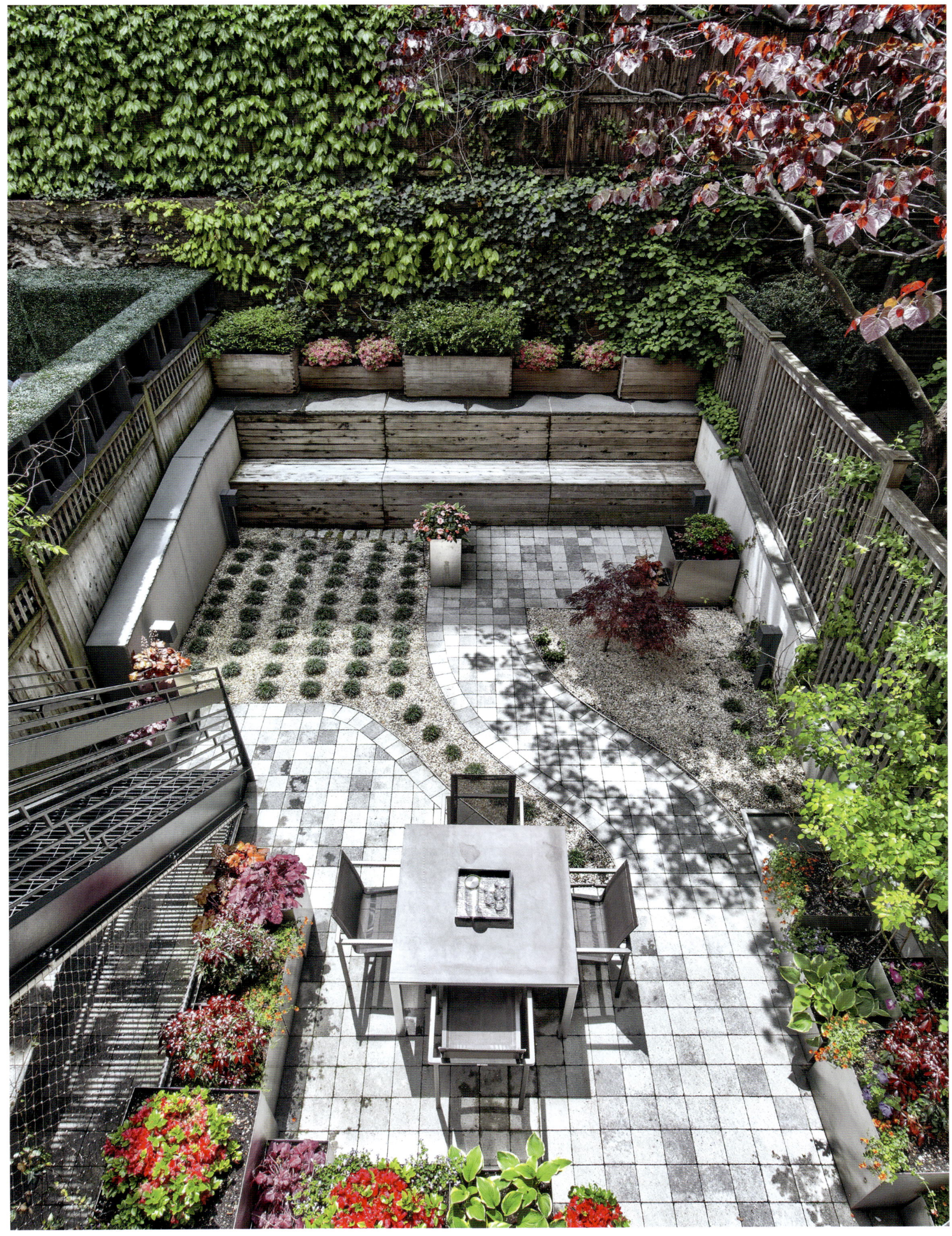

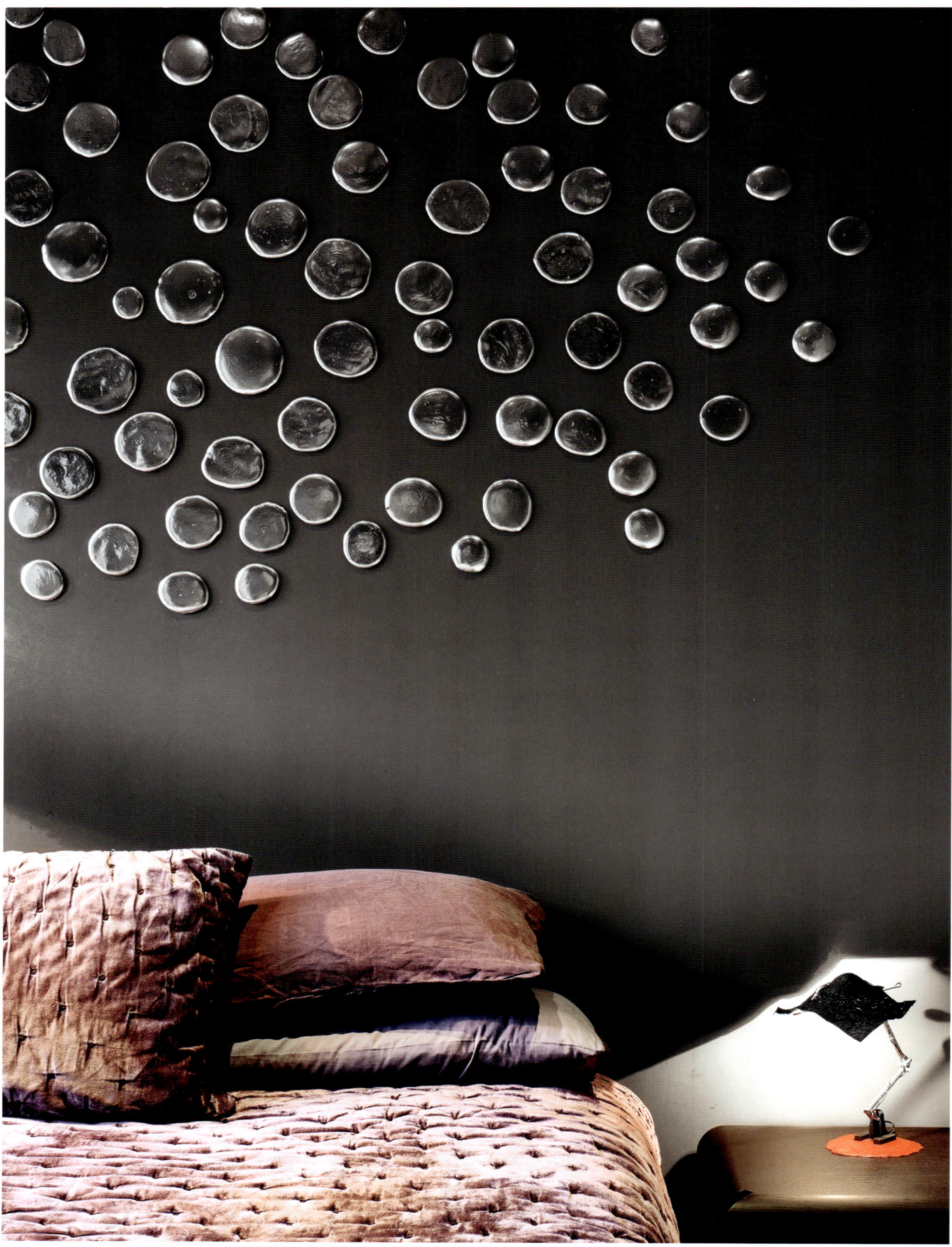

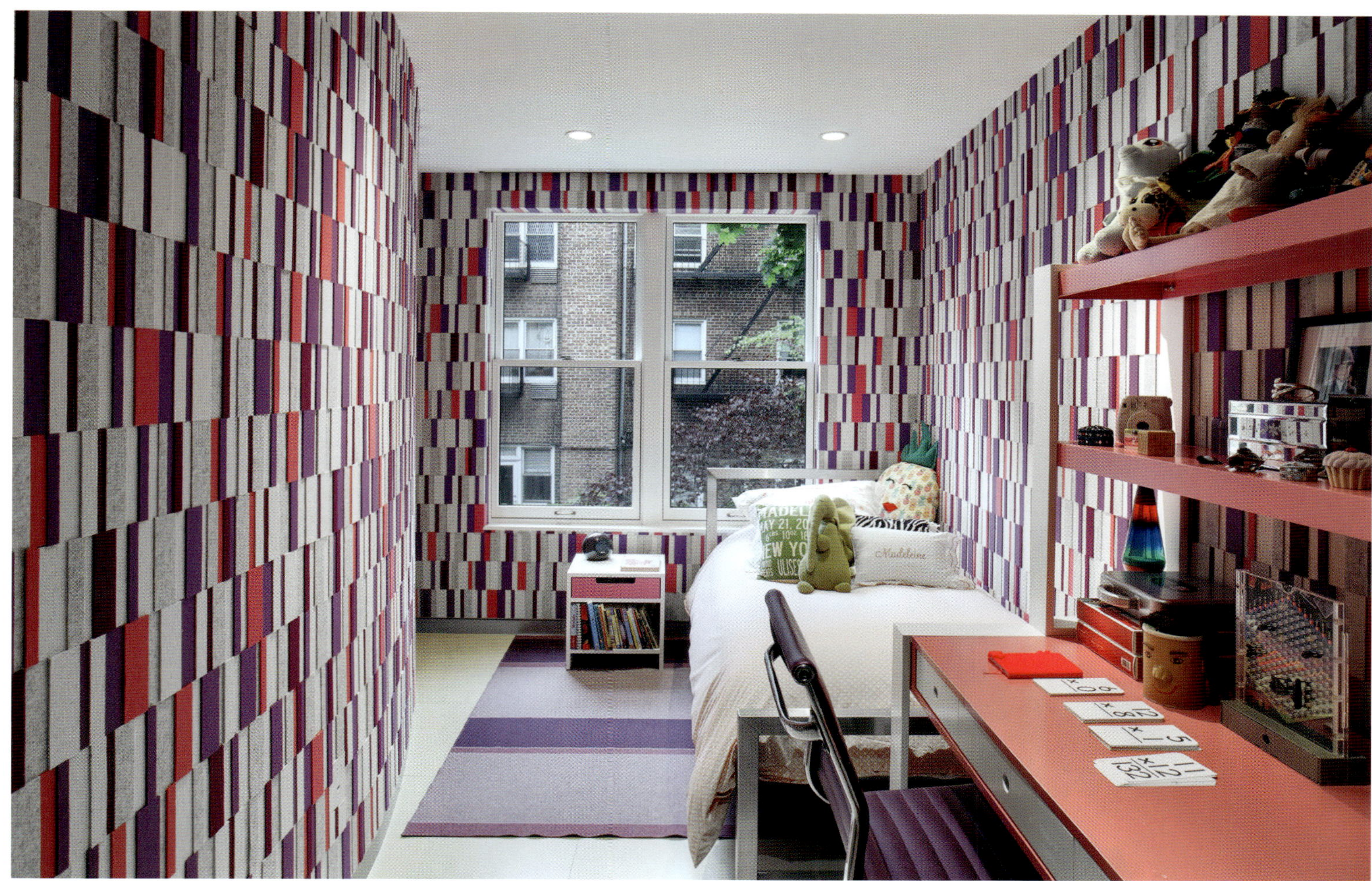

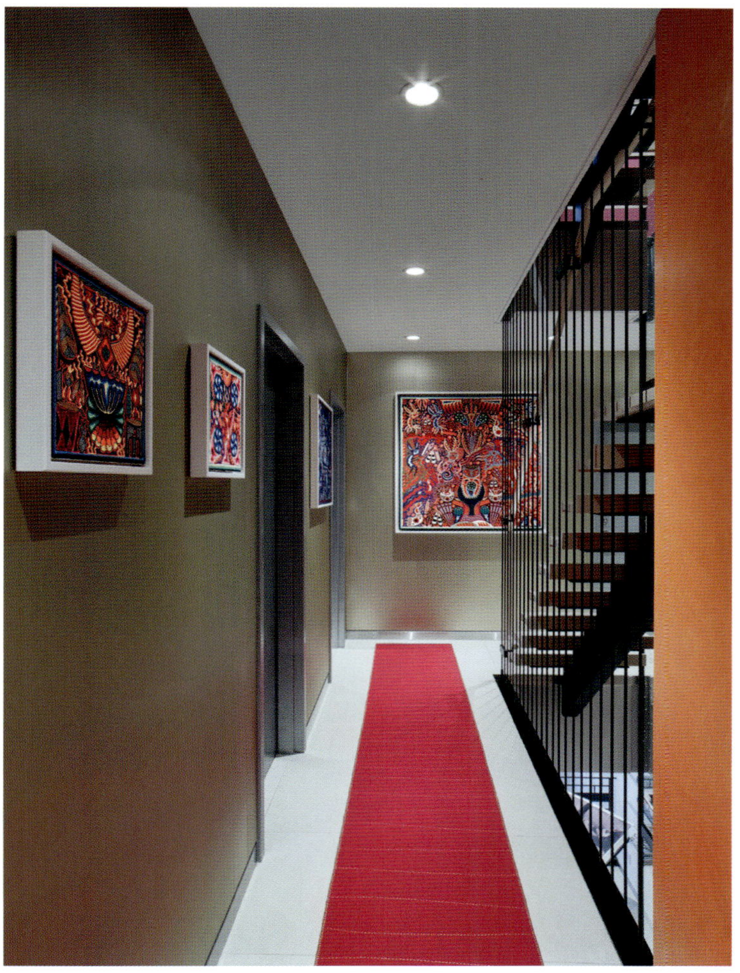

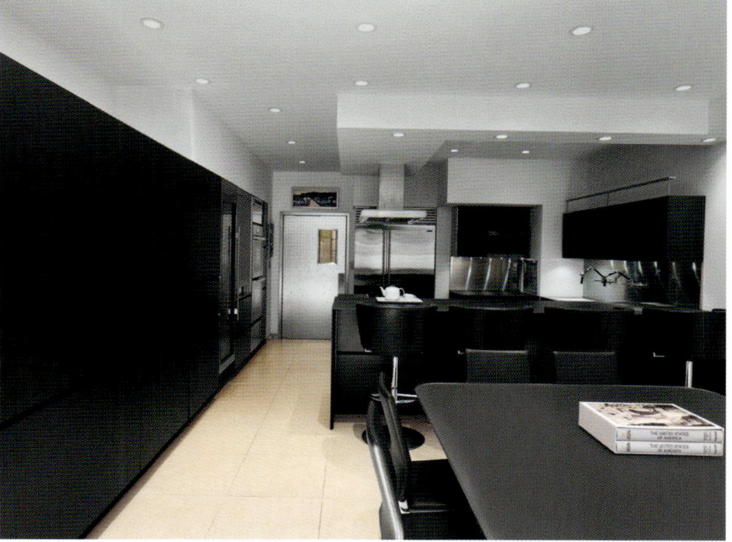

Black vinyl creates a cocoon-like feel in the master suite (left page). Bright colors, in the form of felted, graphic wall coverings, for example, characterize the floors where the children's rooms are to be found. The first-floor kitchen merges directly into the dining area.

Schwarzes Vinyl erzeugt in der Master Suite eine Art Kokon-Gefühl (linke Seite). Die Etagen mit den Kinderzimmern wirken sehr farbenfroh, etwa durch gefilzte grafische Wandverkleidungen. Die Küche im Erdgeschoss geht unmittelbar in den Essbereich über.

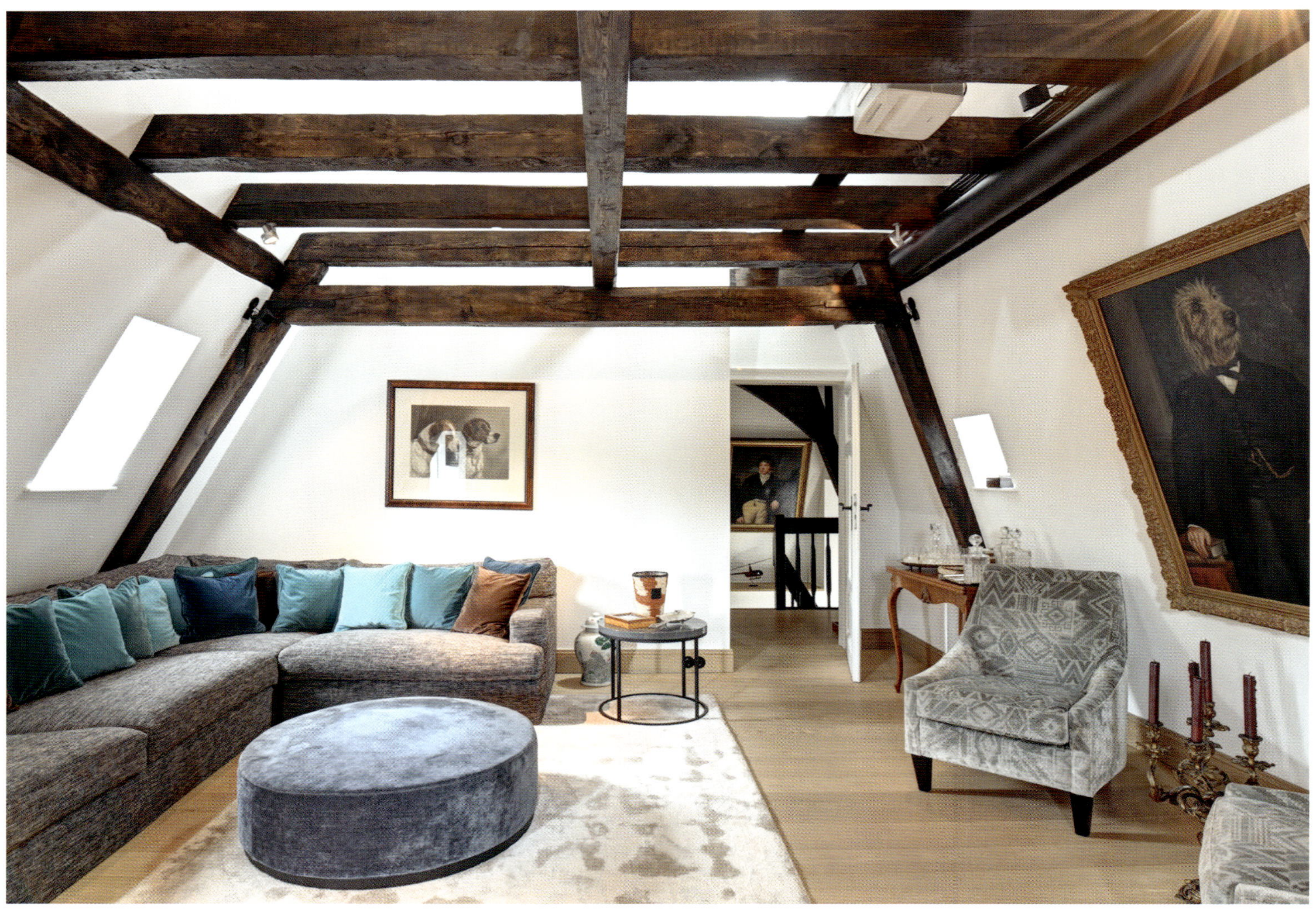

FRESO HOME

MUNICH / GERMANY

Inspiring Ideas for the Home | Inspirierende Wohnideen

A key focus of Maria Brandis' work is the transformation of old spaces and the harmonious blending of new and historic features. The conversion of the apartment in a German castle pictured here, where walls were displaced or removed and beams and gable windows uncovered, is a perfect example. In this way, a bright, naturally-lit living room was created, in which old and new elements merge harmoniously. The work of the art history graduate Brandis, who also studied *trompe-l'œil* art in Madrid, has become known and appreciated by many interior design fans, not least by her furnishing store Freso Home, in the heart of Munich.

Einer der Schwerpunkte von Maria Brandis ist die Umgestaltung alter Räume und die harmonische Verbindung historischer und neuer Elemente. Ein schönes Beispiel dafür ist die hier abgebildete Wohnung in einem deutschen Schloss, bei deren Umbau Wände versetzt oder entfernt sowie Deckenbalken und Giebelfenster freigelegt wurden. So entstand ein lichtdurchfluteter Wohnraum, in dem alte und neue Elemente harmonisch verbunden sind. Die Arbeit der studierten Kunsthistorikerin Brandis, die außerdem in Madrid Trompe-l'œil-Malerei erlernte, kennen und schätzen viele Interior-Fans auch aus ihrem Interior-Store Freso Home im Herzen Münchens.

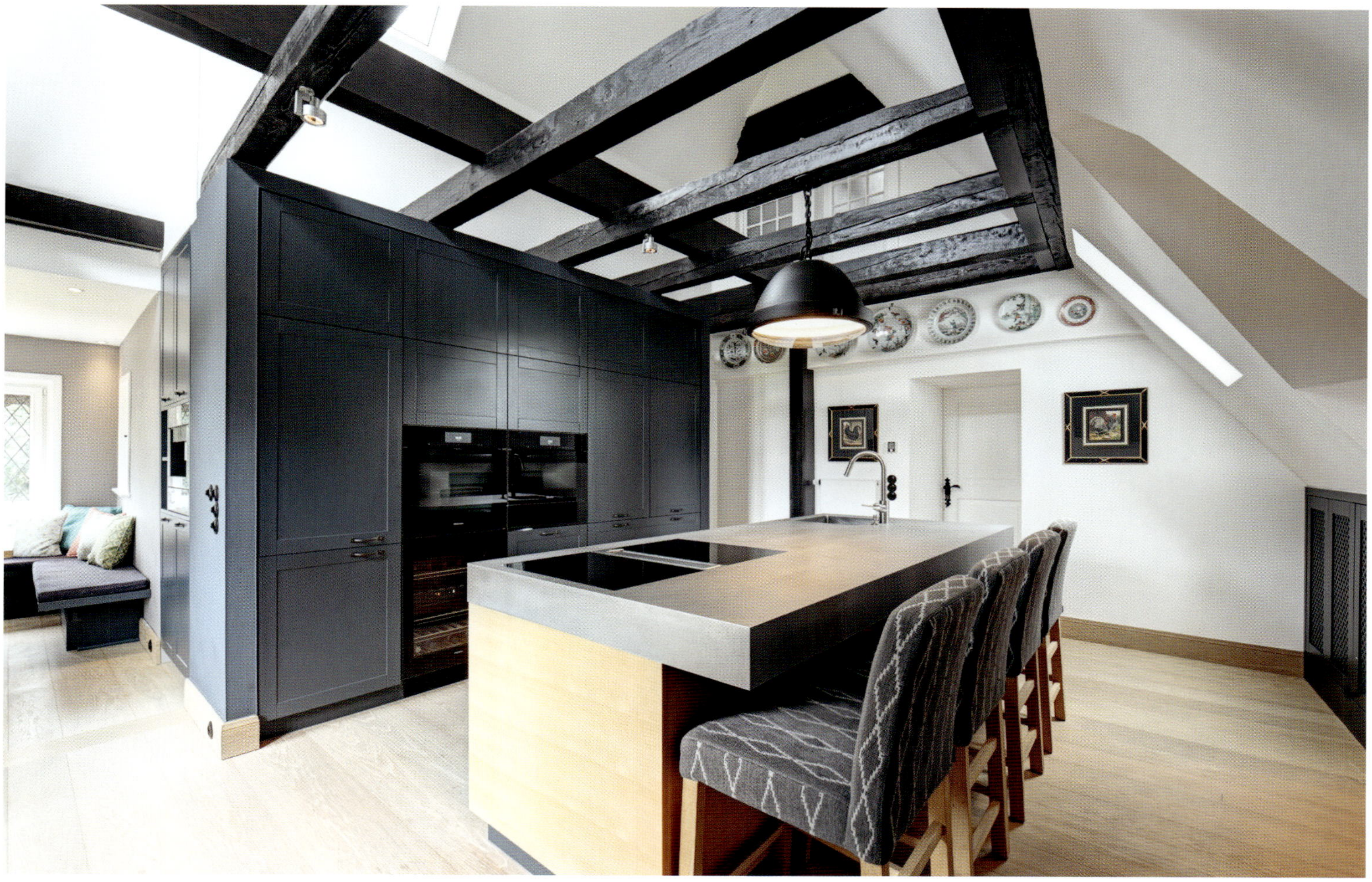

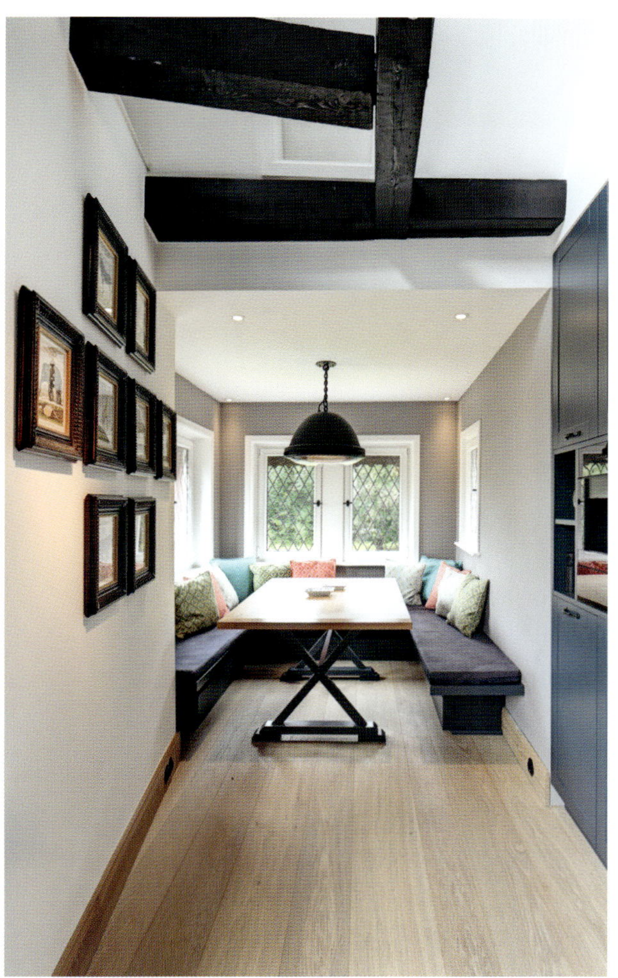

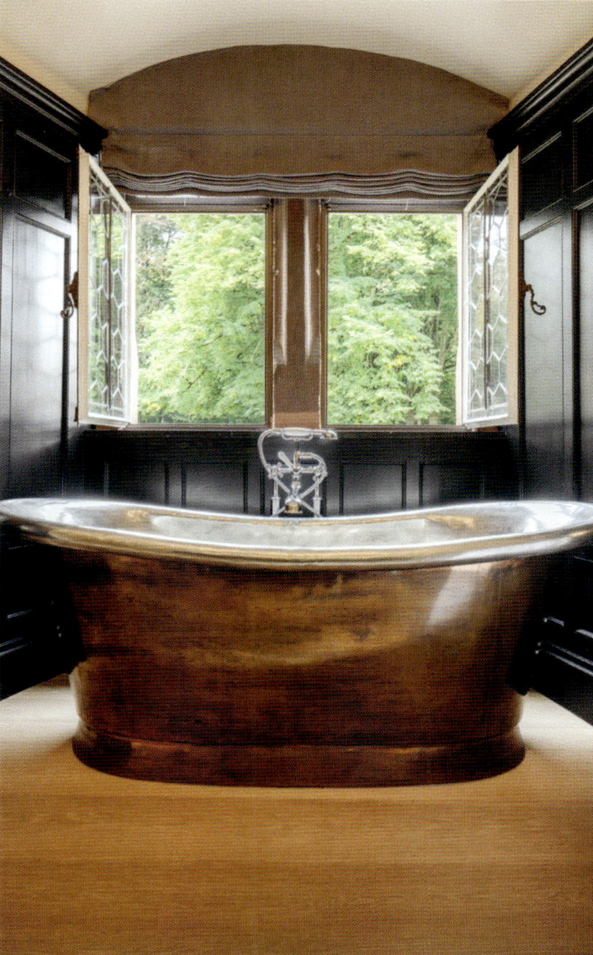

The loft-style kitchen (above) spans a large part of the gable, with a seating area extending into one of the towers (far left). In the newly created bathroom (left), old wood contrasts with modern features.

Die Küche im Loftstil (oben) erstreckt sich über einen großen Teil des Giebels und bezieht durch eine Sitzecke auch einen der Türme mit ein (ganz links). Im neu entstandenen Badezimmer (links) kontrastiert altes Holz mit modernen Elementen.

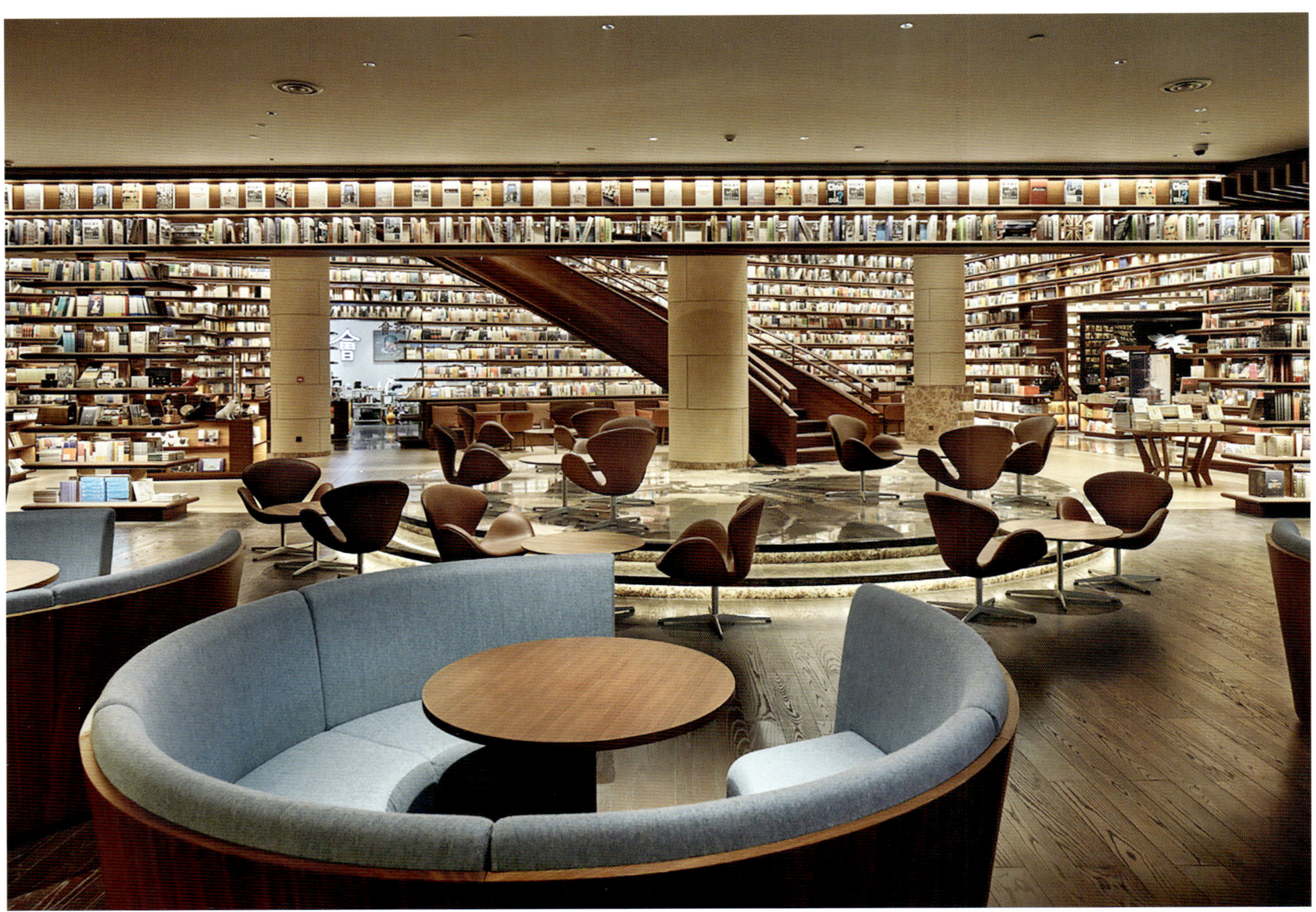

FRITZ HANSEN

ALLERØD / DENMARK

Passion and Tradition | Leidenschaft und Tradition

Fritz Hansen's designs are sold in over eighty-five countries at more than 2000 points of sale, including the flagship stores in Copenhagen, San Francisco, New York, and Tokyo. Founded in Denmark in 1872, the company is a leading designer and manufacturer of furniture, lighting, and accessories. It embodies a modern, Nordic lifestyle and collaborates with visionary artists, designers, and architects, including big names such as Arne Jacobsen, Cecilie Manz, Hans J. Wegner, Piero Lissoni, and Poul Kjærholm. The Fritz Hansen team believes that a single design object can dramatically enhance an entire space, both physically and emotionally.

Über 2000 Verkaufsstellen in mehr als 85 Ländern bieten Fritz-Hansen-Designs an, inklusive der Flagship-Stores in Kopenhagen, San Francisco, New York und Tokyo. Das 1872 in Dänemark gegründete Unternehmen ist führend im Entwerfen und Produzieren von Möbeln, Leuchten und Accessoires. Es verkörpert einen modernen, nordischen Lebensstil und arbeitet mit visionären Künstlern, Designern und Architekten zusammen, darunter große Namen wie Arne Jacobsen, Cecilie Manz, Hans J. Wegner, Piero Lissoni und Poul Kjærholm. Bei Fritz Hansen glaubt man daran, dass ein einzelnes Designobjekt einen ganzen Raum physisch und emotional dramatisch aufwerten kann.

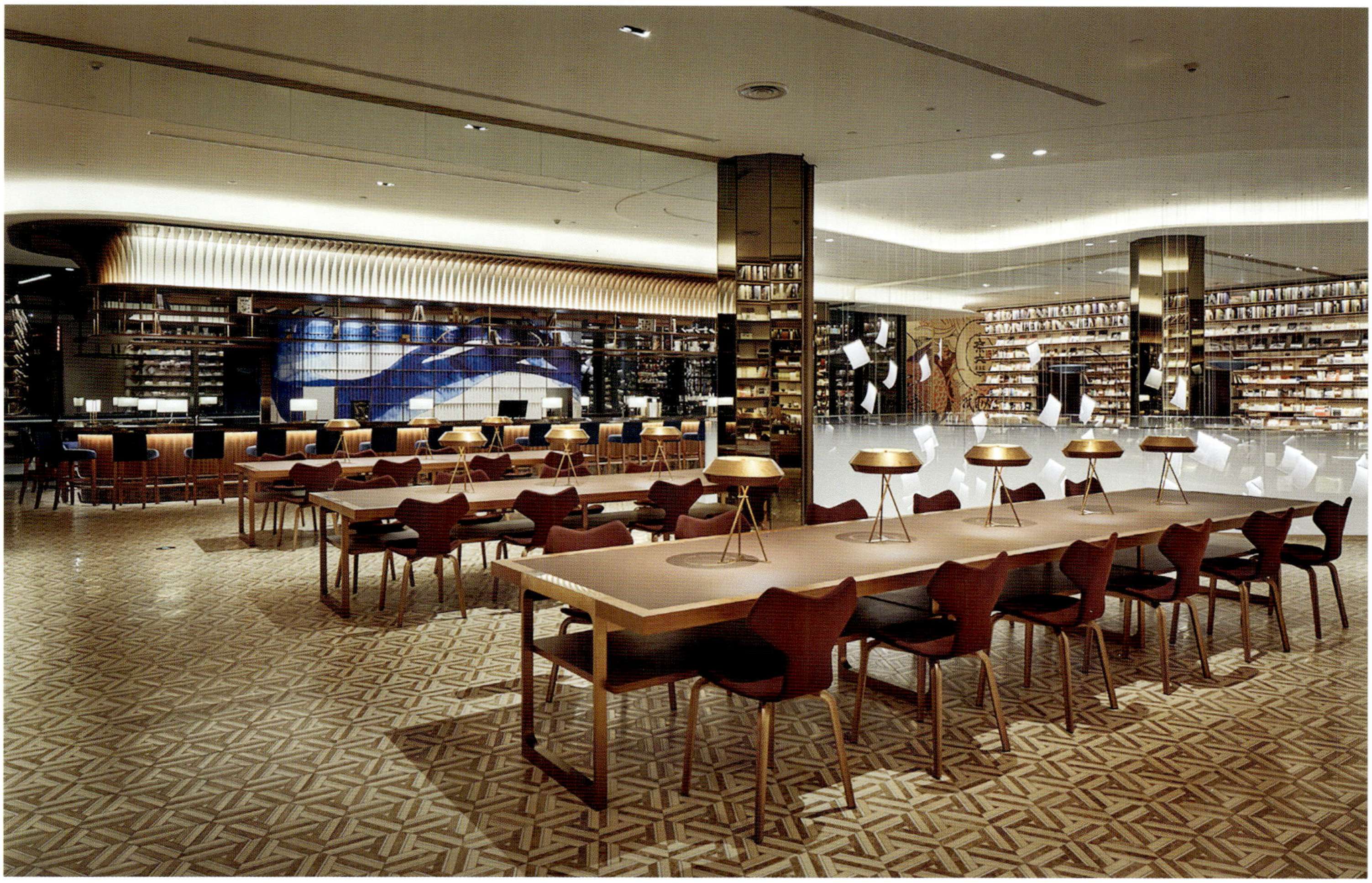

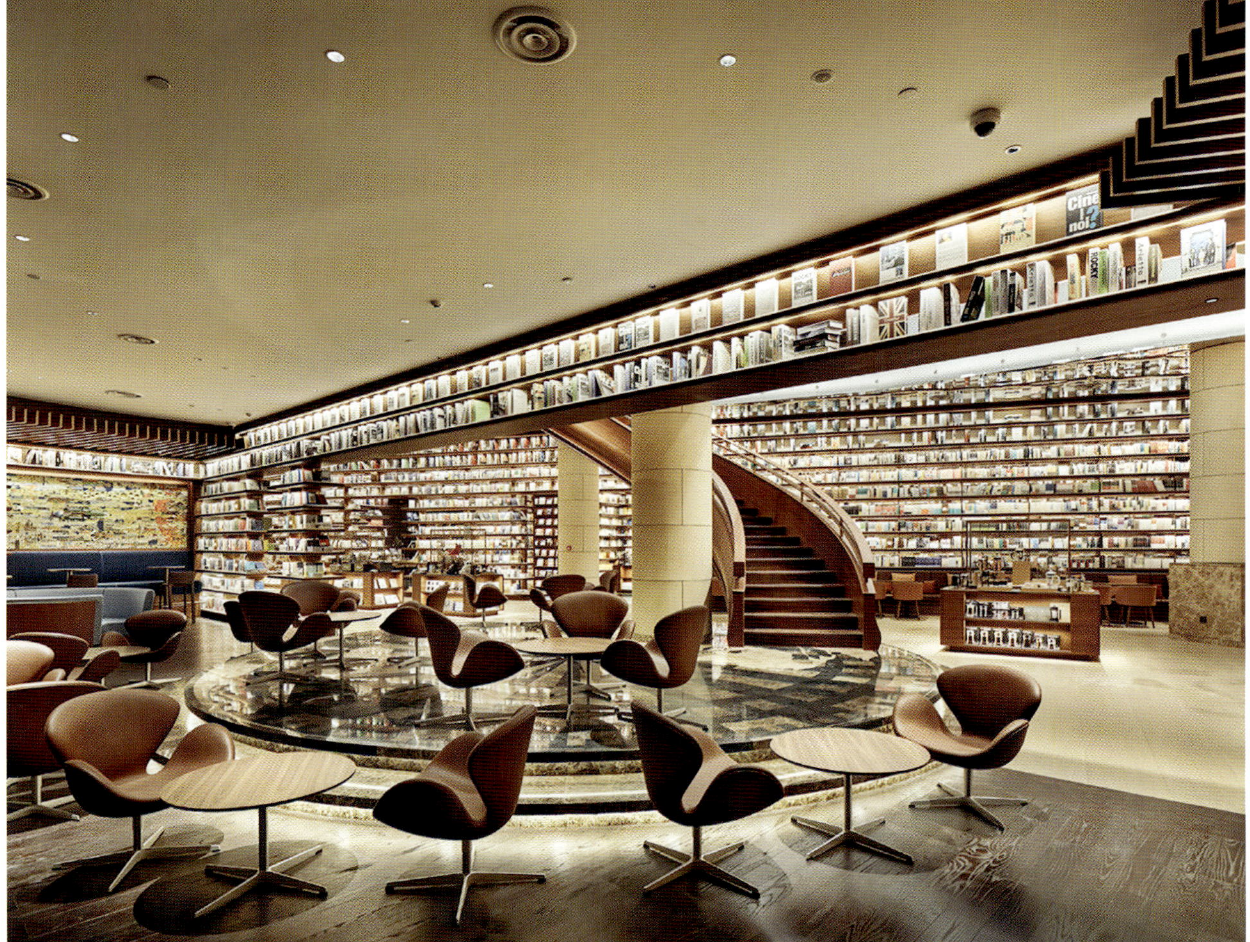

Exceptional interiors require exceptional objects. The Japanese designer Tomoko Ikegai selected the Fritz Hansen chairs Grand Prix™ (above) and Swan™ (left) as the seats in the award-winning YJY Maike Centre flagship store in Xi'an, China. Among other things, the complex houses a large bookstore and a hotel.

Außergewöhnliche Innenräume erfordern besondere Designobjekte, deshalb wählte die japanische Designerin Tomoko Ikegai für die Bestuhlung des preisgekrönten YJY Maike Centre Flagship Store in Xi'an, China, den Stuhl Grand Prix™ (oben) und den Sessel Swan™ (links) von Fritz Hansen. In dem Gebäudekomplex befinden sich unter anderem eine große Buchhandlung und ein Hotel.

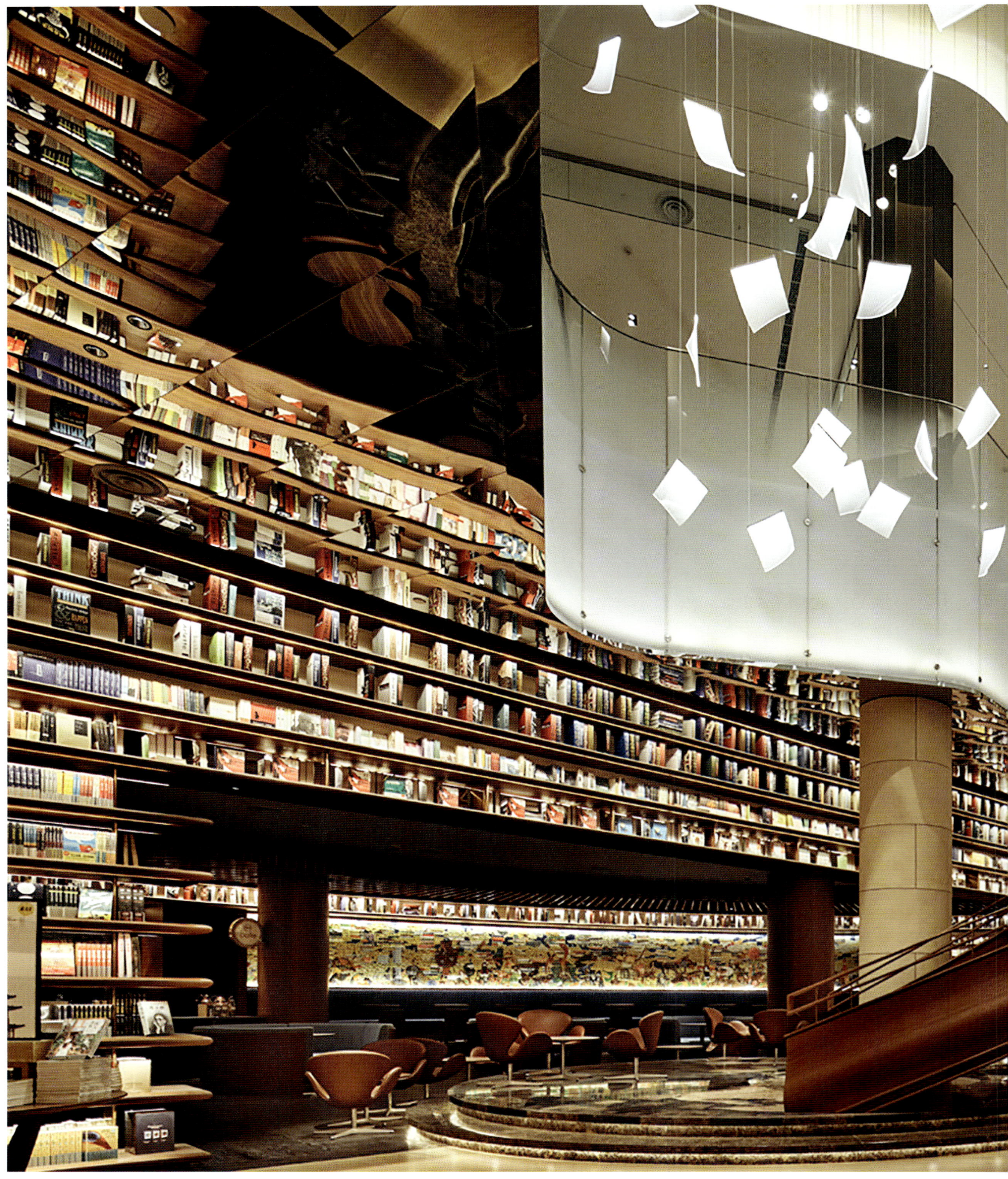

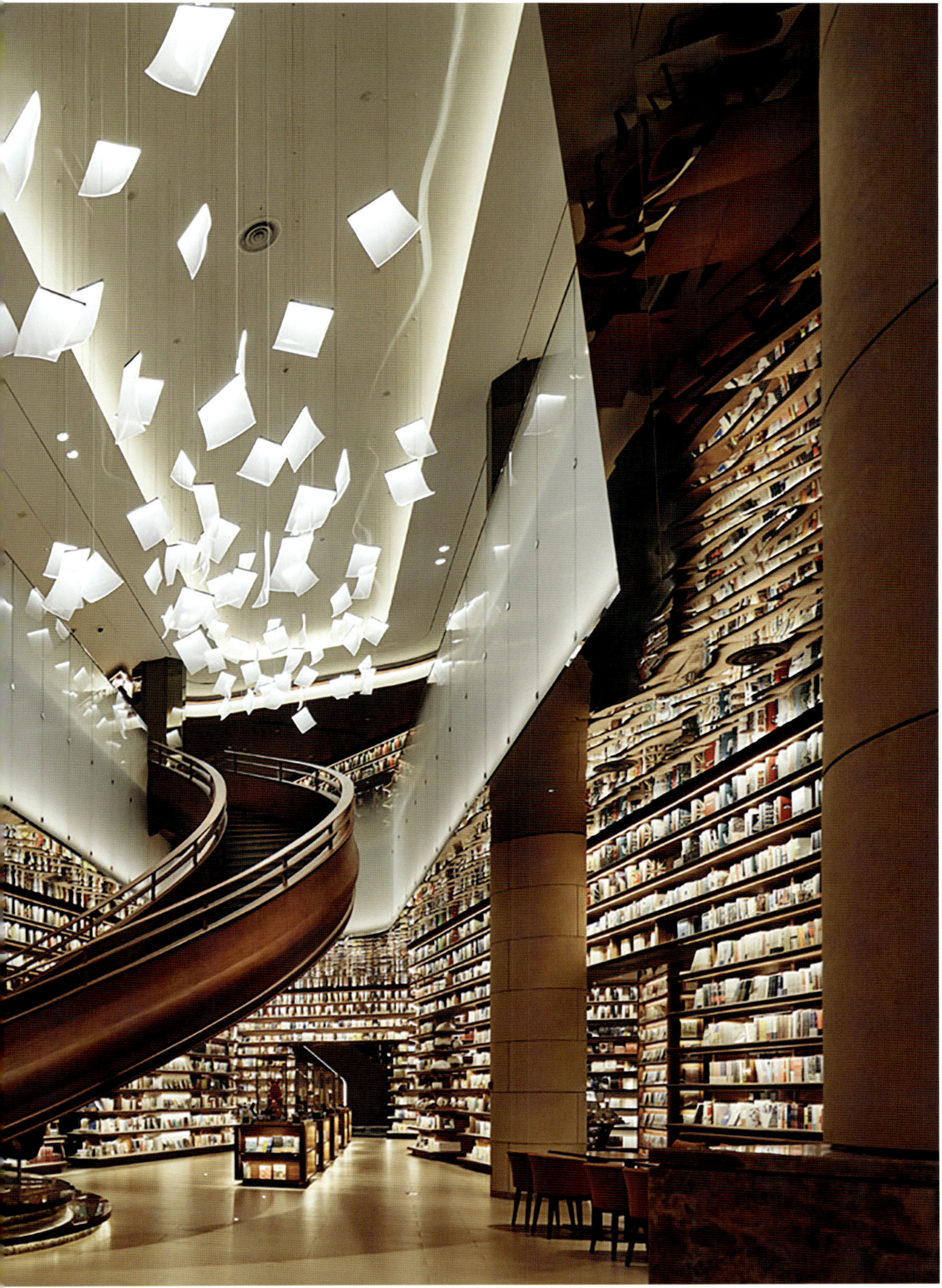

The commercial complex YJY Maike Centre flagship store occupies 4500 square meters in Xi'an's 'Hi-tech Industries Development Zone.' The second floor also serves as a lounge for the neighboring Grand Hyatt Hotel. The guiding principle of 'Library & Gallery' is to promote individual learning and research as well as social interaction. In addition to the vast assortment of books, the spectacularly designed bookstore also provides many sitting and reading areas, as well as boasting countless art objects, all of which are originals. Visitors from throughout the world are invited to relax, unwind, learn, think, and dream.

Der Gewerbekomplex YJY Maike Centre Flagship Store nimmt 4500 Quadratmeter in der „Hi-tech Industries Development Zone" Xi'ans ein. Der zweite Stock dient gleichzeitig als Lounge für das angrenzende Grand Hyatt Hotel. Unter dem Leitgedanken „Library & Gallery" soll hier sowohl individuelles Lernen und Erkunden als auch gemeinschaftliches Zusammenkommen gefördert werden. Neben unzähligen Büchern beherbergt die spektakulär gestaltete Buchhandlung viele Ecken zum Sitzen und Lernen sowie zahlreiche Kunstobjekte, ausnahmslos Originale. Besucher aus aller Welt sind hier zum Entspannen, Erholen, Lernen, Denken und Träumen eingeladen.

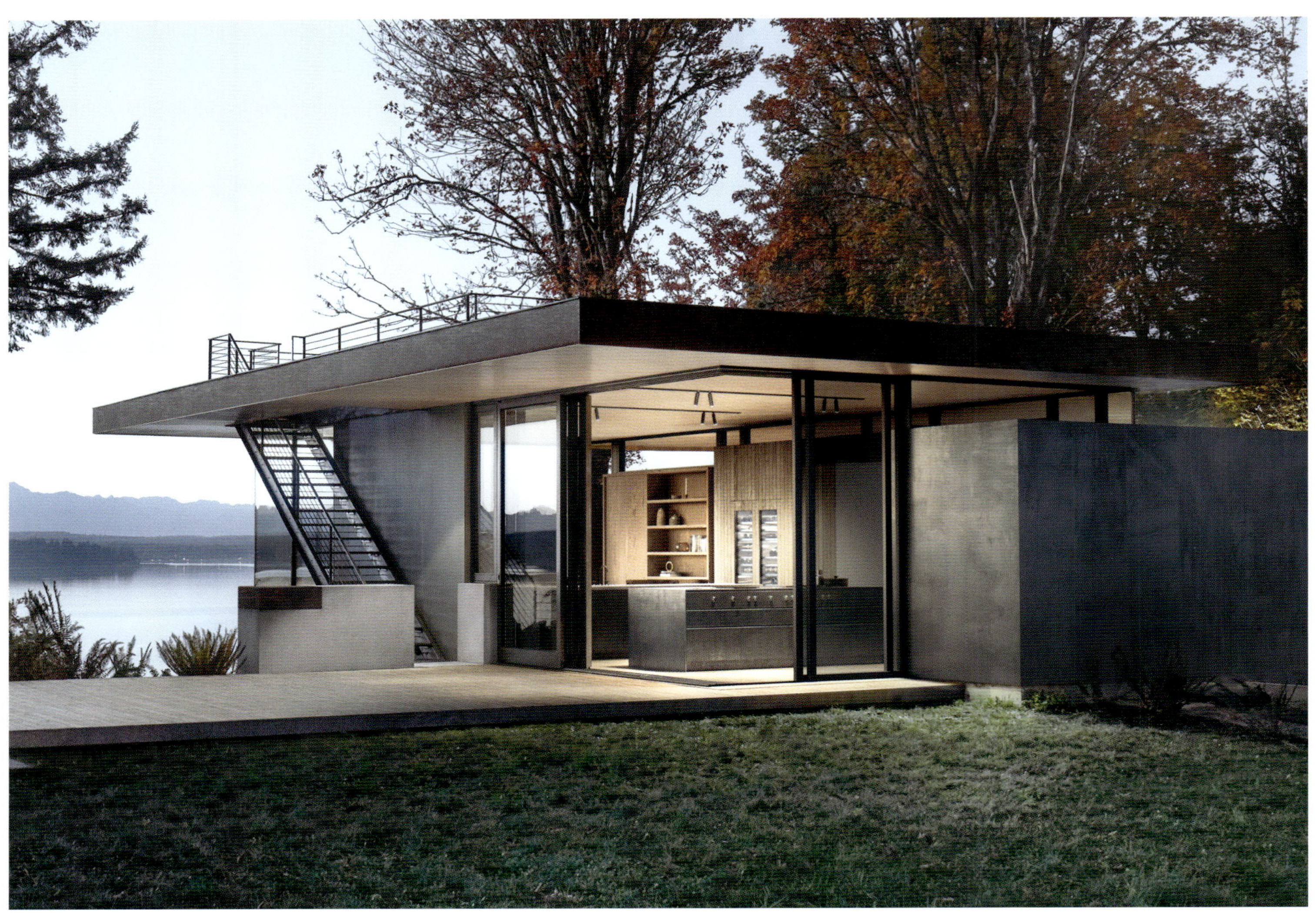

GAGGENAU

MUNICH / GERMANY

Timeless Design for Culinary Greatness | Zeitloses Design für kulinarische Größe

The luxury of limitless possibilities: Gaggenau's integrated kitchen appliances provide the perfect backdrop for exceptional culinary experiences. Inspired by the needs of professional chefs, they impress with both performance and design. The range caters for personal cooking habits, including steam and baking ovens, warming and vacuum-packing drawers, hobs, extractors, refrigerators, and wine climate cabinets, all of which can be combined in a modular way. To guarantee longevity, only the best materials are implemented for the made-to-measure appliances. The particular attention to detail allows uncompromising perfection to become an architectural statement.

Der Luxus grenzenloser Möglichkeiten: Mit seinen Küchen-einbaugeräten bietet Gaggenau die perfekte Kulisse für außergewöhnliche Kocherlebnisse. Inspiriert von den Bedürfnissen der Profiköche sind die Geräte beeindruckend in ihrer Leistung und imposant im Design. Für individuelle Kochgewohnheiten gibt es Dampf- und Backöfen, Wärme- und Vakuumierschubladen, Kochfelder, Lüftungen, Kältegeräte und Weinklimaschränke, die sich modular kombinieren lassen. Um die Langlebigkeit der Gaggenau Geräte zu gewährleisten, werden in Maßarbeit und mit Liebe zum Detail nur beste Materialien verarbeitet. Kompromisslose Perfektion wird so zum architektonischen Statement.

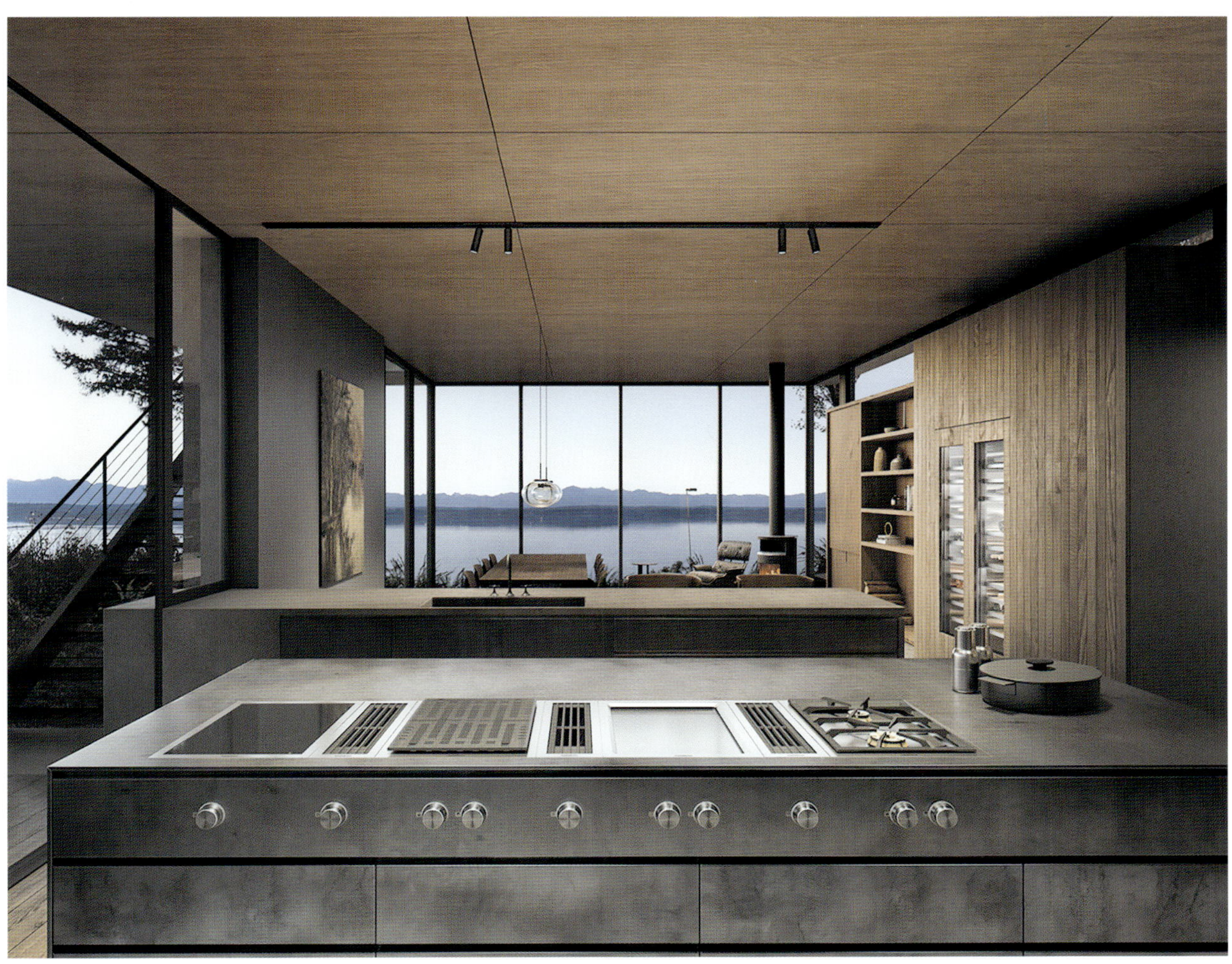

The Gaggenau 400 series appliances are custom-made for the culinary ambitions of private chefs. They can all be easily combined in a single unit. One is convinced not least by the 400 series' high-quality materials and timeless design.

Die Serie 400 der Gaggenau Geräte ist wie maßgeschneidert für die kulinarischen Ambitionen privater Köchinnen und Köche. Alle Geräte lassen sich problemlos zu einer Einheit zusammenstellen. Nicht zuletzt überzeugt die Serie 400 durch besonders hochwertige Materialien und zeitloses Design.

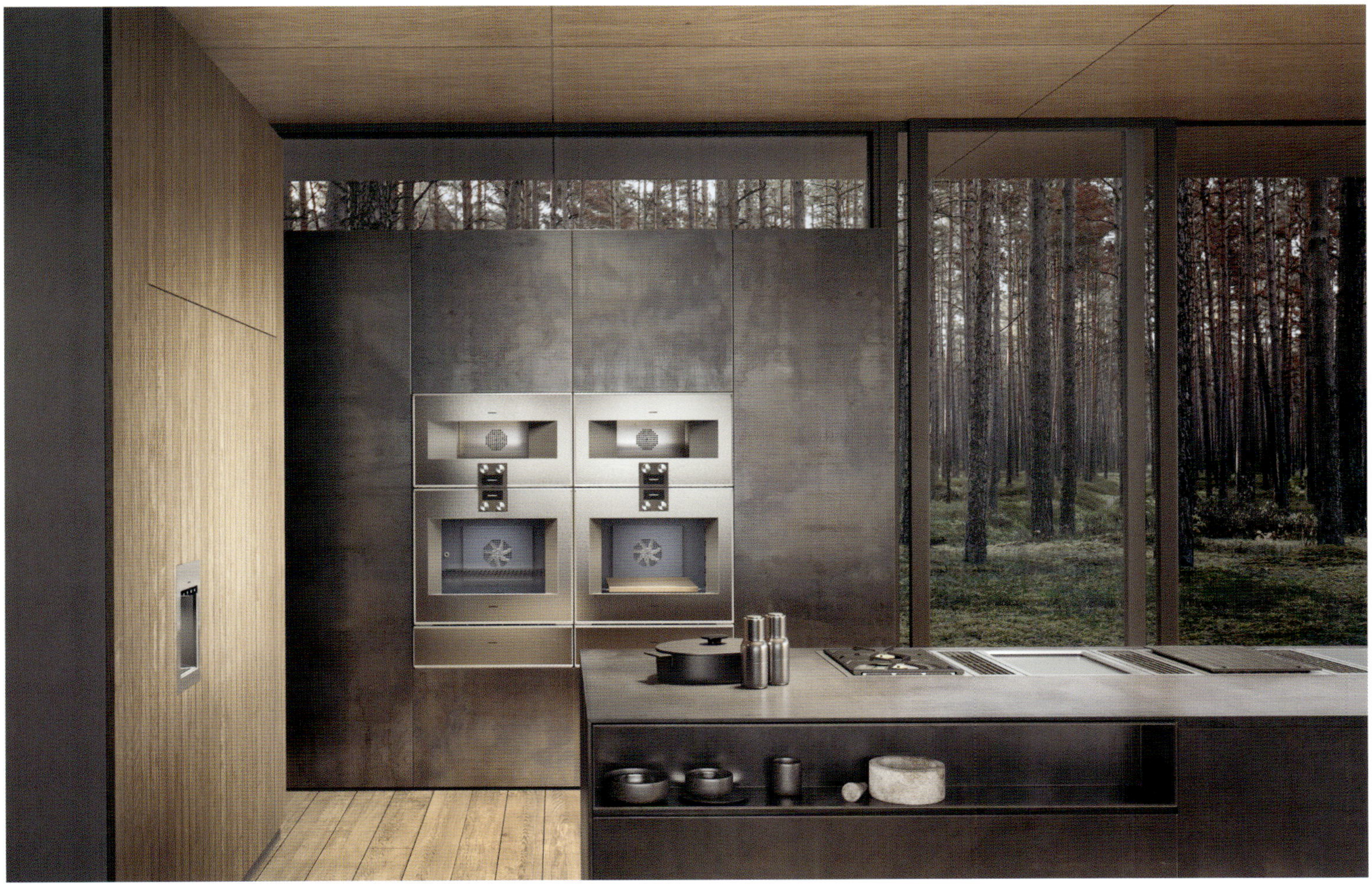

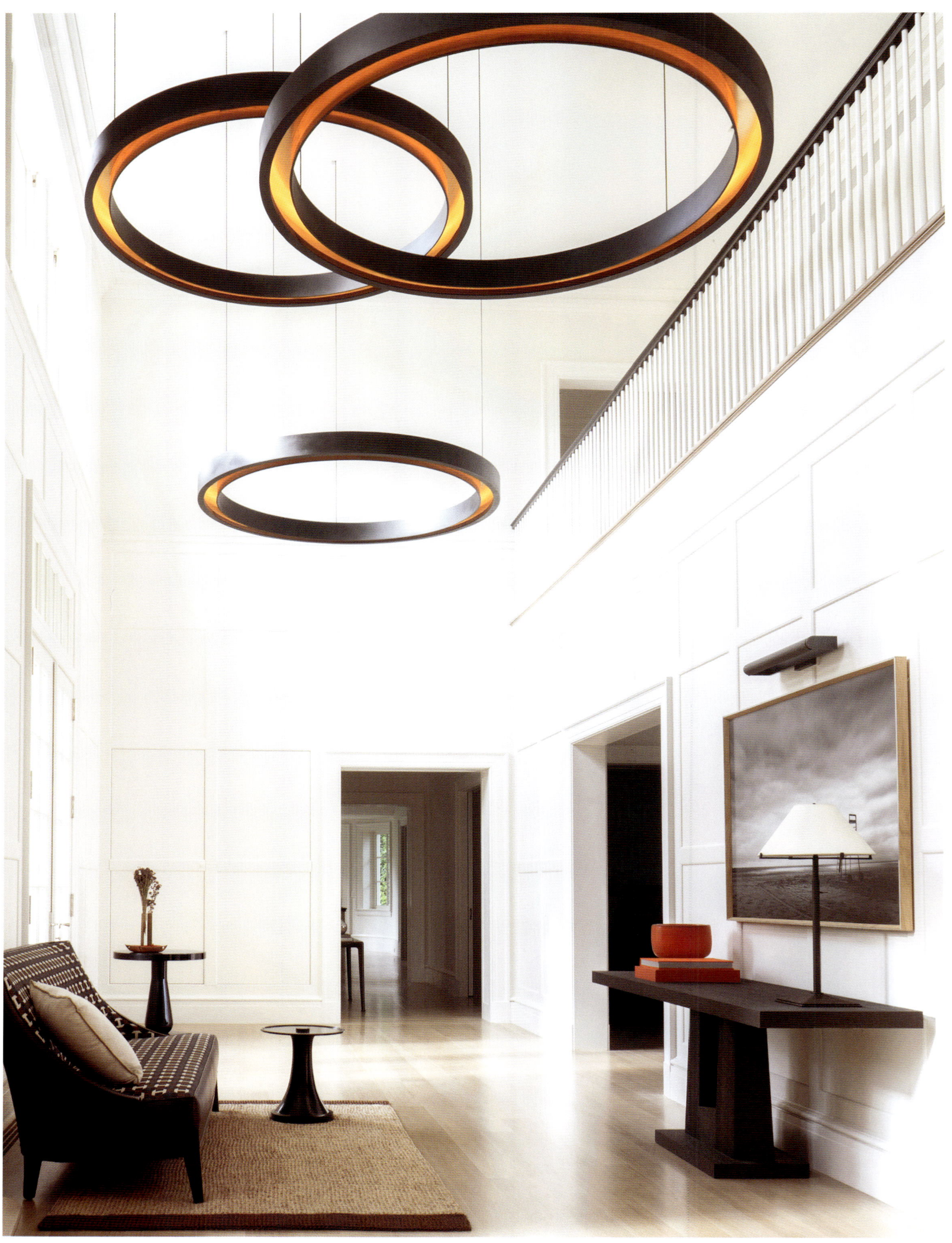

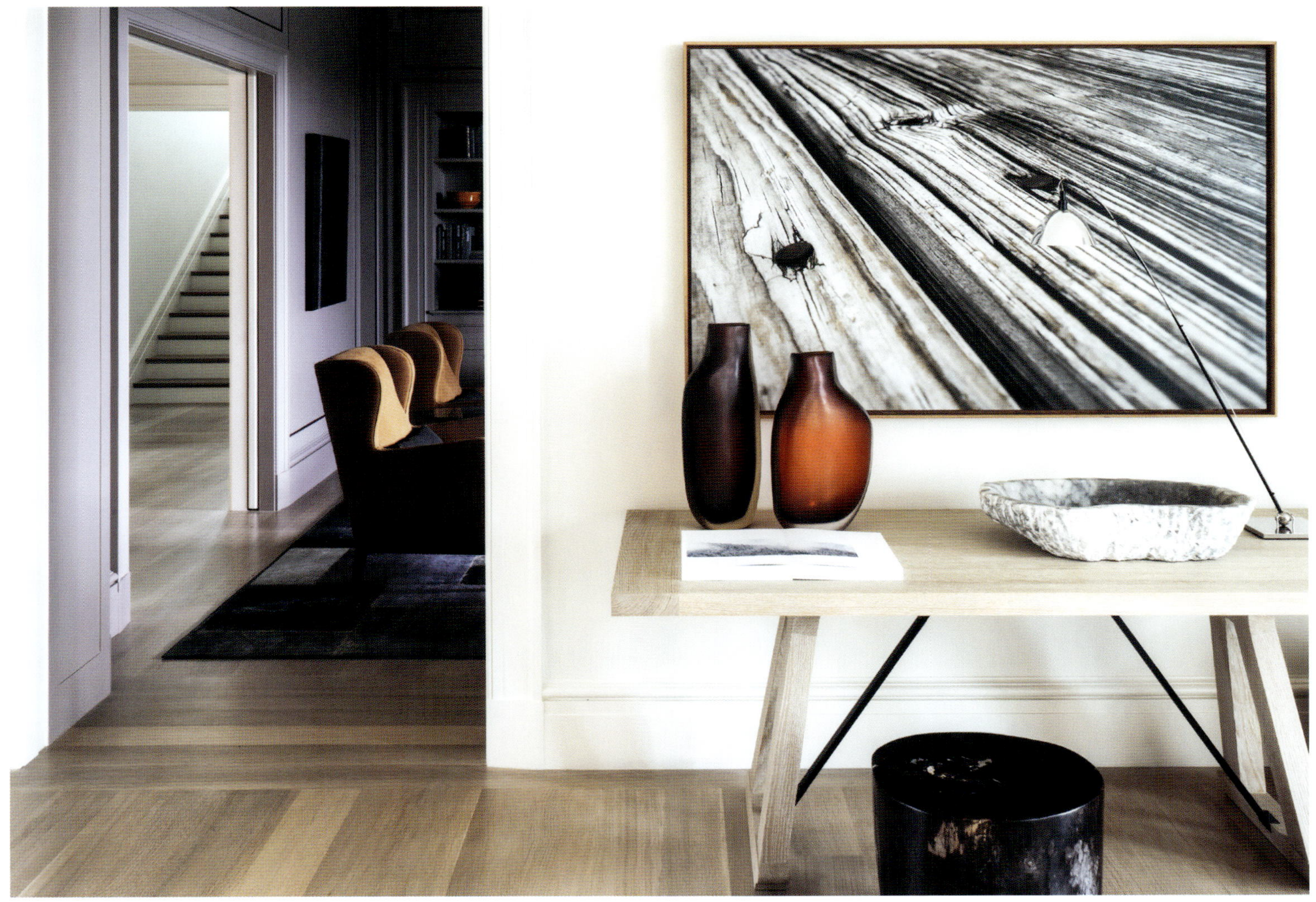

GWdesign

LOS ANGELES & NEW YORK / USA

Integrative Design | Integratives Design

Dominic Gasparoly and Khalid Watson came from different corners of the industry, when they established their integrative studio GWdesign. Since then, they have aimed to combine all aspects of design in their craft. Here in this bucolic residence on the Georgica Pond estuary in East Hampton, NY, and in collaboration with Peter Pennoyer Architects, they have composed an overall experience that ranges from spatial design, to furnishings and accessories, and even extending into lighting and art curation. With the thoughtful placement of elegant motifs and references, each of the rooms has been composed with the intent of triggering specific emotional responses.

Dominic Gasparoly und Khalid Watson kamen aus unterschiedlichen Ecken der Branche, als sie ihr integratives Designstudio GWdesign gründeten. Seitdem haben sie sich zum Ziel gesetzt, alle Designfacetten in ihrer Arbeit zu vereinen. In diesem idyllischen Landhaus am Georgica Pond in East Hampton, NY, haben sie in Zusammenarbeit mit Peter Pennoyer Architects ein Gesamterlebnis erschaffen, das sich nicht auf die räumliche Gestaltung beschränkt, sondern auch Möblierung und Accessoires umfasst, bis hin zur Beleuchtung und der Auswahl von Kunst. Jedes Zimmer wurde mit überlegt platzierten eleganten Objekten so komponiert, dass ganz bestimmte Stimmungen entstehen.

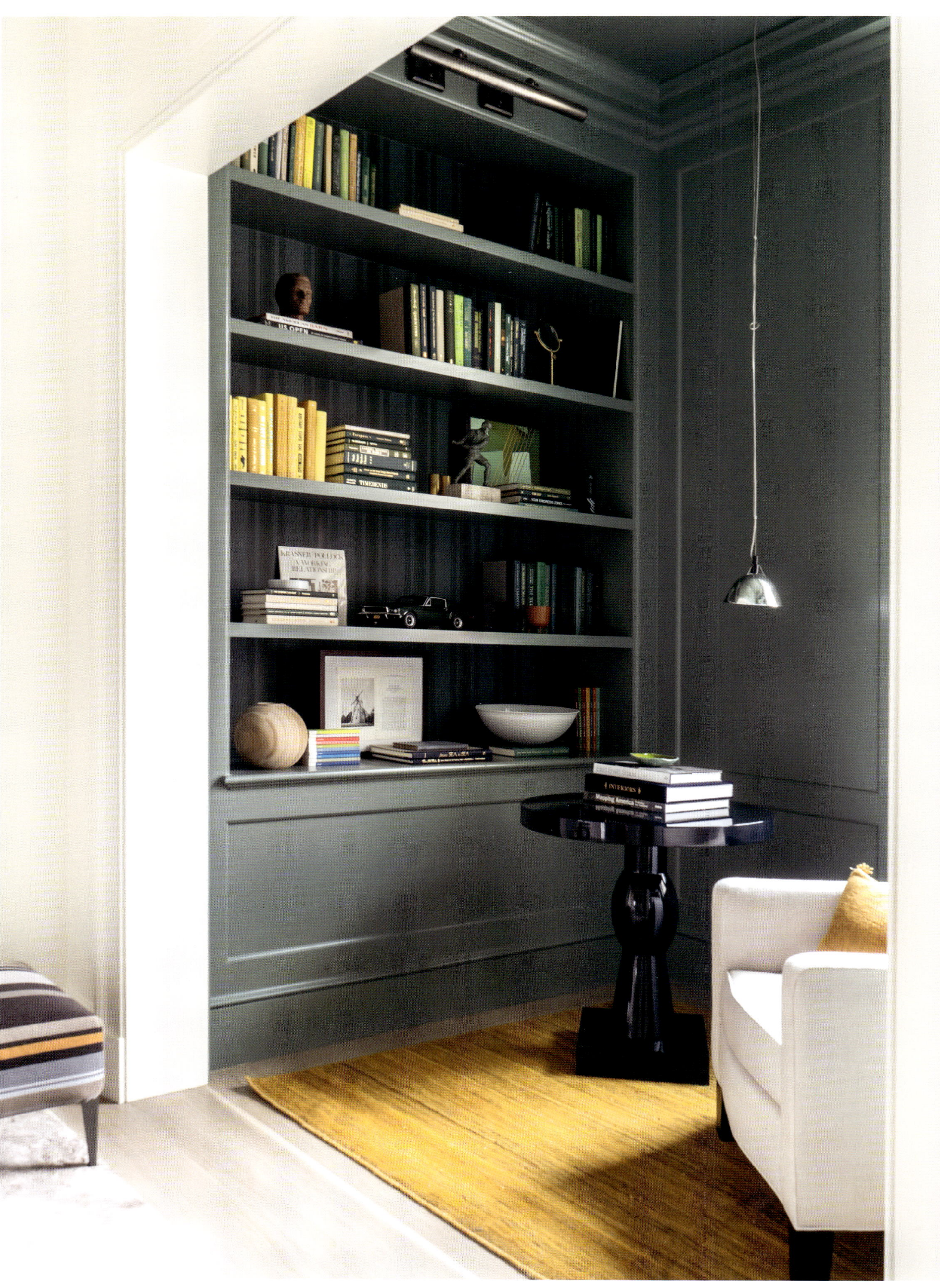

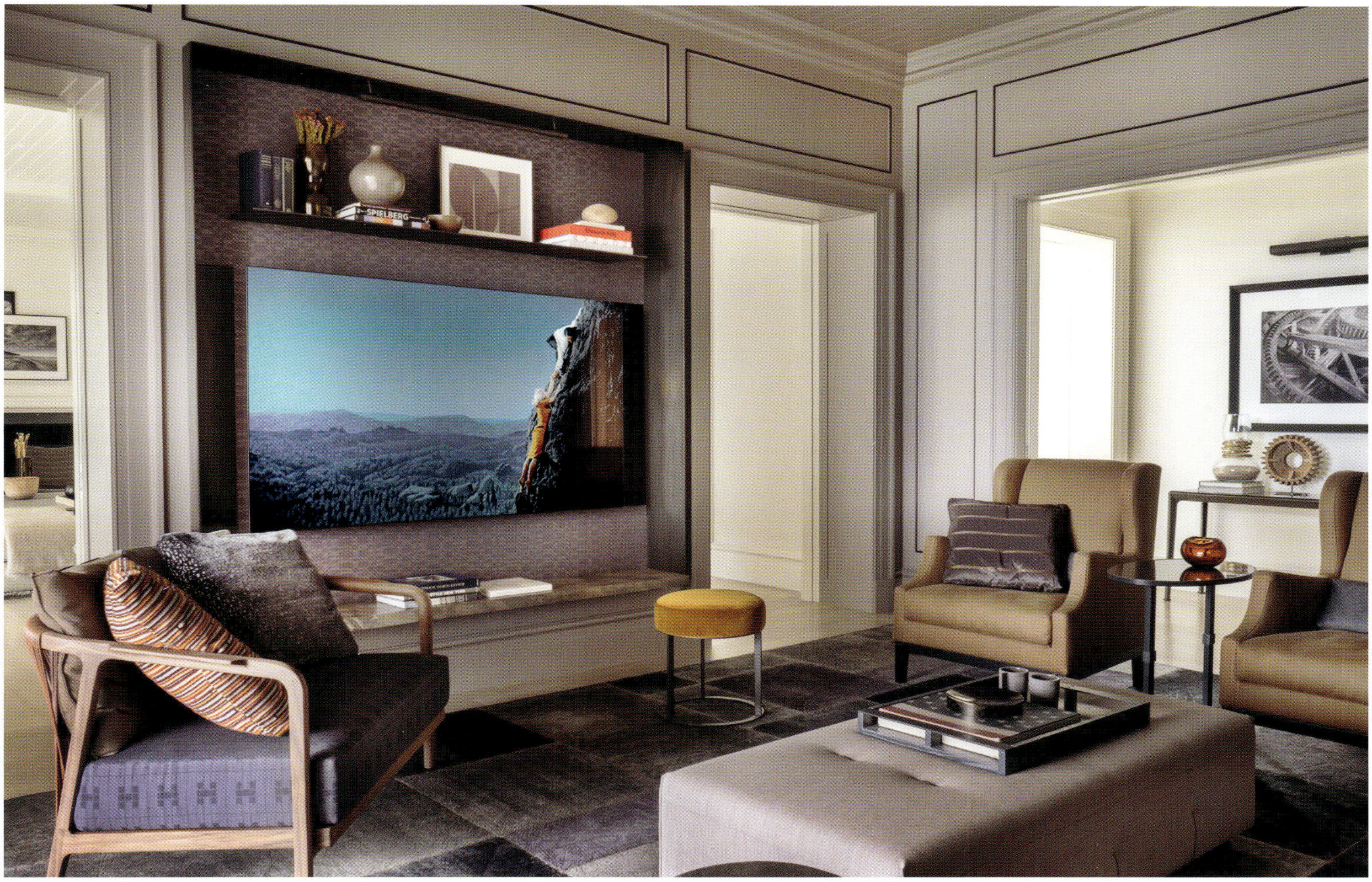

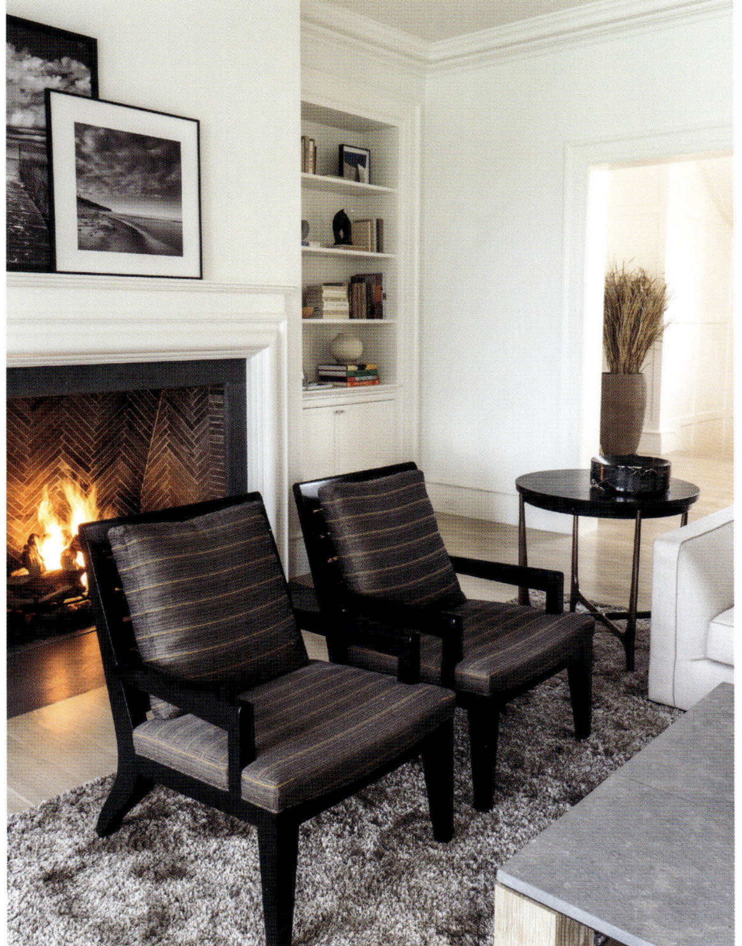

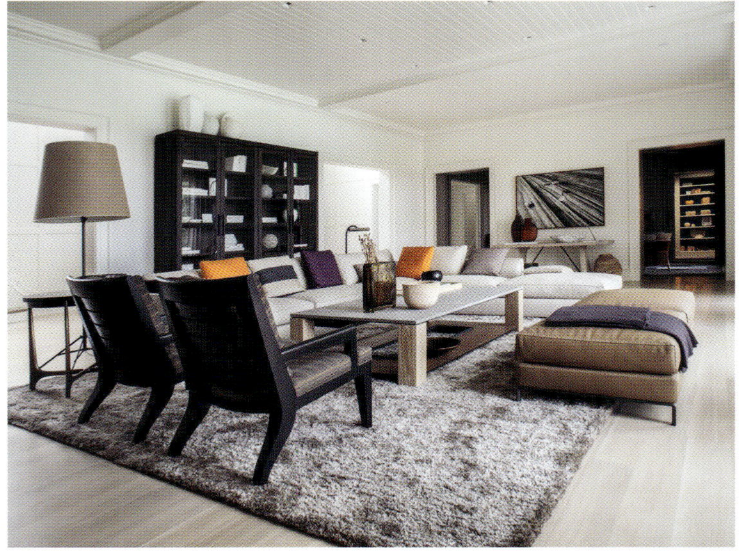

The client's brief was for an aesthetic that is both contemporary and classic. In addition to its stylish and comfortable furnishings, the living and family rooms were designed to promote an atmosphere that harmonizes perfectly with the home's natural surroundings.

Der Kunde wünschte sich einen ebenso zeitgemäßen wie klassischen Stil. Die Wohn- und Familienzimmer wurden so gestaltet, dass sie neben stilvollem Komfort auch eine Atmosphäre bieten, die gut mit der Natur um das Landhaus herum harmoniert.

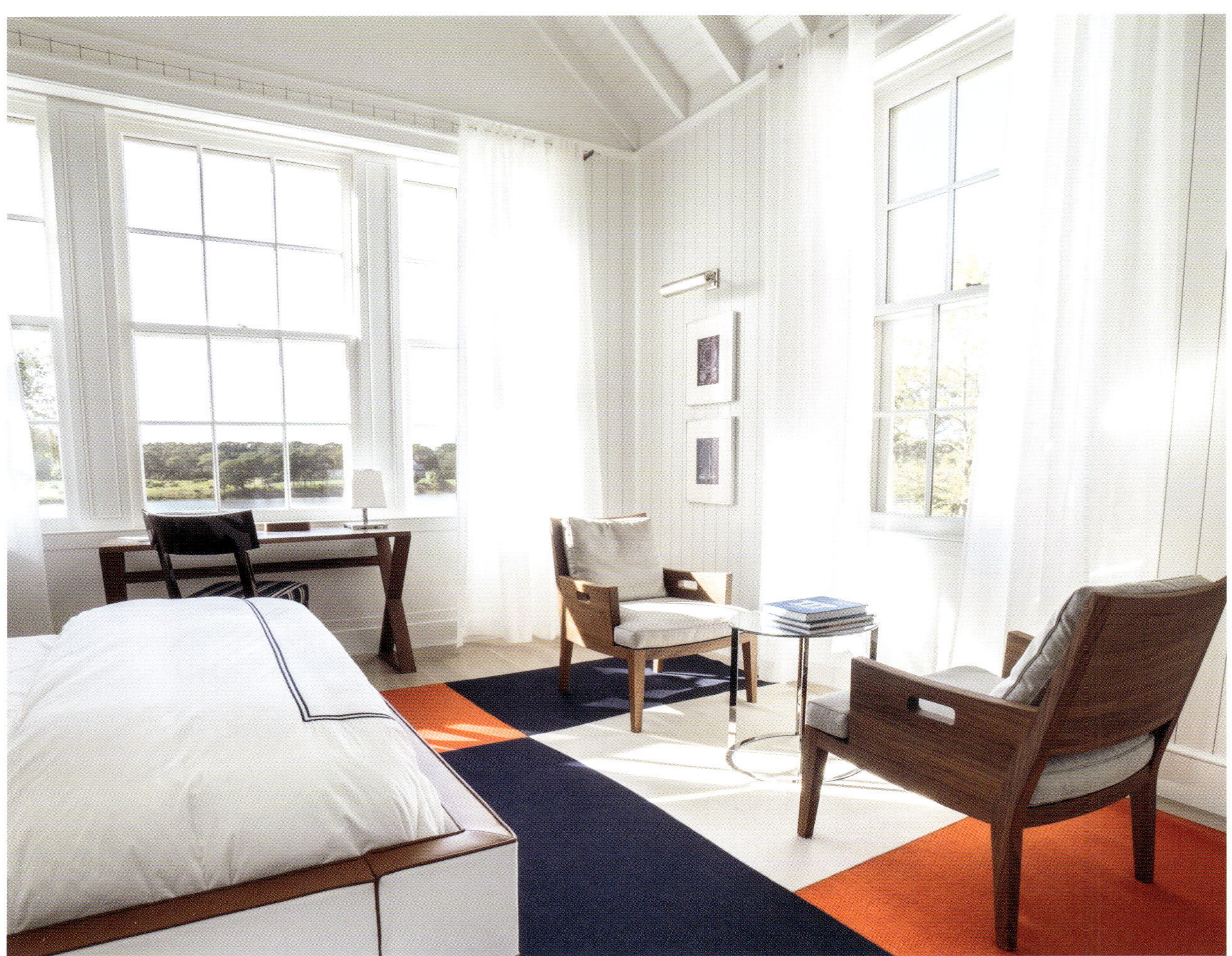

One of the house's nautical-styled guest rooms (left). The crown of this manor is the elegantly conceived master suite (below left), with its fireplace, seating area and marble-wood paneled bathroom (below right). Each of the ten bedrooms have their own fully appointed en-suite.

Eines der maritim gestalteten Gästezimmer des Hauses (links). Ein Glanzstück ist die edel designte Master Suite (unten rechts), unter anderem mit Kamin, Sitzecke sowie einem Marmorplatten-Badezimmer (unten links). Jedes der zehn Schlafzimmer verfügt über ein eigenes, voll ausgestattetes Bad.

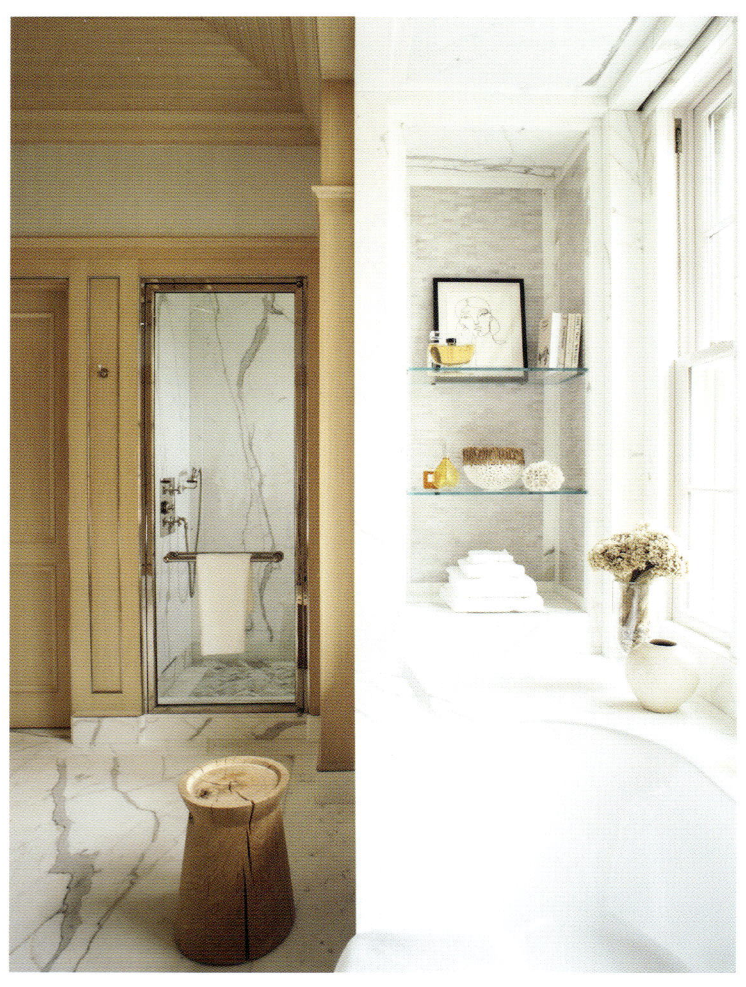

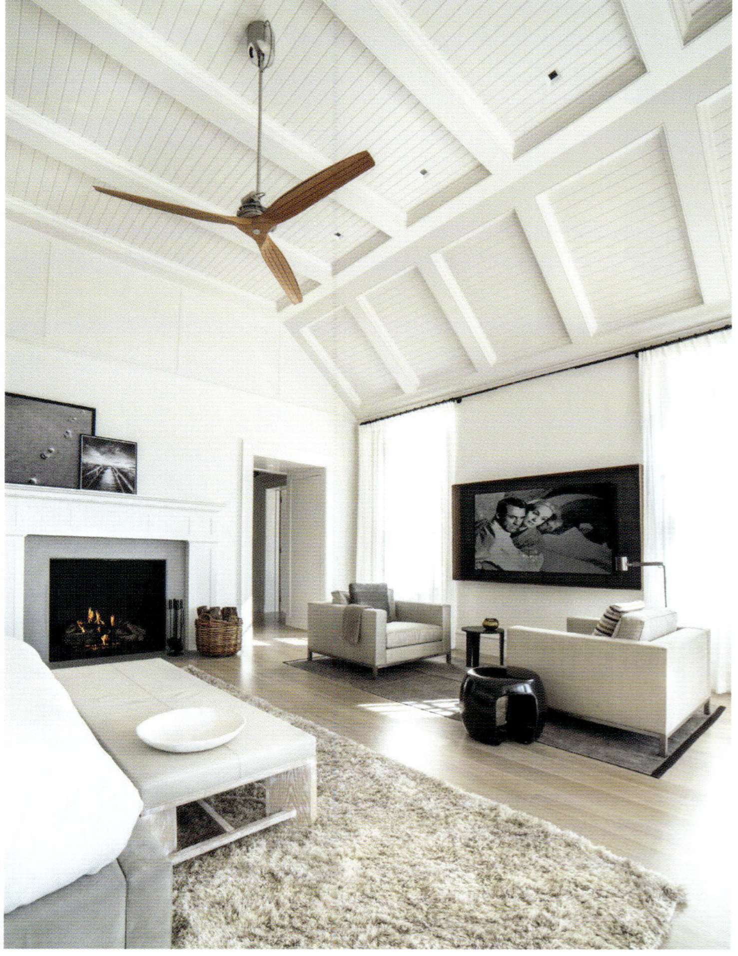

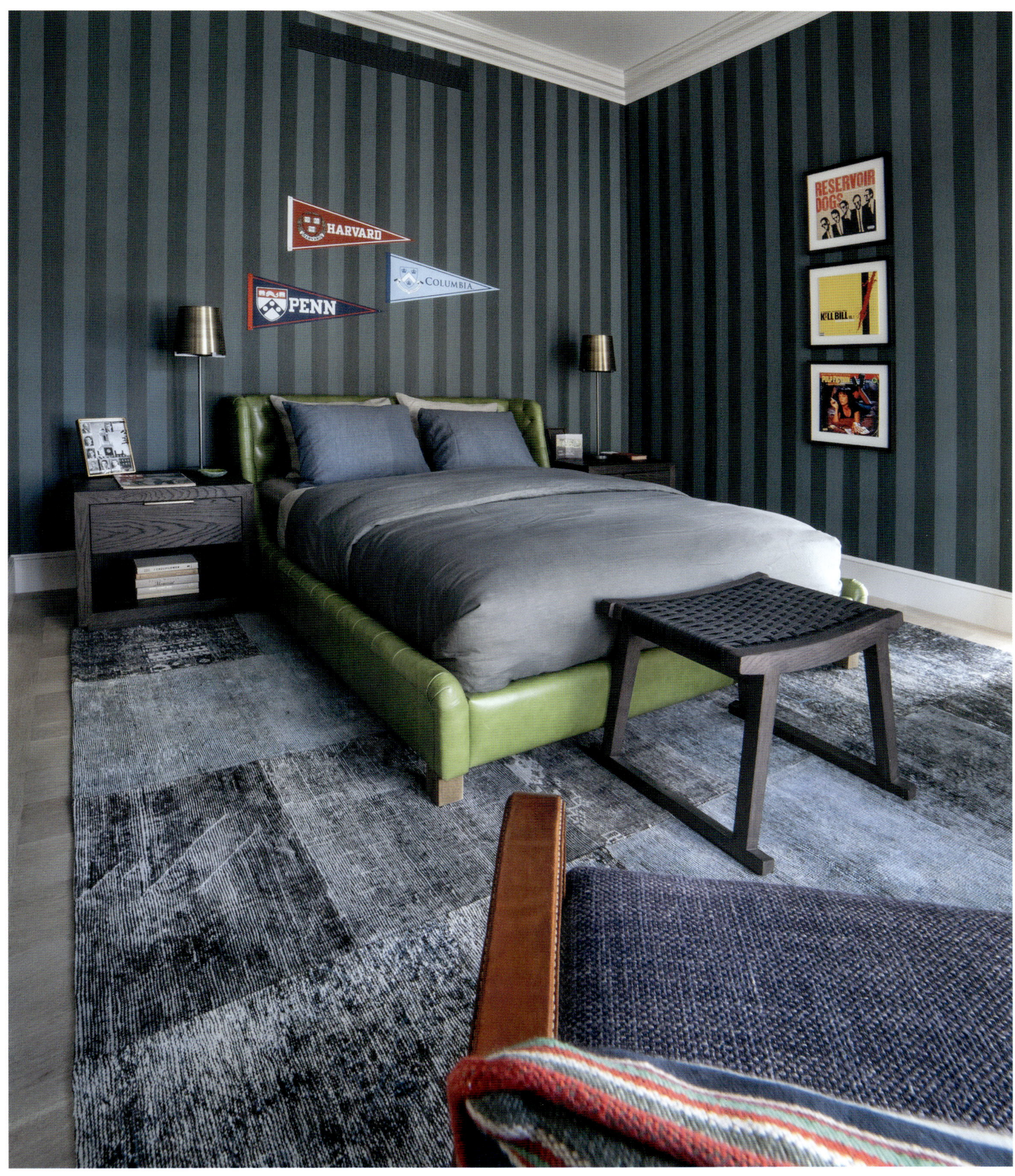

The home's guest rooms were all thematically-rendered: in addition to the maritime, vintage, and coastal motifs found on the upper level (opposite page, top), a collegiate-styled bedroom was handsomely fashioned on the first floor.

Die Gästezimmer des Hauses wurden thematisch gestaltet: Neben maritimen und Vintage-Sujets, die im oberen Stockwerk zu finden sind (Seite gegenüber oben), gibt es im Erdgeschoss ein Zimmer, das liebevoll im US-College-Look eingerichtet wurde.

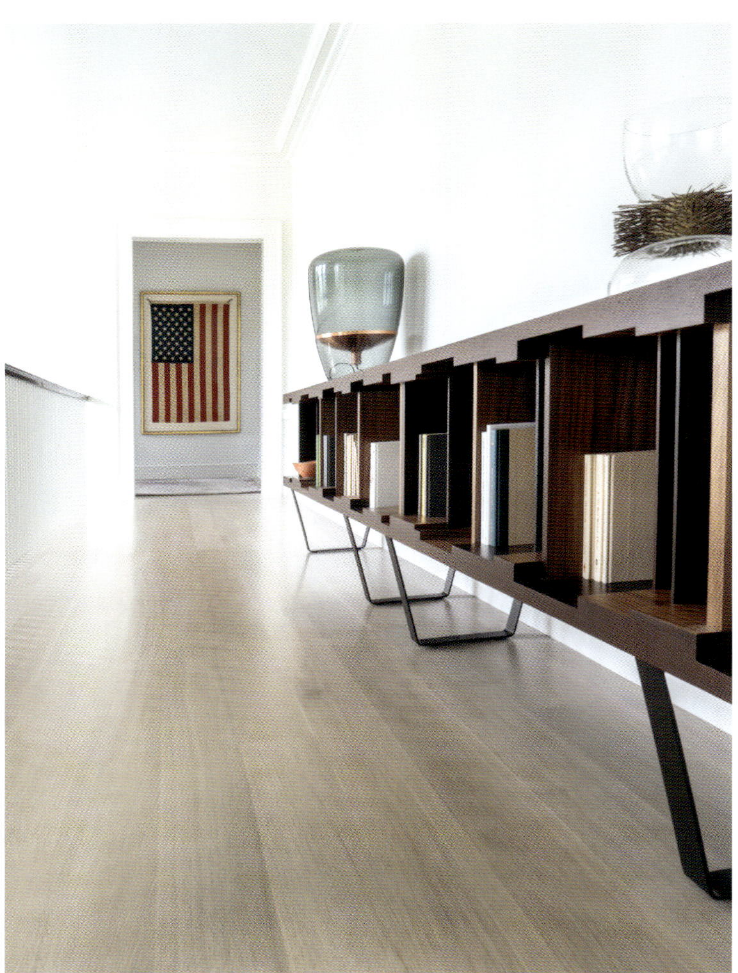

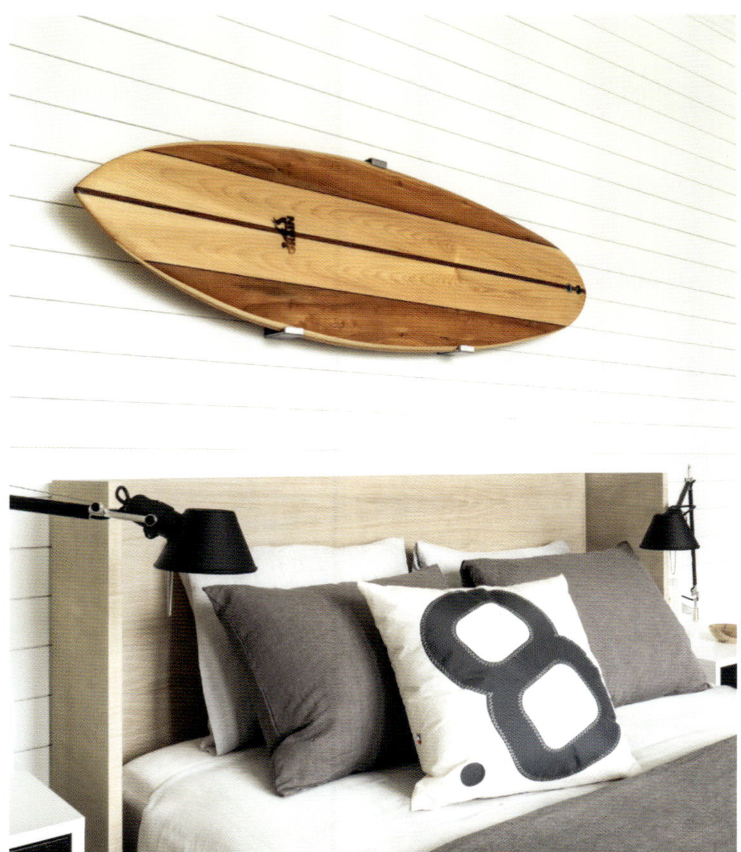

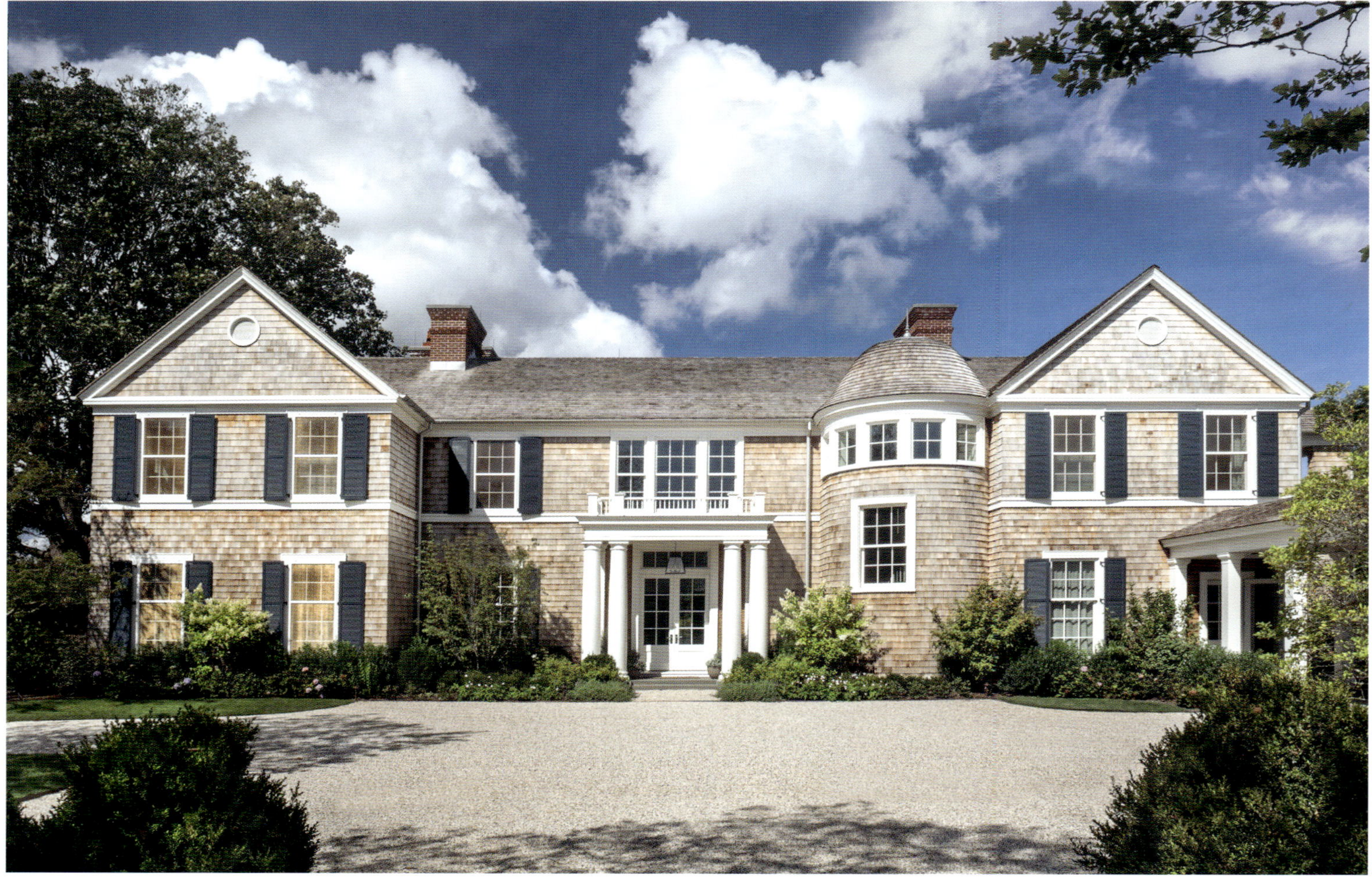

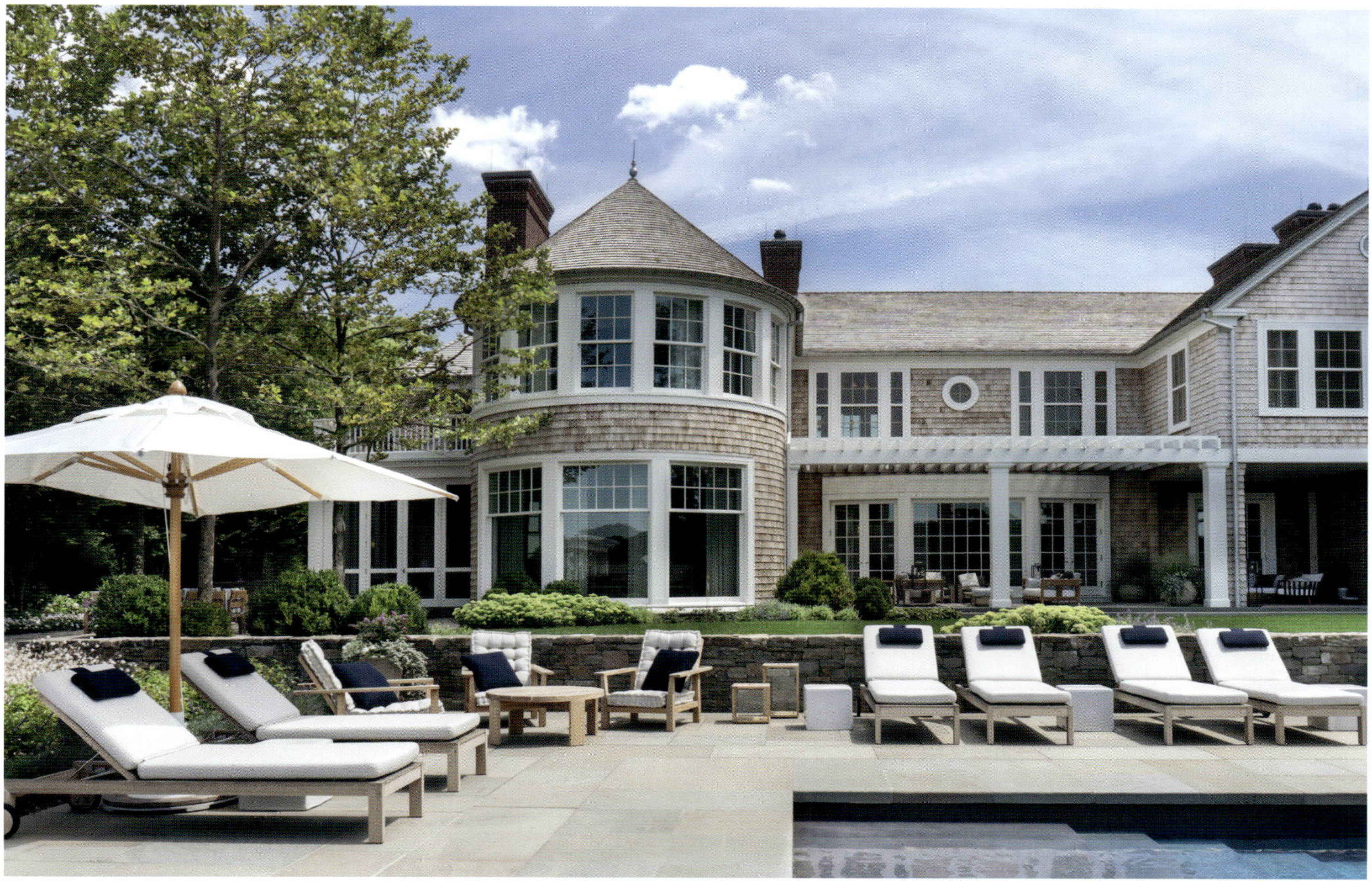

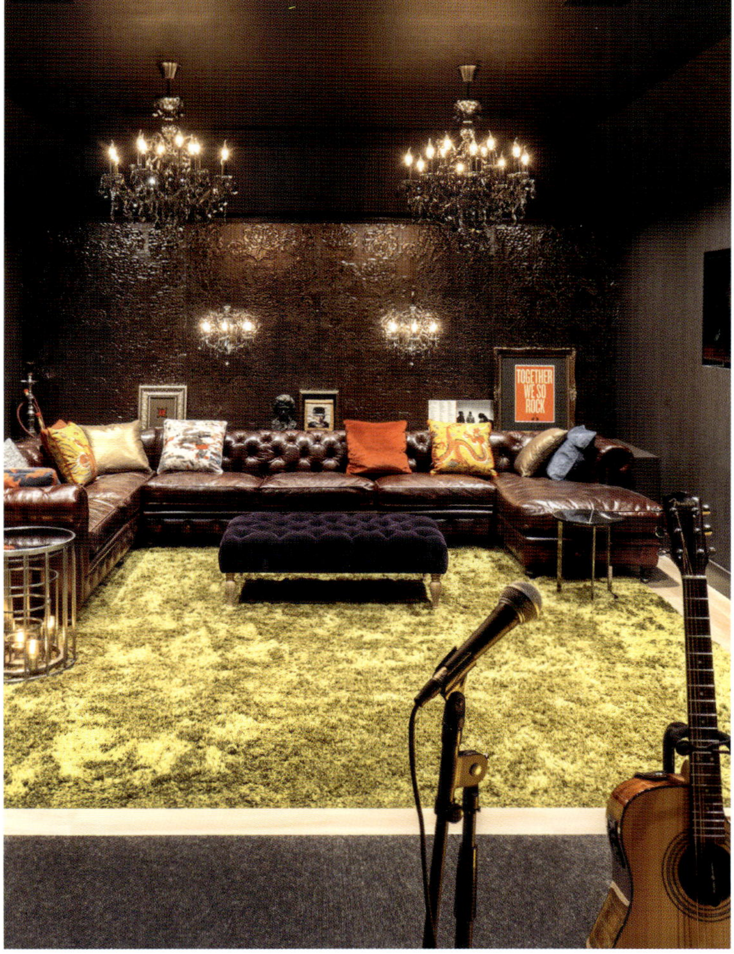

Soft materials were eagerly combined with naturally stained wood and custom steelwork. An unexpected jewel box off from the lounge area (pages 110–111) is a jam session parlor, pushing a chic rock and roll aesthetic, replete with vintage shag carpeting, a distressed leather sectional, black crystal chandeliers and a textured high gloss back wall (left). At the back of the house the pool area (top) can be accessed as well as the landscaped garden from Hollander Design Landscape Architects.

Weiche Stoffe wurden bewusst mit natürlich gebeiztem Holz und maßgefertigten Stahlelementen kombiniert. Hinter dem Lounge-Bereich (Seite 110–111) findet sich ein überraschendes Kleinod: ein Musikzimmer in schicker Rock-and-Roll-Ästhetik mit Vintage-Flokati, Ledersitzgruppe, Kronleuchtern und strukturierter Hochglanz-Rückwand (links). Auf der Rückseite des Hauses kommt man in den Poolbereich (oben) und den von Hollander Design Landscape Architects gestalteten Garten.

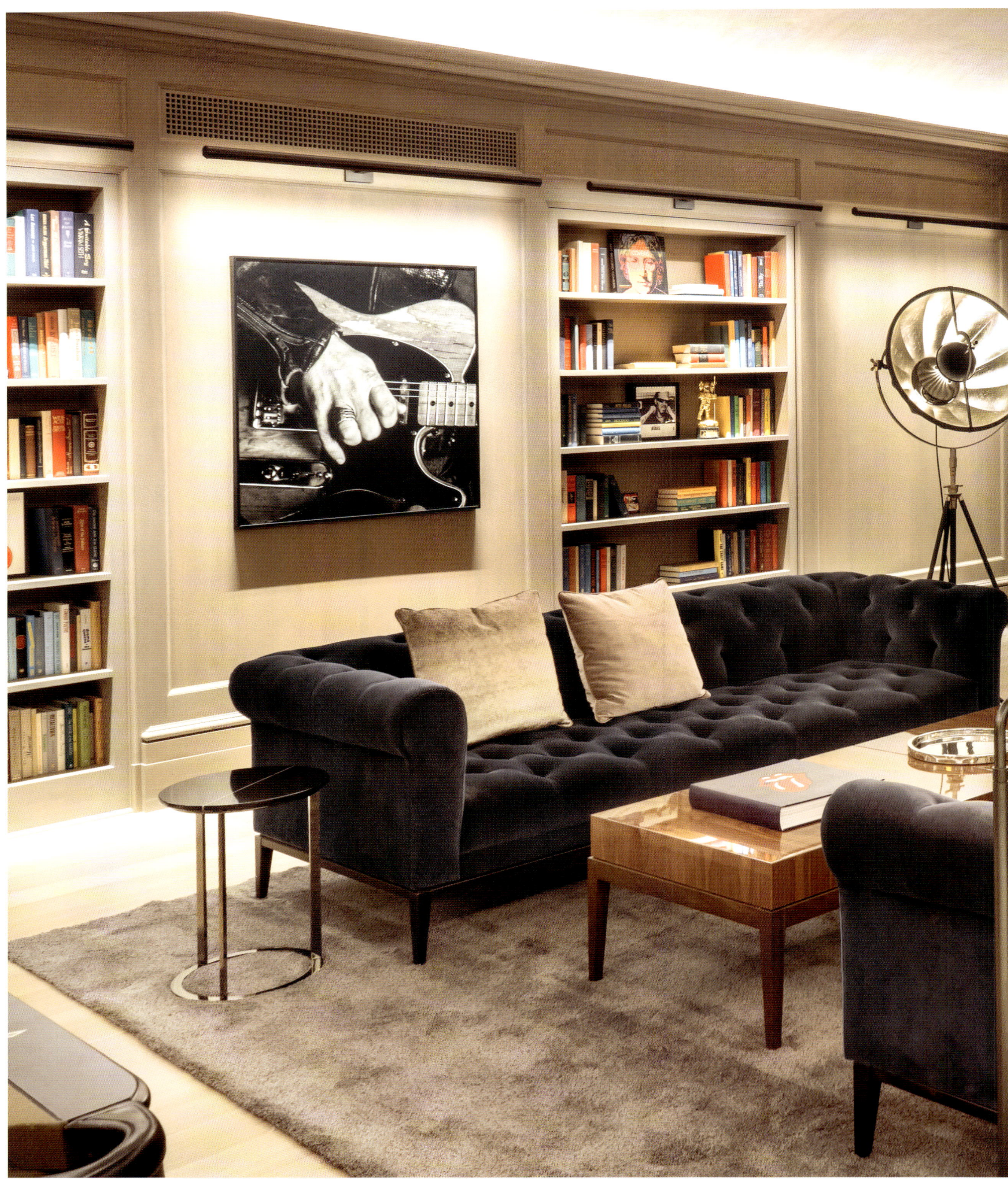

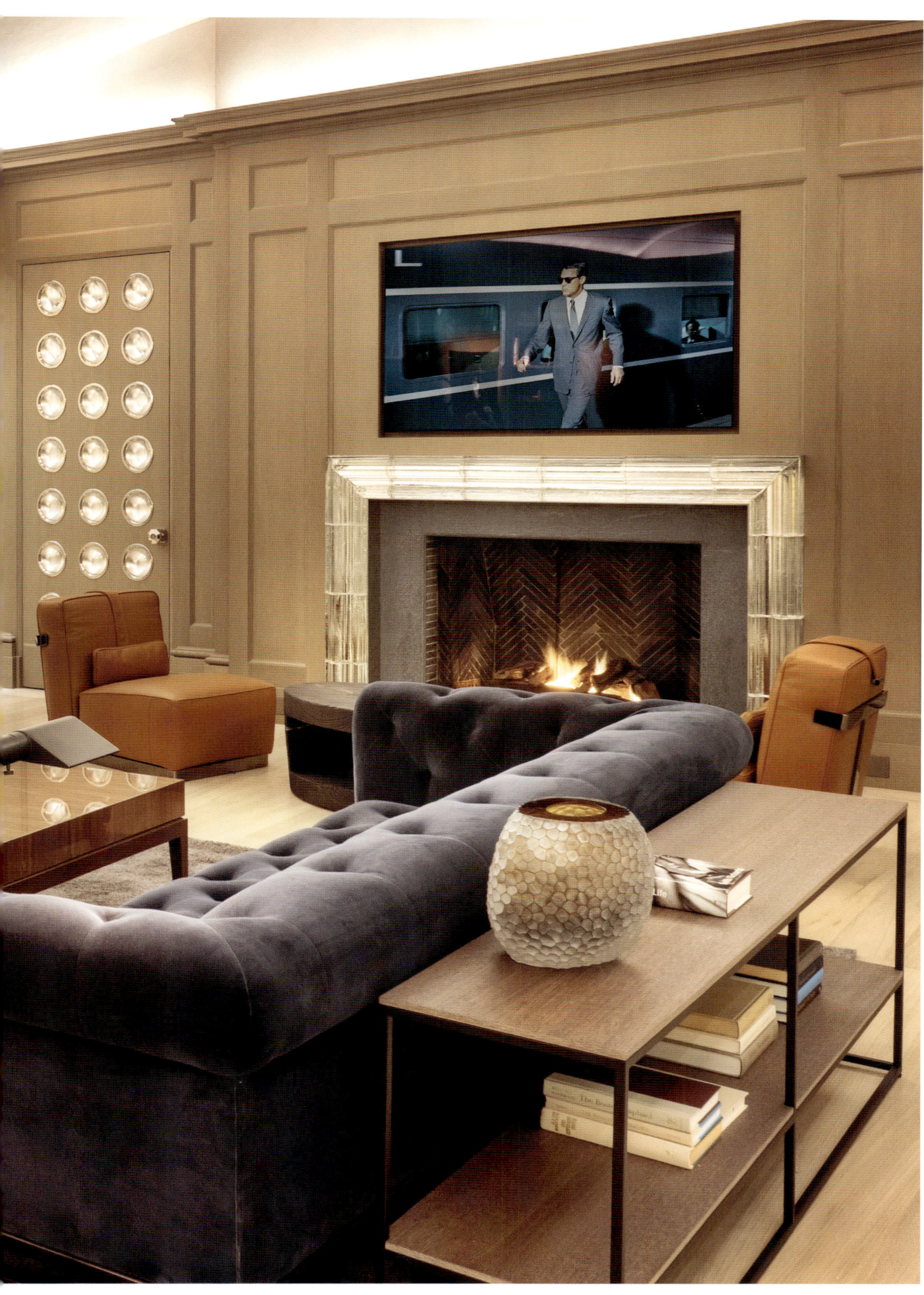

Upon entering the lounge, on the home's lower level, you are struck immediately with the stained oak wall panelling, a silvered-casted glass fireplace surround, and the dimly lit Italian stucco ceiling. And in addition to this communal area with velvet Chesterfield sofas, custom high-gloss coffee table, bar, and billiard table, there is access to a jam session parlor (see page 109).

Unmittelbar Eindruck beim Betreten der Lounge auf der unteren Ebene des Hauses machen die Wandtäfelung aus gebeizter Eiche, die Kamineinfassung aus versilbertem Gussglas und die dezent beleuchtete italienische Stuckdecke. Es ist aber nicht nur ein Wohnraum mit Chesterfield-Samtsofas, maßgefertigtem Hochglanz-Couchtisch und Billardtisch, hier ist auch der Zugang zum Musikzimmer (siehe Seite 109).

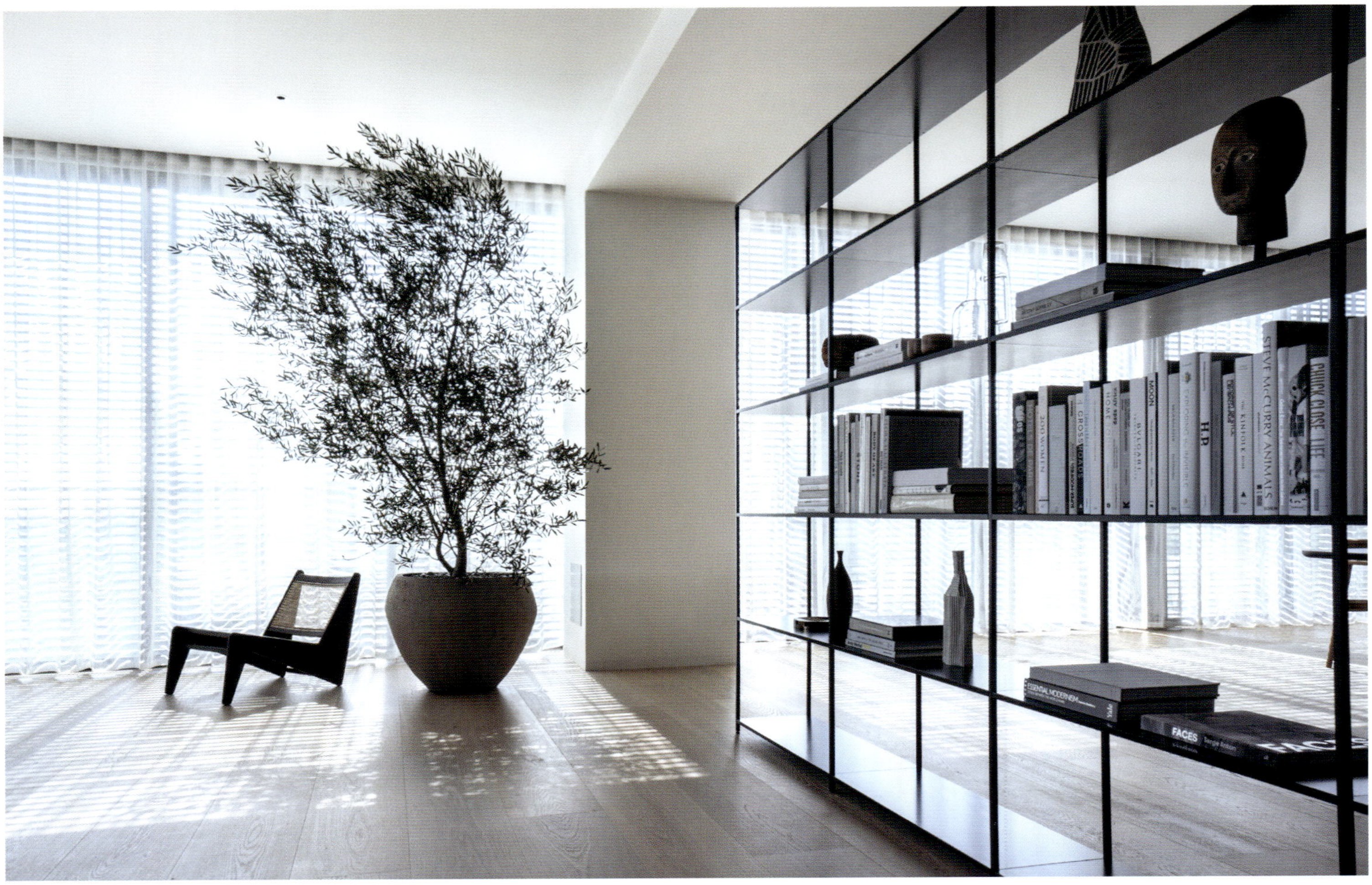

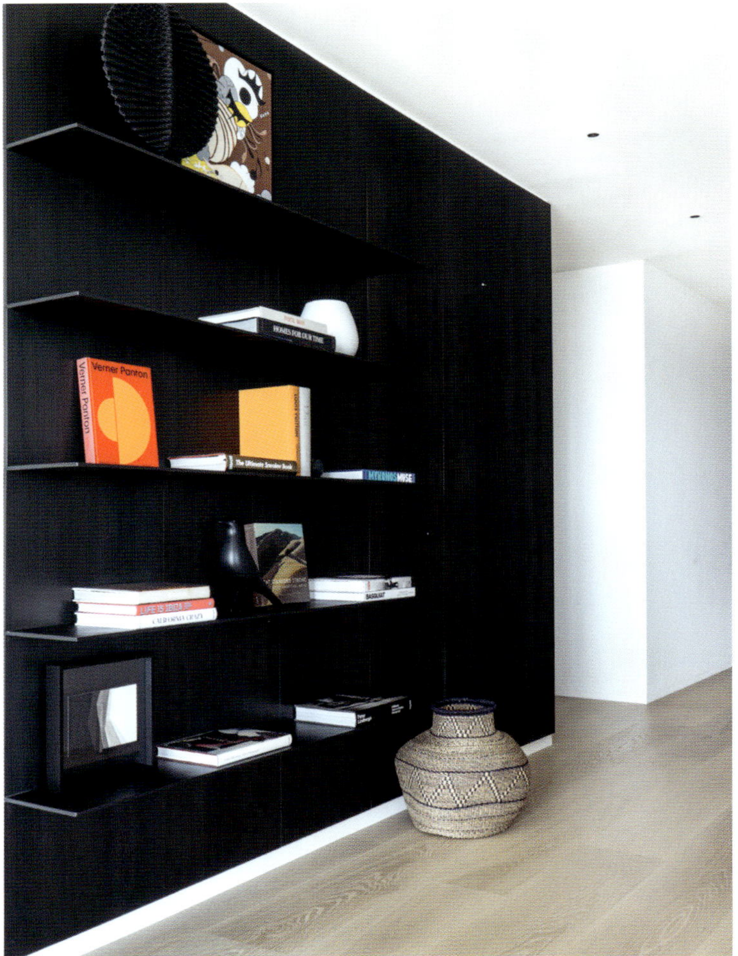

This Los Angeles penthouse sits atop John Pawson's most recent building, commissioned by the famous American hotelier, Ian Schrager. Dominic Gasparoly and Khalid Watson equipped the 3800 square foot apartment with magnificent furniture, accessories, along with customized pieces, including the living room's coffee table, and built-in steel bookshelf. The open floor plan offers a panorama from the Hollywood Hills to Downtown Los Angeles and beyond. A spacious balcony with the atmosphere of a tropical yacht club extends all along one side. An oasis of calm and relaxation in the heart of the beautiful, yet frenetic world of West Hollywood.

Dieses Penthouse in Los Angeles befindet sich in der obersten Etage des neuesten Gebäudes des Architekten John Pawson, gebaut im Auftrag des berühmten amerikanischen Hoteliers Ian Schrager. Dominic Gasparoly und Khalid Watson richteten das über 350 Quadratmeter große Apartment mit grandiosen Möbeln, Accessoires und maßgeschneiderten Einbauten ein, etwa mit dem Couchtisch des Wohnzimmers und dem eingebauten Bücherregal aus Stahl. Der offene Grundriss erlaubt Ausblicke von den Hollywood Hills bis nach Downtown Los Angeles und darüber hinaus. Entlang einer Seite erstreckt sich ein weitläufiger Balkon mit der Atmosphäre eines tropischen Jachtclubs. Eine Oase der Ruhe und Entspannung mitten in der schönen, aber hektischen Welt von West Hollywood.

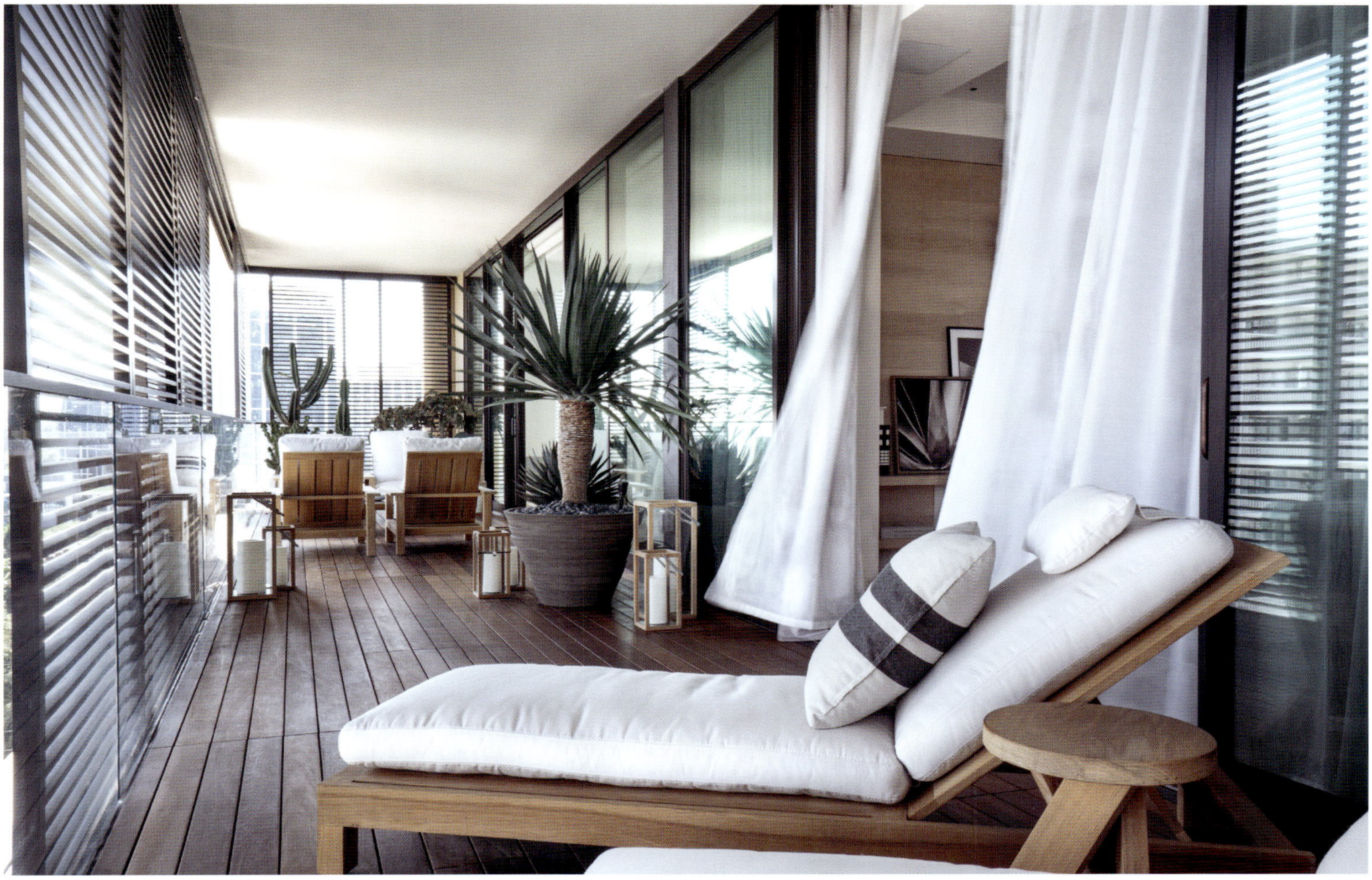

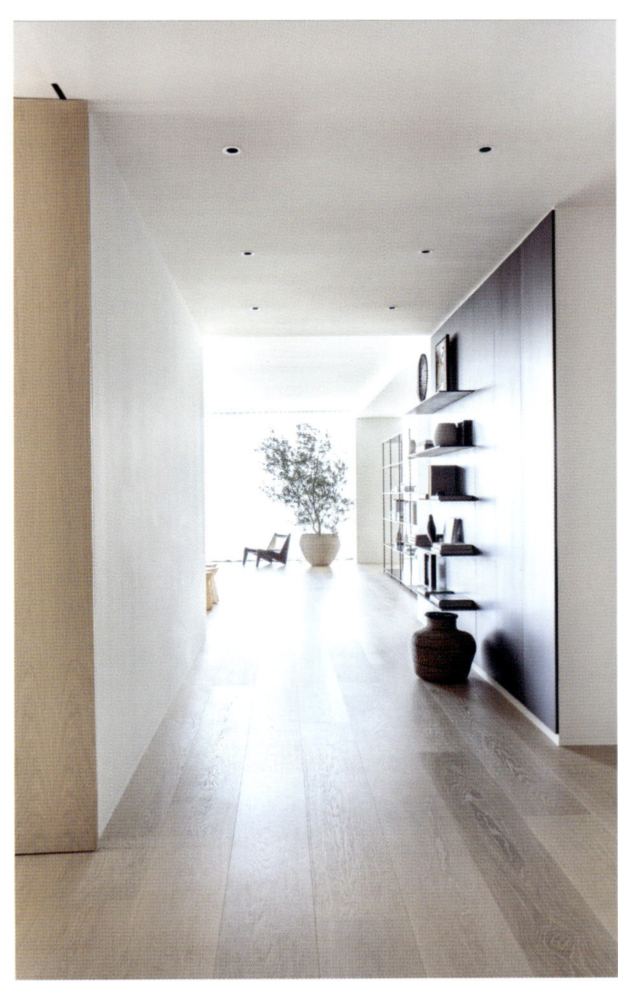

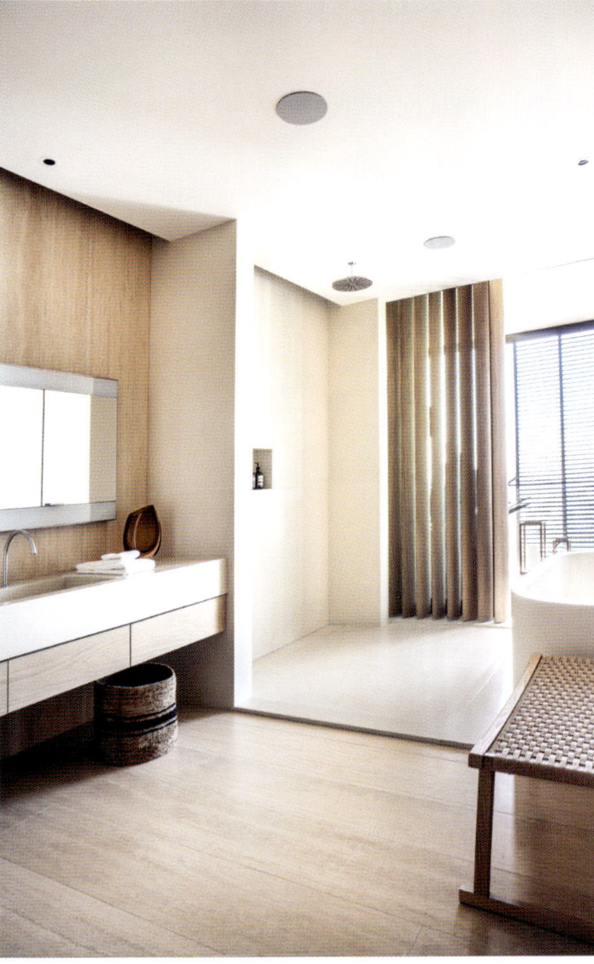

The clean lines of the blackened steel shelving unit immediately catch the eye when entering the long hallway (far left and opposite page). The overriding impression, however, is of light hues and brightness. Floor-to-ceiling windows allow for sun-drenched rooms, creating a sense of peace and tranquility.

Gleich beim Betreten des langen Flurs fallen die klaren Linien des Regals aus geschwärztem Stahl ins Auge (ganz links und Seite gegenüber). Doch insgesamt dominieren eher helle Farbtöne. Raumhohe, vom Boden bis zur Decke reichende Fenster sorgen für sonnendurchflutete Räume, die ein Gefühl von Ruhe und Frieden hervorrufen.

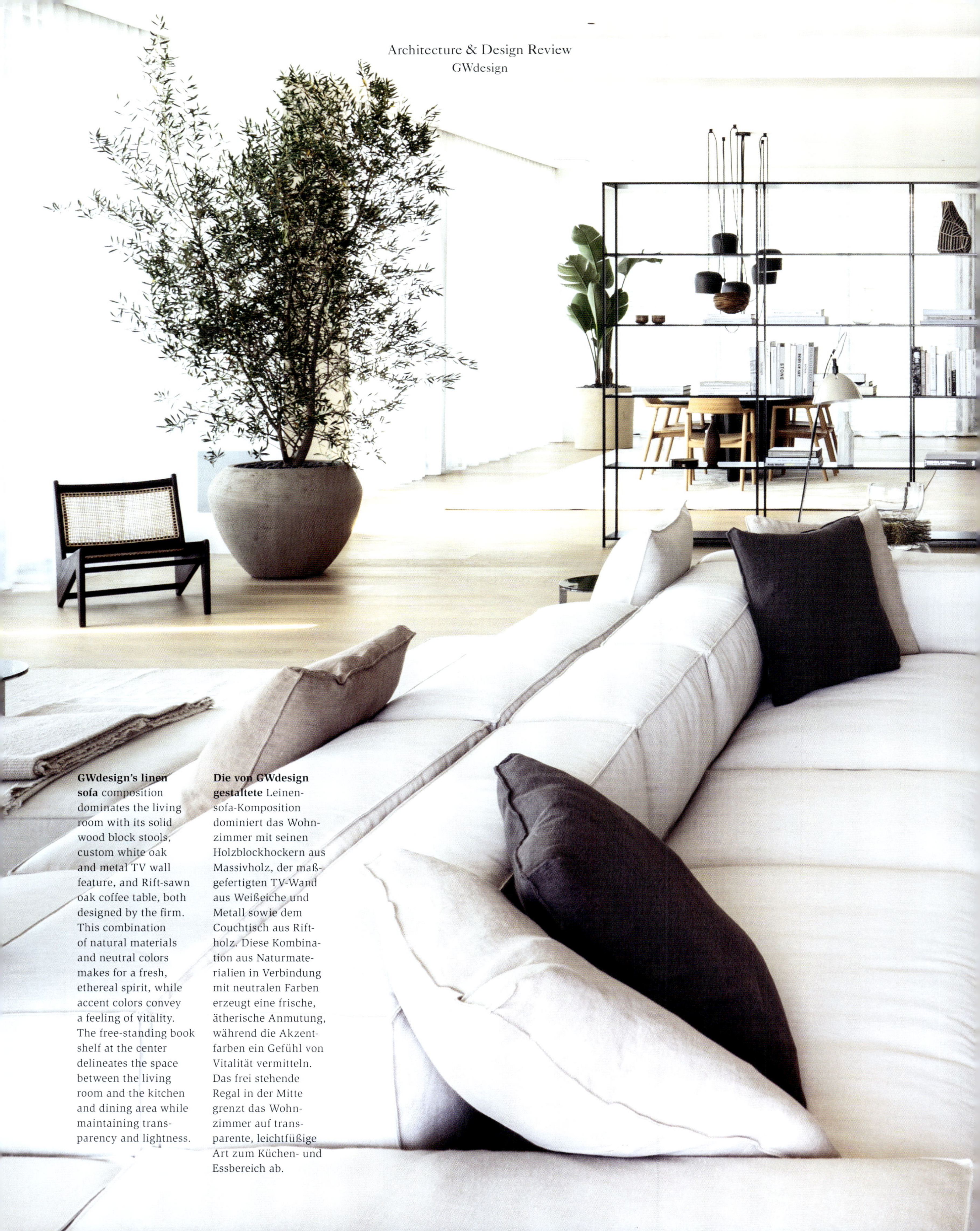

GWdesign's linen sofa composition dominates the living room with its solid wood block stools, custom white oak and metal TV wall feature, and Rift-sawn oak coffee table, both designed by the firm. This combination of natural materials and neutral colors makes for a fresh, ethereal spirit, while accent colors convey a feeling of vitality. The free-standing book shelf at the center delineates the space between the living room and the kitchen and dining area while maintaining transparency and lightness.

Die von GWdesign gestaltete Leinen-sofa-Komposition dominiert das Wohnzimmer mit seinen Holzblockhockern aus Massivholz, der maß-gefertigten TV-Wand aus Weißeiche und Metall sowie dem Couchtisch aus Rift-holz. Diese Kombination aus Naturmate-rialien in Verbindung mit neutralen Farben erzeugt eine frische, ätherische Anmutung, während die Akzent-farben ein Gefühl von Vitalität vermitteln. Das frei stehende Regal in der Mitte grenzt das Wohn-zimmer auf trans-parente, leichtfüßige Art zum Küchen- und Essbereich ab.

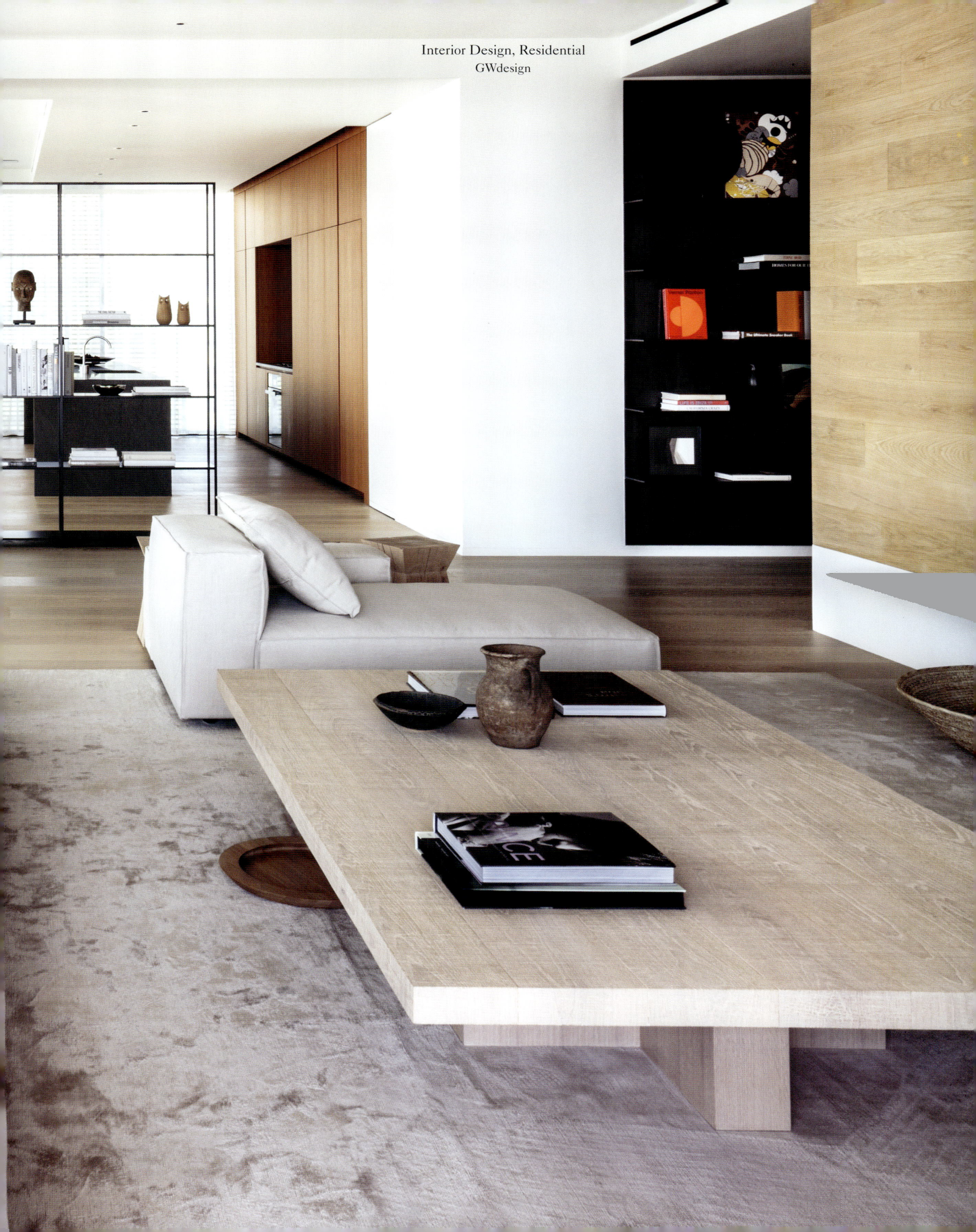

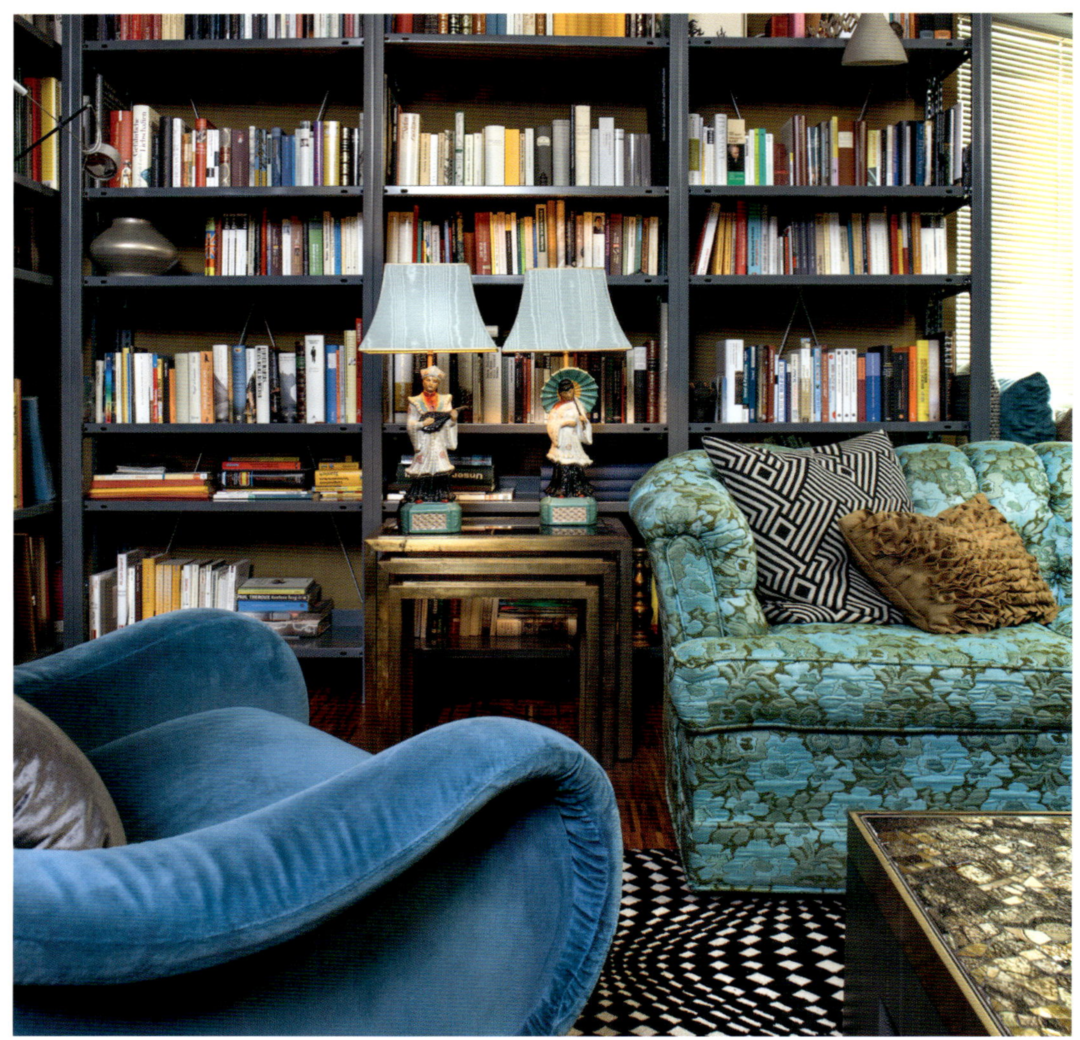

harryclarkinterior

BERLIN / GERMANY

Composition and Creation | Komposition und Kreation

The Berlin-based interior design consultancy, harryclarkinterior, works on national and international projects. Its sophisticated clients appreciate harry clark's artistic, creative concepts and the excellence and precision of his company's execution. The design approach is always the composition and creation of colors, textures, and materials and the way they interact with the architectural and spatial environment, as well as with furniture, design, and art objects. harry clark combines diverse styles and elements from various epochs with contemporary designs and exclusive furniture. His own bespoke furniture is made in Berlin. The results are expressive and elegant interior concepts with a unique ambiance.

Das Berliner Beratungsbüro harryclarkinterior arbeitet in nationalen und internationalen Interior-Design-Projekten. Seine anspruchsvollen Kunden schätzen den künstlerisch-kreativen Ansatz von harry clark und die damit verbundene exzellente und detailgenaue Ausführung. Ausgangspunkt der Gestaltung ist immer die Komposition und Kreation von Farben, Strukturen und Materialien im Zusammenspiel mit der Architektur, den Möbeln, Design-und Kunstobjekten. harry clark kombiniert vielfältige Stile vergangener Epochen mit aktuellem Design und exklusiven, in Berlin handgefertigten Möbeln. So entstehen ausdrucksstarke und elegante Konzepte für Interieurs in einzigartiger Umgebung.

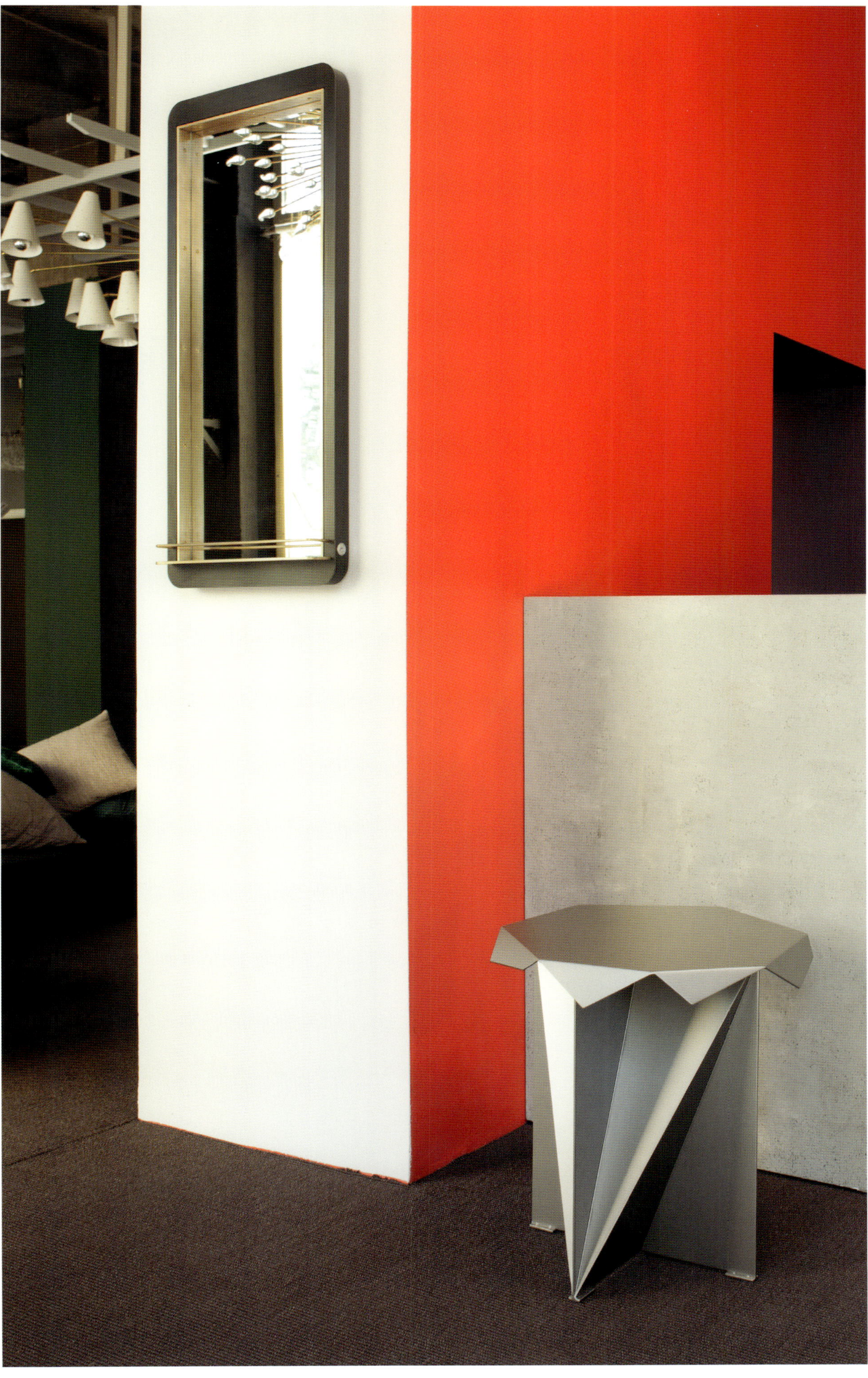

The apartment is located in a listed 1930s Bauhaus villa in Berlin's Tiergarten district. The exquisite color concept creates the backdrop for harry clark's eclectic mix of modernity to evolve. Elements of Functionalism, Art Deco, the sensual elegance of the 1950s, the Pop Art style of the 1970s and contemporary design all combine and ultimately complement each other.

Das exquisite Farbkonzept im Appartement in einer denkmalgeschützten Bauhaus-Stadtvilla der 1930er-Jahre in Berlin-Tiergarten bildet die Plattform, auf der harry clark einen eklektischen Mix der Moderne entstehen lässt. Und so ergänzen sich die Elemente des Funktionalismus, des Art déco, der sinnlichen Eleganz der 1950er, des Pop-Art-Stils der 1970er sowie zeitgenössischen Designs.

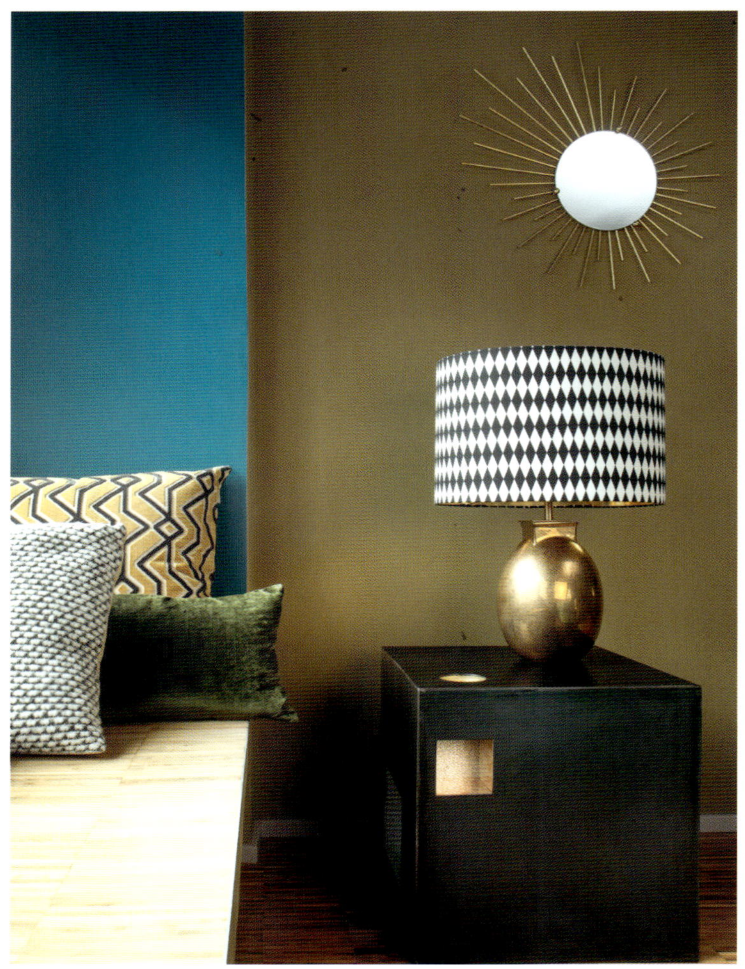

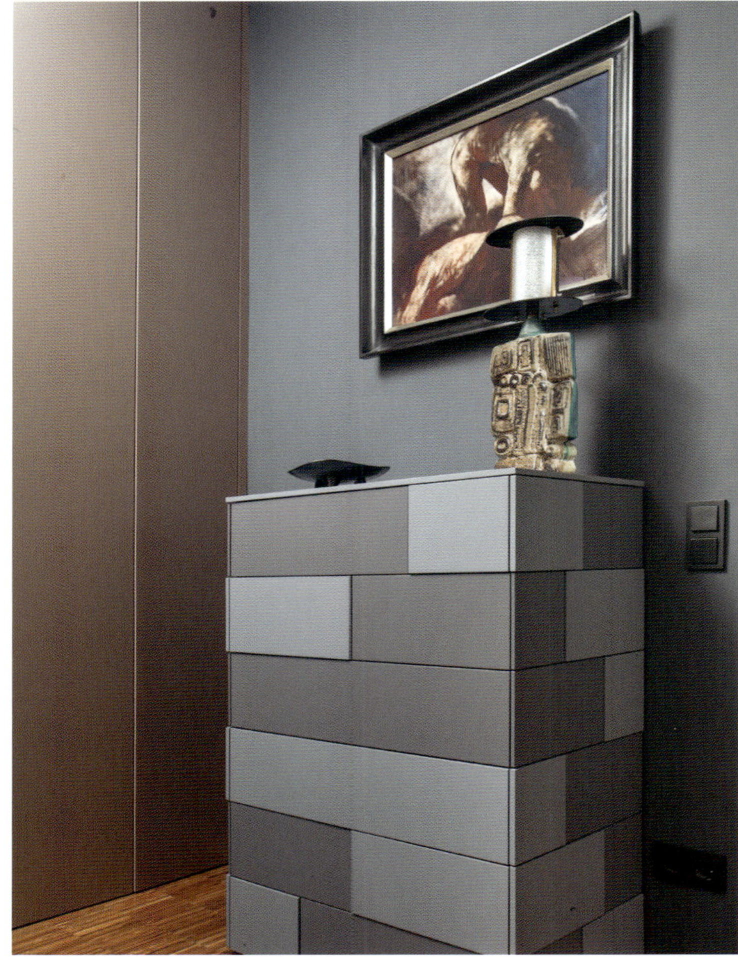

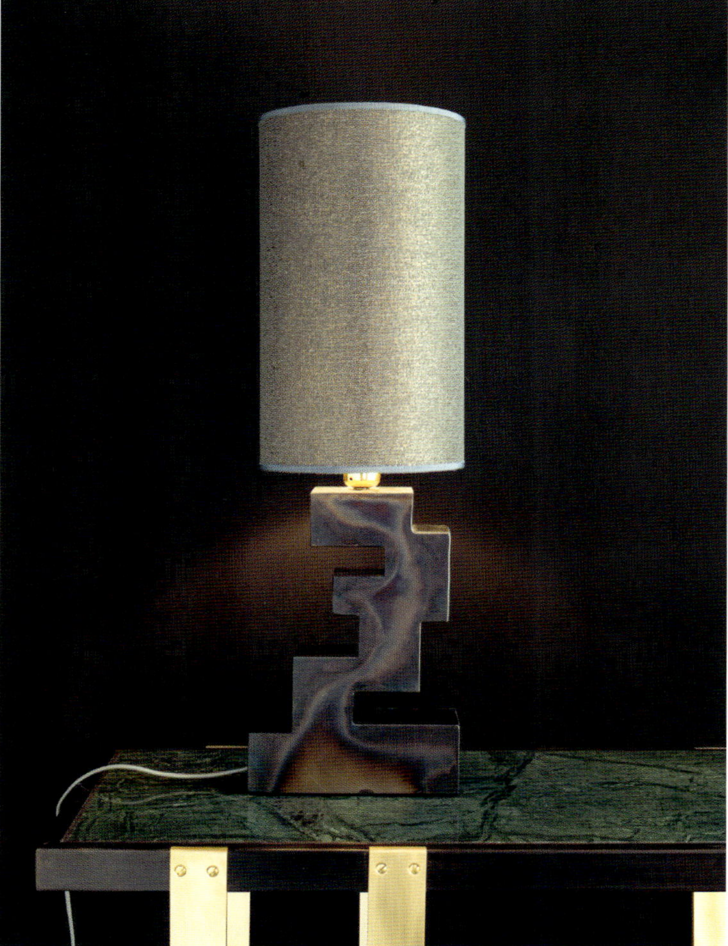

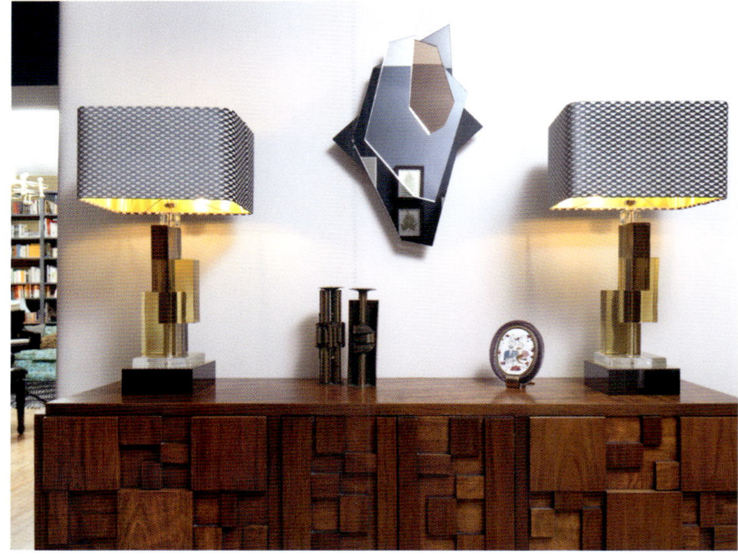

harry clark's furniture, lamps and objects speak a language of their own, and are impressive art objects in their own right. Nevertheless they still function as integral parts of the apartment's generous and spacious layout.

harry clarks Möbel, Leuchten und Objekte haben eine ganz eigene Diktion, sind mitunter eindrucksvolle Solitäre und integrieren sich dennoch in die unterschiedlichsten Raumsituationen des großzügig geschnittenen Appartements.

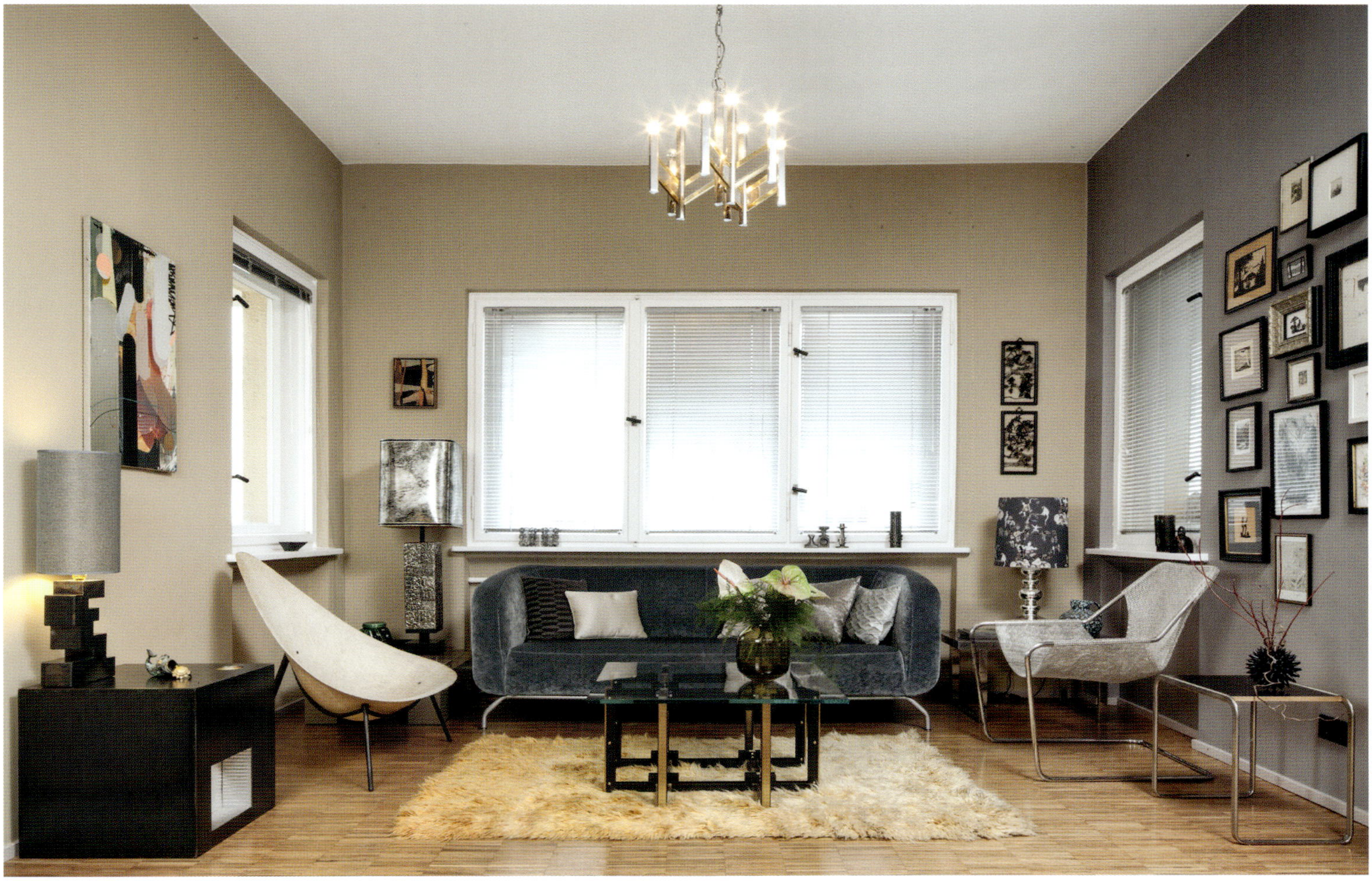

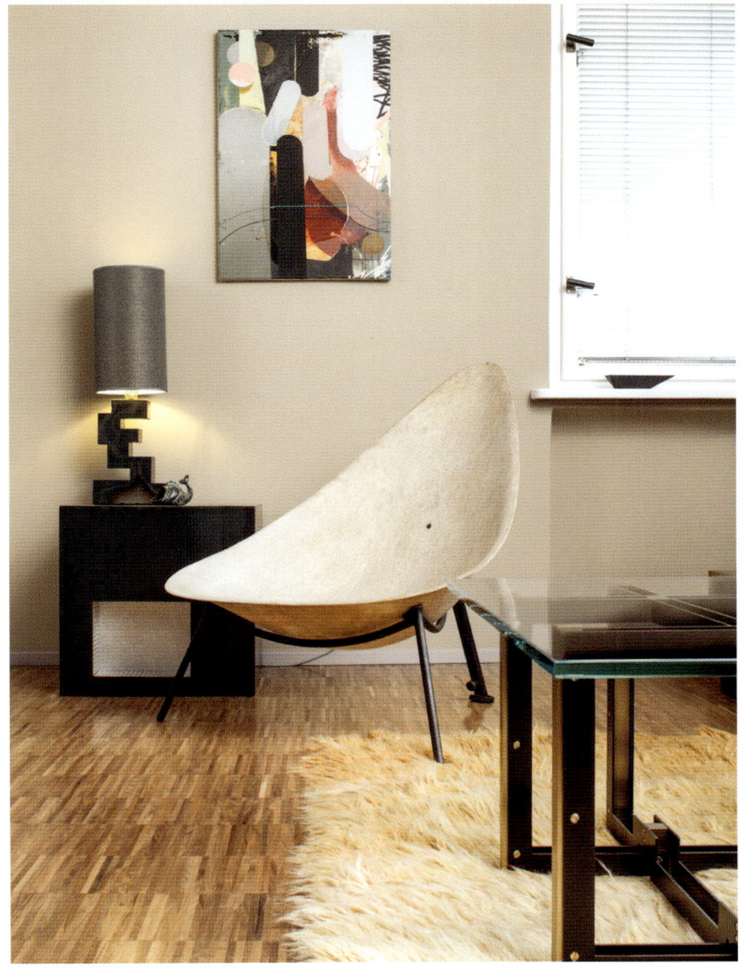
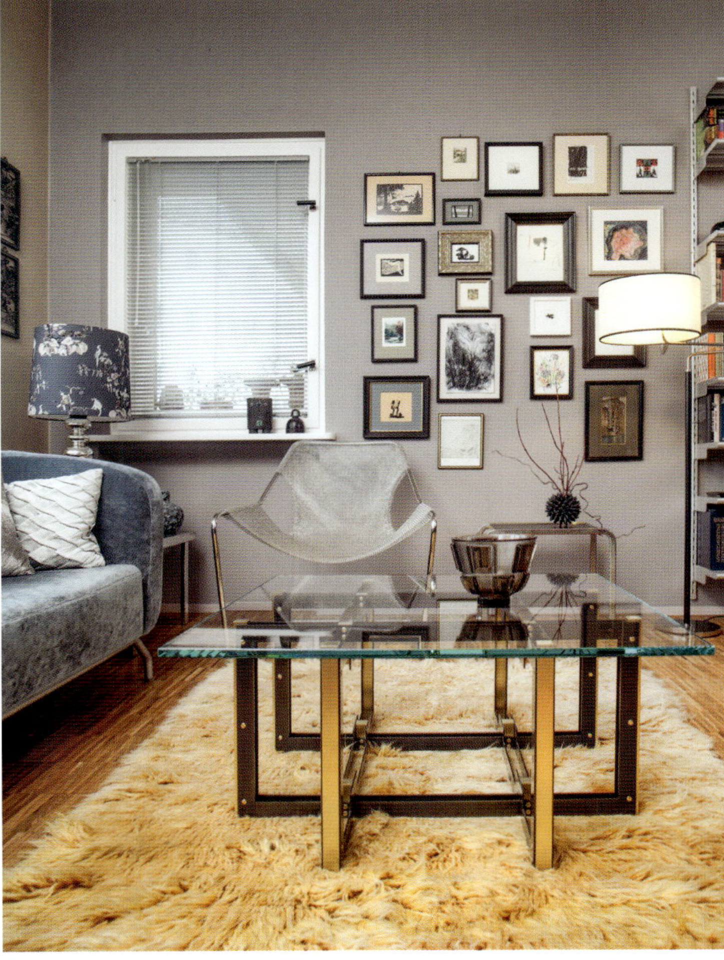

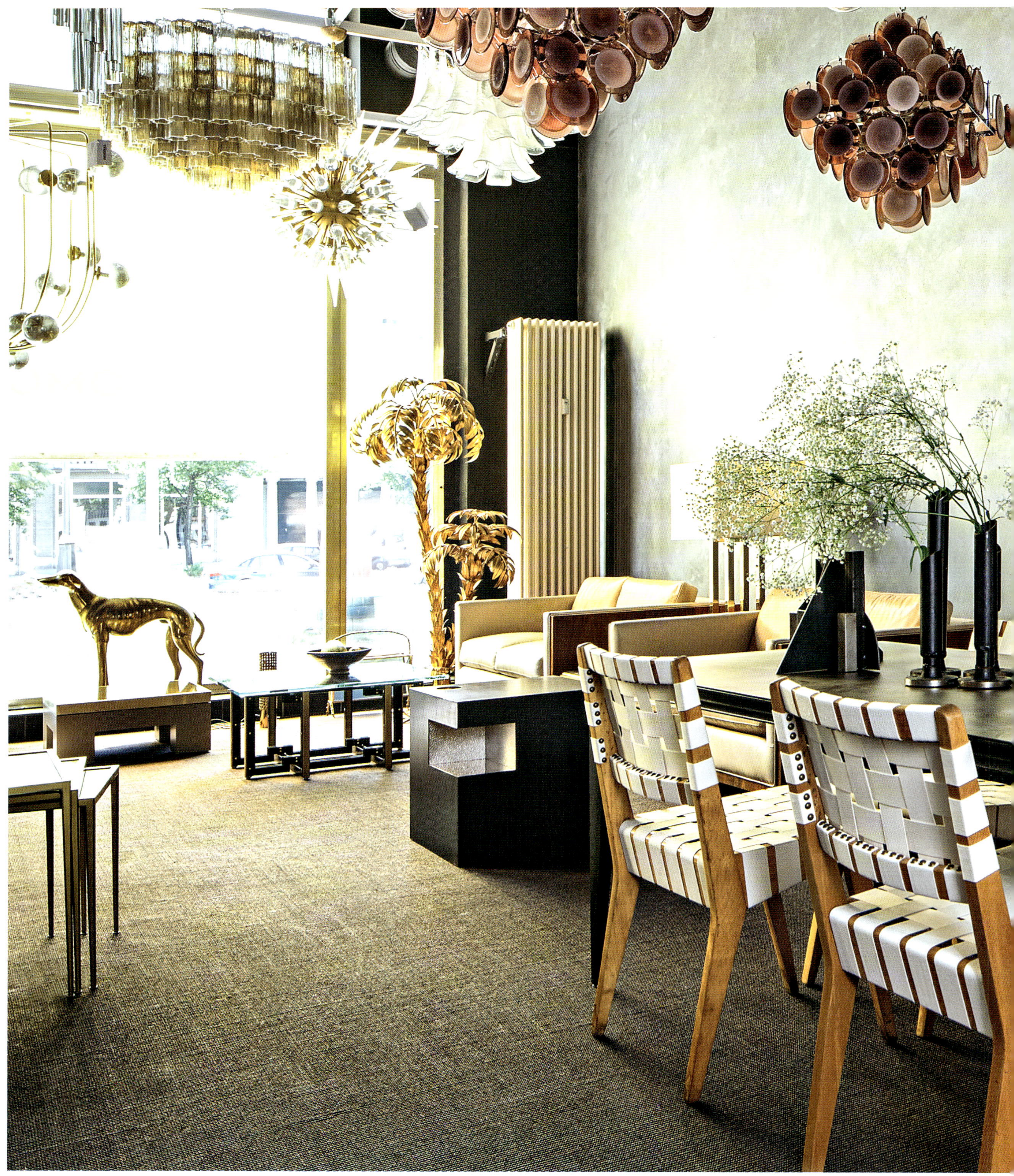

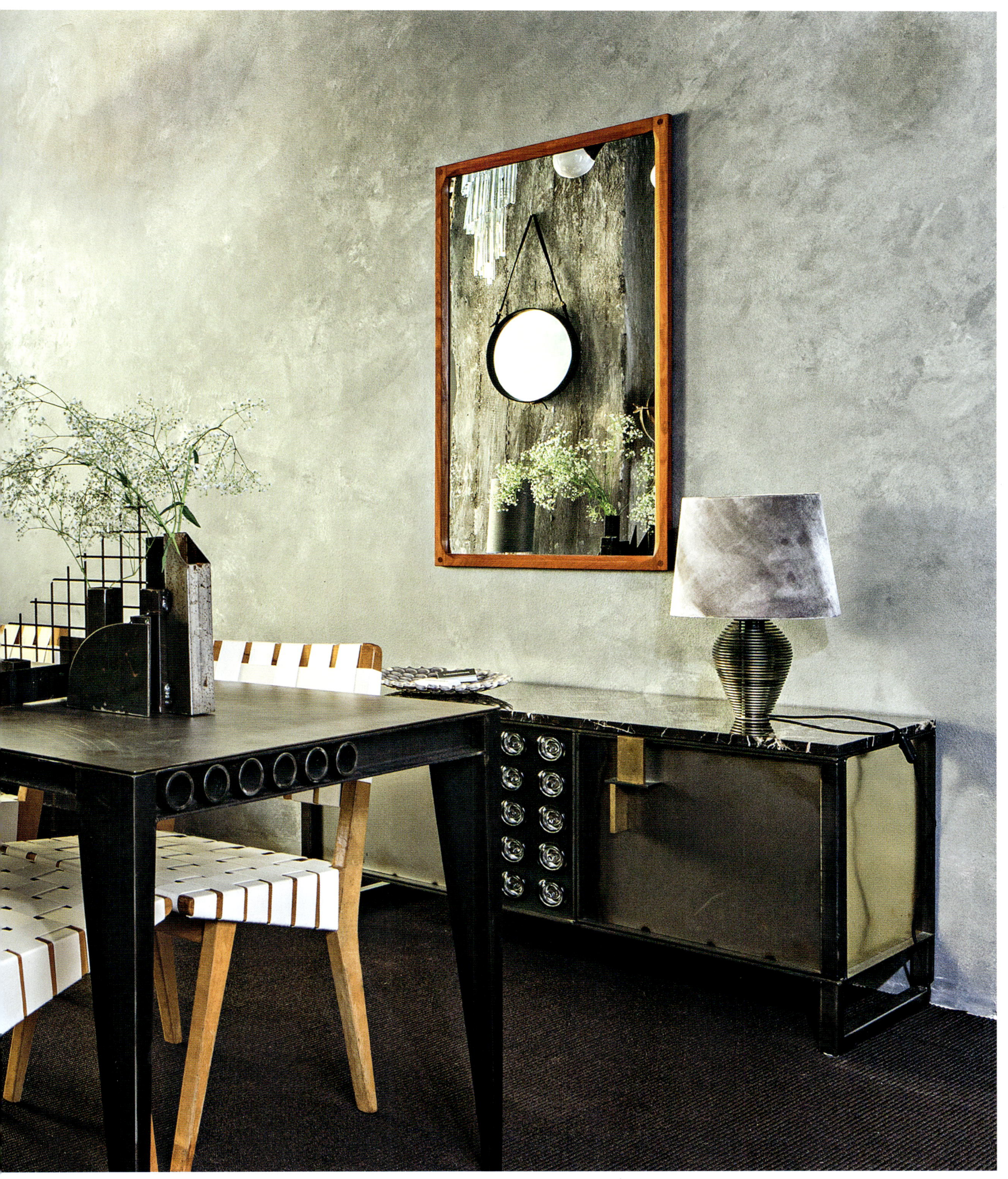

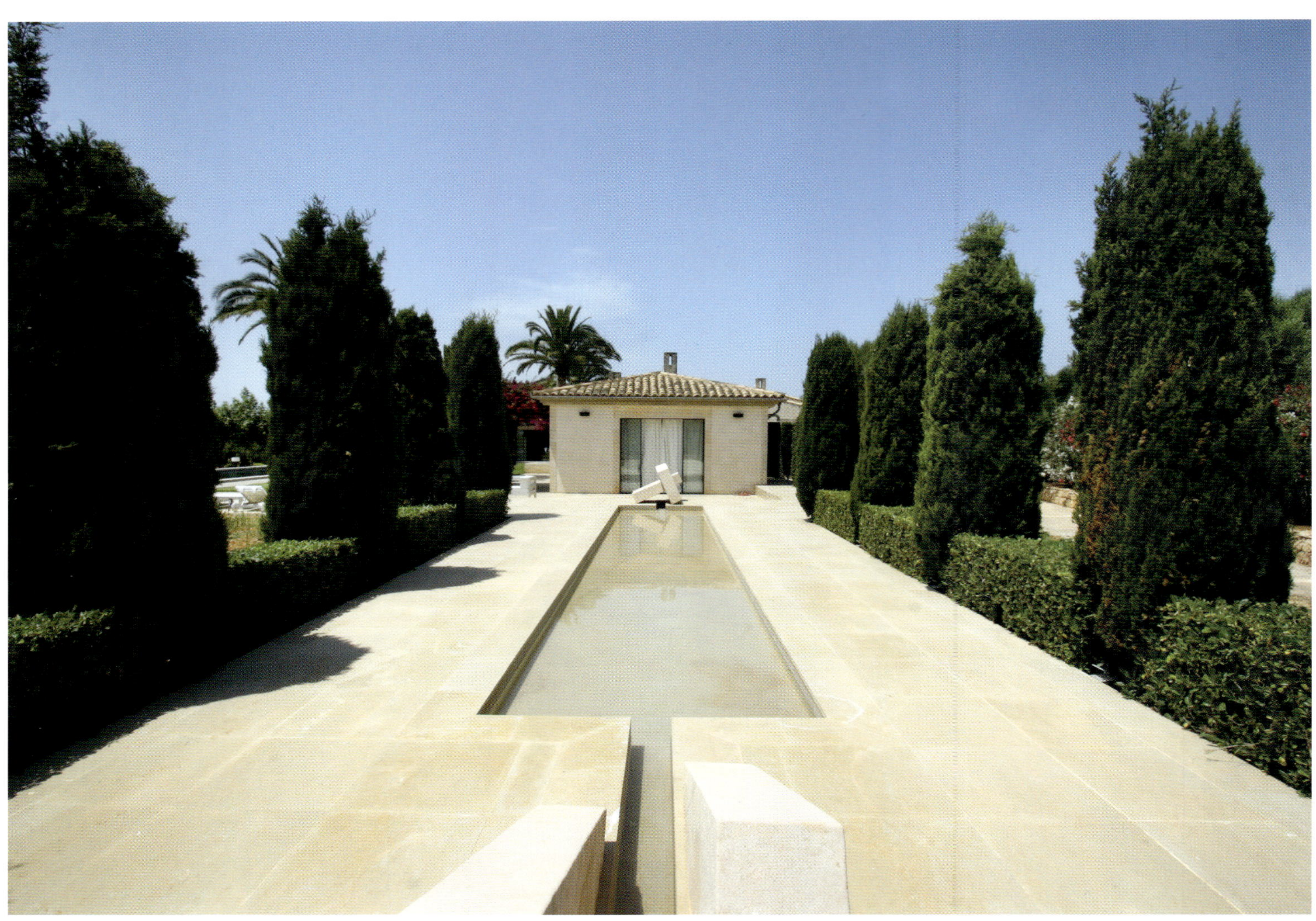

ICAZAR ARCHITECTS

PALMA DE MALLORCA / SPAIN

Obsessive Passion | Obsessive Leidenschaft

Ando Schirmer, the founder and person responsible for all business-related matters, Johannes Kiefer, the firm's inspirational and creative mind, and David Moret, the cool and rational engineer, together form the backbone of ICAZAR Architects. Collectively, they are fulfilling their vision of creating the ultimate architectural and construction experience. The team, which operates internationally, aims to design atmospheric spaces that people can use or enjoy, irrespective of whether the property is a modest country home, a city apartment or a hotel. 'Sometimes it doesn't have to be bigger, just better,' is one of ICAZAR's mottos, with the firm showing a great love for detail in all its projects.

Ando Schirmer, Gründer und zuständig für alle kaufmännischen Fragen, Johannes Kiefer, der emotional-kreative Kopf, und David Moret, der kühl-rationale Ingenieur – sie bilden zusammen das Zentrum von ICAZAR Architects. Gemeinsam leben sie ihre Vision, eine ultimative Erfahrung von Architektur und Bauwesen zu erschaffen. Das international arbeitende Team will atmosphärische Orte gestalten, die von Menschen genutzt und genossen werden können, egal ob bescheidenes Landhaus, Stadtwohnung oder Hotel. „Manchmal muss es nicht größer, sondern nur besser sein", ist einer der Leitsprüche von ICAZAR, das all seine Projekte mit großer Liebe zum Detail entwickelt.

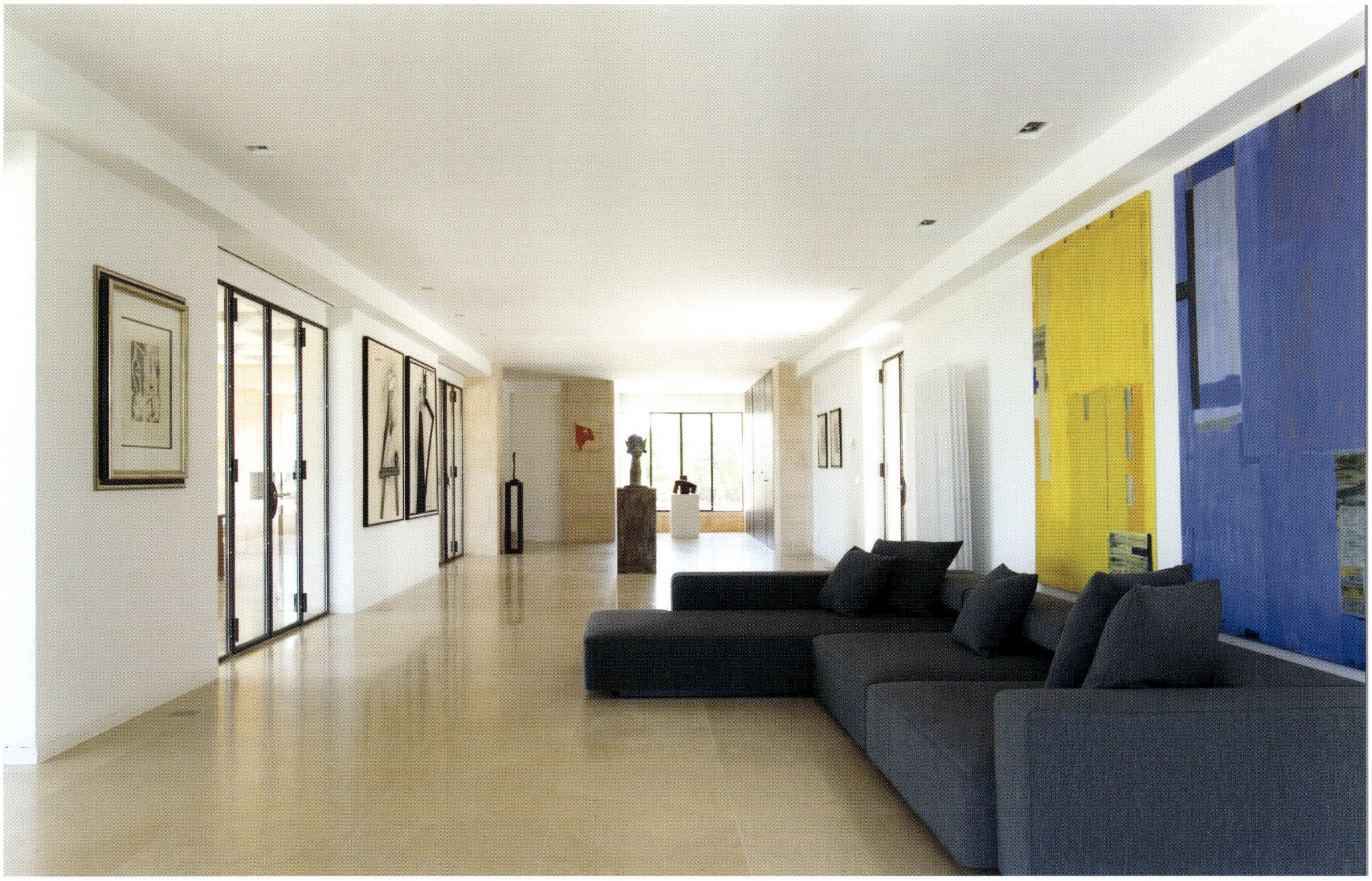

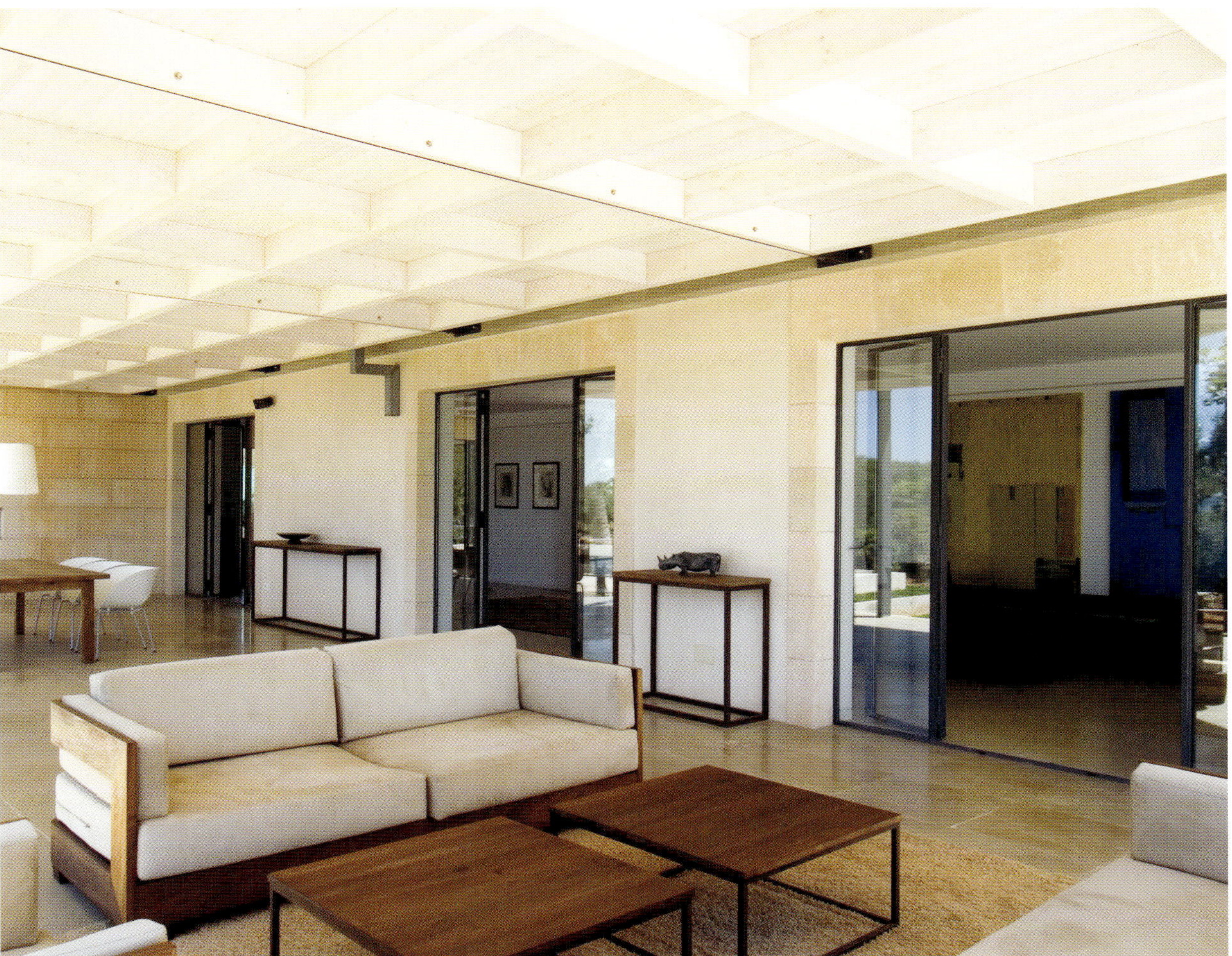

The design of the property S'Avall Petit in the vicinity of Palma de Mallorca is faithful to the typical rural architecture in the area. The interior is sparsely furnished, light can circulate without obstruction and art is the main protagonist. The selected colors provide serenity and balance.

Das Anwesen S'Avall Petit unweit von Palma de Mallorca ist nach der hier typischen ländlichen Architektur gestaltet. Die Innenräume sind sparsam möbliert, das Licht kann ohne Hindernisse zirkulieren, und die Kunst wird zum Hauptprotagonisten. Die verwendeten Farben sorgen für Gelassenheit und Ausgewogenheit.

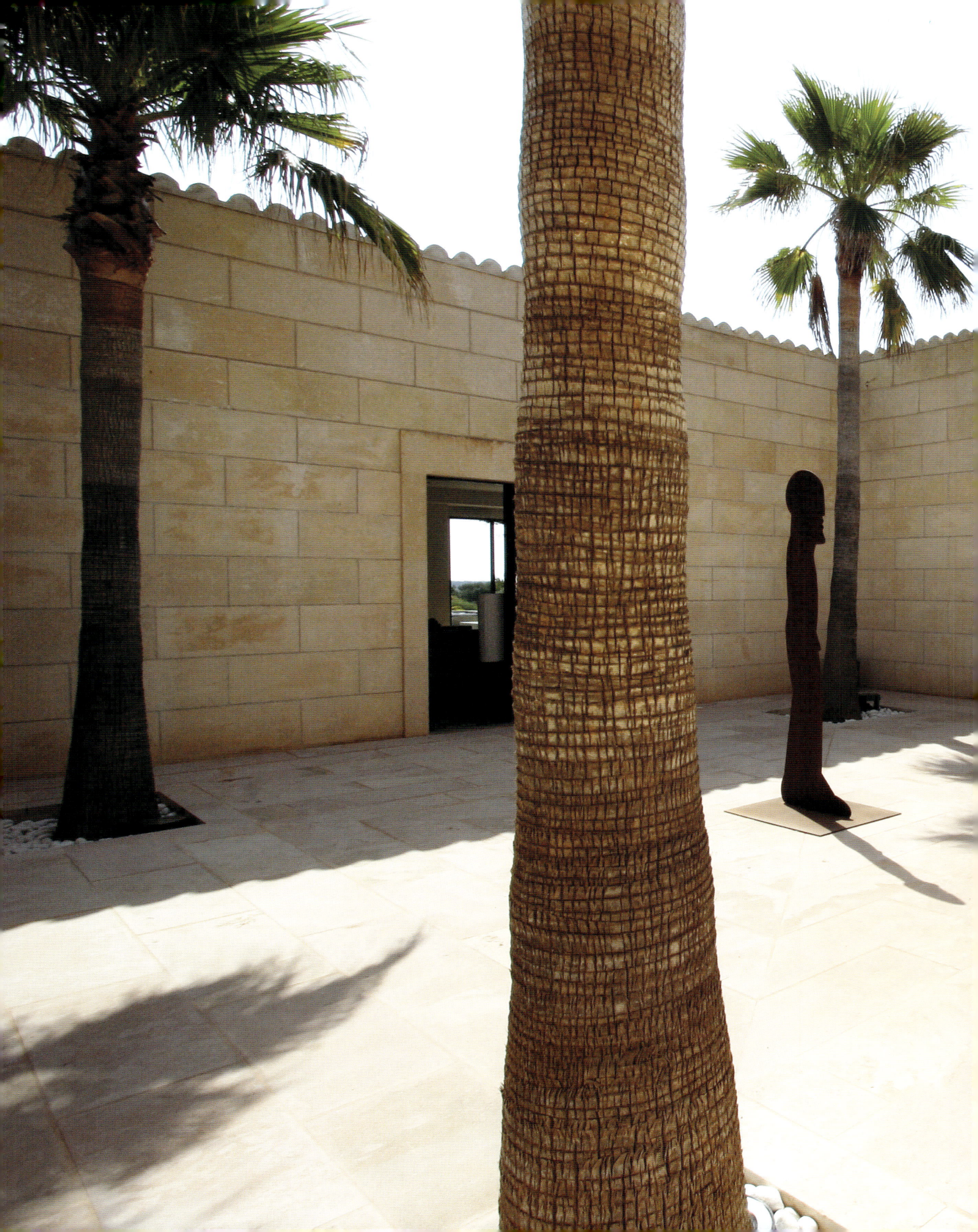

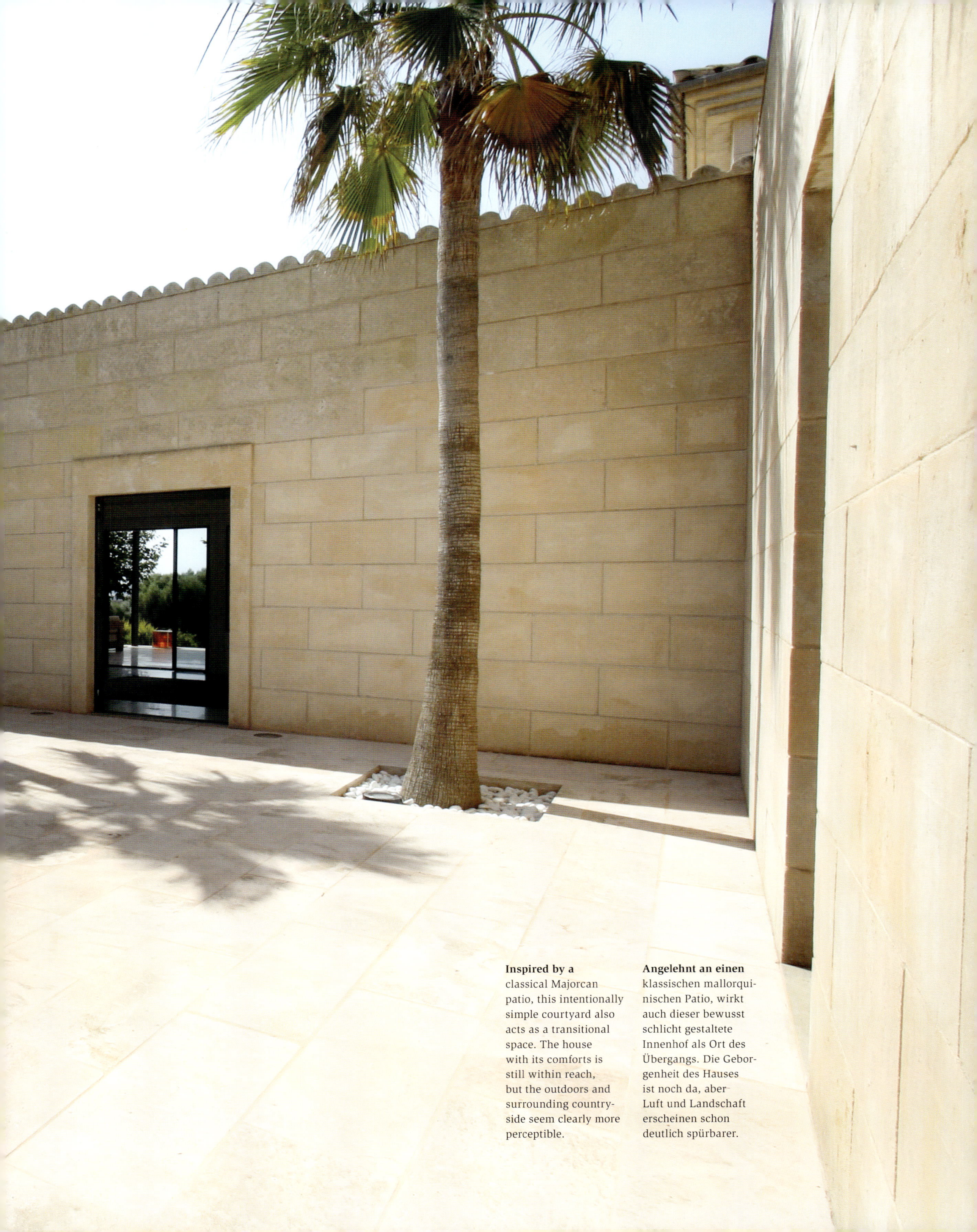

Inspired by a classical Majorcan patio, this intentionally simple courtyard also acts as a transitional space. The house with its comforts is still within reach, but the outdoors and surrounding countryside seem clearly more perceptible.

Angelehnt an einen klassischen mallorquinischen Patio, wirkt auch dieser bewusst schlicht gestaltete Innenhof als Ort des Übergangs. Die Geborgenheit des Hauses ist noch da, aber Luft und Landschaft erscheinen schon deutlich spürbarer.

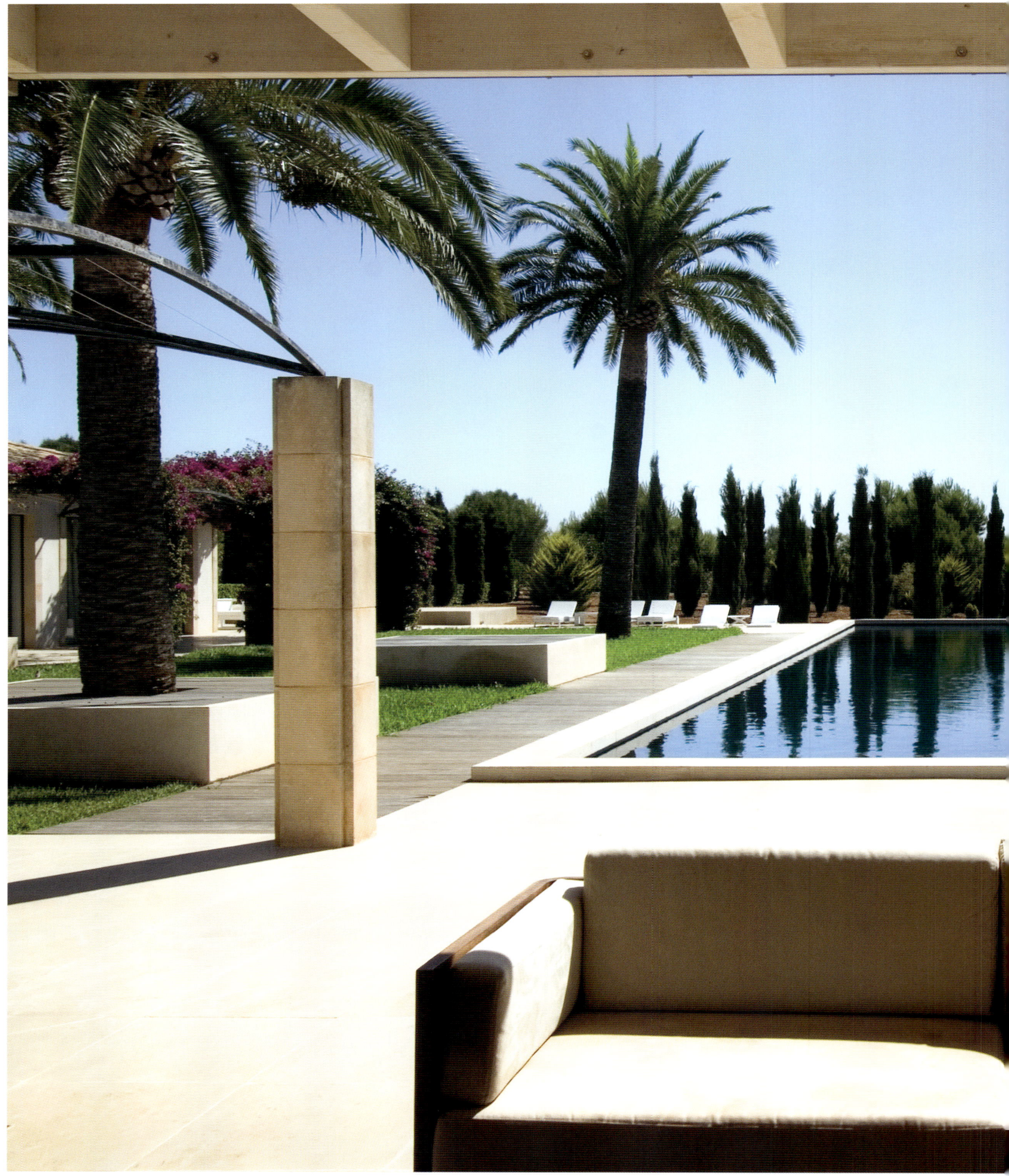

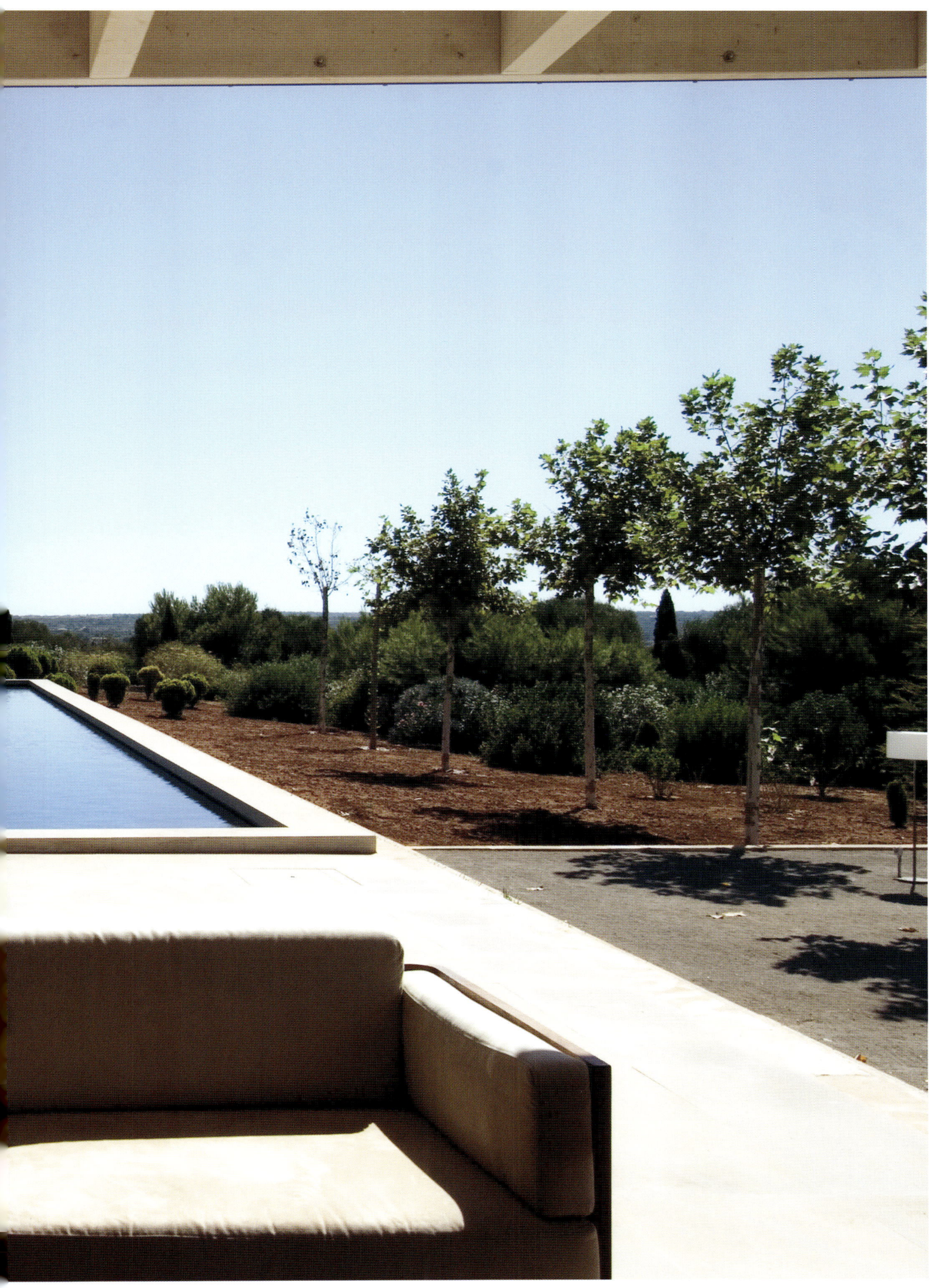

The ambience at S'Avall Petit is imbued with openness. Local vegetation dominates the gardens, with large stone cases serving as planters while protecting the palm trees. The pool area is paved with Marés limestone. The puristic architectural lines are typical of the overall ensemble.

Offenheit prägt die Atmosphäre von S'Avall Petit. In den Gärten dominiert einheimische Vegetation, große Steinumfassungen dienen als Pflanzgefäße und schützen die Palmen. Der Poolbereich ist mit Marés-Kalkstein ausgelegt. Typisch für das gesamte Ensemble sind die puristischen architektonischen Linien.

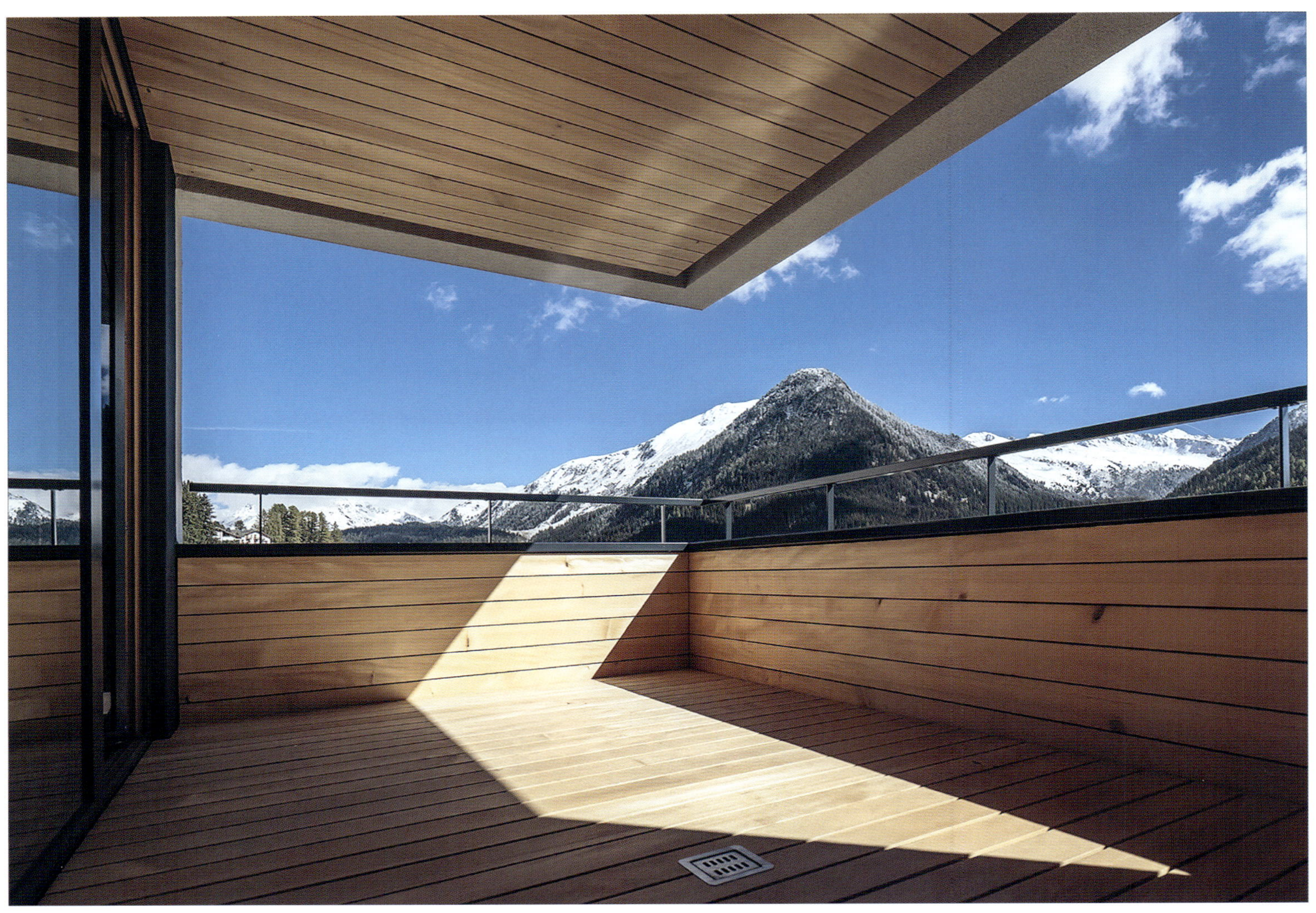

INTERIOR ARCHITECTS MUNICH

MUNICH / GERMANY

High-quality Implementation | Hochwertige Umsetzung

Creating the new and the original, optimizing what already exists, designing spaces—these are the core goals of the interior designer collective Interior Architects Munich (iam). Among other things, iam oversees office, trade show, residential, and catering construction projects. Collaborations with carefully selected craft workshops and fitters cater for clients' most unusual requests. The photographs depict a project in the Swiss winter sport resort Davos. In addition to thirty holiday apartments, the newly constructed Parsenn resort offers direct access to the ski slopes, as well as a wellness area and fitness studio.

Neues schaffen, Bestehendes optimieren, Räume gestalten – das sind zentrale Ziele der Innenarchitektinnen-Gemeinschaft Interior Architects Munich (iam), die unter anderem Projekte in den Bereichen Office, Messebau, Wohnen und Gastronomie betreut. Durch die Zusammenarbeit mit handverlesenen Handwerksbetrieben und Ausstattern können dabei auch außergewöhnliche Wünsche der Bauherren umgesetzt werden. Die Bilder zeigen ein Projekt im Schweizer Wintersportort Davos. Das Parsenn Resort hat direkten Zugang zur Skipiste, und neben dreißig Ferienapartments bietet der Neubau einen Wellnessbereich mit Fitnessstudio.

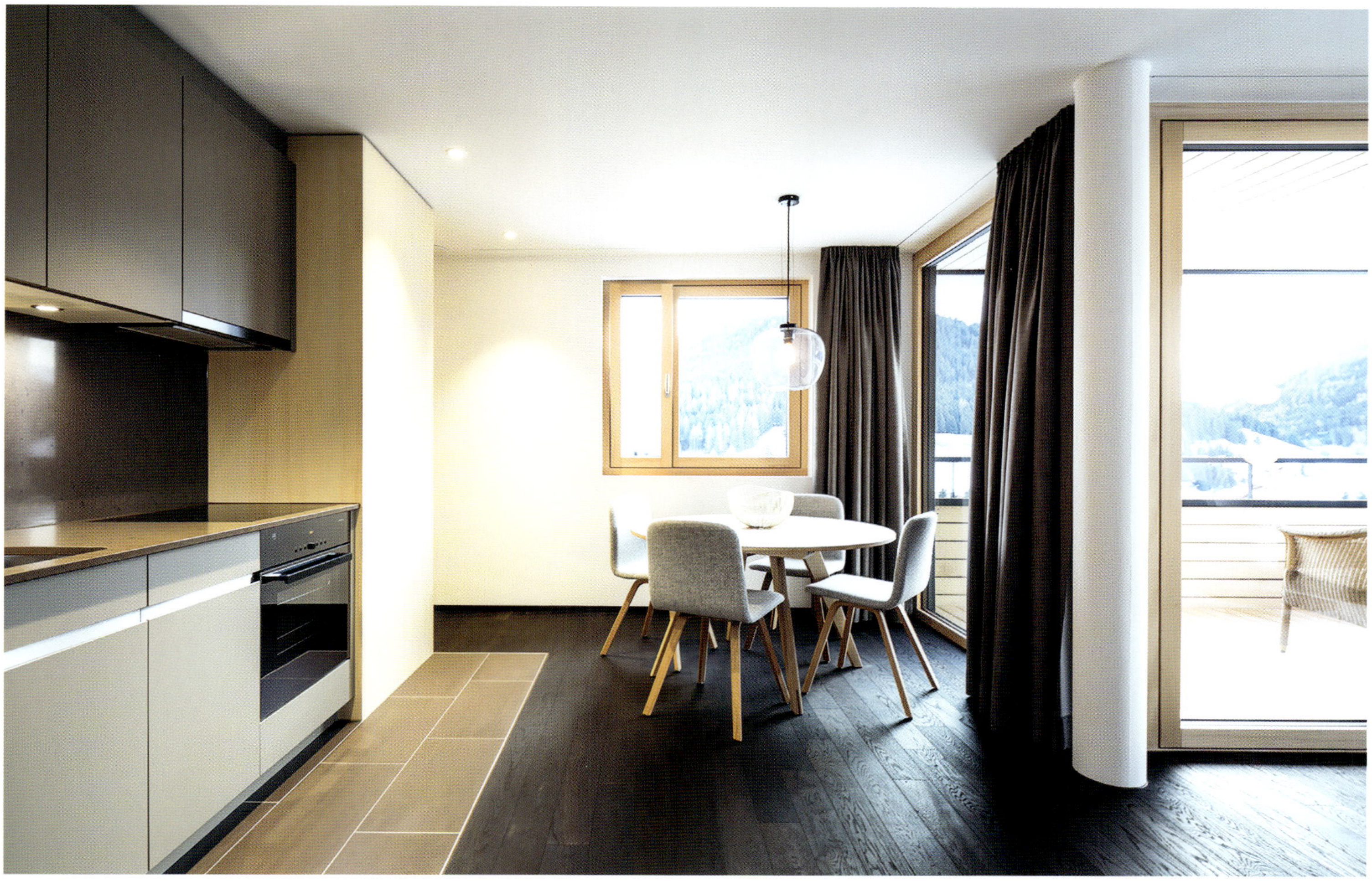

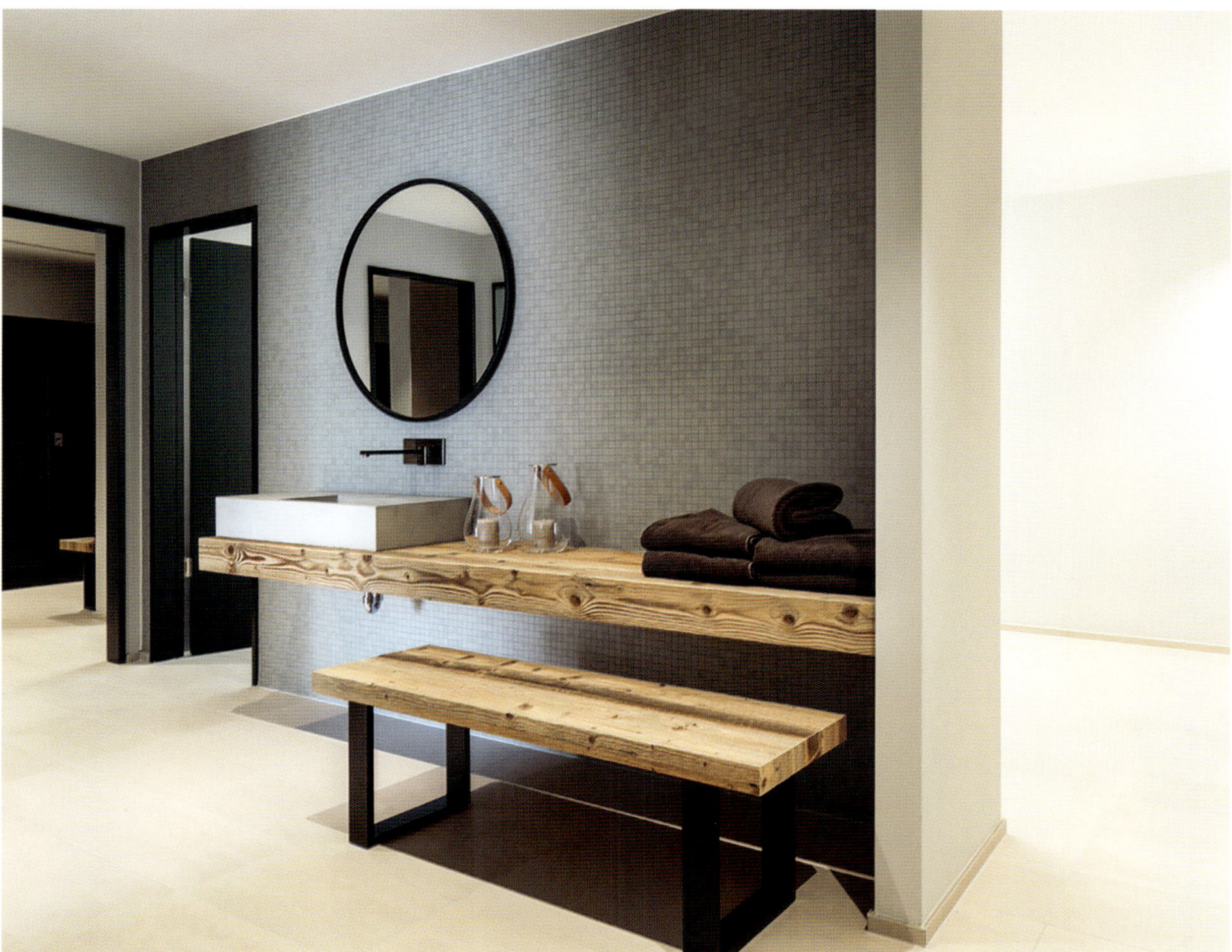

Parsenn Resort, Davos: spacious loggias with Alpine views (opposite page) make the apartments appear larger. Each residence contains high-quality furnishings, with skillfully combined materials creating a special ambience, in which the dark parquet floor contrasts with the overall light wooden character (above).

Parsenn Resort, Davos: Großzügige Loggien mit Bergblick (Seite gegenüber) erweitern die Wohnungen optisch. Jedes Apartment bietet hohe Standards. Der gekonnte Einsatz der Materialien schafft ein außergewöhnliches Ambiente, in dem das dunkle Parkett mit dem hellen Holzkern kontrastiert (oben).

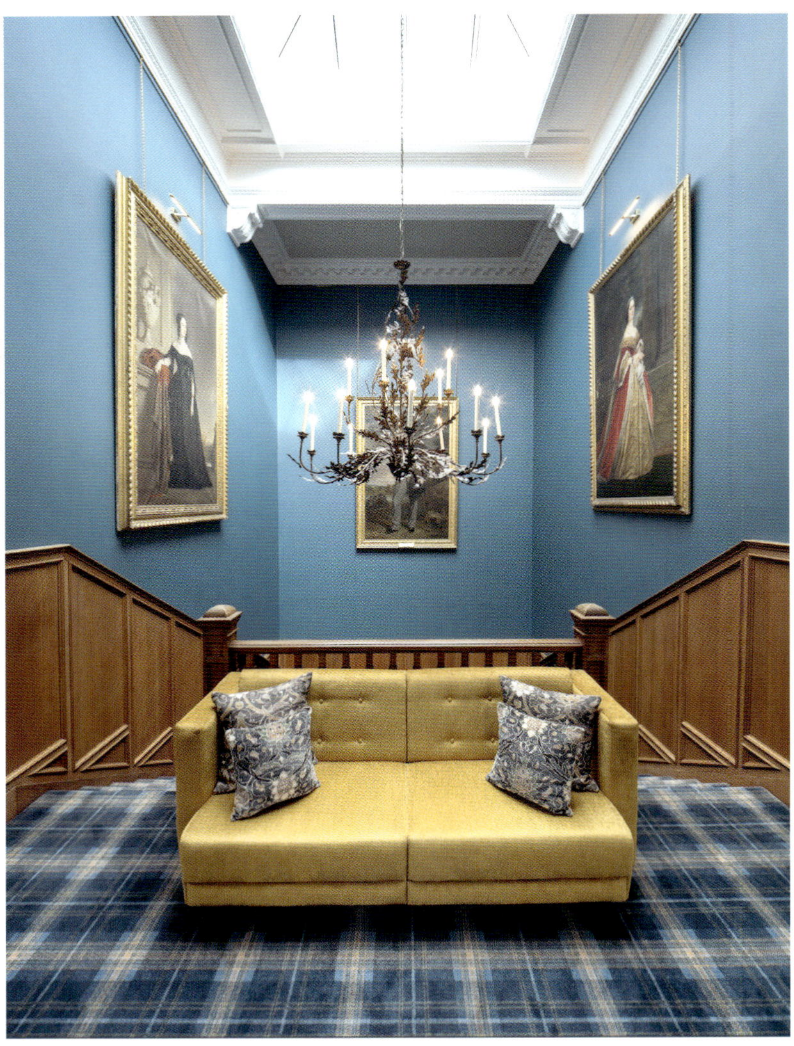

KITZIG INTERIOR DESIGN

LIPPSTADT, MUNICH, BOCHUM & DÜSSELDORF / GERMANY

Living Tradition | Tradition leben

When Kitzig Interior Design takes on a project, it transforms illusions into real dreams. Olaf Kitzig, founder and CEO, and his team of six are well-known for their visionary solutions, even when working on the most challenging properties. A current example is to be found in the Scottish county of Roxburghshire, where Kitzig Interior Design has modernized and extended a seventeenth century manor house and transformed it into a modern, luxurious boutique hotel. When converting the listed building into the Schloss Roxburghe Hotel & Golf Course, the sensitive old structure could mostly be maintained while adopting a contemporary interior design.

Wenn Kitzig Interior Design ein Projekt annimmt, verwandelt es Illusionen in reale Träume. Das etwa sechzigköpfige Team um Gründer und CEO Olaf Kitzig ist bekannt für seine visionären Lösungswege, selbst bei anspruchsvollsten Objekten. Ein aktuelles Beispiel findet sich in der schottischen Grafschaft Roxburghshire, wo Kitzig Interior Design ein Herrenhaus aus dem 17. Jahrhundert modernisiert, erweitert und in ein modern-luxuriöses Boutique-Hotel verwandelt hat. Beim Umbau des denkmalgeschützten Gebäudes zum Schloss Roxburghe Hotel & Golf Course konnte die empfindliche alte Bausubstanz größtenteils bewahrt und gleichzeitig aktuelles Interior Design integriert werden.

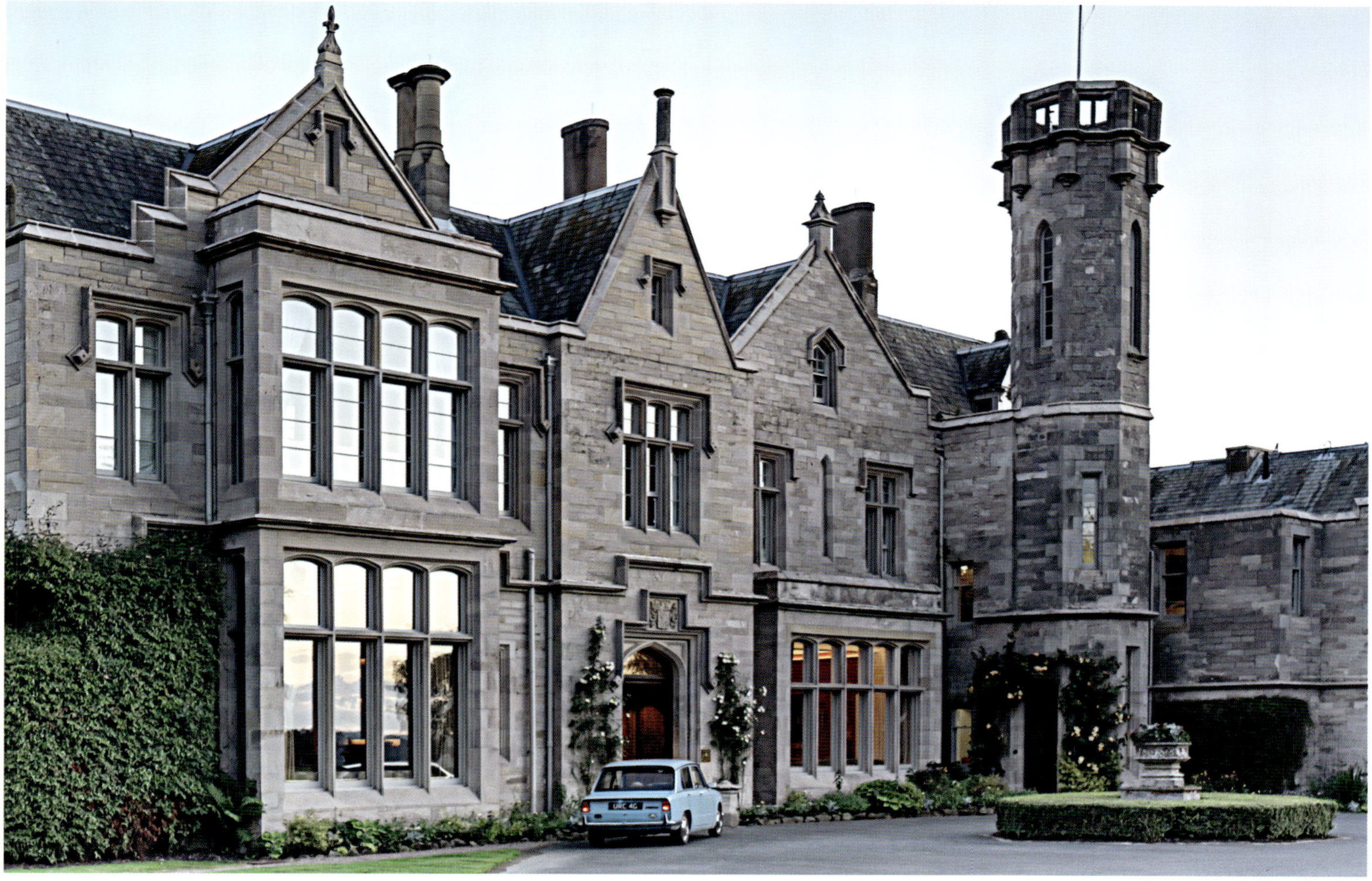

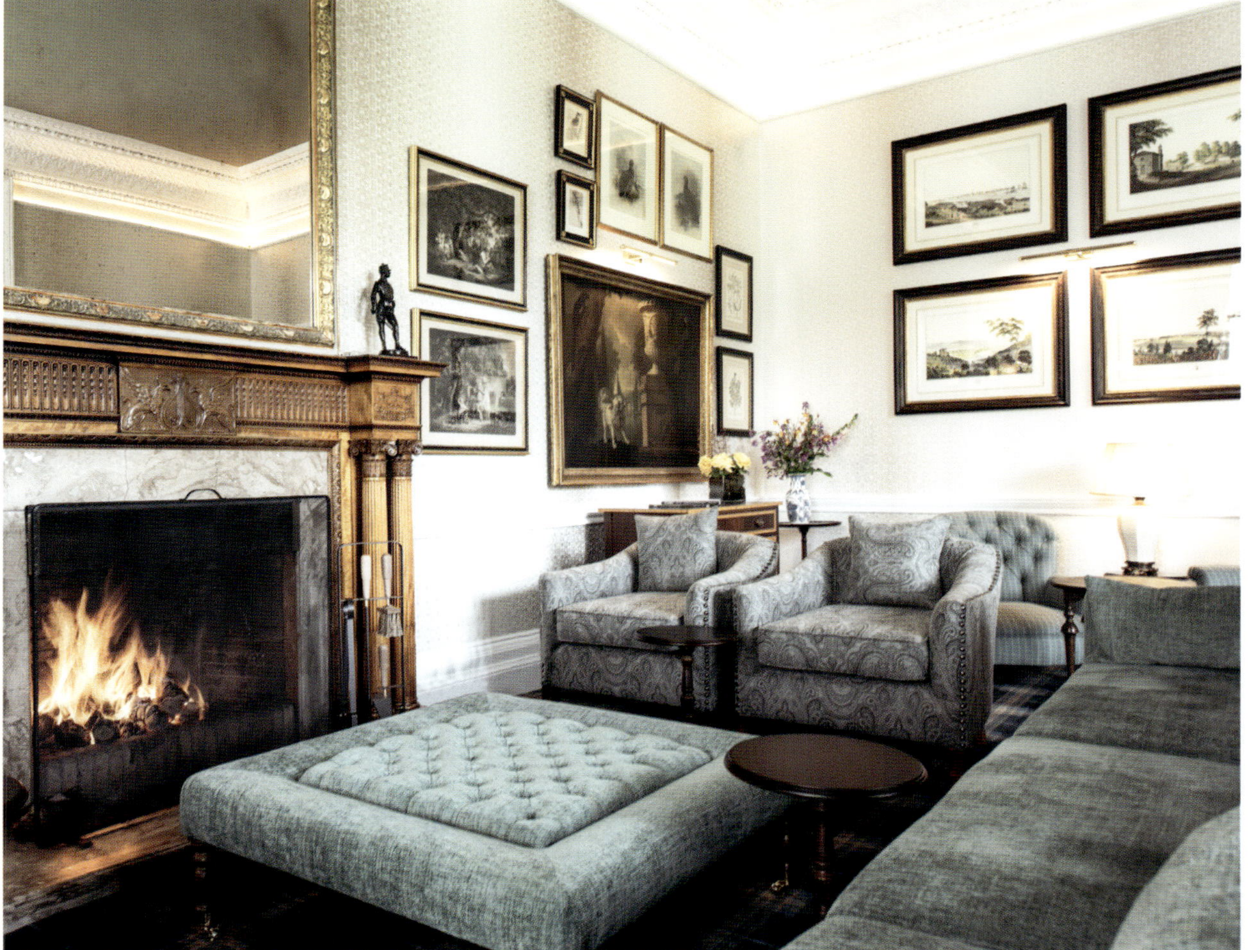

The vestiges of past centuries were consciously preserved in the modernization of Schloss Roxburghe. High ceilings, cornices, fireplaces and bay windows characterize the interior. The classic British furnishing style preserves the property's historic charm and even extends to traditional Scottish tartan carpets.

Die Spuren der Jahrhunderte wurden bei der Modernisierung von Schloss Roxburghe bewusst erhalten. Hohe Decken, Stuckleisten, Kamine und Erker prägen die Innenräume. Bei der Inneneinrichtung bewahrt ein klassisch-britischer Stil den geschichtsträchtigen Charme, bis hin zu Teppichböden im typisch schottischen Karomuster.

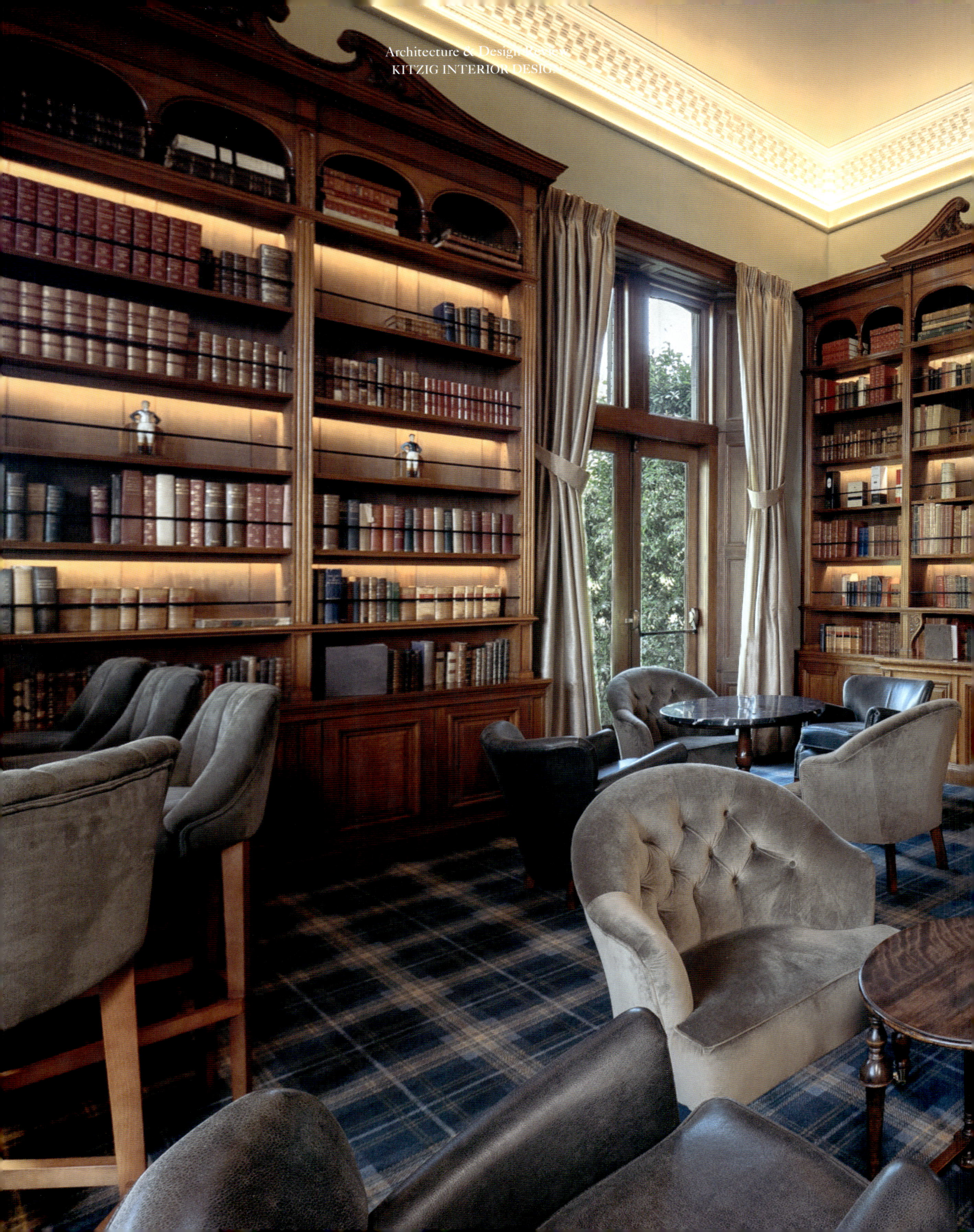

Architecture & Design Projects
KITZIG INTERIOR DESIGN

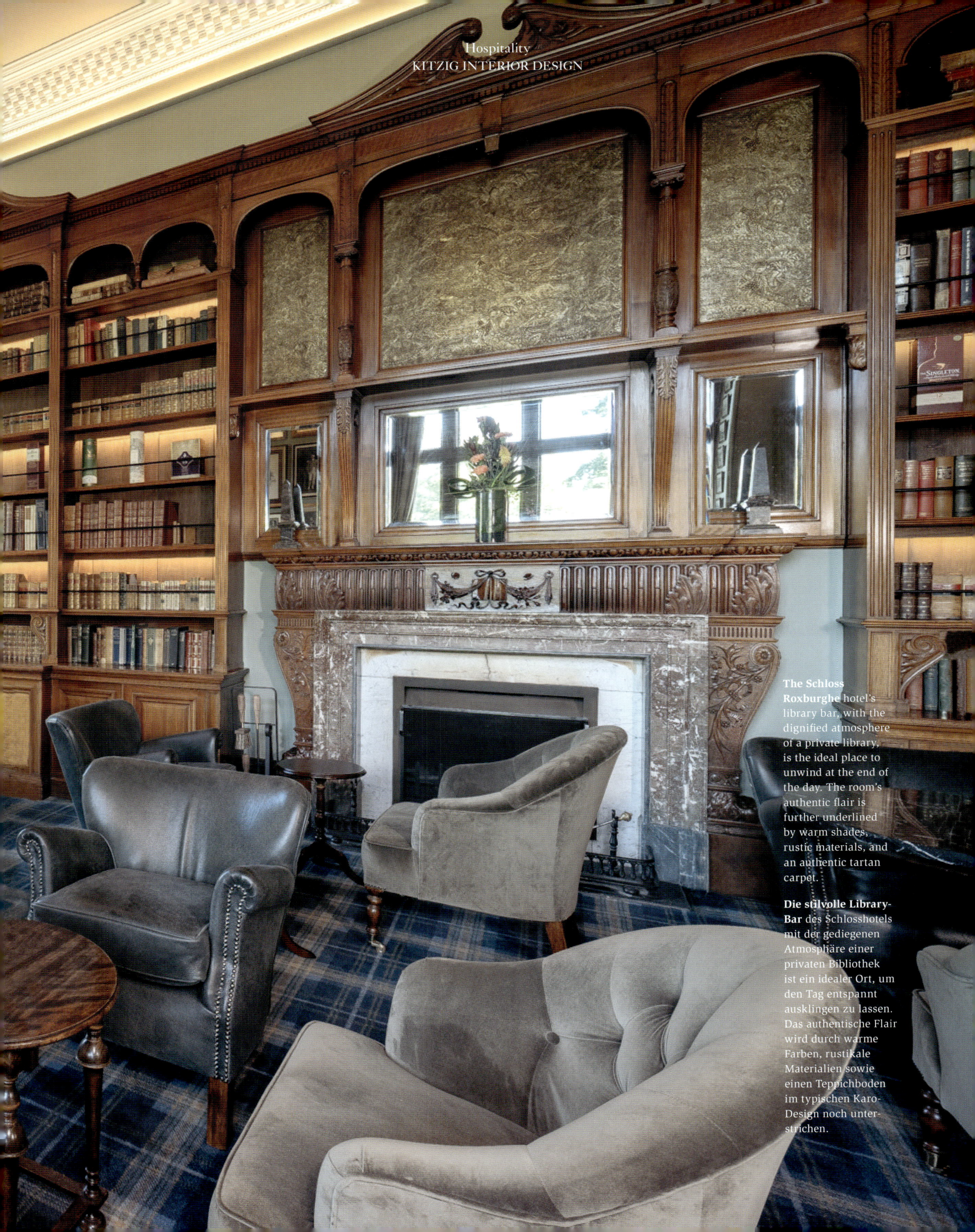

The Schloss Roxburghe hotel's library bar, with the dignified atmosphere of a private library, is the ideal place to unwind at the end of the day. The room's authentic flair is further underlined by warm shades, rustic materials, and an authentic tartan carpet.

Die stilvolle Library-Bar des Schlosshotels mit der gediegenen Atmosphäre einer privaten Bibliothek ist ein idealer Ort, um den Tag entspannt ausklingen zu lassen. Das authentische Flair wird durch warme Farben, rustikale Materialien sowie einen Teppichboden im typischen Karo-Design noch unterstrichen.

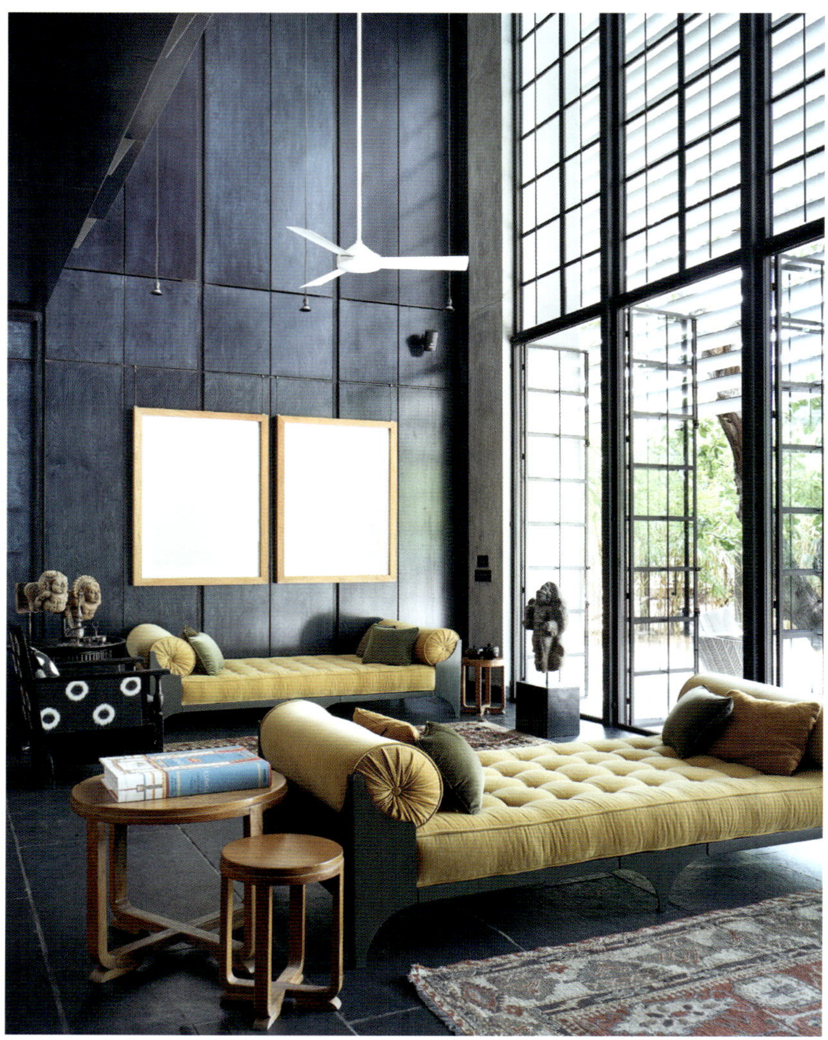

MANCINI ENTERPRISES

KESAVAPERUMALPURAM, CHENNAI / INDIA

Space, Light and Color | Raum, Licht und Farbe

Mancini Enterprises has been working in the field of architecture and interior design since 2004; in recent years, landscaping projects play an increasingly important role. Assignments from private individuals, institutions and companies can, however, vary considerably depending on their scope and location. Even during planning, the team tries to reconcile the project goals with both artistic principles and ecological and cultural concerns. The property shown here at the Bay of Bengal is for three generations, comprising several building sections and an inner courtyard. While offering sufficient space for private rooms, the house also contains delightful spaces for family gatherings.

Seit 2004 arbeitet Mancini Enterprises im Bereich der Architektur und Innenarchitektur; in den letzten Jahren kamen auch vermehrt Projekte der Landschaftsgestaltung hinzu. Je nach Umfang und Standort können sich die Aufträge von Privatpersonen, Institutionen und Unternehmen allerdings deutlich unterscheiden. Bereits während des Entwurfs versucht das Team, die Projektziele mit den Regeln der Kunst sowie ökologischen und kulturellen Fragen in Einklang zu bringen. Die Bilder zeigen ein Drei-Generationen-Haus am Golf von Bengalen mit mehreren Gebäudeteilen und einem Innenhof. Neben ausreichend Platz für private Räume finden sich hier reizvolle Orte der Begegnung.

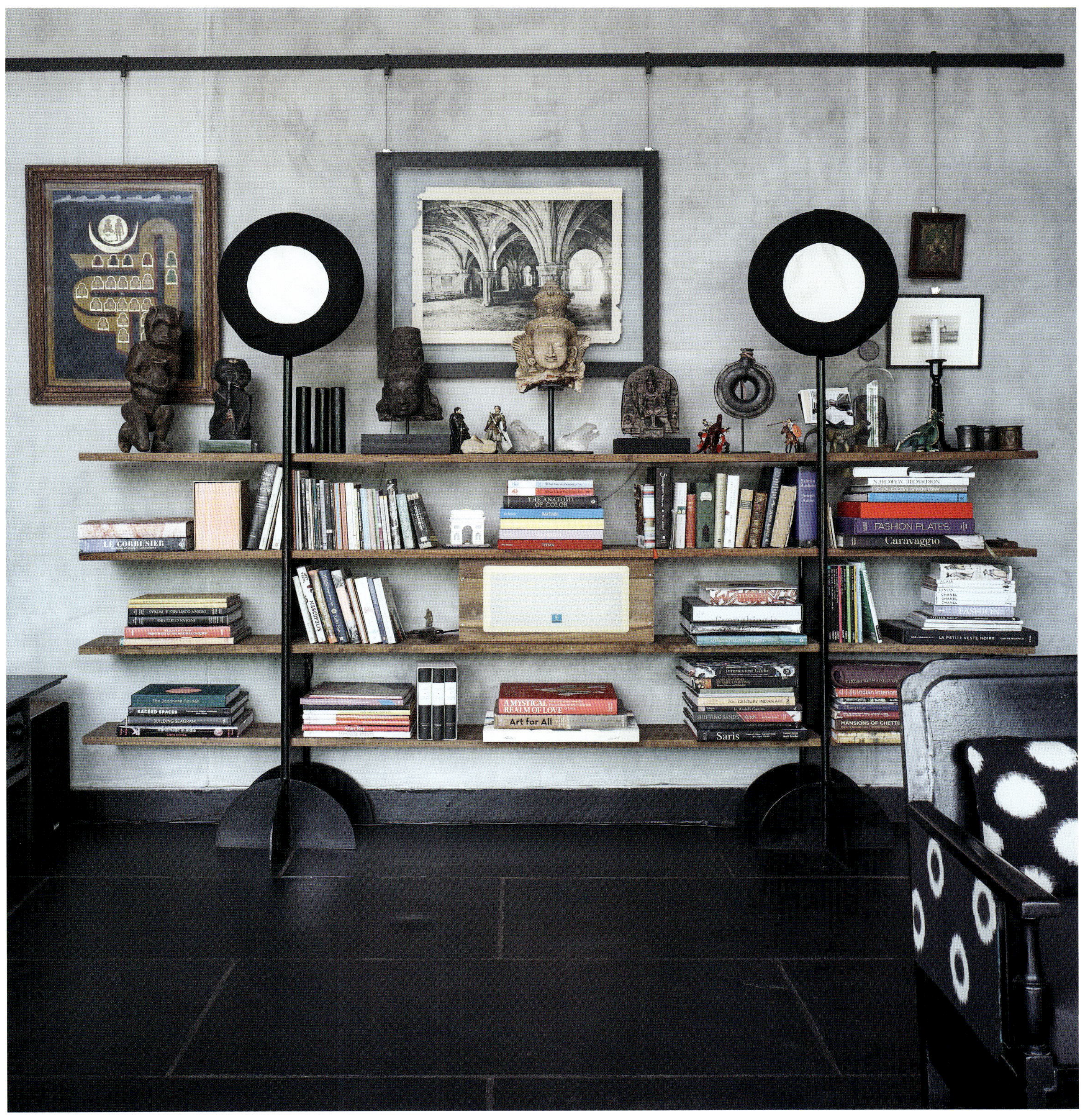

In the west building's
living room, with
its extra-high ceilings
(opposite page), an
aluminum louver
screen filters the light
from the glass façade

and emphasizes the
depth of the indigo
walls (see also
page 137). Custom-
made furniture
(above) reinforces
the overall concept.

**Im extrahohen
Wohnzimmer**
des Westgebäudes
(Seite gegenüber)
filtert eine Alumi-
niumlamellen-
Jalousie das Licht

der Glasfassade
und betont die tief
indigoblauen Wände
(siehe auch Seite 137).
Handgefertigte Möbel
(oben) unterstützen
das Gesamtkonzept.

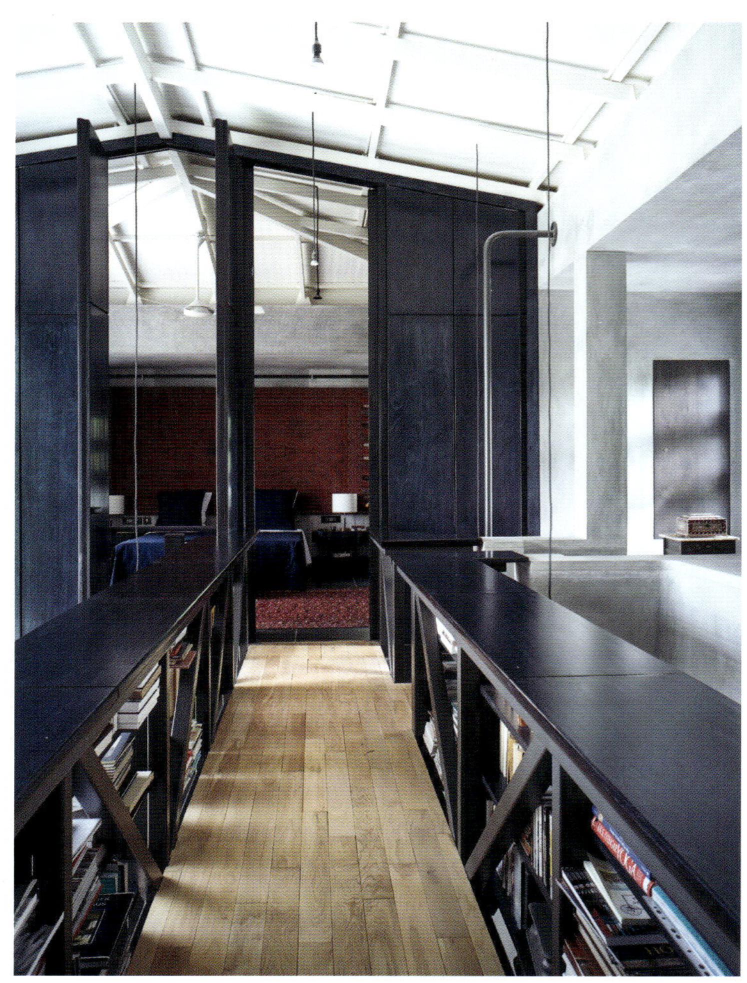

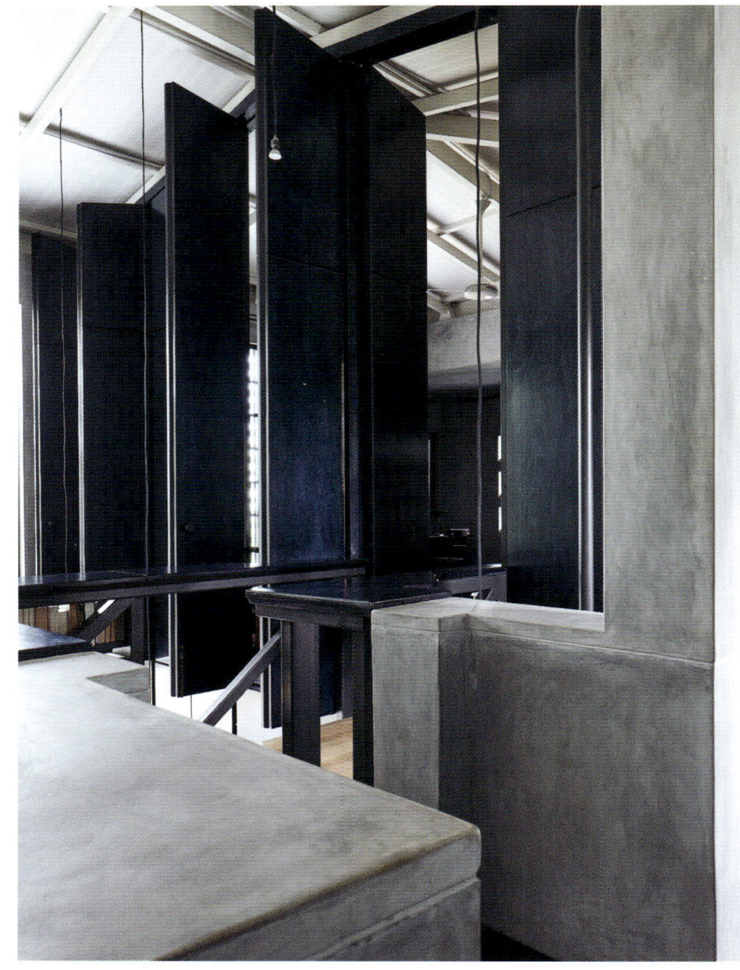

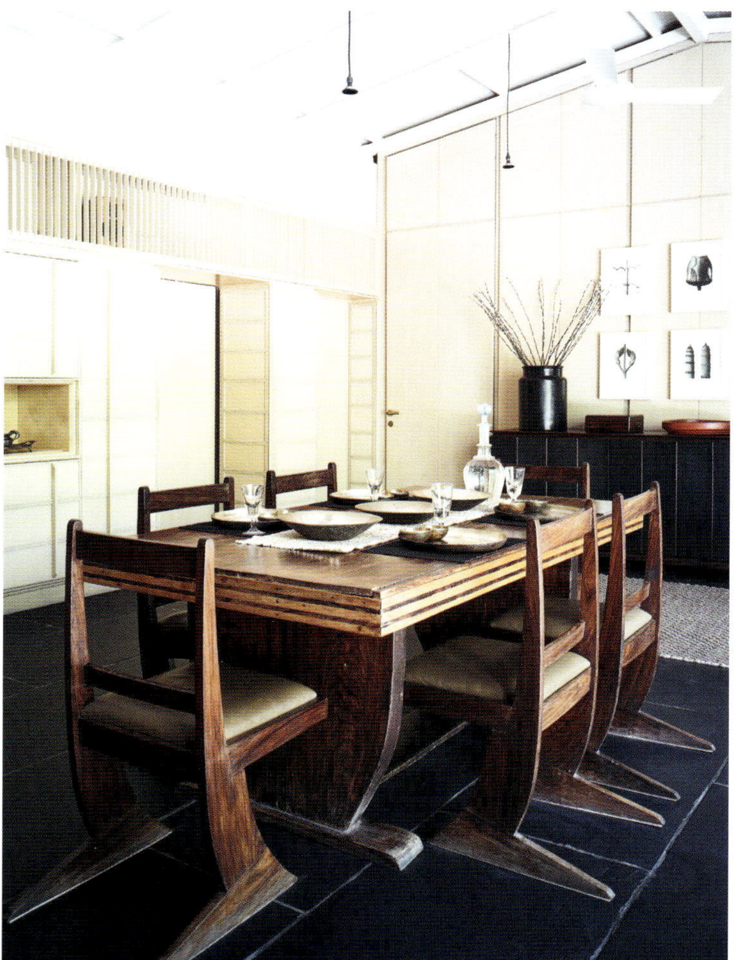

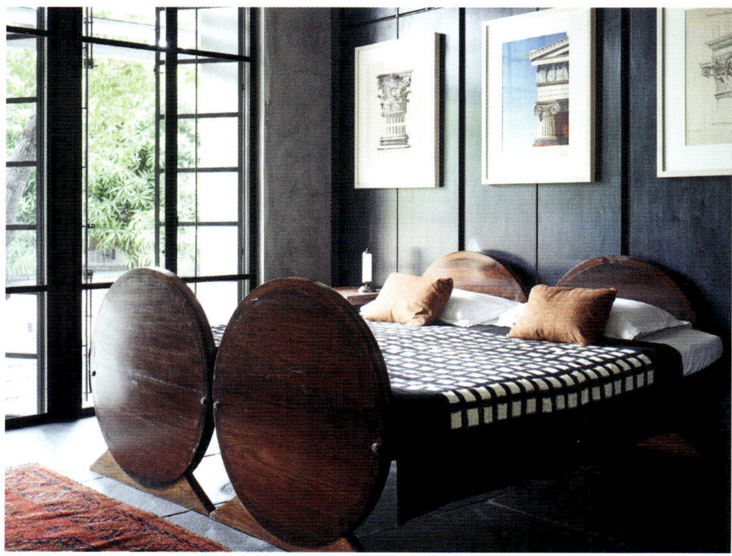

The walls in the dressing room and master bedroom on either side of the library bridge are all composed of floor-to-ceiling panels that can be opened to reveal an airy, loft-like space (above). The east building provides plenty of room for communal meals (left).

Die Wände des Ankleide- und des Elternschlafzimmers auf beiden Seiten der Bibliotheksbrücke bestehen jeweils aus raumhohen Paneelen, die sich zu einem loftartig-luftigen Raum öffnen lassen (oben). Im Ostgebäude ist viel Platz für gemeinsame Mahlzeiten (links).

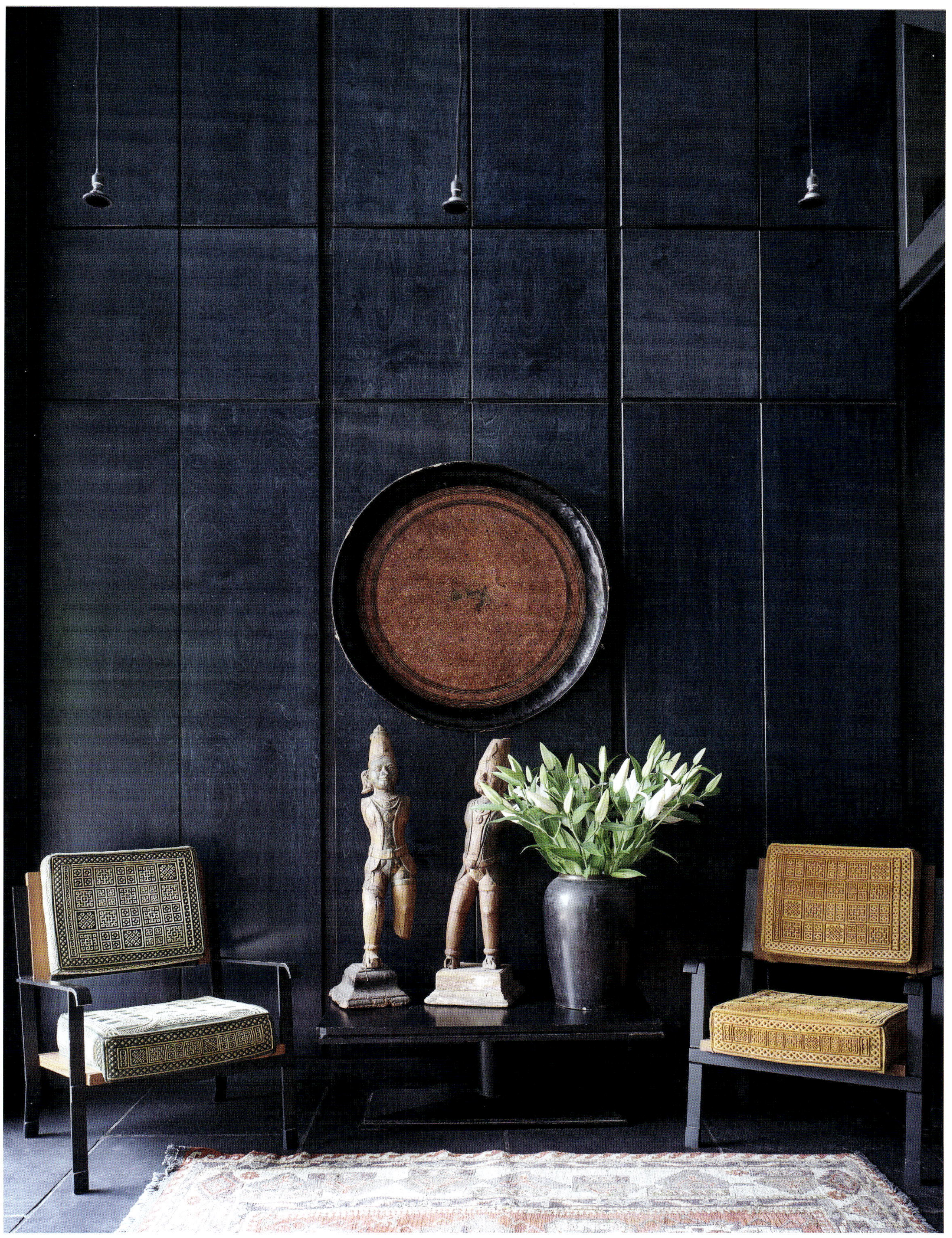

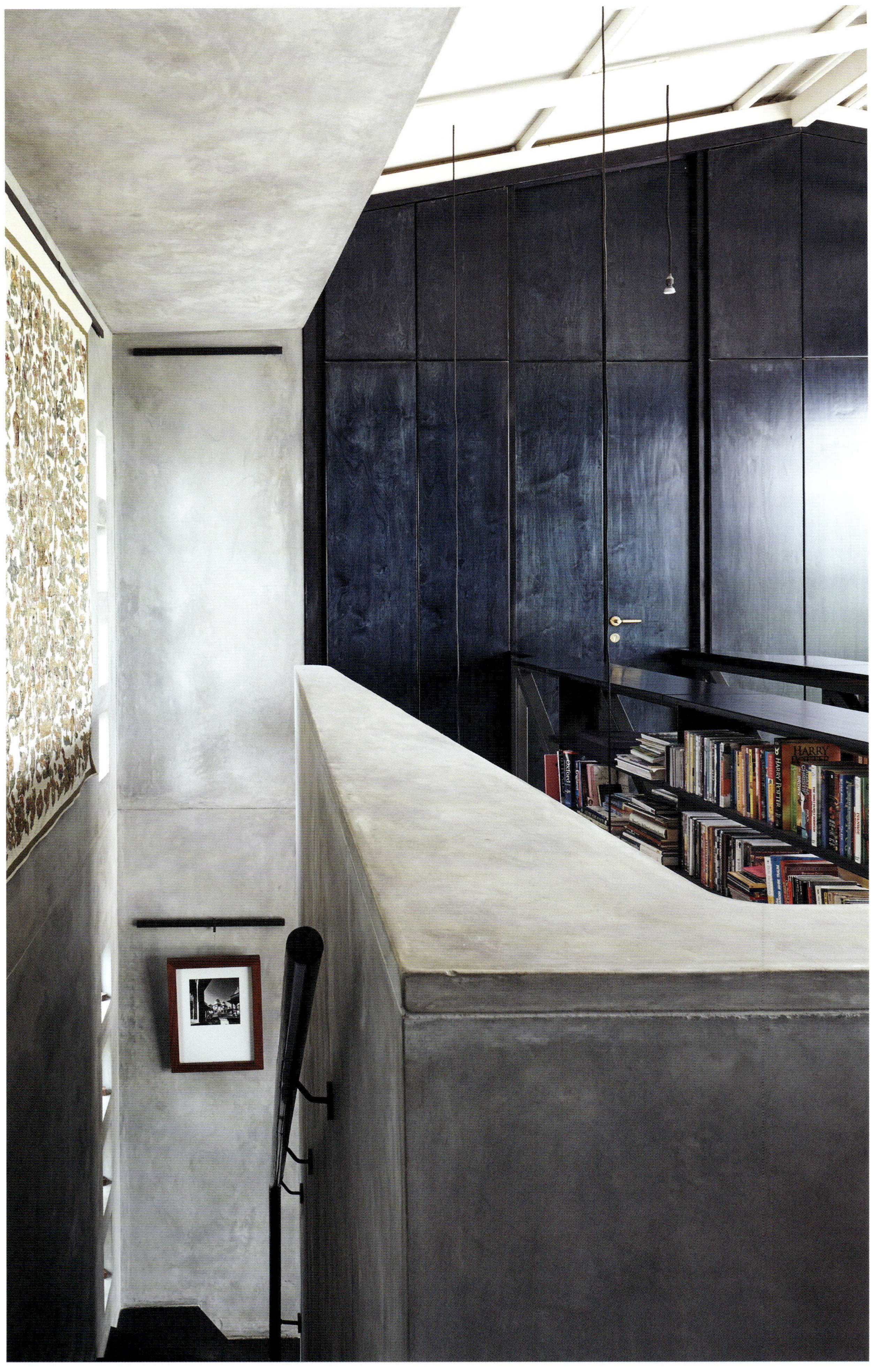

The large, embroidered seventeenth century tapestry contrasts markedly with the simple, modern stairway (left). The previously mentioned library bridge is once again visible on the right. There are numerous places for relaxation and communication in the building's outer areas (opposite page).

Der große gestickte Wandteppich aus dem 17. Jahrhundert steht im deutlichen Kontrast zum schlicht-modernen Treppenaufgang (links). Im rechten Bereich des Bildes ist noch einmal die erwähnte Bibliotheksbrücke zu sehen. In den Außenbereichen des Gebäudes (Seite gegenüber) finden sich viele Orte für Entspannung und Kommunikation.

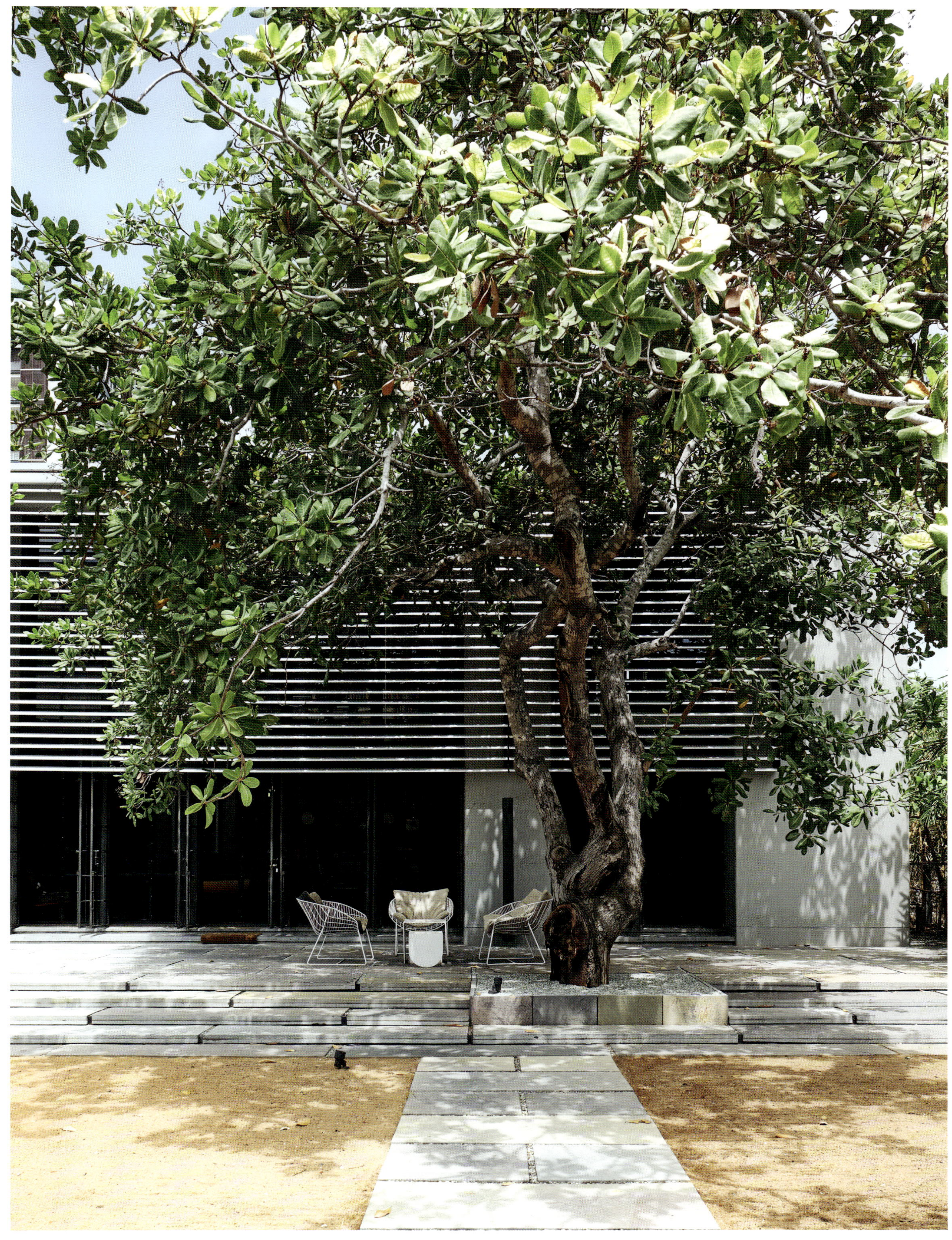

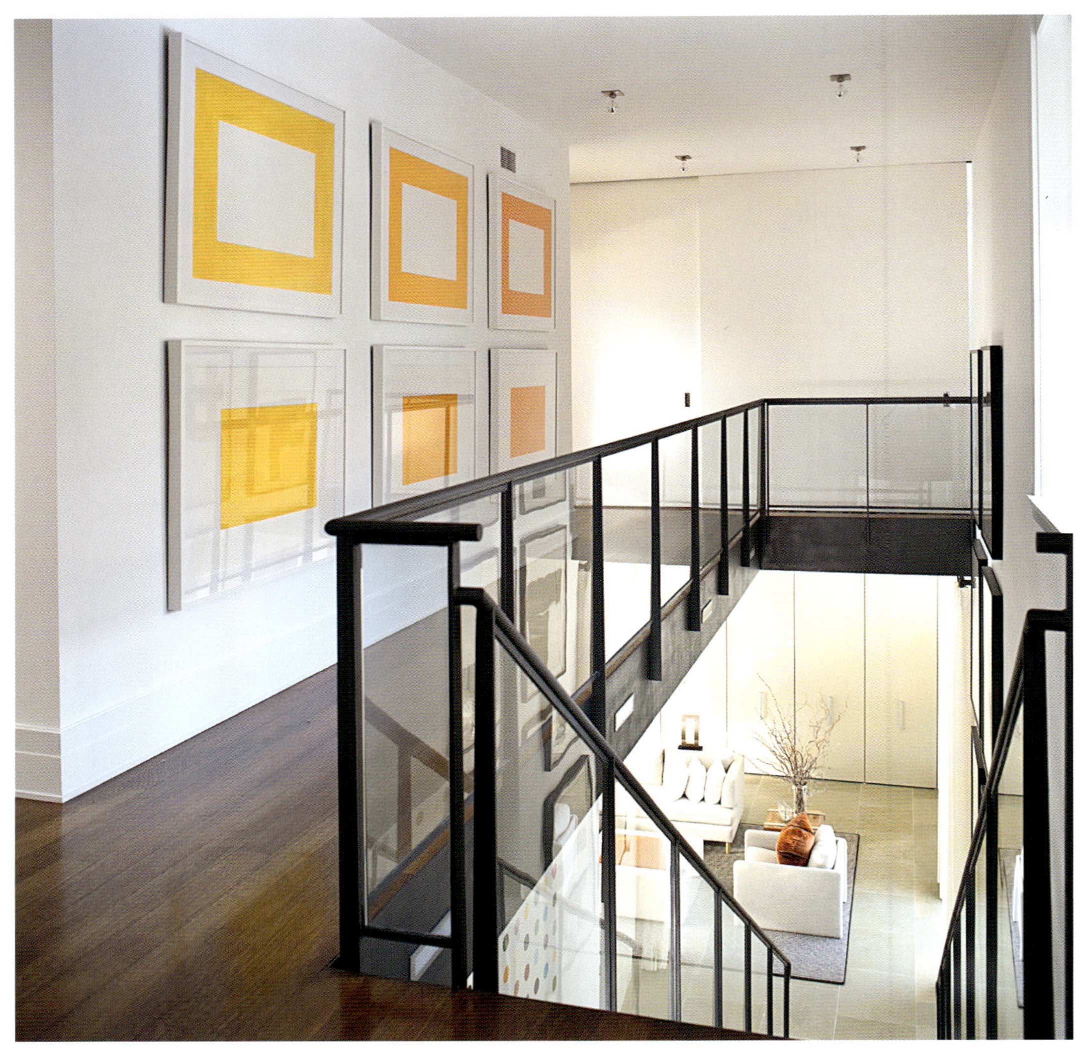

MATTHEW FREDERICK

NEW YORK & FLORIDA / USA

Timeless and Sophisticated | Zeitlos und raffiniert

With offices in New York and Florida, M. Frederick works nationally and internationally on residential projects of all dimensions. The award-winning firm offers multidisciplinary services in the field of interior design and architecture. The owner, Matthew Frederick, has always remained loyal to his principle of 'Elegant Living for Everyday Life' and loves to combine antique and extremely modern pieces. 'This lends them a more timeless and sophisticated quality,' says Frederick. His clients are inspired by the use of art and furnishings emanating from different periods, absent of any preconceived ideas.

Von seinen Standorten New York und Florida aus ist M. Frederick landesweit und international für Wohnprojekte aller Größenordnungen tätig. Das preisgekrönte Unternehmen bietet multidisziplinäre Dienstleistungen der Bereiche Innenarchitektur und Design an. Inhaber Matthew Frederick ist dabei seinem Grundsatz „Elegant Living for Everyday Life" stets treu geblieben und liebt es etwa, antike Objekte mit supermodernen Stücken zu kombinieren. „Das verleiht ihnen einen zeitloseren und raffinierteren Charakter", so der Chefdesigner. Seine Kunden sollen sich vorurteilsfrei von den verschiedensten Kunst- und Einrichtungseinflüssen diverser Epochen inspirieren lassen.

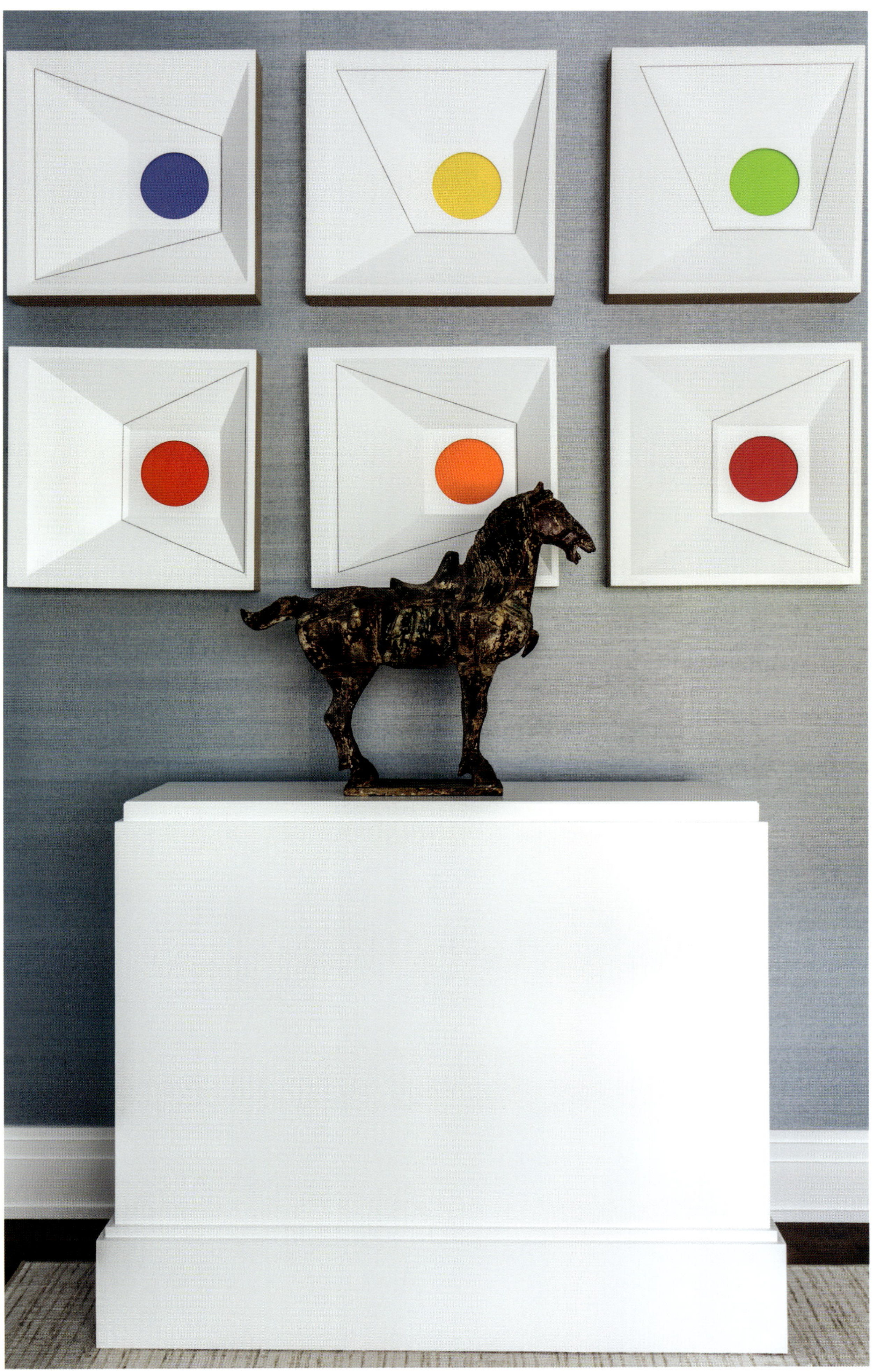

Elegant stairway
(opposite page): an intentionally over-dimensioned modern art composition crowns a dramatic stair landing and helps to unify the first and second floor living spaces. Steel and glass combine to round off the effect.

Horse sculpture
(left): modernity and antiquity are blended into a symmetrical whole. The old wooden horse's special texture provides a welcome contrast to the geometrical circle motifs of crisp and intense color.

Elegante Treppe
(Seite gegenüber): Eine absichtlich etwas überdimensionierte Komposition moderner Kunst krönt ein dramatisches Treppenpodest und hilft dadurch, die Räume des Erdgeschosses und ersten Stocks zu einer Einheit zusammenzuführen. Stahl und Glas ergänzen die Wirkung.

Pferdeskulptur
(links): Modernes und Antikes in einer symmetrischen Kombination. Die besondere Textur des alten Holzpferdes bildet einen willkommenen Kontrast zu den geometrischen Bildmotiven mit den gestochen scharfen Farbkreisen.

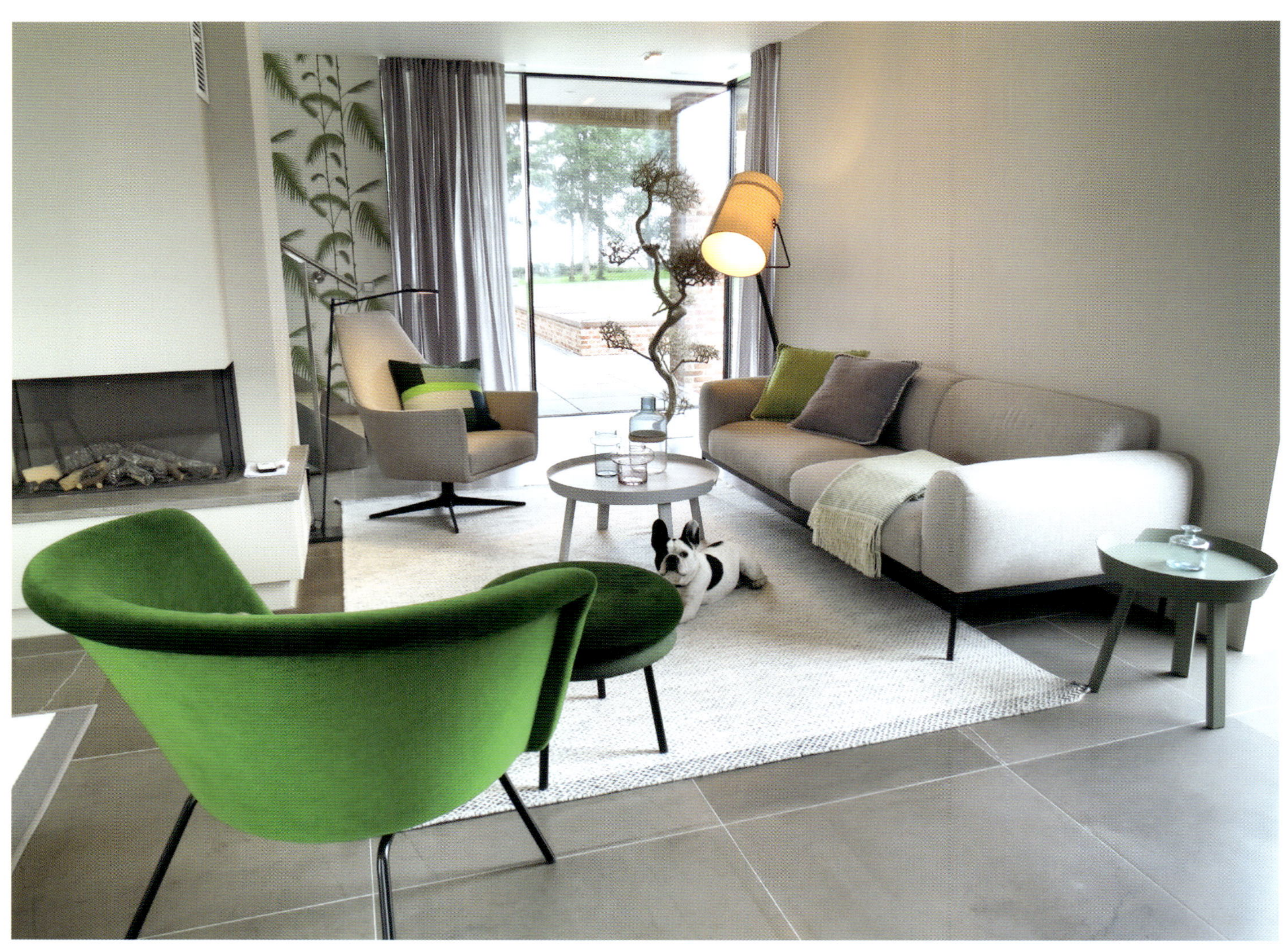

MONICA MARX
INNENEINRICHTUNGEN

MUNICH / GERMANY

Advise, Plan, Implement | Beraten, planen, umsetzen

The work of Monica Marx Inneneinrichtungen is distinguished by a combination of bespoke, high-quality design of both interior and furnishings along with a comprehensive service. The firm designs private living spaces, houses and villas, both at home and abroad. The example shown here is of a retreat belonging to a family of Berlin entrepreneurs in a nature reserve on the island of Rügen. Following the guideline 'A world of its own—peace, harmony and a feeling of spaciousness,' Monica Marx designed and furnished all areas of both houses in detail. A large, custom-made dining table, with special revolving chairs at each end, was conceived as the focal point of family life.

Eine individuelle, hochwertige Planung von Ausstattung und Interieur und ein umfassender Service zeichnen das Unternehmen Monica Marx Inneneinrichtungen aus. Die Firma gestaltet private Wohnräume, Häuser und Villen im In- und Ausland. Ein Beispiel ist der abgebildete Rückzugsort einer Berliner Unternehmerfamilie in einem Naturreservat auf der Insel Rügen. Gemäß der Vorgabe „Eine Welt für sich! Ruhe, Harmonie und das Gefühl von Weite" hat Monica Marx hier alle Bereiche der beiden Häuser detailliert geplant und eingerichtet. Als Mittelpunkt des gemeinsamen Familienlebens wurde eigens ein großer Esstisch mit speziellen Drehstühlen an den Enden entworfen.

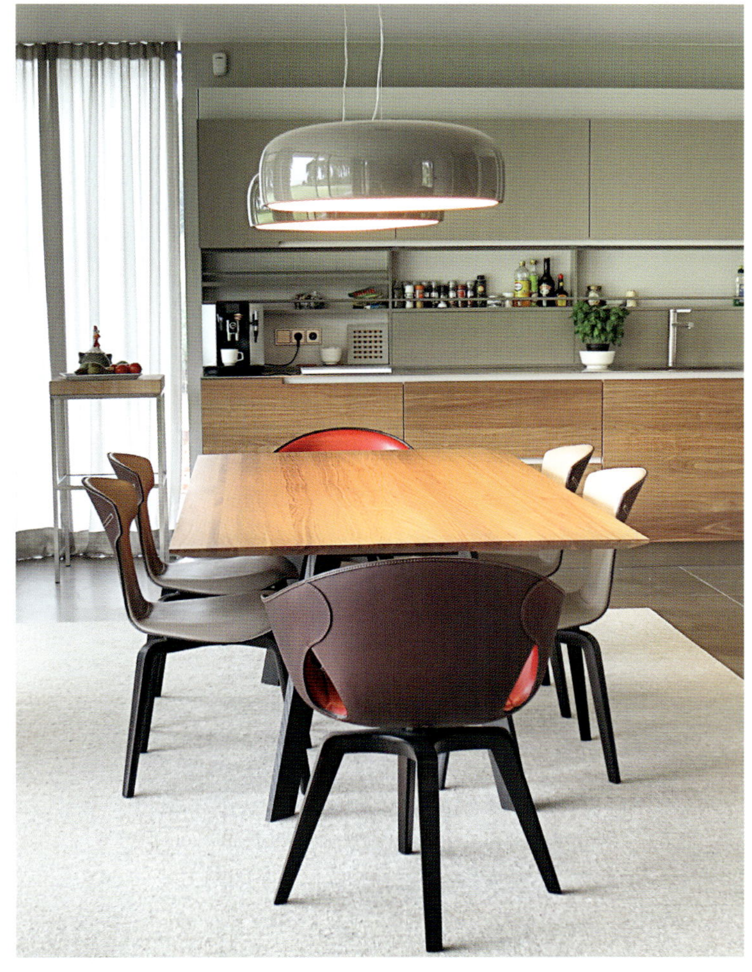

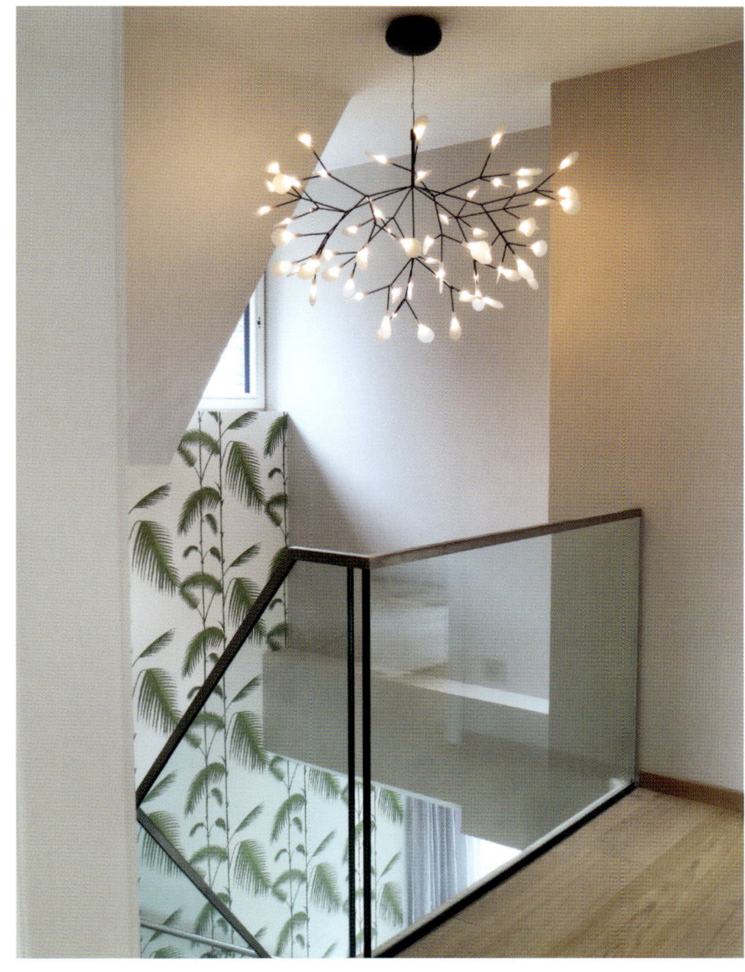

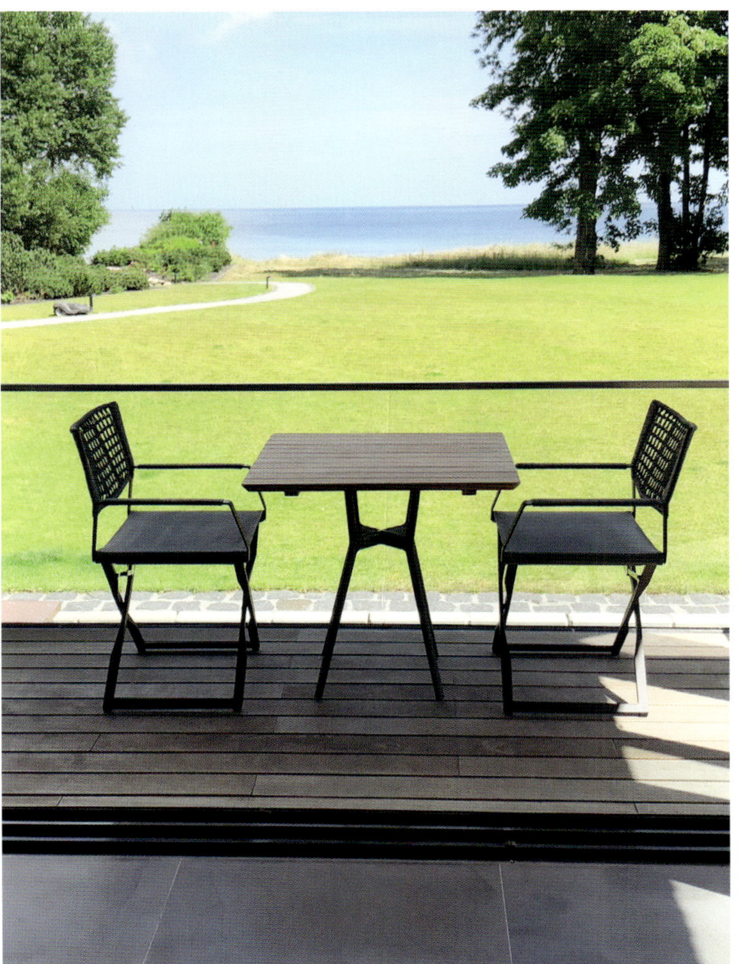

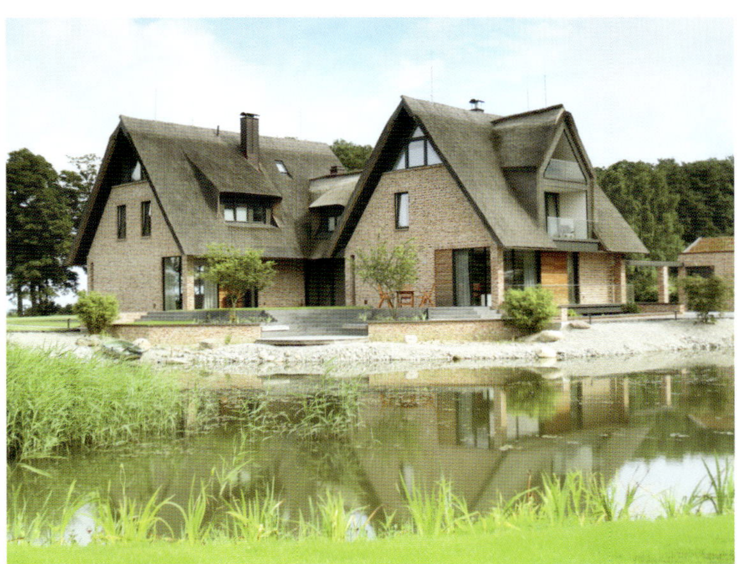

Two houses, two styles—an elegant, international blend of designs in the 'Lake House': dining area with kitchen (top left) and terrace (left). Scandinavian-style 'Pond House': room with fireplace in fresh shades of green (opposite page) and stairway (top right).

Zwei Häuser, zwei Stile – edler internationaler Designmix im „Seehaus“: Essbereich mit Küche (ganz oben links) und die Terrasse (links). Skandinavisch gestaltetes „Teichhaus“: Kaminzimmer mit frischen Grüntönen (Seite gegenüber) und das Treppenhaus (oben rechts).

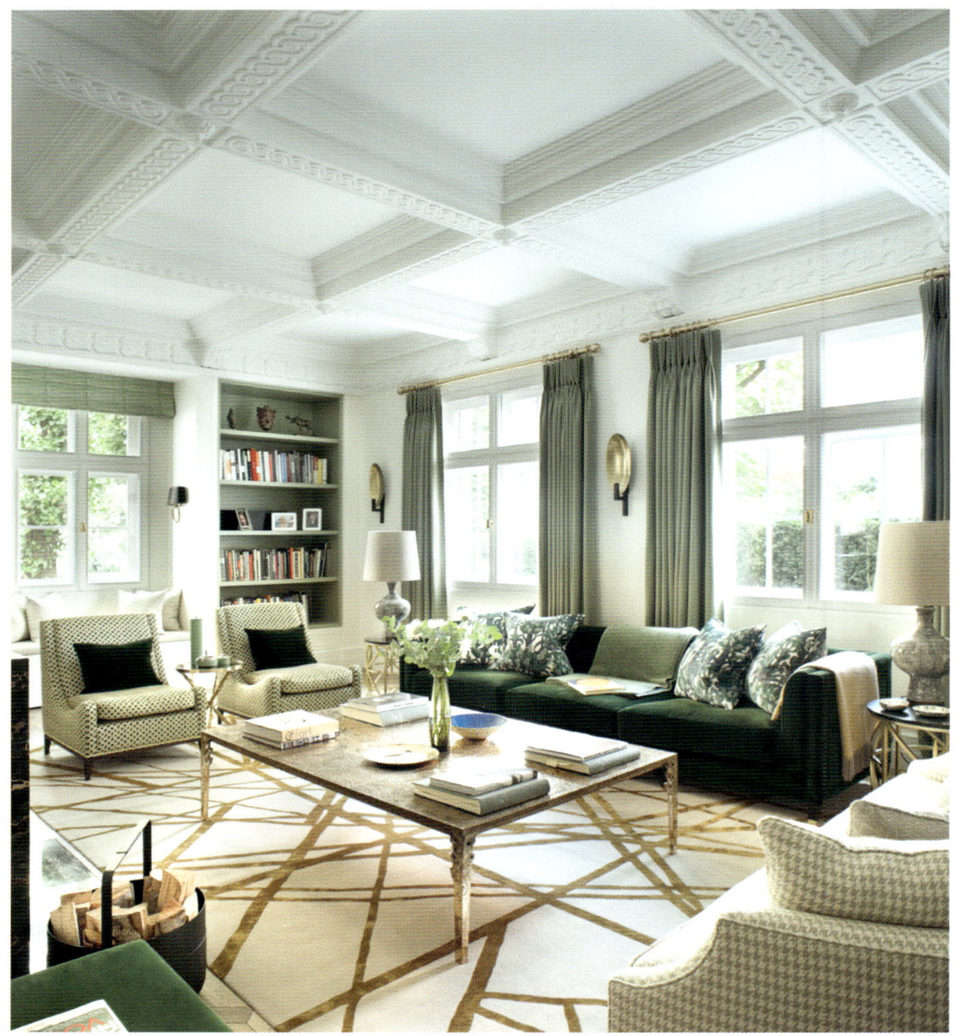

NICKY DOBREE

LONDON / UNITED KINGDOM

Elegant and Timeless | Elegant und zeitlos

For a relocation back to Munich the expertise of London-based interior designer Nicky Dobree was called upon to help with the restoration of the family's 1920's listed villa. The house was stripped back to its bare bones and a basement was dug. Cornices and mouldings were restored or replicated. Panelling inspired by the original was redesigned to work with the new room layouts, and bespoke taller doors were fitted throughout to elevate each space and draw the eye up. Every detail in the renovation of this property was chosen to create a modern home, whilst its individuality, history and stories still remain intact.

Für die Renovierung ihrer denkmalgeschützte Villa aus den 1920er-Jahren engagierte eine Familie die in London ansässige Innenarchitektin Nicky Dobree. Im Zuge der Neugestaltung wurde das Haus in München entkernt und unterkellert, Simse und Stuckleisten wurden rekonstruiert oder nachgebaut. An die Originale erinnernde Täfelungen wurden neu gestaltet, passend zum neuen Zuschnitt der Zimmer und den überall eingebauten höheren Türen, die als Blickfang für ein luftiges Raumgefühl sorgen. Jedes Detail wurde bei der Renovierung des Anwesens so bedacht, dass ein modernes Haus entstand, das dennoch seine Individualität und ganz eigene Geschichte bewahrt hat.

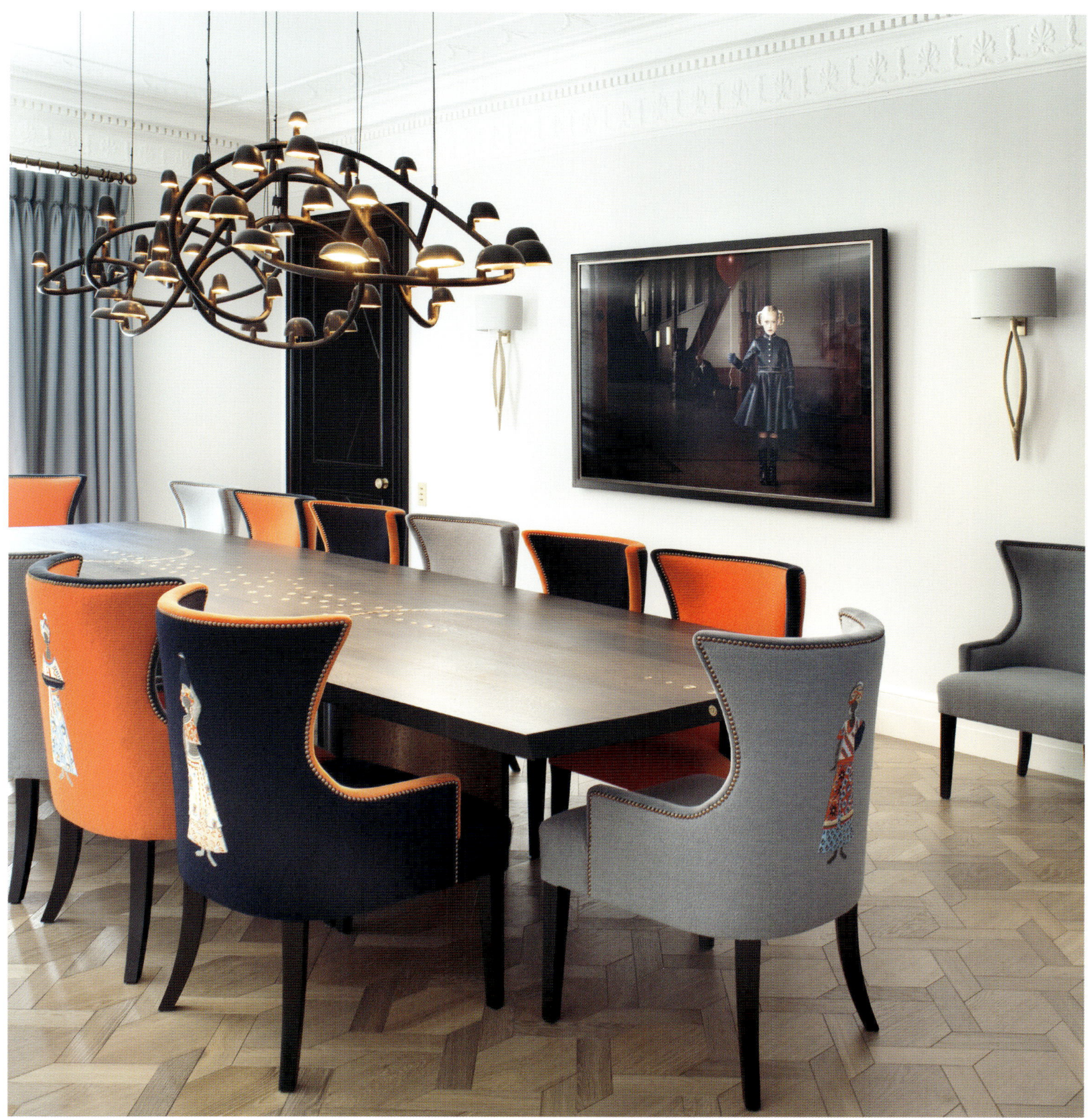

In the dining room
the Nicky Dobree
bespoke chairs were
upholstered in boiled
wool with contrasting
velvet trim. On the
back of each chair
is an embroidered
African lady inspired
by the clients travels
to Africa.

Die von Nicky Dobree
maßgefertigten Stühle
im Esszimmer wurden
mit gekochter Wolle
gepolstert und mit
einem kontrastieren-
den Samtbesatz ver-
sehen. Inspiriert von
den Afrikareisen des
Kunden, sind die Leh-
nen der Stühle mit
afrikanischen Frauen-
figuren bestickt.

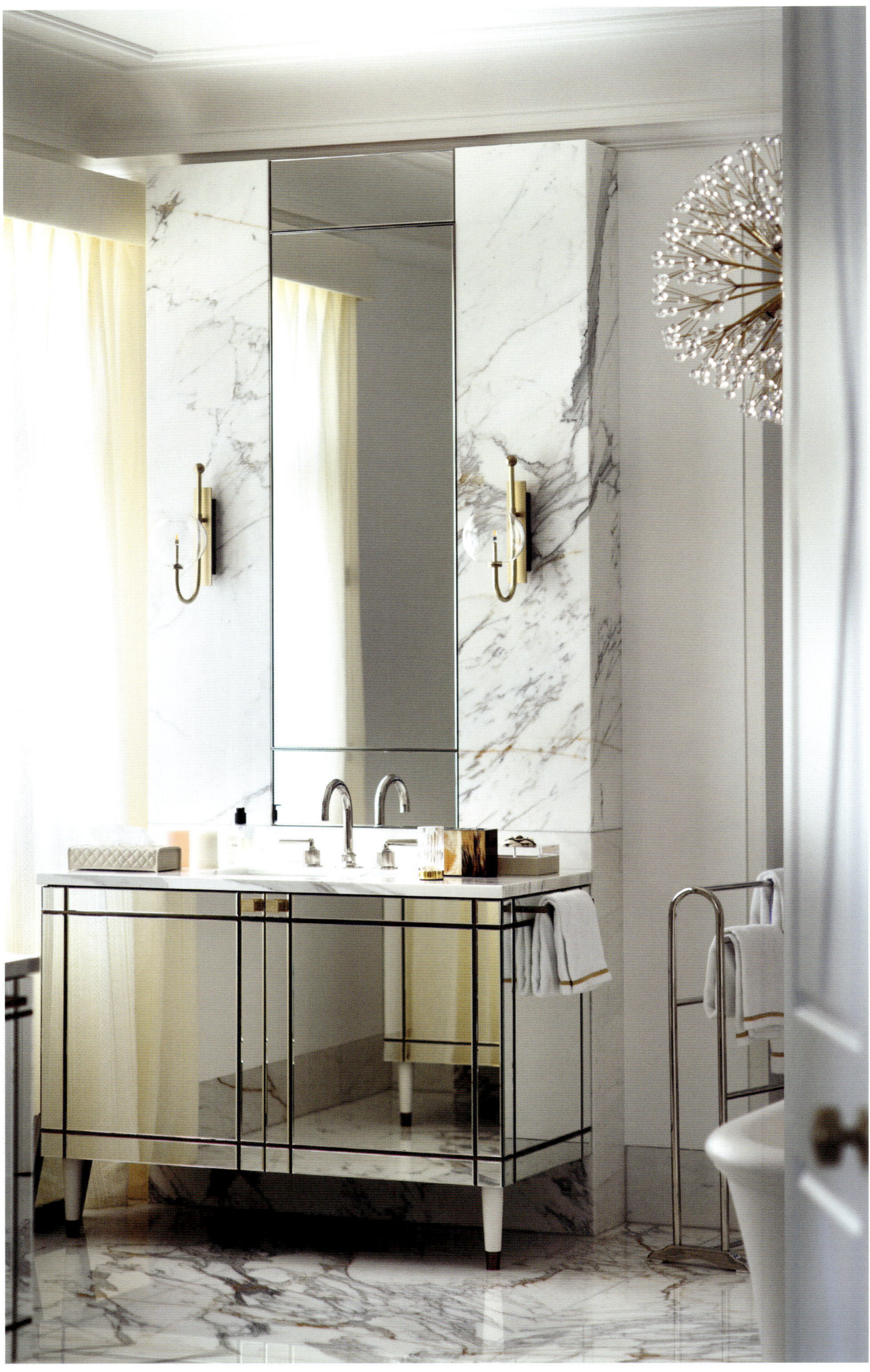

The use of light marble and gold elements in the bathroom (left) hearkens back to the style of the 1920s when the villa was constructed. The color blue dominates in the master bedroom (opposite page), complemented by shades of light brown. The perfect matching of different hues, in combination with carefully selected materials, creates a sense of relaxed, understated luxury.

Der Einsatz von hellen Marmor- und Goldelementen sorgt im Bad (links) für eine stilvolle Erinnerung an die Zeit der 1920er-Jahre, als die Villa erbaut wurde. Im Hauptschlafzimmer (Seite gegenüber) dominiert die Farbe Blau, ergänzt durch hellbraune Akzente. Durch die perfekte Abstimmung der Farbtöne, in Kombination mit ausgewählten Materialien, entsteht hier ein Gefühl von entspanntem, zurückhaltendem Luxus.

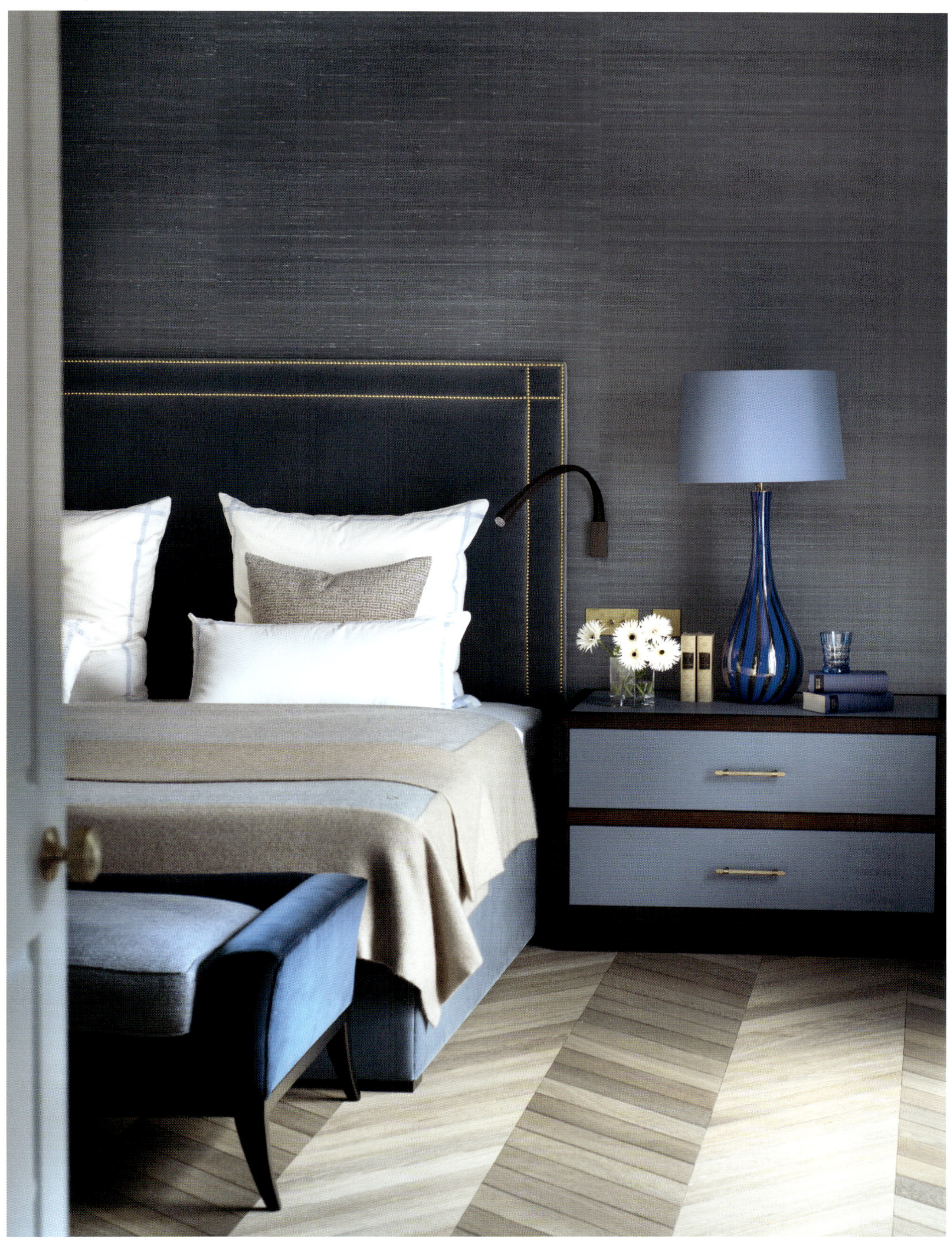

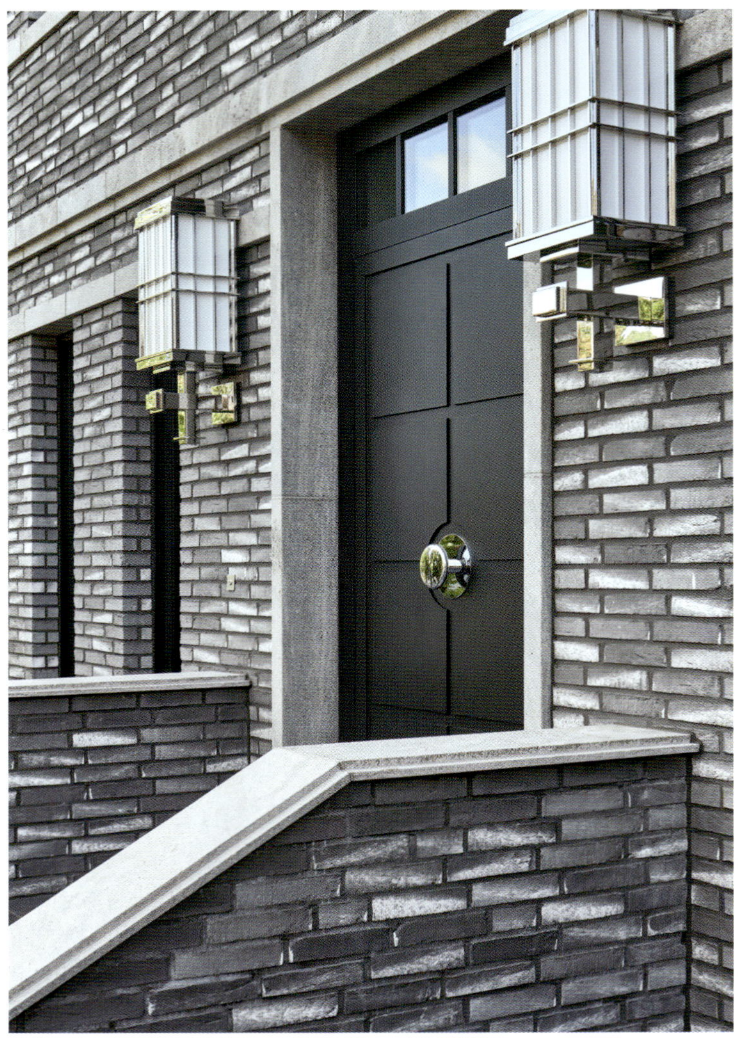

PATRICK TREUTLEIN
INTERIORS

MEERBUSCH / GERMANY

A Designer's Dream | Designertraum

For more than twenty-five years, interior designer Patrick Treutlein's firm has been a byword for style and expertise. He and his team demonstrate this on a daily basis, both in their retail stores in Düsseldorf and Meerbusch as well as in the furniture manufactory and when dealing with independent design orders. Now and again, however, the client's budget or taste stymies the team's creativity. For this reason, Treutlein was particularly happy to design his own personal dream house in his hometown of Meerbusch: an individual new building using the old foundation walls along with perfect gardens and a highly distinguished, aesthetically harmonious interior.

Patrick Treutlein steht seit über 25 Jahren für Stil und Sachverstand. Das Team um den Innendesigner stellt dies auch täglich unter Beweis, in den Ladengeschäften Düsseldorfs und Meerbuschs ebenso wie in der Möbelmanufaktur und bei externen Designaufträgen. Oft jedoch setzen Budget oder Geschmack der Kunden kreative Grenzen. Gerade deshalb war es für Treutlein eine große Freude, in seiner Heimatstadt Meerbusch sein ganz persönliches Traumhaus gestalten zu können. Er hat dabei aus dem Vollen geschöpft: vom individuellen Neubau auf alten Grundmauern über die perfekte Gartenanlage bis zum ästhetisch-harmonischen Interieur auf höchstem Niveau.

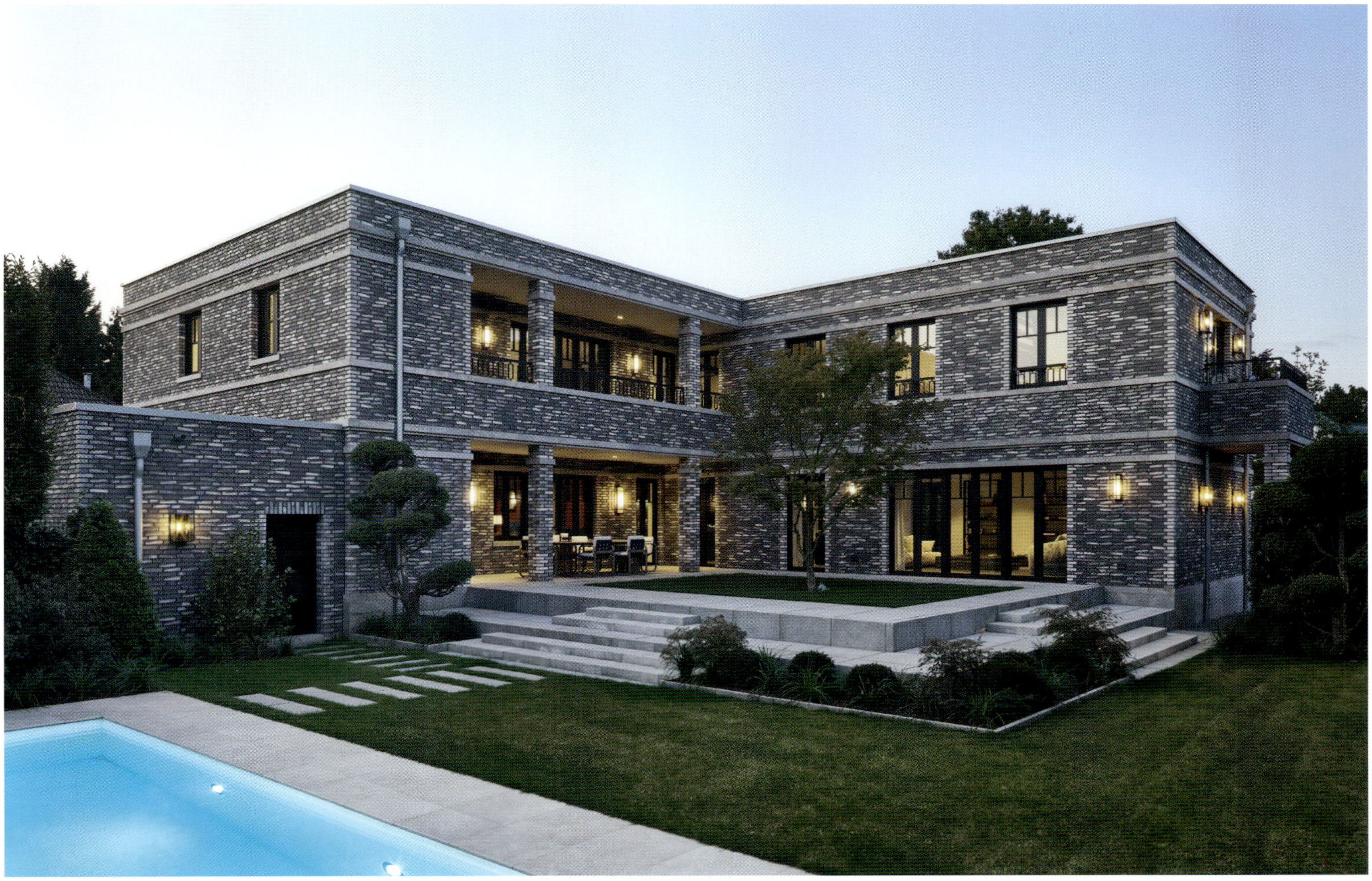

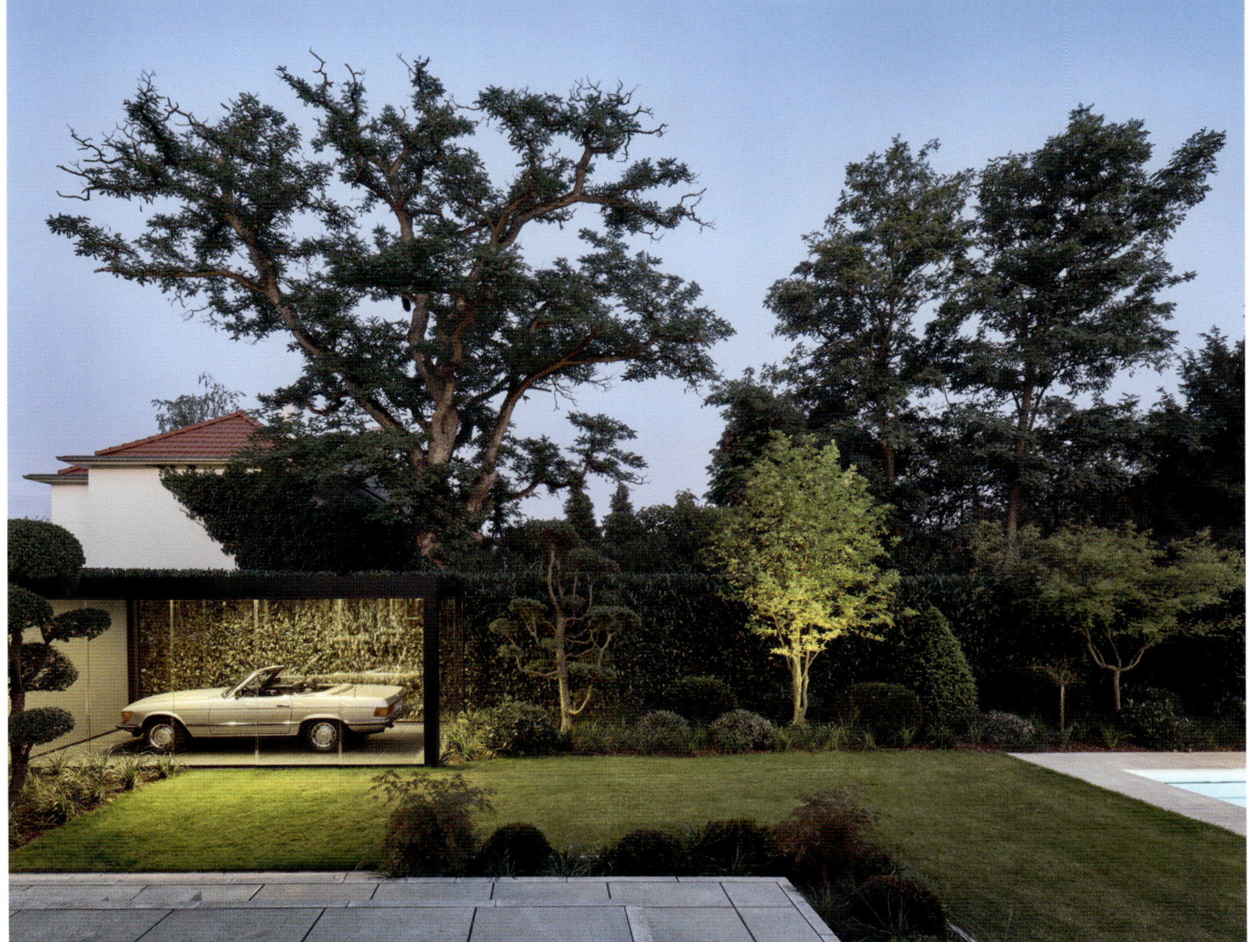

Entrance porch: the polished stainless-steel lamps with their rectilinear design were made at Dornow Masterpieces (opposite page). On the façade, iridescent tiles were fitted in a precise sequence (above). The garden was designed by Ullrich Wantikow – particularly eye-catching is the illumination of the owner's vintage car in a glass cube (left).

Hausportal: Die geradlinigen Lampen aus poliertem Edelstahl wurden bei Dornow Masterpieces gefertigt (Seite gegenüber). In der Fassade wurden changierende Ziegel präzise verbaut (oben). Der Garten wurde von Ullrich Wantikow gestaltet. Besonderer Hingucker: In einem Glaskubus wird der Oldtimer des Hausherrn effektvoll angestrahlt (links).

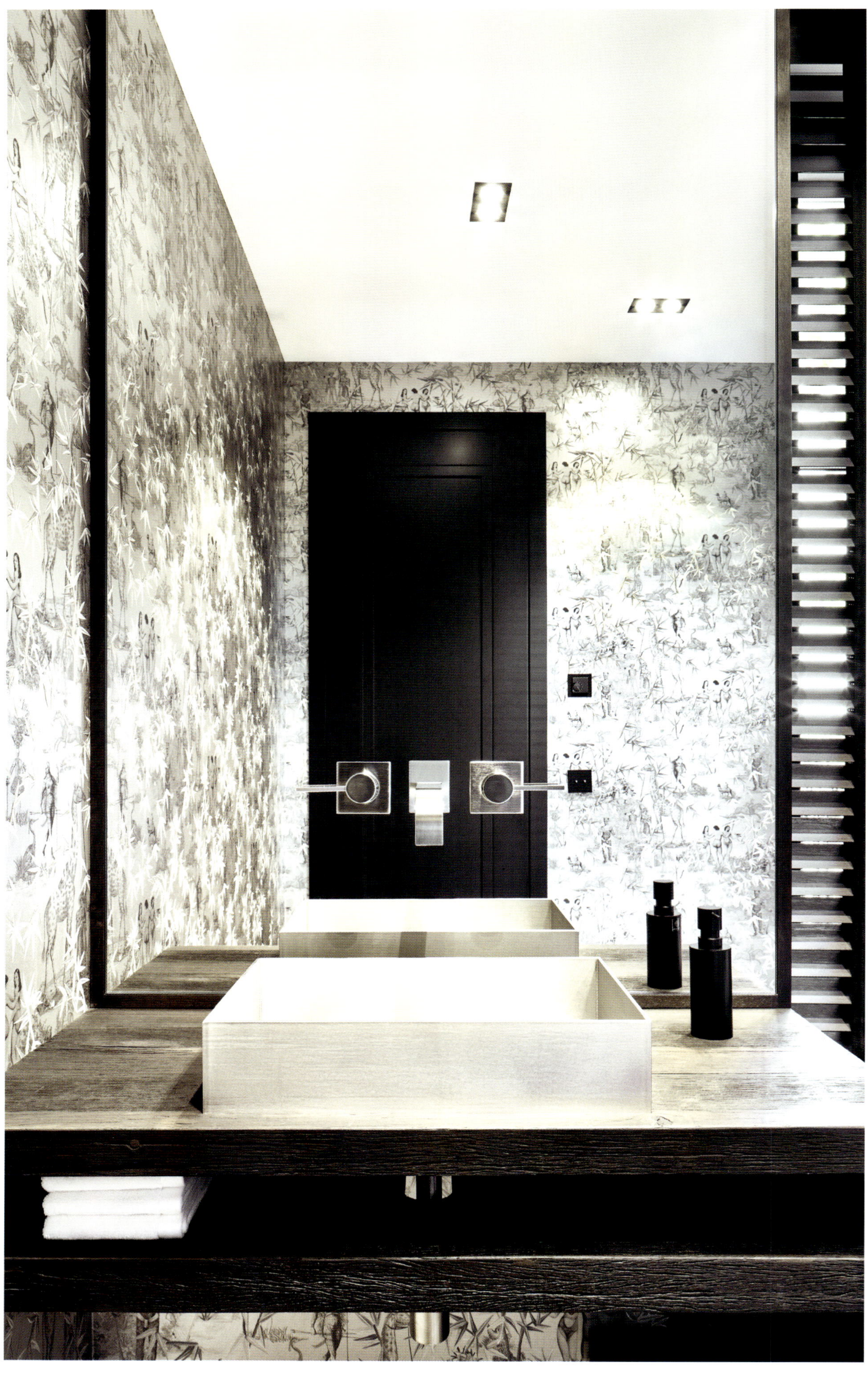

Treutlein has himself designed many of the features in the 380 square-meter living space and has had other items manufactured by hand following close consultation: art objects and other one-off items provide the finishing touches to the interior. As Treutlein explains, apart from the televisions, no single item in his dream house is 'off the shelf'. The impact of a specially harmonized lighting concept in combination with stylishly designed materials is of course also reflected in the house's bathrooms.

Vieles auf den 380 Quadratmetern Wohnfläche hat Treutlein selbst designt, weiteres in enger Abstimmung von Hand anfertigen lassen und das Interieur schließlich mit Kunstobjekten und Unikaten ergänzt. Abgesehen von den Fernsehgeräten, so erklärt Treutlein, ist kein Gegenstand in seinem Traumhaus „von der Stange". Was speziell abgestimmtes Lichtdesign im Zusammenspiel mit edel designten Materialien bewirken kann, zeigt sich natürlich auch in den Badezimmern des Hauses.

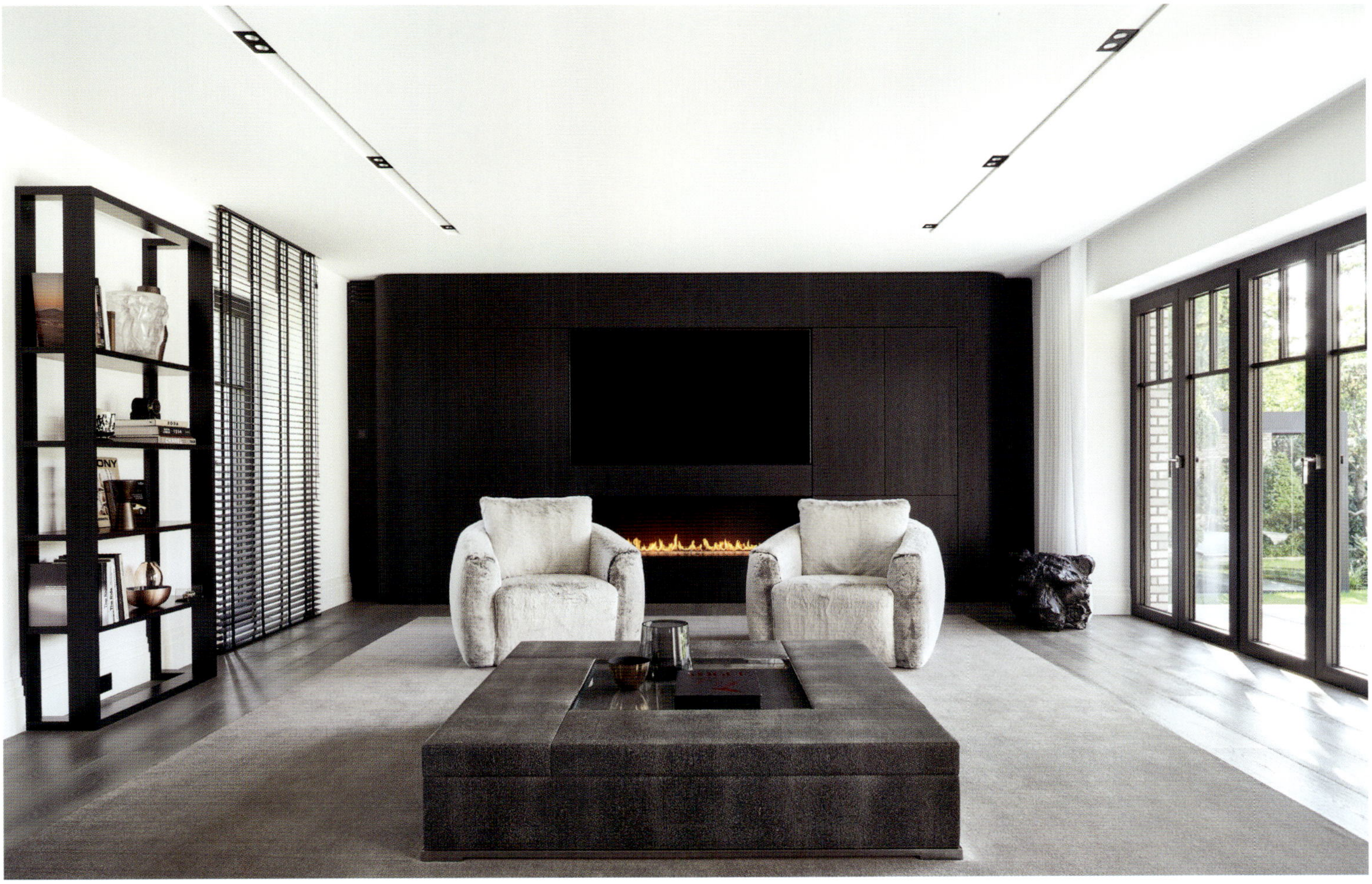

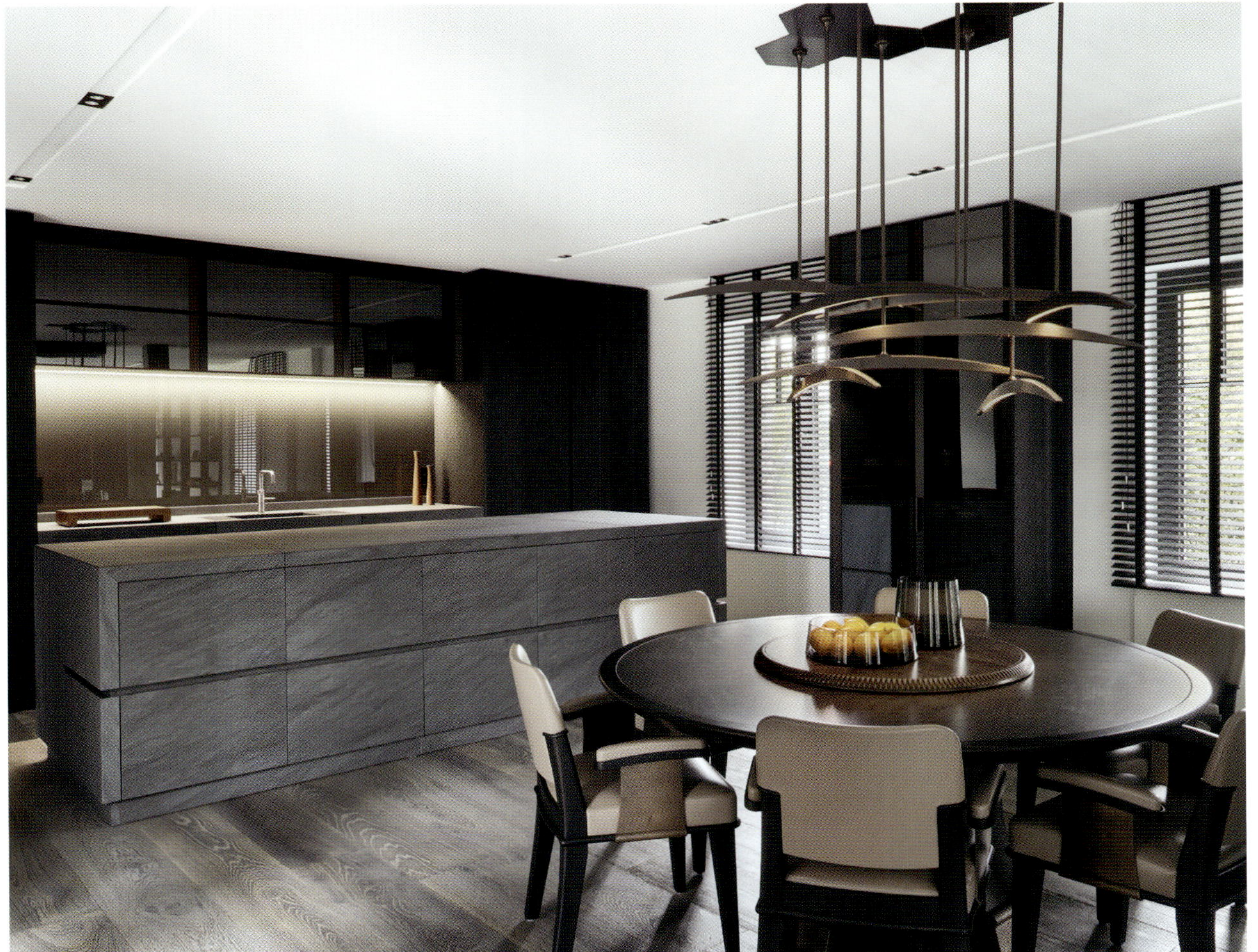

Family meeting point: the fireplace, TV, and bar are integrated in the black oak wall of the large living room (above), which transitions seamlessly into the dining area (left). The work surface of the ingenious slate-gray kitchen island, which conceals hobs and a second sink, can be moved and converted into a cozy breakfast bar.

Der große Wohnraum ist Familientreffpunkt: In der schwarzen Eichenholzwand stecken Kamin, TV und Bar (oben). Nahtlos ist der Übergang zum Essbereich (links). Die Arbeitsplatte des raffinierten schiefergrauen Küchenblocks, unter der sich Kochfelder und eine zweite Spüle verbergen, lässt sich in den Raum verschieben, sodass eine gemütliche Sitztheke entsteht.

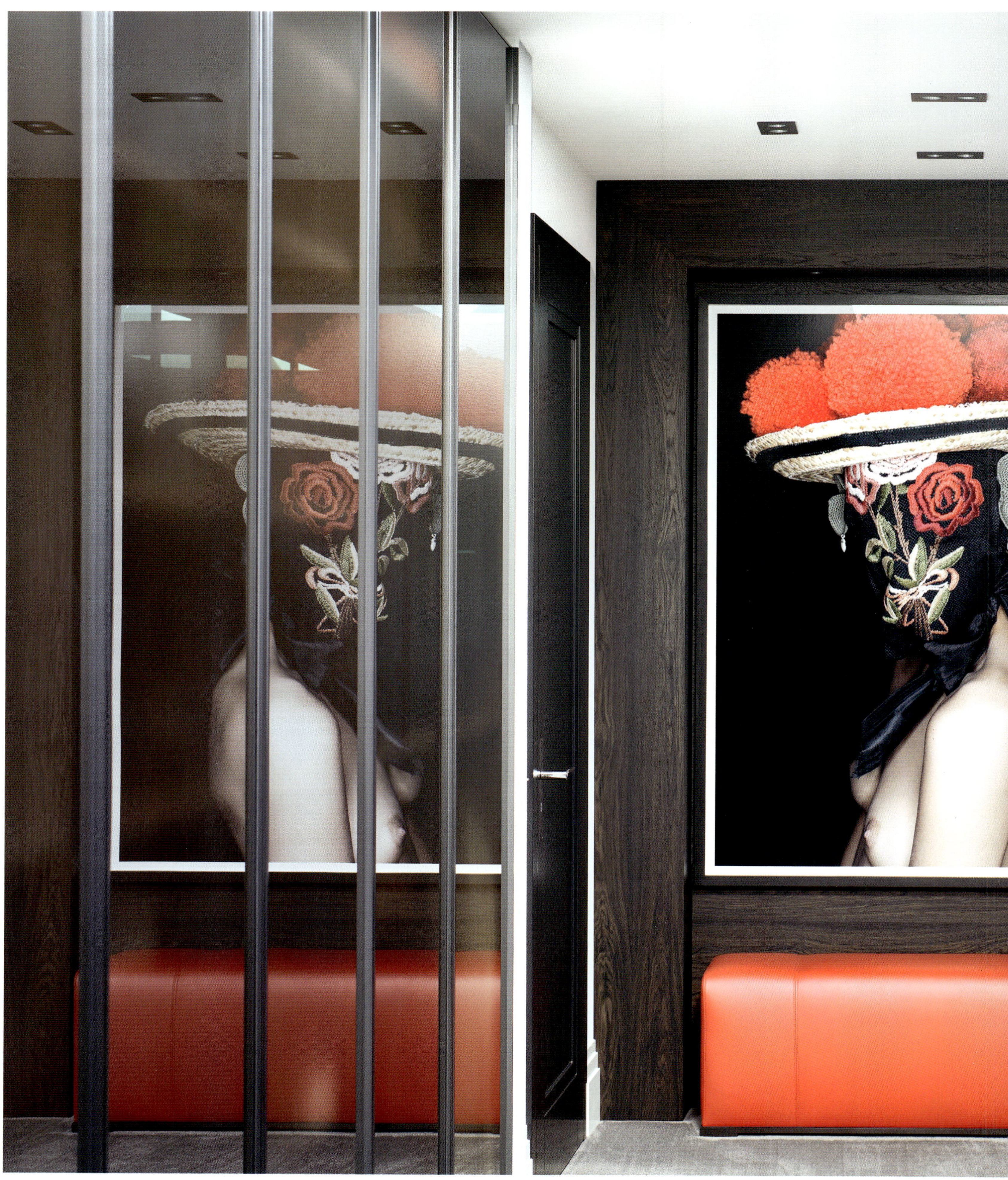

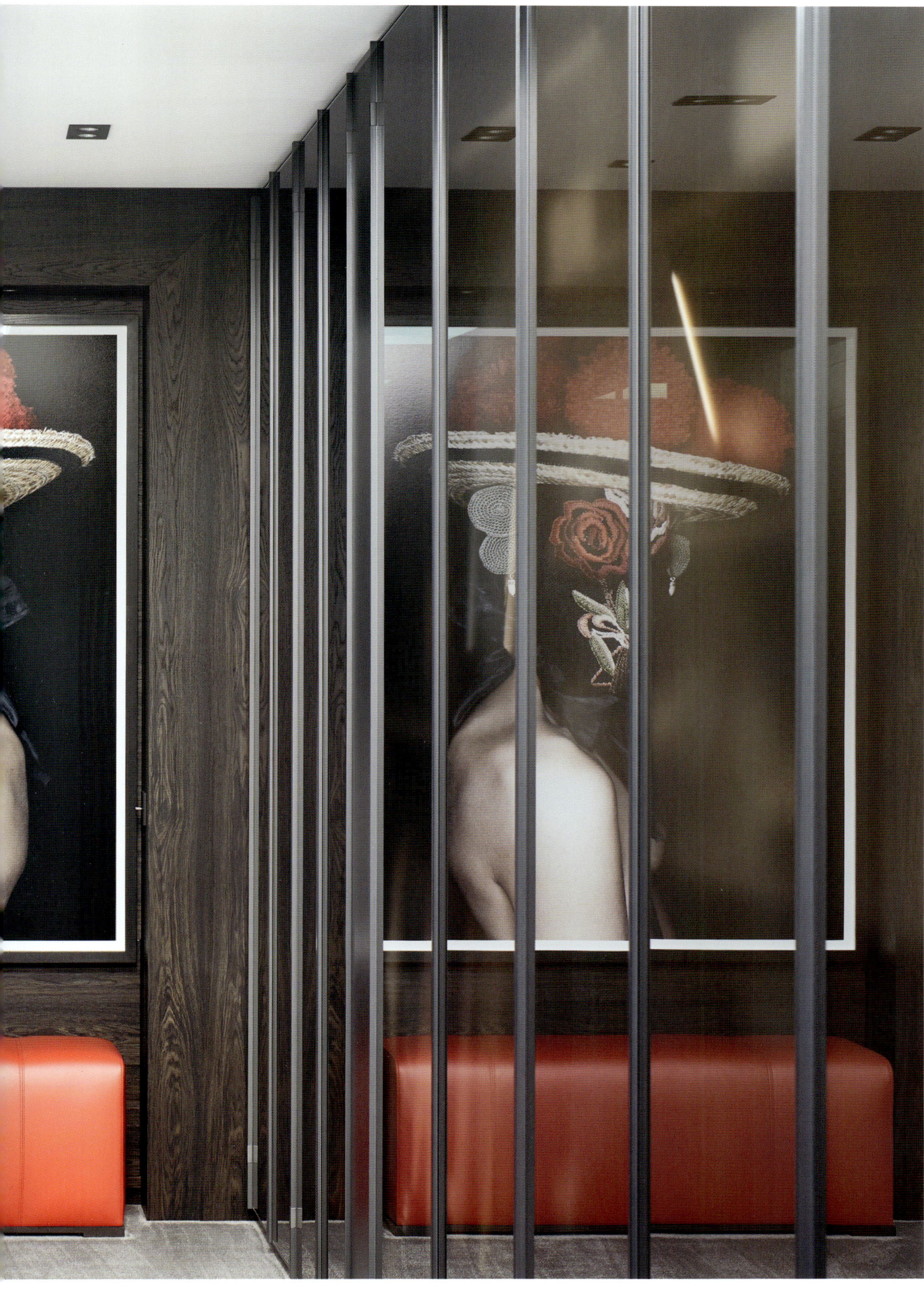

Every piece of furniture, every lamp, almost every object in this unique villa is a one-off that was custom-made for Treutlein's dream house. The works of art were also, of course, commissioned individually for the owner, with careful consideration also given to their placement within the house. The painting hanging directly above the red upholstered couch is the 'Schwarzwaldmädel', or 'Black Forest Girl', by the artist Armin Morbach.

Jedes Möbel, jede Lampe, so gut wie jedes Objekt in dieser einzigartigen Villa ist ein Unikat, das speziell für Treutleins Traumhaus erschaffen wurde. Natürlich sind auch die Kunstwerke individuell für den Hausherrn erstellte Auftragsarbeiten, so wie auch der Ort, an dem das Werk im Haus positioniert wird, stets sorgfältig überlegt ist. Das direkt über der rot gepolsterten Sitzbank platzierte Gemälde ist das „Schwarzwaldmädel" des Künstlers Armin Morbach.

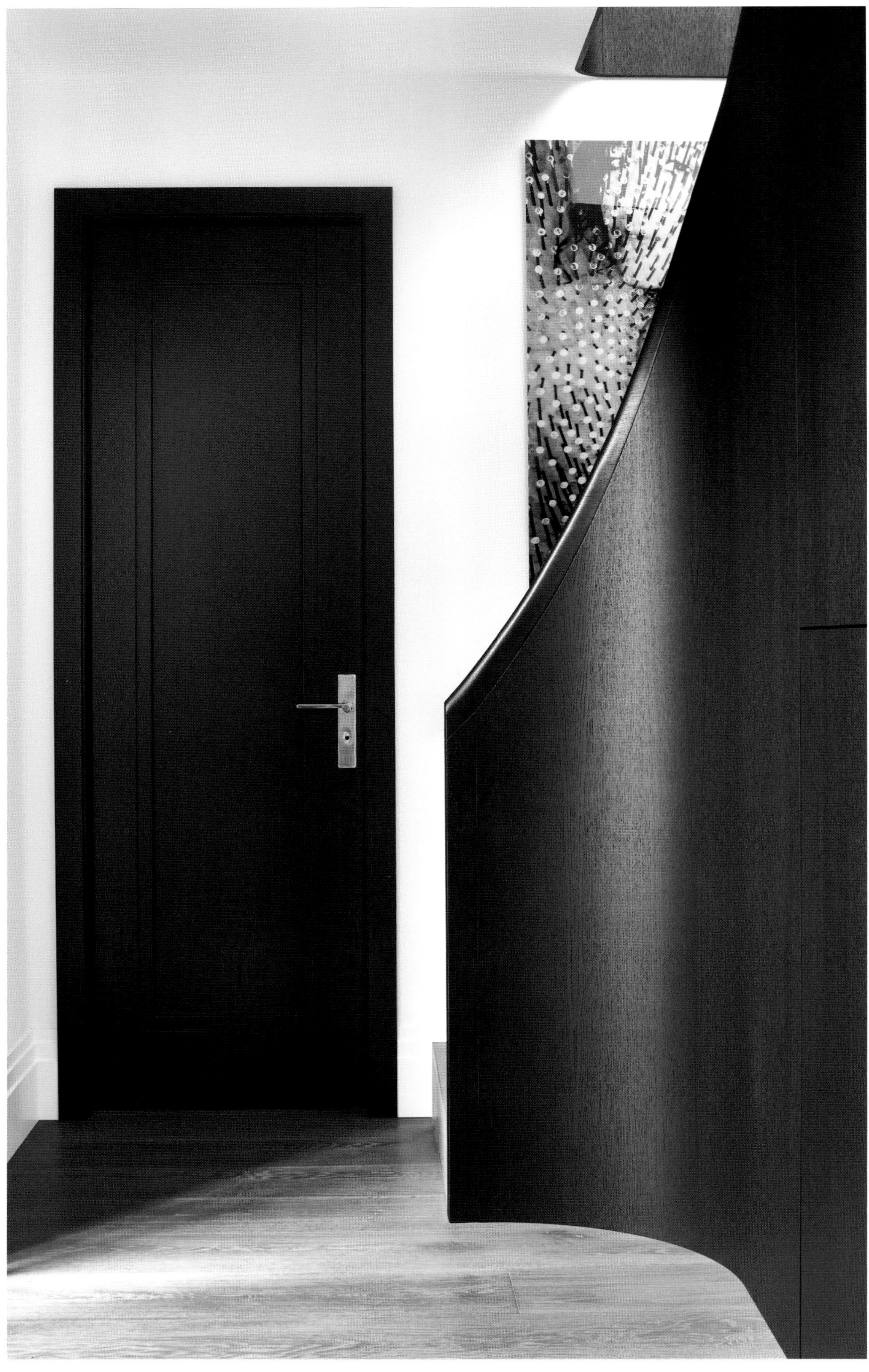

Further, selected art objects, carefully displayed: Partially covered by the curved staircase made of black fumed oak, a 'nail' photograph by Manfred Vogelsänger (left). The impressive portrait of the rock musician David Bowie, who died in 2016, was painted by Benjamin Rayher, a master student from the Düsseldorf Art Academy (opposite page).

Weitere ausgewählte Kunstobjekte, sorgfältig in Szene gesetzt: Durch den geschwungenen Treppenaufgang aus schwarz geräucherter Eiche hier teilweise verdeckt: eine „Nagel"-Fotografie von Manfred Vogelsänger (links). Das eindrucksvolle Porträt des 2016 verstorbenen Rockmusikers David Bowie stammt von Benjamin Rayher, einem Meisterschüler der Kunstakademie Düsseldorf (Seite gegenüber).

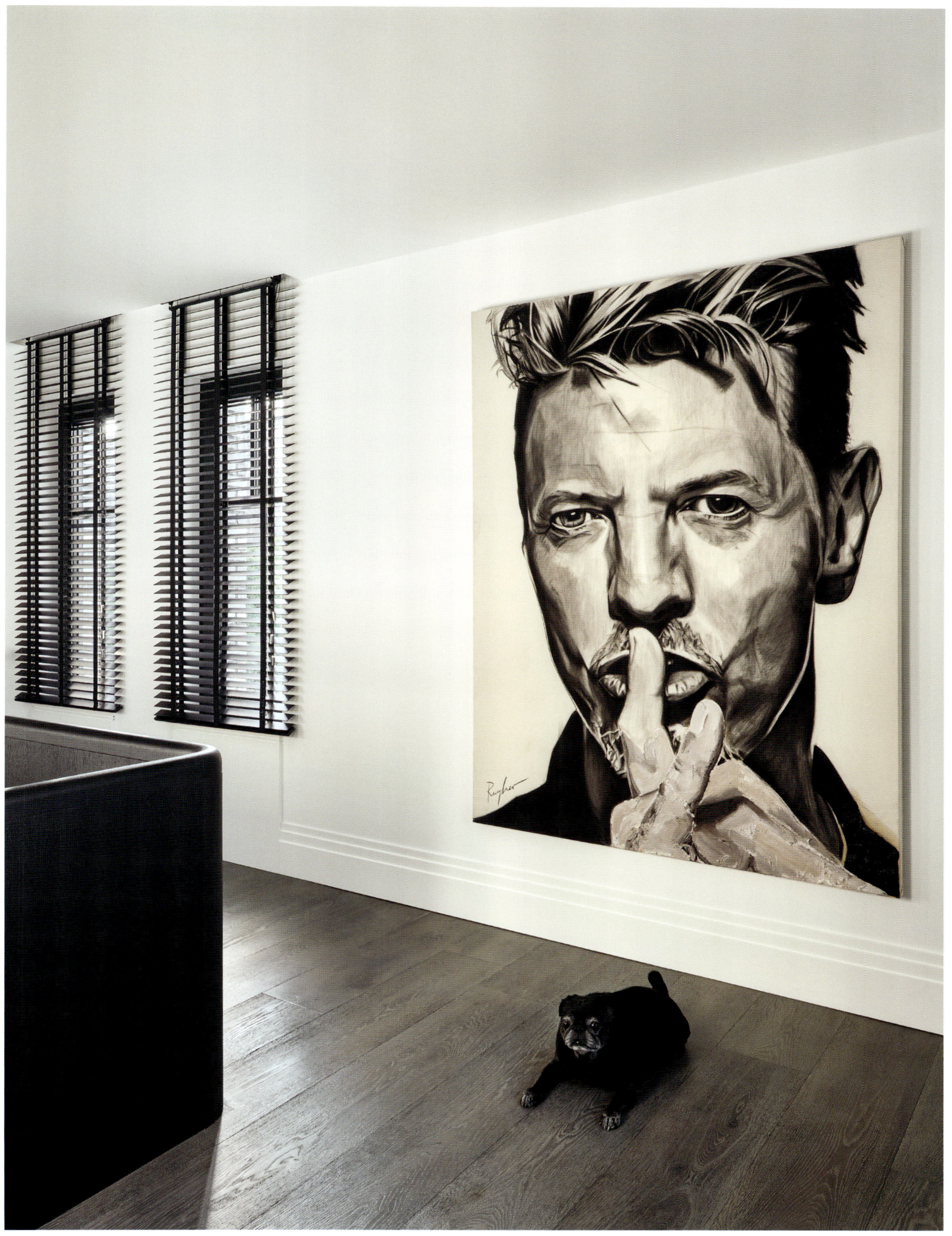

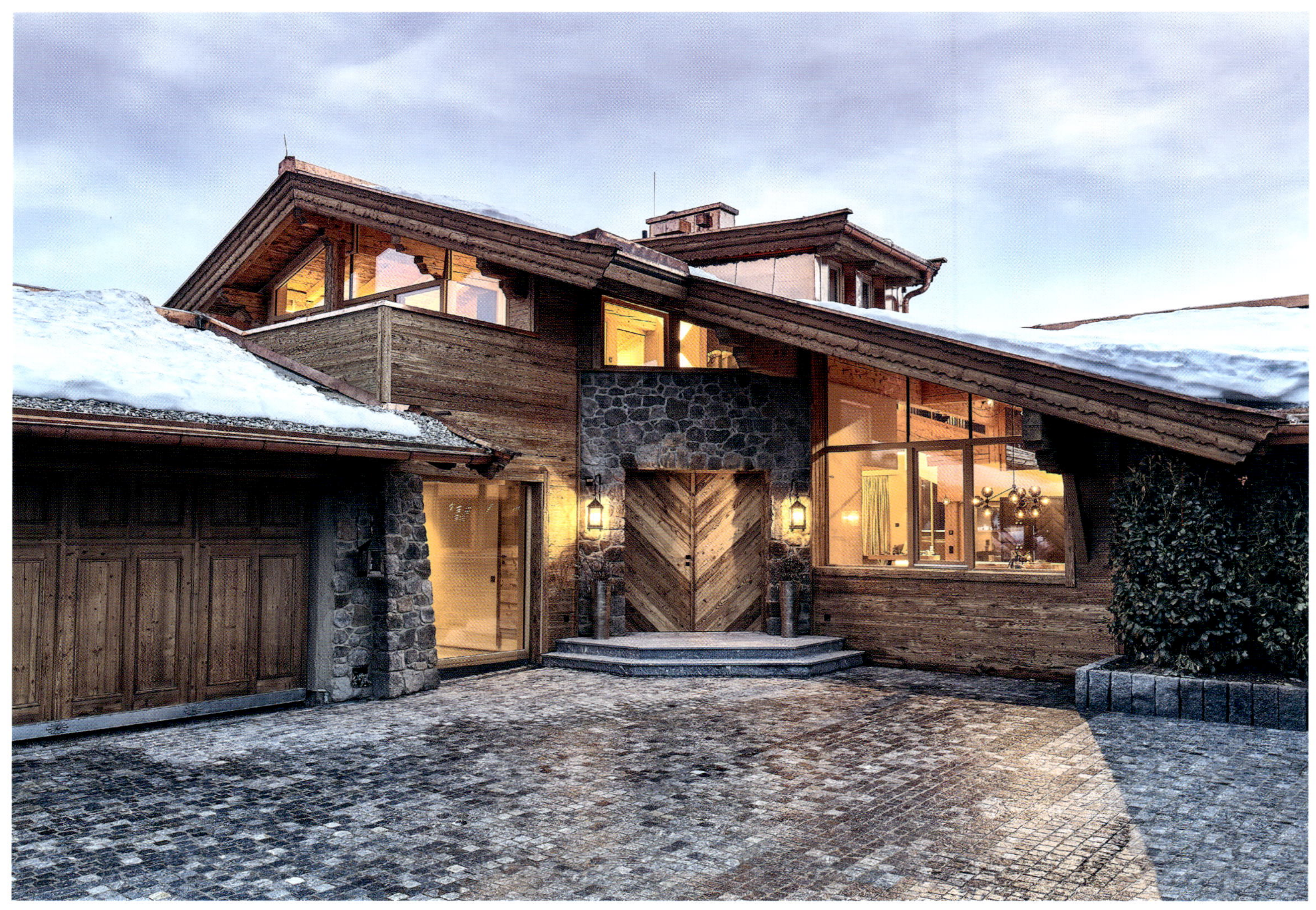

PHILICIMA DESIGN STUDIOS

MUNICH / GERMANY

An intimate and Snug Environment | Geborgenheit und Vertrautheit

The Chalet 1869 is situated in the midst of alpine meadows at the foot of the Wilder Kaiser in Kitzbühel. The villa Bright Blue occupies an imposing location on a cliff on Ibiza's west coast. The two locations could not be more different, yet both of them are unique and full of magic. "Settling in, enjoying a feeling of snugness and familiarity and drawing strength. This is the philosophy we follow when designing our houses," says Philipp Magin, the founder of Philicima Design Studios. From the site's location to its architecture and interior design, from furniture to linen napkins, the Magin siblings design and select each detail individually—always aiming to create a home.

Am Fuß des Wilden Kaisers in Kitzbühel liegt inmitten von Almwiesen das Chalet 1869; auf einer Klippe an Ibizas Westküste thront die Villa Bright Blue – zwei Orte, die unterschiedlicher nicht sein könnten, doch beide einzigartig und voller Magie. „Ankommen, Geborgenheit und Vertrautheit genießen, Kraft schöpfen. Diese Idee leitet uns beim Kreieren unserer Häuser", sagt Philipp Magin, Gründer der Philicima Design Studios. Von der Lage des Grundstücks über die Architektur und das Interior Design, vom Möbelstück bis zur Leinenserviette: Jedes Detail wird von den Magin-Geschwistern individuell konzipiert und ausgewählt – immer mit dem Ziel, ein Zuhause zu schaffen.

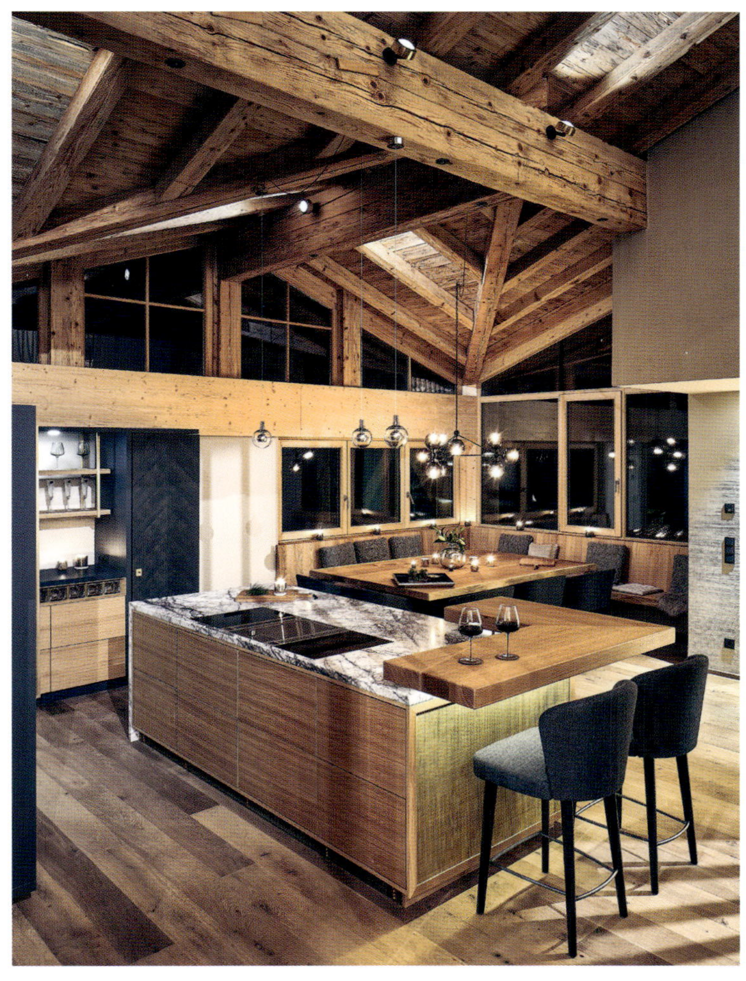

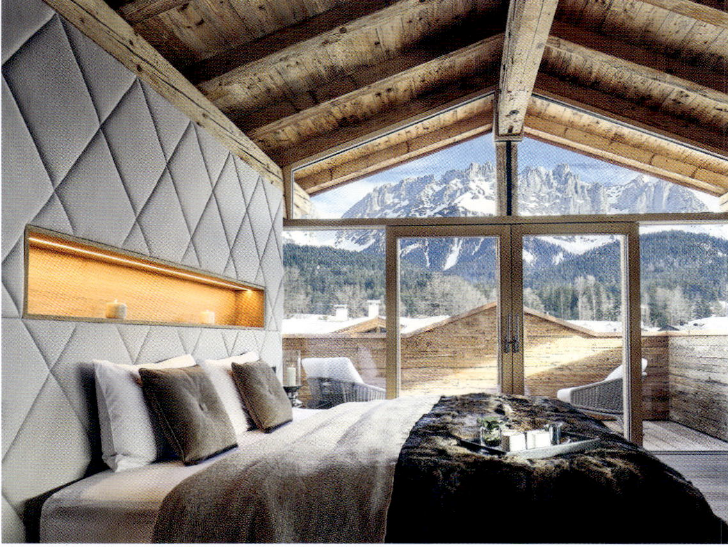

With its large glass façades, the Chalet 1869 is extremely modern, yet still very cozy at the same time. Here the individual seems to be in an amphitheater designed by nature, becoming part of the wonderful alpine world and its magical atmosphere.

Im hochmodernen und gleichzeitig urgemütlichen Chalet 1869 mit seinen großen Glasfronten fühlt man sich wie in einem von der Natur geschaffenen Amphitheater – man wird Teil der traumhaften Bergwelt und ihrer magischen Atmosphäre.

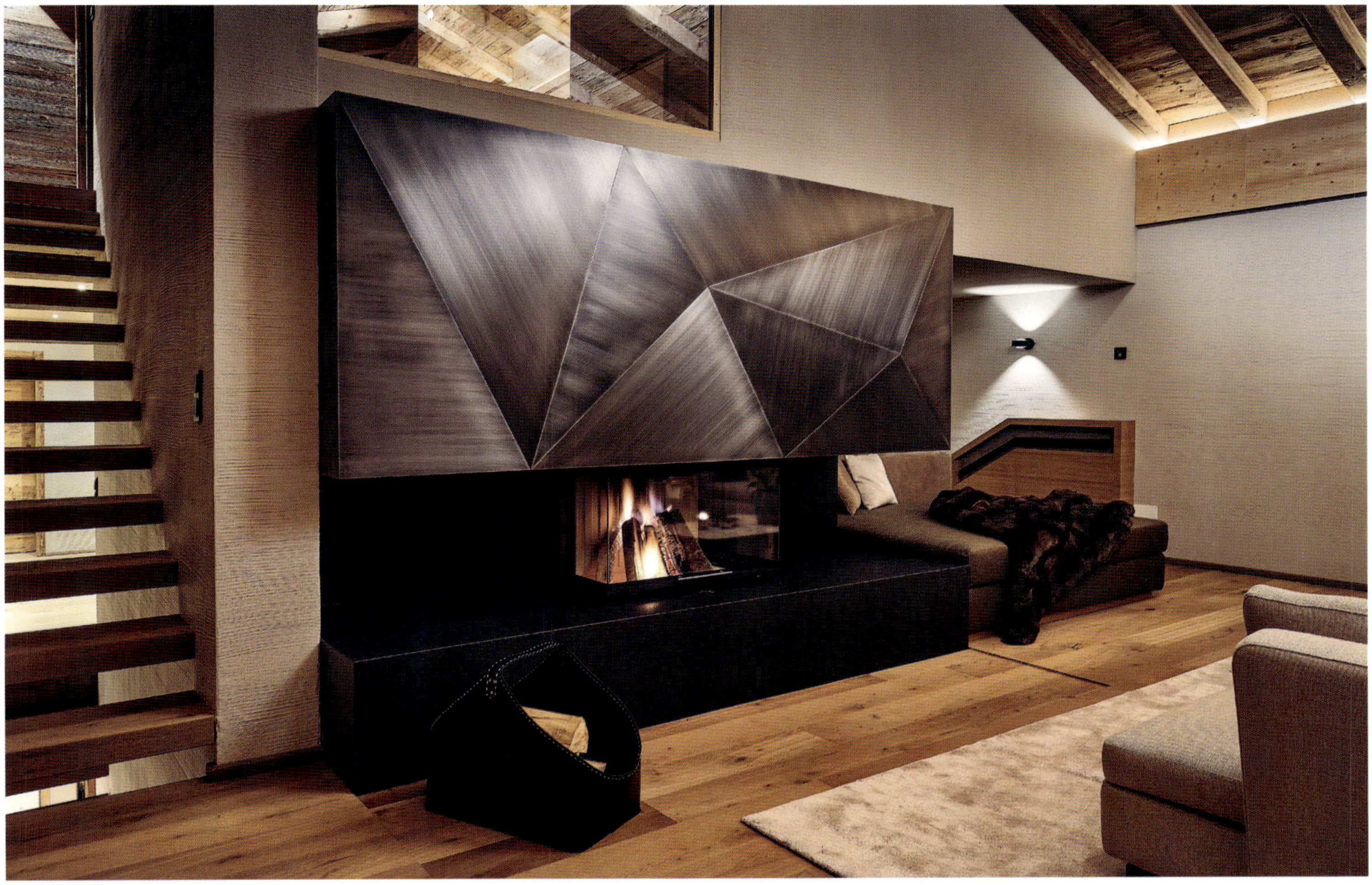

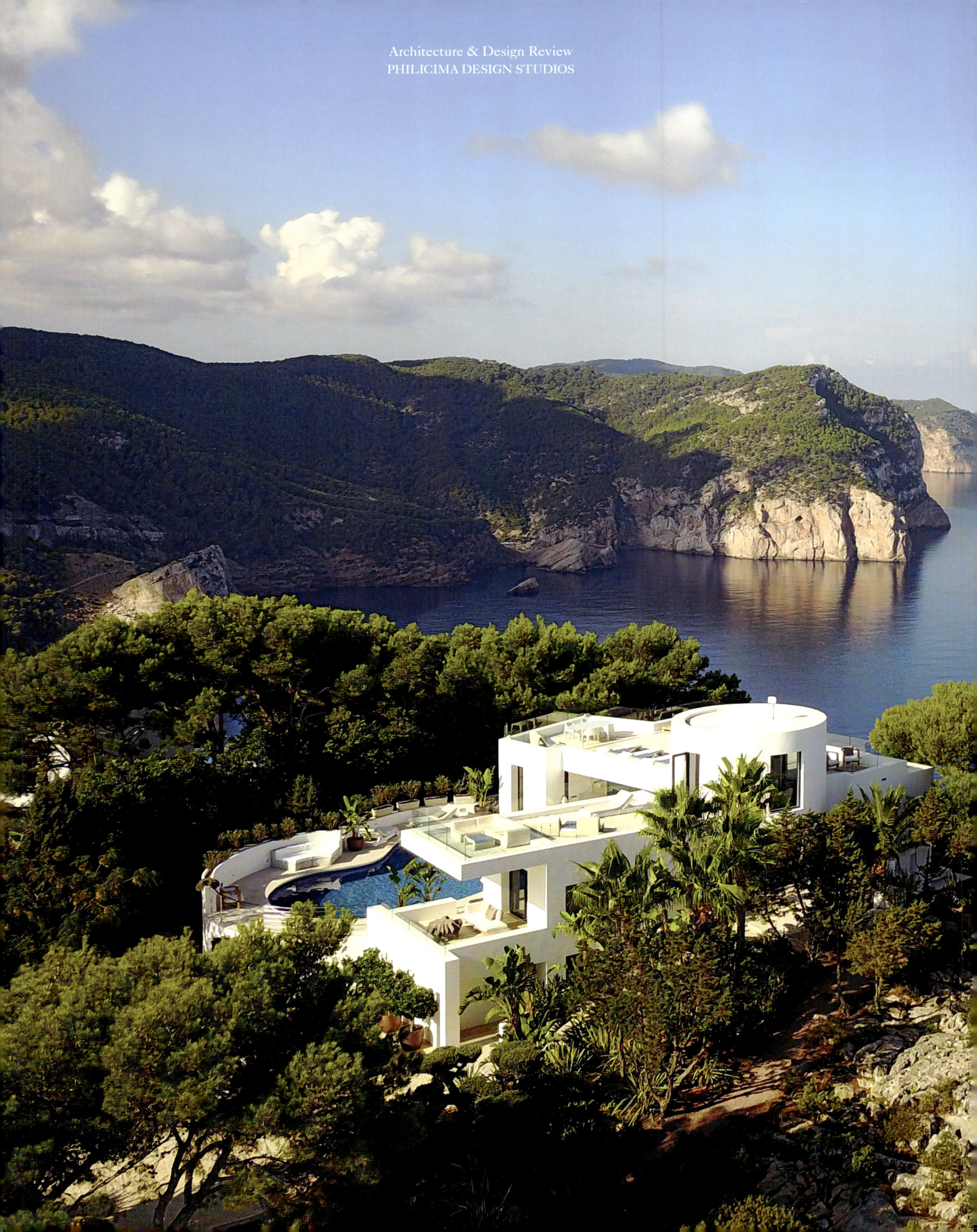
Architecture & Design Review
PHILICIMA DESIGN STUDIOS

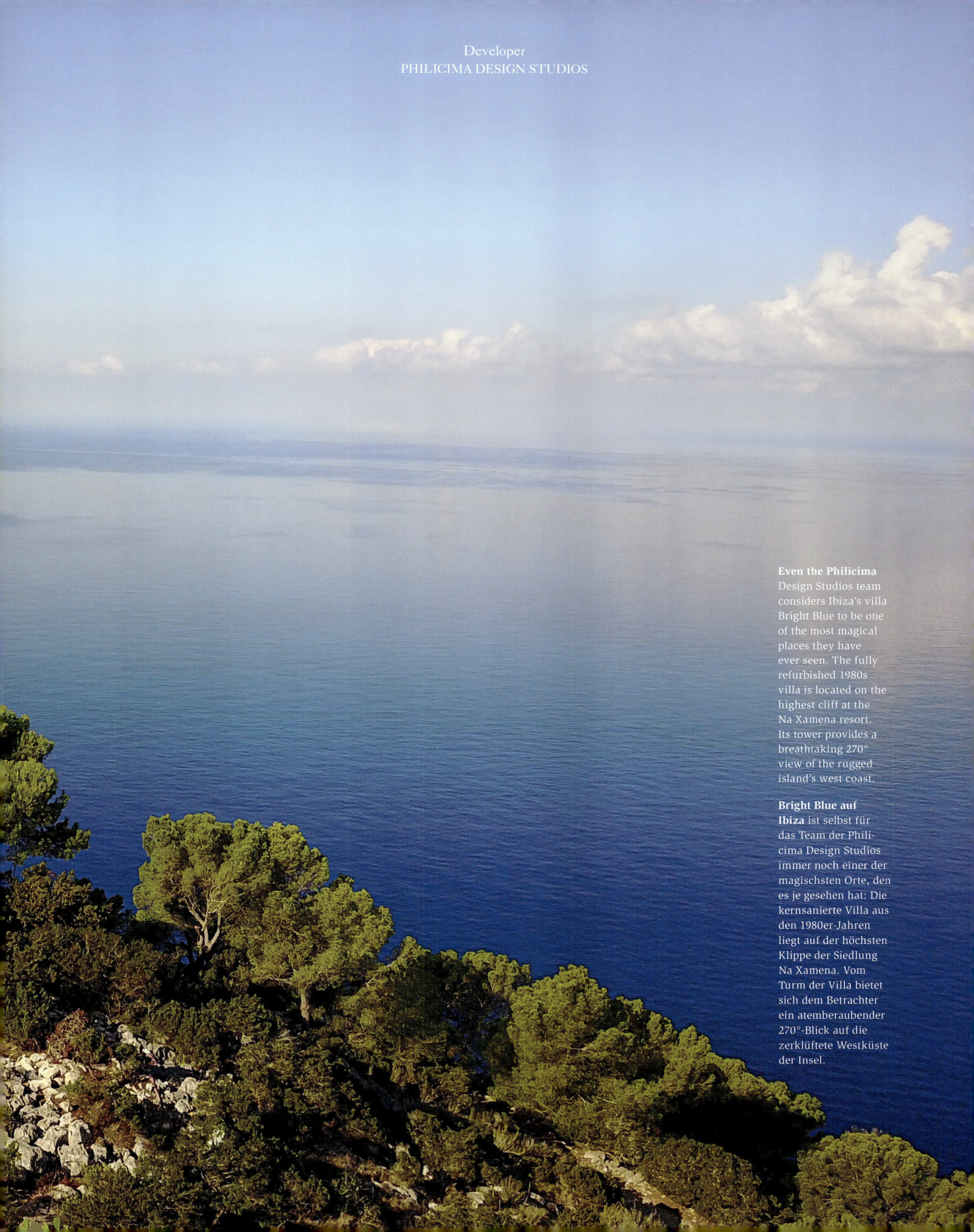

Even the Philicima Design Studios team considers Ibiza's villa Bright Blue to be one of the most magical places they have ever seen. The fully refurbished 1980s villa is located on the highest cliff at the Na Xamena resort. Its tower provides a breathtaking 270° view of the rugged island's west coast.

Bright Blue auf Ibiza ist selbst für das Team der Philicima Design Studios immer noch einer der magischsten Orte, den es je gesehen hat: Die kernsanierte Villa aus den 1980er-Jahren liegt auf der höchsten Klippe der Siedlung Na Xamena. Vom Turm der Villa bietet sich dem Betrachter ein atemberaubender 270°-Blick auf die zerklüftete Westküste der Insel.

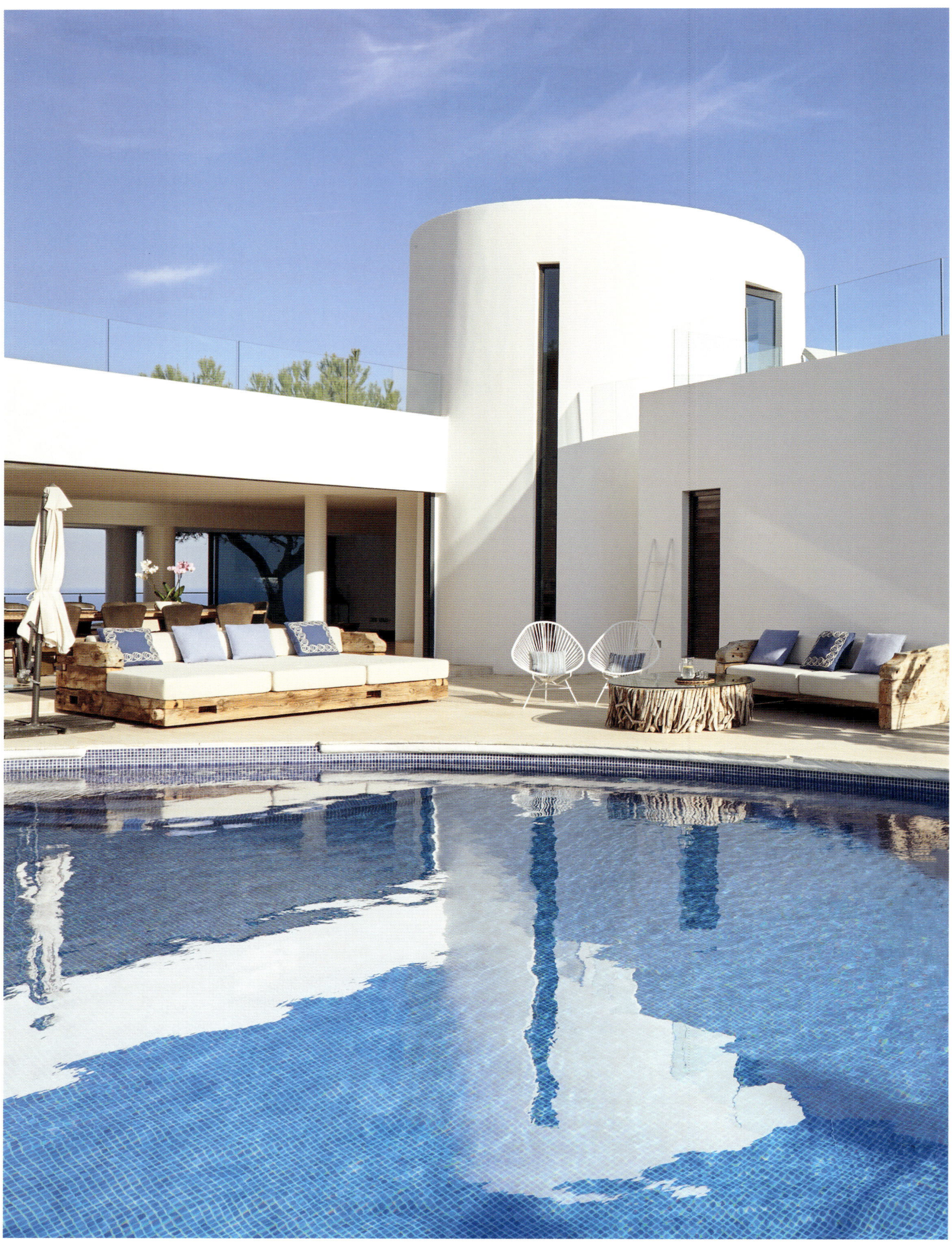

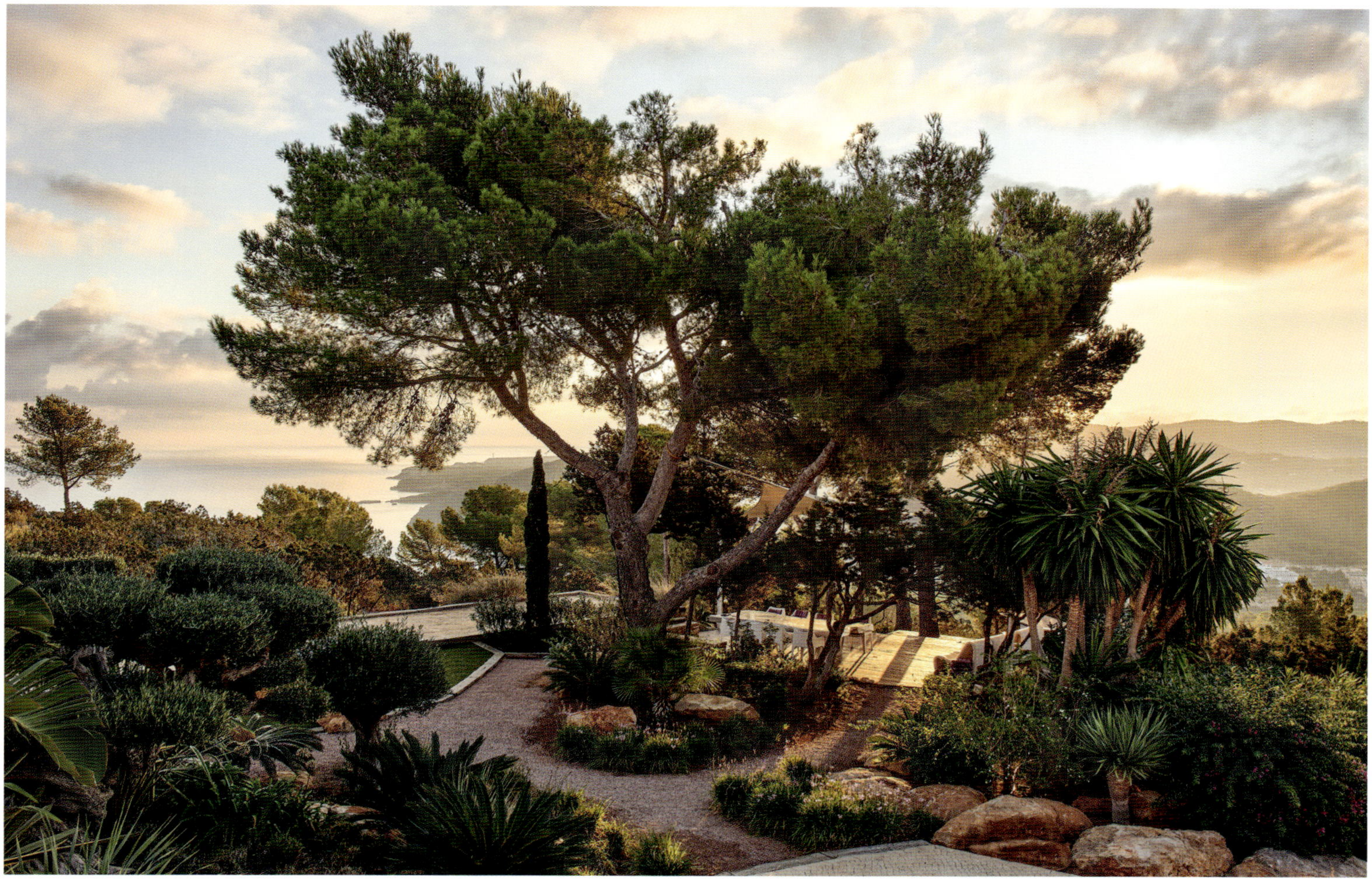

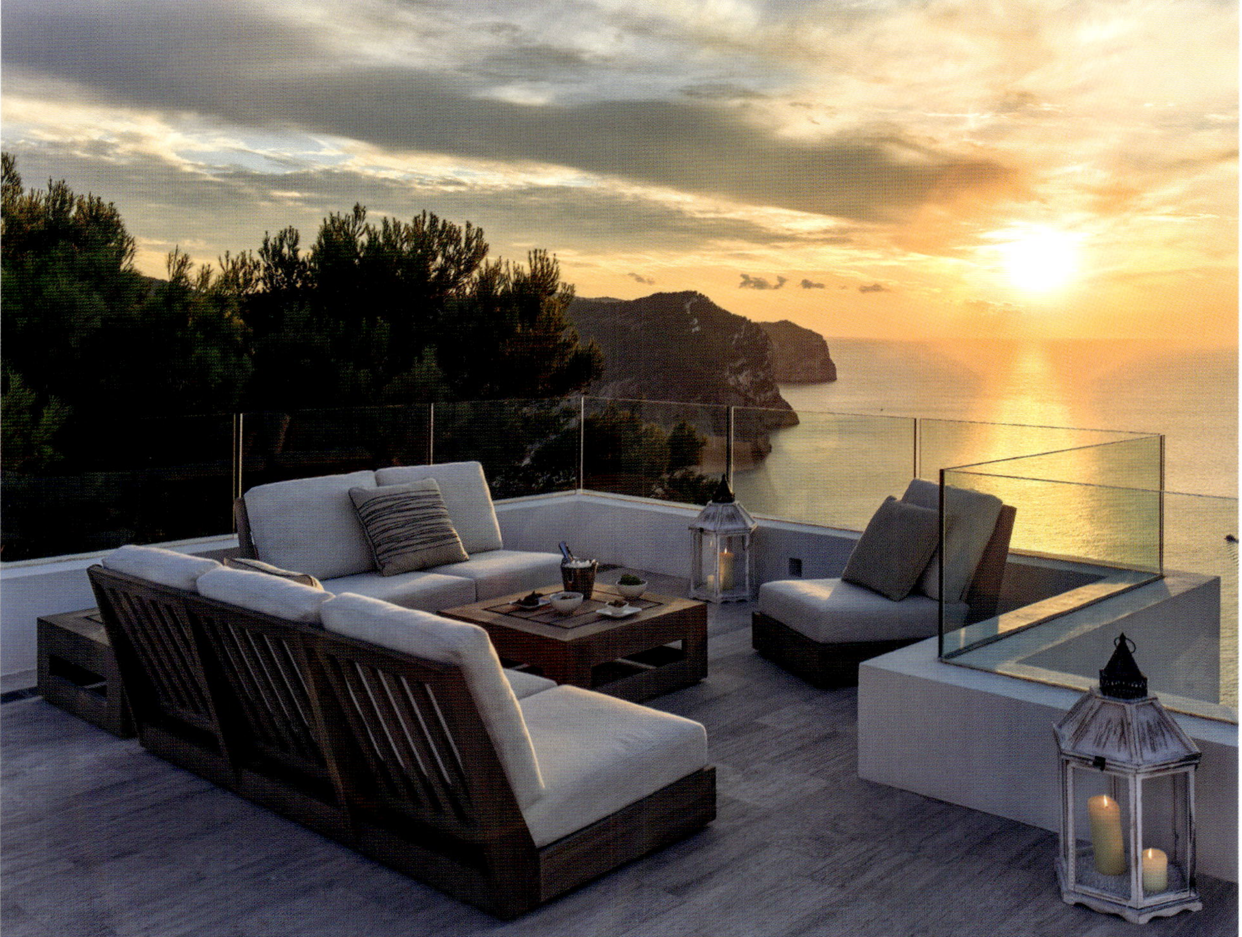

Since 2017, the villa Bright Blue shines in renewed splendor. Purist in its luxury, understated rather than pompous, elegant and close to nature—this is how occupants and visitors alike experience the Philicima Design Studios' interior design. The villa Bright Blue is a unique oasis of peace and harmony.

Seit 2017 erstrahlt die Villa Bright Blue in neuem Glanz. Puristischer Luxus, nicht pompös, sondern zurückhaltend, elegant und naturbelassen – so erleben Bewohner und Besucher hier das Interior Design der Philicima Design Studios. Es macht die Villa Bright Blue zu einer einzigartigen Oase der Harmonie und Ruhe.

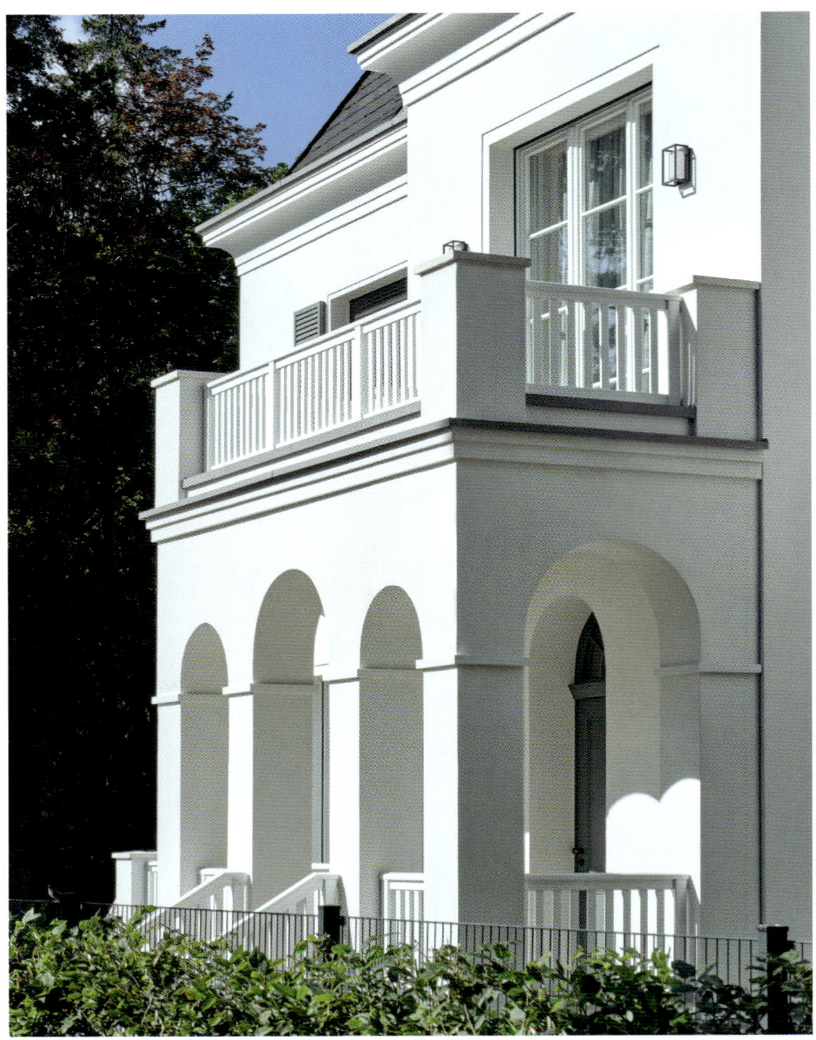

RALF SCHMITZ

BERLIN / GERMANY

Elegant Homes | Elegante Wohnkultur

Classical stylistic details freshly interpreted by prestigious architects and executed by master craftsmen using exclusive materials—these are the hallmarks of RALF SCHMITZ elegant homes. The firm, which was established in 1864, has branches in Kempen, Düsseldorf, Berlin and Hamburg. Its projects include many exquisite, unique items that are custom-made and tailored to the concept of luxurious, newly-built residences. They are created in four locations in desirable residential areas. The striking ensemble presented here of two urban villas in Berlin's Dahlem district are a prime example of green grandeur—a sheen of modernity applied to the *Gründerzeit* style.

Klassische Stildetails, neu interpretiert von renommierten Architekten und mit exklusiven Materialien durch Handwerksmeister umgesetzt – das sind Markenzeichen der eleganten Wohnkultur von RALF SCHMITZ. Das 1864 gegründete Unternehmen hat Niederlassungen in Kempen, Düsseldorf, Berlin und Hamburg. Für seine Projekte werden viele Elemente als erlesene Unikate maßgefertigt und individuell auf das Konzept der luxuriösen Neubaudomizile zugeschnitten. Sie entstehen an vier Standorten in begehrten Wohnlagen. Das hier abgebildete markante Ensemble zweier Stadtvillen in Berlin-Dahlem steht exemplarisch für Grandezza im Grünen – Gründerzeit in modernem Glanz!

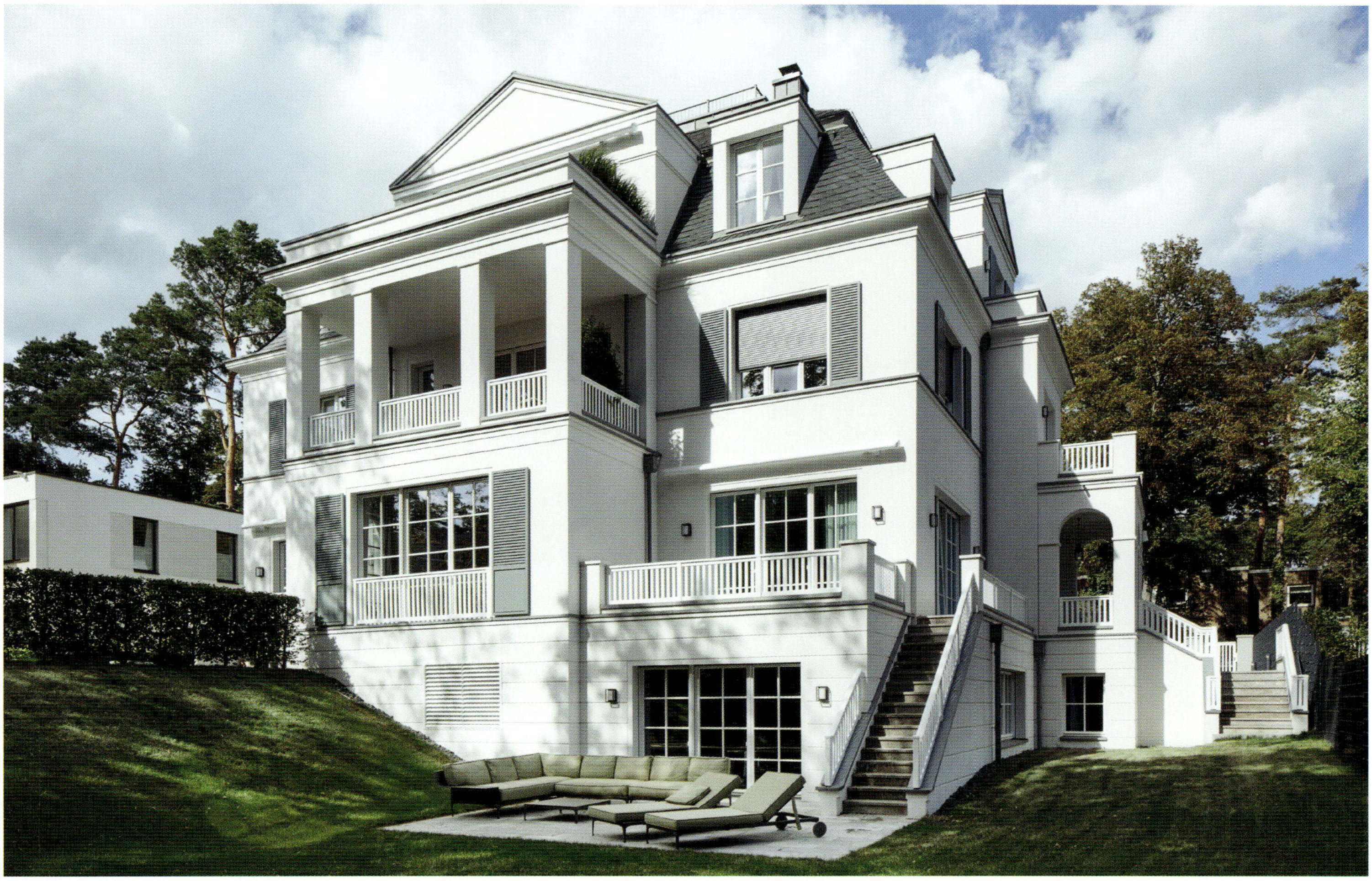

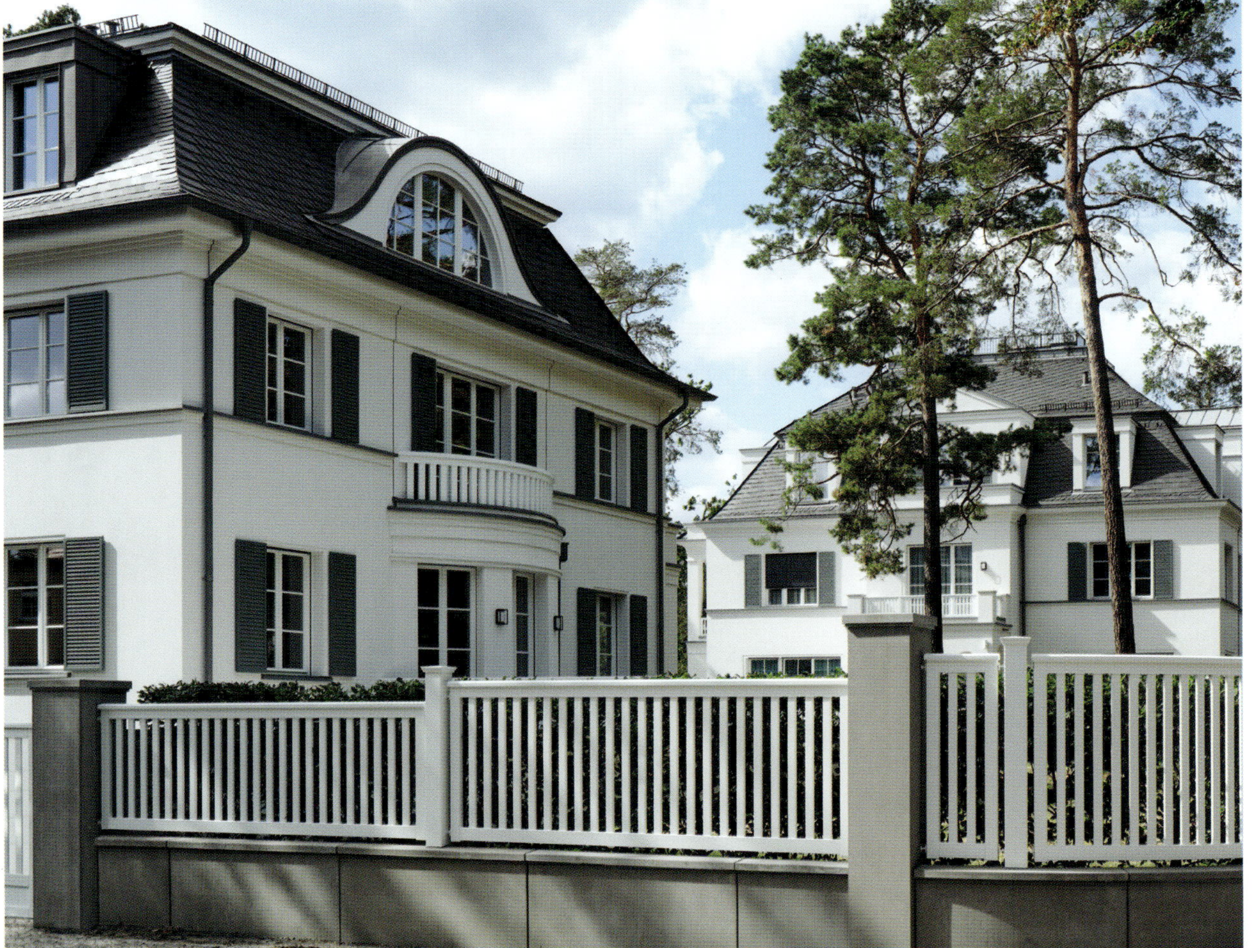

Beautiful Berlin sisters: the 'Dahlem Duo' ensemble consists of a villa with two separate representative homes and four individually designed apartments in the house next door. The garden floor with terrace is particularly charming. Traditional features such as shutters, arches and lattice windows are emblematic of RALF SCHMITZ projects.

Schöne Berliner Schwestern: Das Ensemble „Dahlem Duo" besteht aus einer Villa mit zwei repräsentativen Einheiten sowie vier individuell geschnittenen Wohnungen im Haus nebenan. Besonders charmant: das Gartengeschoss mit Terrasse. Traditionsdetails wie Fensterläden, Rundbögen und Sprossenfenster sind typisch für Projekte von RALF SCHMITZ.

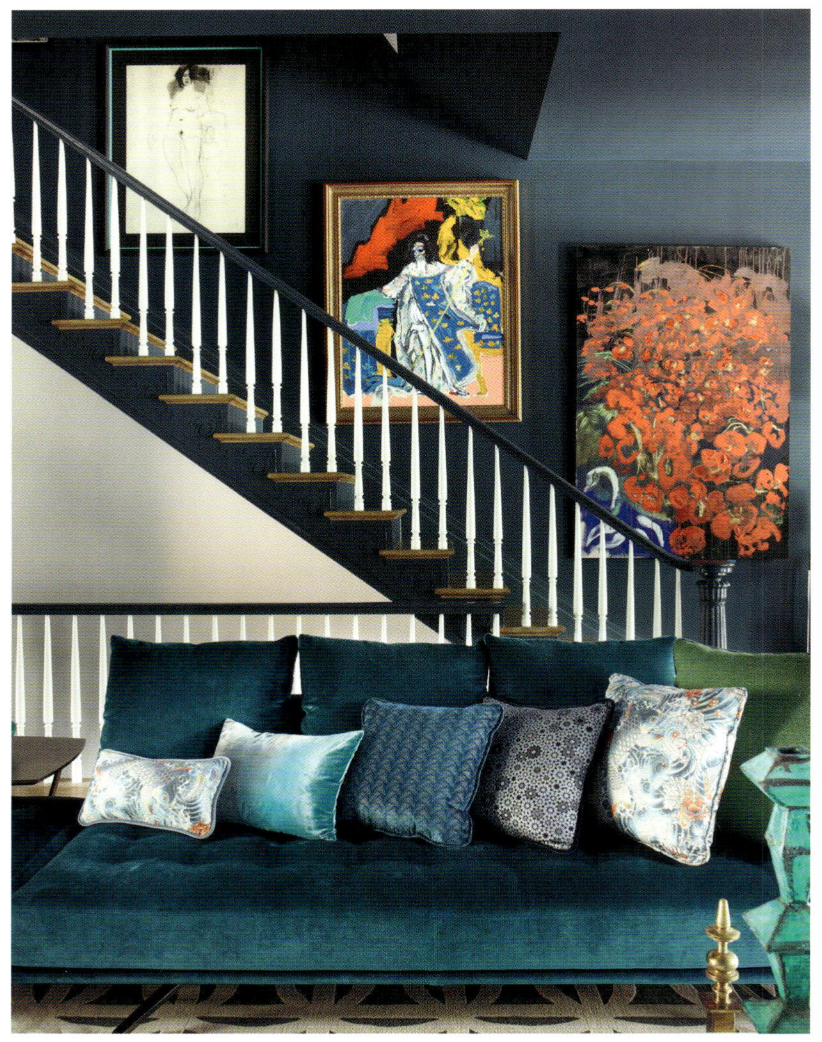

REBEKAH CAUDWELL DESIGN

NEW YORK / USA

Exciting Esthetics | Aufregende Ästhetik

Creating intimate, warm and expressive homes is always the aim of designer Rebekah Caudwell. Describing herself as a 'maximalist', she has, in recent years, executed numerous interesting projects in the United States, the United Kingdom and France. Caudwell established her residential design firm in 2009 with her husband, Nicolas Dupart, coming on-board as Managing Director in 2012. Not averse to taking risks, the company is a byword for bold, exciting aesthetics and has particular strengths in both color and patterns. The property presented here is located in New York City.

Persönliche, warme und ausdrucksstarke Häuser zu gestalten ist stets das Ziel der Designerin Rebekah Caudwell. Sie bezeichnet sich selbst gern als „Maximalistin" und konnte in den vergangenen Jahren zahlreiche interessante Projekte in den Vereinigten Staaten, Großbritannien und Frankreich umsetzen. Caudwell hat ihr Büro für Wohndesign 2009 gegründet; im Jahr 2012 stieg dann ihr Ehemann Nicolas Dupart als Managing Director bei Rebekah Caudwell Design ein. Das Unternehmen steht für kühne, aufregende Ästhetik, scheut keine Risiken und zeigt eine besondere Stärke bei Farben und Mustern. Das hier abgebildete Objekt befindet sich in New York City.

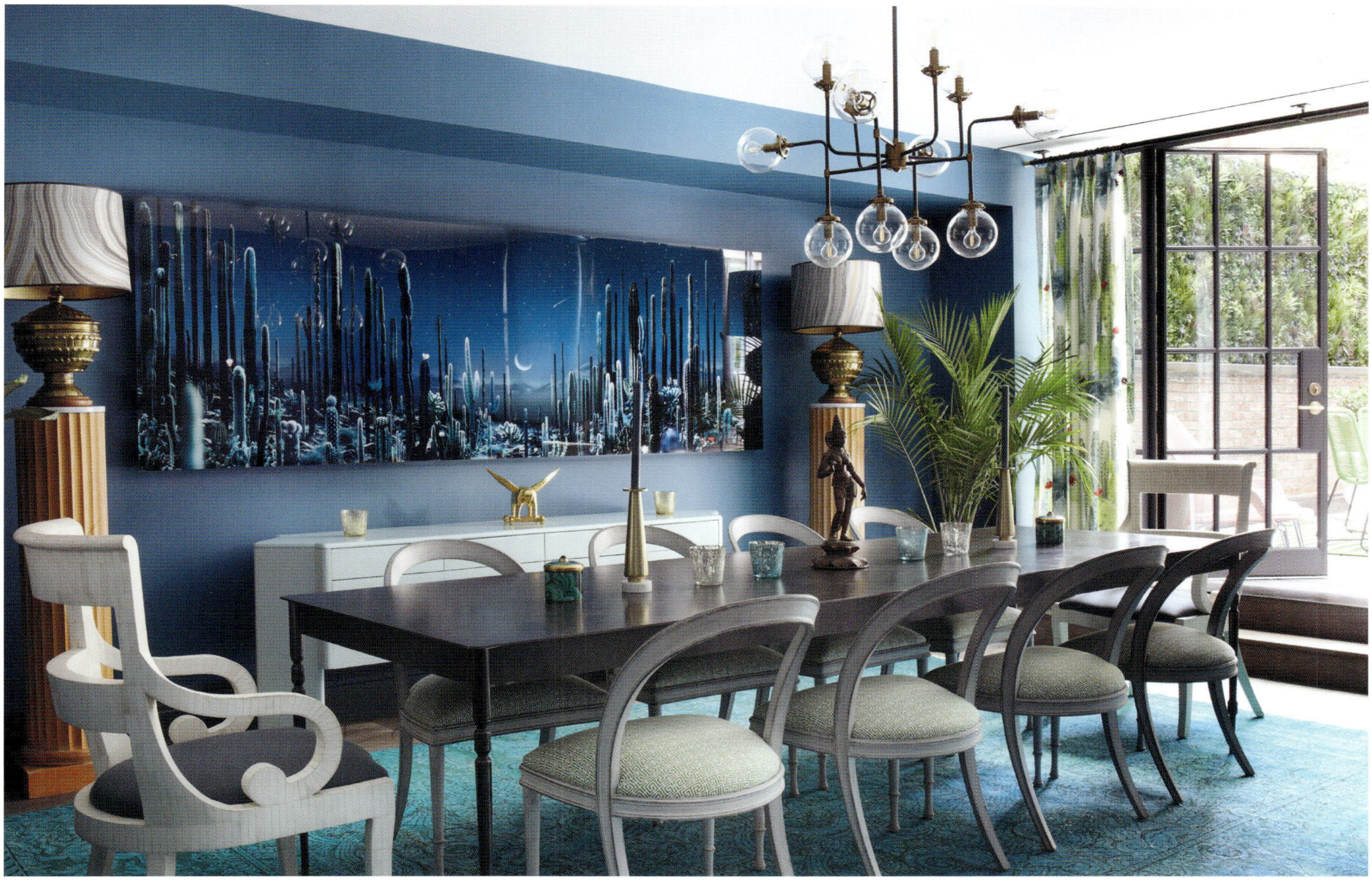

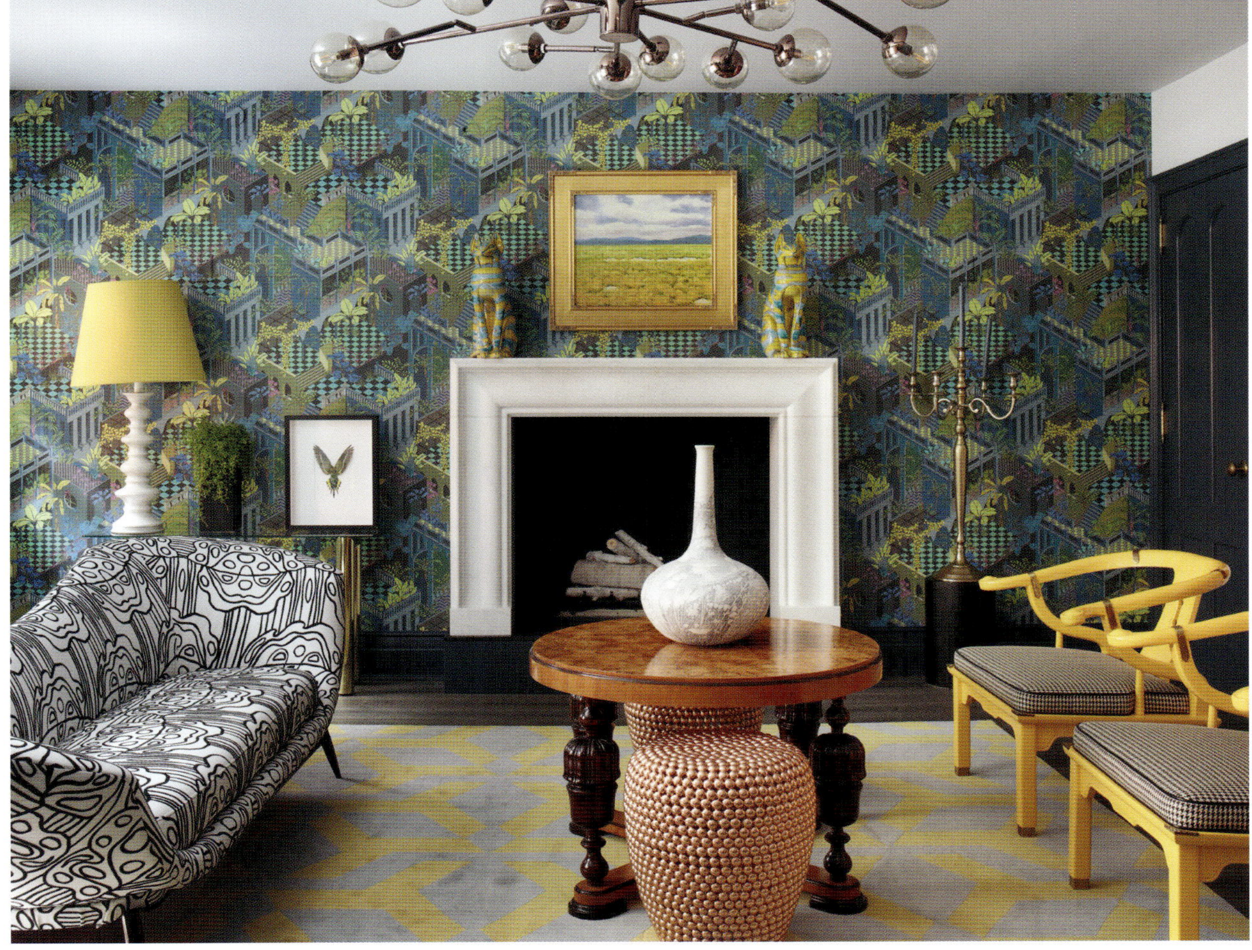

Punchy patterns, vibrant colors and a bold approach to design have completely transformed this New York townhouse: stairway (opposite page), dining room (above) and lounge with fireplace (left). The historical building's original charm was nevertheless maintained.

Ausdrucksstarke Muster, lebhafte Farben und ein mutiger Designansatz haben das New Yorker Stadthaus in etwas wirklich Neues verwandelt: Treppenhaus (Seite gegenüber), Esszimmer (oben) und Kaminzimmer (links). Dennoch wurde der ursprüngliche Charme dieses historischen Gebäudes erhalten.

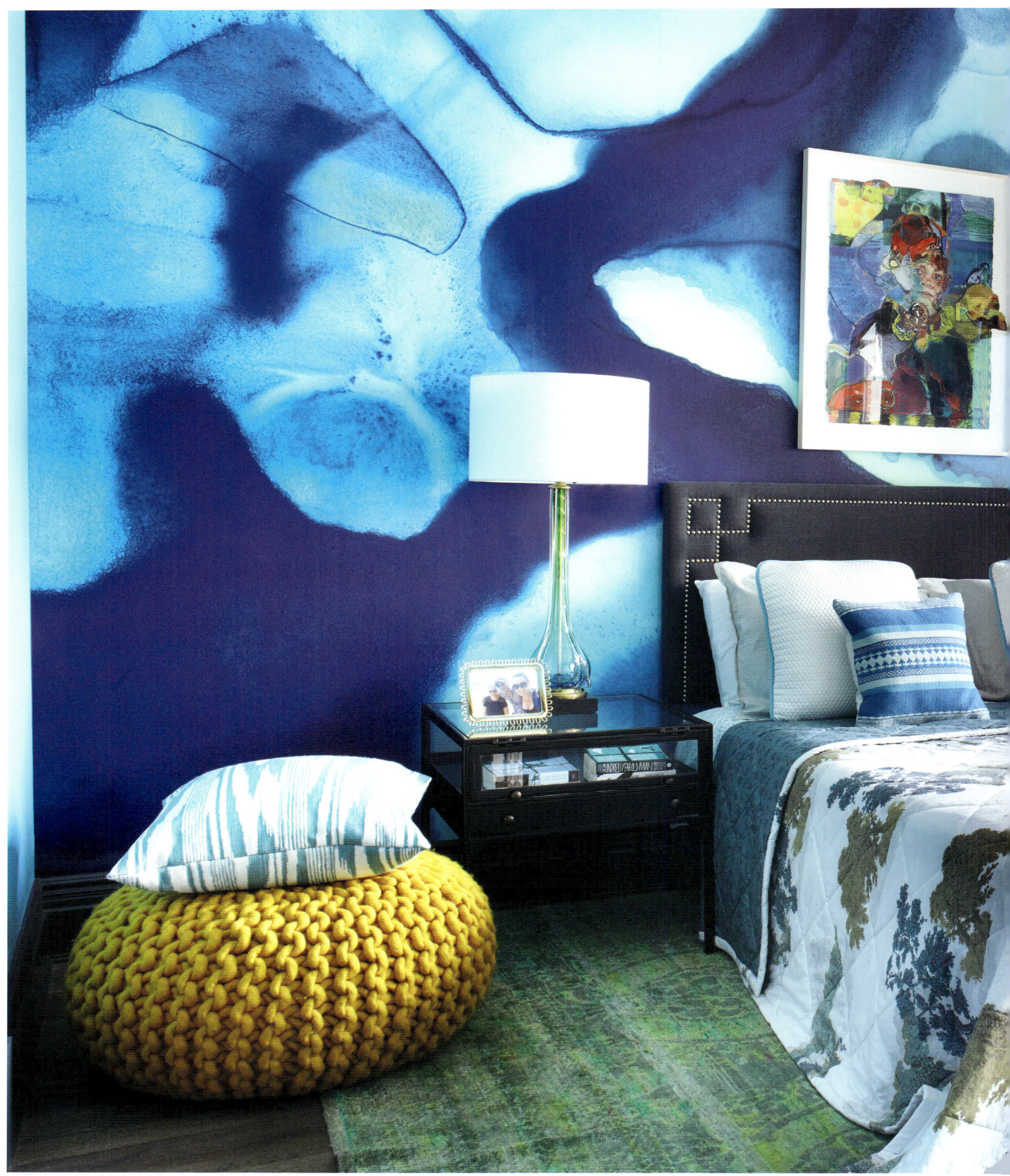

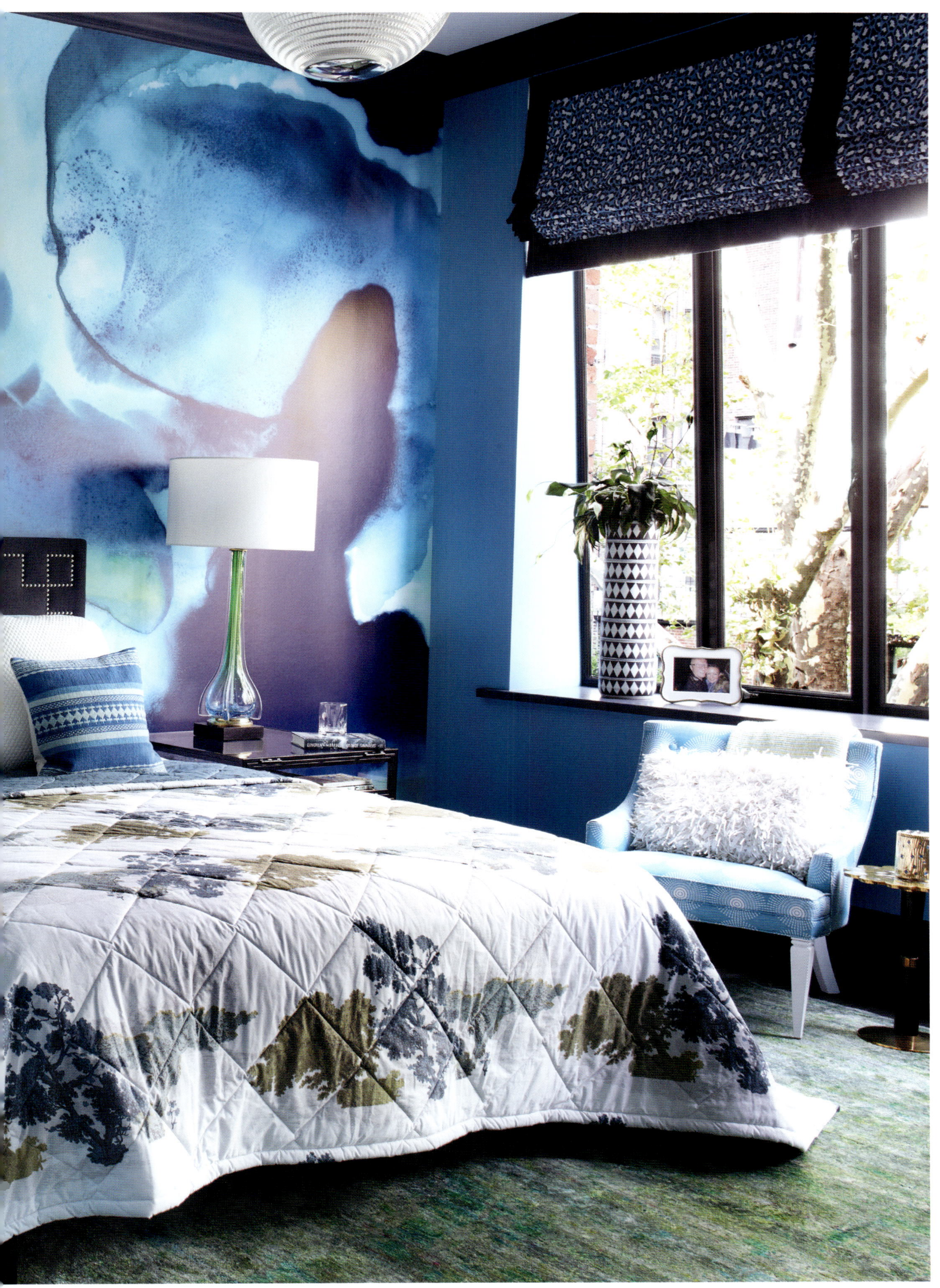

The house's bedrooms were entirely refurbished. The building had been completely neglected for a while and had fallen into serious disrepair. Rebekah Caudwell and Nicolas Dupart's plan was to turn the whole property back into a family home. During the renovations, particular attention was paid to the original features: the aim was to revive the property's earlier glories, while at the same time ushering it into the twenty-first century.

Ganz neu gestaltet wurden die Schlafzimmer des Hauses. Das Gebäude war zwischenzeitlich stark vernachlässigt worden und beinahe verfallen. Der Plan von Rebekah Caudwell und Nicolas Dupart war, das komplette Anwesen wieder zu einem Zuhause für eine Familie zu machen. Bei der Umgestaltung wurde sehr auf die ursprünglichen Details geachtet. Die frühere Pracht sollte wieder aufleben, dem Haus aber gleichzeitig der Sprung ins 21. Jahrhundert gelingen.

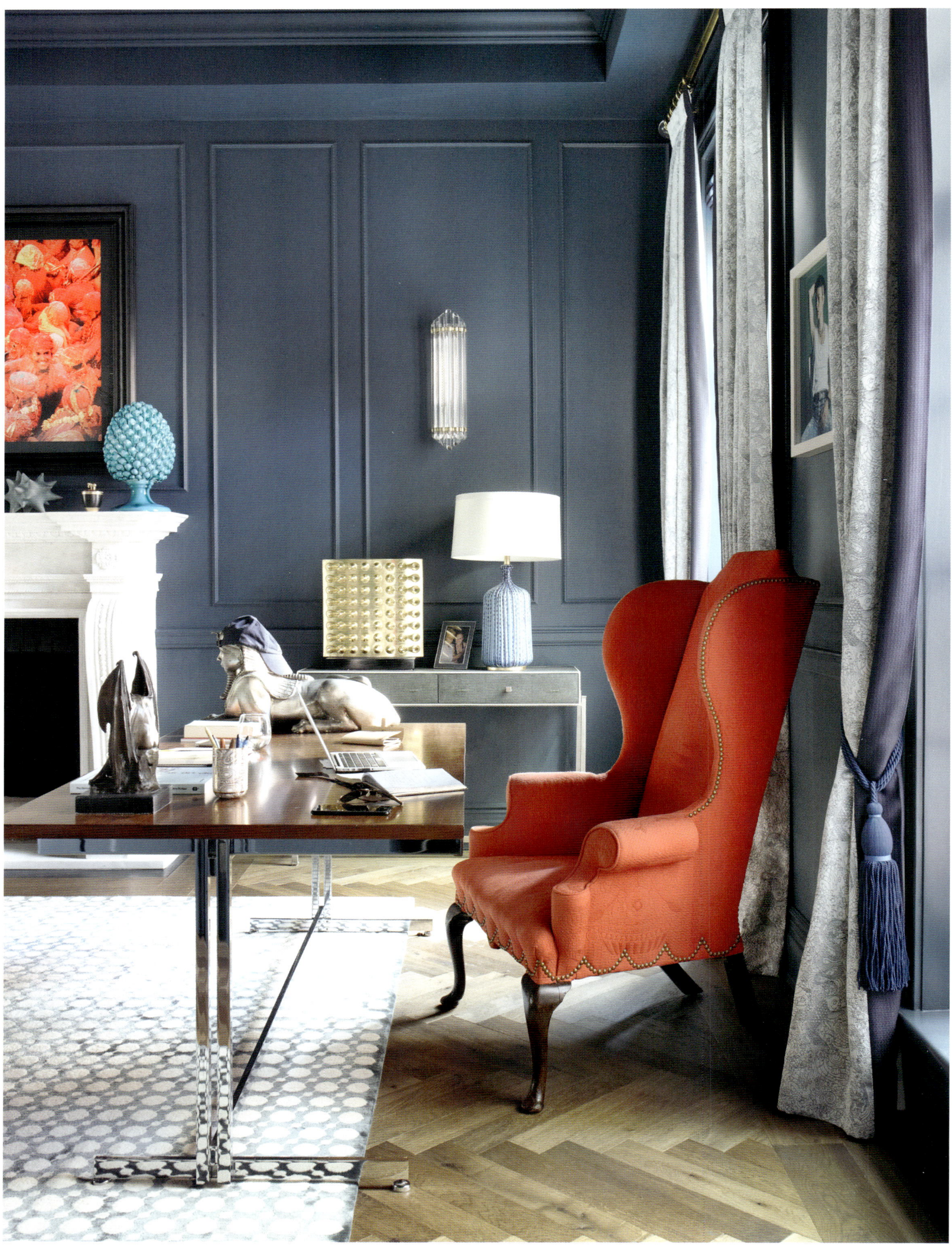

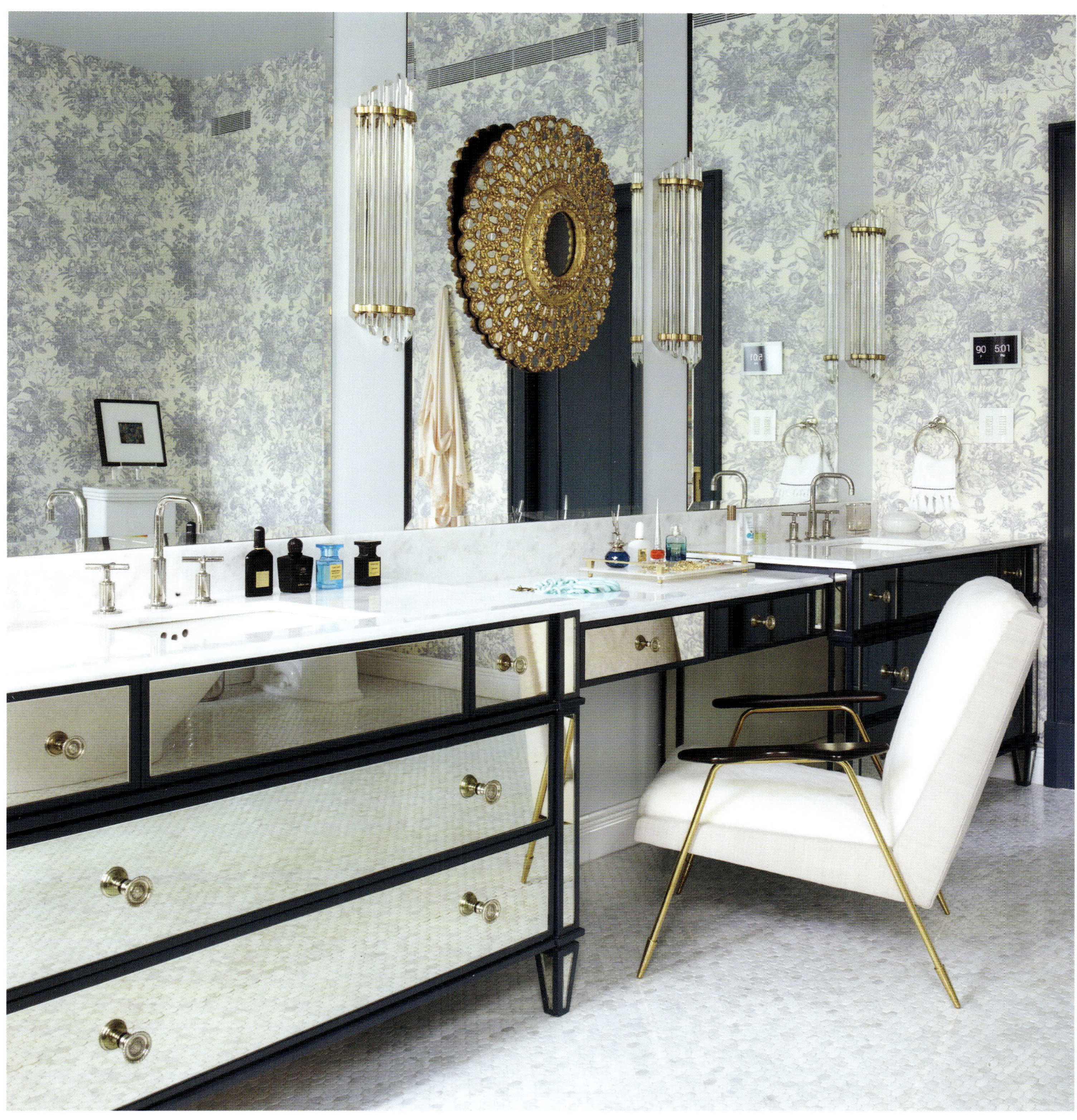

Unexpectedly trendy features provide an intentional contrast to the otherwise traditional furnishings in the study (opposite page) and an ideal stimulus for refreshing ideas. The bright, homely bathroom (above) impresses with its subtle, refined luxury.

Überraschend poppige Elemente schaffen im Arbeitszimmer (Seite gegenüber) einen bewussten Kontrast zur eher seriösen Grundausstattung. Eine gute Basis für erfrischende Ideen. Das wohnliche, helle Badezimmer (oben) beeindruckt durch seinen raffiniert-dezenten Luxus.

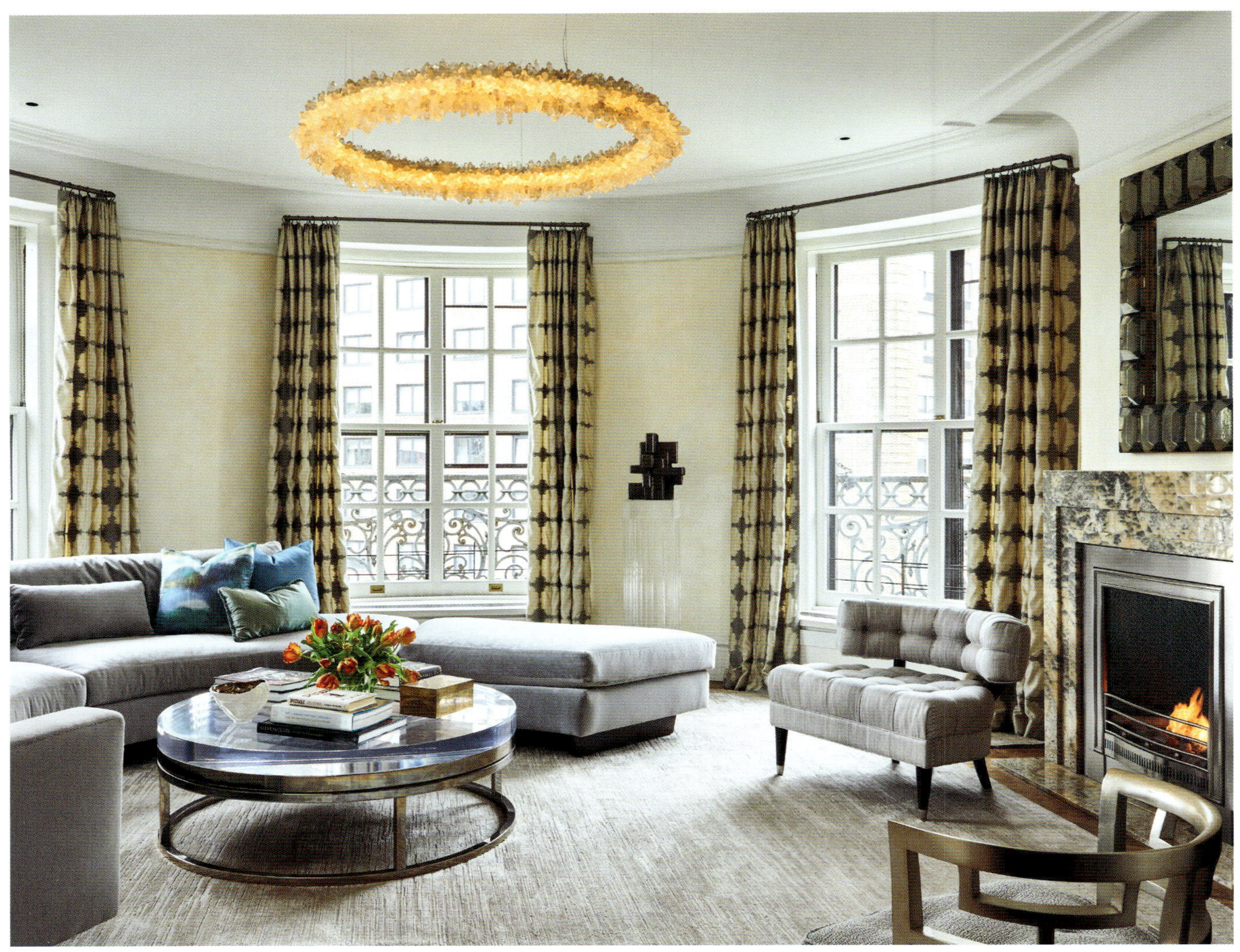

RINEHARDT | MILLER
INTERIORS

EDGEWATER, NEW JERSEY / USA

Transforming Spaces | Räume verwandeln

When Leslie Rinehardt and Marvin Miller founded their firm in 2004, they had already attained many years of experience in the industry. Their intuitive perception when transforming interiors and their passion for design have been delighting numerous clients in the New York metropolitan area and abroad ever since. Rinehardt | Miller's aim is to imbue a certain spirit into each interior and create integral designs. A good example of this is a Manhattan duplex apartment in the historic Ansonia Hotel, which was built between 1899 and 1904 in the Beaux-Arts style. A further referential project is located in a new state-of-the-art building in Prospect Heights, Brooklyn (next double page).

Als Leslie Rinehardt und Marvin Miller 2004 ihre Firma gründeten, blickten sie bereits auf eine lange Branchenerfahrung zurück. Ihr Gespür für die Verwandlung von Räumen und ihre Leidenschaft für Design begeisterten seitdem zahlreiche anspruchsvolle Kunden im Großraum New York sowie im Ausland. Rinehardt | Miller will jedem Raum eine Seele einhauchen und ganzheitliche Designerlebnisse schaffen. Beispielhaft hierfür ist eine Manhattaner Maisonettewohnung im historischen Ansonia Hotel, 1899–1904 im Beaux-Arts-Stil erbaut. Ein weiteres Referenzobjekt findet sich in einem hochmodernen neuen Gebäude in Prospect Heights, Brooklyn (nächste Doppelseite).

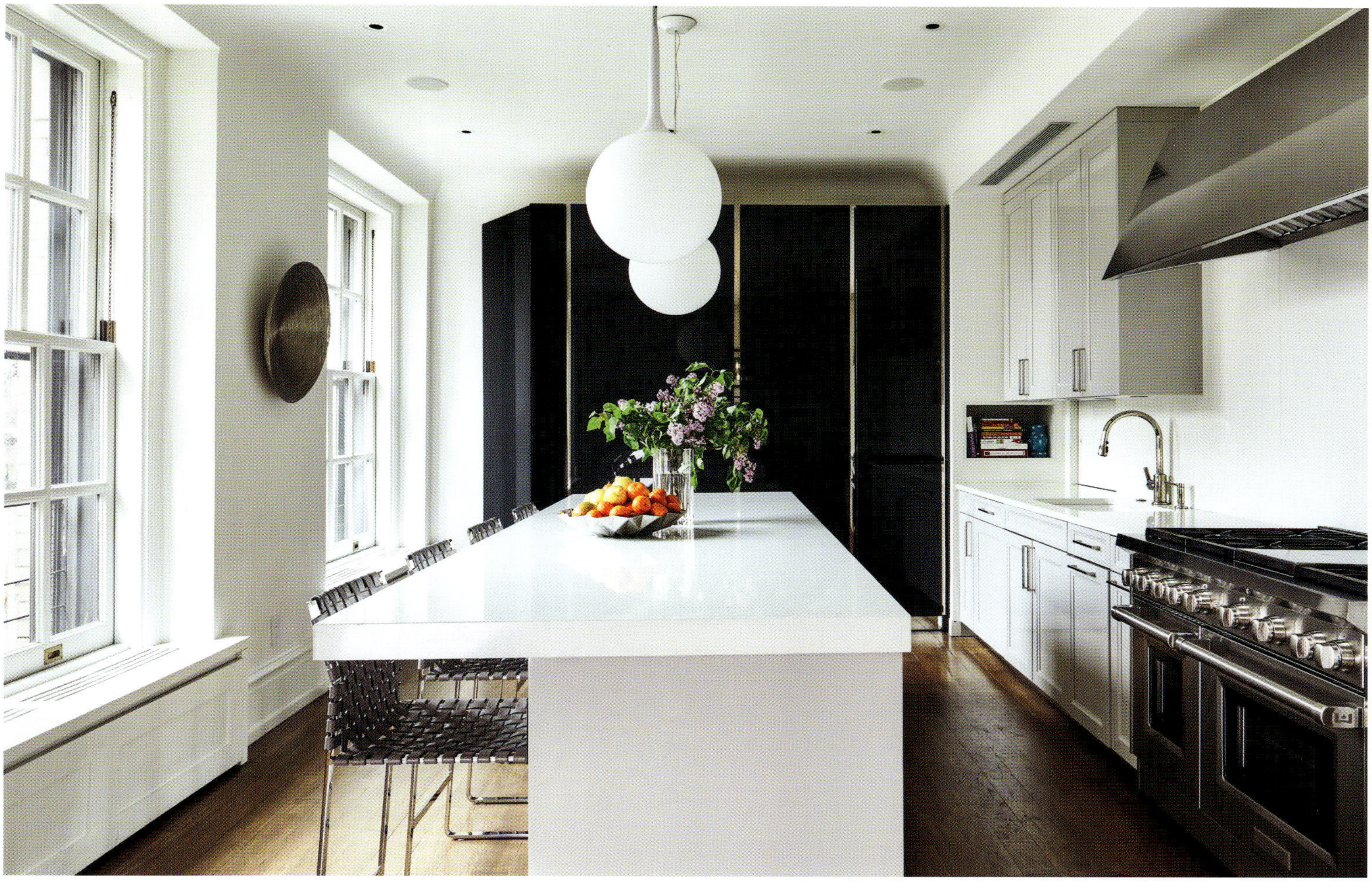

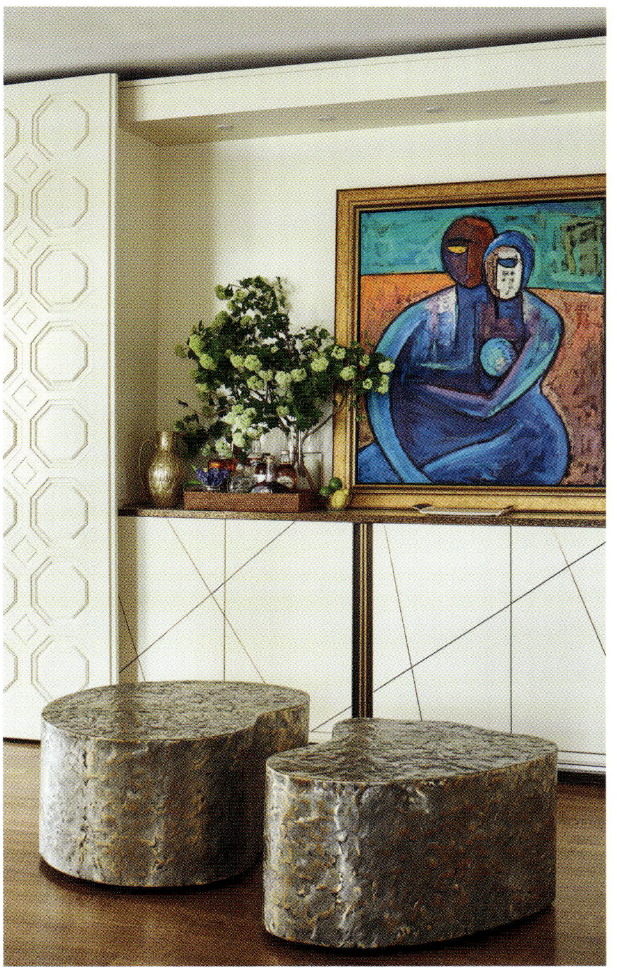

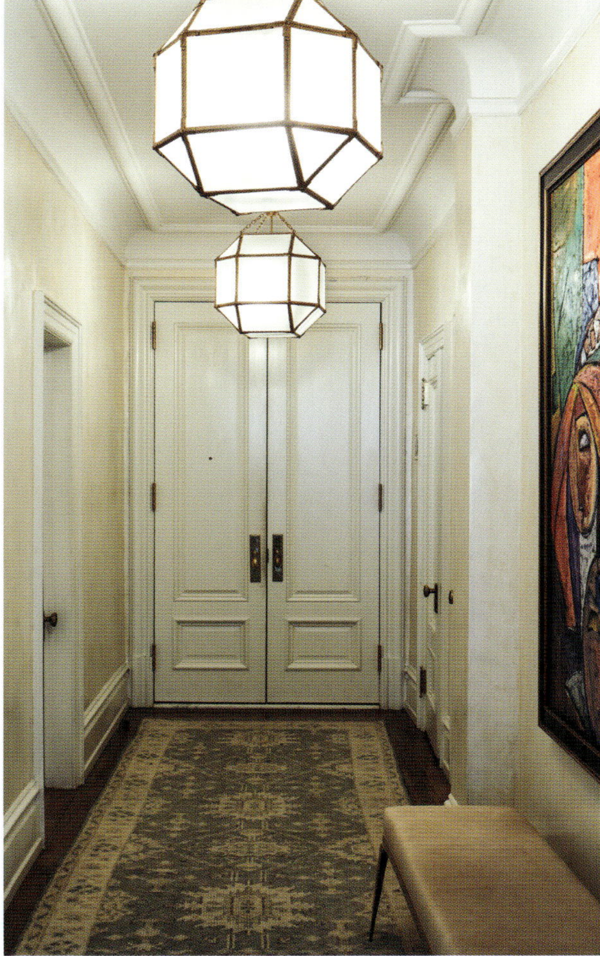

The 'round' living room is situated in one of the turrets of the Ansonia Hotel (opposite page). The kitchen—which is huge by Manhattan's standards—looks out directly onto Broadway. A hallway doubles as a lounge area (left). Among other things, the built-in cupboards contain an entire wet-bar (far left).

In einem Eckturm des Ansonia Hotels liegt das „runde" Wohnzimmer (Seite gegenüber). Aus der für Manhattan sehr großen Küche (oben) blickt man direkt auf den Broadway. Ein Durchgangszimmer der Wohnung dient als Lounge-Bereich (links). In den großen Einbauschränken befindet sich unter anderem eine komplette Bar (ganz links).

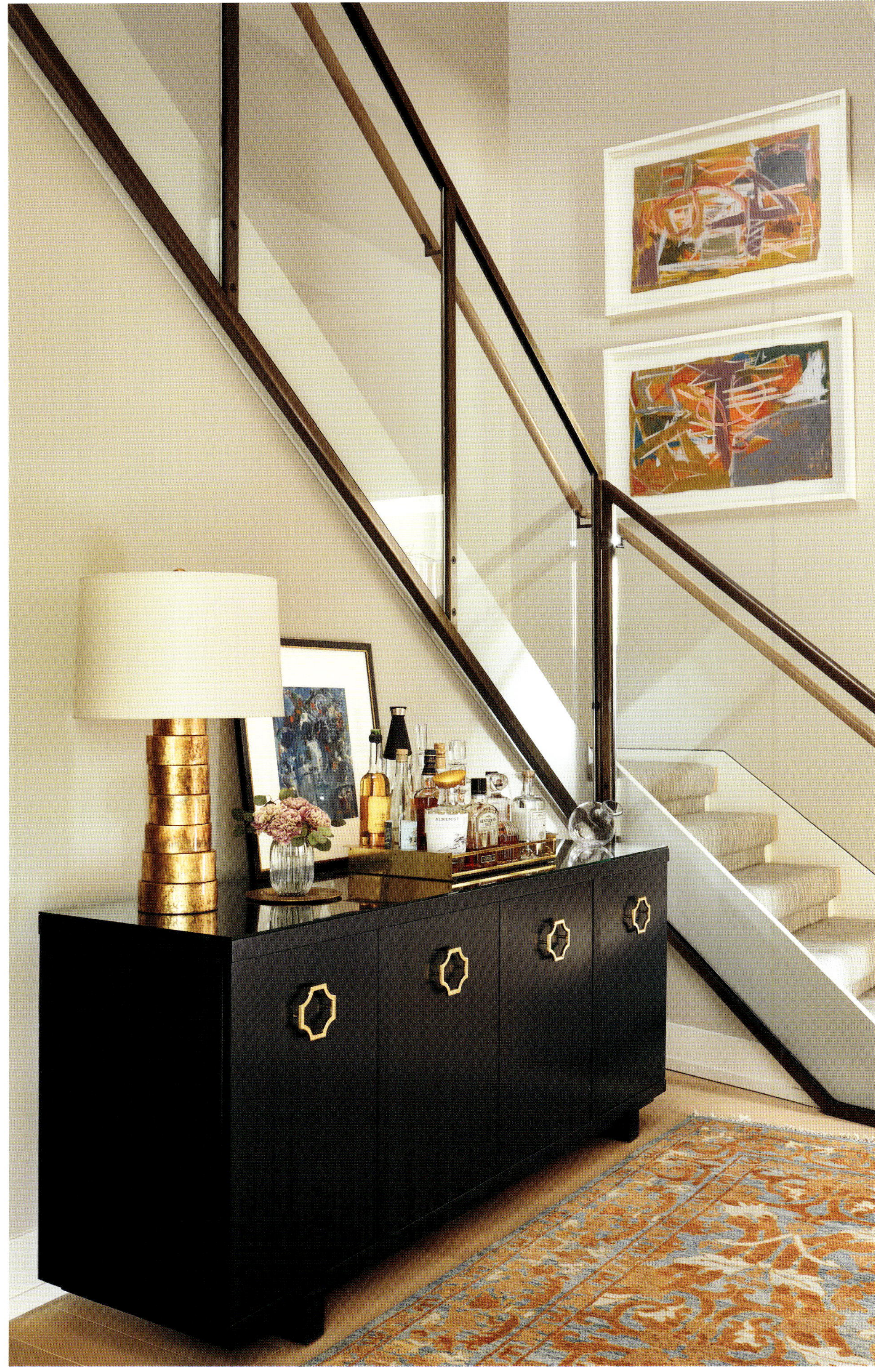

This 'townhome' property in Brooklyn's Prospect Heights has its own private elevator with direct street access. The images show the duplex apartment's hallway and stairs (left) as well as the living room with its adjoining lounge area (opposite page). Rinehardt | Miller's team has fitted the interior with high-quality furniture, unique antiques and various art objects. Individual recessed lighting, custom-designed cupboards, ceiling fixtures and a fireplace have also been added.

Dieses „Townhome"-Objekt in Prospect Heights, Brooklyn, besitzt einen privaten Aufzug mit direktem Straßenzugang. Die Bilder zeigen Flur und Treppenaufgang der Maisonettewohnung (links) sowie das Wohnzimmer mit dem angrenzenden Lounge-Bereich (Seite gegenüber). Das Team von Rinehardt | Miller hat die Räume mit hochwertigen Möbeln, antiken Einzelstücken sowie diversen Kunstobjekten ausgestattet. Außerdem wurden unter anderem individuelle Einbauleuchten, maßgefertigte Schränke und Deckenelemente sowie ein Kamin hinzugefügt.

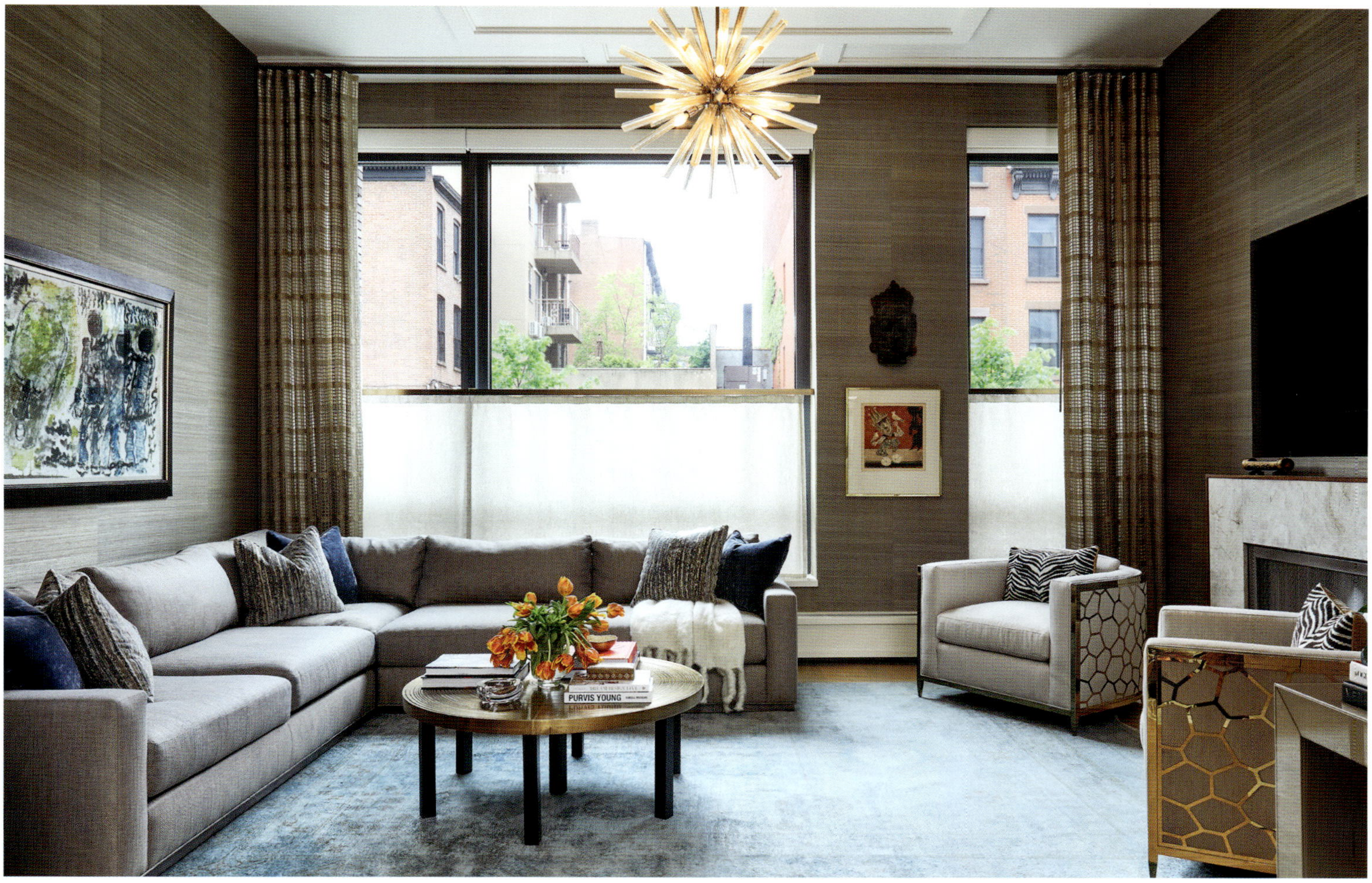

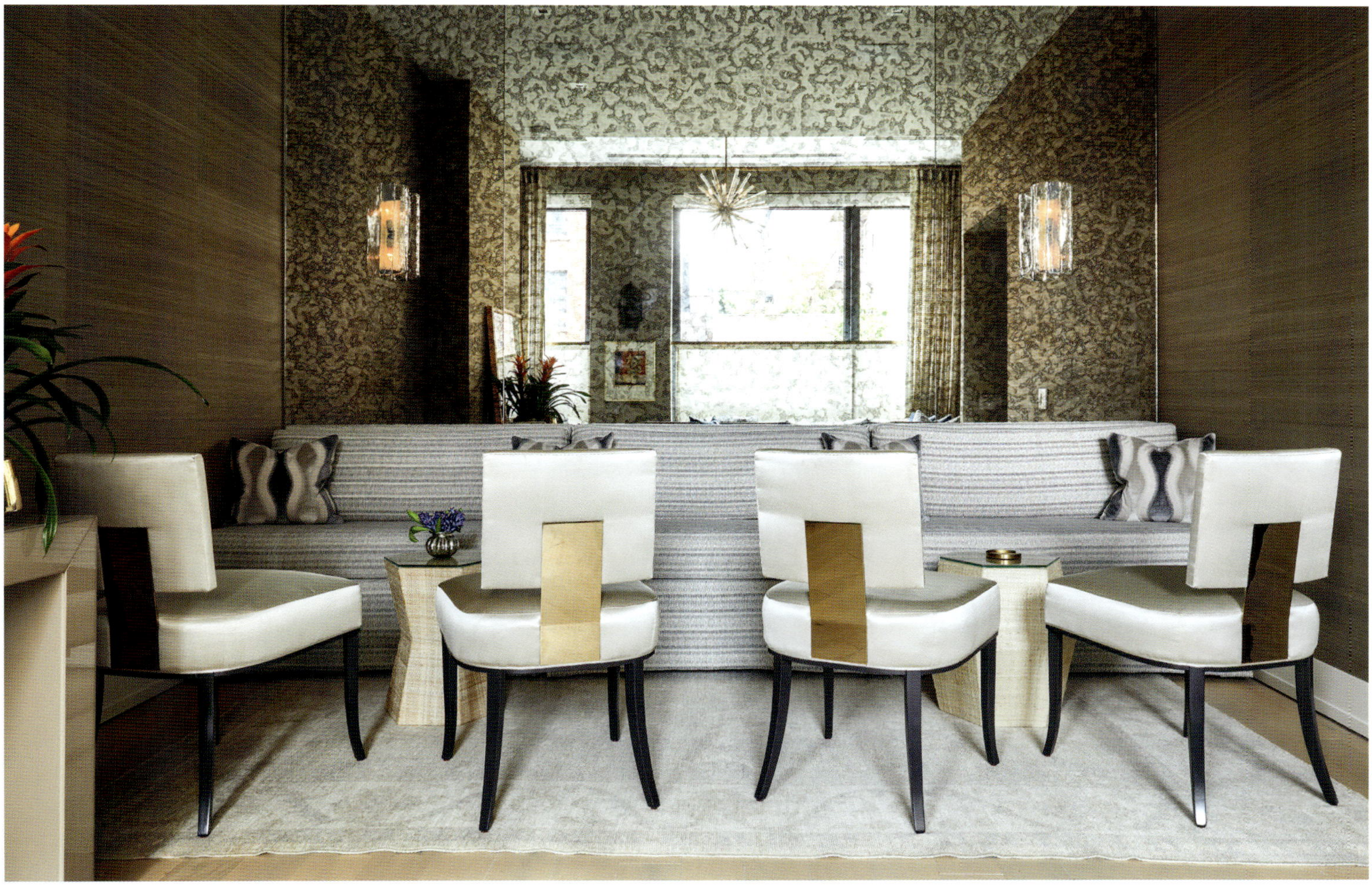

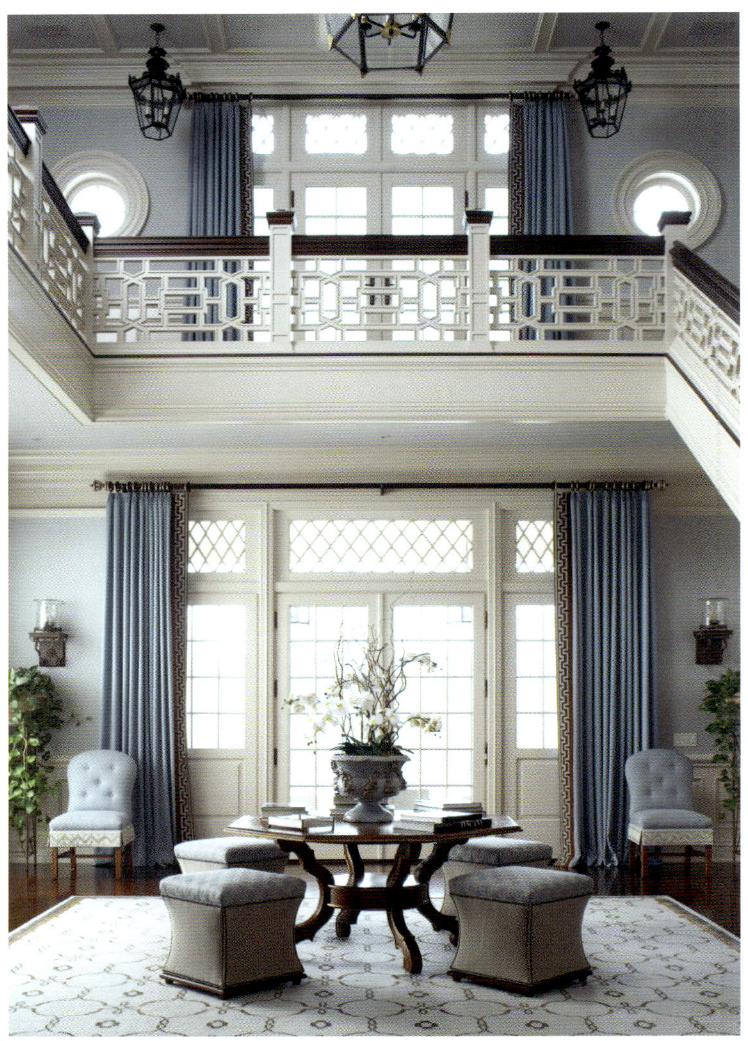

RINFRET, LTD.

CONNECTICUT & FLORIDA / USA

Luxurious and Comfortable | Luxuriös und komfortabel

Cindy Rinfret, principal designer of Rinfret, Ltd. is recognized across the world for creating classically elegant residences for the most discerning clients. Best known for her luxurious yet comfortable aesthetic, as illustrated in her two Rizzoli books on 'Greenwich Style', Rinfret is a renowned designer, having completed a wide range of projects, including the Kips Bay Palm Beach Show House and numerous Greenwich estates that have graced the covers of magazines. Rinfret, Ltd. is highly respected by its peers and is consistently honored with important design awards and editorial coverage in the best interior design magazines every year.

Vielen anspruchsvollen Interior-Design-Fans, die klassisch-elegante Wohnungen lieben, ist Cindy Rinfret ein Begriff: Die Chefdesignerin von Rinfret, Ltd. ist weltweit für ihre ebenso luxuriöse wie komfortable Designästhetik bekannt und über ihren „Greenwich Style" wurden bereits zwei Bildbände veröffentlicht. Zu den Arbeiten der vielfach ausgezeichneten Designerin und Autorin gehören Projekte wie das Kips Bay Palm Beach Show House oder Anwesen in Greenwich, Connecticut, die auch Titelthema großer Innenarchitektur-Magazine waren. Rinfret, Ltd. genießt großes Ansehen in der Branche und gewinnt regelmäßig wichtige Designpreise.

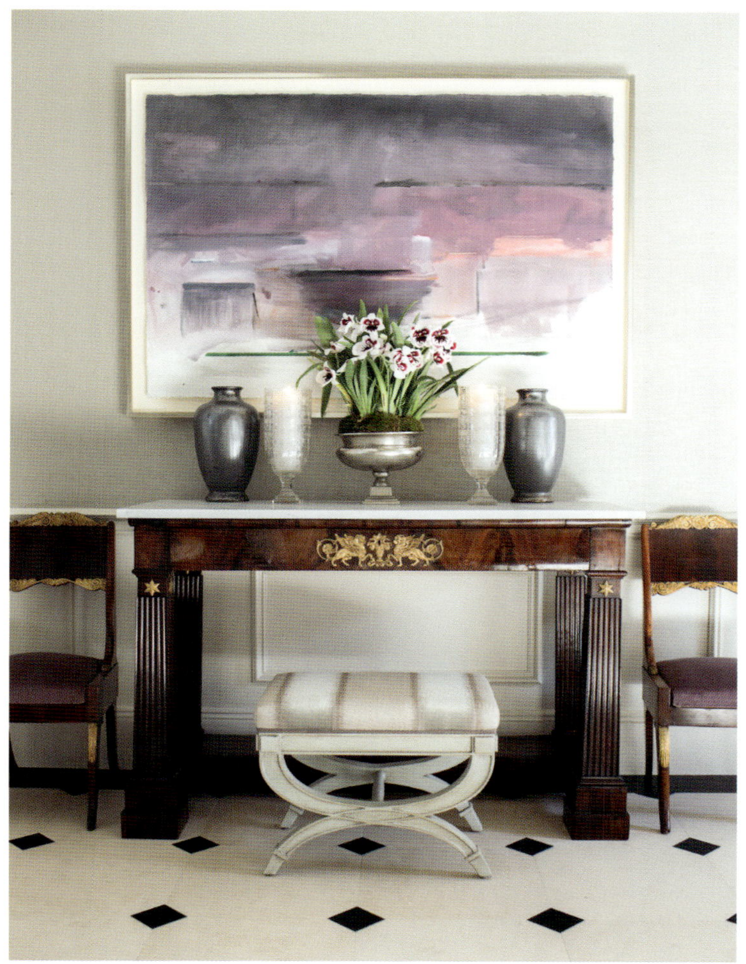

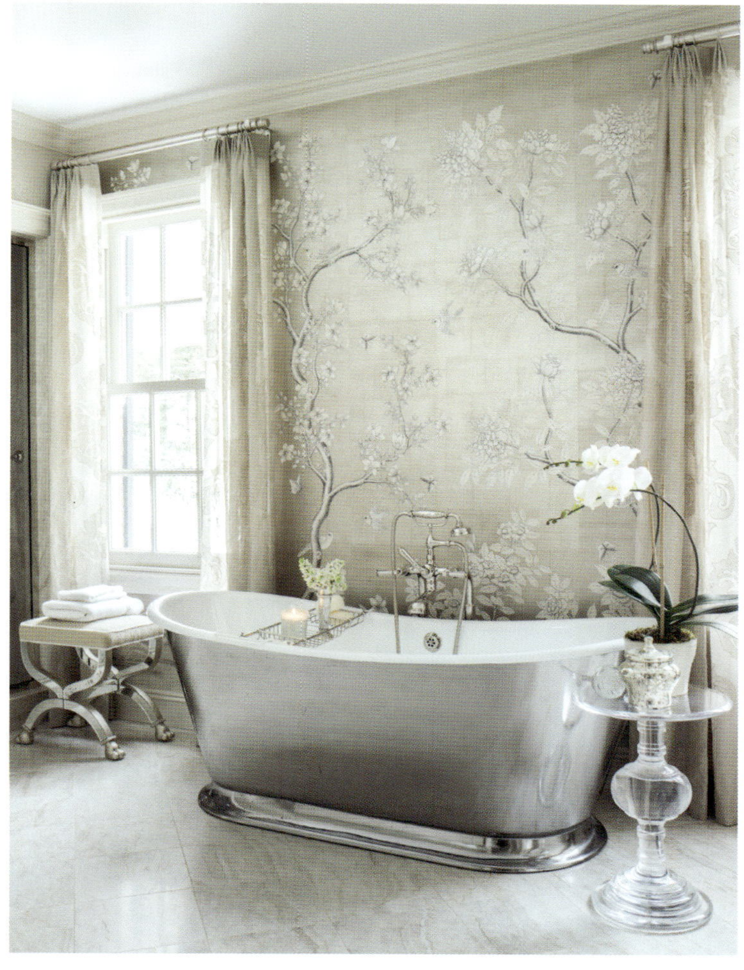

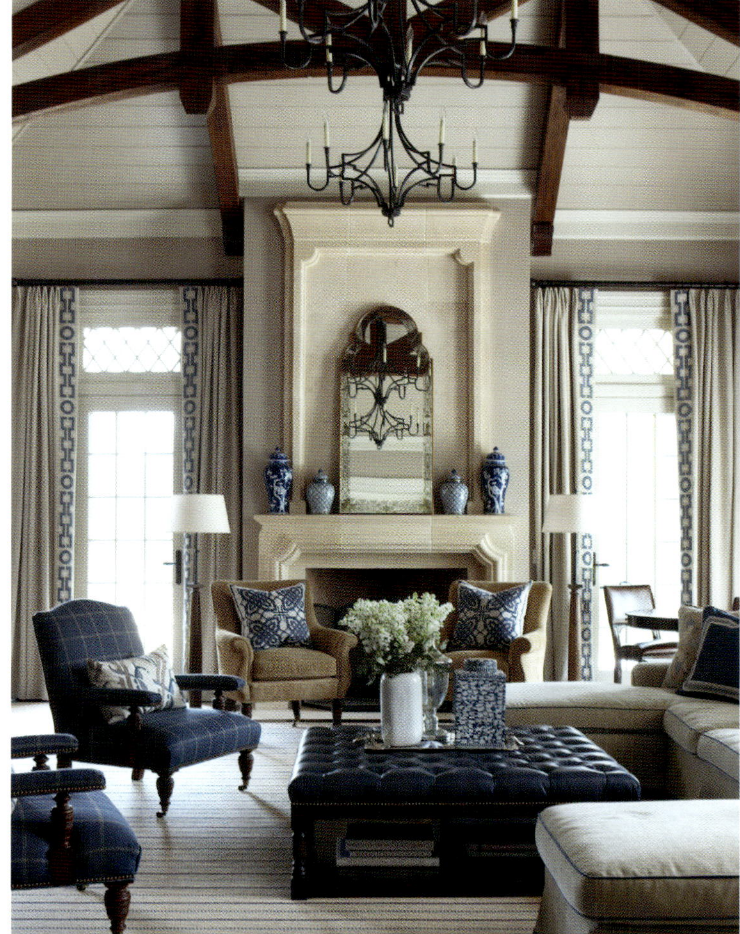

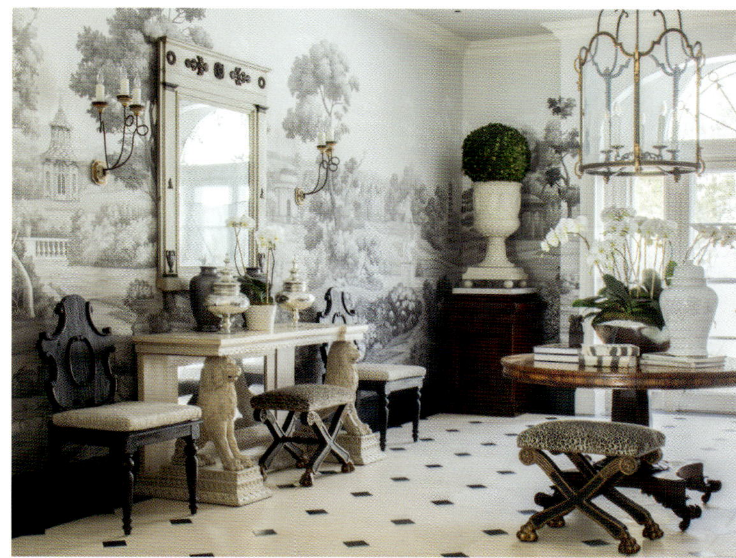

The large foyer (opposite page) and a living room (left) with open fireplace in the Jacobean Country House in Greenwich, CT. Rinfret's project 'Neoclassical Greenwich', in the same location: views of the main bathroom (top right) and the foyer (above and top left).

Das große Foyer (Seite gegenüber) und ein Kaminzimmer (links) des Jacobean Country House in Greenwich, CT. Das Rinfret-Projekt „Neoclassical Greenwich" am gleichen Ort: Ansichten vom Hauptbadezimmer (ganz oben rechts) und vom Foyer (oben und ganz oben links).

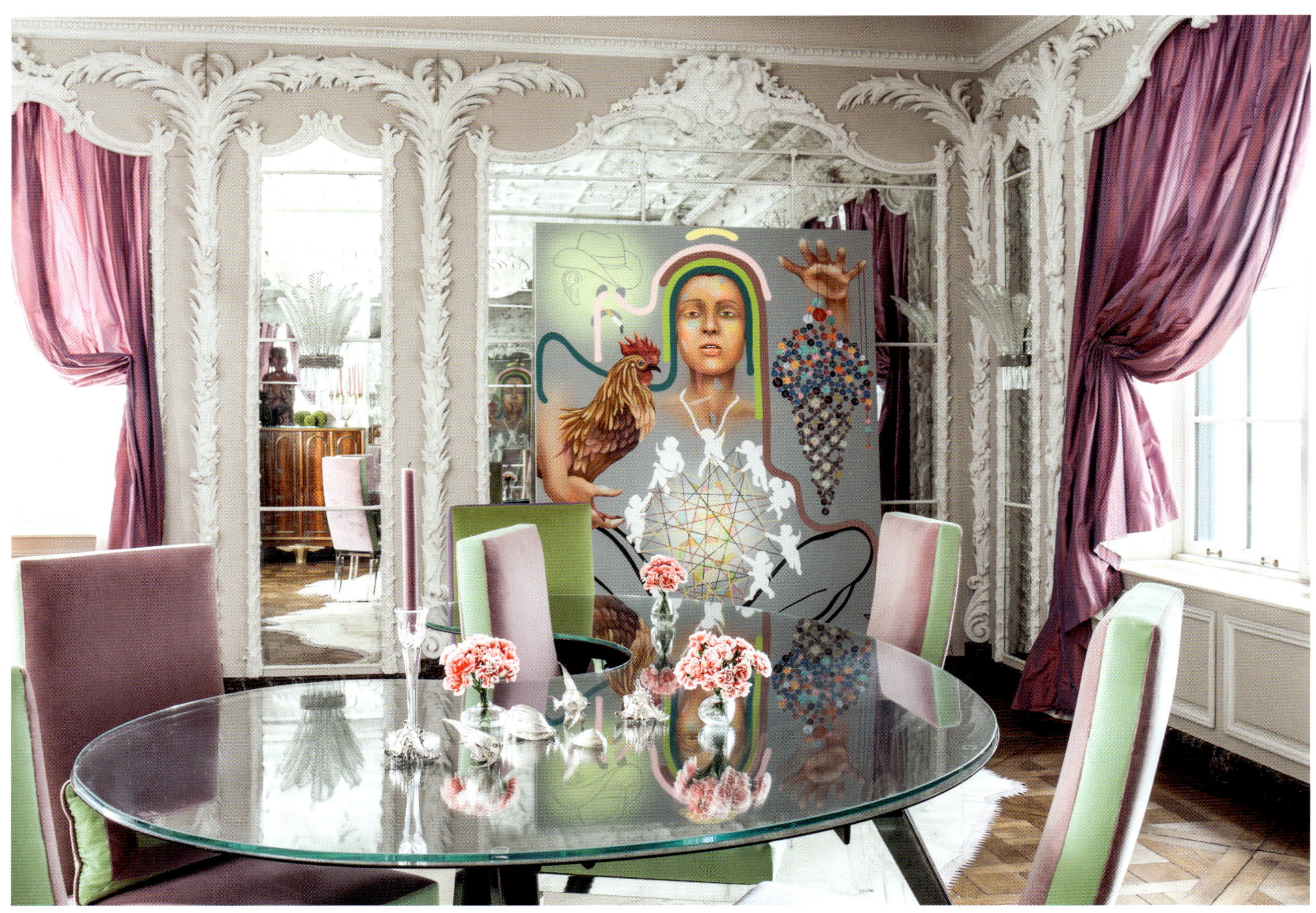

ROBERT COUTURIER INC.

NEW YORK / USA

Think Big | Groß denken

In 1987, billionaire industrialist James Goldsmith commissioned the then 32-year-old Couturier to redesign his Mexican west-coast property La Loma, which covers an area of more than 8000 hectares. It was to be a spectacular success, enabling the French designer to claim his place among the world's best. Today, Couturier's name is a byword for an international style that blends a profound understanding of classicism with an original, contemporary perspective. For the designer, the decor should not only be in keeping with the architecture and surroundings but also with the client and their needs. Couturier's interiors are not stage sets but residential spaces for everyday living.

Im Jahr 1987 beauftragte der milliardenschwere Industrielle James Goldsmith den damals 32-jährigen Robert Couturier, sein über 8000 Hektar großes Anwesen La Loma an der Westküste Mexikos grundlegend umzugestalten. Es wurde ein spektakulärer Erfolg, der den französischen Designer an die Weltspitze führte. Heute steht Couturiers Name für einen internationalen Stil, der ein tiefes Verständnis von Klassik mit einer originellen, heutigen Betrachtungsweise verbindet. Décor, so das Credo des Designers, müsse nicht nur der Architektur und Umgebung, sondern auch dem Kunden angemessen sein. Couturiers Interieurs sind keine Bühnenbilder, sondern Räume für lebendige Menschen.

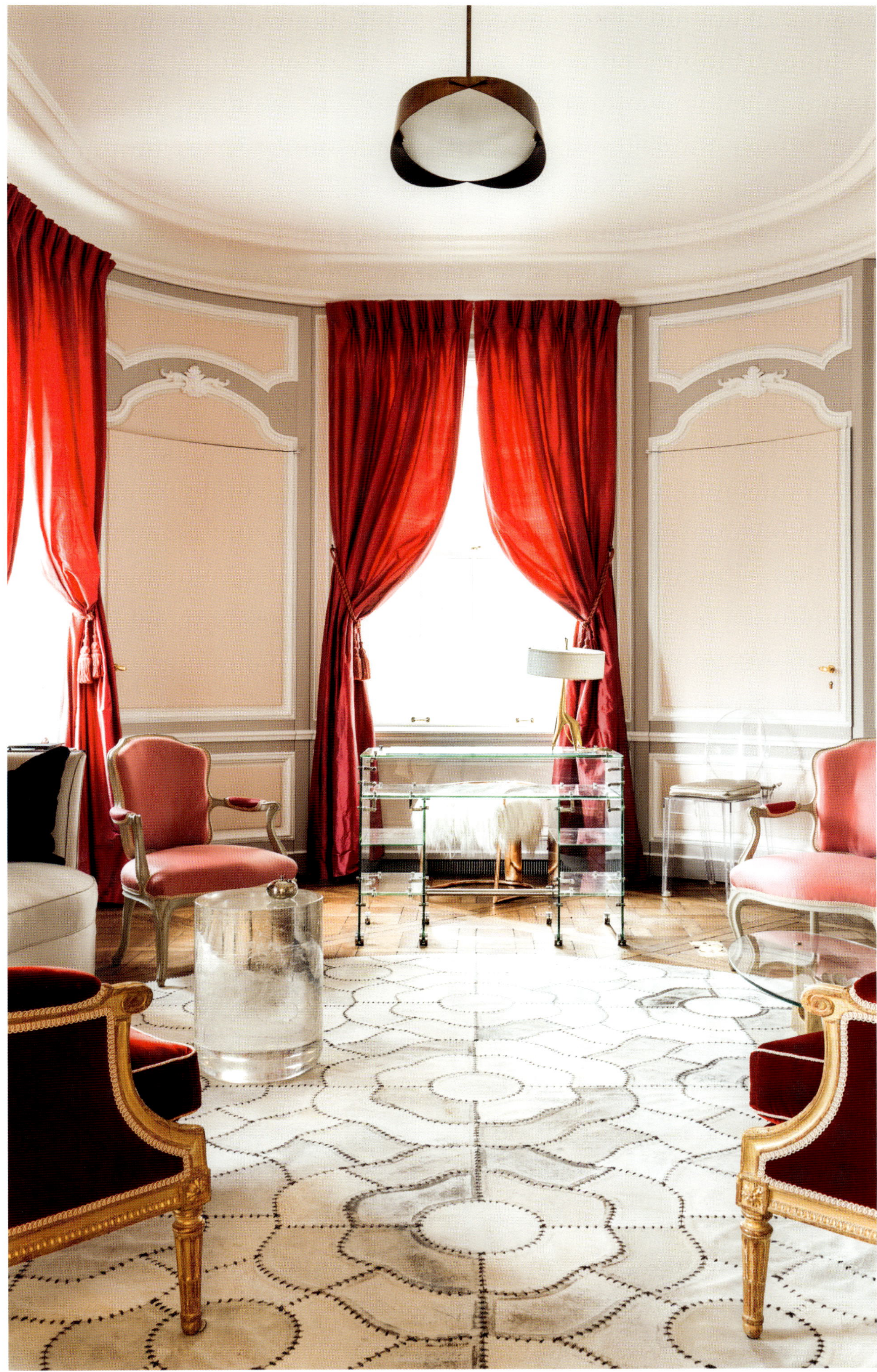

Robert Couturier designed this apartment in New York City's Upper East Side in 2011: in the dining room with its original stucco ceiling (opposite page), Ron Arad's glass and stainless-steel dining table blends with Charles Hollis Jones chairs from the 1970s. The Italian sconces date from the 1940s. In the wife's office (left), gilded Louis XVI chairs were combined with a 1930's glass desk by René-André Coulon and a crystal side table by Martin Szekely. The FontanaArte light fixture originates from the 1950s and the rug was designed by the Rug Company.

Diese Wohnung gestaltete Robert Couturier 2011 in der Upper East Side, New York City: Im Esszimmer mit Original-Stuckdecke (Seite gegenüber) harmoniert Ron Arads Esstisch aus Glas und Edelstahl mit Charles-Hollis-Jones-Stühlen aus den 1970er-Jahren. Die italienischen Wandleuchter stammen aus den Vierzigerjahren. Im „Wifes Office" (links) wurden vergoldete Louis-XVI-Stühle mit einem Dreißigerjahre-Glasschreibtisch von René-André Coulon und einem Kristall-Beistelltisch von Martin Szekely kombiniert. Die Fontana-Arte-Leuchte ist aus den Fünfzigern, der Teppich wurde von der Rug Company hergestellt.

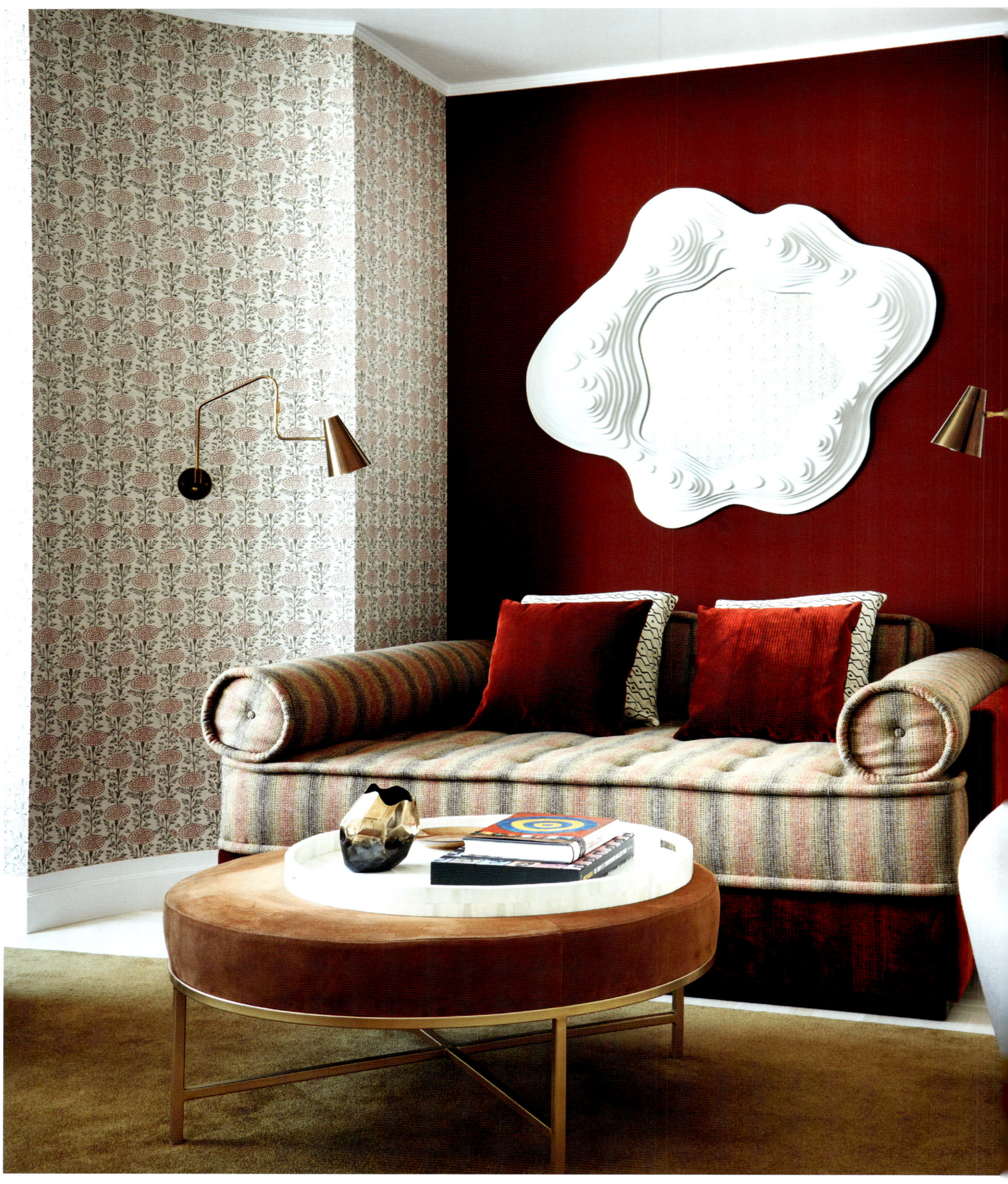

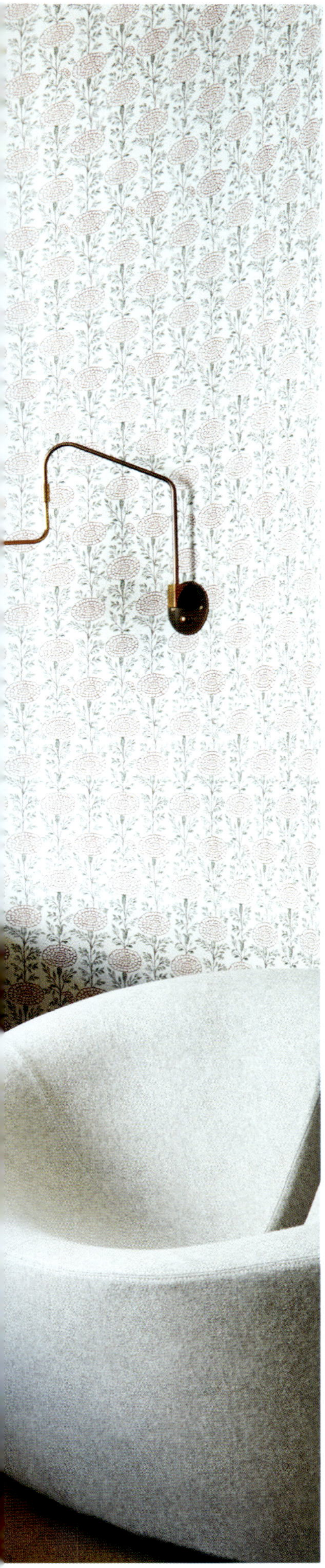

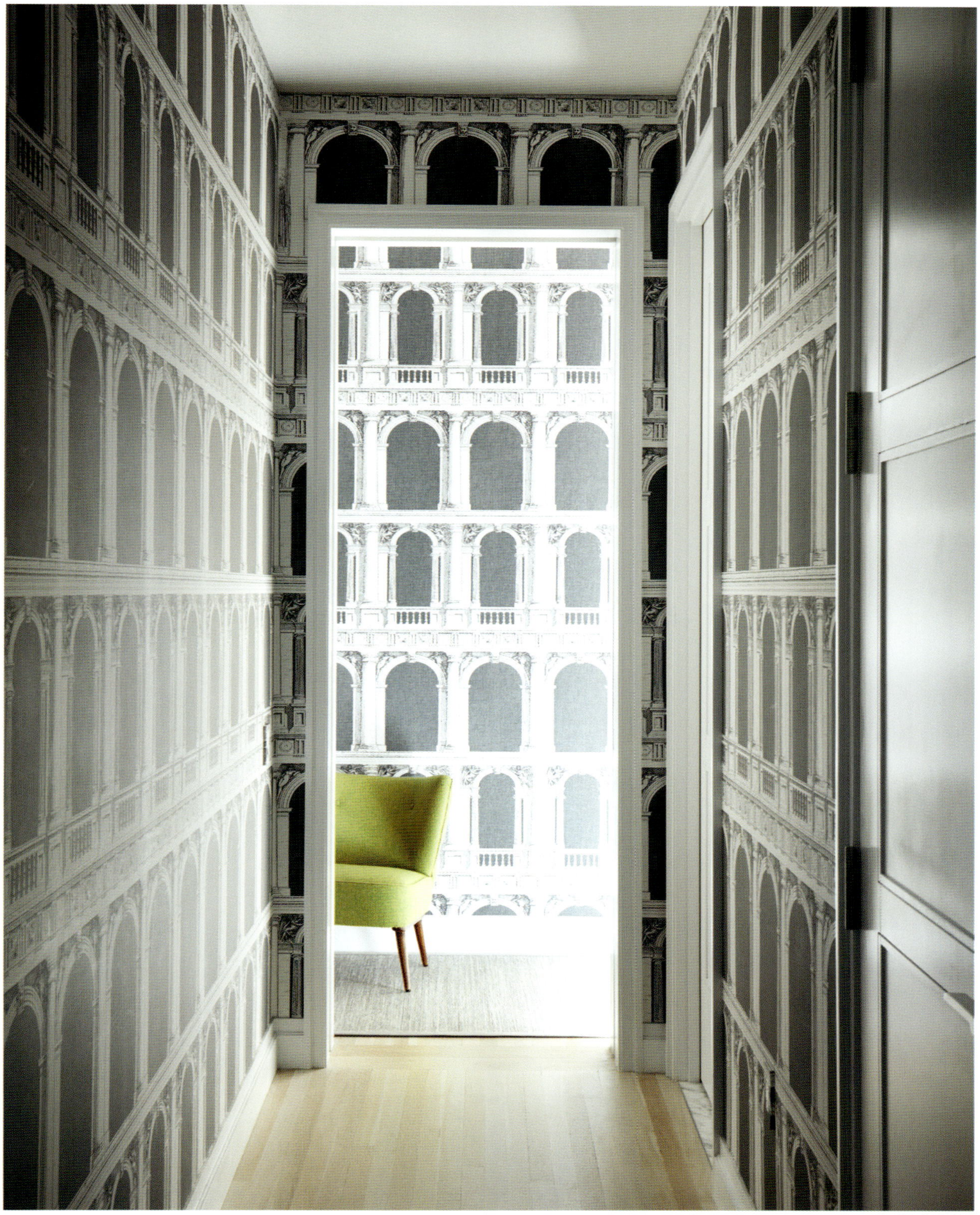

A penthouse apartment at 432 Park Avenue in NYC (2016): The study (left) contains a daybed conceived by Couturier and upholstered with fabrics by Maharam and Loro Piana. The custom rug was designed by ALT for Living. In the hallway (above), the Fornasetti wallpaper with its Roman columns creates a unique spatial sensation.

Penthouse-Wohnung in der 432 Park Avenue in NYC (2016): Im Arbeitszimmer (links) steht diese von Couturier entworfene Schlafcouch, bezogen mit Stoffen von Maharam und Loro Piana. Der handgefertigte Teppich stammt von ALT for Living. In der Diele (oben) sorgt die Fornasetti-Tapete mit römischen Säulen für ein besonderes Raumgefühl.

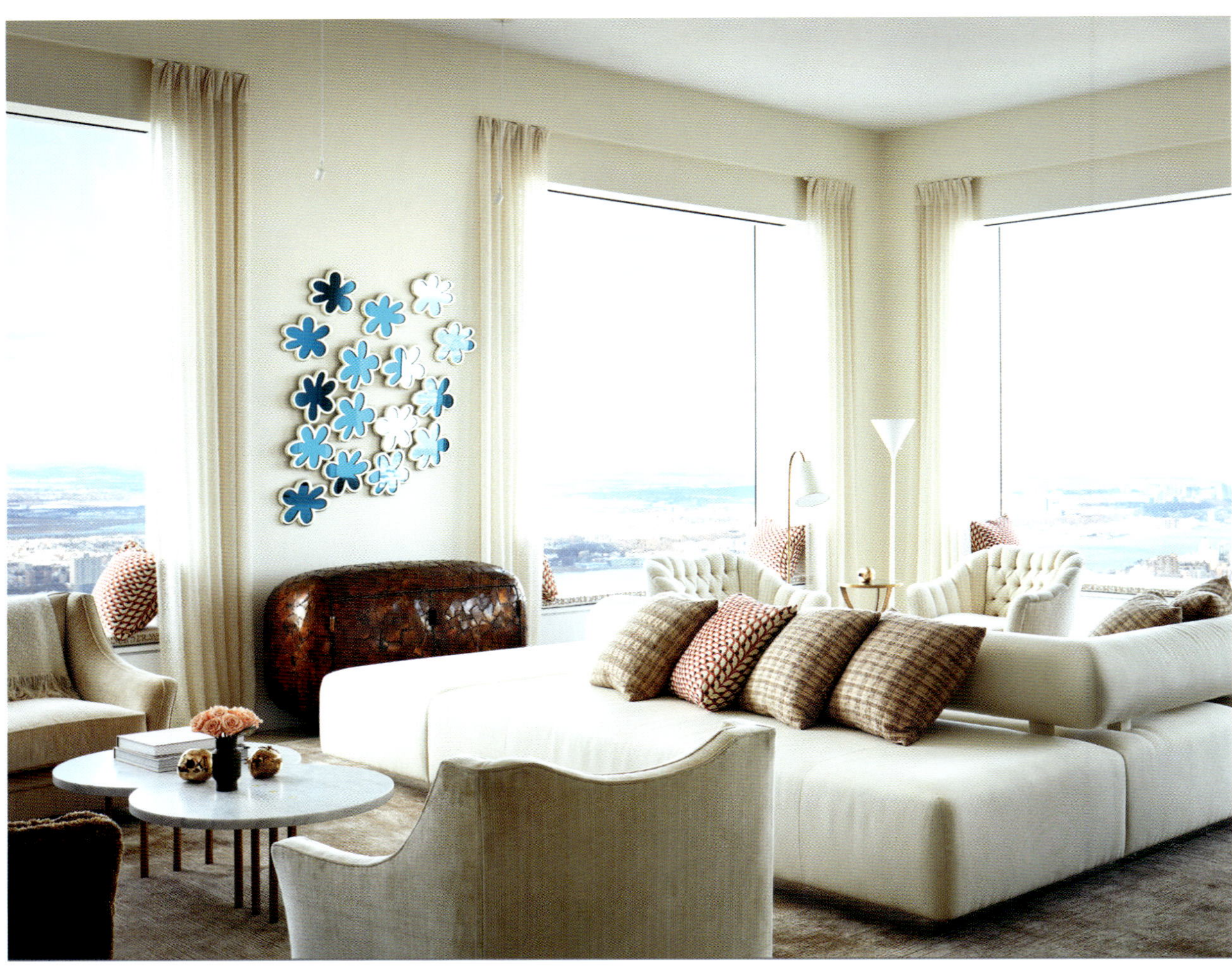

In the hallway of the penthouse an antique Persian carpet and a custom-made bench upholstered with Pierre Frey fabrics cater for a hospitable ambiance (opposite page). In the bright living room, the blue mirrors by Hubert le Gall are particularly striking (left). The view from the windows takes in vast areas of New York.

Im Flur des Penthouses schaffen ein antiker Perserteppich und die maßgefertigte Sitzbank mit Pierre-Frey-Stoffen eine gastfreundliche Atmosphäre (Seite gegenüber). Im hellen Wohnzimmer fallen die blauen Spiegel von Hubert le Gall ins Auge (links). Aus den Fenstern kann man den Blick weit über New York schweifen lassen.

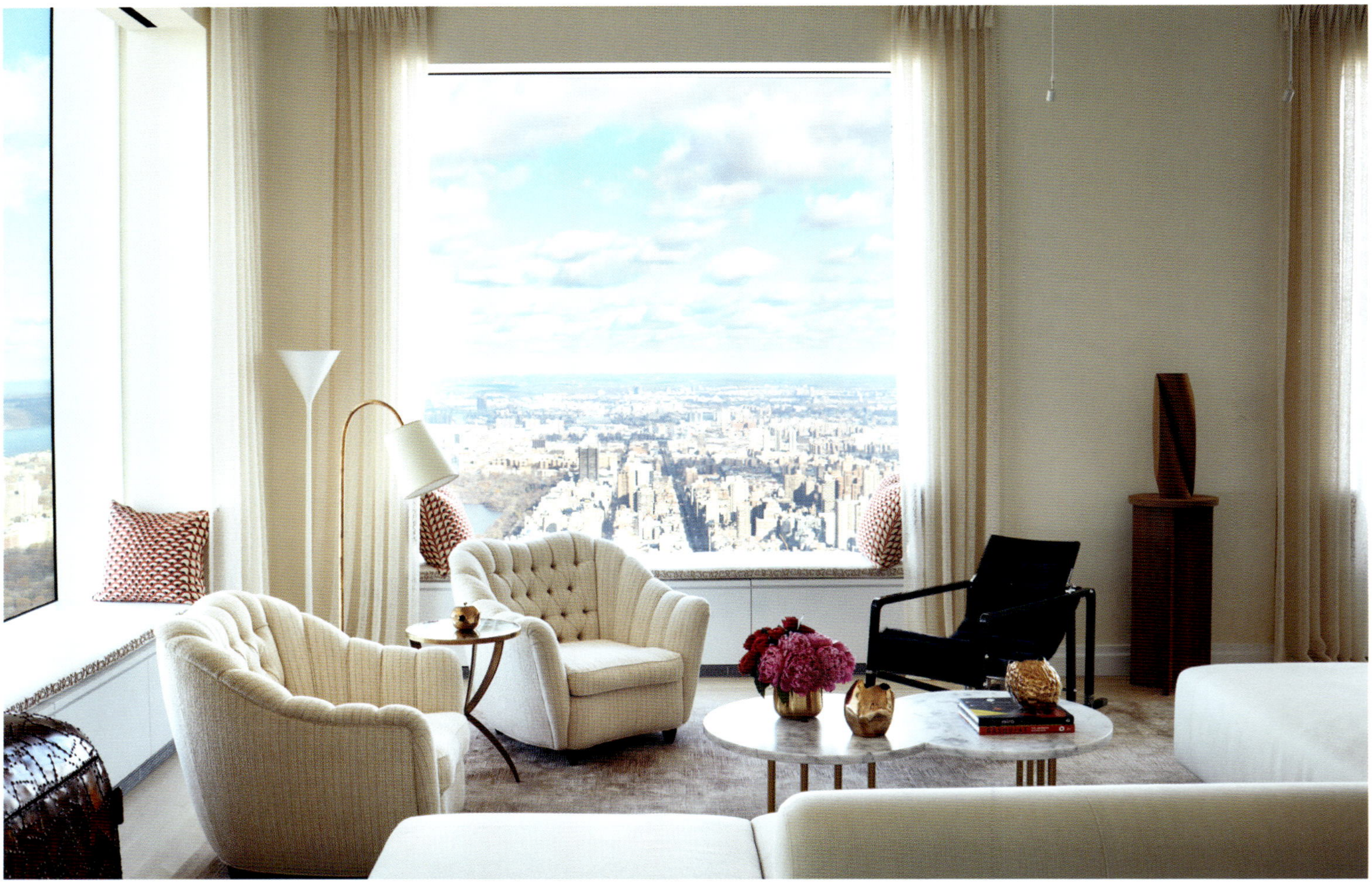

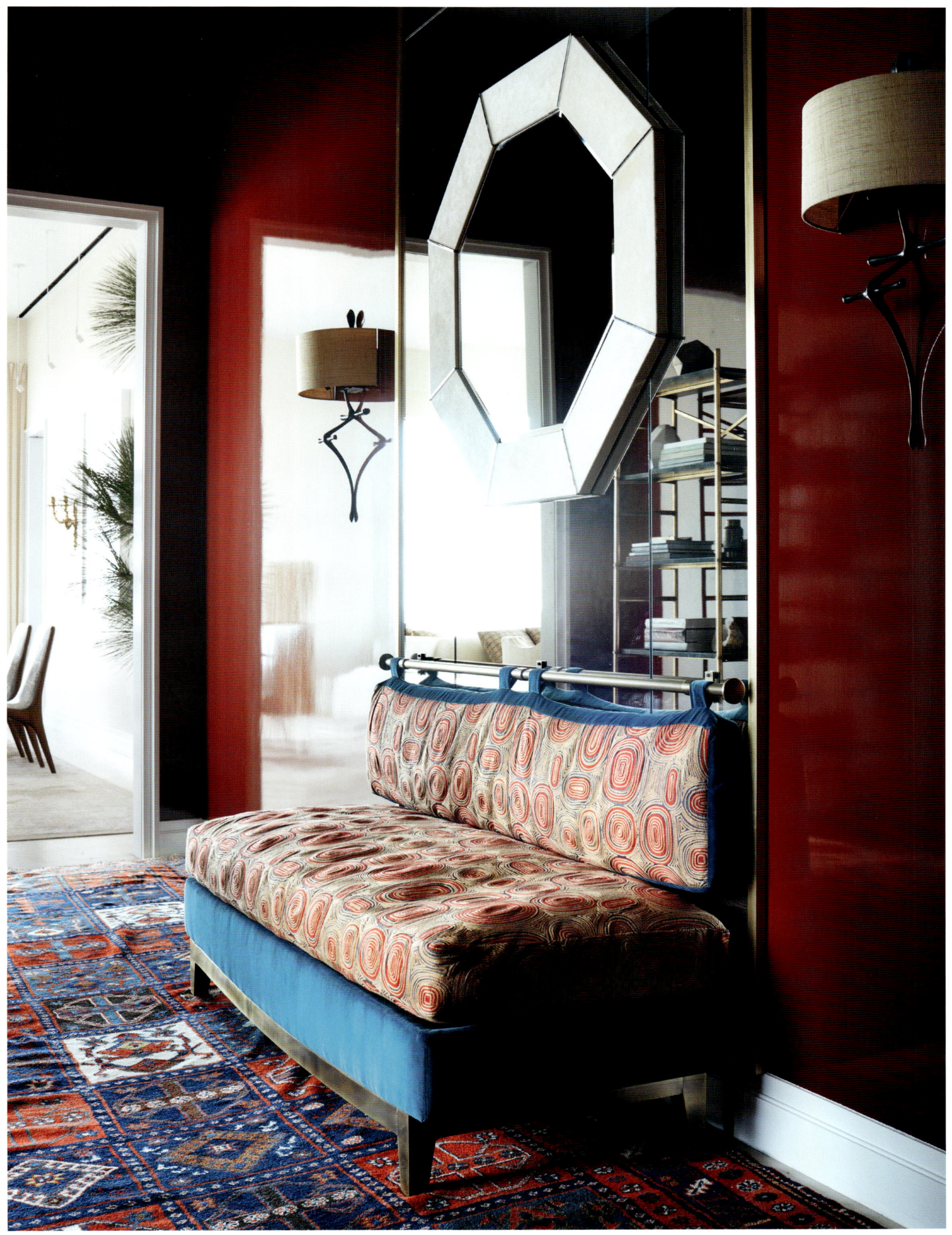

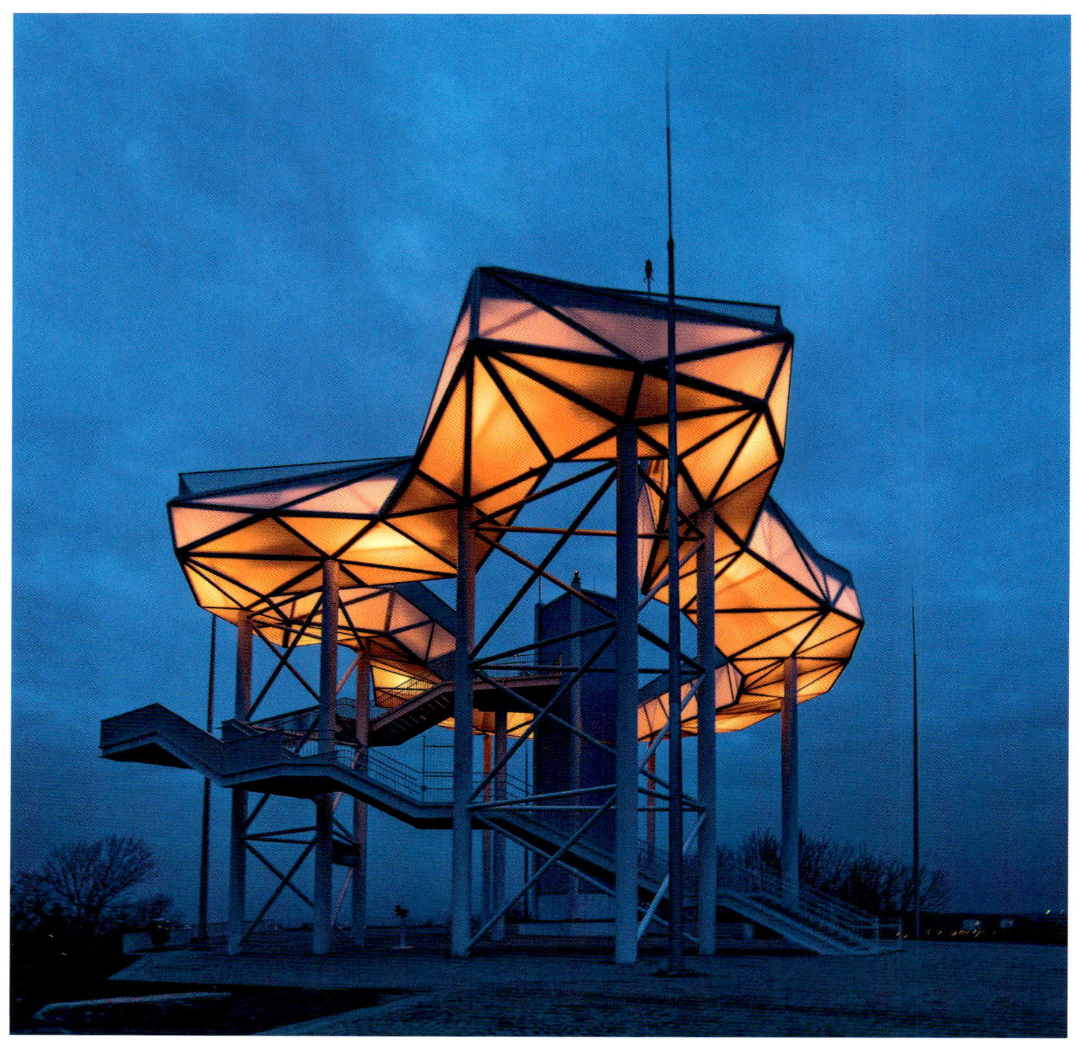

SCHLOTFELDT LICHT

HAMBURG / GERMANY

Atmospheric Effects | Atmosphärische Wirkung

Schlotfeldt Licht, a Hamburg-based lighting design firm for architectural projects, collaborates with builders and architects to plan appropriate lighting concepts. The team's goal is to consistently implement its creative vision based on the given technical possibilities. The individual, with his visual and emotional needs, is at the heart of every project. The effect of both daylight and artificial light on the surrounding architecture is determined, visualized and given due expression in the lighting concept. Schlotfeldt Licht has already successfully completed more than 400 national and international projects and has a number of design awards to its credit.

Das Hamburger Lichtplanungsbüro für Architekturprojekte, Schlotfeldt Licht, entwirft zusammen mit Bauherren und Architekten Konzepte zur Lichtwirkung von Architektur. Ziel des Teams ist eine konsequente Umsetzung der kreativen Visionen auf der Grundlage technischer Möglichkeiten. Im Mittelpunkt der Projekte steht immer der Mensch mit seinen visuell-emotionalen Bedürfnissen. So wird etwa die Wirkung von Tages- und Kunstlicht auf die umgebende Architektur erarbeitet, visualisiert und im Lichtkonzept umgesetzt. Schlotfeldt Licht hat bereits über 400 nationale und internationale Projekte erfolgreich abgeschlossen und wurde mit etlichen Designpreisen ausgezeichnet.

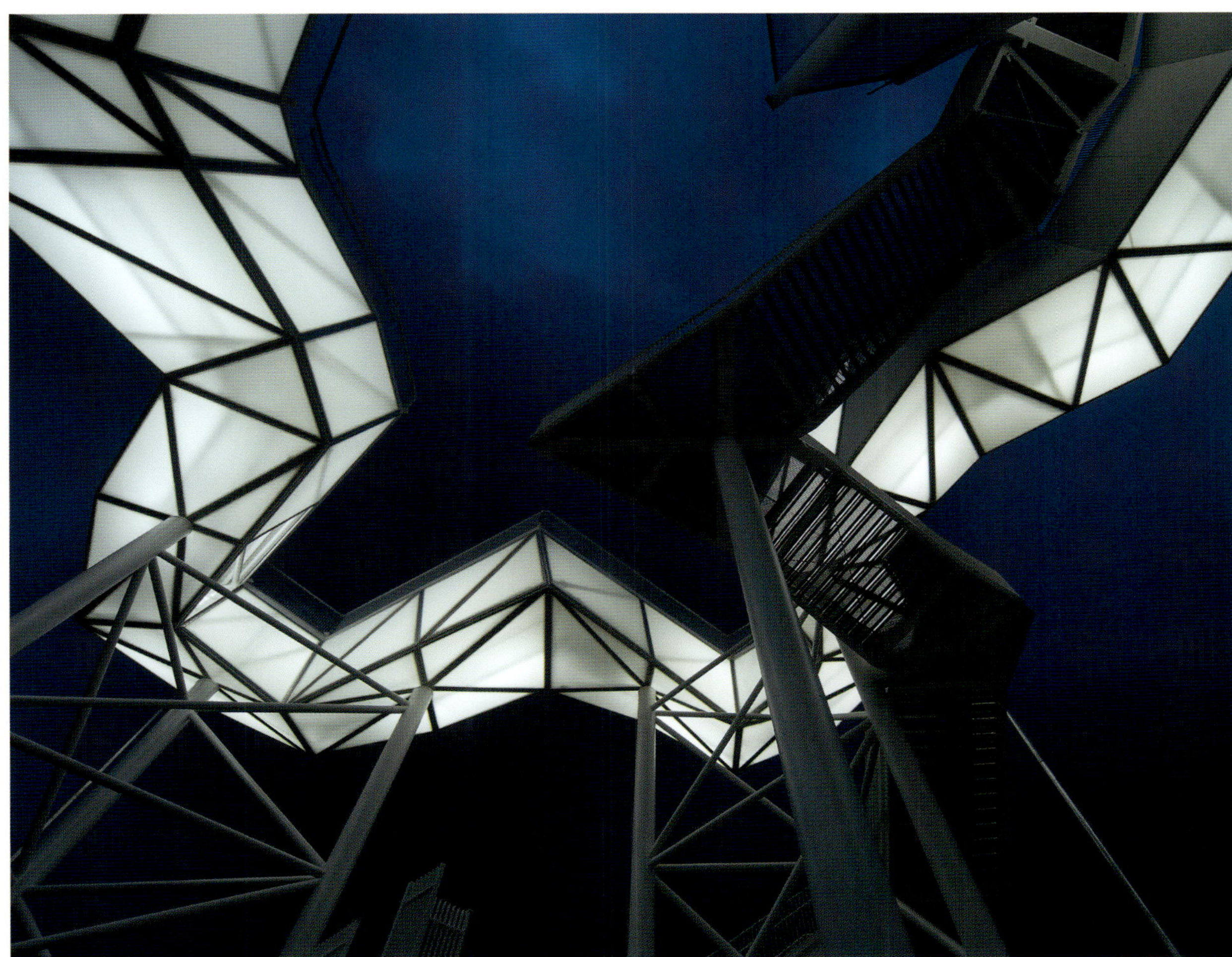

The Wolkenhain Viewing Platform, Kienbergpark, Berlin: the 'cloud' was the reception center for the International Garden Show (IGA). The polygonal steel building is equipped with a fiberglass diaphragm and controllable LEDs, which set the floating 'cloud' off impressively at nighttime.

Aussichtsbauwerk Wolkenhain, Kienbergpark, Berlin: Die „Wolke" war das Empfangszentrum der Internationalen Gartenausstellung (IGA). Das stählerne polygonale Bauwerk ist mit einer Glasfasermembran und steuerbaren LEDs versehen. So lässt sich die schwebende „Wolke" nachts stimmungsvoll in Szene setzen.

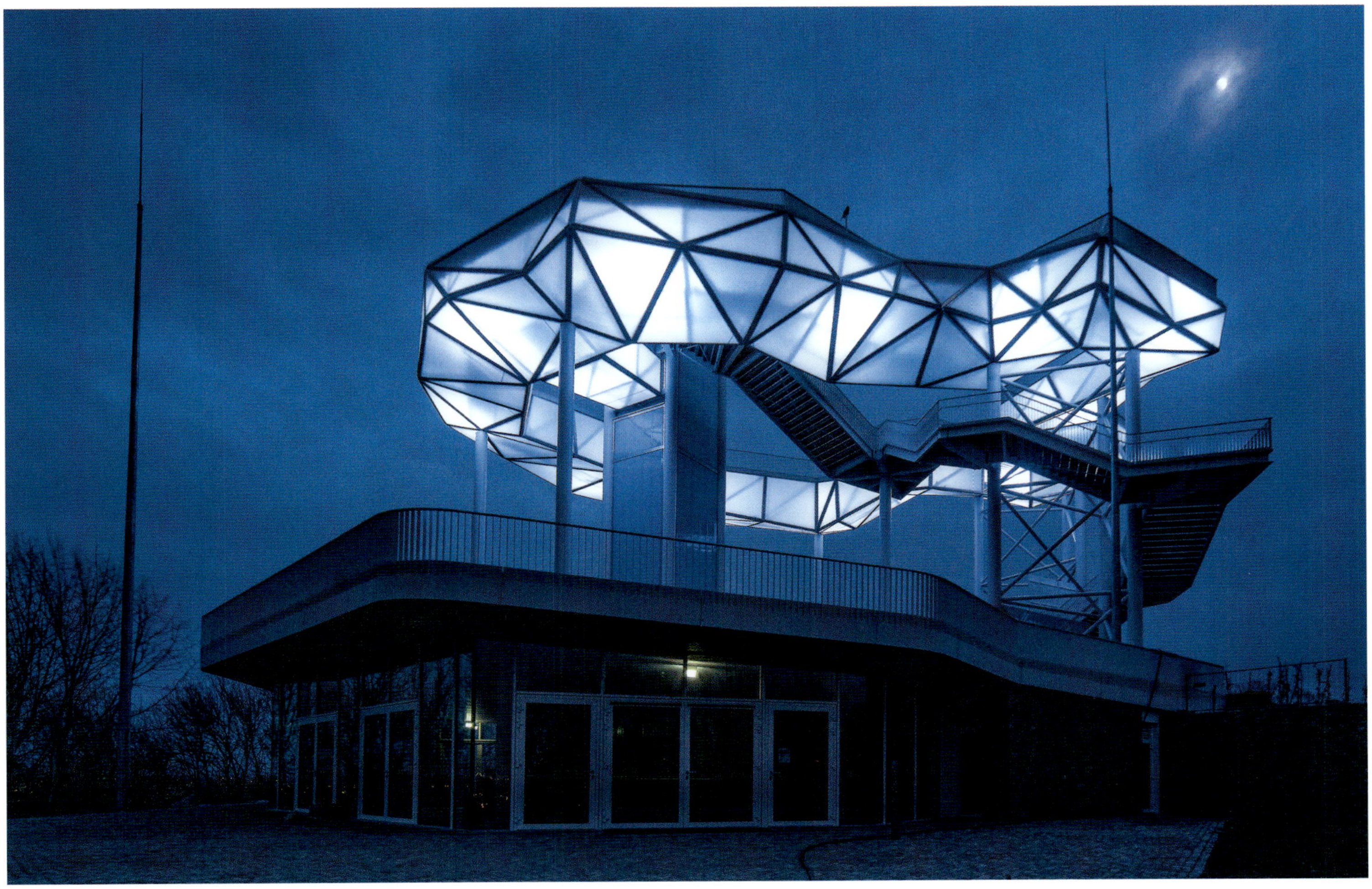

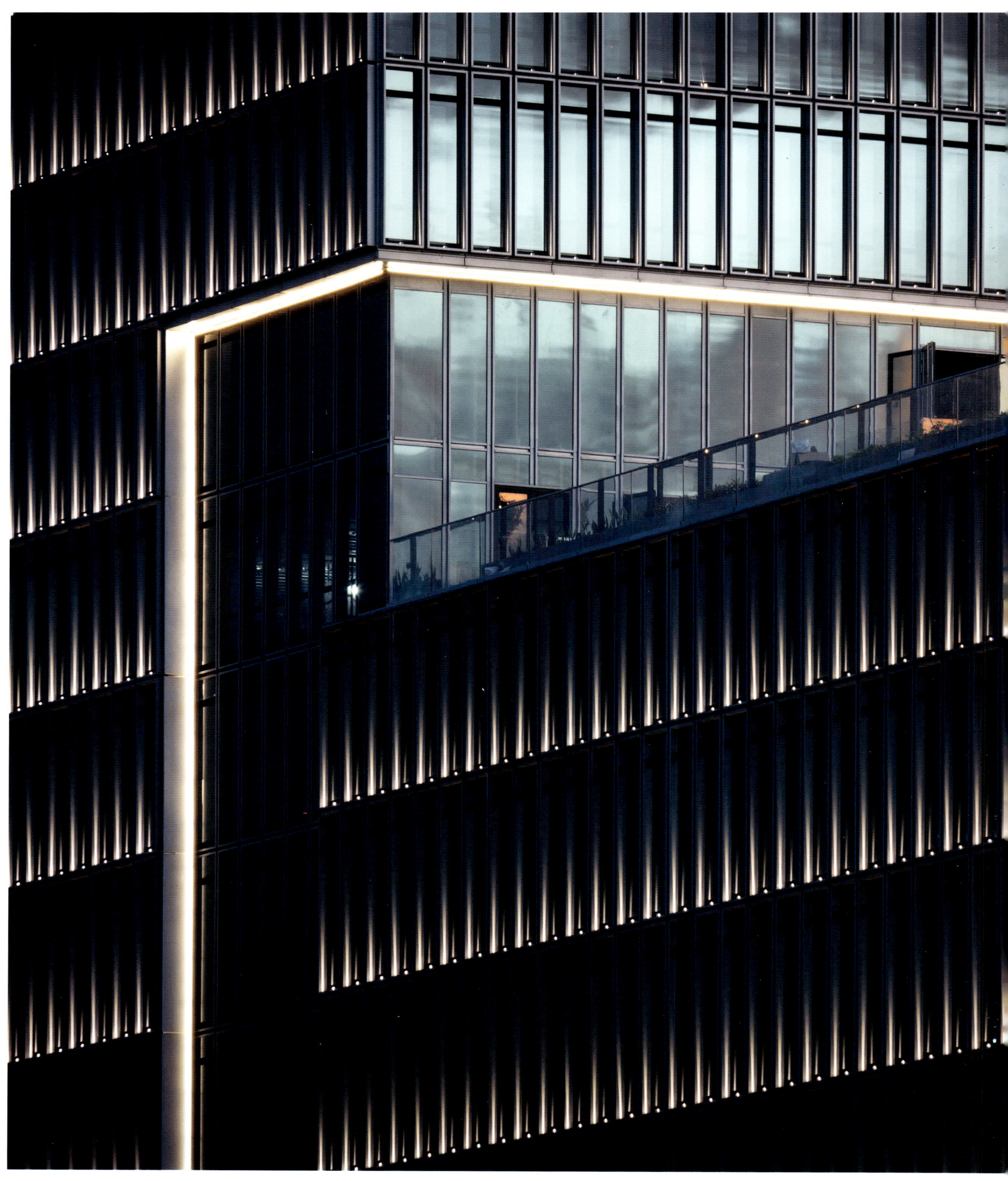

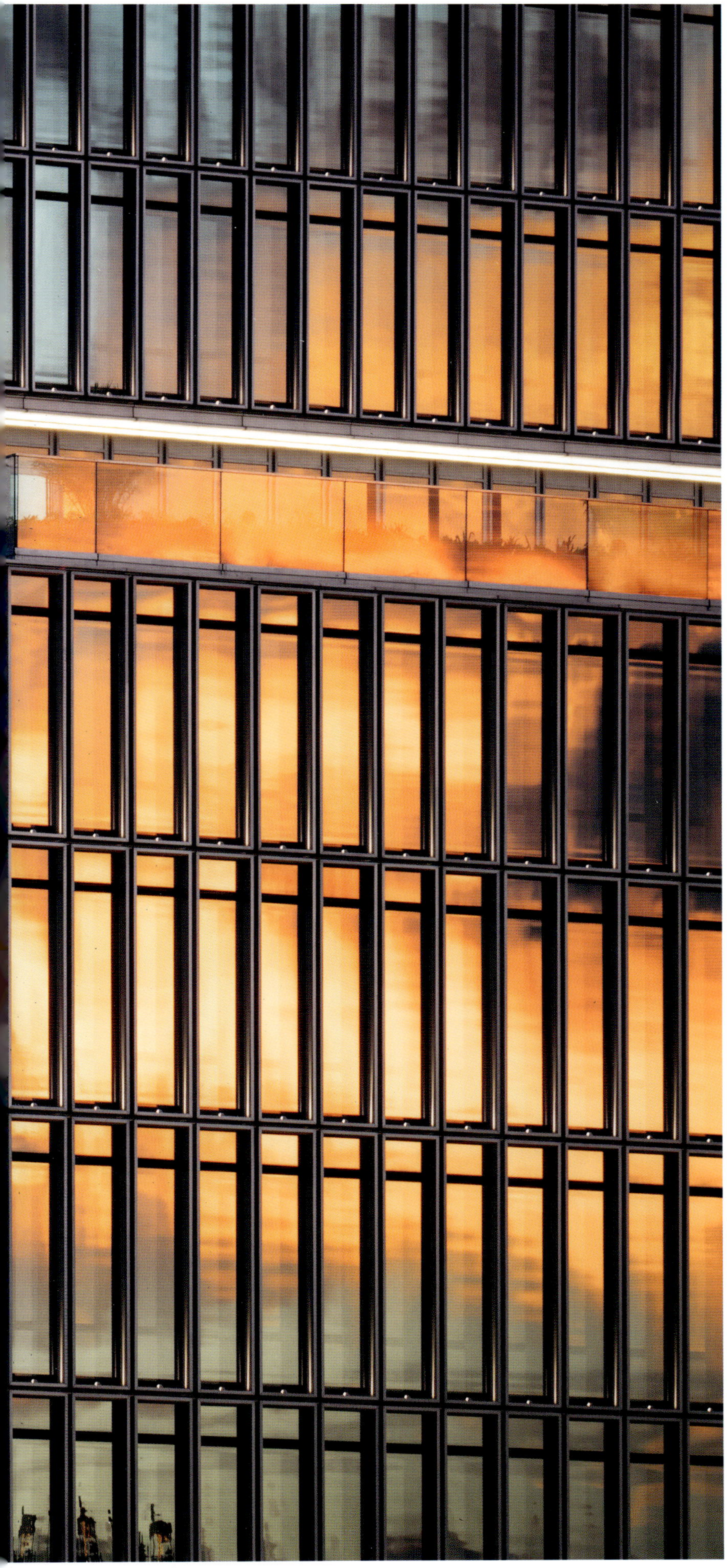

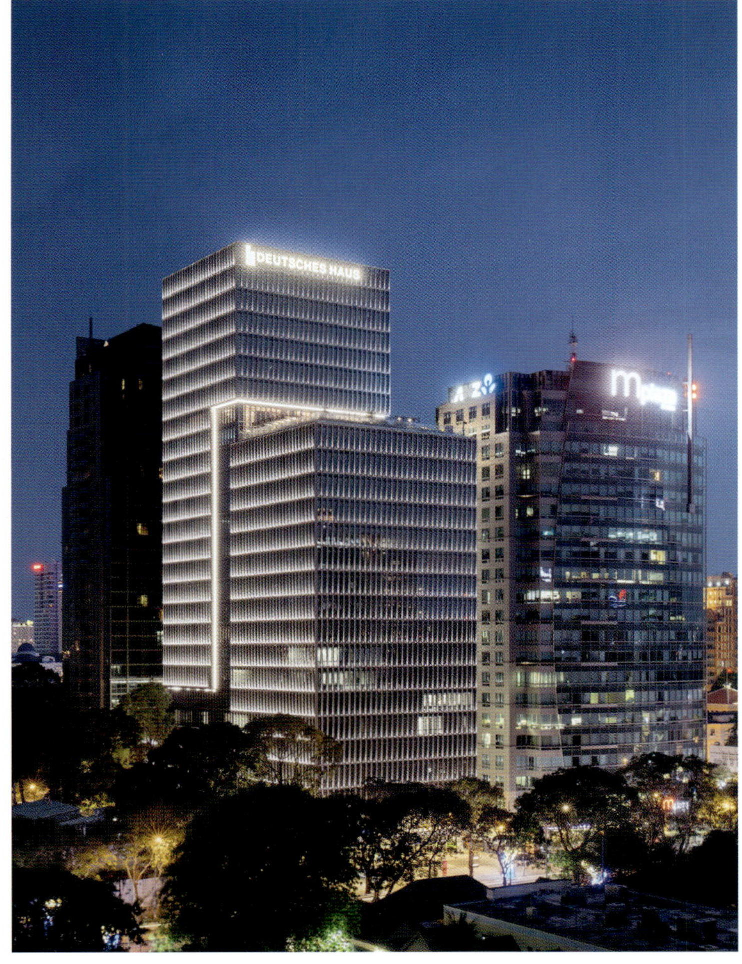

The German House
in Ho Chi Min City, Vietnam, houses a number of institutes and companies, in addition to the German Consulate General. Schlotfeldt Licht's lighting concept highlights the façade against the urban landscape distinctly, and accentuates the building's architecture with vertical and horizontal strips of light.

Das Deutsche Haus
in Ho-Chi-Minh-Stadt, Vietnam, beherbergt neben dem deutschen Generalkonsulat auch diverse Institute und Unternehmen. Die Lichtplanung von Schlotfeld Licht stellt die Fassade deutlich im Stadtbild heraus und betont die Gebäudearchitektur mit vertikalen und horizontalen Leuchtstreifen.

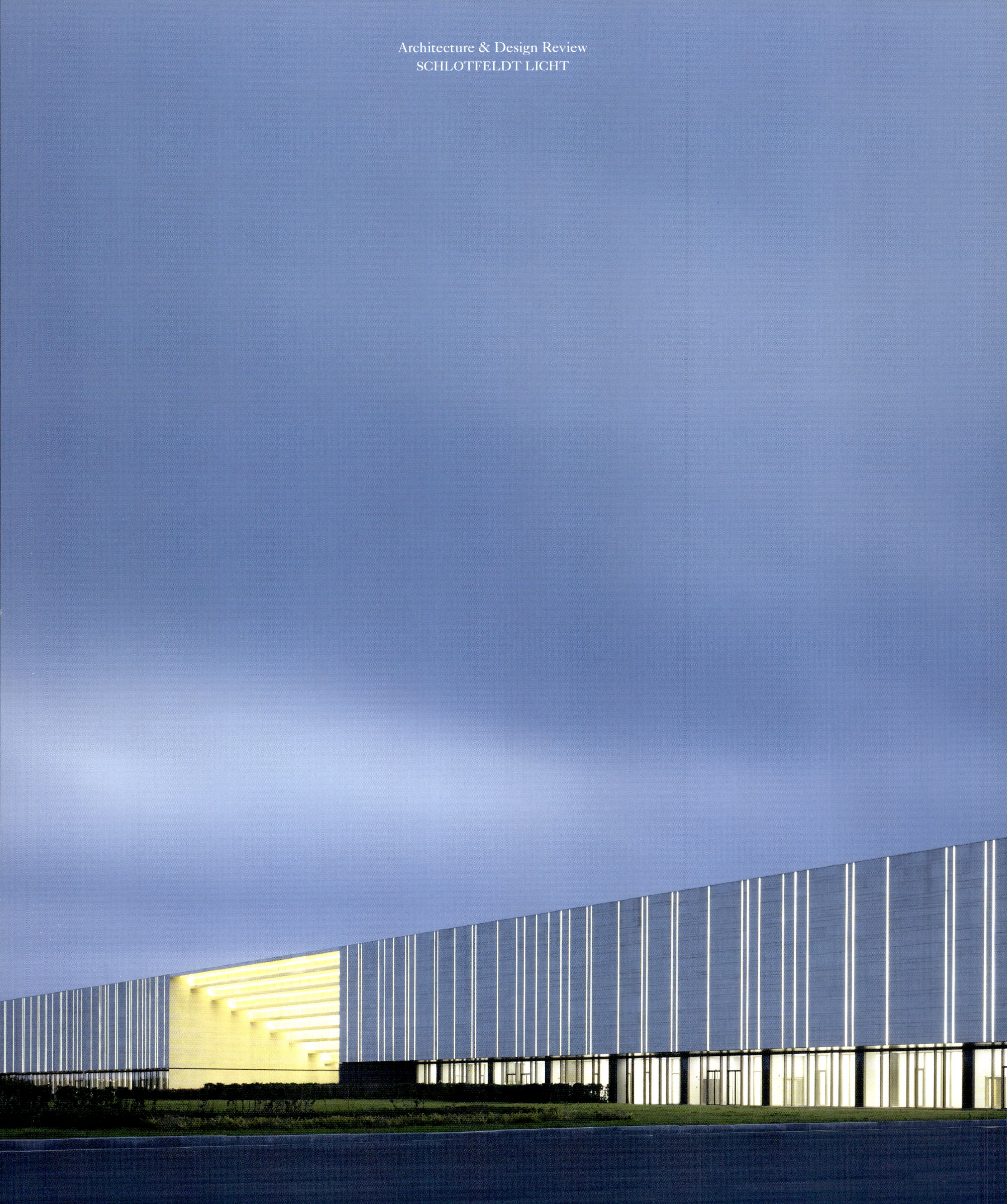
Architecture & Design Review
SCHLOTFELDT LICHT

Trade Show and Congress Center in Lianyungang, China: dynamically spaced vertical caesuras provide structure to large closed surfaces made of light granite. The resulting barcode image alludes to the building's function as a place of trade and business. The lighting concept underlines this idea by highlighting the façade's openings at nighttime.

Messe- und Kongresszentrum in Lianyungang, China: Große geschlossene Flächen aus hellem Granit sind durch dynamisch verteilte vertikale Zäsuren strukturiert. Als Referenz an die Funktion des Gebäudes als Ort des Handels und des Gewerbes entsteht so das Bild eines Barcodes. Die Lichtarchitektur unterstreicht diesen Gedanken, indem sie nachts die Öffnungen der Fassade betont.

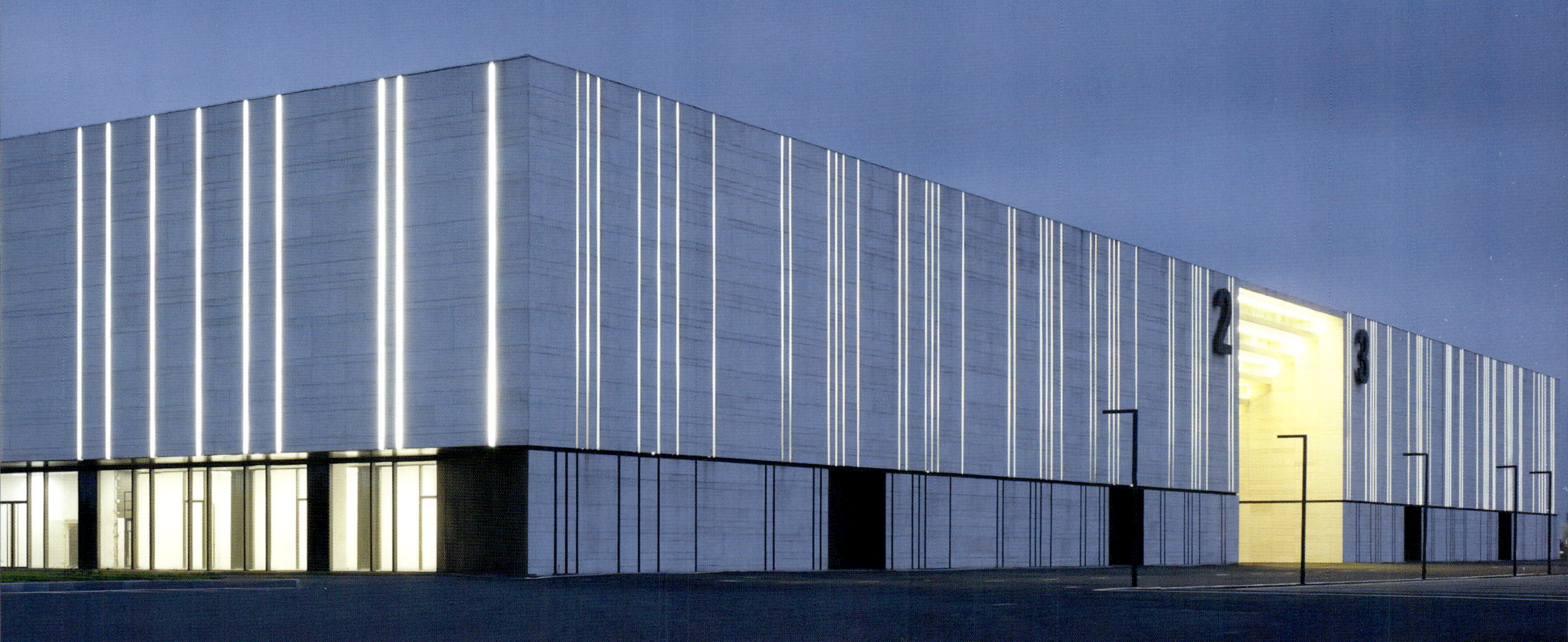

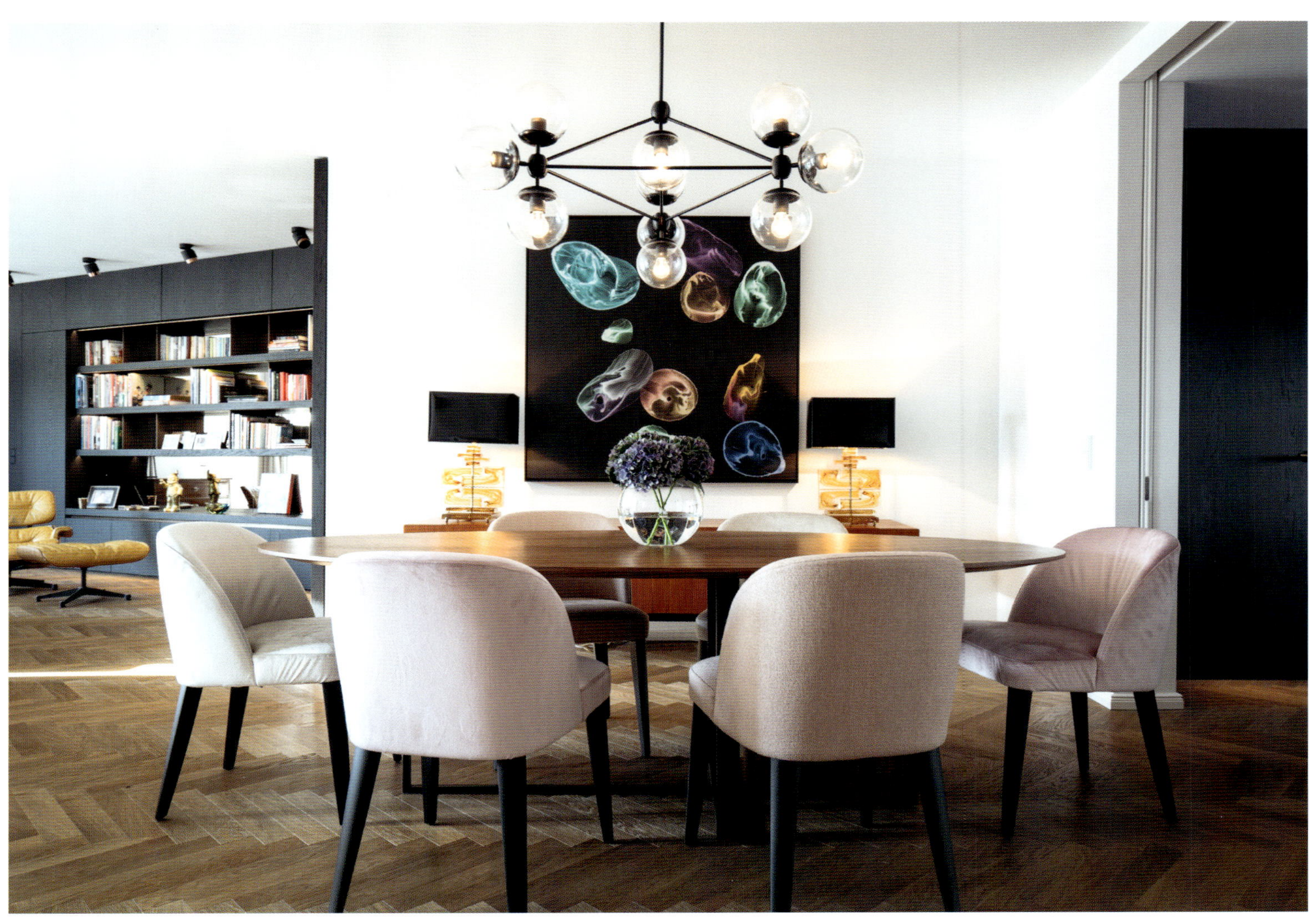

SEBASTIAN ZENKER
INTERIOR DESIGN

MUNICH / GERMANY

Light and Color | Licht und Farbe

The studio Sebastian Zenker Interior Design focuses primarily on private residential and hospitality projects. Together with his team, Sebastian Zenker refurbishes private residences, luxury hotels, up-market restaurants, exclusive retail stores and company boardrooms. A strong sense of style and aesthetics, combined with a drive for perfection and a preference for vivid colors and contrasts, are the hallmarks of his work. The project presented here is that of a spacious Munich roof terrace apartment, which he refurbished in an elegant yet relaxed style. His approach blends Mid-century modern, jazzy colors and high-quality fittings with classical elements and carefully selected furniture.

Der Fokus des Studios Sebastian Zenker Interior Design liegt auf privaten Residential- sowie Hospitality-Projekten. Gemeinsam mit seinem Team richtet Sebastian Zenker private Wohnträume sowie Luxushotels, gehobene Gastronomie, exklusive Stores und Vorstandsetagen ein. Stilsichere Ästhetik und Perfektion, gepaart mit klaren Linien, starken Farben und Kontrasten, sind seine Markenzeichen. Das hier gezeigte Projekt, ein großzügiges City-Apartment mit Dachterrasse in München, richtete er elegant und gleichzeitig lässig in einem spannenden Mix aus Mid-Century, poppigen Farben und hochwertigen Einbauten ein, kombiniert mit klassischen Elementen und erlesenem Mobiliar.

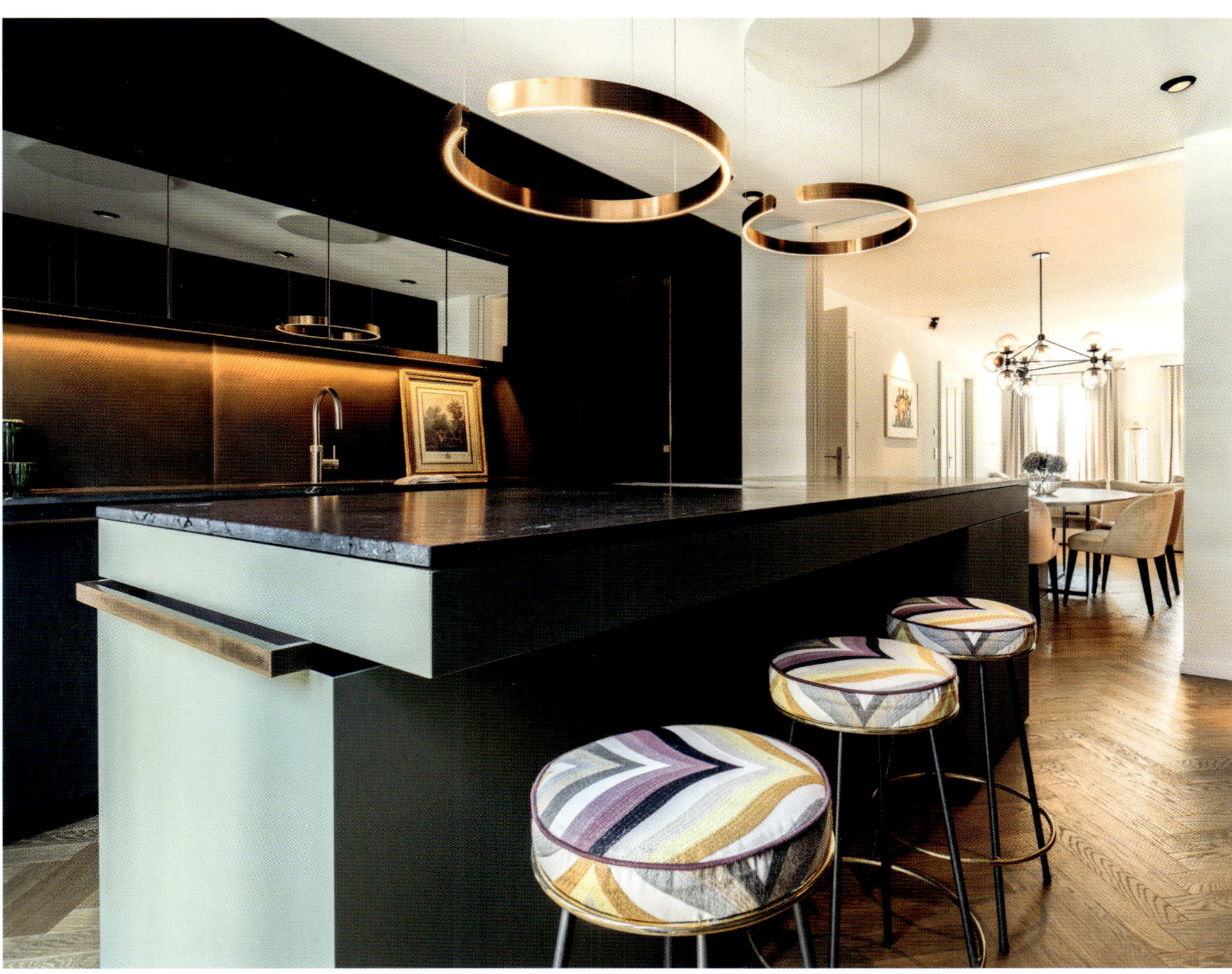

In the tastefully and yet informally refurbished Munich apartment, Zenker combined elegant flooring and fittings, from brands such as Holzrausch (below), with vintage and bespoke furniture. Also included are *en vogue* items such as Occhio light fittings and a Meridiani dining table and chairs (opposite page).

In der lässig-eleganten Münchner Stadtwohnung kombinierte Zenker edle Böden und Einbauten, etwa von der Marke Holzrausch (unten), mit Vintage-Möbeln oder Sonderanfertigungen. Dazu kommen Design-Must-haves wie Leuchten der Marke Occhio (links) oder ein Esstisch mit Sitzmöbeln von Meridiani (Seite gegenüber).

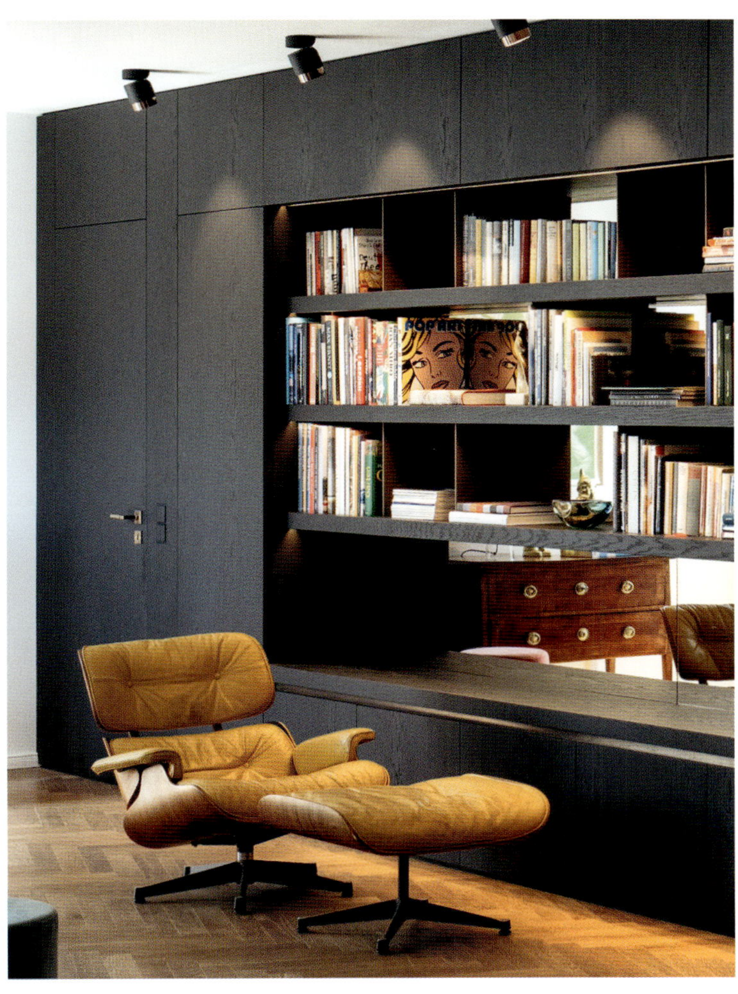

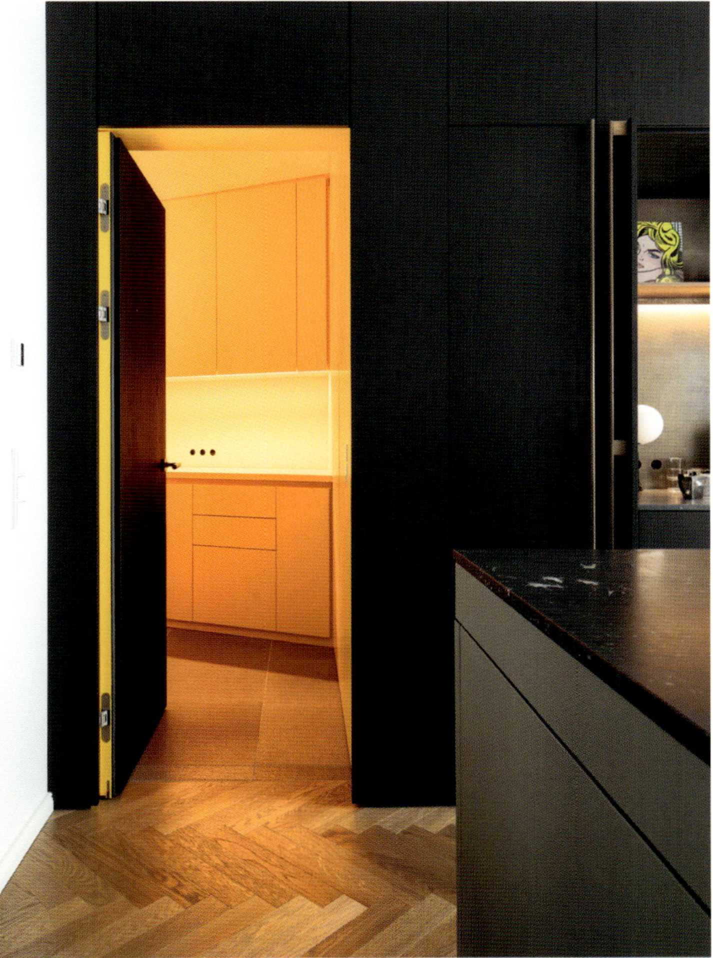

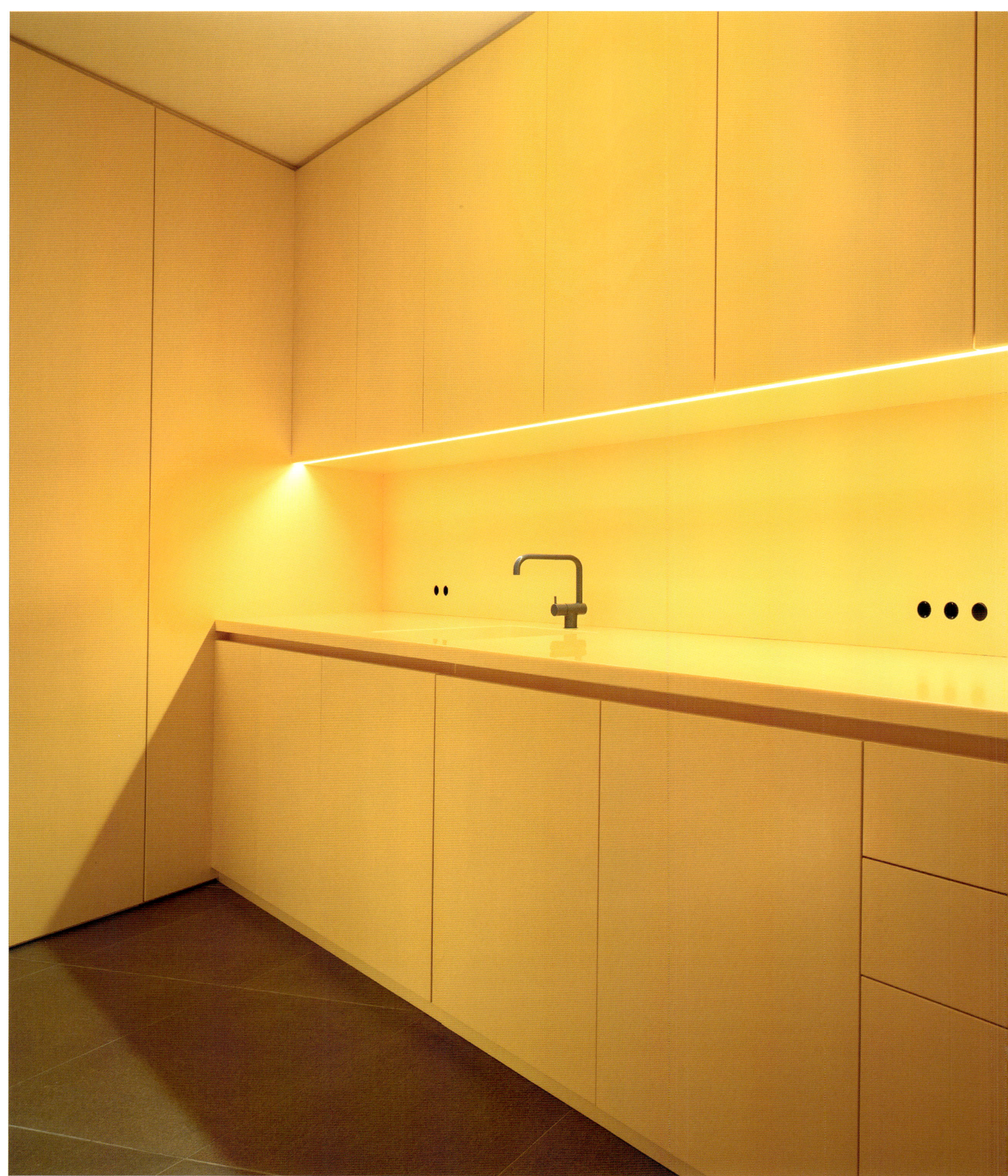

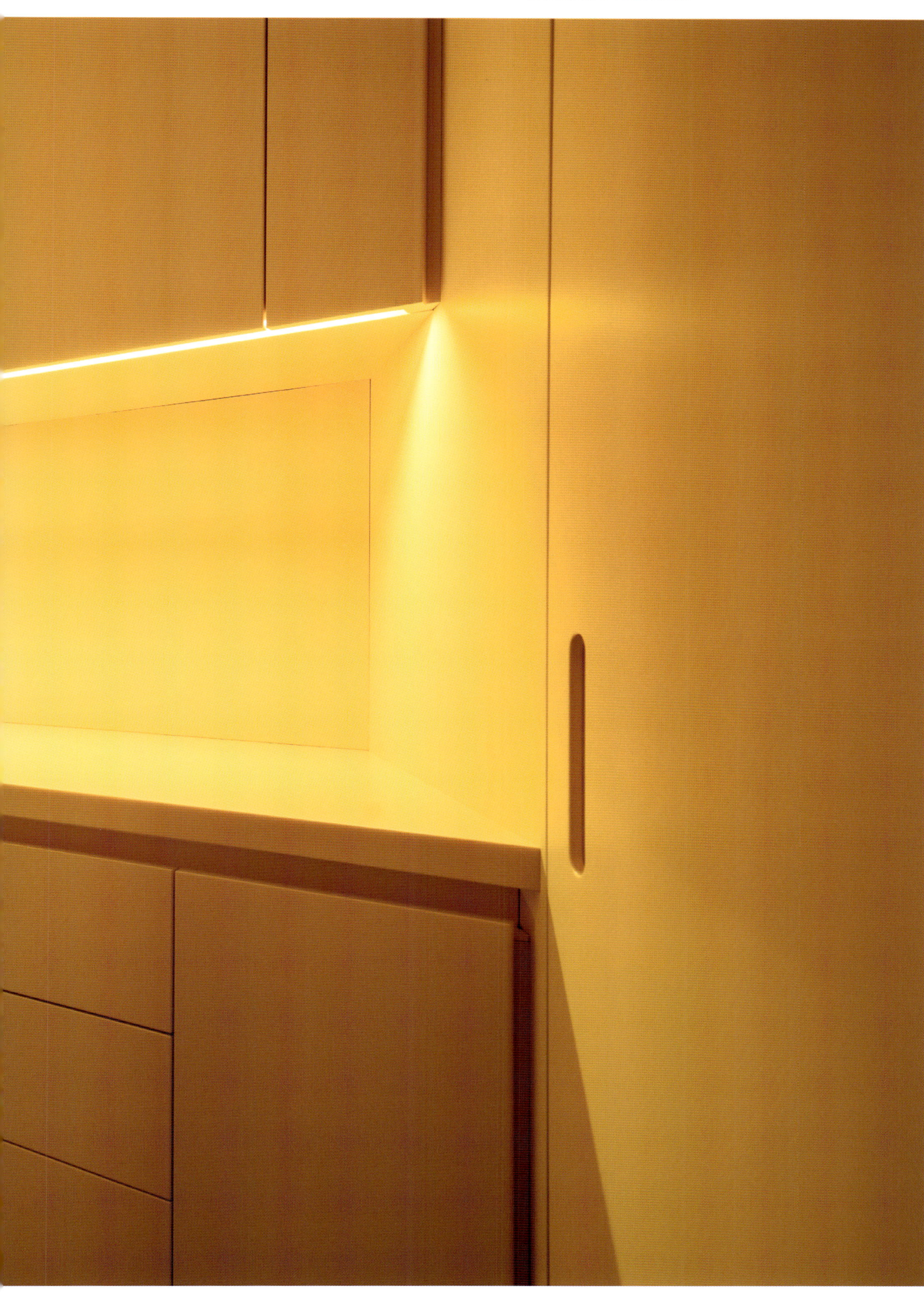

This utility room, which directly adjoins the Munich apartment's kitchen, allows Sebastian Zenker to create additional space—more room for working and for everything that should not be left lying around in the cooking and dining area. The bright yellow turns this artificially lit room into a hidden jewel. Puristic design and functionality are perfectly united.

Mit diesem Hauswirtschaftsraum, der direkt an die Küche der Münchner Wohnung angrenzt, schafft Sebastian Zenker zusätzlichen Raum: mehr Platz zum Arbeiten und für alles, was im Koch- und Essbereich nicht herumstehen soll. Das knallige Gelb macht diesen tageslichtlosen Raum zu einem versteckten Juwel. Puristische Formensprache und Funktionalität bilden hier eine ideale Einheit.

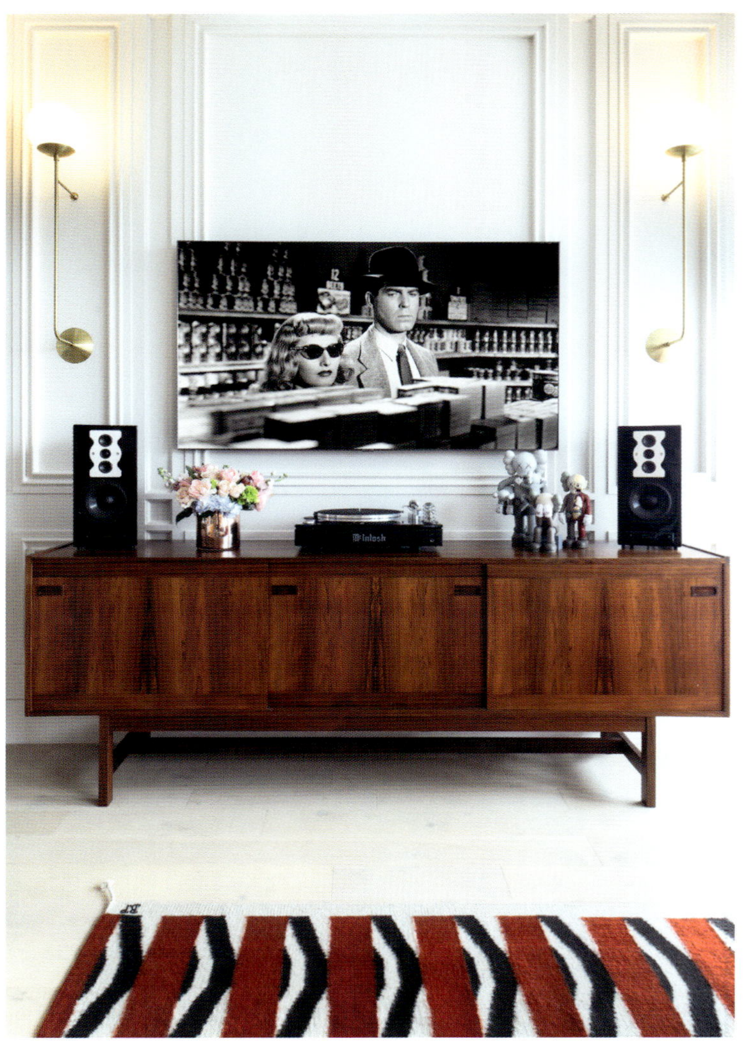

SOFÍA ASPE

MEXICO CITY / MEXICO

Artistic Blends | Kunstvolle Mischungen

Sofía Aspe is renowned for creating eclectic, colorful and comfortable spaces which blend different styles, eras, colors, materials and artistic elements. She established her firm Sofía Aspe Interiorismo in 2011. Since then, Aspe and her team have made a name for themselves with high-end residential projects in Mexico and the US. For the interior design of an apartment in a luxury sky rise in Austin, Texas, Mid-Century Modern was blended with contemporary design, but not at the expense of coziness and functionality. The team combined colorful wallpapers, white boiseries, wood flooring and selected vintage furniture to achieve this effect.

Eklektische, farbenfrohe und komfortable Räume, in denen sich ganz unterschiedliche Stile, Epochen, Farben, Materialien und Kunstelemente mischen – das ist typisch Sofía Aspe. Ihre Firma Sofía Aspe Interiorismo gründete sie 2011. Seitdem haben sich Aspe und ihr Team vor allem mit hochwertigen Wohnprojekten in Mexiko und den USA einen Namen gemacht. Für die Innengestaltung einer Wohnung in einem exklusiven Hochhaus in Austin, Texas, sollte Mid-Century- mit heutigem Design kombiniert werden, ohne Verlust an Funktionalität und Wohnlichkeit, was mit bunten Tapeten, weißer Wandtäfelung, Parkett und ausgewählten Vintage-Möbeln erreicht wurde.

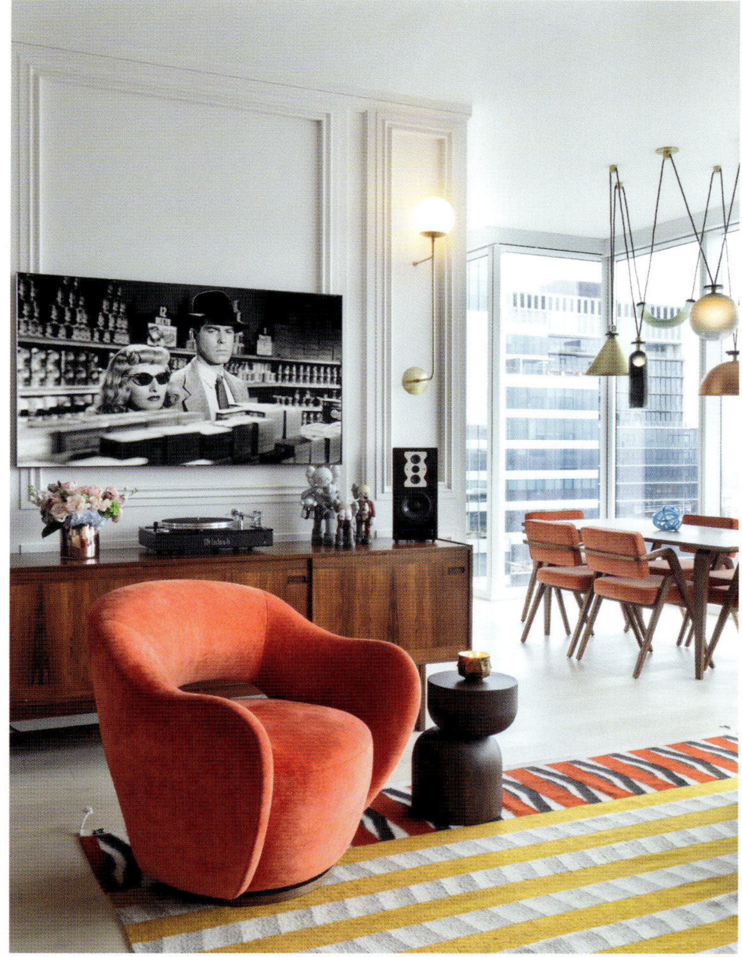

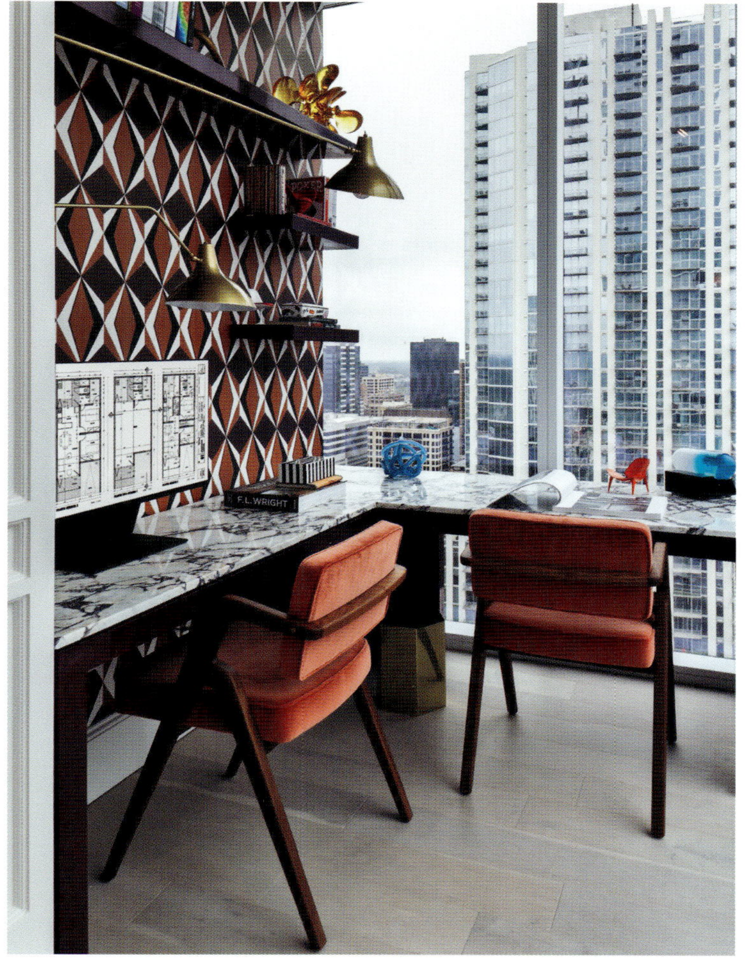

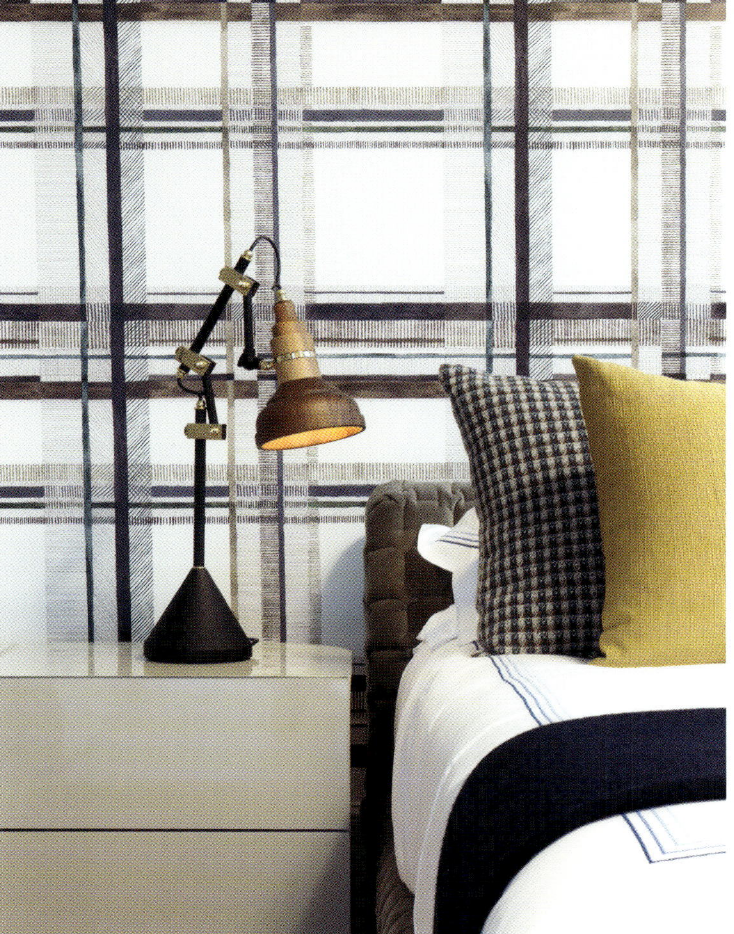

Elegant retro touches
in a modern ambience:
In the living and
dining room (opposite
page and top left),
Vladimir Kagan's red
'WYSIWYG chair'
is placed in front
of a 1stdibs vintage
sideboard; the dining
chairs are from Luteca.
Pierre Frey designed
the wallpaper in the
study (top right), while
the bedroom table
lamps (left) are from
1stdibs.

Edle Retro-Anklänge
in moderner Atmo-
sphäre: Im Wohn-
und Esszimmer (Seite
gegenüber und oben
links) steht der rote
„WYSIWYG Chair"
von Vladimir Kagan
vor einem Vintage-
Sideboard von 1stdibs;
die Stühle am Esstisch
sind von Luteca. Die
Tapete im Büro (oben
rechts) ist von Pierre
Frey, die Tischleuchte
im Schlafzimmer
(links) von 1stdibs.

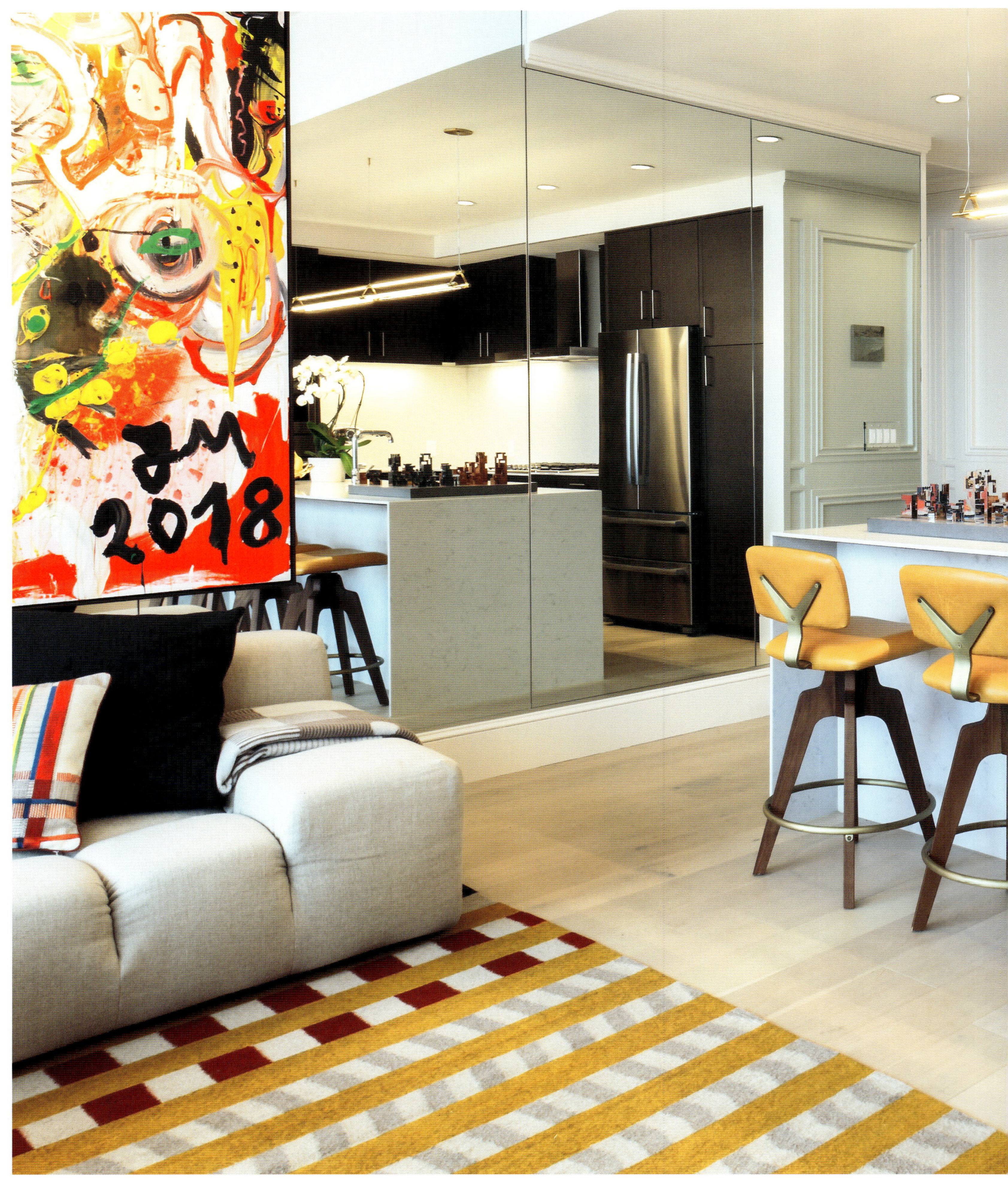

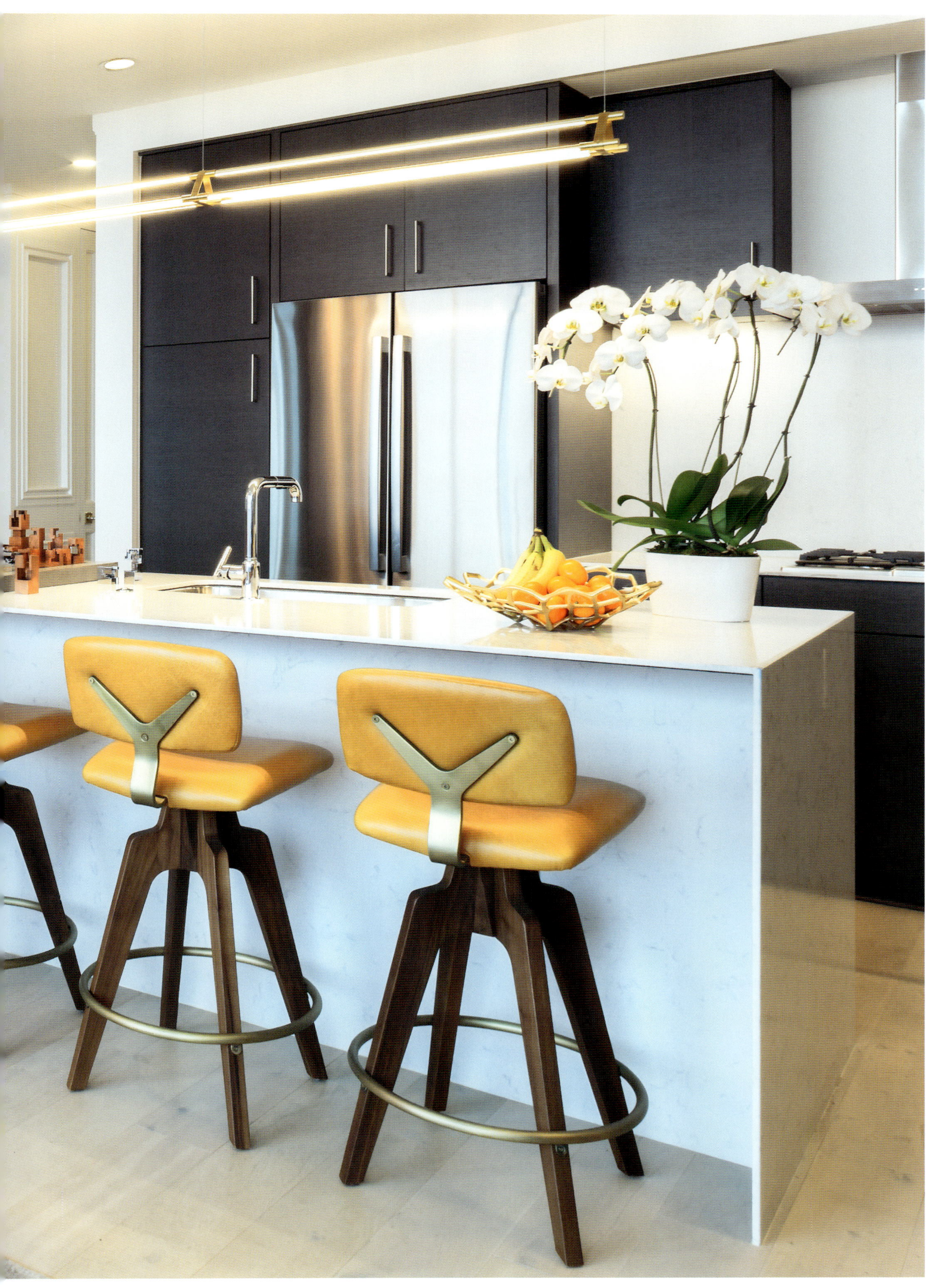

Homely designer kitchen with a bar and four stools from 1stdibs. The long ceiling lamp was created by Juniper Design Lighting and the fruit bowl in front of the flowers by Tom Dixon, while the chessboard on the left of the bar was designed by Jorge Yázpik. The German artist Jonathan Meese painted the picture above the sofa; the woolen carpet in front of it was handcrafted in Teotitlán del Valle, Oaxaca, Mexico.

Wohnliche Designerküche mit Tresen und vier Counter Stools von 1stdibs. Die längliche Deckenleuchte wurde von Juniper Design Lighting gefertigt, die Obstschale vor den Blumen ist von Tom Dixon und das Schachspiel links auf dem Tresen von Jorge Yázpik. Das Gemälde über den Sofa stammt von dem deutschen Maler Jonathan Meese, der Wollteppich davor wurde in Teotitlán del Valle, Oaxaca, Mexiko, handgefertigt.

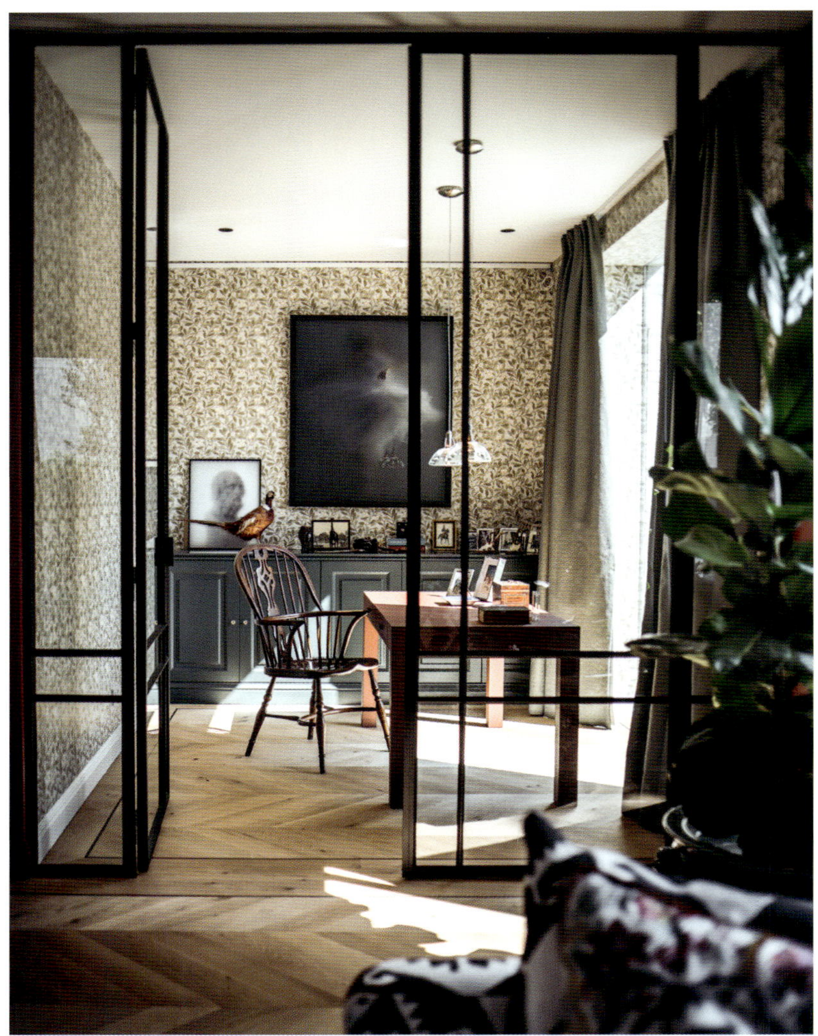

STOCK DUTCH DESIGN

OVERVEEN / NETHERLANDS

Harmonies and Contrasts | Harmonien und Kontraste

Leonie Hendrikse and Jeroen Stock, the founders of Stock Dutch Design, and their team are advocates of timeless design. The projects presented here are typical examples of the special Stock 4.0 signature: in a newly constructed, majestic townhouse here, the Stock designers and their partners were able to give free rein to their creativity in matters of color. And in a traditional Amsterdam villa (pages 200–202), the charm of high ceilings was to be preserved while, at the same time, ensuring a cozy ambience. A well-conceived lighting design provides a path of light from the living room through to the kitchen, emphasizing the contrast between traditional and modern.

Leonie Hendrikse und Jeroen Stock, die Gründer von Stock Dutch Design, stehen mit ihrem Team für zeitlose Gestaltung. Die abgebildeten Projekte sind typische Beispiele für die spezielle Stock-Signatur 4.0: In einem neu erbauten majestätischen Stadthaus durften die Stock-Designer und ihre Partner ihre farbenfrohe Kreativität ausleben. Und in einer traditionellen Villa in Amsterdam (Seite 200–202) sollte der Reiz der tiefen Räume erhalten bleiben und gleichzeitig Gemütlichkeit entstehen. Ein durchdachter Lichtplan schafft dort vom Wohnzimmer bis zur Küche eine Lichtverbindung, die den Kontrast zwischen Tradition und Moderne elegant betont.

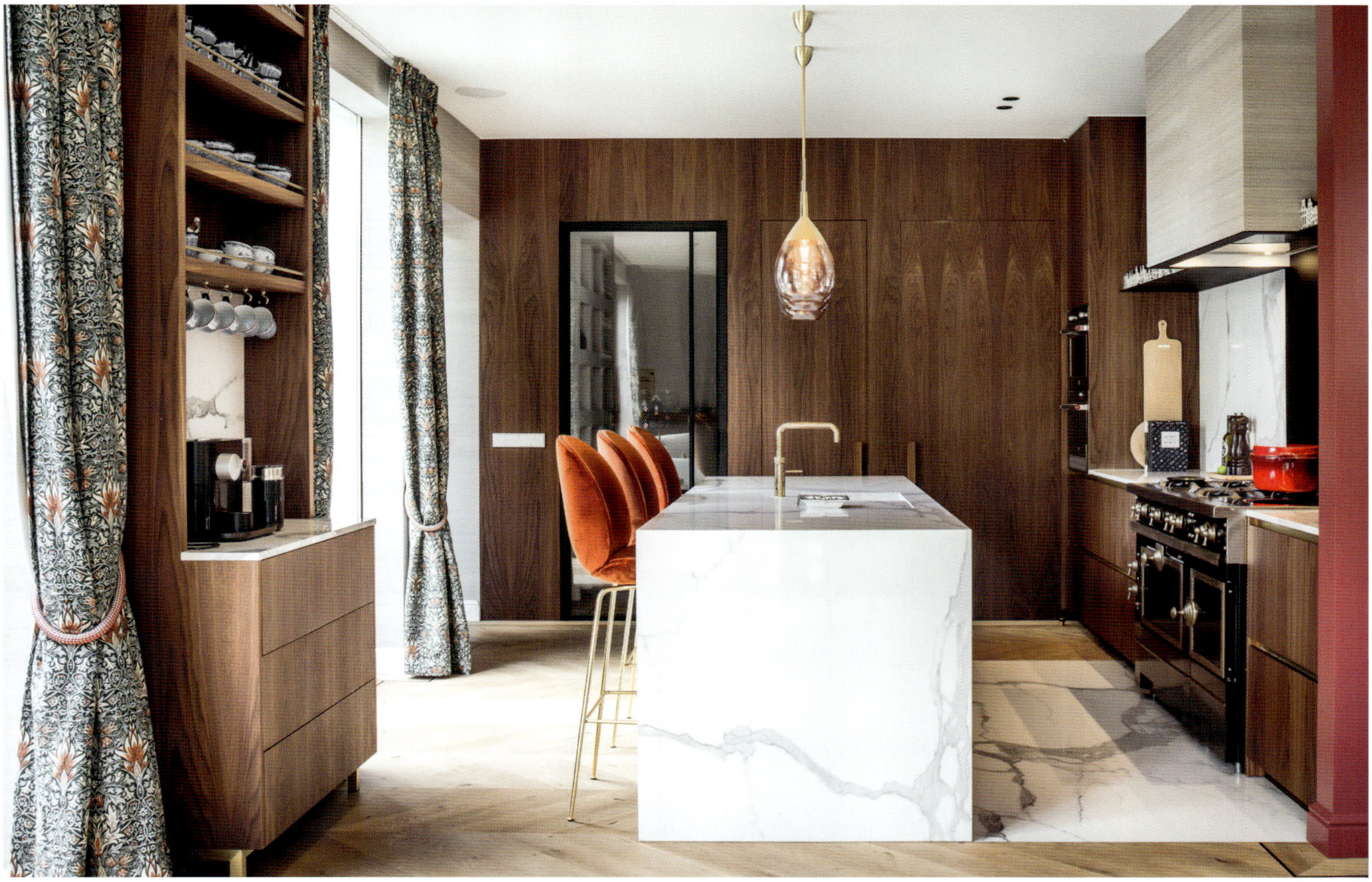

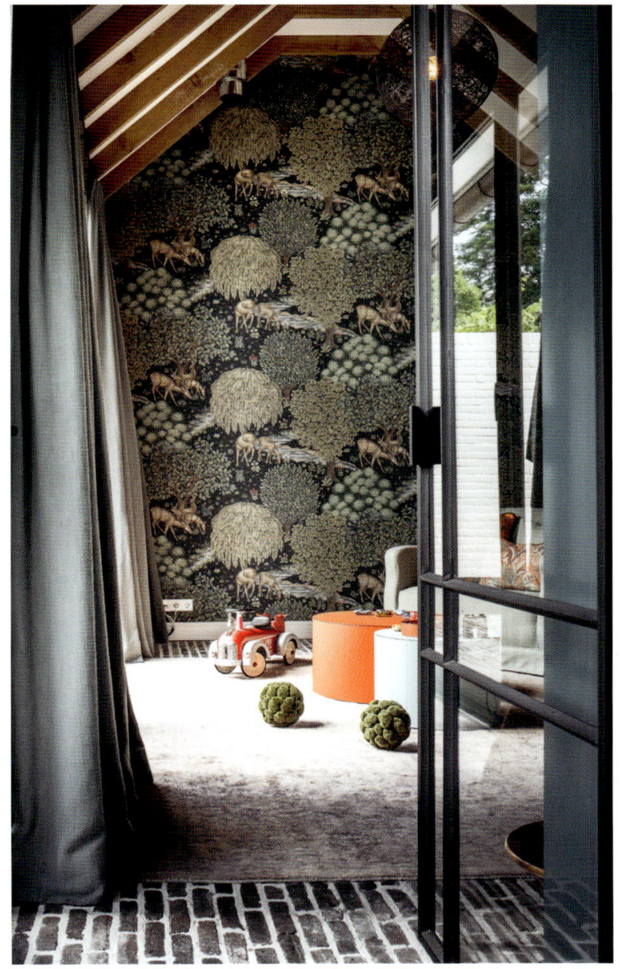

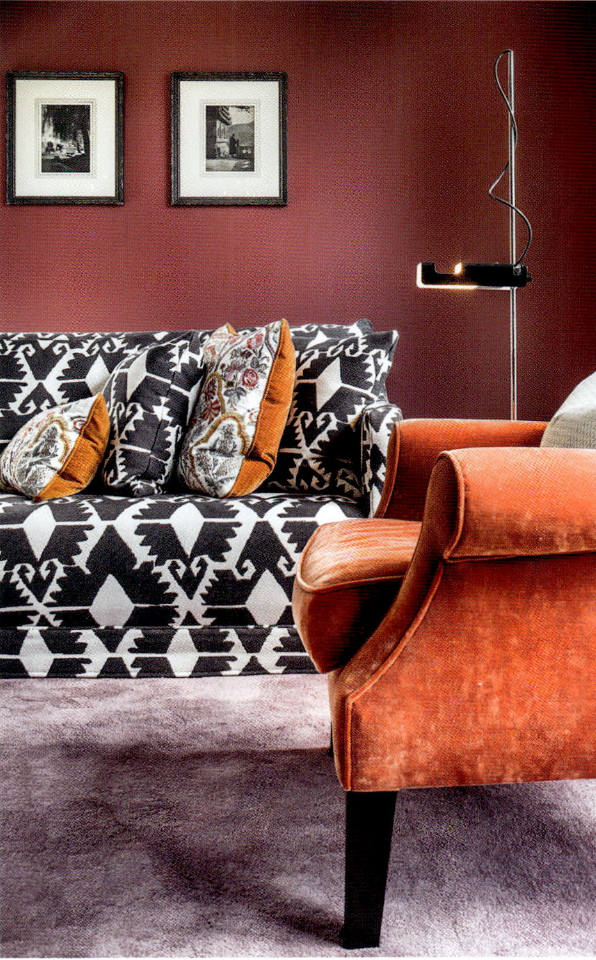

The beautiful English wallpaper in the study sets off the photographs by the artist Casper Faassen to their best advantage (opposite page). The small kitchen (above) thrives on the contrast of classical and modern design features; in the colorful living room (left), the black and white couch adds a special touch.

Die schöne englische Tapete im Arbeitszimmer bringt die Fotografien des Künstlers Casper Faassen besonders gut zur Geltung (Seite gegenüber). Die kleine Küche (oben) lebt vom Gegensatz klassischer und moderner Designelemente; im farbenfrohen Wohnzimmer (links) setzt die schwarz-weiße Couch einen besonderen Akzent.

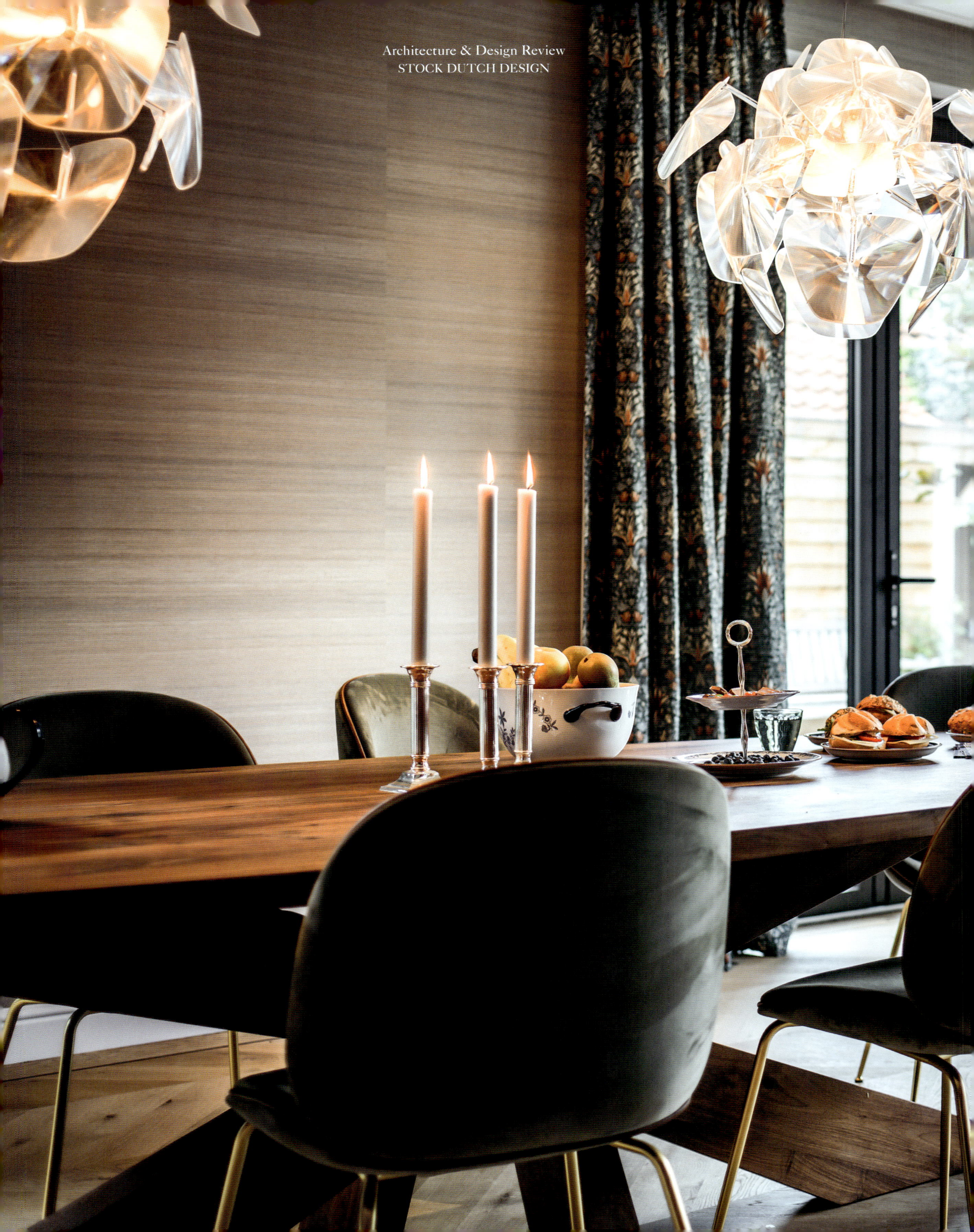

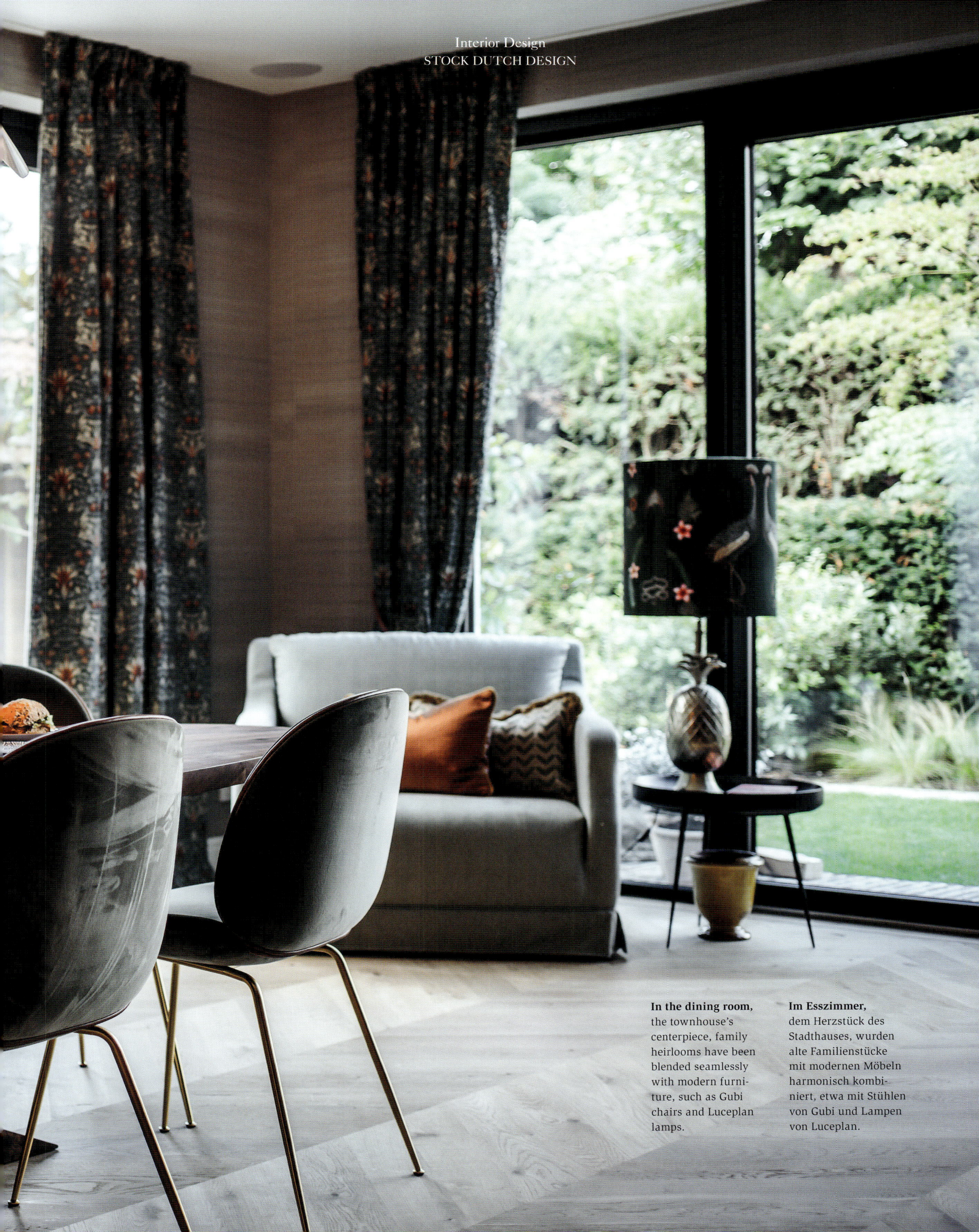

In the dining room, the townhouse's centerpiece, family heirlooms have been blended seamlessly with modern furniture, such as Gubi chairs and Luceplan lamps.

Im Esszimmer, dem Herzstück des Stadthauses, wurden alte Familienstücke mit modernen Möbeln harmonisch kombiniert, etwa mit Stühlen von Gubi und Lampen von Luceplan.

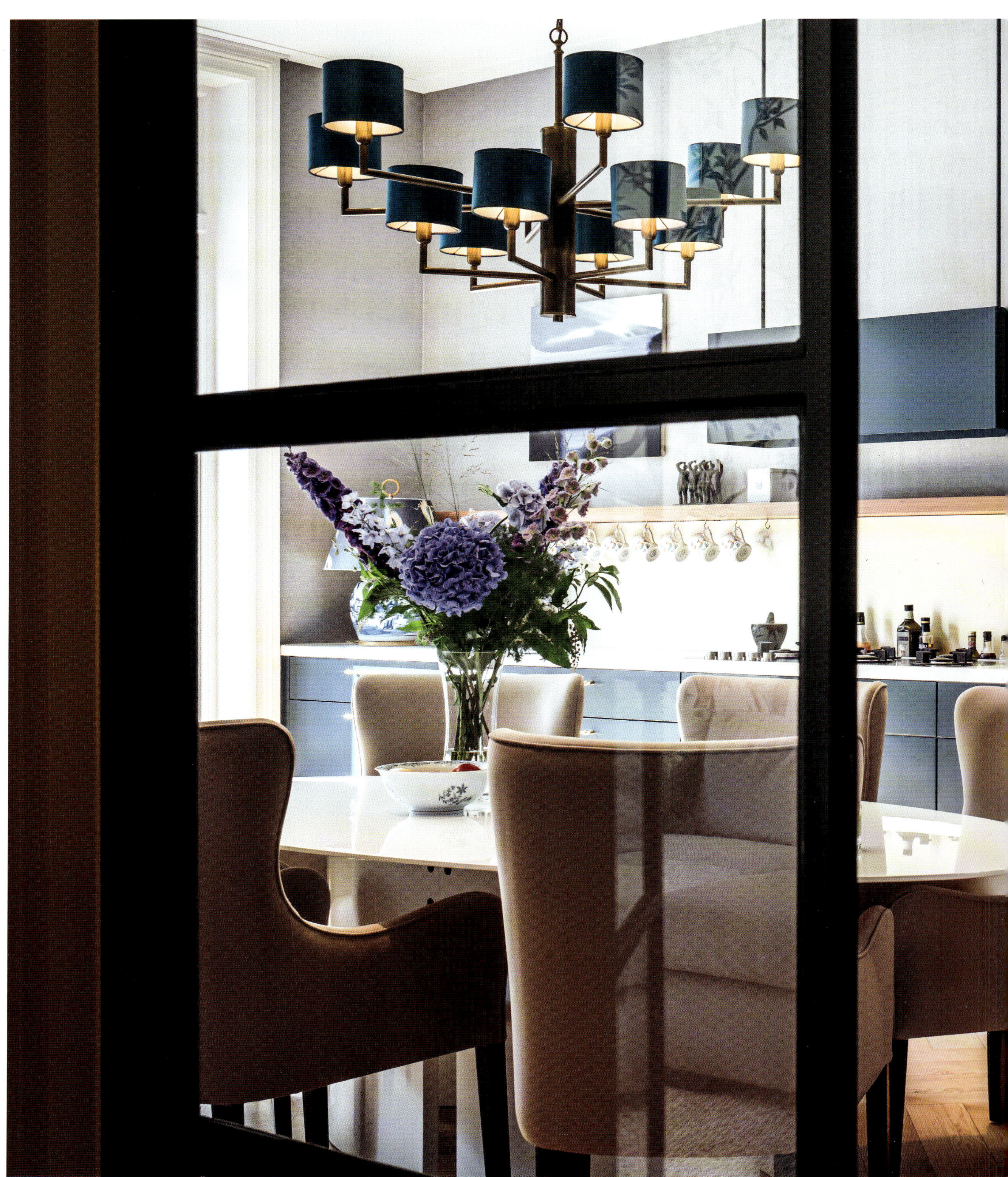

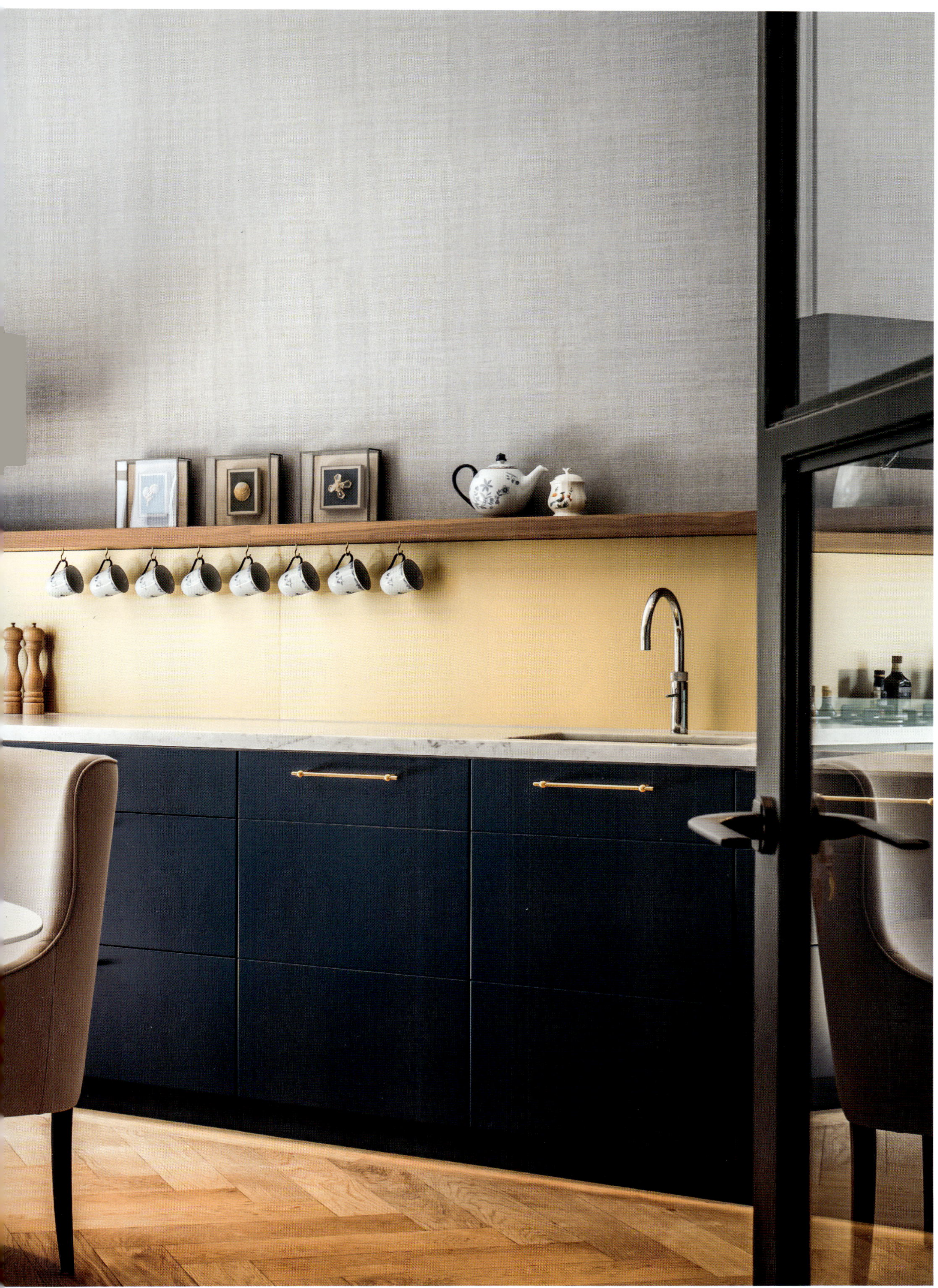

Upon entering the kitchen in the Amsterdam villa, it is striking how well the wooden floor's natural material blends in with the modern, black door. 'The Leonie', a hanging lamp designed by Stock, perfectly matches the blue cupboard fronts.

Beim Betreten der Küche der Amsterdamer Villa fällt auf, wie gut das natürliche Material des Holzbodens mit der modernen schwarzen Tür harmoniert. Auch passt der von Stock designte Kronleuchter „The Leonie" perfekt zum Blau der Schrankfronten.

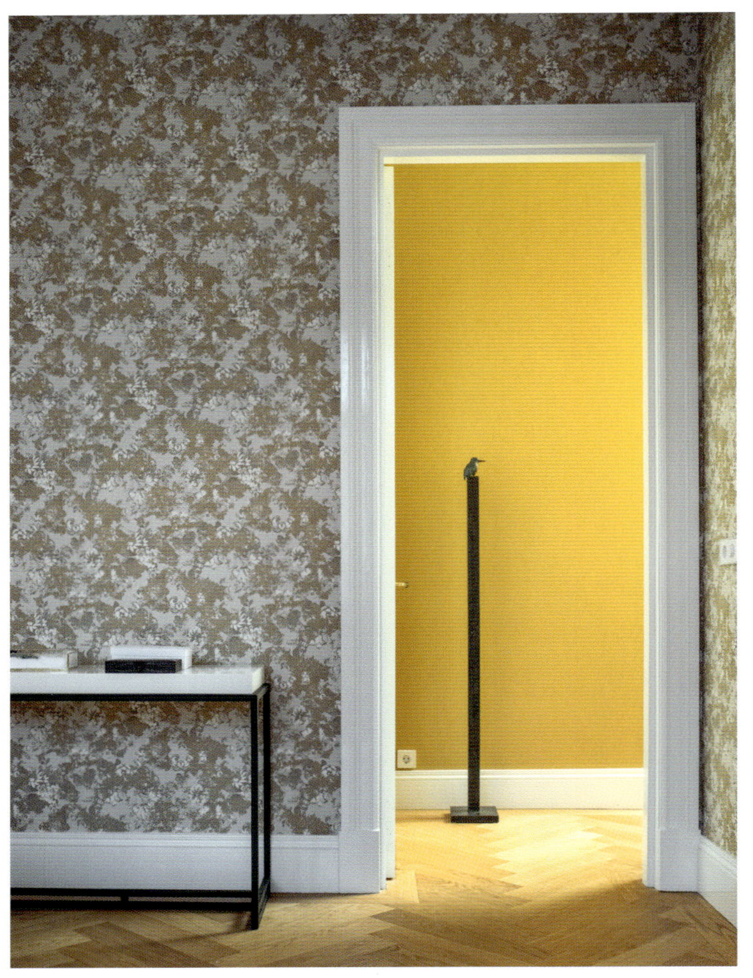

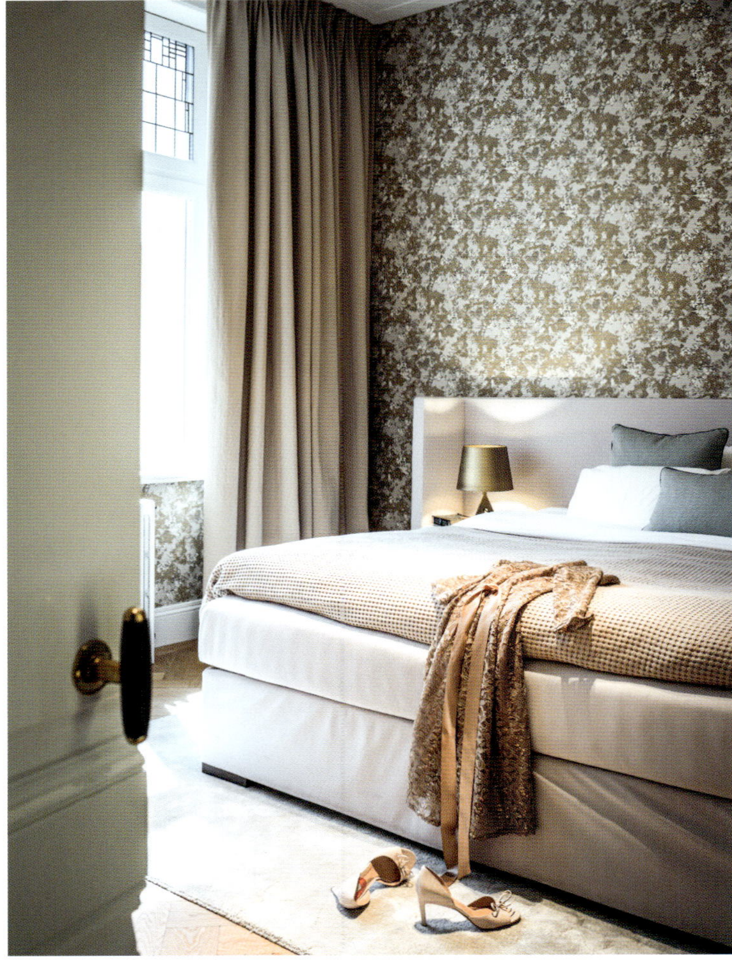

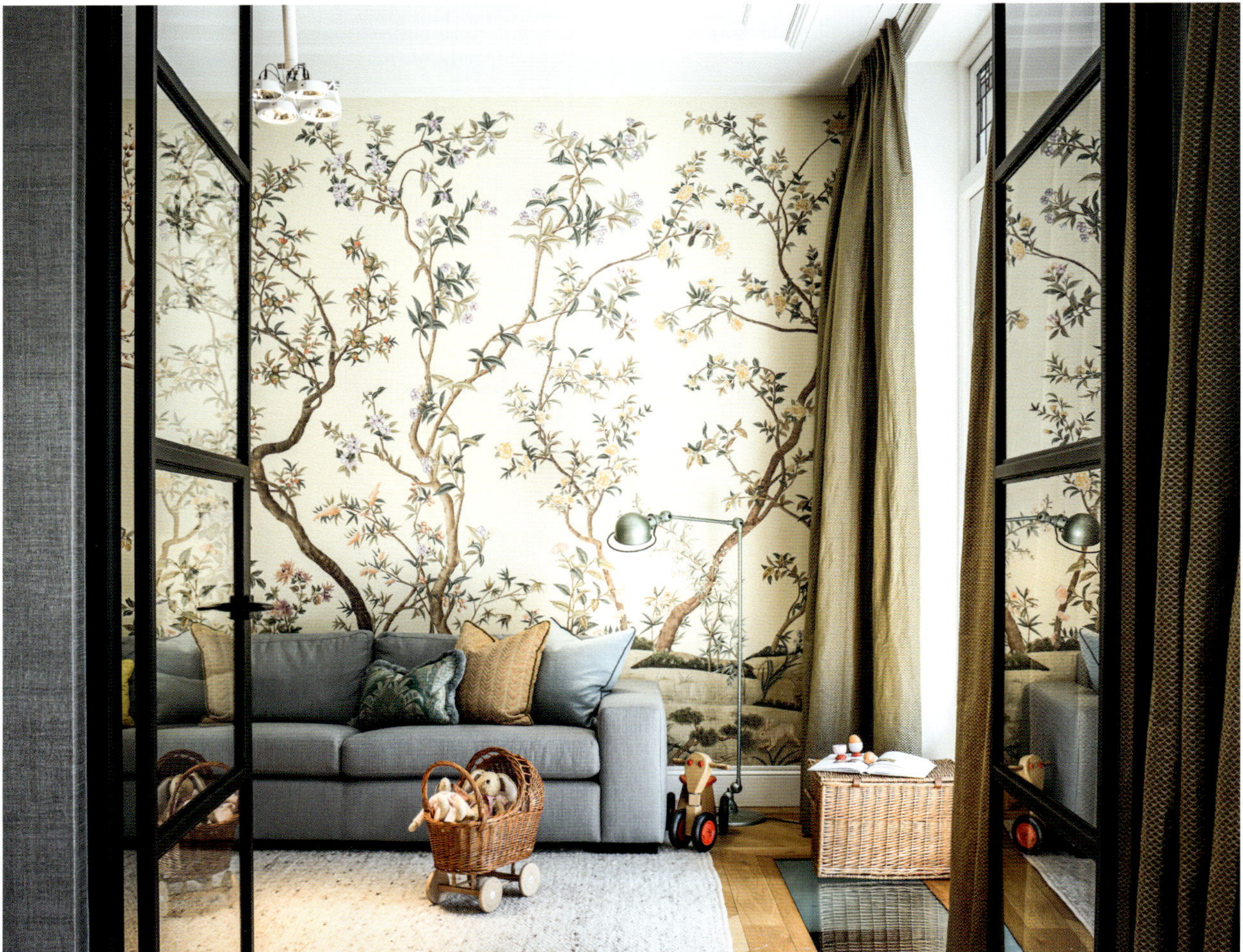

In the bedroom
of the Amsterdam
villa, subtle shades
and an elegant
carpet provide a cozy
ambience (above).
Playful and colorful
best describe the
children's room (left).
The English wallpaper
is by Morris & Co.

Im Schlafzimmer
der Amsterdamer
Villa schaffen sanfte
Töne und eine edle
Tapete ein gemütliches
Ambiente (oben).
Verspieltheit und bun-
tes Design prägen das
Kinderzimmer (links).
Die englische Tapete
ist von Morris & Co.

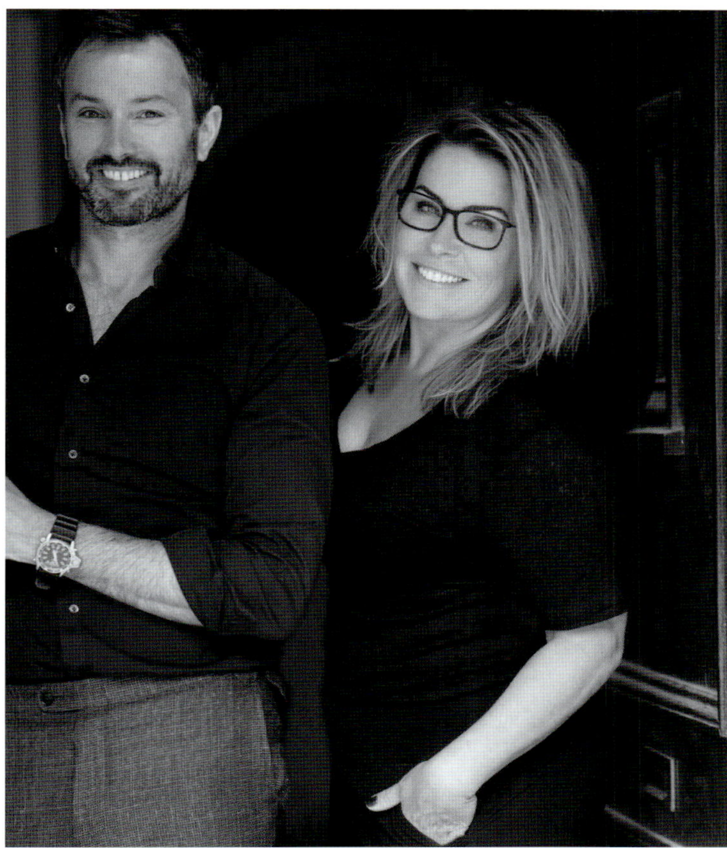

The founders of Stock Dutch Design, Leonie Hendrikse and Jeroen Stock
Die Gründer von Stock Dutch Design Leonie Hendrikse und Jeroen Stock

Stock Dutch Design was founded in 2005. With regards to your work, what has changed during this time and what has stayed the same?

Over the years we have grown from being an interior design shop and hands-on consultant to an integral interior design studio. In all of our work, however diverse and focused on matching our clients wishes, our key values have remained the same: lively colors and patterns, future-proof designs, and placing heritage in a contemporary context. 'Making enchanting memories' is still our highest ambition.

What role does light play when re-designing spaces?

Light is a very important factor in all of our designs. We start the process by determining the best use of natural light, followed by deciding where the light-spots and fixtures will be, and then completing with extra light sources such as table lamps and candles.

Do you have a favorite material which you particularly like?

We love beautiful and rich wallpaper. At home we even have wallpaper in our garage. And, as said before, placing family heirloom furniture (re-upholstered in stunning fabrics) in an unexpected context is our specialty.

You collaborate closely with your clients. Do you sometimes have avid discussions with them about which specific design solution is the best?

Yes, that does happen sometimes. But the first step is to truly listen to our clients issues before making up our minds. Our experience is that clients often come forward with an idea of how to solve a design challenge without truly understanding their own wishes or questions. This is where we come in. We help them to clarify their thought processes and to visualize the solutions. When both sides have understood one another, we then put forward a number of ways of approaching the issues.

Stock Dutch Design wurde 2005 gegründet. Was hat sich seitdem an Ihrer Arbeit geändert und was ist gleich geblieben?

Mit der Zeit sind wir von einem Inneneinrichtungsshop mit praktischer Beratung zu einem umfassenden Studio für Interior Design gewachsen. In unserer ganzen Arbeit, so vielfältig und kundenbezogen sie auch ist, sind unsere zentralen Werte unverändert: flotte Farben und Muster, zukunftsträchtige Designs und traditionelle Dinge in einen modernen Kontext zu setzen. Unser Leitbild ist nach wie vor „verzaubernde Erinnerungen schaffen".

Welche Rolle spielt Licht bei der Umgestaltung von Räumen?

Licht ist stets ein entscheidender Gestaltungsfaktor. Zunächst versuchen wir, das Tageslicht optimal einzusetzen, dann wird die Platzierung der festen Beleuchtungskörper bestimmt, und schließlich kommen noch Lichtquellen wie Tischlampen und Kerzen dazu.

Gibt es ein Lieblingsmaterial, das Sie besonders gern verwenden?

Wir lieben schöne Tapeten. Zu Hause ist sogar unsere Garage tapeziert. Und, wie gesagt, Familienerbstücke – alte, mit tollen Stoffen aufgepolsterte Möbel – in einen unerwarteten Kontext zu stellen ist unsere Spezialität.

Sie arbeiten eng mit Ihren Auftraggebern zusammen. Gibt es mit diesen auch schon mal leidenschaftliche Diskussionen, welche Designlösung im Detail die beste ist?

Ja, das kommt vor. Wir hören dann erst einmal gut zu, was die Kunden wollen. Oft erleben wir, dass sie eine Idee für die Gestaltung haben, ohne aber ihre eigenen Wünsche oder Fragen selbst genau verstanden zu haben. Hier steigen wir ein. Wir helfen den Kunden, klarer in ihren Überlegungen und bei der Visualisierung der Lösungen zu werden. Wenn auf beiden Seiten Klarheit besteht, zeigen wir unsere verschiedenen Lösungsvorschläge.

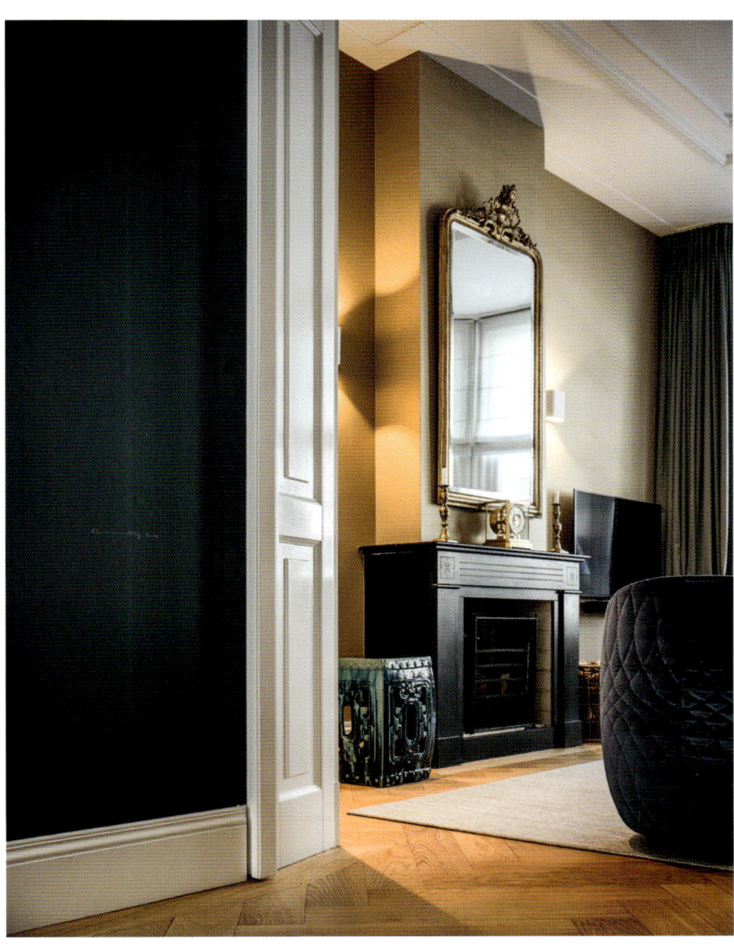

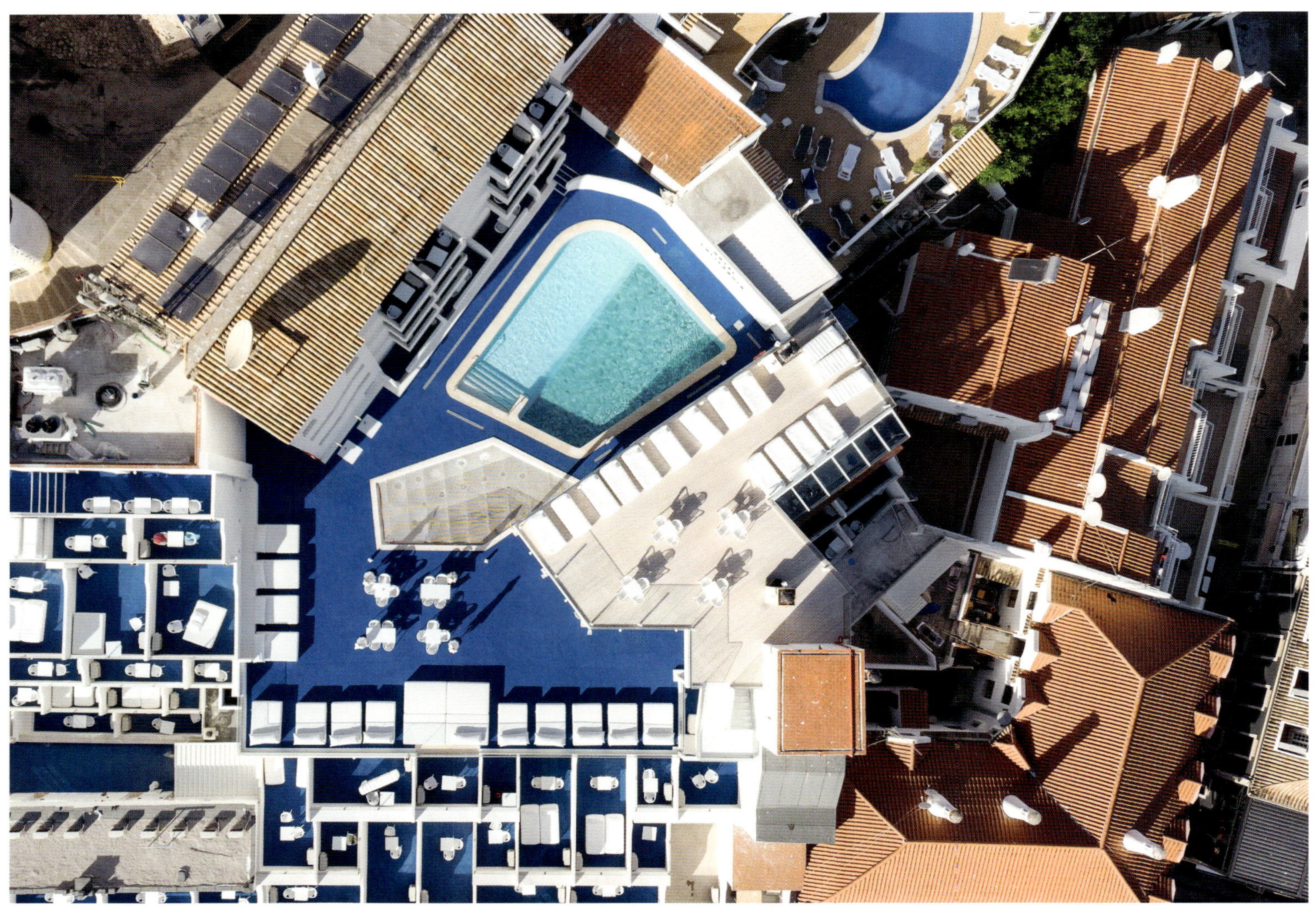

STUDIO ARTE

PORTIMÃO / PORTUGAL

Beyond All Norms | Jenseits des Normalen

Creating environments that astound, fire the imagination and exceed all expectations is the motto of the Studio Arte designer team. The firm, which is located in Portugal and the Netherlands, offers its clients architectural expertise that surpasses all norms. The four-star Hotel California, close to the city of Albufeira, was redesigned with a particular goal in mind: the existing site was to be transformed into a 'playground for adults', exclusively for guests aged eighteen and over. Studio Arte accepted the challenge and redesigned the hotel resort with a blend of minimalism and comfort.

Umgebungen schaffen, die erstaunen, die Fantasie beflügeln und alle Erwartungen übertreffen – das ist das Motto des Designerteams Studio Arte. Die in Portugal und den Niederlanden ansässige Firma bietet ihren Kunden Fachwissen in Verbindung mit Architekturideen, die über das Normale hinausgehen. Bei der Umgestaltung des Viersternehotels California nahe der Stadt Albufeira gab es ein besonderes Ziel: Die bestehende Anlage sollte in einen „Spielplatz für Erwachsene" verwandelt werden, ausschließlich für Gäste ab 18 Jahren. Studio Arte nahm die Herausforderung an und gestaltete das Hotelresort in einer Mischung aus Minimalismus und Komfort ganz neu.

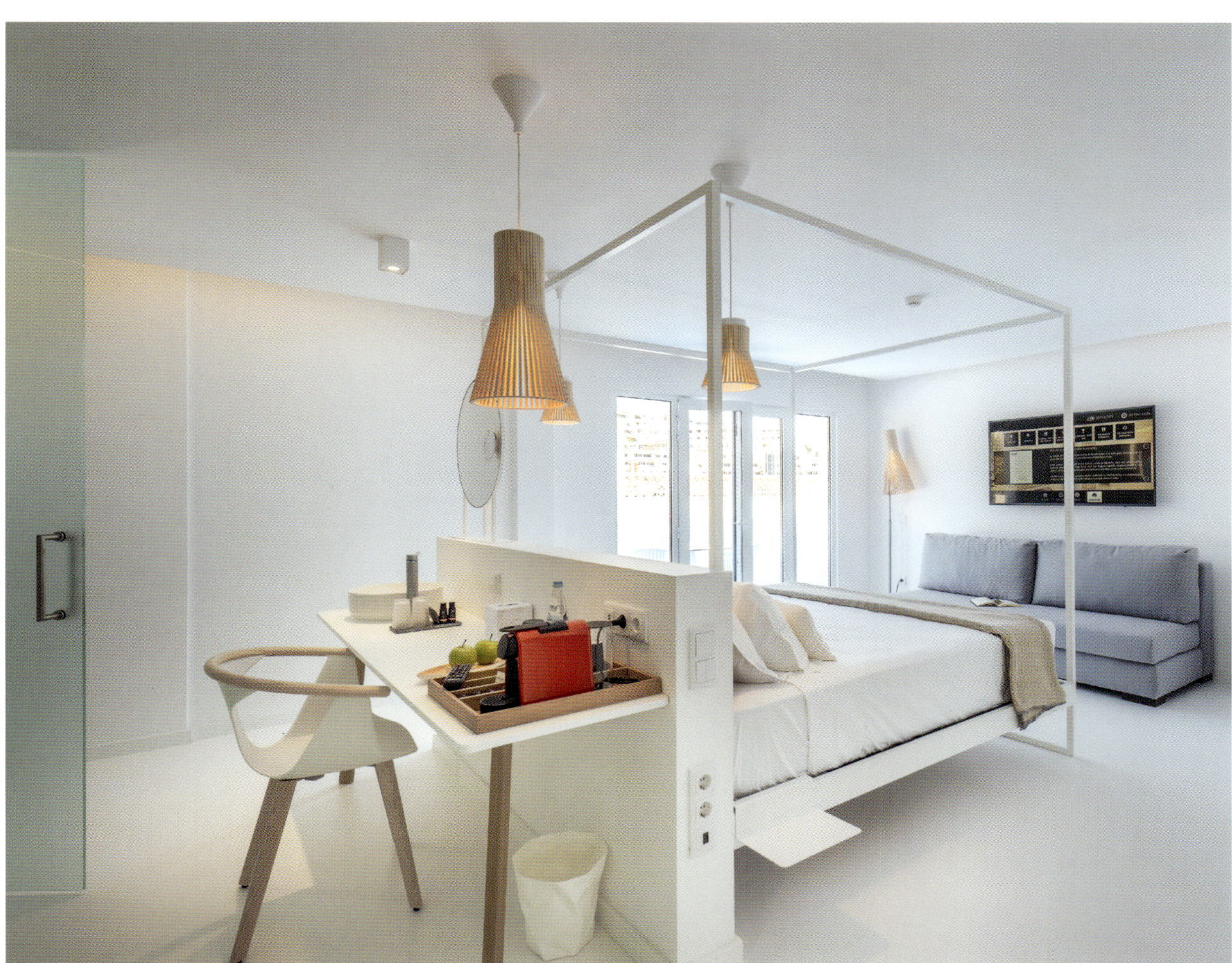

The Hotel California at the Praia dos Pescadores viewed from above (opposite page). The furnishings of the five different room types include special resin acoustic flooring, custom-made furniture—such as the Gelderland leather couch (left)—and hanging lights by Secto Design.

Das Hotel California an der Praia dos Pescadores von oben gesehen (Seite gegenüber). In der Ausstattung der fünf verschiedenen Zimmertypen finden sich spezielle Harz-Akustikböden, handgefertigte Möbel – wie etwa eine Ledercouch von Gelderland (links) – und Designer-Pendelleuchten von Secto Design.

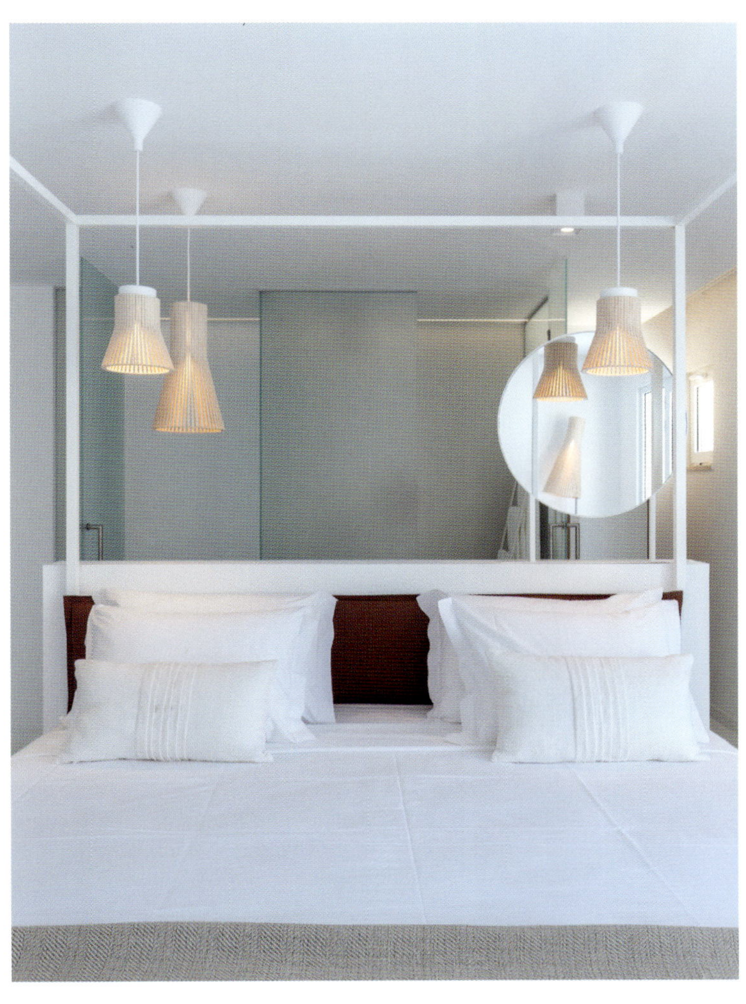

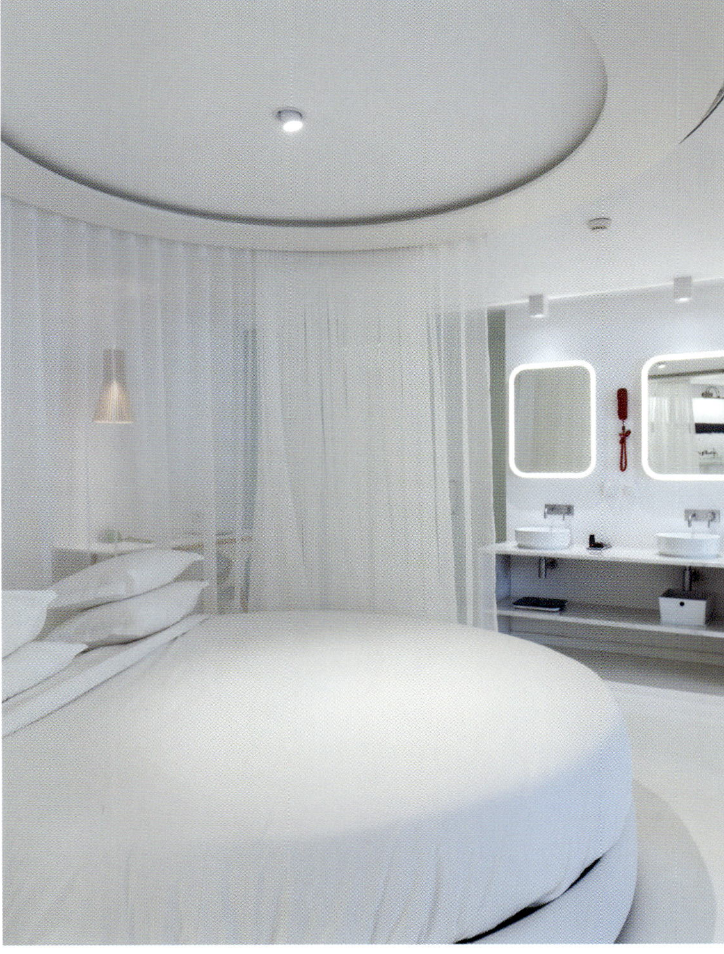

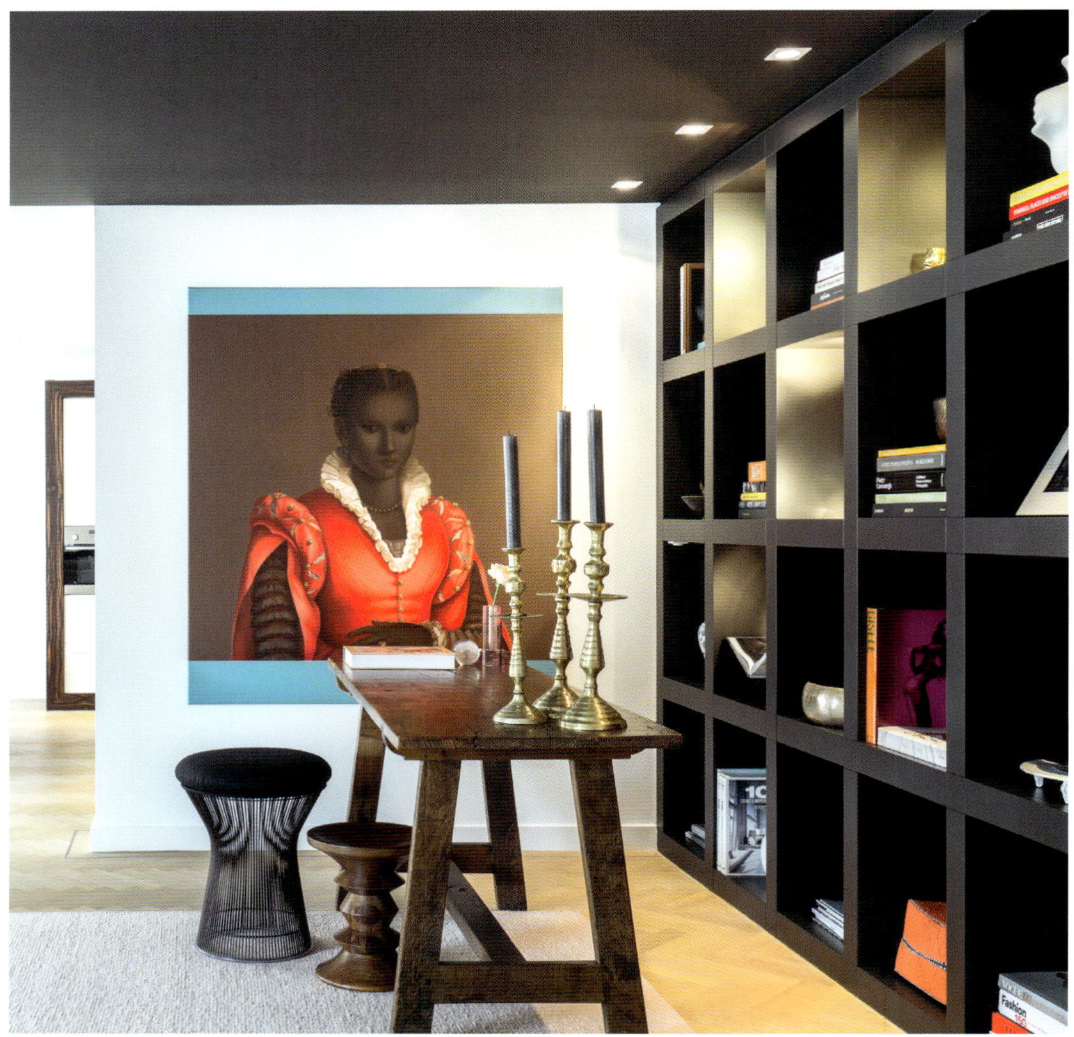

STUDIO HERMANIDES

AMSTERDAM / NETHERLANDS

Timeless Eclecticism | Zeitloser Eklektizismus

After Jeroen Machielsen had worked for a number of well-known interior designers, he established his Studio Hermanides in 2008, which rapidly acquired a formidable reputation in the fields of interior decoration and design. The firm's portfolio extends from private properties and yachts to office premises and events; its style combines classical elements with a broad contemporary approach. This 'timeless eclecticism' is reflected, for example, in the use of pure materials blended with eye-catching stylistic elements and a fresh color palette—and provides the foundation for harmonious, symmetrical spaces with a true feeling of luxury.

Nachdem Jeroen Machielsen für diverse namhafte Innenarchitekten gearbeitet hatte, gründete er 2008 sein Studio Hermanides, das sich schnell international einen guten Ruf in den Bereichen Innenarchitektur und Gestaltung erarbeitet hat. Das Portfolio reicht von Privatimmobilien und Jachten über Büroräume bis zu Veranstaltungen. Der Stil lässt sich als Kombination klassischer Elemente mit einem breiten modernen Ansatz beschreiben. Dieser „zeitlose Eklektizismus" zeigt sich etwa in der Verwendung reiner Materialien in Verbindung mit auffälligen Stilelementen und einer frischen Farbpalette – die Basis für harmonische, symmetrische Räume mit wahrem Luxusgefühl.

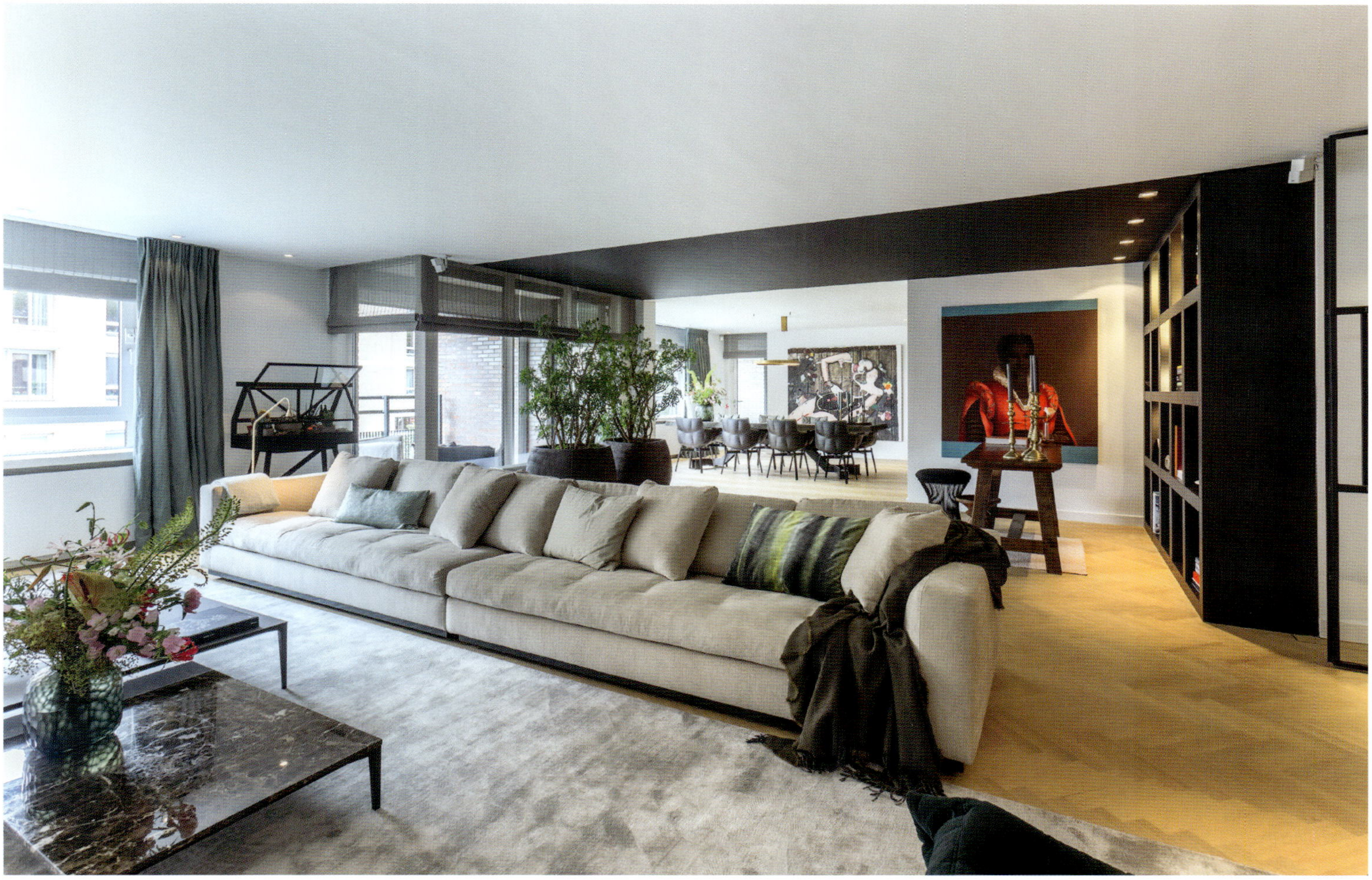

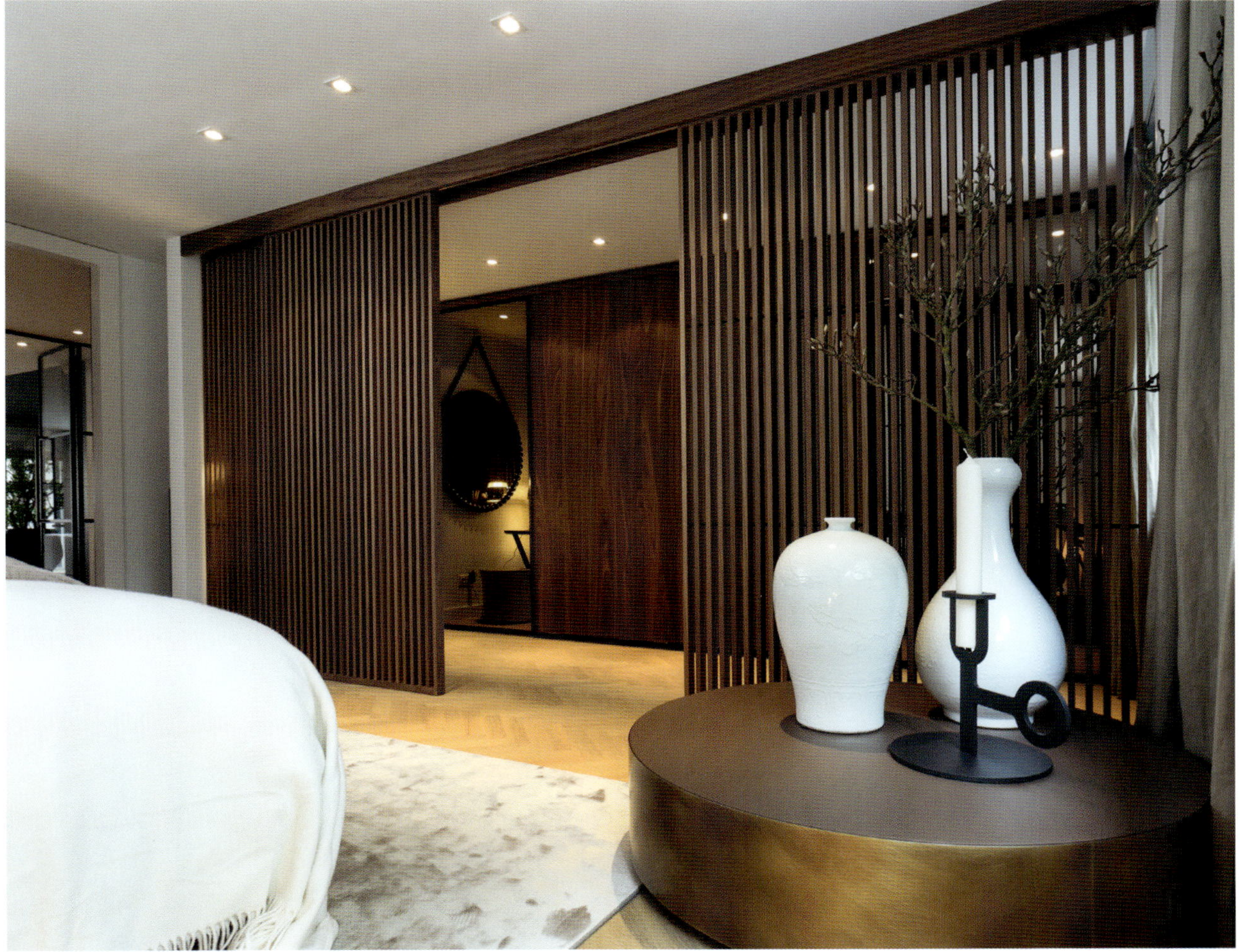

The 'Art Apartment' in Amstelveen, North Holland: As genuine art enthusiasts, the owners wished for an environment combining cozy living with art, while avoiding the creation of a museum-like ambience. To that end, various materials were allied with Italian design and a fresh color palette.

„**Art Apartment**" in Amstelveen, Nordholland: Die kunstbegeisterten Auftraggeber wünschten sich eine Umgebung, die Gemütlichkeit mit Kunst verbindet, ohne dabei eine museale Atmosphäre zu schaffen. Dafür wurden verschiedene Materialien mit italienischem Design und lebendigen Farben kombiniert.

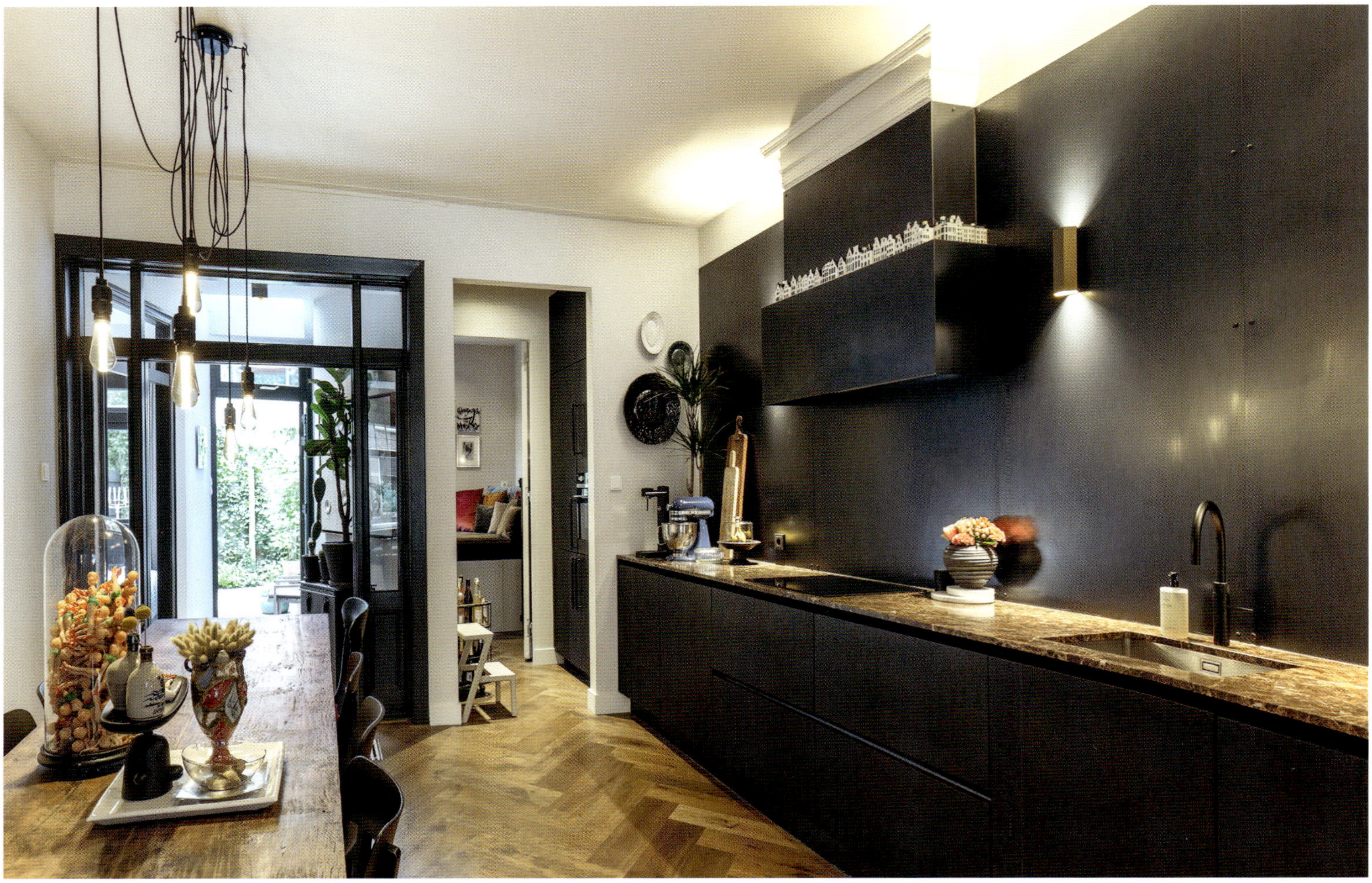

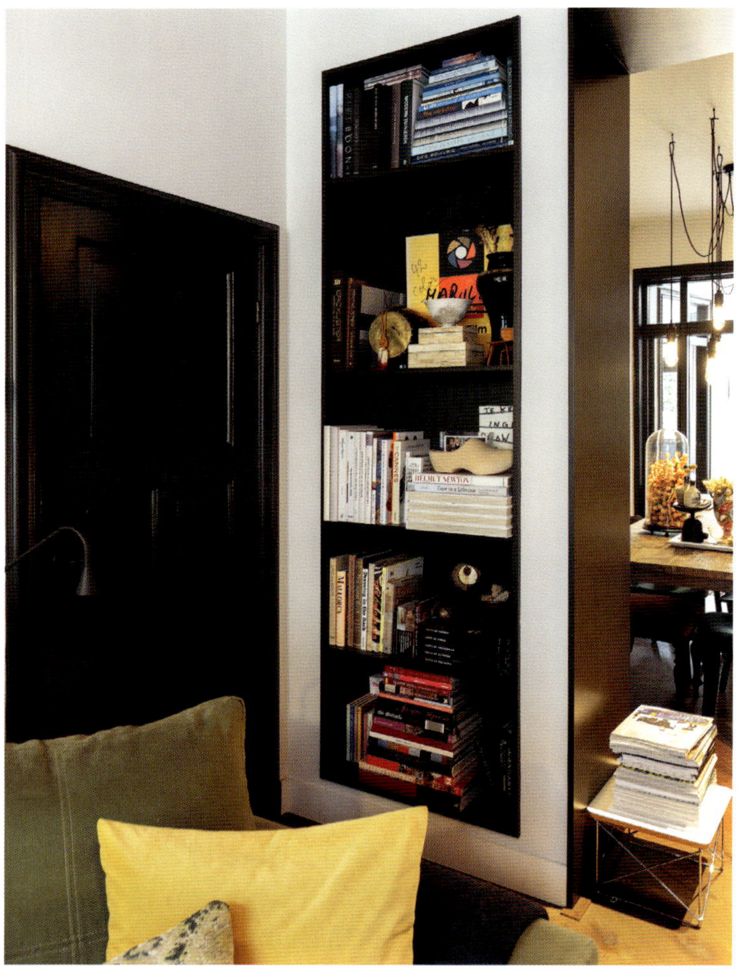

The client for this project in the eastern part of Amsterdam had some specific requests: the kitchen (above) was to be a place in which large dinners with friends could take place, hence the long narrow table. The Studio Hermanides team also had to create considerable space for the large collection of books, stylish antique objects, and works of art. This resulted in charming areas, such as the one on the left. Even the small rooms are cozy (opposite page below). And above all, the red ceiling in the living room was intended to create a particular 'wow' effect (opposite page above and page 210–211).

Die Auftraggeber dieses Projekts im Osten Amsterdams hatten besondere Wünsche: Die Küche (oben) sollte zu einem Ort werden, an dem große Essen mit Freunden stattfinden können, daher der lange schmale Tisch. Auch musste das Team von Studio Hermanides viel Platz für die große Sammlung von Büchern, Antik-Stil-Objekten und Kunst schaffen. So entstanden charmante Ecken (links). Selbst kleine Zimmer wurden sehr wohnlich (Seite gegenüber unten). Mit der roten Zimmerdecke im Wohnzimmer schließlich sollte ein besonderer „Wow-Effekt" erzielt werden (Seite gegenüber oben und Seite 210–211).

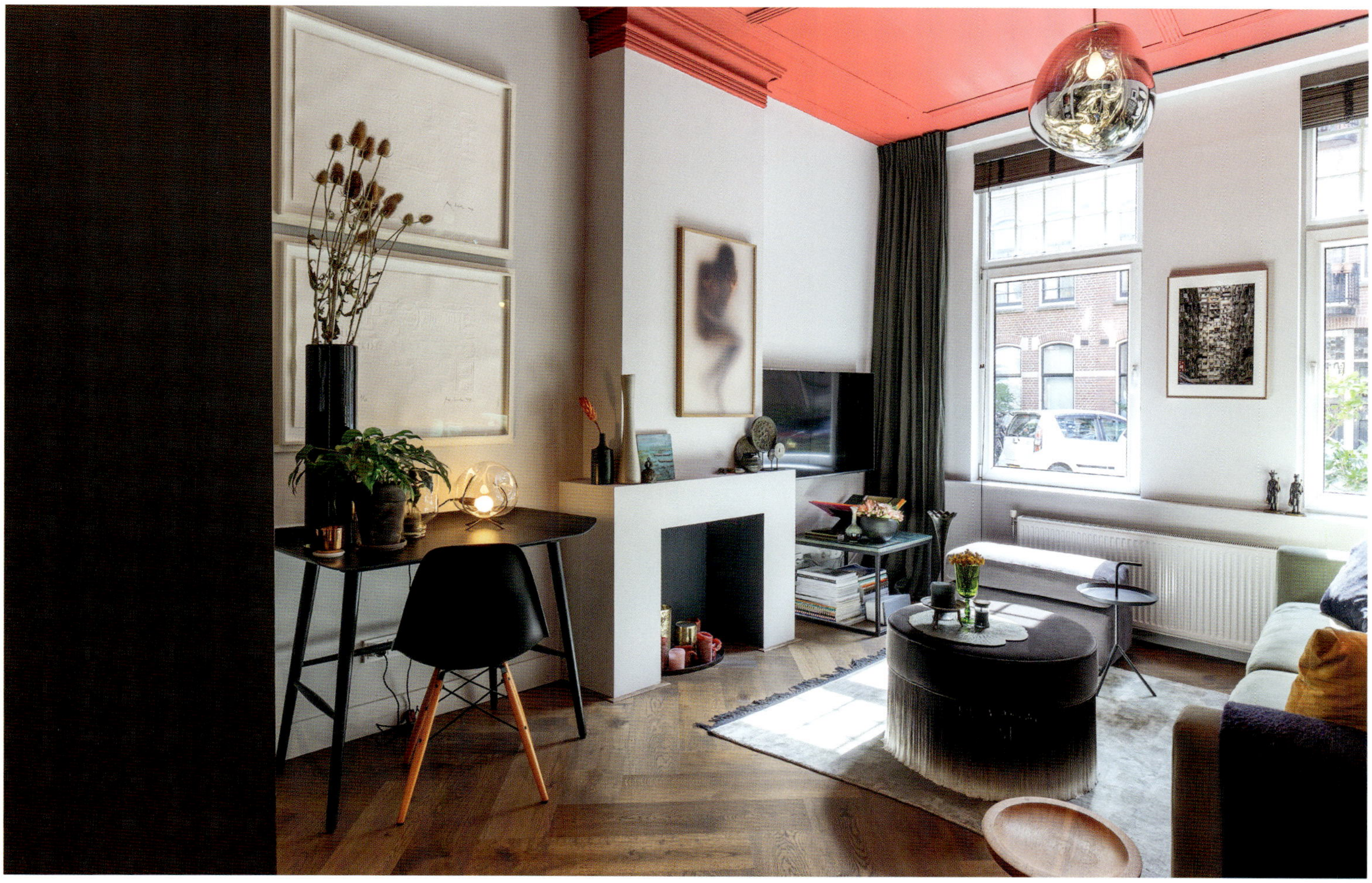

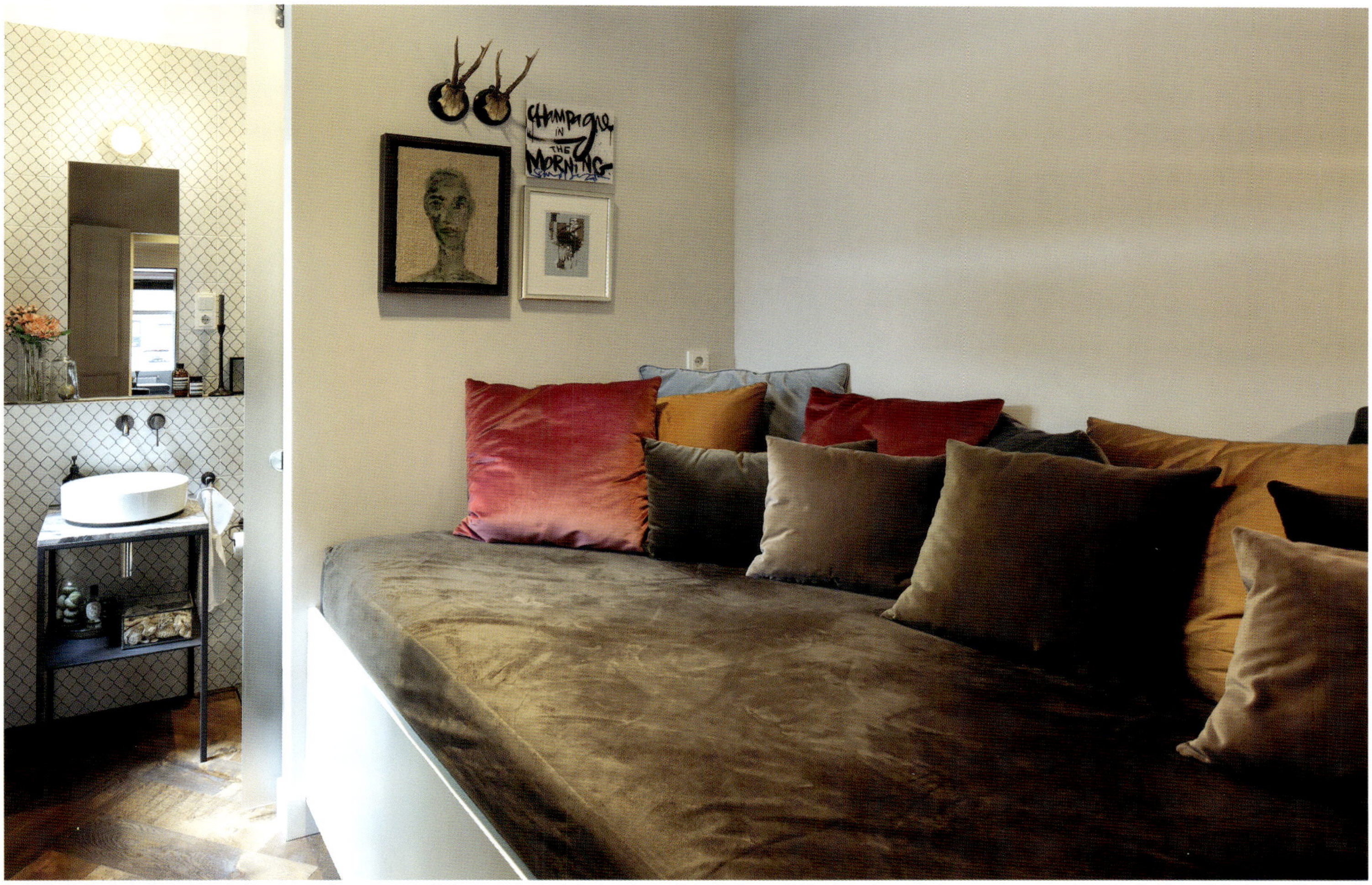

Another glimpse into
the living room of the
Amsterdam house.
Despite the bright
red ceiling, highly
modern ceiling lamp
and rather puristic
fireplace, a near tradi-
tional, very cozy space
has been created. Any
family member can
feel at home here,
anytime.

Hier noch ein Blick
ins Wohnzimmer des
Amsterdamer Hauses:
Trotz knallig-roter
Decke, sehr moderner
Deckenleuchte und
eines eher puristischen
Kamins entstand
ein fast traditionell
anmutender, sehr
gemütlicher Raum.
Hier können sich alle
Familienmitglieder
zu jeder Tageszeit
wohlfühlen.

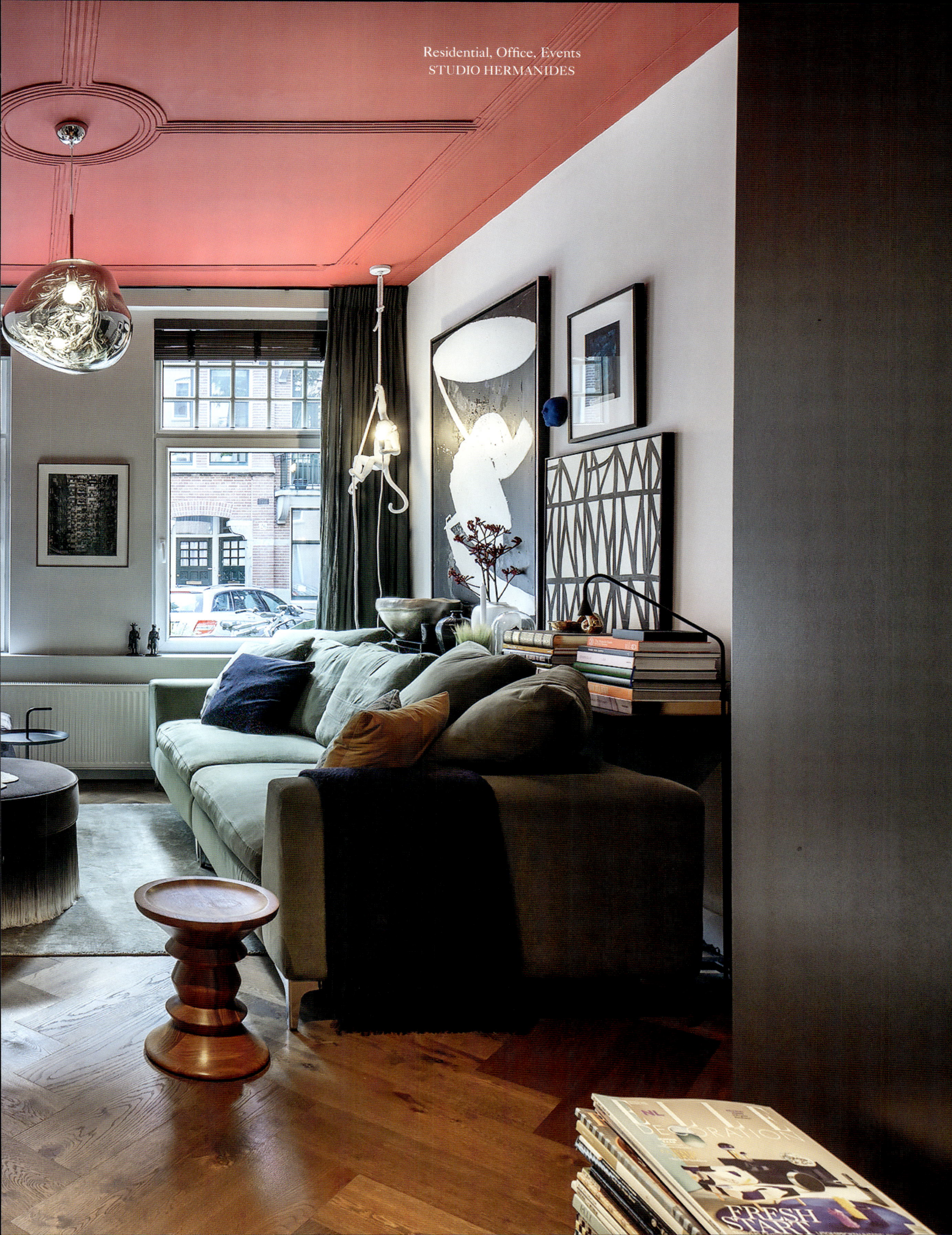
Residential, Office, Events
STUDIO HERMANIDES

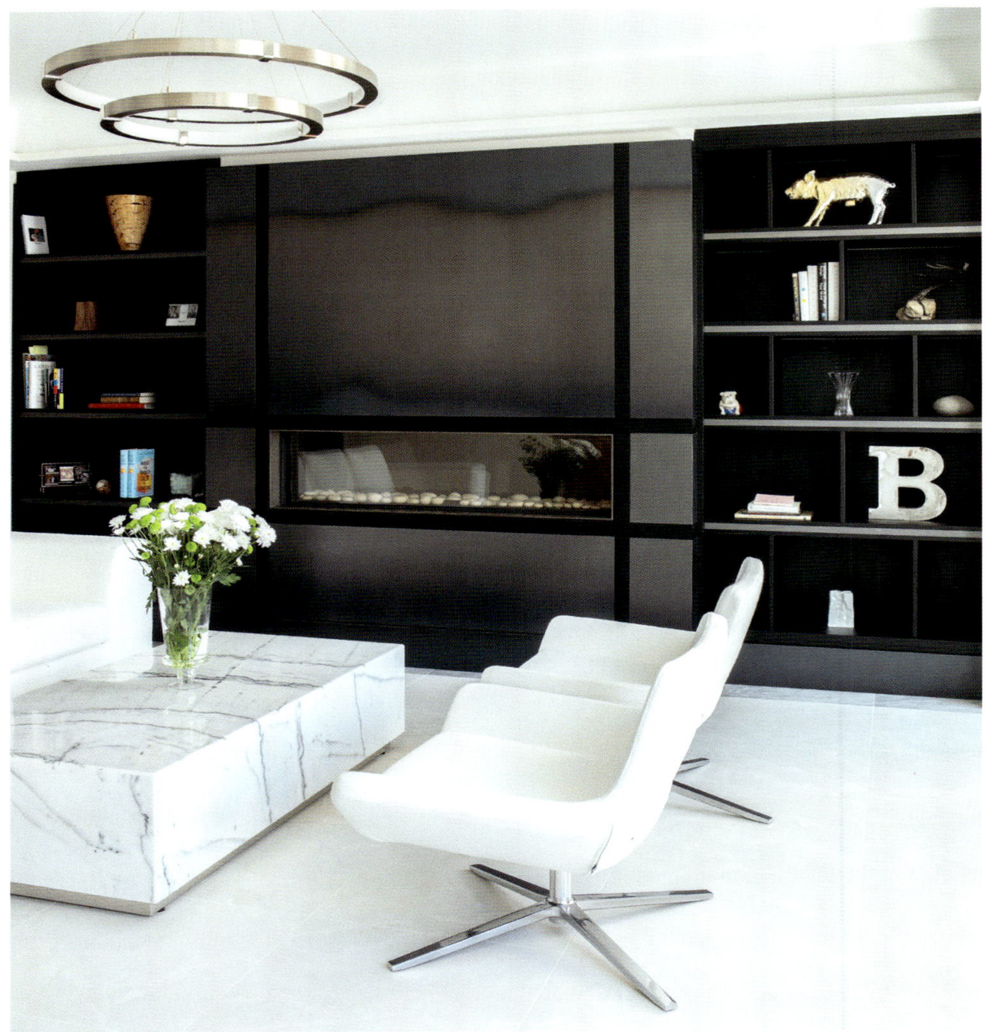

TAYLOR HANNAH ARCHITECT

TORONTO / CANADA

Timelessly Elegant | Zeitlos elegant

Following her studies at the University of Toronto's Faculty of Architecture, Dee Dee Taylor Eustace established her firm Taylor Hannah Architect Inc. in Toronto. A member of both the Ontario Association of Architects and the Royal Architecture Institute of Canada, the architect and interior designer specializes in a timelessly elegant style. The firm draws many of its assignments from the residential, office and hospitality sector. Dee Dee and her team have executed hundreds of residential and commercial projects, often at premier addresses both in and outside Canada. The photos shown here of newly designed offices, apartments and houses convey an impression of the designer's work.

Nach dem Studium an der University of Toronto School of Architecture gründete Dee Dee Taylor Eustace das Unternehmen Taylor Hannah Architect Inc. in Toronto. Die Architektin und Innenarchitektin ist Mitglied der Ontario Association of Architects sowie des Royal Architecture Institute of Canada und steht für einen zeitlos eleganten Stil. Viele ihrer Aufträge stammen aus dem Wohnungs-, Büro- und Gastronomiesektor. Dee Dee und ihr Team haben Hunderte von Wohn- und Geschäftsprojekten umgesetzt, oft an Top-Adressen in und außerhalb Kanadas. Die hier abgebildeten Fotos neu gestalteter Büros, Wohnungen und Häuser vermitteln einen Eindruck von der Arbeit der Designerin.

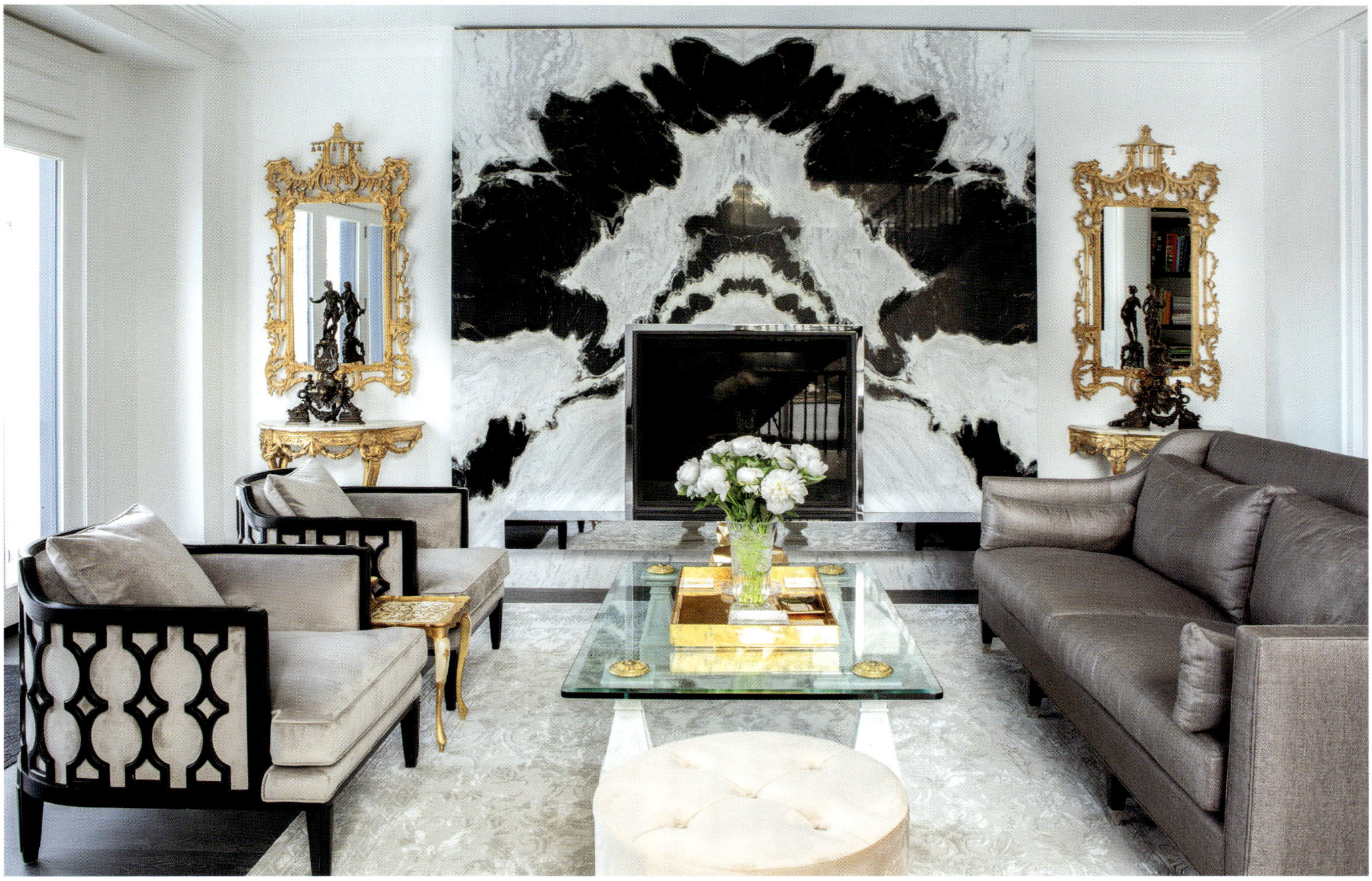

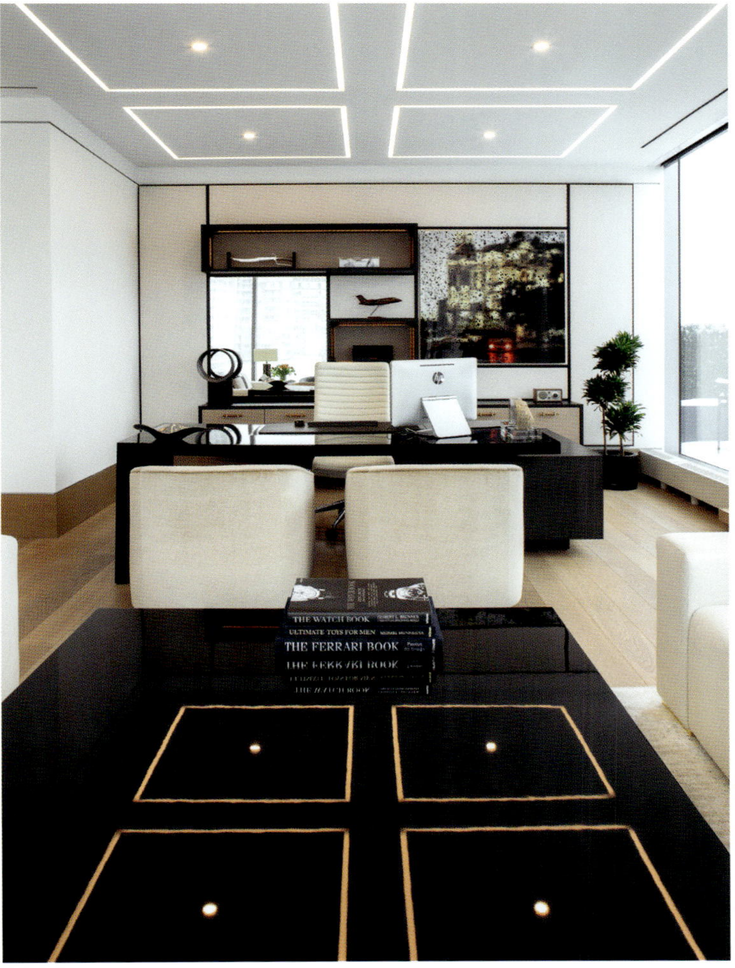

The large marble fireplace has sophisticated backlighting, its modern design providing a deliberate contrast to the antique mirrors, consoles, and small tables. Two types of seating furniture add the finishing touches to the interior design (above). Graphic LED lighting in the newly designed offices of an investment bank (left). A contemporary condo with a metal-clad fireplace and custom lighting (opposite page).

Der große Marmorkamin hat eine raffinierte Hintergrundbeleuchtung, die moderne Gestaltung kontrastiert bewusst mit antiken Spiegeln, Konsolen und Tischchen. Zwei Arten Sitzmöbel runden die Raumgestaltung ab (oben). Grafische LEDs im neu gestalteten Büro einer Investmentbank (links). Moderne Eigentumswohnung mit metallverkleidetem Kamin und maßgefertigten Leuchten (Seite gegenüber).

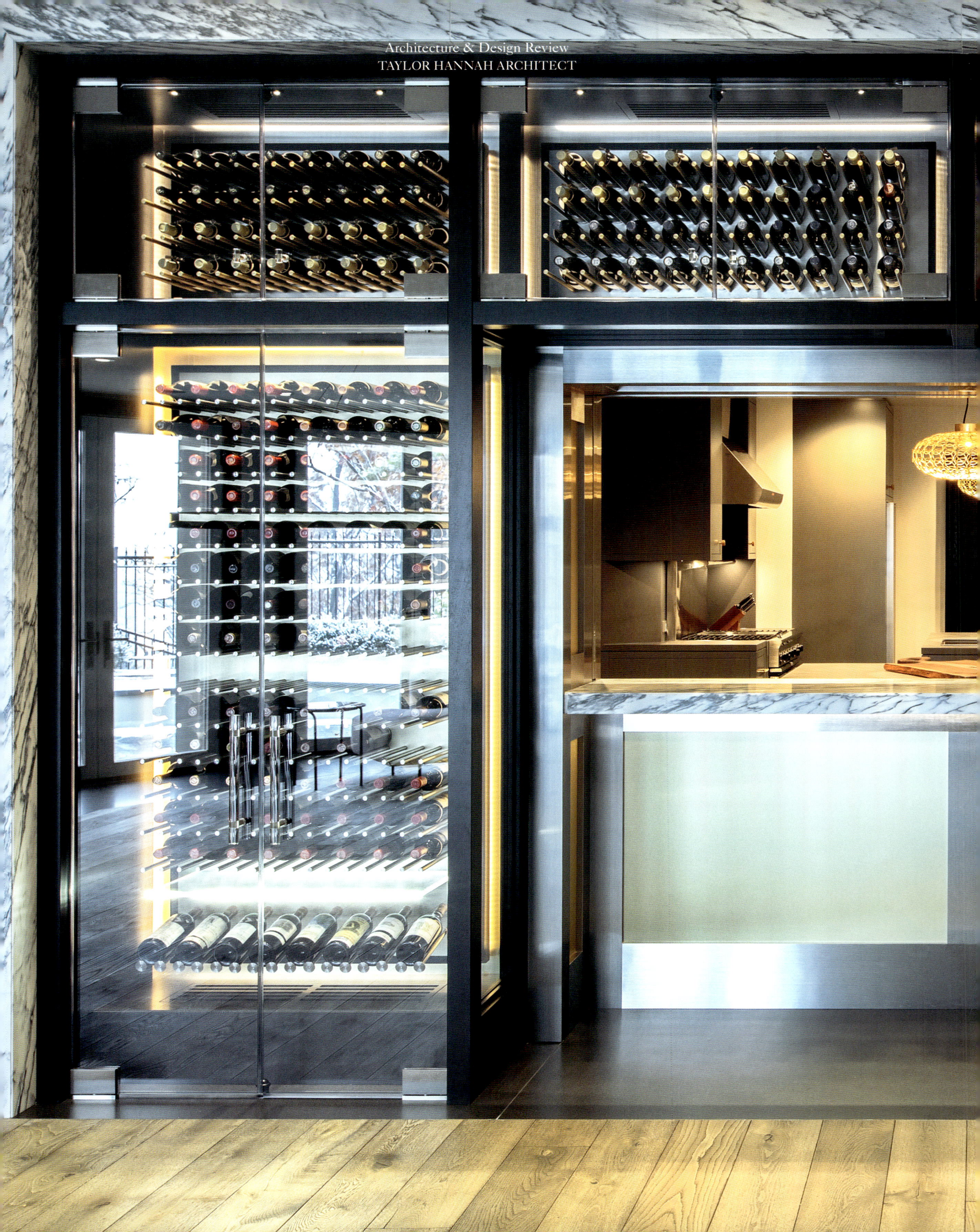
Architecture & Design Review
TAYLOR HANNAH ARCHITECT

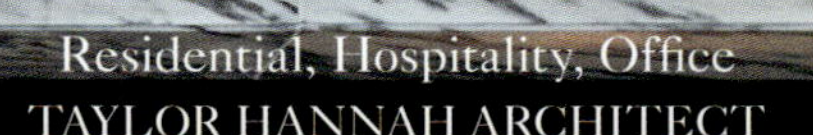

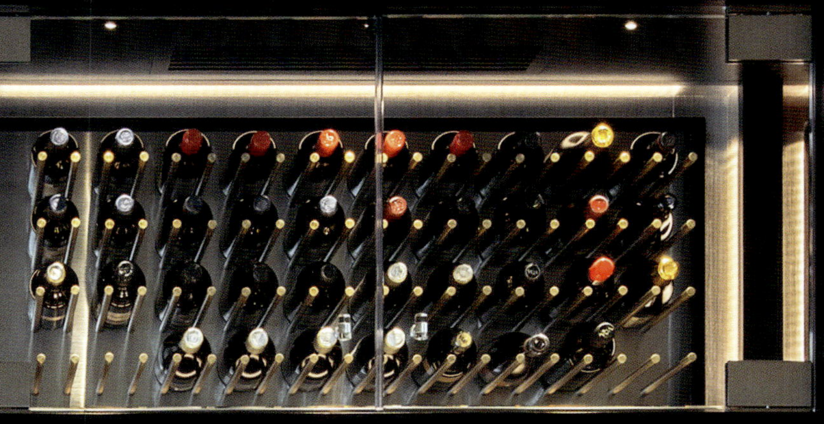

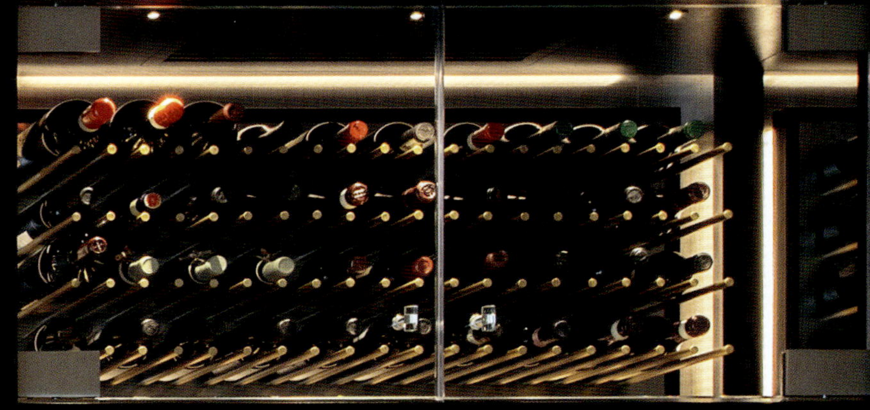

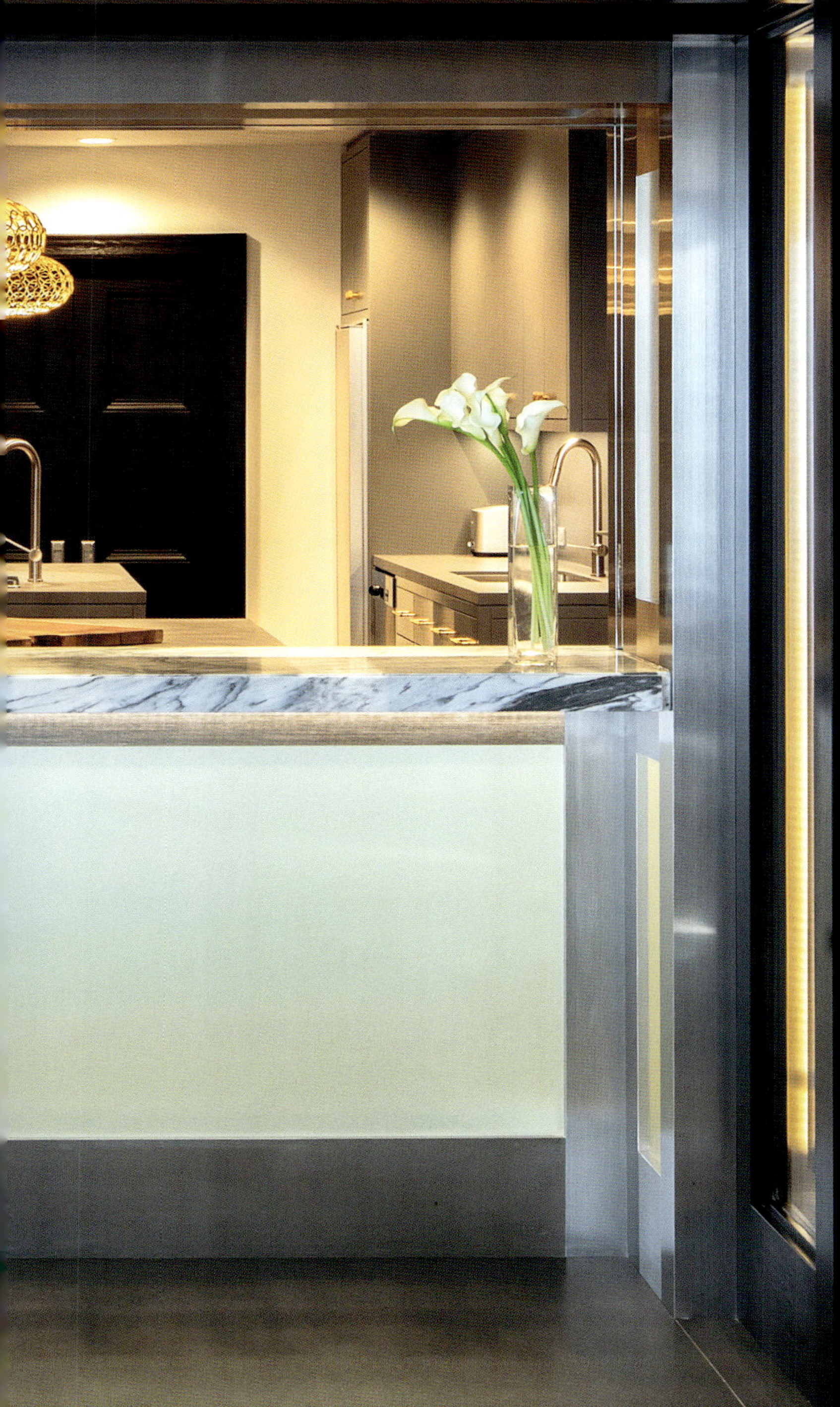

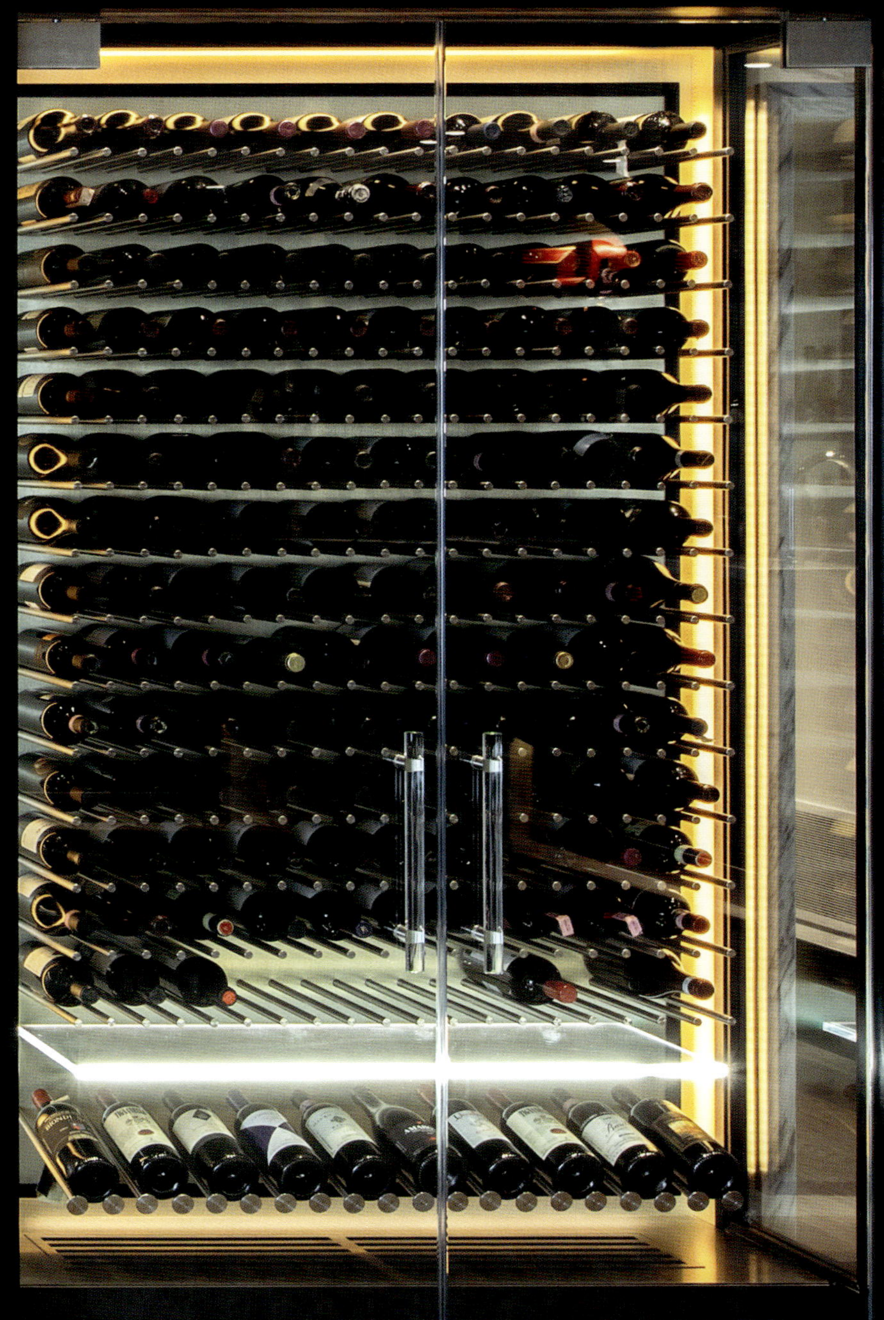

This private 'wine cellar wall' was custom designed for the client and, in conjunction with the catering kitchen located behind it, fulfills every connoisseur's dream.

Diese private „Weinkeller-Wand" wurde individuell für den Auftraggeber gestaltet. Zusammen mit der dahinter gelegenen Catering-Küche lässt das Ensemble Genießerträume wahr werden.

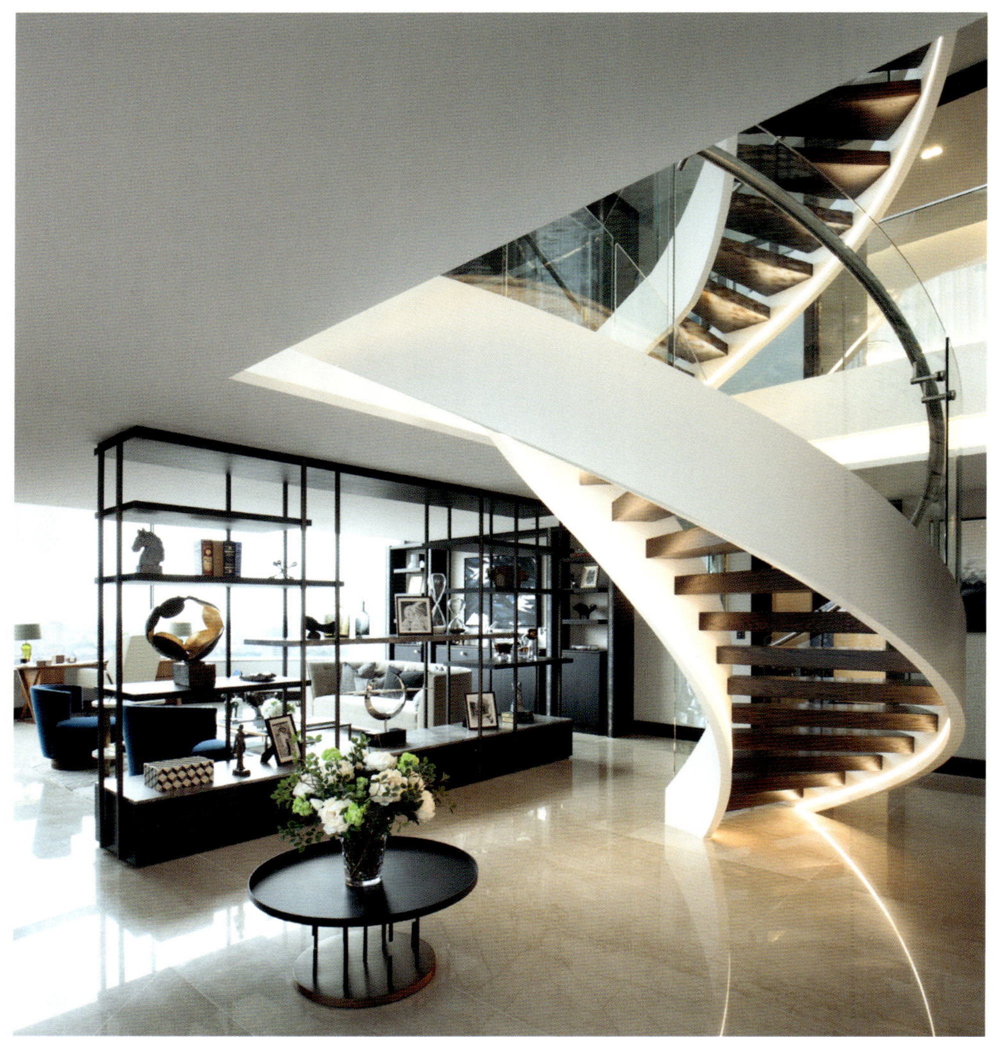

TG STUDIO

LONDON / UNITED KINGDOM

Spectacular Views | Spektakuläre Ausblicke

Following his studies in Berlin and London, the graduate of architecture, Thomas Griem, co-founded the interior design firm Target Living. After making his mark in the field of design, Griem established TG Studio in 2011. The project presented here is particularly spectacular: the furnishing of a 500 square meter residential unit in London's 'Corniche.' Conceived by the architects Foster + Partners, this high-rise ensemble was constructed directly on the banks of the Thames in 2019. The penthouse designed by TG Studio extends from the twenty-second to the twenty-fourth floor and boasts a 185 square meter roof terrace.

Nach seinem Studium in Berlin und London trat der diplomierte Architekt Thomas Griem unter anderem als Mitbegründer des Innenarchitekturbüros Target Living in Erscheinung. Nach sehr erfolgreichen Jahren im Designbereich gründete Griem dann 2011 das Unternehmen TG Studio. Das hier gezeigte Projekt ist besonders spektakulär: die Ausstattung einer 500 Quadratmeter großen Wohneinheit im Londoner „Corniche". Dieses Hochhausensemble der Architekten Foster + Partners wurde 2019 direkt am Themse-Ufer erbaut. Das von TG Studio gestaltete Penthouse erstreckt sich vom 22. bis zum 24. Stockwerk und hat eine etwa 185 Quadratmeter große Dachterrasse.

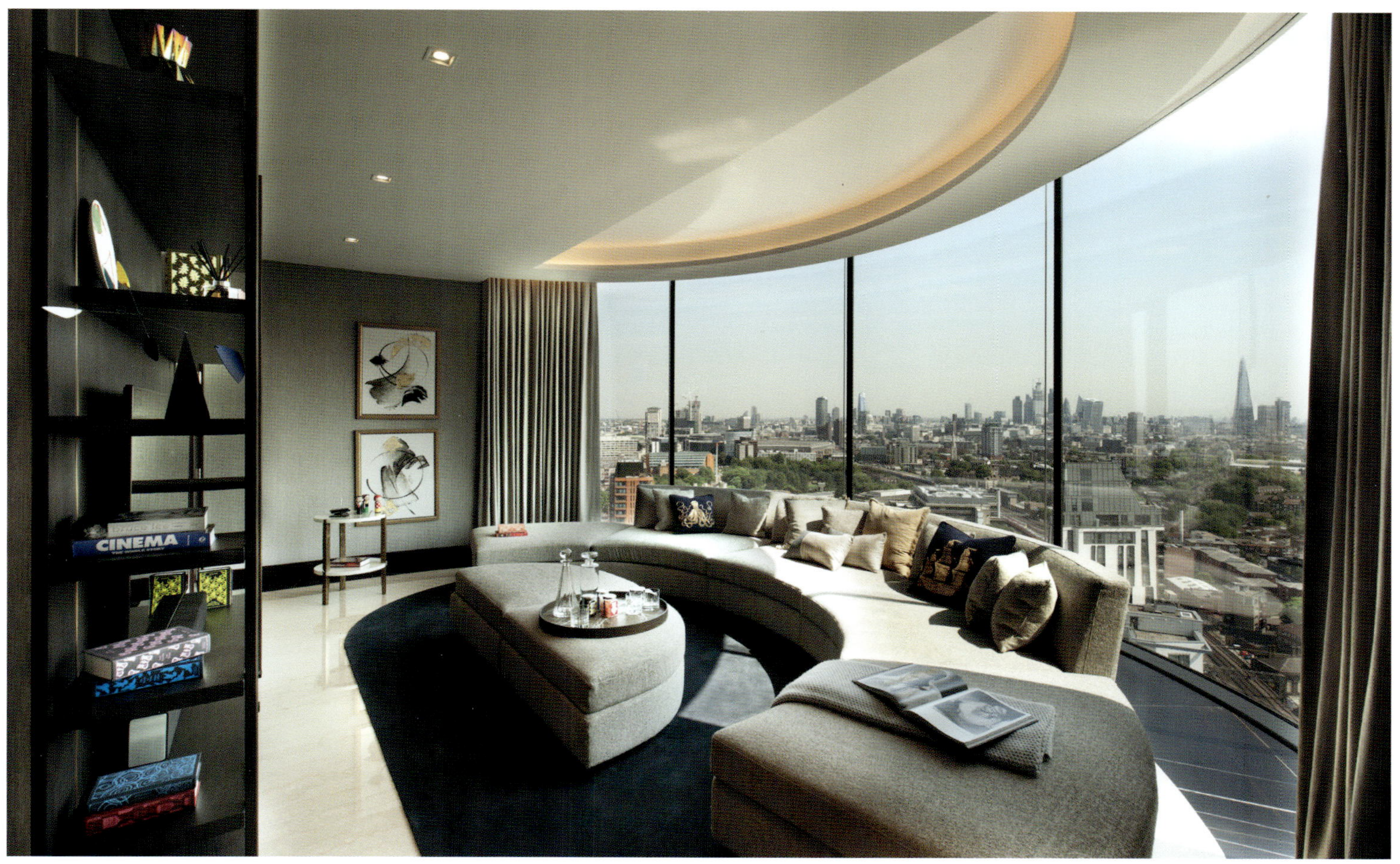

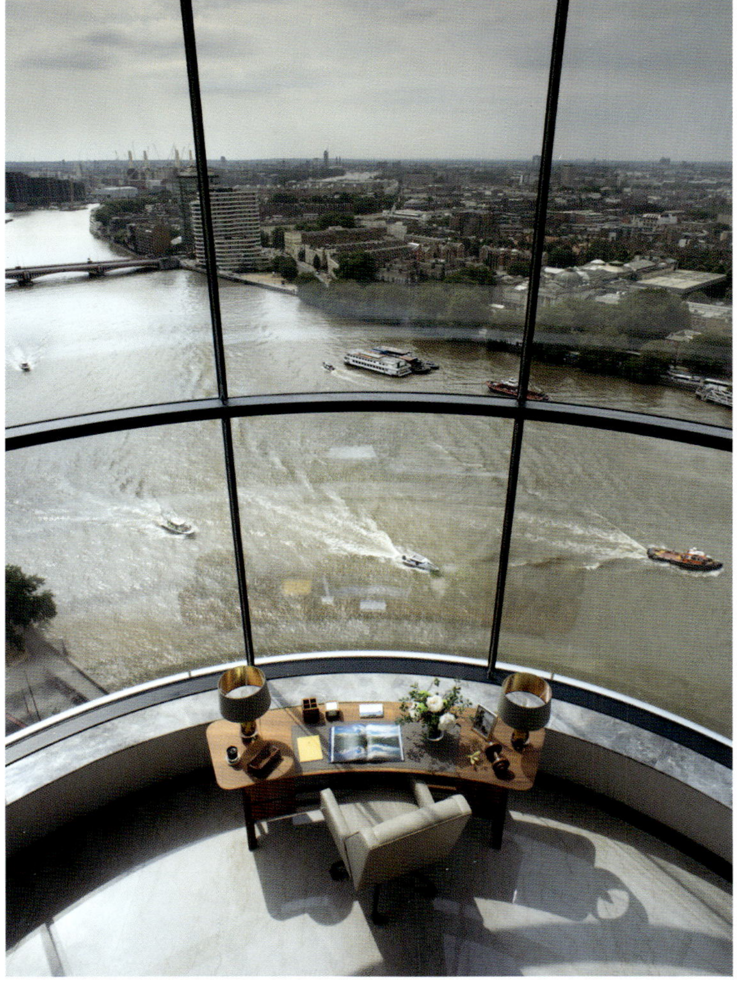

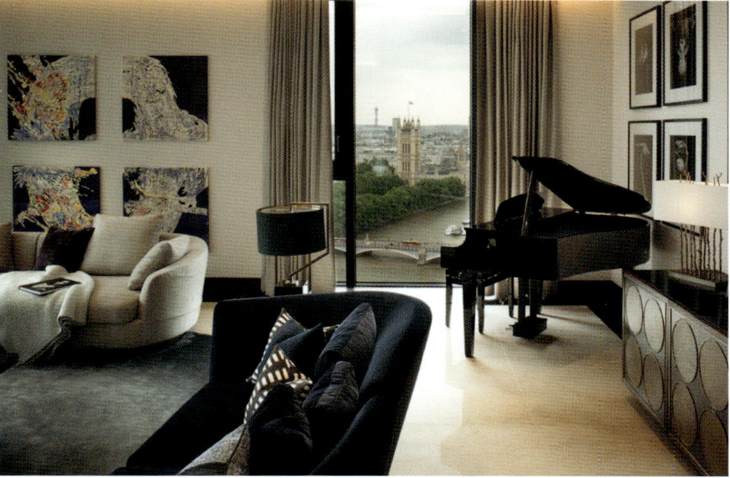

The 'Corniche' penthouse: three floors offer plenty of space for all residents as well as a grand piano (above). The curves of the walls and windows are echoed perfectly in the custom-made furniture. The panoramic outlook is only surpassed by the view from the roof terrace, which can be reached via the impressive interior staircase (opposite page).

Penthouse „The Corniche": Drei Ebenen bieten viel Platz für alle Bewohner sowie einen Flügel (oben). Maßgefertigte Möbel stehen im kongenialen Dialog mit den Rundungen der Wände und Fenster. Der Panoramablick lässt sich nur noch durch die Aussicht von der Dachterrasse steigern, zu der die eindrucksvolle Innentreppe führt (Seite gegenüber).

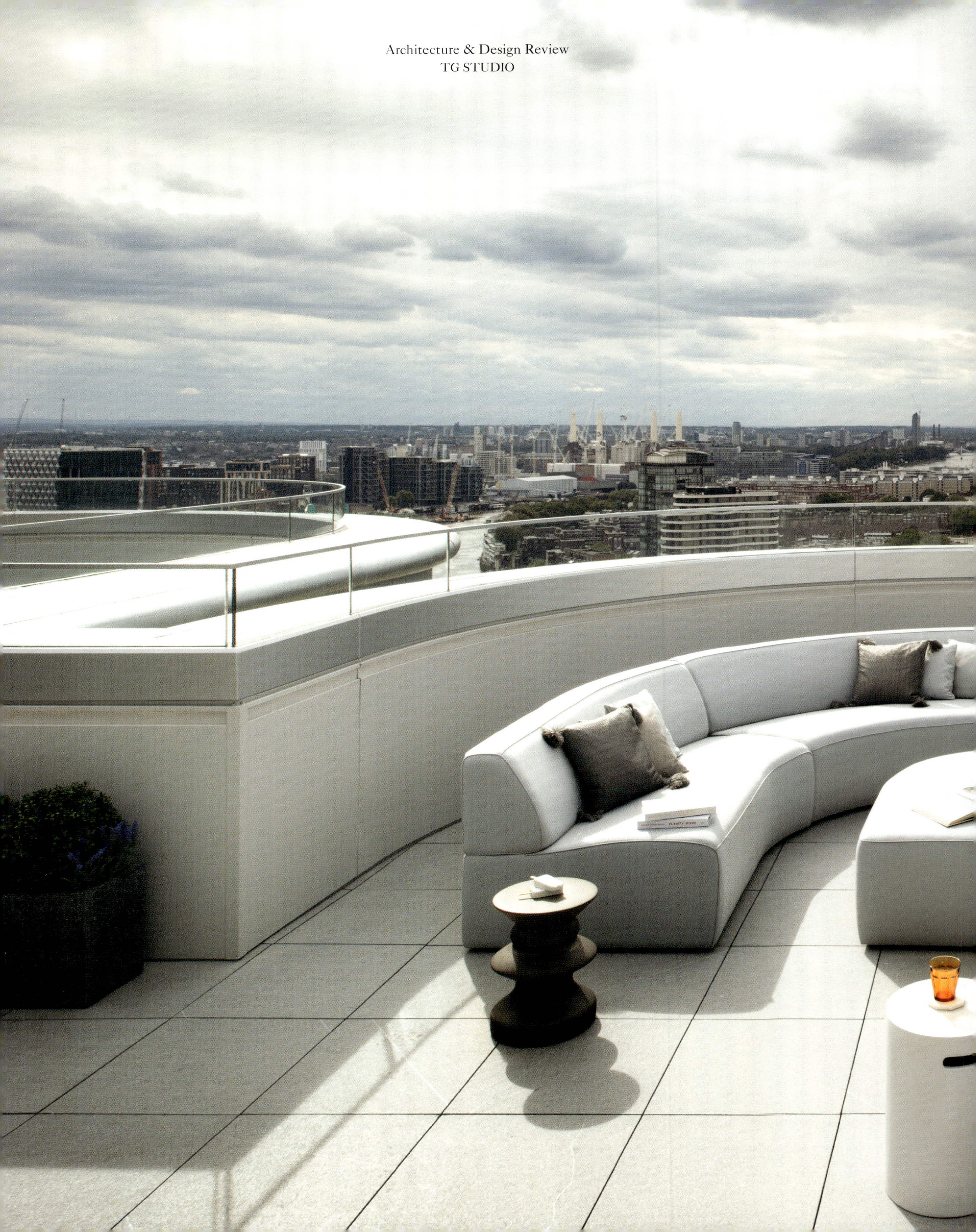

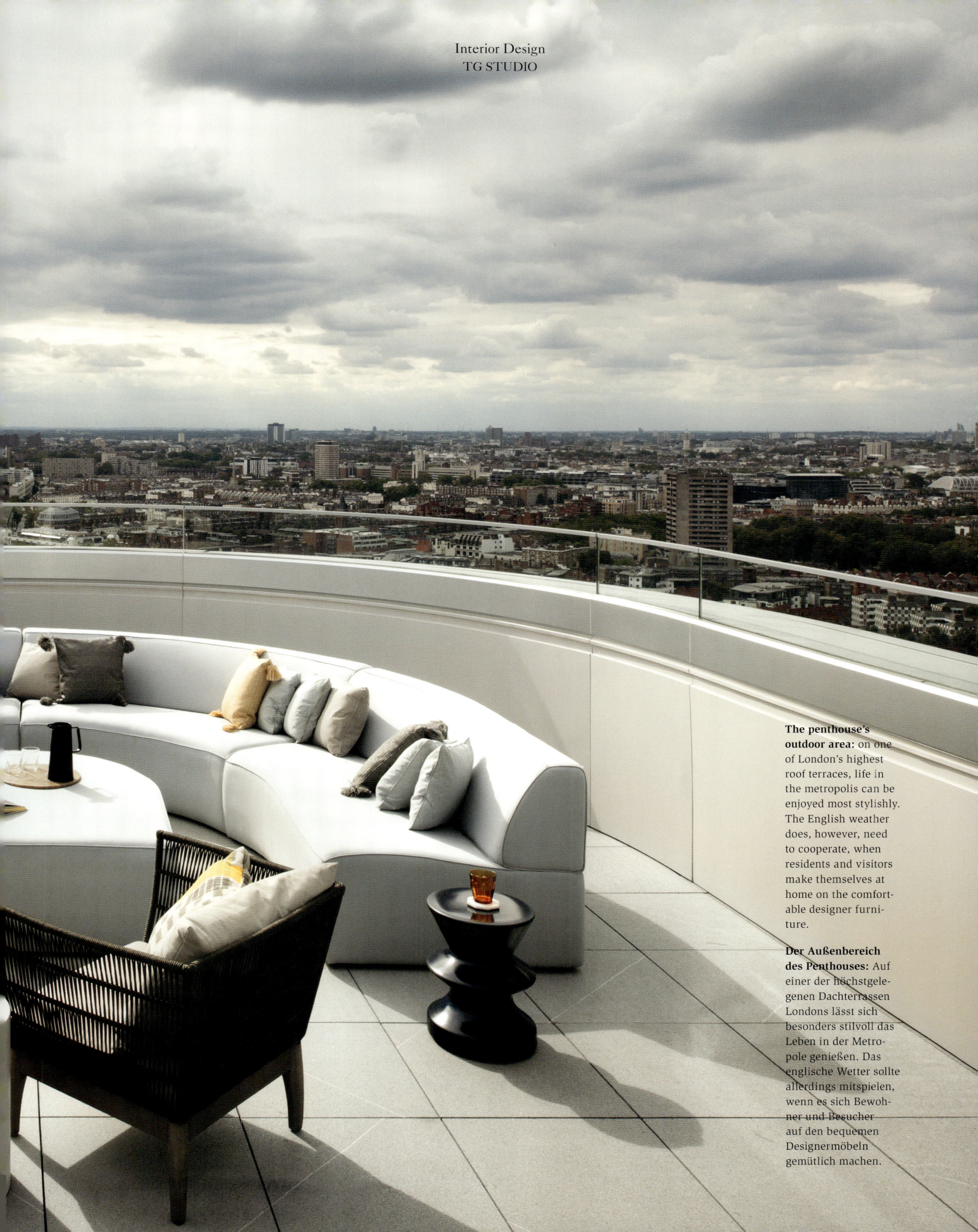

The penthouse's outdoor area: on one of London's highest roof terraces, life in the metropolis can be enjoyed most stylishly. The English weather does, however, need to cooperate, when residents and visitors make themselves at home on the comfortable designer furniture.

Der Außenbereich des Penthouses: Auf einer der höchstgelegenen Dachterrassen Londons lässt sich besonders stilvoll das Leben in der Metropole genießen. Das englische Wetter sollte allerdings mitspielen, wenn es sich Bewohner und Besucher auf den bequemen Designermöbeln gemütlich machen.

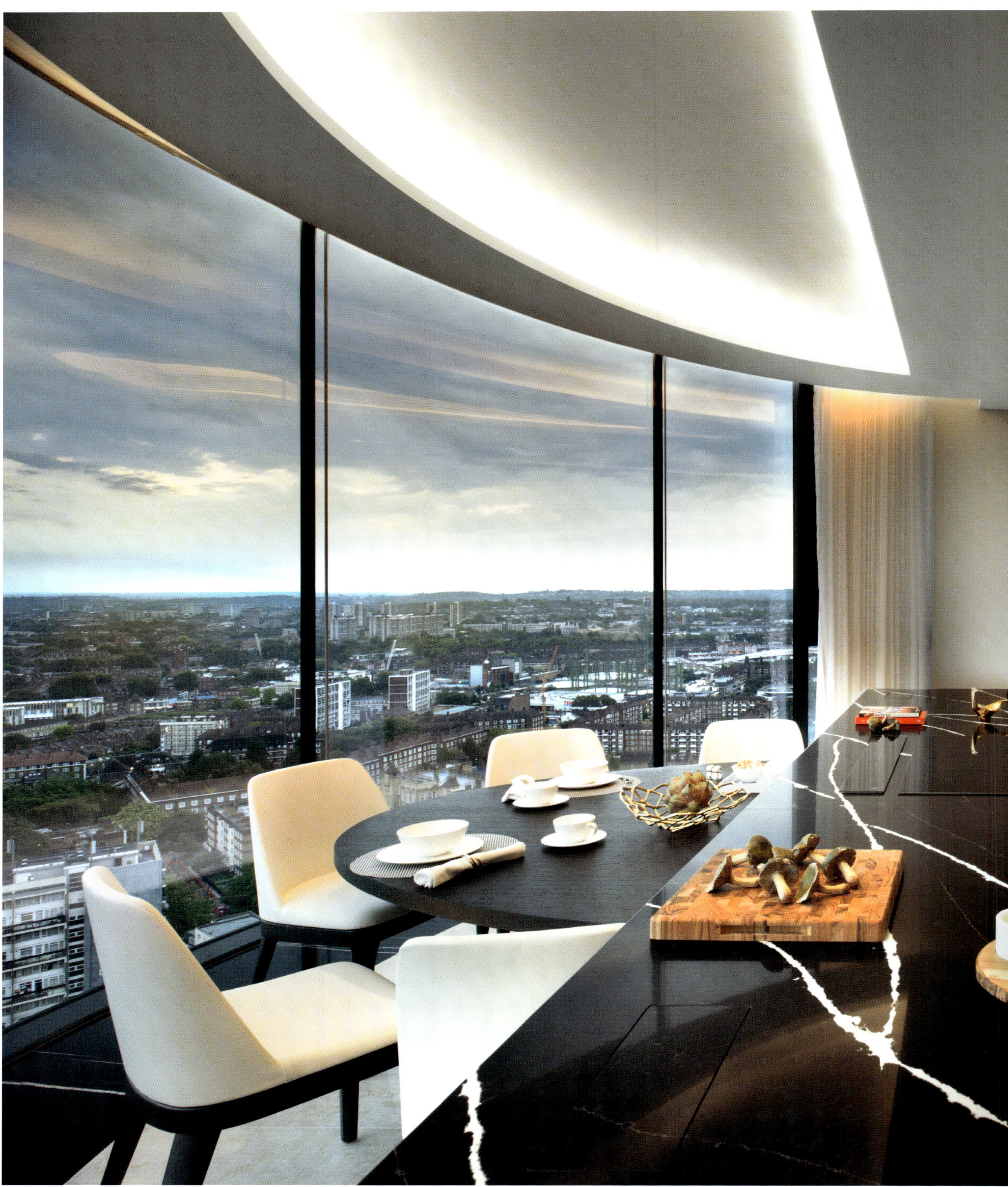

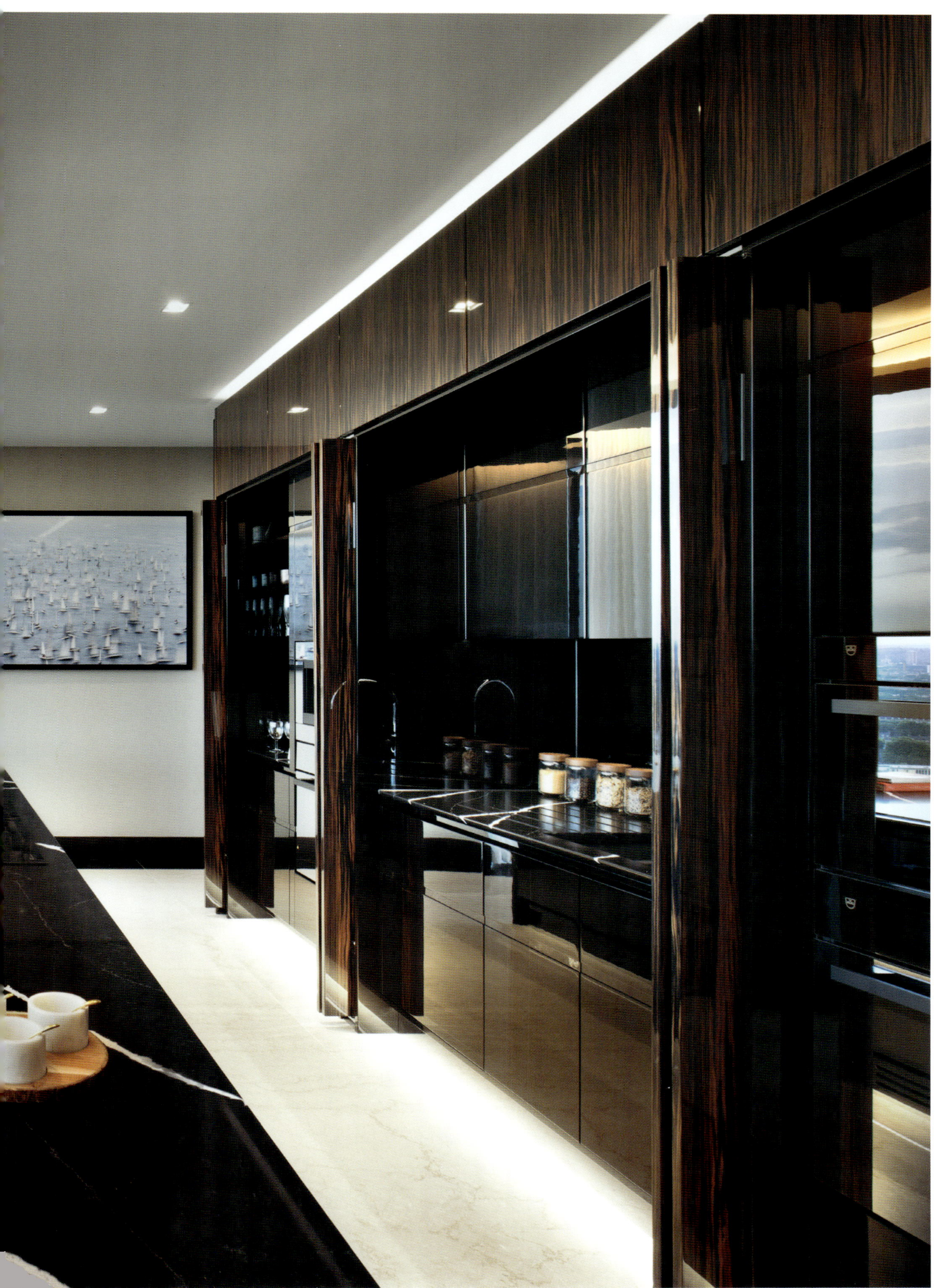

If the weather puts the terrace off-limits, this cozy kitchen-cum-dining room offers a more than adequate substitute. Even here, of course, no one needs to forego select furnishings, state-of-the-art kitchen technology or panoramic views of the capital.

Erlaubt die Witterung einmal keinen Aufenthalt auf der Terrasse, bietet diese komfortable Küche mit Essecke mehr als angemessenen Ersatz. Denn natürlich muss auch hier niemand auf ausgewähltes Mobiliar, modernste Küchentechnik oder das Großstadtpanorama verzichten.

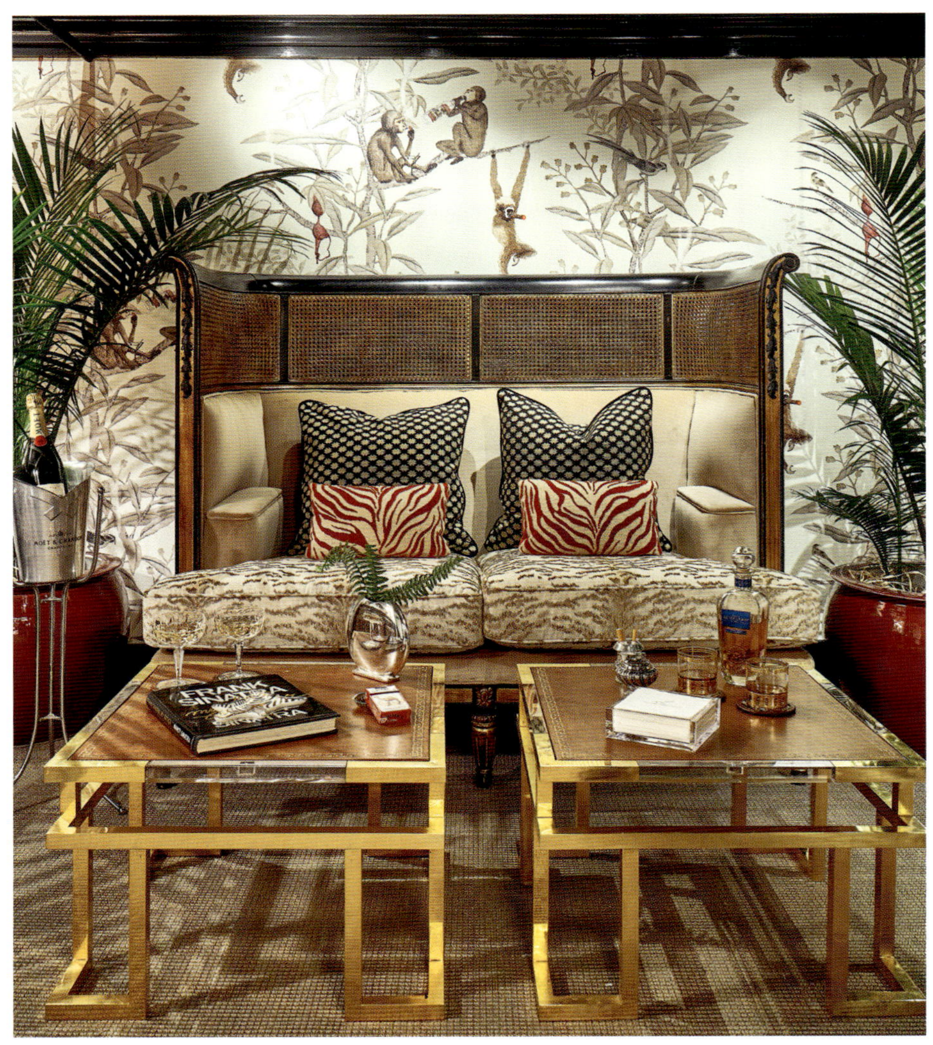

THE LEWIS DESIGN GROUP

CONNECTICUT & NEW YORK / USA

Classic Yet Current | Klassisch, und doch aktuell

Barbara Lewis, principal and owner of The Lewis Design Group is known for her in-depth understanding of fine interiors, which maintain the delicate balance between current trends and timeless style. The Lewis Design Group has earned critical acclaim for residential design and prominent showhouses with global influence displaying her work: Rooms with a View in Connecticut (founded by design icon, Albert Hadley) as well as Holiday House, Hamptons and New York. The company has design studios in Connecticut and New York and finds inspiration across the globe.

Ein tiefes Verständnis für feine Inneneinrichtungen, die das sensible Gleichgewicht zwischen aktuellen Trends und zeitlosem Stil wahren – das ist typisch für Barbara Lewis' Arbeit. Die Direktorin und Inhaberin der Lewis Design Group begeisterte mit ihrer Gestaltung von Wohnungen und Häusern längst Kritiker auf der ganzen Welt. Auch bedeutende Showhouses zeigen Lewis' Arbeiten, etwa Rooms with a View in Connecticut – gegründet von Designikone Albert Hadley – oder Holiday House in den Hamptons und New York City. Die Lewis Design Group besitzt Designstudios in Connecticut und New York, findet ihre Inspirationen aber natürlich weltweit.

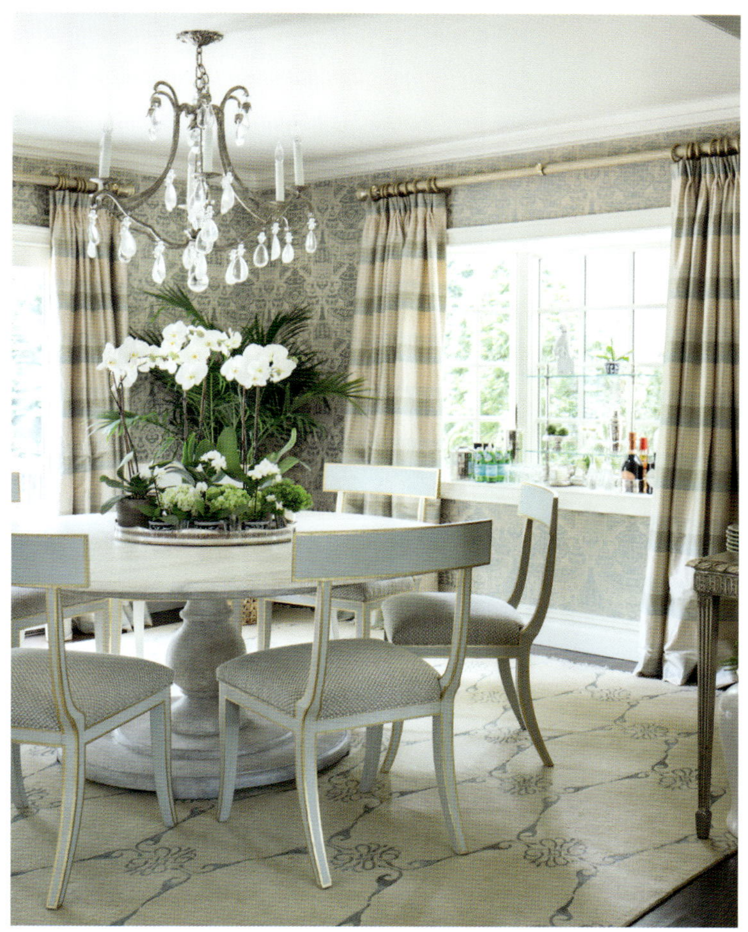

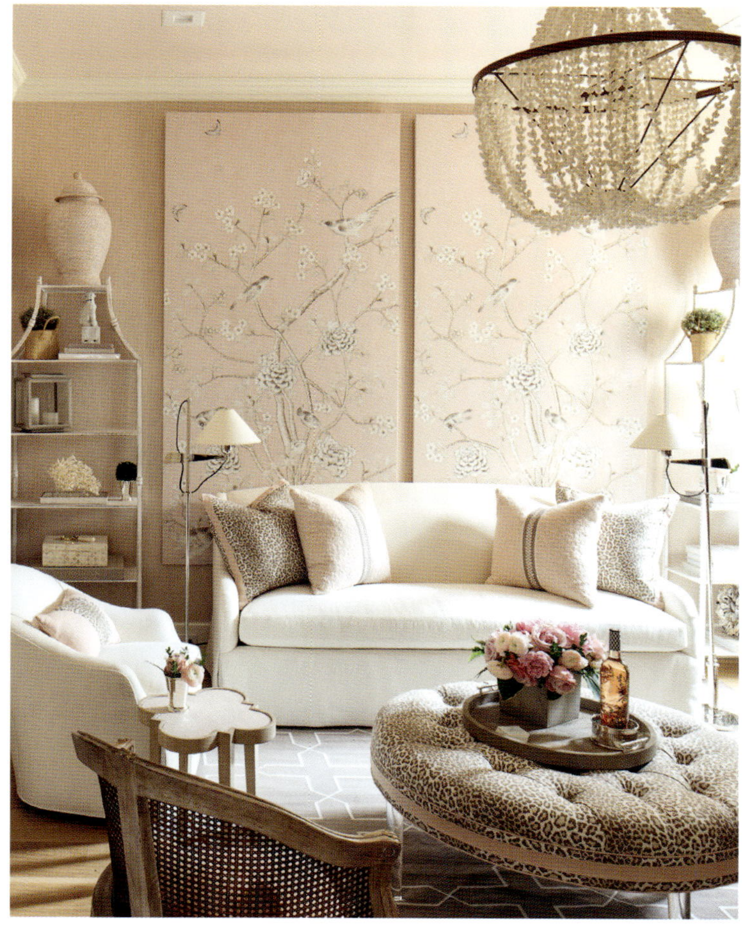

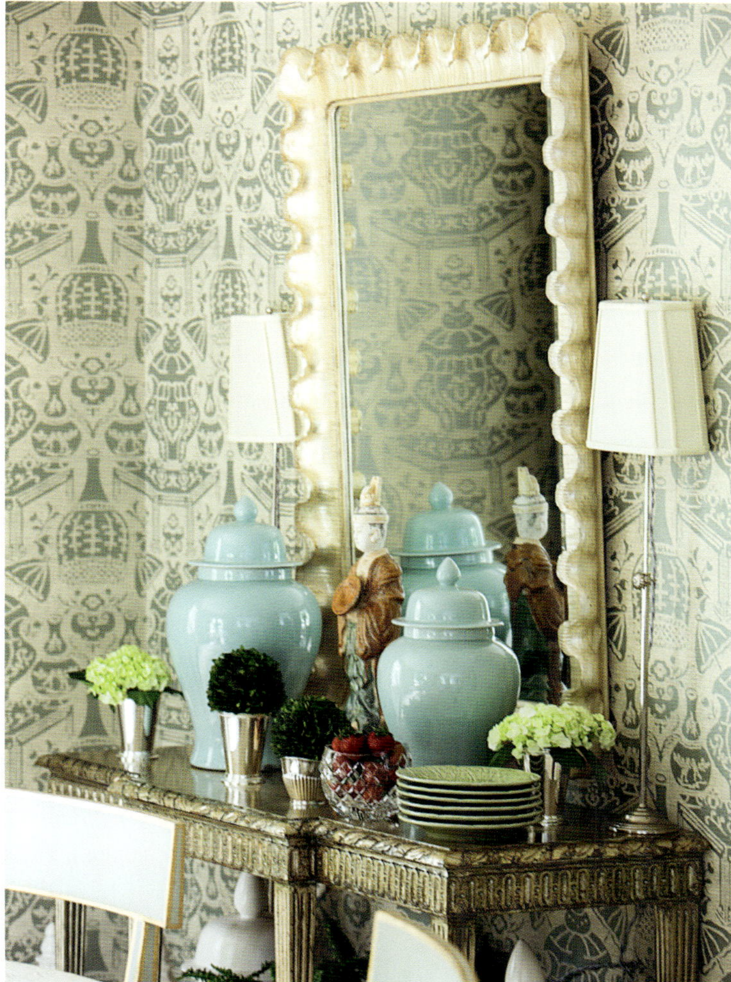

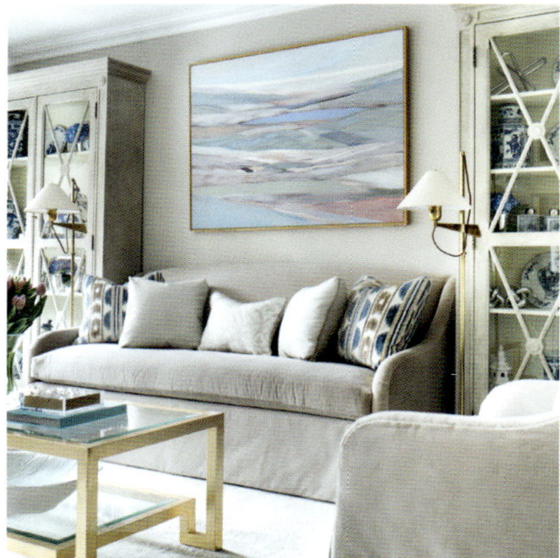

An impression of the design style of Barbara Lewis and her team is conveyed by these photos of private properties and public showhouses. The sitting area with its individual bar ambiance (opposite page) was photographed at Holiday House in New York. The blue room with the curtain (left) was on display at Rooms with a View in 2019.

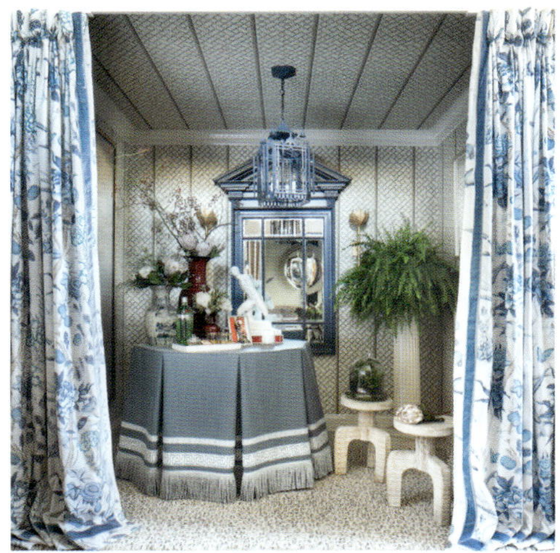

Einen Eindruck vom Designstil Barbara Lewis' und ihres Teams vermitteln diese Fotos aus privaten Anwesen und öffentlichen Showhouses. Die Sitzecke mit individueller Bar-Atmosphäre (Seite gegenüber) wurde im Holiday House New York fotografiert. Der blaue Raum mit Vorhang (links) war 2019 bei Rooms with a View zu sehen.

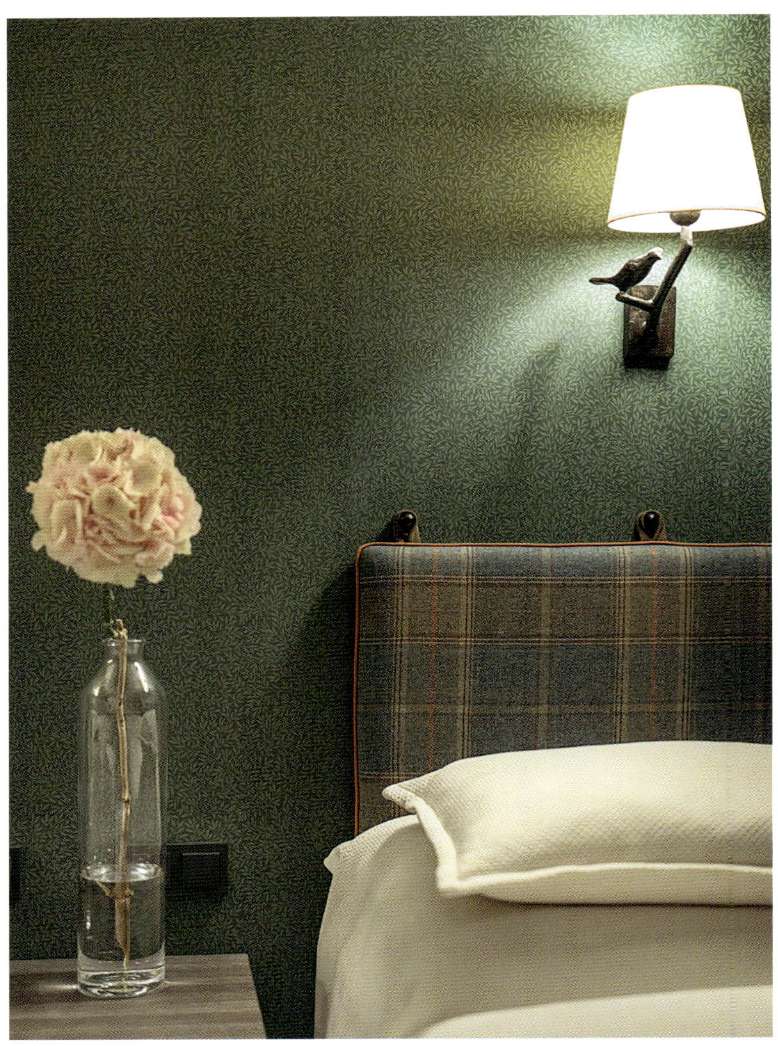

WEBER INTERIORS

ZELL AM SEE / AUSTRIA

Individual Concepts | Individuelle Konzepte

Highly individual furnishing concepts are at the heart of the work carried out by the Austrian family-owned company Weber Interiors, from Zell am See. All of the designs are executed with the highest quality materials, applying craftsmanship handed down from generation to generation. For the redesign of a room in the luxury Hotel Unterschwarzachhof, traditional forms of rural baroque were combined with the materials of festive costumes, such as velvet and silk, and given new meaning. Here, in the peace and tranquility of the Glemm valley, surrounded by idyllic mountain scenery, particular attention was paid to meticulously creating a design concept with a strong affiliation to the region.

Im Mittelpunkt allen Schaffens des österreichischen Familienunternehmens Weber in Zell am See stehen immer äußerst individuelle Einrichtungskonzepte. Alle Projekte werden mit Materialien höchster Qualität und durch über Generationen überlieferte Handwerkskunst ausgeführt. Bei einer Zimmerneugestaltung im Luxushotel Unterschwarzachhof wurden so zum Beispiel traditionelle Formen des Bauernbarocks mit Materialien der Festtagstracht wie etwa Samt und Seide kombiniert und neu interpretiert. Hier, in der Ruhe des Glemmtales, umgeben von idyllischen Bergpanoramen, wurde besonderes Augenmerk auf sorgfältigste, der Region verbundene Gestaltung gelegt.

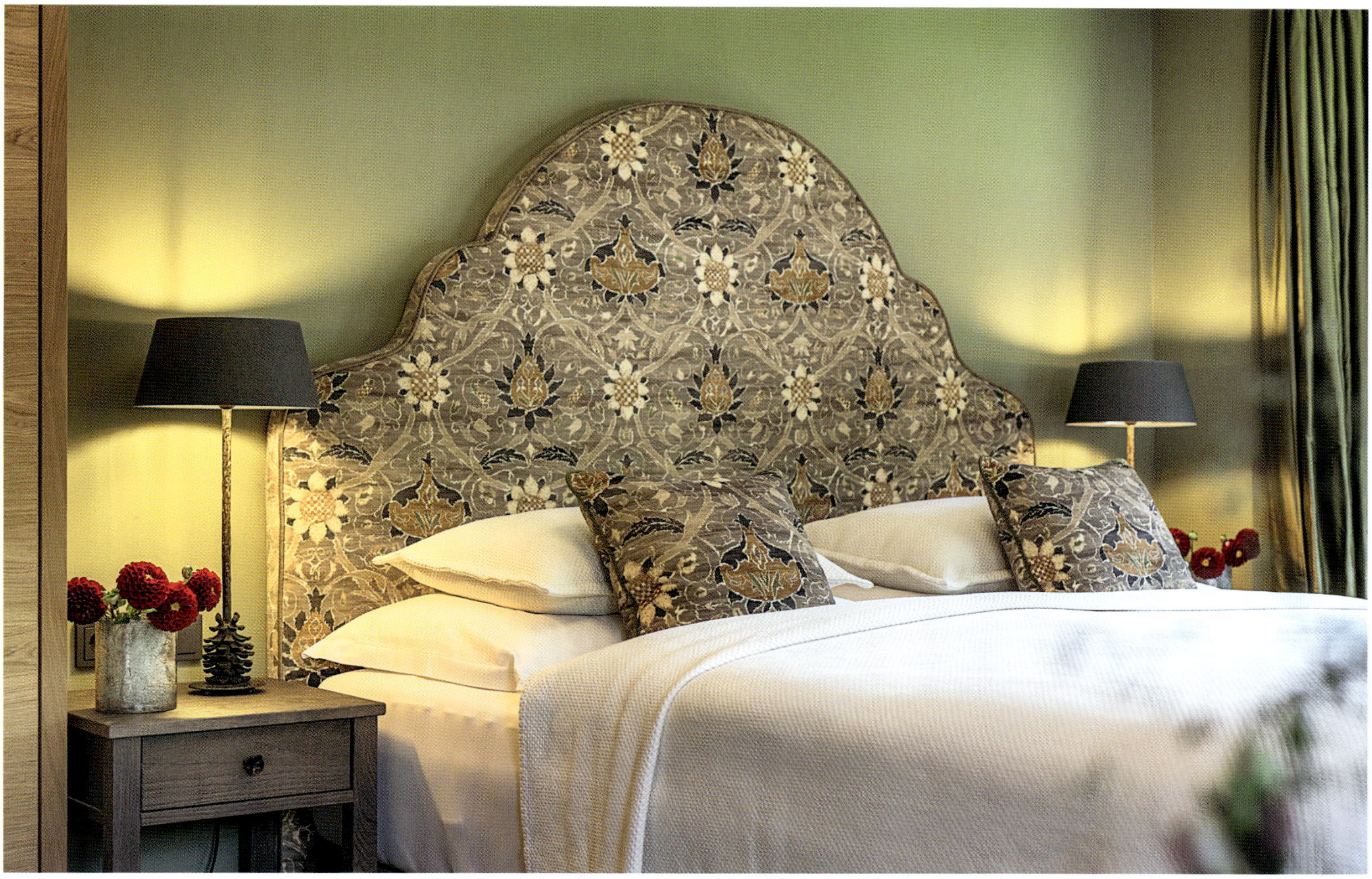

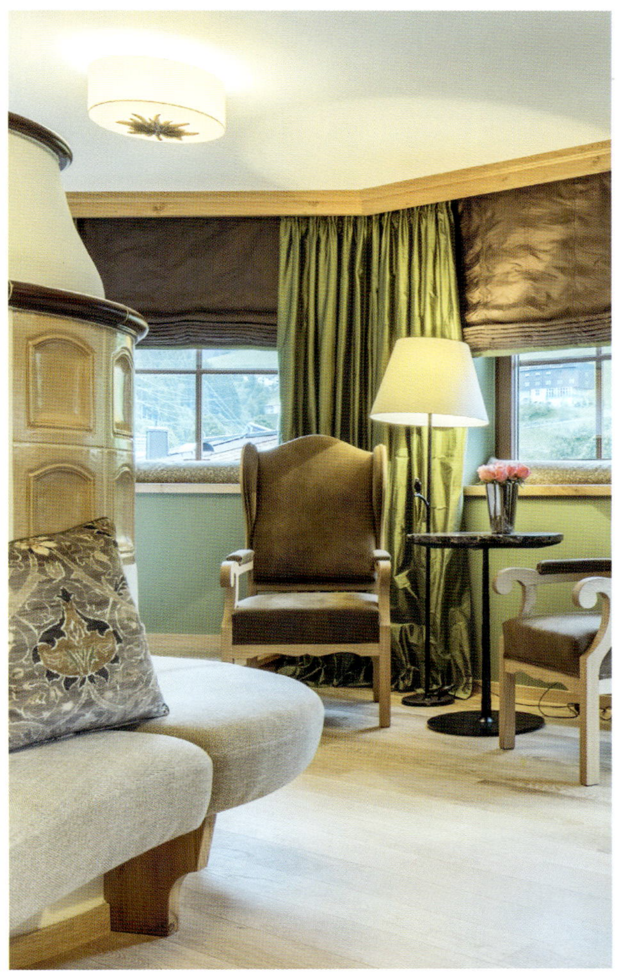

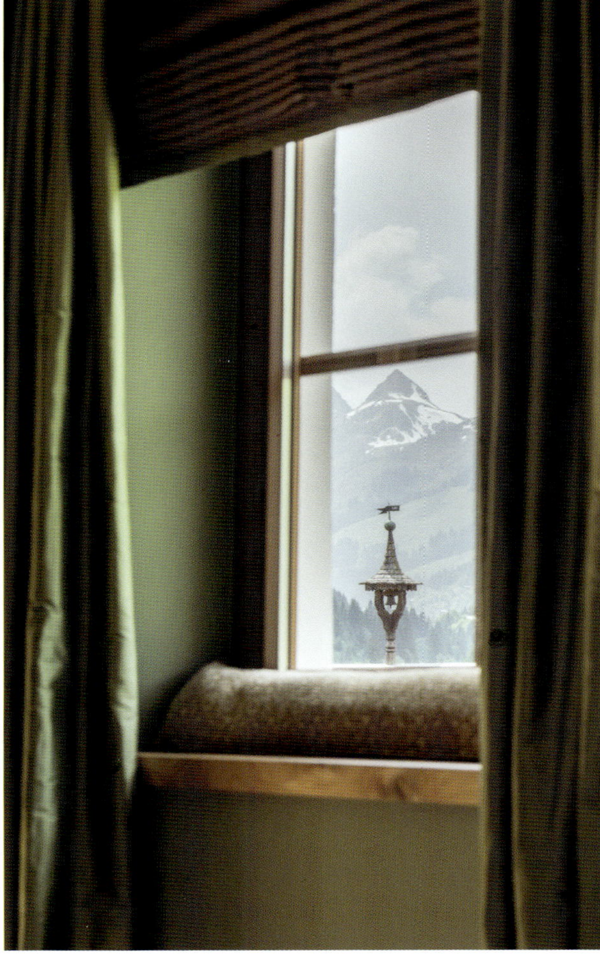

Shades of color, which are intensive but never loud, create a harmonious aura in the rooms. The fabric covers of custom-designed, oversized headboards for the beds serve as signature pieces for the color themes. Individual items of oak furniture with a linear design, in combination with black iron and stone, complete the crossover of design epochs.

Intensive, aber niemals laute Farbnuancen schaffen ein harmonisches Gesamtkonzept in den Zimmern. Die Stoffbezüge maßgefertigter, überdimensionierter Betthäupter fungieren jeweils als „Signature Piece" für die Farbthemen. Geradlinige Einzelmöbel aus Eiche in Kombination mit Schwarzeisen und Stein ergänzen das Crossover der Designepochen.

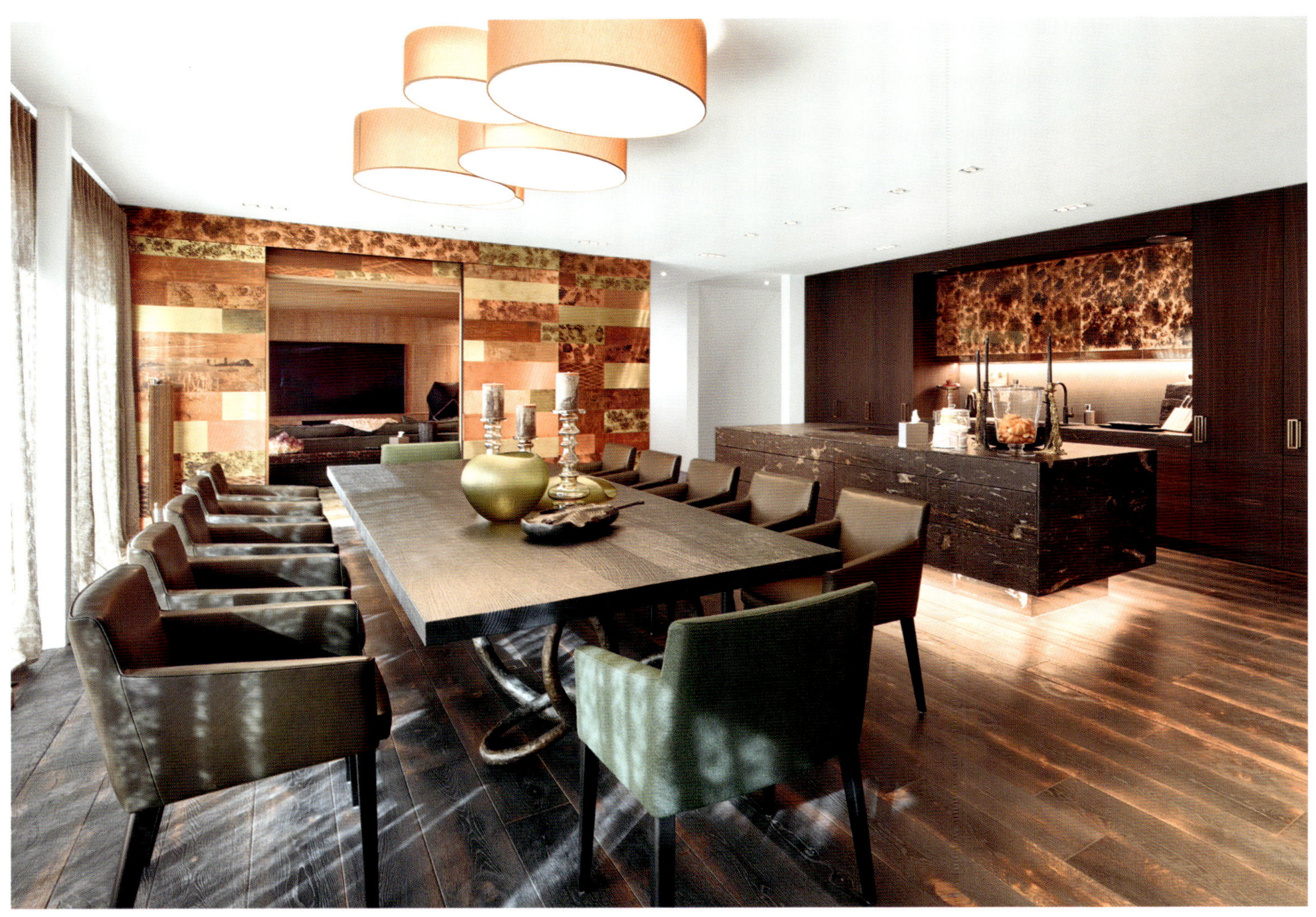

WIDMER WOHNEN

GOSSAU / SWITZERLAND

Unique Craftsmanship | Einzigartige Handwerkskunst

Objects made from exceptional materials, striking in-house creations and eclectic surfaces are just some of the exciting options that Widmer Wohnen AG offers its private and business clients. The family company, which was founded in 1970, has long since made a name for itself both at home and abroad with its realization of highly individual furnishing requests. Widmer Wohnen particularly excels at employing refined craftsmanship to create spaces for specific requirements. A visit to the Zurich showroom provides further insight into these unique worlds of design and the opportunities they present (exceptis.ch).

Objekte aus außergewöhnlichen Materialien, überraschende Eigenentwicklungen und eklektische Oberflächen, wie sie nirgendwo sonst zu finden sind, solche Erlebnisse bietet die Widmer Wohnen AG ihren Privat- und Geschäftskunden. Der 1970 gegründete Familienbetrieb hat sich mit der Umsetzung sehr individueller Einrichtungswünsche längst einen Namen im In- und Ausland gemacht. Nicht zuletzt mit hoch entwickelter Handwerkskunst gelingt es Widmer Wohnen, Räume für besondere Ansprüche zu schaffen. Weitere Einblicke in die Möglichkeiten dieser einzigartigen Designwelten ermöglicht auch ein Besuch im Züricher Showrocm (exceptis.ch).

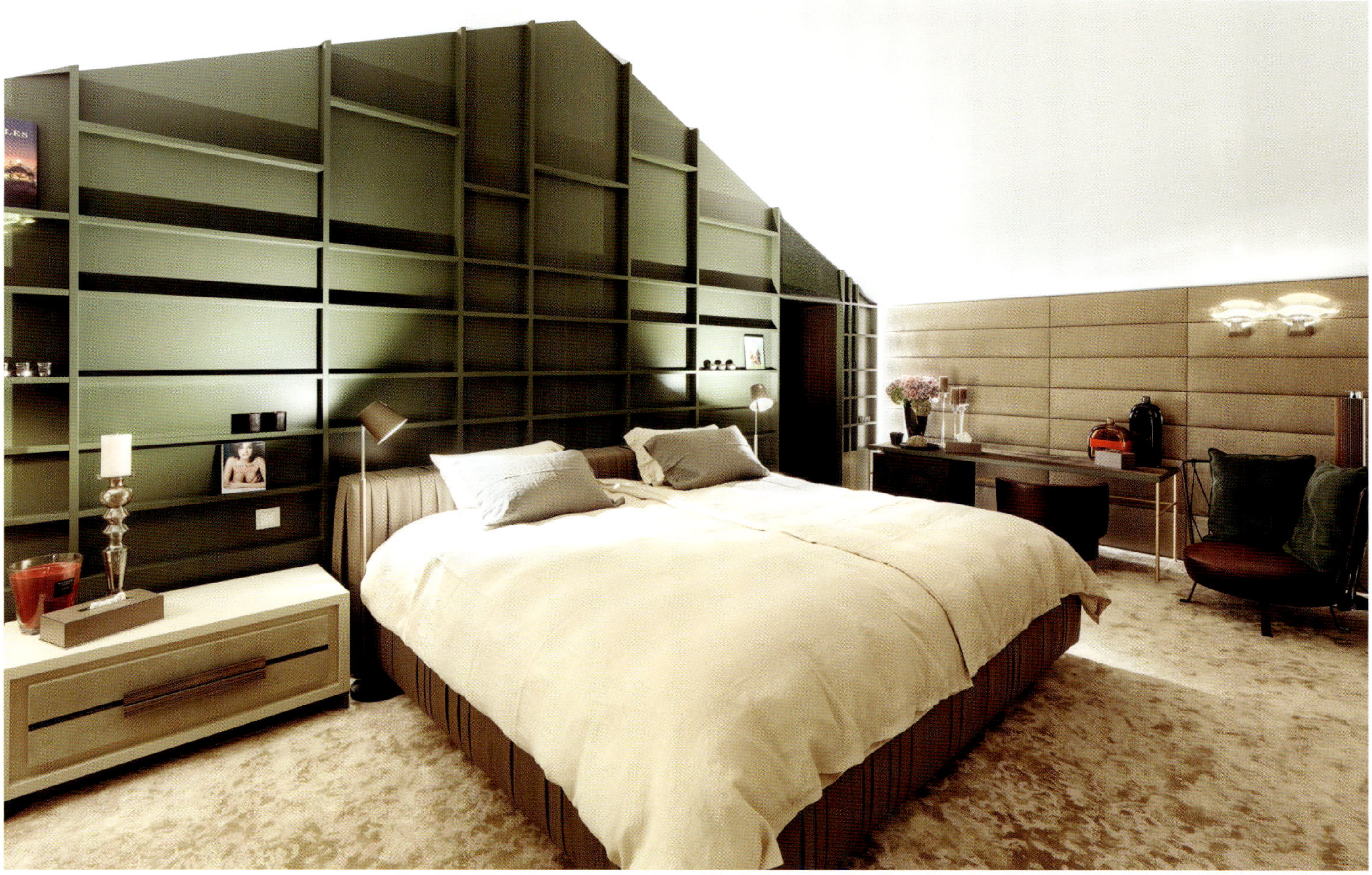

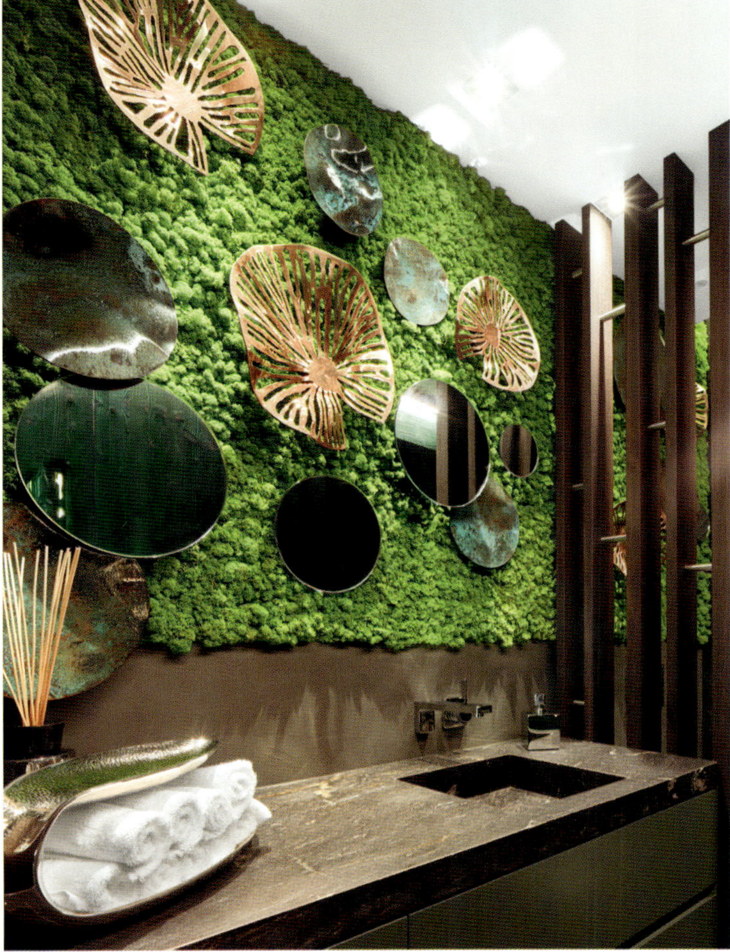

In the open-plan kitchen (opposite page), the cooking and dining areas are separated from the living room located behind. The wall covering and matching sliding doors are composed of a colorful mix of different metals. The bathroom (left) and bedroom (above) are furnished with bespoke wall coverings and shelving.

In der Wohnküche (Seite gegenüber) sind Koch- und Essbereich vom dahinter liegenden Wohnzimmer abgetrennt. Wandverkleidung und dazu passende Schiebetüren bestehen aus einem bunten Mix verschiedener Metalle. Das Bad (links) und das Schlafzimmer (oben) sind mit individuellen Wandverkleidungen und Regalen ausgestattet.

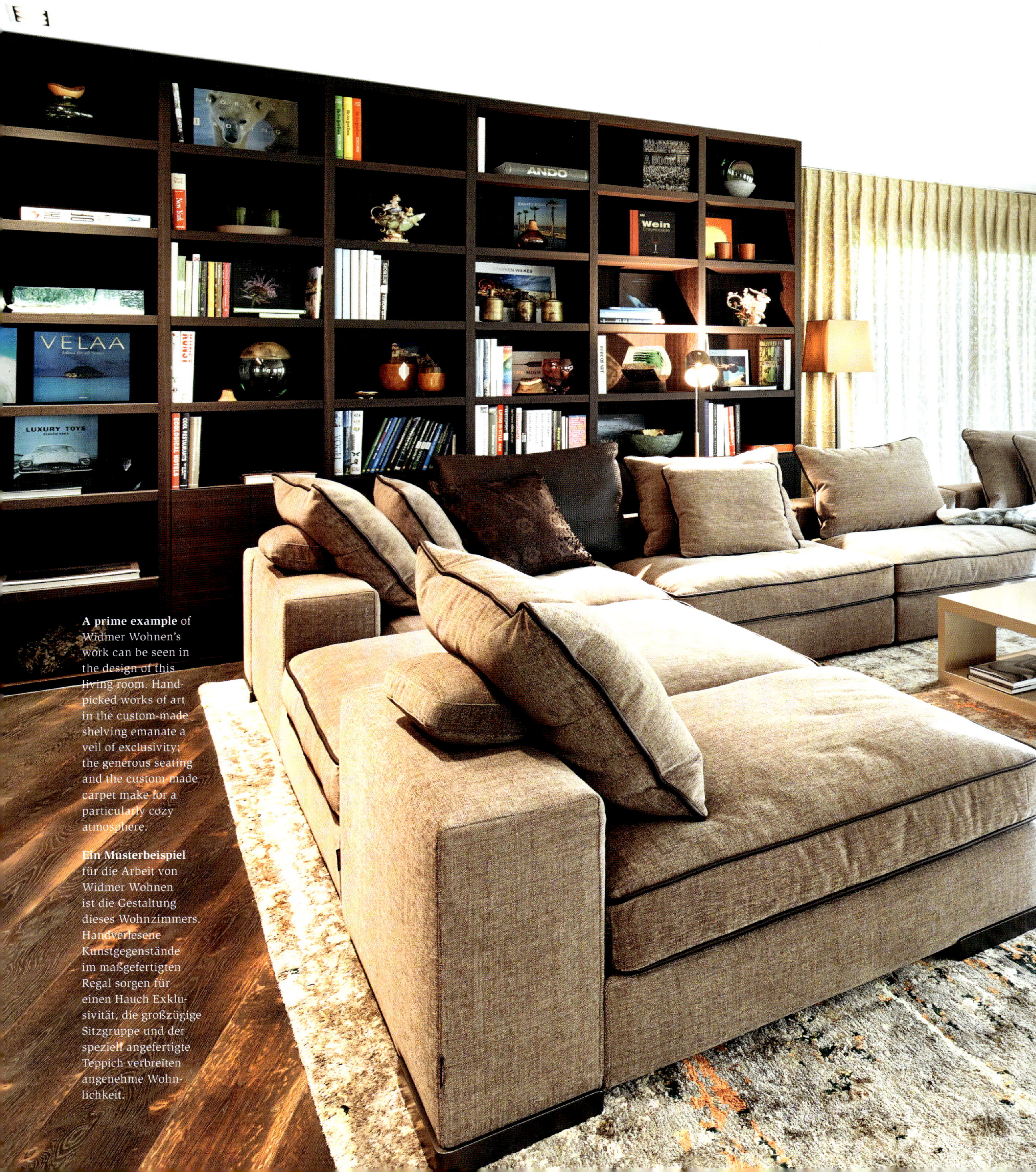

A prime example of Widmer Wohnen's work can be seen in the design of this living room. Hand-picked works of art in the custom-made shelving emanate a veil of exclusivity; the generous seating and the custom-made carpet make for a particularly cozy atmosphere.

Ein Musterbeispiel für die Arbeit von Widmer Wohnen ist die Gestaltung dieses Wohnzimmers. Handverlesene Kunstgegenstände im maßgefertigten Regal sorgen für einen Hauch Exklusivität, die großzügige Sitzgruppe und der speziell angefertigte Teppich verbreiten angenehme Wohnlichkeit.

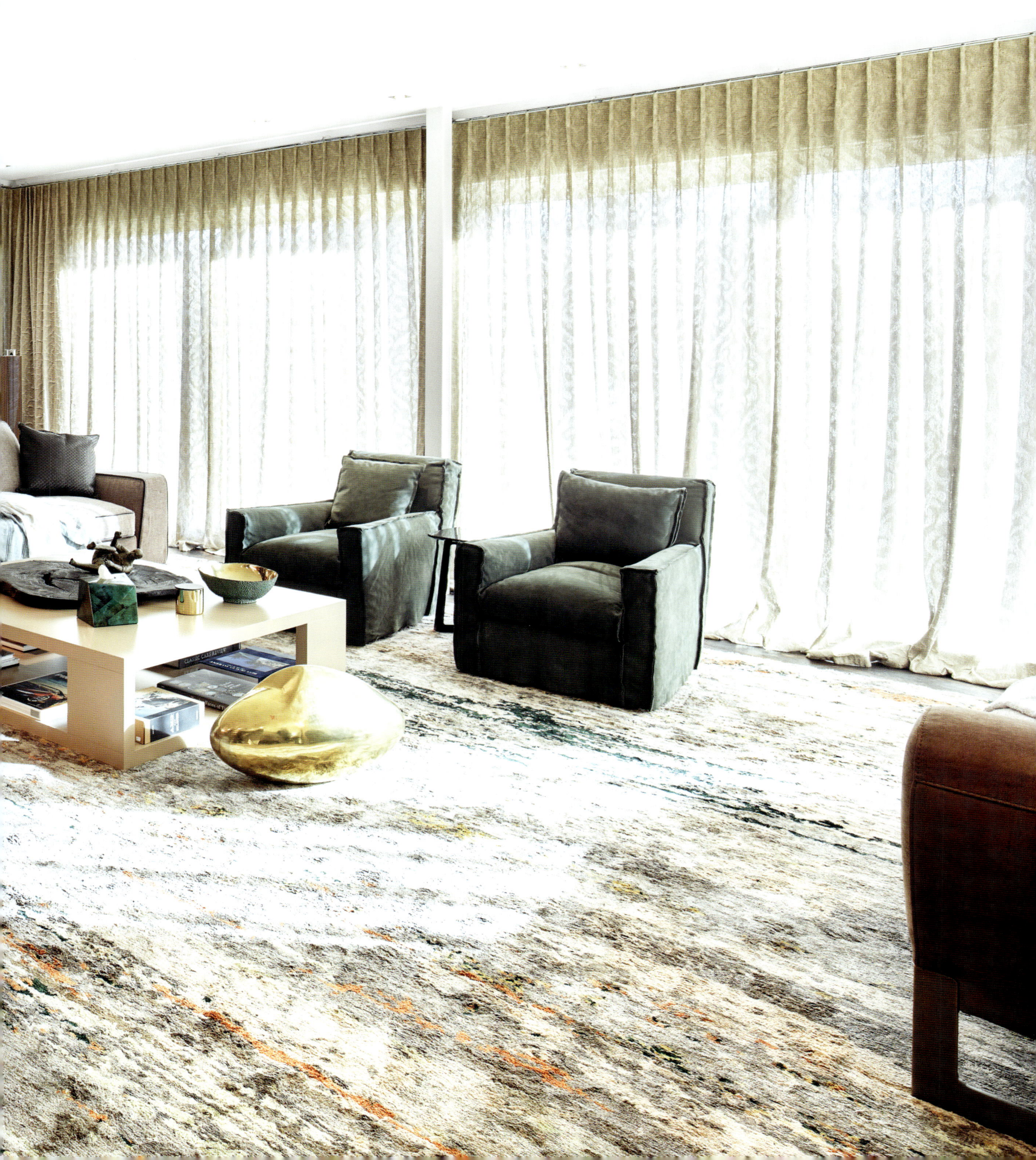

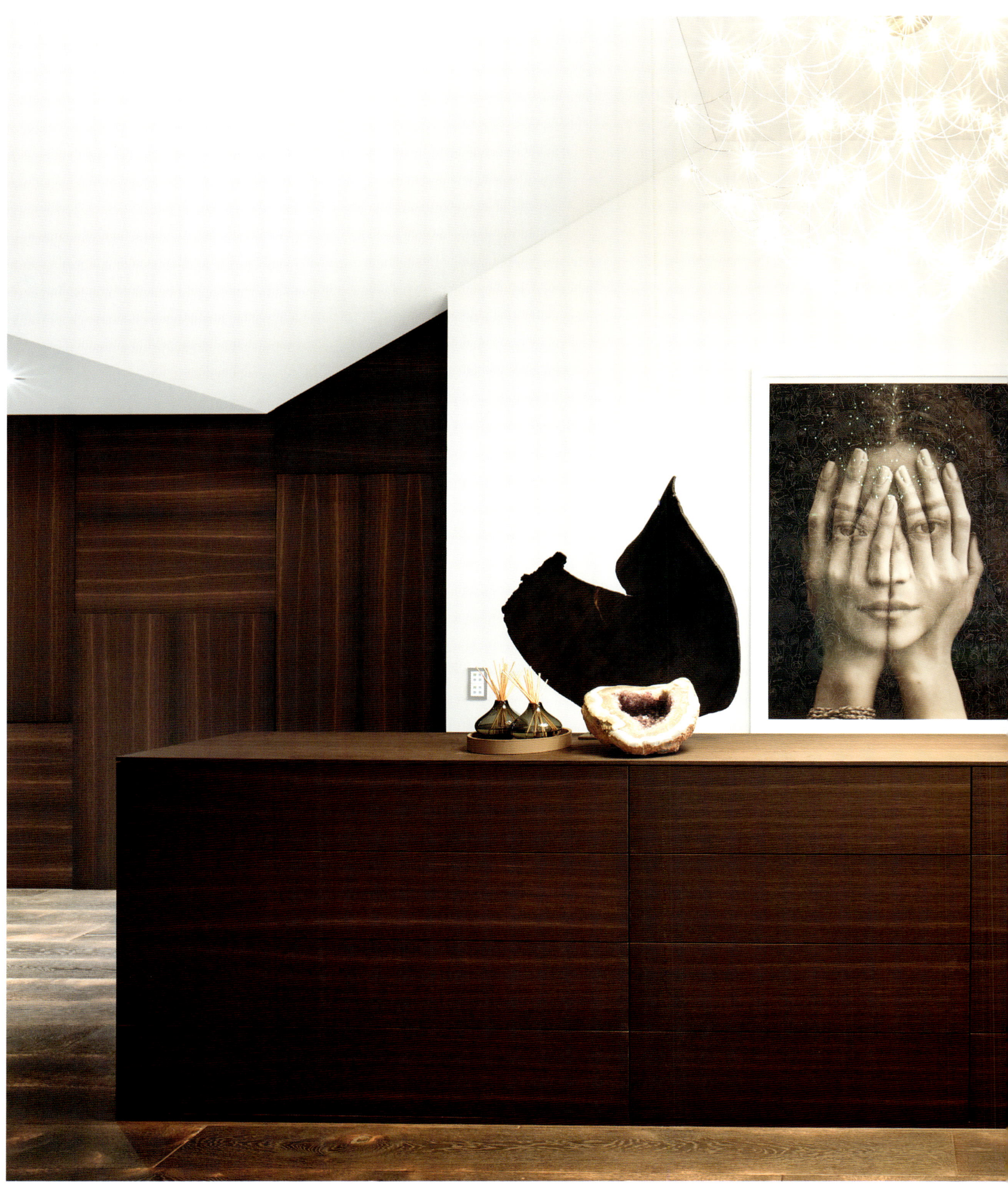

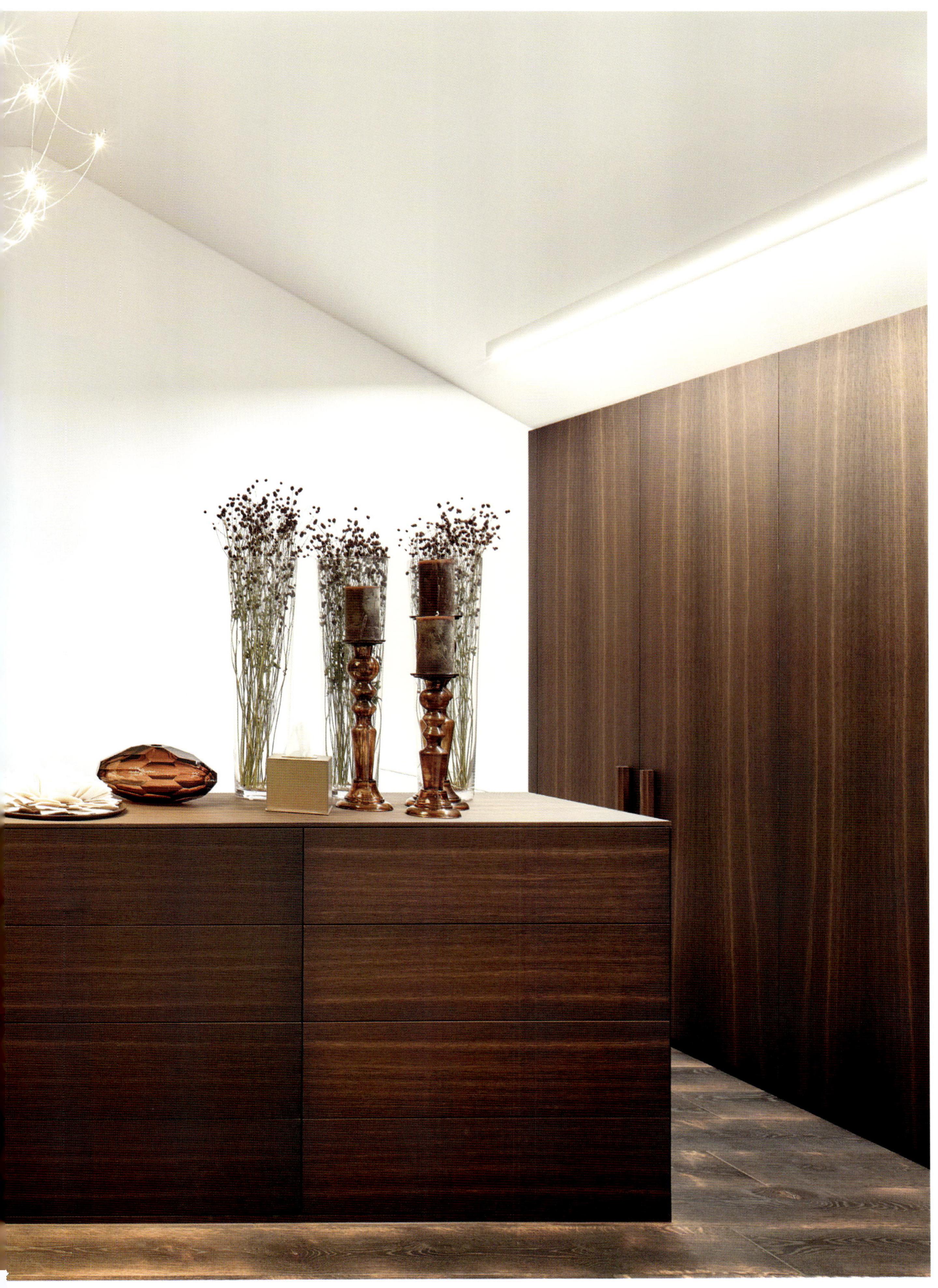

This foyer is, on the one hand, a display of the Widmer Wohnen design-philosophy's discreet elegance while portraying original functionality, on the other. A door to a secret room, conceived according to the highest safety standards, is hidden by the wooden oak panels on the left side of the room. The parquet, which alone required eleven passes, is an in-house creation designed exclusively for this project. Finally, the large chest of drawers in the foreground doubles as a balustrade for a stairway leading behind it to the floor below.

Dieser Eingangs-bereich zeigt das unaufdringlich-elegante und gleichzeitig originell-funktionelle Design der Firma Widmer Wohnen. So verbirgt sich innerhalb der Eichenholzpaneele im linken Bereich des Raums eine nach höchsten Sicherheits-standards gefertigte Tür, die in ein Geheimzimmer führt. Das Parkett, für das allein elf Arbeits-durchgänge nötig waren, ist eine exklu-sive Eigenkreation für dieses Projekt. Der Schubladen-korpus im Vorder-grund schließlich ist gleichzeitig Brüstung für eine dahinter in den unteren Stock führende Treppe.

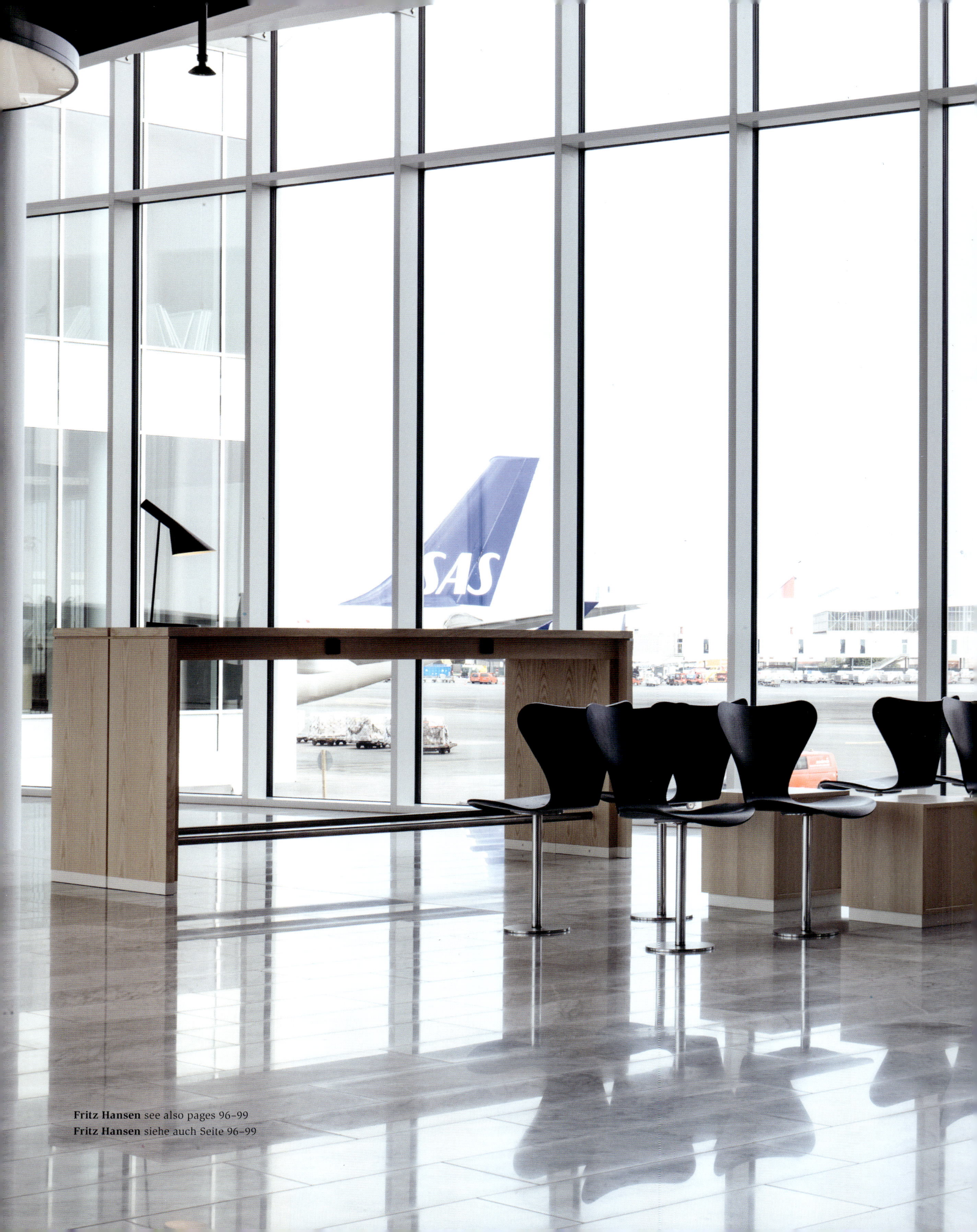

Fritz Hansen see also pages 96–99
Fritz Hansen siehe auch Seite 96–99

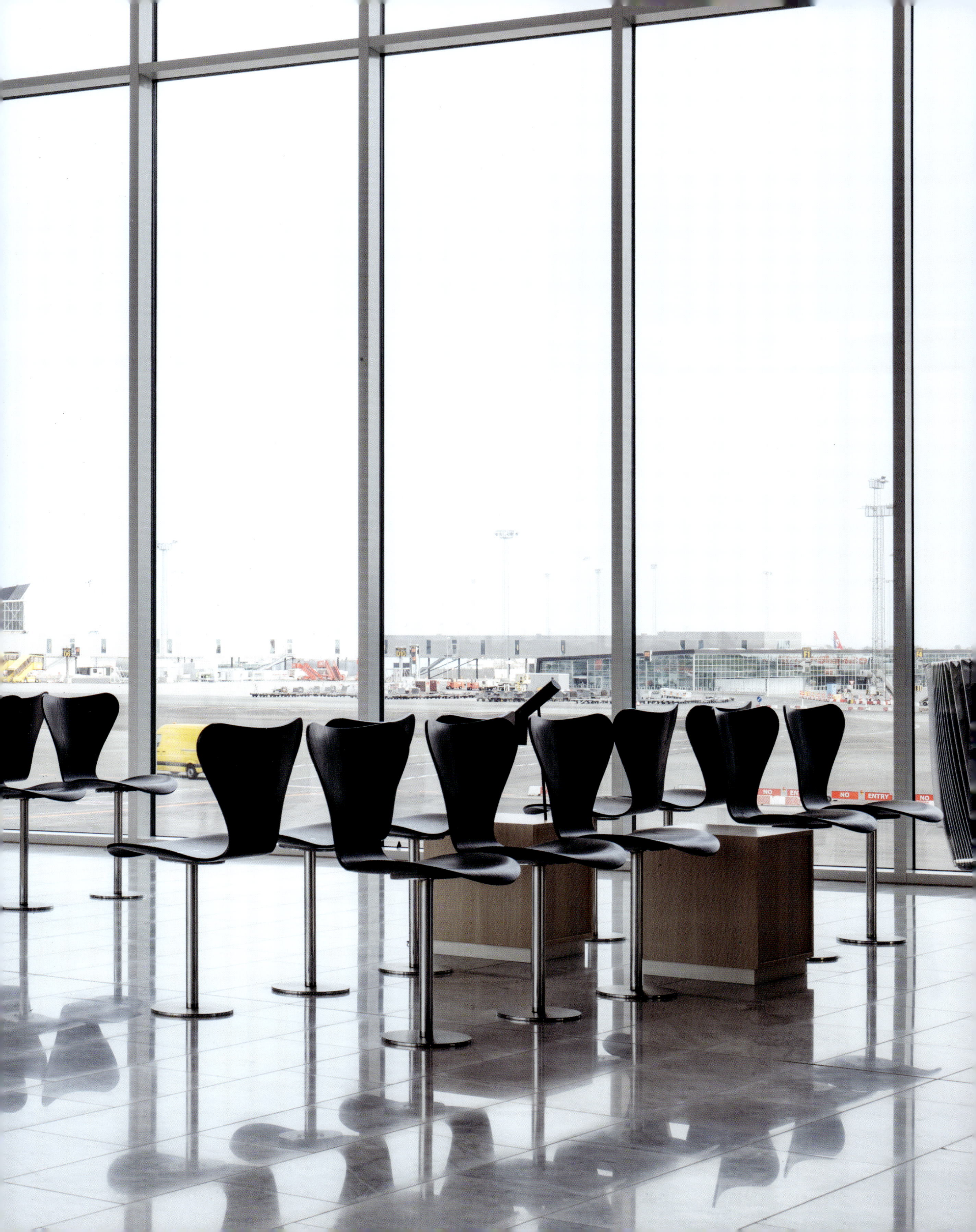

INDEX

Mancini Enterprises
(pp. 134–139)
17 Crescent Avenue
Kesavaperumalpuram,
Chennai, 600 028, India
www.mancini-design.com

Matthew Frederick
(pp. 140–141)
12 Mendham Road
Far Hills, New Jersey 07931, USA
www.mfrederick.com

Monica Marx Inneneinrichtungen
(pp. 142–143)
Nymphenburger Str. 185
80634 Munich, Germany
www.monicamarx.de

Nicky Dobree Interior Design
(pp. 144–147)
39 Moreton Street
London, SW1V 2NY, United Kingdom
www.nickydobree.com

Patrick Treutlein Interior Design
(pp. 148–155)
Dorfstr. 13
40667 Meerbusch, Germany
www.patrick-treutlein.de

Philicima Design Studios
(pp. 156–161)
Jochberger Str. 8
6370 Kitzbühel, Austria
www.philicima-design.com

RALF SCHMITZ GmbH & Co. KGaA
KEMPEN · DÜSSELDORF ·
BERLIN · HAMBURG
(pp. 162–163)
Moorenring 29
47906 Kempen, Germany
www.ralfschmitz.com/berlin

Rebekah Caudwell Design
(pp. 164–169)
Flat 4, 2 Hyde Park
London, W2 2LT, United Kingdom
www.rebekahcaudwelldesign.com

Rinehardt | Miller Interiors
(pp. 170–173)
115 River Road, Suite 112
Edgewater, New Jersey 07020, USA
www.rinehardtmillerinteriors.com

Rinfret, Ltd.
(pp. 174–175)
39 Lewis Street
Greenwich, CT, USA
www.rinfretltd.com

Robert Couturier Inc.
(pp. 176–181)
271 Madison Avenue, Suite 1108
New York, NY 10016, USA
www.robertcouturier.com

Schlotfeldt Licht
(pp. 182–187)
Mühlenkamp 31
22303 Hamburg, Germany
www.schlotfeldtlicht.de

Sebastian Zenker
(pp. 12, 188–191)
Theresienstraße 23
80333 Munich, Germany
www.sebastianzenker.com

Sofía Aspe
(pp. 10–11, 192–195)
Monte Libano 335
Col. Lomas de Chapultepec
CP 11000 Mexico City, Mexico
www.sofiaaspe.com/en/home

Stock Dutch Design
(pp. 14, 196–203)
Bloemendaalseweg 200
2051 GL Overveen, Netherlands
www.stockdutchdesign.com

Studio Arte
(pp. 204–205)
Rua 5 de Outubro 49 RC
8500-581 Portimão, Portugal
www.studioarte.info

Studio Hermanides
(pp. 206–211)
Panamalaan 1A
Amsterdam 1019 AS, Netherlands
www.studiohermanides.nl

Taylor Hannah Architect
(pp. 212–215)
354 Davenport Rd #101
Toronto, ON, M5R 1K6, Canada
www.taylorhannaharchitect.com

TG Studio
(pp. 216–221)
10 Rathbone Place
London, W1T 1HP, United Kingdom
www.tg-studio.co.uk

The Lewis Design Group
(pp. 222–223)
Long Island Design Studio,
40 Highland Road
Glen Cove, NY 11542, USA

Connecticut Design Studio
66 Pipers Hill Road
Wilton, CT 06897, USA
www.thelewisdesigngroup.com

WEBER Interior Design &
Decoration GMBH
(pp. 224–225)
Anton Wallner Str. 11–13
5700 Zell am See, Austria
www.weber-deco.com

Widmer Wohnen
(pp. 226–231, 236–237)
St. Gallerstr. 71
9200 Gossau, Switzerland
www.widmer-wohnen.ch

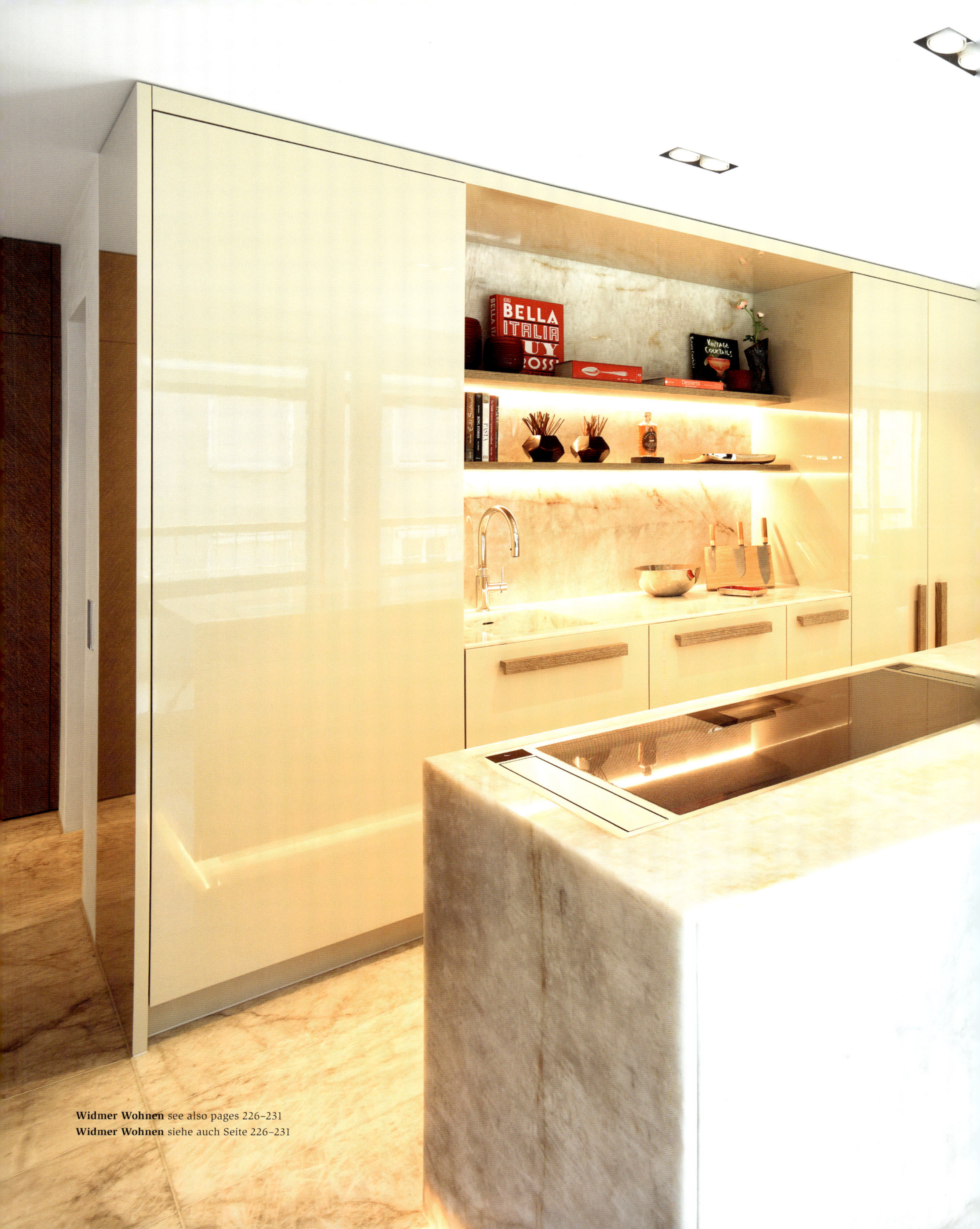

Widmer Wohnen see also pages 226–231
Widmer Wohnen siehe auch Seite 226–231

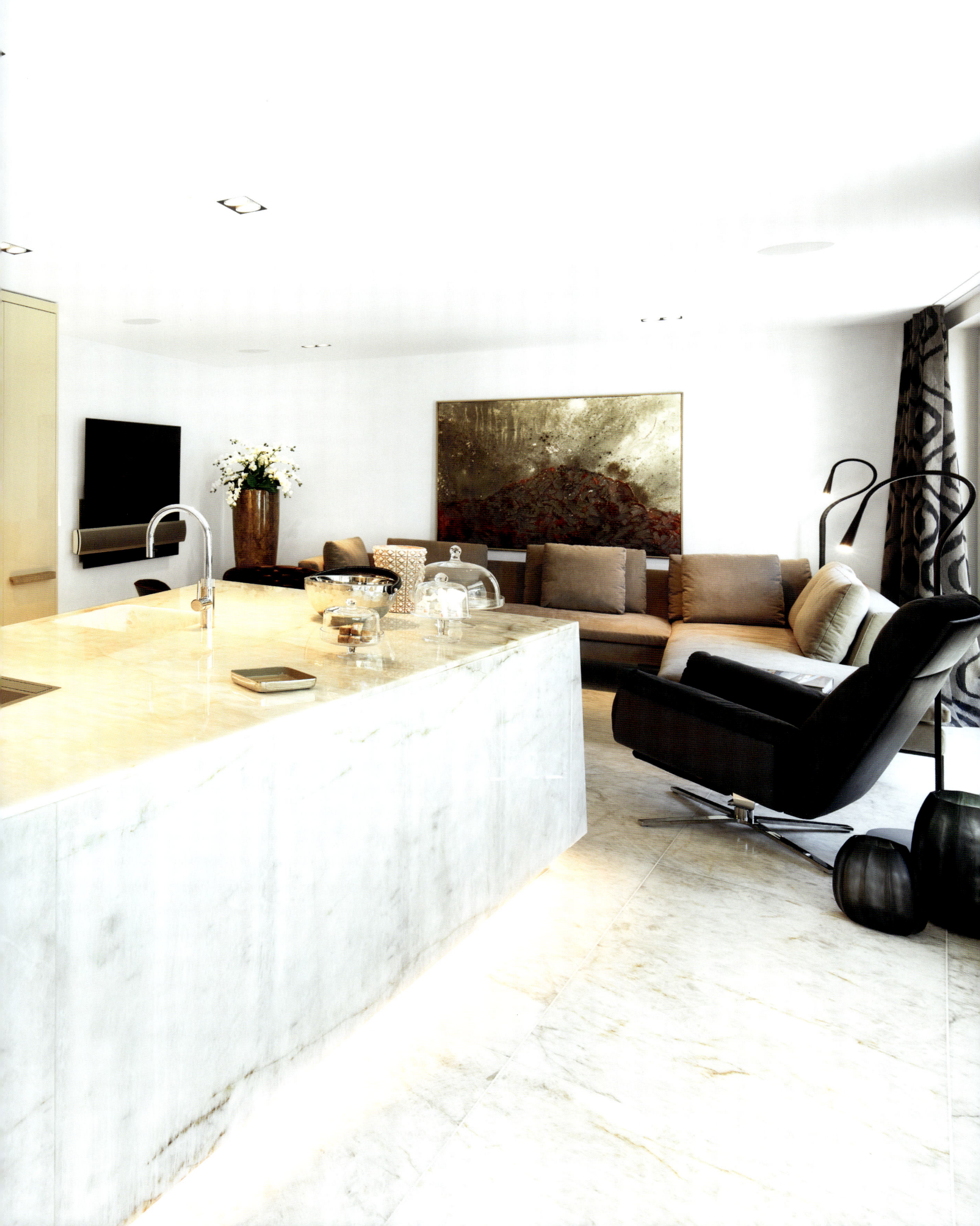

CREDITS

Coverphoto © Richard Koek; pp. 4–5, 9 © SergioGhetti/KeremSanlıman/Secilmi Press; pp. 10–11 © Jaime Navarro; p. 12 © Ortwin Klipp; p. 14 © Peter Baas; pp. 16–19 © Thébaïde; pp. 20–23 © Sergey Ananiev; pp. 24–27 © Paterakis Vangelis; p. 28 © Fabrice Dall'Anese; p. 29 (top image) © Shayne Thomas; p. 29 (bottom image) © Booyeah; pp. 30–31 © Fabrice Dall'Anese; pp. 32–37 © Nick Johnson; pp. 38–39 © Keith Williams; pp. 40–49 © SergioGhetti/KeremSanlıman/Secilmi Press; p. 50 © Roman Kuhn; pp. 51–55 © Mauricio Fuertes; pp. 56–61 © Bernardi + Peschard Arquitectura; pp. 62–67 © Alexander van Berge, Styling: Bergje Nix; pp. 68–71 © Toto Labrador; pp. 72 –73 (top and bottom left images) © Gieves Anderson; p. 73 (bottom right image) © Classic Kids; pp. 74–77 © Panoramic Studio Bangkok; pp. 78–79 (top image) © Marco Menghi, Milano; p. 79 (bottom image) © Wolfgang Pulfer, Munich; pp. 80–81 © Roland Halbe; pp. 82–83 © Jaime Navarro; pp. 84–87 © Gerhard Groger Photography; p. 88 © Jacob Sadrak; pp. 89–90 © Eric Laginel; p. 91 © Jacob Sadrak; pp. 92–93 © Eric Laginel; pp. 94–95 © Christine Dempf Photography; pp. 96–99 © Tomoko Ikegai ikg inc. (Design) / Nacasa&Partners Inc. (Photo); pp. 100–101 © Gaggenau Hausgeräte GmbH; pp. 102–115 © Richard Koek; pp. 116–121 © Ludger Paffrath Fotografie Berlin; pp. 122–127 © Icazar Architects; pp. 128–129 © Interior Architects Munich; pp. 130–133 Christian Laukemper, © Kitzig Design Studios GmbH & Co. KG; pp. 134–139 © Björn Wallander; pp. 140–141 © John Bessler; pp. 142–143 © Monica Marx; pp. 144–147 © Philip Vile; pp. 148–155 © Annika Feuss; pp. 156–161 © Jamie McGregor Smith; pp. 162–163 © NOSHE/RALF SCHMITZ; pp. 164–169 © Simon Upton; pp. 170–173 © Kelly Marshall Photography (NYC); pp. 174–175 (bottom left image) © Michael Partentio; p. 175 (all images except bottom left) © Neil Landino; pp. 176–177 © Zach Desart; pp. 178–181 © Kent Johnson; pp. 182–183 © Hans Joosten/iGuzzini; pp. 184–185 © Marcus Bredt; pp. 186–187 © Christian Gahl; pp. 188–191 © Ortwin Klipp; pp. 192–195 © Jaime Navarro; pp. 196–203 © Peter Baas (except 203 top left image); p. 196 © (fotos displayed in the image) Casper Faassen; p. 203 (top left image) © Brenda van Leeuwen; pp. 204–205 © Studio Arte; pp. 206–211 © Monde Photography; pp. 212–215 © Costas Picadas; pp. 216–221 © Philip Vile; p. 222 © Marco Ricca Studio; pp. 223 (all images except top right) © Neil Landino, p. 223 (top right image) © JJ Jetel; pp. 224–225 © Christoph Schöch Photography; pp. 226–231 © Widmer Wohnen; pp. 232–233 © Fritz Hansen; pp. 236–237 © Widmer Wohnen; p. 239 © Mauricio Fuertes; Backcover (top left image) © Mauricio Fuertes, (top right image) © Marco Menghi, Milano, (bottom image) © SergioGhetti/KeremSanlıman/Secilmi Press

© VG Bild-Kunst Bonn, 2021

p. 32 Artwork in background by Damien Hirst, Dipalmitin
p. 32 Sculptural floor lamp by Paul Evans
p. 33 (top image) Table lamps: "Iseo Bronze" by Mattia Bonetti
p. 33 (bottom left image) Glazed lava stone cabinet by Christophe Come
pp. 34–35 Cube sculpture "Cube without a Cube" by Sol Lewitt
pp. 34–35 Coral sculpture by Eva Zethraeus
p. 51 (top image) Artwork in the background by Bill Max and Tom Wesselmann
p. 71 (bottom image) Artwork in the background by Richard Serra
p. 119 (top and bottom left images) Sebastian Menzke (abstract painting)
p. 188 Artwork in the background by Jiri Georg Dokoupil
p. 194 Artwork in the background by Jonathan Meese
p. 211 Artwork in the background by Rob Scholte

bconnected see also pages 50–55
bconnected siehe auch Seite 50–55

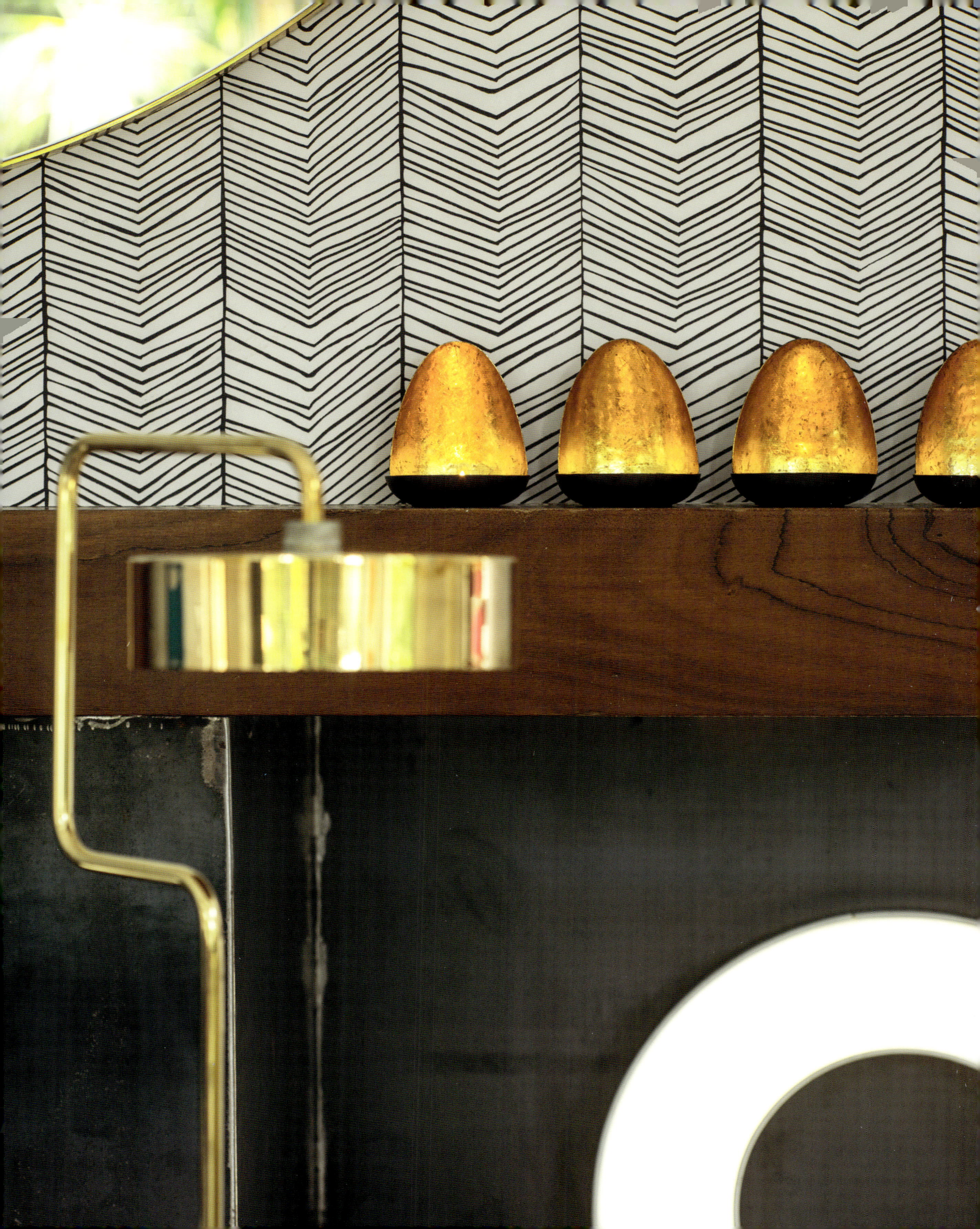

IMPRINT

© 2021 teNeues Verlag GmbH

Texts: © Frank Wagner, Hamburg. All rights reserved.

Editorial Coordination by Marc Strittmatter for Werkstatt München GbR;
Berrit Barlet, Inga Wortmann-Grützmacher, teNeues Verlag
Production by Sandra Jansen-Dorn, teNeues Verlag
Produced by Werkstatt München GbR, Munich
Photo Editing, Color Separation by Jens Grundei, teNeues Verlag
Design by Robin John Berwing; Anja Dengler,
Werkstatt München GbR, Munich
Cover design by Eva Stadler; Jens Grundei, teNeues Verlag
Copyediting by Vanessa Magson (English), Martin Waller (German)
Proofreading by Werkstatt München GbR, Munich; So to Speak, Icking

Translations by Werkstatt München GbR, Munich:
Richard Bishop (English), Martin Waller (German)

ISBN: 978-3-96171-247-2

Library of Congress Number: 2020935922

Printed in the Czech Republic by PBtisk a.s.

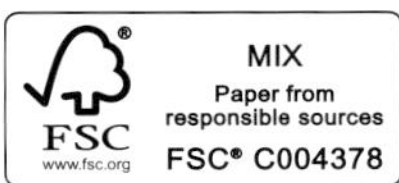

Picture and text rights reserved for all countries. No part of this
publication may be reproduced in any manner whatsoever.

While we strive for utmost precision in every detail, we cannot be
held responsible for any inaccuracies, neither for any subsequent
loss or damage arising.

Every effort has been made by the publisher to contact holders of
copyright to obtain permission to reproduce copyrighted material.
However, if any permissions have been inadvertently overlooked,
teNeues Publishing Group will be pleased to make the necessary
and reasonable arrangements at the first opportunity.

Bibliographic information published by the
Deutsche Nationalbibliothek:
The Deutsche Nationalbibliothek lists this publication
in the Deutsche Nationalbibliografie; detailed bibliographic
data are available on the Internet at dnb.dnb.de.

Published by teNeues Publishing Group

teNeues Verlag GmbH
Werner-von-Siemens-Straße 1
86159 Augsburg, Germany

Düsseldorf Office
Waldenburger Straße 13
41564 Kaarst, Germany
e-mail: books@teneues.com

Augsburg/München Office
Werner-von-Siemens-Straße 1
86159 Augsburg, Germany
e-mail: bbarlet@teneues.com

Berlin Office
Lietzenburger Straße 53
10719 Berlin, Germany
e-mail: ajasper@teneues.com

Press department Stefan Becht
Phone: +49-152-2874-9508 / +49-6321-97067-99
e-mail: sbecht@teneues.com

teNeues Publishing Company
350 Seventh Avenue, Suite 301, New York, NY 10001, USA
Phone: +1-212-627-9090
Fax: +1-212-627-9511

teNeues Publishing UK Ltd.
12 Ferndene Road, London SE24 0AQ, UK
Phone: +44-20-3542-8997

www.teneues.com

teNeues Publishing Group
Augsburg / München
Berlin
Düsseldorf
London
New York

teNeues